D1131837

Hitler's Northern War

Hitler's Northern War
The Luftwaffe's Ill-Fated Campaign, 1940–1945

Adam R. A. Claasen

 University Press of Kansas

Published by the University Press of Kansas (Lawrence, Kansas 66049), which was
organized by the Kansas Board of Regents and is operated and funded by Emporia
State University, Fort Hays State University, Kansas State University, Pittsburg State
University, the University of Kansas, and Wichita State University.

Library of Congress Cataloging-in-Publication Data

Claasen, Adam R. A., 1964–
    Hitler's northern war : the Luftwaffe's ill-fated campaign, 1940–1945 / Adam R. A.
Claasen.
        p. cm. — (Modern war studies)
    Includes bibliographical references and index.
    ISBN 0-7006-1050-2 (cloth : alk. paper)
    1. World War, 1939–1945—Campaigns—Norway.   2. World War, 1939–1945
—Aerial operations, German.   3. Norway—History—German occupation, 1940–
1945.   I. Title.   II. Series.
D763.N6 C53 2001
940.54'4943—dc21   00-043651

British Library Cataloguing in Publication Data is available.

Printed in the United States of America
10 9 8 7 6 5 4 3 2 1

The paper used in this publication meets the minimum requirements of the American
National Standard for Permanence of Paper for Printed Library Materials Z39.48-1984.

To Sandra, Nicholas, Josiah,
Nathanael, and Isaac

Contents

Illustrations

26. Heinkel He 115 floatplane
27. Heinkel He 177
28. Focke-Wulf Fw 200
29. Stumpff and commander of the Finnish air force
30. Junkers Ju 88 over PQ 17
31. Torpedo-laden He 111
32. Luftwaffe strike on an Allied freighter in Arctic waters
33. Successful hit on a cruiser during convoy attacks
34. Recovery of downed air crew by air-sea rescue
35. Focke-Wulf Fw 190
36. German Würzburg-Riese radar

While nearly all illustrations were provided by the USAFHRA, other photographs are from the National Archives, Washington, D.C. (no. 1); the Centre of Military Study, Carlisle Barracks (2); the private collection of James S. Corum (3); the Norwegian National Military Museum, Oslo (7, 16); and the author's own collection (4, 5, 6, 8, 9, 10, 14, 15, 17).

MAPS

Abbreviations

AMB	Air Ministry, Great Britain
AWM	Australian War Memorial
BdU, KTB	*Befehlshaber der Unterseeboote, Kriegstagebuch* (Commander U-Boats, War Diary)
DGFP	*Documents on German Foreign Policy*
IMT	*International Military Tribunal*
KTB OKW	*Kriegstagebuch des Oberkommando der Wehrmacht* (War Diary, High Command of the Armed Forces)
KTB Skl	*Kriegstagebuch der Seekriegsleitung, Teil A* (War Diary, High Command of the Navy)
NA	National Archives, Washington, D.C.
OKH	Oberkommando des Heeres (High Command of the Army)
OKL	Oberkommando der Luftwaffe (High Command of the Luftwaffe)
OKM	Oberkommando der Kriegsmarine (High Command of the Navy)
OKW	Oberkommando der Wehrmacht (High Command of the Armed Forces)
USAFHRA	United States Air Force Historical Research Agency, Maxwell Air Force Base, Montgomery, Alabama
USAFHSO	United States Air Force Historical Support Office, Bolling Air Force Base, Washington, D.C.

Designation and Structure of Operational Units and Commands

Luftflotte. Although at the outbreak of hostilities the Luftwaffe's operational units were divided into four *Luftflotten* (air fleets) numbered *1* through *4*, it soon became evident that these would be insufficient to cover the operational theaters into which the war spread. By the end of the Second World War, a further three air fleets had been added: Luftflotten 5, 6, and Reich. Each of these *Luftflotten* was composed of a wide range of machines and personnel necessary for a "stand-alone" operational air force along the lines of those deployed overseas by the Royal Air Force (RAF) and the U.S. Army Air Force (USAAF), and as such included not only strike units of bombers, fighters, and close air support aircraft but also the requisite reconnaissance, transport, and flak units. Maintenance and supply services for each *Luftflotte* were carried out by one or more *Luftgaue* (air districts), enabling the air fleets to concentrate combat duties.

Fliegerkorps. Numbering between 300 and 750 aircraft, the *Fliegerkorps* (Air Corps) was the largest operational command within the air fleet, usually subordinated to the regional *Luftflotte*. Its strength and composition were dependent on its function and the importance of the theater into which it was deployed. On occasion, individual air corps operated independently of regional air fleets when the need arose. Like Fliegerkorps X, which spearheaded the German invasion of Norway in April 1940, all air corps were differentiated by Roman numerals.

Geschwader. Within the *Fliegerkorps*, the *Geschwader* (wing) was the largest single air formation. Each wing was usually composed of three *Gruppen* (groups) numbering some ninety aircraft in all—though later in the war a fourth was added—of a single type of aircraft. For instance, a *Kampfgeschwader* (KG) was made up of bombers, a *Jagdgeschwader* (JG) and *Zerstörergeschwader* (ZG) single- and twin-engined fighters, respectively, and a *Stukageschwader* (StG) dive-bombers.

Each independent *Geschwader* was numbered with Arabic numerals, for example, two prominent bomber wings to serve under Luftflotte 5 at various times were KG 26 and KG 30. In addition to these units, so-called *Lehrgeschwader* (LG), or training wings, existed to test new types of aircraft under operational conditions.

Gruppe. Generally composed of three *Staffeln* (squadrons) of nine aircraft plus a headquarters staff of three additional aircraft, a *Gruppe* (group) contained thirty machines. Individual *Gruppen* were designated by Roman numerals prefixing their respective *Geschwader*. Thus the 3rd Group of the 26th Bomber Wing was III.KG 26. Independent *Gruppen* were not common in the Luftwaffe, but they did exist and on occasion made an appearance over Norway, such as Kampfgruppe 100 (KGr 100) in 1940. More commonly, reconnaissance and naval squadrons were also collected into *Gruppen* and numbered consecutively with an Arabic numeral, which in turn was followed by designation type. Thus the 1st *Staffel* of the long-range *(Fern)* 121st reconnaissance group was known as 1.(F)/121.

Staffeln. Typically numbering only nine aircraft, the *Staffel* was the Luftwaffe's lowest formation and within each *Geschwader* was consecutively numbered with Arabic numerals prefixing their parent wing. By way of illustration, the 1st Squadron of KG 40 was abbreviated to 1./KG 40.

Note: Although this work follows the traditional practice of translating *Geschwader, Gruppen,* and *Staffeln* as "wings," "groups," and "squadrons," these designations in no way resemble the RAF or USAAF units of the same names in size, composition, or function.

Equivalent Officer Ranks

Luftwaffe	USAAF	RAF
Generalfeldmarschall	General (five-star)	Marshal of the RAF
Generaloberst	General (four-star)	Air Chief Marshal
General der Flieger	Lieutenant General	Air Marshal
Generalleutnant	Major General	Air Vice-Marshal
Generalmajor	Brigadier General	Air Commodore
Oberst	Colonel	Group Captain
Oberstleutnant	Lieutenant Colonel	Wing Commander
Major	Major	Squadron Leader
Hauptmann	Captain	Flight Lieutenant
Oberleutnant	First Lieutenant	Flying Officer
Leutnant	Lieutenant	Pilot Officer

Preface

Physically, Scandinavia can be an uncompromising environment. And it was here, upon Norway's rough-hewn landscape and frigid Arctic waters, that the resourcefulness and resilience, as well as foibles and follies, of Adolf Hitler and his Luftwaffe were laid bare. In examining the northern war, this present work is unique in a number of ways. In the first instance, although a large body of literature in English, German, and Norwegian has been published in the last fifty years on the invasion of Norway (code-named *Weserübung*), no single work in English exists that attempts to survey the entire panorama of Luftwaffe experience (and Hitler's interest) in Norway from April 1940 until May 1945. In attempting to do this, I have cast the discussion within the traditional paradigm of campaign history covering four main components: genesis, planning, operational execution, and consequences. In other words, why did Hitler decide to invade Norway, in what manner did the German armed forces propose to carry this out, how was this actually achieved, and, once accomplished, were the short- and long-term objectives of the campaign attained?

Unlike a good number of histories in which the origins of *Weserübung* are briefly skimmed over as a necessary evil before diving into planning and execution, I discuss the campaign's causes in some detail in chapter 1, because to determine the success or otherwise of any endeavor it is essential to understand its initial goals. In this chapter and those that follow, it may appear odd in a history centered on the Luftwaffe to spend, as I do, a considerable amount of time discussing the role of the navy. I make no apologies for this. Not only is it clear from the inception of the invasion until the loss of *Tirpitz* in 1944 that the navy was the primary mover and shaker in matters Norwegian; the navy also remained the Luftwaffe's main operational partner in the theater throughout the war. The successes and failures of this relationship are a central theme of this book.

Rather than merely dealing with the nuts and bolts of the planning process, chapter 2 also provides a case study of Germany's often ad hoc approach to campaign warfare and illustrates the powerfully destructive influence of interservice rivalry that thwarted attempts to establish a true supreme theater commander with authority over all the services involved in 1940 and would characterize Hitler's approach to making war in later years. In addition to these considerations, the invasion of Norway was groundbreaking in a number of ways. For example, it was the first time that paratroops were used in war; objectives were secured solely by airpower; large quantities of men, equipment, and supplies were delivered to the forefront of battle by air; and the Luftwaffe engaged in large-scale operations over the sea. Given the innovative nature of the undertaking, therefore, the way in which the Luftwaffe proposed to carry out these tasks and the organizational framework under which it would operate deservedly receives a good deal of attention here.

Chapters 3 and 4 are devoted to the campaign itself. Although popular perception would have us believe that the campaign was over within twenty-four hours, in fact it lasted for nearly a full two months: from 9 April until 8 June. The air campaign over this period has been broken into three distinct phases: first, the initial assault on 9 April until the end of the Second Battle of Narvik five days later; second, the Allied landings in central Norway in the week that followed until their ejection on 2–3 May; and third, the final phase running from early May until 8 June, when the Luftwaffe's attention centered on supporting the isolated German forces in and around Narvik in northern Norway. Within this chronicle are woven recurring threads dealing with the leadership of Erhard Milch and his successor, Hans-Jürgen Stumpff; the singularly decisive role of the Luftwaffe in the first two phases and its declining importance in the last; the significance of the campaign in the evolution of airpower as a potentially potent force in maritime warfare; and controversies surrounding the use of aircraft in support of ground forces, to name but a few.

One of Hitler's main reasons for invading his Nordic neighbor was to utilize it as a base of operations for the Luftwaffe and navy against Britain. How well the post-*Weserübung* reality measured up to the pre-*Weserübung* expectations is broadly the focus of the remaining three chapters. Of these, chapter 5 provides the analytic fulcrum of the book. It is here that I explain in some detail why German hopes of using Norway in the Battle of Britain and the Battle of the Atlantic were never realized. In particular, the lack of a coherent air-maritime strategy meant Germany entered the war without a force of purpose-built long-range reconnaissance and antishipping aircraft. Alongside this analysis, the actual involvement of Luftflotte 5 in the war over Britain and the war at sea is examined at length to show the unrealized potential of Germany's Norwegian conquest. The part played by Hitler, Hermann Göring, and Erich Raeder, plus a number of important bit-part players such as Ernst Udet, Karl Dönitz, and Ernst Heinkel, in these proceedings is also examined in relation to the exploitation of Norway in the war against Britain.

If Luftflotte 5's part in the war against Britain was to prove abortive, the air fleet's operational strength and fortunes soared for a season against the PQ convoys, as described in chapter 6. In one of the Second World War's most demanding theaters, the Luftwaffe found itself at the forefront of the war against Arctic convoys. Stumpff's clever use of limited resources and his continual tussle with the navy over the use of airpower in support of the latter's remaining big ships highlight the conflicting demands and constraints facing Luftflotte 5's commander. Although the assault on PQ 17 revealed what might have been achieved earlier in the Battle of the Atlantic had the Germans had adequate numbers of long-range aircraft and U-boats, German success against this ill-fated convoy was really determined more by the British Admiralty's misguided order scattering the convoy than by any intrinsic advantages held by the Luftwaffe over the enemy vessels. This was a point made abundantly clear by the heavy losses sustained by Luftflotte 5 for very little gain against the resolutely escorted PQ 18 convoy.

The seventh and final chapter chronicles the final drawn-out gasps of an underequipped and ailing air fleet attempting to operate against increasingly impossible odds. Stripped of the bulk of its bomber strike force after the Allied *Torch* landings in North Africa in late 1942 and defensively weakened by the slow withdrawal of fighters to the Reich for Home Defense in 1943, the Luftwaffe in Norway was unequal to the tasks at hand. Luftflotte 5's role in the loss of *Scharnhorst* and *Tirpitz,* the appallingly poor resistance put up against Allied bombers raiding Norway, and the final halfhearted efforts against the Arctic convoys following the PQ 17 and PQ 18 assaults are charted in the pages of chapter 7.

Chapter 7 also chronicles Hitler's enduring and unrequited love affair with Norway. To the bitter end, and despite the fact that the Third Reich was being squeezed from both sides after D-Day, the Führer remained steadfast in his resolve never to relinquish his northern conquest. Even as the Red Army and Anglo-American forces converged on Germany, and for purposes as diverse as retaining a source of fish protein and bases for his U-boats, Hitler accumulated large numbers of men and material in Norway and had plans drafted for the assembly of a large Luftwaffe presence should the Allies finally attempt to emulate his own audacious 1940 Norwegian operation.

The work concludes with a detailed discussion of what can be learned about the importance of airpower during *Weserübung* and subsequently in the war against Britain and Arctic convoys, Hitler's leadership and strategic vision, Germany's way of war, and the Third Reich's joint-service operations.

Acknowledgments

Of all the people who had a hand in this book, I must first thank my loving and long-suffering wife, Sandra, who over the last few years has bravely survived the stresses and strains of a husband immersed in academic endeavor. It would be impossible to catalog the sacrifices made by my beautiful wife in what has truly been a team effort, and this completed book is a testimony to her supportive companionship and her care of our four children. Thanks to Sandra, the journey was much more enjoyable and rewarding than I had the right to expect.

Vincent Orange, my doctoral supervisor (this work began its life as a thesis), has been an encouragement from the inception of the idea through the research stage, then into the "writing-up" phase of my work, and finally the presentation of the completed work. One could not ask for a better guide and mentor. Vincent provided not only skilled supervision that kept me on track but also a much needed intellectual sounding board for my ideas and a critical eye for my "jeweled prose."

During the course of my work, James S. Corum, Professor of Comparative Military Studies at the School of Advanced Airpower Studies, Air University, most generously supplied me with large quantities of documents and photos. In addition, Jim's expert advice on some of my earlier chapters and his thoughts on what would be my later chapters have been extremely beneficial to the finished work. Jim has been unfaltering in answering any questions and concerns put to him. In 1997 he greatly aided my efforts in giving a paper based on the first chapter of this book to the Society for Military History, which in turn enabled me to get a good deal of research completed at the United States Air Force Historical Research Agency (USAFHRA) at Maxwell Air Force Base, Montgomery, Alabama.

At the USAFHRA I was well looked after by Colonel Richard S. Rauschkolb and his staff, among whom Ann Webb and Archie DiFante were of immense importance in helping a "Kiwi" get as much done in an all too short space of time. Meanwhile, the School of Advanced Airpower Studies provided me with a base camp from which to carry out my research. The southern hospitality was greatly appreciated and made my brief sojourn in Alabama very rewarding. At the same time as I was engaged in research at the USAFHRA, I had the good fortune to meet Nils Naastad, a Lecturer at the Royal Norwegian Air Force Academy who, then and in later correspondence, offered some very helpful insights into the problems faced by the Germans during the 1940 invasion.

One of the most important assets to my work was a Short-Term Fellowship I was able to take up with the Smithsonian Institution's National Air and Space Museum (NASM), Washington, D.C. At the NASM my sponsor, and most gracious host, Von Hardesty, Curator, Department of Aeronautics, not only took time out of his own considerable workload to see that I settled in successfully but also, along with Michael Neufeld, Curator and the NASM's scholarship director, was only too willing to answer my questions and make me feel part (if all too briefly) of what is truly a great "Institution." Thanks to the support of Dr. Hardesty and the funding provided by the Smithsonian, I was able to explore the considerable collection of materials at the Air and Space Museum's own fine library and also a number of important repositories in and around Washington, including the National Archives II, College Park, and the USAF Historical Support Agency, Bolling Air Force Base. At the former, James Kelling, Archives Specialist, proved indefatigable in helping in my search for relevant documents among an extensive microfilm collection, while at the latter Yvonne Kinkaid and Diane T. Putney were most generous in aiding one of Vincent's students a long way from home.

Horst Boog, the retired Scientific Director of the Bundeswehr's Militärgeschichtliches Forschungsamt (Military History Research Office), is without doubt one of the most influential contributors to our understanding of Second World War German airpower, so it was my good fortune that while he was in New Zealand some four years ago he was kind enough to give some sound advice to a "newcomer" to the field. In the years that followed, he has continued to be most helpful as this work progressed. Dr. Borg's insights and knowledge were gratefully received.

Also important in the formative stages was the direction provided by Joel Hayward, a good friend and presently Senior Lecturer in Defence and Strategic Studies at Massey University. He not only was willing to share a great deal of his own collected Luftwaffe materials but also, having already "cut a track" in this field, imparted some sound advice on research and preparation. Much of his publication *Stopped at Stalingrad* also served as a template for the layout of this book. I am also greatly indebted to another good friend and a fellow thesis writer, Andrew Conway, who, while working on his own magnum opus, gave willingly of his valuable time to aid in the editing of this text during the latter part of the project.

At the University of Canterbury a number of persons within the Department of History have played a part in this endeavor, in particular Ian Campbell, the department's bursar, who made funds available for me to carry out research, and the successive heads of department, W. David McIntyre and John Cookson, both of whom encouraged an atmosphere conducive to research and postgraduate work. On a more relaxed level, the collegiality and good sense of humor of the "morning-tea crew" of Tim Cooper, Tracy Tulloch, Jean Sharfe, Rosemary Goodyear, and Annie Stuart provided a much needed foil to the more trying aspects of the writing process. In addition, a host of other people contributed to the completion of this work, including Sebastian Cox, Wing Commander David A. Proven, Sönke Neitzel, Christina J. M. Goulter, Brian Hewson, Randy Papadopoulos, Karl Mueller, James H. Kitchens, Donald F. Bittner, David M. Glantz, Richard R. Muller, Dennis Showalter, Edward L. Homze, Henry L. DeZeng, Joel Williams, Greg Alford, Nina B. Anderssen, Olve Dybvig, and cartographer Jan Kelly.

Of course, any errors, omissions, or misinterpretations are mine alone.

1

Blood and Iron, and
the Spirit of the Atlantic

Nobody can say for certain that our fleet will not anchor in Nordic fjords as protector for instance of Norway.

Wolfgang Wegener, 1915

On 24 April 1942, Hitler declared that there had been only two decisive events thus far in the entire war. While many historians may well guess at least one of these, the German "defensive battle" outside Moscow during the previous winter, only a few would discern that the other crucial event the Führer had in mind was "the Norwegian campaign of 1940."[1] "If the Norwegian campaign had failed," he continued during his midday monologue, "we would not have been able to create the conditions for the success of our submarines." Additionally, without control of the Norwegian coast, strikes against northern Britain and operations in the Arctic against Allied convoys bound for the Soviet Union would not have been possible. Hitler then went on to lambaste Germany's military leaders of the First World War for their lack of "daring and far-sightedness" because, unlike himself, they had not foreseen the advantages of occupying Norway.

With these words in mind, we might well suppose that Hitler had long planned to occupy Norway and, when given the chance in 1940, was merely following a carefully calculated prewar plan. Nothing, however, could be further from the truth. In marked contrast to his comments above, Adolf Hitler, chief of state and, since February 1938, Supreme Commander of the Wehrmacht (armed forces), had sincerely desired the maintenance of Norwegian (and general Scandinavian) neutrality in the unfolding conflict, a fact he repeatedly made known before the war and during the course of its first few months. On 1 September 1939, while German soldiers stormed across the Polish frontier, Hitler's diplomatic staff in Oslo, Helsinki, and Stockholm were conveying "in clear, but decidedly friendly terms"

1

the German government's intention to respect the integrity of the Scandinavian states "in so far as they maintain strict neutrality."[2] In a lengthy speech to the Reichstag on 6 October, Hitler reassured his northern neighbors that "Germany has never had any conflict of interest . . . with the northern states." Furthermore, despite Germany's offer of nonaggression pacts, none had accepted, "because they do not feel threatened in any way."[3] This was no orchestrated ruse: as Hitler realized, the Reich had much to gain from continued neutrality on its Scandinavian flank.[4] For example, it enabled German shipping to make use of the Leads, the protected channel running down the Norwegian coast, to transport Swedish iron ore from the northern Norwegian port of Narvik to the Fatherland. Additionally, the Leads provided shelter for blockade-runners and greatly extended their choice of exit points into North Atlantic and Arctic waters. Considering the devastating effects of the Allied blockade of Germany during the First World War, in which approximately 700,000 people died of starvation and hypothermia during the "Turnip Winter" of 1916–1917 alone, it is not surprising that Hitler felt Norway's continued neutrality was worth encouraging.[5]

Historically, Germany's approach was in harmony with the Scandinavian nations' own policy of avoiding entanglement in Continental conflicts. With the exception of Denmark's loss on the battlefield to Prussia and Austria in 1864, this policy had been successfully pursued since the mid–nineteenth century. Such an outlook was reinforced further by their experiences in the First World War, when neutrality had been sorely tested. Imperial Germany successfully coerced the Danish government to mine portions of the Great Belt to protect its vital naval base at Kiel. Germany had also received the lion's share of Swedish iron ore from the rich Kiruna-Gällivare fields and the bulk of Sweden's industrial exports. The Allies, on the other hand, had pressed the Norwegian merchant fleet into their service, at a cost of almost 50 percent of its vessels lost to German U-boats. In the latter stages of the Great War, they had also forced the Norwegians to agree to mine their territorial waters off Karmøy in order to complete the British North Sea minefield.[6] Consequently, at the outbreak of the Second World War, all the Scandinavian nations immediately declared, in the words of Halvdan Koht, the Norwegian foreign minister, their wish to maintain *"stricte neutralité."*[7]

Yet in mid-December, only two and a half months into the Second World War, Hitler began the planning process that would engulf Norway in the greatest conflict the world has ever known. In the following pages, in order to make sense of this apparently inexplicable change in Hitler's strategic thinking regarding Norway, I will chart the development of Norwegian entanglement in German military planning up until December 1939, when he made the fateful decision to establish a planning group to investigate occupying this Nordic nation. The purpose of this chapter is not simply to provide a narrative description of the early planning process but rather to weigh the relative influence of the three main components involved in the decision to invade Norway: geostrategy, economics, and National Socialist racial ideology. With this in mind, the importance of major actors (especially Erich Raeder, Alfred Rosenberg, and Vidkun Quisling) and significant events (particularly the relevance of German naval experience in the First World War, the German-Soviet pacts, and the outbreak of the Soviet-Finnish Winter War) will all be examined in attempting to explain Hitler's change of heart and what he hoped to achieve by a Norwegian operation.

THE SPIRIT OF THE ATLANTIC

During the euphoria of late September 1939, Hitler established his headquarters at the spacious Kasino Hotel in the town of Zoppot, overlooking Danzig's Baltic coastline. Irrepressible in victory, Hitler on 23 September met *Großadmiral* Erich Raeder, the most influential individual in the planning process that eventually led to the decision to invade Denmark and Norway.[8] It was during this meeting with Hitler and *Generaloberst* Wilhelm Keitel, chief of the High Command of the Wehrmacht, that Raeder "broached the question of the measures to be adopted *in case* the war against France and Britain should have to be fought out to the finish."[9] Although Hitler clearly still hoped to "drive a wedge" between France and Britain, he discussed the possibility of a "siege of Britain" carried out by the navy and the Luftwaffe. In the following days, Hitler's intention to strike westward began to take form, and on 2 October, at Keitel's behest, Raeder discussed with his Naval Staff alternative strategies for future German operations.[10] Raeder considered that the best of these options lay with the "siege of Britain" by submarine and air warfare. A siege, however, presented the Germans with substantial difficulties. Apart from the small number of oceangoing U-boats available, the Führer had to be made aware of the need to extend the navy's area of operational bases to the north and in particular, Raeder added, of the "possibility of gaining bases in Norway with the object of fundamentally improving our strategic and operational position."[11] This last concern was not a new idea from a navy merely under the capricious and expansionist influence of Nazi leadership; it represented the culmination of German naval experience in the First World War and subsequent interwar planning.

Kaiser Wilhelm II had actually shown interest in annexing portions of Norway in the crisis preceding the 1905 breakup of the Dual Monarchy that had united Norway and Sweden for nearly a century. However, it was not, as the naval historian Carl-Axel Gemzell has pointed out, until the First World War and its aftermath that German military planners seriously began to consider the strategic importance of Norway.[12] This development originated principally from the German naval theorist Wolfgang Wegener, who systematically attacked what he considered a shortsighted German maritime strategy and incorporated the idea of

German bases in Norway as a fundamental prerequisite for success in a future conflict with Britain.

Wegener's ideas first found expression while he was serving as an *Admiralstab* officer with the First Battle Squadron. In a trilogy of private, but widely circulated, memorandums drafted in 1915, and perhaps inspired by the recent Dogger Bank debacle, in which the heavy cruiser *Blücher* was lost, he pointed out the folly of the current policy of waiting for a decisive battle in the North Sea when the British already controlled the trade routes and were therefore only likely to seek "battle in the open sea with superiority, far from our coasts, without any risk."[13] Additionally, wrote Wegener, Britain was able to block German naval activity and trade "merely by its geographical position." Wegener's solution was to expand Germany's operational base so that it would be able to use its fleet in the struggle for control of the seas. In addition to occupation of the Skagerrak, Germany would be able to achieve "the world power position of a German fleet" *(die Weltmachtstellung einer deutschen Flotte)* by the acquisition of bases on the Danish Faroe Islands and on the French Atlantic coast from which to outflank the British completely. To dominate the Atlantic's South American sea routes, Wegener suggested the Portuguese Atlantic Islands, the Azores, and Cape Verdes.[14] In hindsight this may seem rather grandiose, but in 1915, when a German victory was still in the cards, he envisaged these possibilities being achieved by way of a settlement plan at the successful cessation of hostilities. However, before that happy day, Wegener concluded that Germany must be ready to seize any passing opportunities "because nobody knows today what political surprises this war might still have in store, nobody can already know today what attitude the Nordic countries will take if the English ravishing at sea further presses them. Nobody can say for certain that our fleet will not anchor in the Nordic fjords as protector for instance of Norway."[15]

As the First World War drew to its close in November 1918, however, it became clear that the German surface fleet had been powerless. In the only major naval battle of the entire war, the Battle of Jutland, Germany won a tactical victory when it sank fourteen British vessels totaling 111,000 tons for a loss of only eleven ships totaling 62,000 tons. Yet strategically Germany was the loser because Jutland showed not only that the British could win a battle of attrition but also, as Wegener had pointed out, that Britain had neutralized the Imperial Fleet merely by its geographic position. Despite rattling its cage in the Battle of Jutland, the High Seas Fleet remained imprisoned by a superior force and by its poor strategic position vis-à-vis the British Isles.

Wegener's work reached a much wider audience in 1929 with the publication of his maritime classic, *Die Seestrategie des Weltkrieges (The Sea Strategy of the World War)*. Going beyond simply pouring scorn on what he called Germany's "coastal navy" *(Küstenmarine)* defending the "dead angle of the dead sea"—that is, German North Sea ports under British blockade—Wegener, now a *Vizeadmiral,* elaborated on the extension of the fleet's operational base.[16] From strategically important bases, German naval forces could range against British merchant traffic while defending their own routes in the Atlantic. His suggestions closely parallel those made in his 1915 memorandums but with a new heightened emphasis on Norway. In 1915, Norway had been included almost as an afterthought, but by 1929 it featured prominently in Wegener's thinking.

In Wegener's eyes, during the First World War the North Sea had been little more than a northern European "Caspian Sea," in which the battle of two navies would be "totally immaterial" to the outcome of the war because not a "single ship in the world's sea lanes will thereby be forced off its course." This stifling strategic position could have been broken after the failure of the Battle of the Marne. Instead of accepting the resultant stagnation on the western front, Germany should have swung the initiative northward to Denmark and Norway. Reflecting on this possibility, and foreshadowing events that would take place in 1942, Wegener asked:

> What might have been the repercussions for the land war against Russia had we been able, operating from Norway, to interdict the stream of transports and supplies that passed over from the Scandinavian peninsula and through the Arctic Ocean? Much less our influence on overseas trade! Would the neutrals have surrendered so unconditionally to England's orders and placed at her disposal all their available shipping?[17]

Positions in Norway would, moreover, prevent the British from maintaining their Shetlands-Norway blockade line and force them to "withdraw roughly to the line Shetlands-Faroes-Iceland." This situation would have made it extremely difficult for the British to maintain a blockade when considerably outflanked to the north.[18] Nevertheless, Wegener noted that Norway itself would not give the Germans a "conquering" geographic position, but it was essential as a jumping-off point to the Shetlands. Along with the Faroes and Iceland, it was here, not Norway, that Germany would take mastery of the North Sea's northern gate to the Atlantic—a point that would be overlooked in the eventual planning for the invasion of Norway in early 1940 and which became of considerable importance after the British occupation of Iceland in the same year.

Wegener's work was widely read in naval circles, and its themes became the center of much lively debate.[19] His ideas were often incorporated in officers' training papers at the Marine Academy (Marineakademie), and the relative merits of his thesis were discussed in numerous articles in naval journals and magazines. Additionally, naval war games held during the 1920s and 1930s consistently indicated that if Germany were to have any influence beyond its short 240-kilometer North Sea coastline, it needed to expand its operational bases; and consensus more often than not lay with Norway. Despite Raeder's long-standing personal dislike of Wegener, the commander in chief of the navy was also caught up in the stream of expansionist and offensive ideas, including the acquisition of bases, that characterized this period.[20]

In speeches given in 1935 and 1937, Raeder acknowledged Germany's "unfavorable position" and demanded a strategy infused with Wegener's "spirit of the Atlantic" *(Geist des Atlantiks).*[21] For example, in his February 1937 oration "Basic Thoughts of Naval Leadership," presented to a gathering headed by the Führer and including such Nazi illuminaries as Hitler's deputy führer, Rudolf Hess, and master of propaganda, Joseph Goebbels, Raeder's thoughts closely followed those of Wegener.[22] In typical Wegenerian rhetoric, Raeder pronounced that in any future war "the operational use of the fleet is determined by bases." It was this very argument, resting on wartime experience and afterward developed by Wegener and others, that Raeder once again presented to Hitler only a month into the new war. On 10 October 1939, when Raeder had an audience with Hitler, he pressed forcefully for the immediate and ruthless implementation of the "siege of Britain" in order to shorten the duration of the war.[23] To pursue this objective successfully, Raeder pointed out the importance of obtaining bases on the Norwegian coast to aid submarine warfare and suggested the central Norwegian port of Trondheim.[24] Hitler offhandedly replied that he would consider the matter.

Clearly, at this point the German leader was not committed to an occupation of Norway, and evidently he still hoped to preserve the Nordic states' neutrality, despite a groundswell of support from the navy for improving its strategic position. What would change his mind? The answer lies within a statement Hitler made regarding the Scandinavian nations the day before his meeting with Raeder. "Their neutrality, provided no unforeseen circumstances arise, may be assumed for the future," he declared in this secret memorandum of 9 October 1939; moreover, "the continuation of German trade with these countries appears possible, even if the war is of long duration."[25] Although these words held out the promise of continued Norwegian neutrality, within them lay the barbs that would ultimately hook Norway into the conflict. As the Führer had not unreasonably noted, neutrality was conditional on the absence of "unforeseen circumstances" and was tied to Germany's continued trade with the region. On the one hand, this prospect seemed possible at first, as western Europe drifted aimlessly on the beguilingly calm waters of the sitzkrieg; on the other hand, gnawing at German confidence was the threat to its vital Swedish iron ore supplies. As early as 2 November 1934, the Führer, in a conversation with Hermann Göring, Prussian minister of the interior and Reich commissar for aviation, considered "a buildup of the navy . . . absolutely vital, because it would not be possible to wage war at all if the navy was unable to protect the ore shipments from Scandinavia."[26] Before detailing the "unforseen circumstances" that could affect the supply of this material and the relevance of Norway to this dilemma, it is necessary to outline Germany's position with regard to this important raw material and the German assessment of threats to it.

SWEDISH IRON ORE

Since the National Socialists came to power in 1933, Hitler had attempted to progress along a path of rearmament and autarky because he believed that the prerequisites for a successful future war were a prepared military machine and a Reich self-sufficient in strategically important raw materials. By 1936, however, the Führer had grown impatient with the slow progress toward these dual aims and, in order to hasten Germany's preparedness, he composed one of the Reich's defining documents. Dictated in August at Obersalzberg, the typically rambling memorandum cast Germany in an apocalyptic struggle against Bolshevism and worldwide Jewry—a struggle it dare not lose, considering the result would lead not merely to another Versailles but to "the final destruction, indeed to the anni- hilation of the German people."[27] Reflecting on Germany's eternal burden, Hitler stressed the importance of the ruthless subordination of the needs of the individual to the interests of the state. There could be "only one interest and that is the inter- est of the nation, and only one single view, which is that Germany must be brought politically and economically into a state of self-sufficiency." At the forefront of his mind were oil, rubber, and iron ore supplies.[28] In his opinion, "nearly four precious years" had been allowed to slip by, and Germany was still completely dependent on foreign countries for these war-winning materials. "Just as we have stepped up the production of iron ore from two and a half million tons to seven million tons," Hitler intoned, "so we could be processing twenty or twenty-five million tons of German iron ore, and if necessary even 30 million." He elaborated on the iron ore problem at length:

> It is further necessary to increase the German production of iron to the ut- most. The objection that we are not in a position to produce from the German iron ore, with a 20 percent content, as cheap a pig iron as from the 45 percent Swedish ores, etc., is irrelevant because we are not in fact faced with the question of what we would *rather* do but only of what we *can* do. . . . In any case, for a thousand years Germany had no foreign iron ores. Even before the [Great] War, more German iron ores were being processed than during the period of our worst decline. *Nevertheless, if we still have the possibility of importing cheap ores, well and good. But the future of the national economy and, above all, of the conduct of war, must not be dependent on this.*

Concluding with a magisterial flourish, he pronounced that the German army "be operational within four years" and that the German economy must also "be fit for war within four years."[29]

Hitler had rightly singled out mineral resources as a weak link in the German economy.[30] Although Germany possessed large reserves of coal, it was lacking in nearly every other important raw material necessary for a modern armaments in- dustry, including chrome, nickel, tungsten, molybdenum, manganese, zinc, lead, copper, and tin. Moreover, as a result of the loss of the rich Lorraine iron fields to the French at Versailles, German iron ore production had remained below pre–Great War levels well into the 1920s.[31] Additionally, despite having significant reserves in the Hannover region, Germany was hampered by the fact that its domestic ores had a relatively low iron content, averaging only 30 percent. This combination meant that Germany could meet only a paltry 20 percent of its burgeoning steel consumption. Therefore, by far the larger part of Germany's iron ore requirements—80 percent—was imported, and, as economic historian Martin Fritz states, of the major nations only Japan and Italy were less self-sufficient than Germany.[32] This overreliance on imported ores not only strained Germany's balance of payments but also made its steel industry—one of the world's largest producers of crude steel—vulnerable in the event of war, and therefore a real concern to Nazi planners in the 1930s.[33]

The Four-Year Plan attempted to increase Germany's self-sufficiency in iron ore through the opening of new mines and an increase in the output of old fields. Indeed, these measures were spectacularly successful, as domestic output climbed from 7.5 to 14.7 million tons from 1936 to 1939. Production was further bolstered by the incorporation of Austria into Greater Germany in 1938. As a result of the Anschluß, 2.7 million tons of Austrian ore were added to Germany's total output in 1939 alone. Nevertheless, these remarkable increases did not significantly reduce dependency on imported ore. The reasons were twofold. First, at the same time as raw material production was stepped up, industrial demand was increasing to meet Hitler's other main requirement: rapid rearmament. Hence, any increase in domestic ore production was offset by escalating industrial output. For example, the consumption of iron ore in 1938 had increased to 38 million tons: that is, 10 million tons more than in 1936.[34] Second, although the total amount of domestic ore being produced appears impressive, it proved less so when the relatively poor iron content of German ore was taken into consideration. As already noted, the Four-Year Plan demanded the opening of new fields, but these often produced a markedly inferior grade of ore.[35] By way of illustration, although the new Salzgitter mine (located east of Hannover and one of the model mines under the Four-Year Plan's drive for autarky) increased its production by leaps and bounds, the iron content of its ore languished at around only 20 percent.[36] Overall, from the latter part of the 1920s until the end of the 1930s, the iron content in German ores fell from an uninspiring 32 percent to about 27 percent.[37] The lower quality and more costly iron ore produced by these mines had a detrimental impact on German steelworks, resulting in impaired productivity, which in turn led to lower profits and increased prices for steel. Therefore, despite Germany's iron ore production increasing nearly one and a half times from 1935 to 1939, foreign imports also increased sharply, if at a slightly lower rate.[38] In the four years from 1935 to 1938, German imports rose from 14 million tons to nearly 22 million tons; of this, the most significant portion was sourced from only one country: Sweden. In 1935, Sweden had accounted for 5.5 million tons of the iron ore imported by the Reich, and by 1938 this had grown to 9 million tons.[39]

Sweden was the most important source of iron ore for Germany not only because of the sheer volume of iron ore imported but also because its ore had a very high iron content.[40] The significance of Sweden's high-quality ore can be demonstrated by a comparison with the iron content of the ores produced by other importers. As noted, the iron content of Germany's own ore hovered around the 30 percent mark in the 1930s. Foreign ore, on the other hand, possessed an average iron content of up to 50 percent, although with considerable variation from country to country. The ores of France and Luxembourg had an iron content that ranged from 28 to 37 percent, while those of Spain averaged 50 percent. The Swedish ores were superior to all others, with an iron content of about 60 percent.[41] In the period 1936–1938, Sweden's contribution to imports of ore on the basis of quantity was already substantial, representing about 40 percent of Germany's total incoming iron ore; when the high iron ore content is included in the equation, this amount jumped to nearly 60 percent of Germany's imports.[42] Quantitatively and qualitatively, Swedish ores were of great strategic importance to the Third Reich's war economy (a fact not unnoticed by military planners), and as the 1930s drew to a close and the likelihood of war increased, German concerns were naturally heightened.

In the latter stages of the Four-Year Plan, it became increasingly obvious that autarky in iron ore was nowhere close to being attained. Ever conscious of the impending crisis, Wehrmacht planners looked anxiously at likely threats to their most important source of iron ore. "The maintenance of Swedish iron ore imports during a war," began a report of April 1939 by the economic staff of the Oberkommando der Wehrmacht (OKW), "is a fundamental demand of the Wehrmacht."[43] In the gray tones of bureaucratic vernacular, the report calculated that in spite of increasing domestic production, Germany faced a shortfall of 9.2 million tons of high-quality iron ore (that is, ore with an iron content of 60 percent). In peacetime this was not particularly daunting because any deficiency could be made good by imports. In the event of war, however, OKW's economic staff pointed out that Germany would probably lose its imports from Spain and France and their respective colonies, and from Luxembourg, resulting in an import shortfall of 11.6 million tons.[44]

A realistic appraisal of Sweden's ability to make up this difference was not encouraging. The assessment took into account the likely loss of the northern Norwegian port of Narvik as a conduit point during hostilities and the limited ability of the Swedish rail network to transport the ore that would normally pass through Narvik to other Swedish ports. Therefore, in addition to 3 million tons from central and southern Sweden, the Germans could expect only 2.5 million tons from the northern Swedish port of Luleå, giving a total of 5.5 to 6 million tons. To this equation, the Wehrmacht added the estimated mobilization requirements of 14 million tons for the beginning of 1939 and 9 million tons for 1940. The result was an expected import shortfall in time of war of 8.5 million tons in early 1939 and 3.2 million tons in 1940. Although the latter figure was admittedly an improvement, the Wehrmacht stressed that "even a shortfall of 3.2 million tons of ore was not bearable for the German war economy during a war lasting more than half a year."[45]

This report echoed another of 22 December 1938, which concluded that unless a two- to three-year stocking-up period could be achieved, "the iron ore problem can only be brought about by military intervention during a war."[46] Both reports recognized that, because the 5.5 to 6 million tons of iron ore from northern and central Sweden remained the "sole possibility for supplementing Germany's iron ore in a time of war," it was vitally important that they be protected at all costs.

Initially, many planners saw the Soviet Union as a potential threat to Germany's supplies from Sweden. For example, on 14 January 1939, a concerned War Economy Office (Wehrwirtschaftsstab) requested an assessment of the threat posed by a buildup on the Soviet Union's Arctic Kola Peninsula to "German iron ore imports from Sweden."[47] The reply prepared by the Luftwaffe on 25 January soberly confirmed that the Soviet Union had indeed made great efforts to build up its fleet and air bases on the peninsula.[48] Moreover, the Luftwaffe saw not only deep incursions by Soviet aircraft as a threat but also that the deployment of relatively small numbers of paratroops and airborne forces could bring "about a complete disruption to iron ore exports for a considerable duration." By way of illustration, the capture of the Åland Islands, which form a natural gate to the Gulf of Bothnia between Sweden and Finland, would effectively sever Swedish iron supplies via the Baltic. Also, the insertion of Soviet airborne forces against the main northern Swedish power station at Porjus would bring iron ore production to a grinding halt, especially if carried out in the long winter months of perpetual darkness.[49] A minor, but nonetheless significant, threat in the eyes of Luftwaffe analysts was the possibility of Soviet airborne operations against the rail line linking the northern Swedish iron ore mines with Narvik. Admittedly, the mountainous terrain—particularly in the western part of the region—would make it difficult for the Red Army to extract its forces once operations had been concluded, but the fact that the region was sparsely populated and that the line was the linchpin of ore transportation in the north made it a prime target. In August 1939 the concerns of the War Economy Office and the Luftwaffe were laid to rest, at least for the next two years, by the signing of the German-Soviet nonaggression pact. Ironically, this same pact, which eased German insecurity in eastern Europe, brought about a fresh threat to Swedish ore supplies, this time from Britain and France in the West. Their target was Narvik.

THE GERMAN-SOVIET NONAGGRESSION PACT AND NARVIK

Although vehemently opposed to each other, ideologically, Hitler and Stalin found common ground in their mutual deep-rooted hatred of the Versailles settlement, in particular, the establishment of an independent Poland at the end of the Great

War. The nonaggression pact of 23 August 1939 established a framework for the dismemberment of the Polish state and, as laid out in supplementary secret protocols, gave both parties free rein in their own spheres of influence without fear of intervention from the other party.[50] The rough dividing line separating the two signatories followed the Polish Narev, Vistula, and San Rivers. Consequently, the eastern portion of Poland and the Baltic States, excluding Lithuania but including Finland, fell within the Soviet sphere.

This agreement and the subsequent German-Soviet Treaty of Friendship, Cooperation and Demarcation of 28 September 1939 not only tidied up the eastern region but also threw Finland to the wolves.[51] The Finns remained in the Soviet sphere, while Germany secured a sizable slice of Poland between the Vistula and Bug Rivers in exchange for Lithuania. Doubtless, Germany potentially could lose some of the valuable commodities it imported from Finland, but these would be more than compensated for by the raw materials that would flow into Germany from the Soviet Union under the economic provisions of the protocols.[52] More important, bolting the Reich's back door allowed Hitler to concentrate his attentions westward.

Indirectly, the agreements reached between the two parties also facilitated negotiations for a naval base on the Soviet Union's Arctic coast near Murmansk. Barely a month had passed since the signing of the first agreement when Raeder informed the Führer that the navy would like the use of Soviet bases, especially at Murmansk. The outcome of talks between the Germans and Soviets resulted in the offer of a base in Zapadnaya Litsa Bay on the Murman Coast in mid-October 1939, which was subsequently code-named *Basis Nord* (Base North).[53] Located near Murmansk, the base appeared well situated for the navy's long-term goal of outflanking Britain, and unlike at the other Soviet bases, Germany could do "whatever it wished" there, including servicing pocket battleships, submarines, and supply vessels. However, many of the concerns expressed by naval staff at the time regarding the suitability of the base, such as its isolation and lack of adequate communication and logistical support, were borne out during the following year. In addition to the extreme difficulty experienced in maintaining adequate radio contact with Germany, materials and supplies had to be brought in almost exclusively by sea because the base had no rail access.[54] Moreover, the lack of adequate repair facilities hindered its operational usefulness as a base for naval surface vessels and U-boats in the war against British shipping. Although a failure in terms of its workability, *Basis Nord* did show the German navy's continued insistence on improving its strategic options, and if this base proved unsuitable, all the more reason to look toward Norway for bases that would meet its needs. Likewise, the securing of a Soviet base illustrated the ability of the Germans and Soviets to work together in accordance with the secret protocols and to labor toward the implementation of their cozy agreement—the division of Europe.

Yet what neither Hitler nor his Bolshevik partner in crime was able to foresee was Finland's intransigence in the face of Soviet coercion and German desertion. Although by 10 October all three Baltic states had been enveloped into a Soviet "security zone" in accordance with the secret protocols, Finland's membership was by no means a fait accompli. In fact, Finland's failure to give in to Stalin's territorial demands ultimately led to a Soviet invasion along the Finnish-Soviet border on the last day of November 1939. Remarkably, the small Nordic nation, although militarily outnumbered by three to one, thwarted the Red Army at every turn by taking advantage of the thick snow that blanketed the deep tree-clad gullies and frozen lakes making up most of the border region. Highly mobile and resourceful Finnish forces brought the Red Army, demoralized by Stalin's purges of senior officers, to an icy halt in nearly all sectors of the front.

The outbreak of war in the Far North had repercussions for Norway because of the threat of an Anglo-French landing via Narvik. As already noted, prior to the signing of the nonaggression pact with Stalin, Germany's concern regarding its supply of Swedish iron ore had centered on the Baltic shipping routes. Once these were secured, the focus of German concern shifted to Narvik. In December 1939, in the lengthy report "The Iron Ore Supply of Greater Germany during the Present War Entanglement," the Institute for World Economics (Institut für Weltwirtschaft) drew attention to the significance of Narvik. The report suggested that securing the sea route between Narvik and German harbors was an important prerequisite for ensuring "trouble-free" ore imports to Germany because the predominant share of Germany's Swedish iron ore supplies came via Narvik.[55] Neither Gävle nor Oxelösund, on Sweden's central and southern coast, had the "favorable handling facilities" of Narvik; on the other hand, the northern port of Luleå was frozen during the winter months between December and April. Consequently, Narvik, on Norway's ice-free northwestern Atlantic coast, handled about 50 percent of Germany's ore imports, which reached the Reich's home ports via the Norwegian Leads despite the proximity of Britain and the supremacy of the Royal Navy.[56] This narrow stretch of water allowed German freighters to snake their way between the Norwegian coast and Norway's numerous outlying islands all the way from Narvik to the safety of the Skagerrak without leaving Norwegian territorial waters. Yet the tenuous nature of the link between Narvik and German ports was laid bare in the fallout from the Soviet-Finnish War because the significance of controlling northern Norway, and thus the bulk of Germany's Swedish iron ore imports, was not lost on Allied planners—especially Winston Churchill, First Lord of the Admiralty.

NORWAY IN ALLIED CONSIDERATIONS

In the first few weeks of the Second World War, Churchill put a proposal before the British cabinet that called for the laying of mines in Norwegian territorial waters.[57] This action—repeatedly promoted by the First Lord and eventually carried out on the eve of the German invasion in 1940—would force ore-laden German freighters into international waters to risk capture or sinking by the Royal Navy. Severing the main iron ore artery leading to the Reich's industrial heart would, he believed, have a paralyzing effect on Germany's military capabilities, especially if carried out in winter when ice closed the Gulf of Bothnia to shipping. "Nothing would be more deadly . . . to the German war-making capacity, and to the life of the country," enthused Churchill late in November 1939, than to stop ore exports to Germany "for three or even six months."[58] In short, controlling the Leads would place Britain's foot on the throat of the German ore supplies. Aggressive action of this nature, though, had to be weighed against the loss of respect Britain could incur—especially from the United States—by breaching Norwegian neutrality. As Lord Halifax, Britain's foreign secretary, wondered, might not the advantages of stopping the flow of iron ore to Germany via Narvik be offset by distancing Britain and France from their potential war-winning partner?[59] However, the outbreak of the Soviet-Finnish War on 30 November pushed these concerns aside because, in the interests of aiding a small, neutral nation, the British and French could justify sending a force to Narvik and then on by rail to secure the Gällivare ore fields. "Thus, and with a little luck," as the British historian David Dilks put it, "a small nation could be defended, morale uplifted, neutrals emboldened, and the stalemate broken and Germany thwarted."[60]

Needless to say, though, if Britain had its raison d'être for action in Norway, so did Germany. Securing Norway not only would protect Germany's shipments but also would stop the considerable amount of vital raw materials and foodstuffs Britain received from the Baltic region via Norway. Notwithstanding the fact that this latter point barely receives a mention in the vast majority of analyses of the Norwegian campaign, German naval staff in this period were acutely conscious of its implications for their "siege of Britain."

In late October—at the same time as British intelligence was evaluating the significance of German imports of Swedish iron ore—the German naval attaché in Stockholm reported that twelve British iron ore steamers had left Narvik, no doubt bound for British ports. Even though Britain was not as heavily dependent for its survival on the products of the Scandinavian and Baltic nations as Germany, the movement of goods from this region to the British Isles was a significant factor in the war against British and French merchant traffic. In this period, the German navy was receiving a "large number of reports" which revealed that goods from Finland, Estonia, Latvia, and Lithuania were being shipped to Sweden, and from there transported by rail to the Norwegian port of Bergen or Sweden's southern port of Göteborg for "transshipment to Britain."[61] "Exports from the Baltic States to Sweden and Norway," continued a 13 October entry in the naval war diary, "have definitely increased absolutely out of all proportion to peacetime traffic." That these goods were destined for Britain was confirmed by the German legation in Stockholm, the navy's own attaché, and even the Swedish press, which, for example, reported that the exchange of goods between Sweden and Latvia had reached "a volume never hitherto expected." The goods transported via this route ranged from food products (such as Latvian butter and bacon) to raw materials, such as Swedish and Norwegian ores and Finnish pitprops, which the Germans believed were vital to the British coal mining industry. These props were carried overland from northern Finland to Narvik for shipment to Britain.[62] In mid-November, in an attempt to plug this gap, the German navy sent its remaining U-boats—a mere handful—to operate against the "northern trade routes from Murmansk and Narvik."[63] Nevertheless, this northern supply conduit to Britain was particularly difficult to sever because the British, like the Germans, made full use of the lengthy Norwegian Leads.[64]

Fully aware of this dilemma, *Großadmiral* Raeder once again brought Norway to the Führer's attention on 8 December 1939. In his discussion of economic warfare Raeder reiterated the significance of Norway: "Transport via Sweden and Norway over Trondheim to England is extremely active. Points of departure from the Norwegian coast are very numerous and therefore difficult to control. It is very important to occupy Norway."[65] While Hitler had let matters drift during October and November, hoping that Norwegian neutrality could be maintained, events were pushing the two themes discussed so far—geostrategic and economic—into one great confluence. As noted, initially the navy had seen the acquisition of bases in Norway in terms of improving the "strategic and operational position" of Germany vis-à-vis Britain. Now, in addition to this, the navy and elements of the Wehrmacht considered that military operations in Norway were essential to maintaining Germany's vital iron ore supplies and blockading the British Isles from Scandinavian and Baltic sources of raw materials. Moreover, they feared that these possibilities would be frustrated should the British and French occupy Norwegian bases under the guise of aiding Finland. Clearly, as Raeder had discussed with Admiral Rolf Carls, naval commander Baltic, in early October—even before the outbreak of the Soviet-Finnish War—Germany needed to look at the "possibility of forestalling such an action."[66] All that was required to do this was to persuade Hitler, who had been relatively ambivalent until early December, to agree to Raeder's urgings for operations on Germany's Nordic flank. Not only did the outbreak of the Soviet-Finnish War on 30 November and the threat this posed to German interests in the north bring about a sense of urgency, but in the second week of December Raeder was introduced by Alfred Rosenberg to an unlikely ally who aroused the Führer's interest: Vidkun Quisling.

NORDIC BLOOD

Quisling was the leader of the Norwegian Nasjonal Samling (National Union Party)—a pale imitation of the German Nazi Party. Despite being a small and electorally insignificant participant in Norwegian politics, Quisling was the protégé of *Reichsleiter* Alfred Rosenberg, the Nazis' so-called philosopher and head of the Außenpolitisches Amt der NSDAP (Foreign Policy Office of the Nazi Party;

as distinct from the traditional Foreign Office of the German state: the Auswärtiges Amt).[67] Rosenberg, who had been born in Reval (now Tallin), Estonia, of Baltic Germanic parentage, had fled Moscow for Munich during the Russian Revolution in 1917. For Rosenberg, who saw history primarily along racial lines, Scandinavia was an integral part of Germany's Nordic bulwark against the Slavic and Asiatic peoples of the East. In one of the more popular attempts to systematically synthesize the divergent themes of National Socialism—Rosenberg's best-seller, *Der Mythus der 20 Jahrhunderts (The Myth of the Twentieth Century)*—the Nazi ideologue saw two alternatives for Europe: either a racially impoverished "Franco-Jewish pan-Europe" or one in which Germany, bolstered by a second league made up of the "Scandinavian states and Finland," would be "the central power of the continent." These nations would "secure the northeast," while Britain safeguarded the west and overseas in the places where it was required to do so in the interests of "Nordic man."[68] There will be "a German-Scandinavian block whose aim will be . . . the prevention of the formation of a Mongolian threat in the East."[69]

The Außenpolitisches Amt, established in April 1933 by the Führer, was designed to focus on groups inclining toward National Socialism in states bordering the Soviet Union in order to create an isolating ring *(Isolierungsring)* around Germany's Bolshevik enemy.[70] Of these nations, the Scandinavians were in the first rank. However, because of the strong pro–Anglo Saxon bias that had existed in Scandinavia since the end of the First World War, Rosenberg set his Außenpolitisches Amt the task of wooing these nations through closer cultural relations.[71] To this end, the Außenpolitisches Amt absorbed and continued the work of the fledgling Nordische Gesellschaft (Nordic Society), founded in 1921 by a German businessman in Lübeck, to rekindle Germany's cultural ties with its Nordic neighbors.[72] The means by which Rosenberg tried to achieve this, and his success or otherwise, can be gauged from the Außenpolitisches Amt's most visible cultural event: the yearly conferences of the Nordische Gesellschaft held in picturesque Lübeck, on the Baltic coast.

For example, in the summer of 1935, the program for the "Second Convention of the Nordische Gesellschaft" (from 23 to 30 June) began on Monday with "youth and sport" activities, which included gymnastic groups from Denmark and Sweden; this was followed on Tuesday by Thilo von Trotha—Rosenberg's most able assistant—who addressed the subject of "tradition and art"; Wednesday saw not only Rosenberg himself talking on the subject of the "rebirth of the Nordic concept" *(Die Wiedergeburt des nordischen Gedankens)* but also the beginning of the three-day *Nordisches Musikfest,* which included a suitably Nordic-Germanic mix of works by Brahms, Sibelius, Beethoven, and Nielsen.[73]

That this cultural extravaganza in Lübeck was not all that it appeared to be was only too readily appreciated by many Scandinavians. One of Oslo's newspapers, *Dagbladet,* gives a glimpse of how at least some Norwegians perceived the activities in sunny Lübeck.[74] While the conference's Thursday itinerary called for an innocuous introductory concert by young Nordic artists, followed by Nordic folk dancing, that day's edition of the *Dagbladet* drew a more sinister picture by pointing out that this "propaganda institute" was headed by none other than Hinrich Lohse, the leader of the Nazi SA in Kiel. Of course, this confirmed the belief held by some that the Nordische Gesellschaft in Lübeck was nothing more than a "National Socialist propaganda undertaking," which served as the connecting link between National Socialists in Germany and those in the north, and as a "subtly disguised propaganda institute for fascist ideas." The writer informed the reader that the keynote speaker at the conference, Alfred Rosenberg, the worldview dictator *(Weltanschauungsdiktator),* was perhaps the most radical champion of German expansion in the East and, to this end, ardently worked to achieve a "Nordic-German alliance." That this is not an atypical assessment of the Nordische Gesellschaft is supported by the fact that of the 750 to 800 people who the conference attended in 1935, only 96 were from Scandinavia.[75] Moreover, at the previous year's conference all the Nordic nations snubbed the event by not sending official representatives, much to the chagrin of Rosenberg.[76] The Außenpolitisches Amt, though, was not the only Nazi agency actively seeking to infiltrate Scandinavian society.

As Rosenberg's star began to descend and effectiveness of the Nordische Gesellschaft declined in the wake of Trotha's death in 1936, the Außenpolitisches Amt had to contend with other ideologically driven organizations muscling into Nordic affairs. These included the Nordische Verbindungsstelle (Nordic Liaison Office) of Goebbels's Propaganda Ministry and the Auslandsorganisation der NSDAP (Organization for Germans Abroad).[77] Added to this clutch of competing Nazi agencies was Heinrich Himmler, the *Reichsführer SS,* who in early 1938 declared to a group of his high-ranking officers his intention to man the *SS-Standarte Germania* (the "Germania" element of the SS police forces) solely with "non-German Germanic people."[78] Furthermore, once these Nordics had completed their service and returned to their home nations—spreading the ideology of National Socialism—Himmler believed they would provide the material for the "Führer to create a greater Germanic Imperium, a pan-Germanic Reich, the largest Reich that ever has been established by mankind and the largest the globe has ever seen."[79] Yet, despite the rhetoric and the obvious effort devoted to infiltrating and influencing Scandinavian nations throughout the 1930s, these competing bodies were unable to make any significant inroads into bringing their Nordic neighbors politically closer to Germany. Only in the last frantic year of the decade did it appear that some success might be achieved in Norway.

Despite the jostling between these contending groups, it was Rosenberg's Außenpolitisches Amt that could claim to have bagged the Norwegian prize. Although Rosenberg had to admit that he had failed to have any substantial success in Denmark and Sweden, he boasted of an association within Norway that could be based on "Greater Germany ideology."[80] The Nazi ideologue and Quisling shared many fundamental beliefs. Quisling, like Rosenberg, had had firsthand experience of Russia, having been an eyewitness to the Russian Revolution and an aid worker there with the League of Nations, and had developed a strong racial explanation for the rise of Bolshevism. Like his German counterpart, who held that "originally Russia was the creation of Vikings," Quisling reminisced that he had often seen "really fine types in Russian villages—men who remind one of the best type of peasant in the Norwegian highlands, and sometimes have a Viking air about them."[81] However, both men concurred that an adulteration of this Nordic stock in Russia by an Asiatic-Slav movement led by Jews had taken place. Quisling believed that "the sharpest antagonism in the world today, especially, perhaps, in my own country of Norway and in Germany, amount in the last resort to a duel between the Nordic-European principle and the Asiatic-Oriental principle, ie Bolshevism."[82] "When, however, the truth comes to be realised that Bolshevism is a conspiracy against Western civilisation of the Nordic type," Quisling proclaimed, drawing the threads of his argument together, "the remedy . . . will be found in a closer cultural, economic and political co-operation between those peoples which are the main supporters of Western civilisation." He concluded that a "Northern Coalition" of these Nordic supporters, including the Scandinavian countries, Holland and Flanders, the British Empire, Germany, and the United States, would "render innocuous any Bolshevist combination."[83]

Given the ideological similarities between the two men as expressed in works published within a year of each other at the beginning of the 1930s, and the obvious aping of the German National Socialist party by Nasjonal Samling, one might assume that the Nazis would have actively courted Quisling's fascist party soon after the birth of the Third Reich. Nevertheless, nothing could be further from reality, for reasons that lie at least partially with the insignificance of Nasjonal Samling in the Norwegian parliamentary system. At its height of electoral support in the 1936 general election, the party secured a miserable 1.8 percent of the vote—insufficient to gain a single seat in the Parliament—and it was downhill thereafter.[84] Given the strong historical link between parliamentarianism and nationalism associated with the struggle for Norwegian independence, it is hardly surprising that Nasjonal Samling's fascist antiparliamentary platform did not have the same populist appeal that it did in other European countries.[85] In addition, the party was facing an uphill battle against the middle classes' general affinity with Britain rather than Germany. In short, Quisling's party did not represent a credible entity in Norway. Therefore, it is not surprising that Nasjonal Samling had to fight for any recognition from its disinterested big brother in Germany.

It is difficult to determine exactly when Rosenberg first became aware of Nasjonal Samling or came into contact with Quisling. Clearly, in the early 1930s he knew of Quisling because of the latter's tenure as Norway's minister of war (as a member of the Peasants Party), and it appears that at least by 1935 Rosenberg had heard of Nasjonal Samling. Nevertheless, although following the successful occupation of Norway in 1940 Rosenberg alluded to a lengthy association with this political fighting group "taken by the idea of a Greater-German Community," he notes that it was not until the winter of 1938–1939 that Nasjonal Samling was visited by a member of the Außenpolitisches Amt.[86] Hence it was only belatedly in 1939 when the European political situation—as Rosenberg euphemistically noted—"came to a head," and after Quisling made an appearance at the annual conference of the Nordische Gesellschaft in June that Nasjonal Samling had a look-in with Rosenberg. Using the connections of a Norwegian businessman living in Dresden, Quisling met with Rosenberg in the summer of 1939. At this meeting, he successfully secured funding for Nasjonal Samling from the Nazis. Quisling once again appeared in Berlin in December, by which time his importance was growing in German military circles as naval staff pushed for action in Norway to secure bases for the "siege of Britain" to preempt any Anglo-French attempt to cut off Germany's vital iron ore supply. Quisling met with Rosenberg and Raeder in the second week of December, and both the "philosopher" and the sailor were able to turn Quisling's visit to their own ends.

On 11 December, Raeder listened intently to Quisling's description of the situation in Norway and heard much to his liking. The following day he made his report to the Führer. In his summation to Hitler, the *Großadmiral* repeated the discussion of the previous day, including Quisling's claim that the Norwegian government, under the "influence of the well-known Jew [Carl] Hambro," had signed a secret agreement with Britain regarding a possible occupation of Norway. Consequently, there was a "very real danger that Norway may be occupied by the British, possibly soon." Quisling's alternative was a coup d'état supported by officers in the Norwegian army and coconspirators working at strategically important facilities, such as railways; if needed, Germany would provide the military assistance to complete the job. "It must be made impossible for Norway to fall into British hands," Raeder stressed, because "this could be decisive for the outcome of the war." Once Norway was lost, Sweden would fall prey to British influence, and if the war was extended into the Baltic, German hopes of playing a part in the war of the Atlantic would be gone. Having laid out this grim prospect, Hitler agreed that "the occupation of Norway by Britain was unacceptable"; he decided to speak with Quisling himself in order to take his own measure of the man.[87]

The would-be Norwegian dictator met with the German Führer twice during the following week.[88] It was in this crucial third week of December that Hitler took his first tentative steps toward invading Norway. Although at both meetings he repeatedly stressed that he preferred Norway—and in fact the whole of Scandinavia—to remain neutral because he did not wish to enlarge the theater of war, he was not prepared to sit idly by and allow the enemy to further "throttle" *(Abschnürung)* and threaten the Greater German Reich.[89] In the event that this should be the case, he would have no alternative but to "arm against such actions." Hitler promised to provide financial backing for Quisling's movement to combat the increasing pro-British propaganda of the enemy. More significantly, he commissioned a small staff to carry out an investigation on "how one might occupy Norway."[90]

It was at this point that Hitler moved, if somewhat falteringly, from strict adherence to the idea of Nordic neutrality to including Norway in his military considerations. To discover how much this decision centered on racial ideology and Nordic affinity—as opposed to the geostrategic and economic factors already detailed—it is useful to first appraise Hitler's worldview (Weltanschauung) with regard to the Nordic race and Scandinavia.

That Hitler was interested in the iron ore mines of Sweden is in little doubt. However, a more accurate picture of his thinking on matters "Nordic" can be gleaned from *Mein Kampf* and, more important, Hitler's so-called *Zweites Buch (Second Book)*. In his first work Hitler had comparatively little to say on future foreign affairs and even less to say on Germany's relationship with its Scandinavian neighbors because in the mid-1920s, when he was still far from the corridors of power, his ideas on the subject were in embryonic form. Nevertheless, he certainly believed that nature did not want "a higher race to intermingle with a lower one" because history shows "with startling clarity, that wherever Aryans have mingled their blood with that of a lower race the result has been the end of the people who were the standard-bearers of a higher culture."[91] Germany should avoid at all cost the corruption of its German racial stock by a Jewish adulteration of its blood and take note of how, through immigration, French blood was becoming "progressively negroid."[92] Hitler lamented that, should the German spirit ever be forced to make its contribution to civilization through individuals under foreign rule, it would do so until, finally, the "last residue of Aryan-Nordic blood would become polluted or obliterated."[93] This rather isolated reference to Nordic blood was developed more fully in his *Zweites Buch,* written in the spring and summer of 1928 but not published until 1961.[94]

In a similar vein to Rosenberg and Quisling, Hitler claimed that since the time of Peter the Great it was the "many Germans (Balts!) who formed the skeleton and brains of the Russian state."[95] Nevertheless, as the Nordic blood element waned and the Slavic waxed ever stronger in Russia, their lack of commonality became evident. For example: "If as a test of the two spiritual natures we were to take a purely Nordic German, from, let us say, Westphalia, and place a purely Slavic Russian opposite him, between these two representative peoples an infinite gulf would open."[96] Now, however, the purity of German blood itself was under threat. "The German people," Hitler bemoaned, "will slowly descend to the level of an equally inferior race and hence to that of an incompetent and worthless people" because of the "bastardization systematically carried out by the Jews" and because it "also lets its best blood bearers be taken away by a continuation of emigration."[97] Germany could learn from the United States, which through its vices had brought about the slow elimination of its most racially valuable element, the "Nordic blood bearers," which he later described as being made up of the "Scandinavians, that is, Swedes, Norwegians, further Danes, then Englishmen, and finally Germans."[98] Additionally, permanent emigration from Germany often took away the "boldest and most resolute," and "these above all, like the Vikings of the past, will also today be bearers of Nordic blood."[99]

It may well be that the obvious strong similarities evident in the Weltanschauungen of Hitler, Rosenberg, and Quisling with regard to "Nordic blood bearers" and the desire to "tie Norway's fate to that of Greater Germany as the new center of strength of a Nordic-Germanic . . . community" eased the way for the meetings with Hitler. Yet there is no evidence to suggest that this was the fundamental reason for beginning the planning process for the occupation of Norway.[100] All surviving documents surrounding the meetings of December, including those of the ideologically driven Außenpolitisches Amt, barely make reference to racial kinship as a motivating force or justifying reason for the Führer's decision. Rather, it was the complementary assessment of Quisling by the militarily minded Raeder and the emphasis the *Großadmiral* laid on strategic matters that led to Hitler's meeting with the Norwegian fascist. In fact, once these meetings were under way, it became clear that Hitler's decision to consider violating Norwegian neutrality was based on what, in early October 1939, he had called "unforeseen circumstances."

At the outbreak of the Second World War, Weizsäcker's memorandum to the German legations in Norway, Sweden, and Finland had stated that Germany would respect the Scandinavian nations' "integrity insofar as they maintain strict neutrality."[101] Yet, he had added, "we would naturally be compelled to safeguard our interests" should a breach of Norwegian and Swedish neutrality by third parties take place.[102] What made Hitler sit up and take notice in December 1939 was the possibility of just such a breach of Norwegian neutrality, namely, Anglo-French intervention in Norway under the guise of aiding Finland in the Soviet-Finnish Winter War.

The preceding analysis reveals that this threat posed to Germany's "interests"—in particular its iron ore interests—forced Hitler away from a relatively hands-off approach to Norway toward direct action that coincided with Raeder's naval demands, Rosenberg's ideological-political aims, and Quisling's self-serving political aggrandizement. Of these three, it was Raeder's arguments, bolstered by Quisling's own claims of imminent Anglo-French operations, that were the most compelling and corresponded most closely to Hitler's own thinking at the time—that is, geostrategic and economic rather than ideological. If Britain were able to establish itself in Norway, it not only would be able to sever ore shipments to Germany and bring pressure to bear on Sweden but also could extend its operations into the Baltic. On the other hand, if Germany were able to occupy Norway first, Hitler realized that he would kill not just two birds with one stone but a veritable flock. Economically, this would secure Germany's iron ore shipments and provide a firm grasp on the Baltic, with access to all the goods that had previously gone to Britain. On top of thwarting Britain's attempt to outflank Germany, Hitler could also do his own outflanking by providing the navy with much-needed bases for the "siege of Britain." Overall, the case for securing the Nordic flank appeared very strong, and this twin geostrategic and economic focus would be reflected in the preamble of Hitler's war directive of 1 March 1940 for *Weserübung:*

> The development of the situation in Scandinavia necessitates the commencement of preparations for the occupation of Denmark and Norway by formations of the armed forces *(Fall Weserübung)*. This would anticipate English action against Scandinavia and the Baltic, secure our supplies of iron ore from Sweden, and provide the navy and the Luftwaffe with the expanded bases for operations against England.[103]

2

Planning for *Weserübung*

I cannot and will not begin the offensive in the west before this [Norwegian] affair has been settled.

Adolf Hitler, 21 February 1940

Both Hitler and Raeder described the invasion of Norway as one of the "cheekiest operations" in recent history, one that broke all "the rules of naval warfare."[1] Yet as the Führer and his naval commander brooded over maps of the elongated and deeply fjorded Norwegian coastline, they agreed that the audacity of the proposal was its greatest strength. Under the very noses of the Royal Navy's mighty juggernauts, the German invasion of Norway would be almost wholly contingent upon surprise and speed if it was to have any hope of success. Therefore, given that the Norwegian blitzkrieg was dependent on the rapid deployment of forces over a lengthy operational theater, German planners immediately saw that this could be achieved only by delivering the initial assault troops by fast men-of-war and the aircraft of the Luftwaffe. Yet, although much is known of the high price paid by the German naval forces, and even the heroic efforts of the army in northern Norway, the Luftwaffe's story remains little known. Nevertheless, the invasion of Norway was the first German campaign in which the Luftwaffe was less the handmaiden of the German army—that is, merely playing a supporting role—and more an equal partner among the three services in achieving final success. In aerial assaults by paratroopers and airborne forces, forays against threatening British naval vessels, a massive airlift operation, and logistical and tactical support of far-flung German ground forces, the men of the Luftwaffe, alongside those of the army and navy, passed (in Hitler's view) "into history as the best representatives of the highest German soldiership."[2]

To make sense of the Luftwaffe's pivotal role within the framework of this triservice campaign, it is essential to examine the forces and events that pushed German preparations forward. The period leading up to the invasion can be split into three distinct phases, beginning with the introductory planning phase in late December 1939, ultimately producing *Studie Nord* (Study North); followed by an intermediate phase involving the deliberations of *Kapitän* Theodor Kranke's staff in early February 1940; and culminating in the final phase initiated by the *Altmark* incident in mid-February, resulting in the appointment of *General der Infanterie* Nikolaus von Falkenhorst as overall commander of the campaign. I will follow this account with an examination of how the Germans planned to carry out the invasion, with special emphasis on the role of the Luftwaffe, crucial to the success of the Norwegian blitzkrieg.

QUISLING'S ABORTIVE INITIATIVES

Adolf Hitler's order of 13 December 1939 to establish a "small staff" to carry out an investigation of "how one might occupy Norway" set political and military wheels in motion for tentative planning work. "In order to counter the increasing enemy propaganda activity," noted a memorandum prepared by the Außenpolitisches Amt of the National Socialist Party, "the Führer promised Quisling financial assistance" for a "Pan-Germanic movement."[3] Accordingly, Alfred Rosenberg's Außenpolitisches Amt retained oversight of Norwegian political activity. Expenses, though, were to be met by the German state's Auswärtiges Amt.[4] In early January 1940, during a meeting attended by Rosenberg and *Reichsaußenminister* Joachim von Ribbentrop, both men agreed that a sum of 200,000 gold marks—made in several separate payments—would be made available for Vidkun Quisling's activities in Norway. As with all enterprises involving Norwegian "affairs," the two installments had to be delivered to Quisling under the greatest secrecy, and in the Auswärtiges Amt only one senior official (other than Ribbentrop, of course) was made aware of this clandestine arrangement.

Not only did the Germans establish close "official" liaison with Quisling, but the Norwegian himself reported to his Nazi associates through Wiljam Hagelin, his deputy living in Germany. For the most part, few Norwegians within Norway were aware of the close relationship between Quisling and Hagelin. Consequently, the latter successfully infiltrated the Nygardsvold government. From this position, Hagelin was able to overhear the uncolored opinions of government members, whom he considered conducted themselves like a secret "Norwegian-Anglophile society" *(norwegisch-anglophile Gesellschaft).*[5] Although his inside information often contradicted assessments made by the German legation in Oslo—which believed the Norwegian government meant to maintain its neutral position—it became the stock of Quisling's reports to Berlin. For example, in a memorandum of 13 January, Hagelin reported the observations of two Norwegian ministers who felt that Germany had little hope of winning the war and therefore believed that Norway, because of its large merchant fleet, had little option but to "favor Britain in politics during the war, even more than it did in peacetime." Reports such as these, conveyed to Rosenberg's Außenwartiges Amt, reached the ears of Hitler and the *Großadmiral* (via a specially appointed naval attaché) in the following weeks and increasingly fueled Hitler's demands for action in Norway.[6]

Quisling also offered his own plan for bringing his country within the German sphere. A number of his followers would be given intensive military training in Germany, thus providing a nucleus of loyal and highly skilled supporters who would act as area specialists and interpreters when a special German force arrived undercover in coal barges. Their aim: the capture of the most prominent individuals in the government (including the king) to forestall military resistance, after which Quisling would assume political control of the nation and officially call for German troops. To German planners, though, Quisling's quasi-military coup had the hallmarks of a disaster waiting to happen. Neither Hitler nor his subordinates ever gave much credence to Quisling's ability to carry out such a risky enterprise, and they were always far more interested in his and Hagelin's ability to gather political and military intelligence. Real military planning would be carried out by experts.

GERMAN AND ALLIED PLANNING BEGINS: *STUDIE NORD* AND *AUSTER*

As in the early months of the war, the German navy was the main driving force behind the Norwegian planning. It was none other than Raeder who reminded the Führer on 30 December 1939 that it was "essential that Norway does not fall into British hands."[7] On 10 January 1940, the military deliberations of the small OKW staff, instructed by Hitler in mid-December to "determine how one might occupy Norway," were released to the three armed services as *Studie Nord*.[8] Three days later, Raeder's naval staff assembled to scrutinize the Wehrmacht's rough preliminary survey. The meeting covered many of the major concerns raised previously, while at the same time making a number of recommendations. From the outset, the study made it clear that should Britain establish itself "in the Norwegian area it would create an impossible situation for Germany in its military strategy."[9] The only way to ensure this did not take place was for Germany to "anticipate a British move and occupy Norway first." The *Großadmiral* voiced his own support of this assessment, adding that he was firmly convinced that Britain intended to occupy Norway in the "near future" to deprive its Continental enemy of imports, particularly those of Swedish origin. Moreover, once installed in Norway—with the assistance of the "Jewish" pro-British prime minister, Hambro—Britain could lean on Sweden, choking the flow of all merchant traffic and possibly bringing it into the Western Powers' own sphere of influence.

Raeder's assessment met with a measure of disagreement from members of his operations staff. In their view, an imminent invasion by Britain was not probable. Furthermore, even if the British had the requisite resources to carry out such an action (which the operations staff doubted), it would not be without risks—specifically, the possibility of Britain running into "strong and extremely undesirable opposition" from the Soviet Union on the one hand and severe countermeasures from Germany on the other hand, namely, the occupation of bases in Denmark, and if need be, in Sweden. All in all, the operations division remained skeptical about the idea that Britain would, or could, release a large enough force with which to occupy Norway merely to counter Germany's threat. While Raeder agreed that the maintenance of Norwegian neutrality remained the best means of ensuring the continued use of Norwegian territorial waters for German merchant traffic, especially iron ore imports, he warned that the Norwegian political situation and the war in general were not predictable. "It is therefore necessary, on principle," noted Raeder as he wrapped up the Norwegian segment of the meeting, "to include the occupation of Norway in the op-erational preparations for the general war strategy."

In fact, on the other side of the Maginot Line and across the Channel, the respective French and British planners were seriously examining the possibility of just such an initiative themselves. Since the beginning of the war, both London and Paris had seen the possibilities open to them for operations in Scandinavia, but these opportunities were accentuated after the outbreak of the Soviet-Finnish War. Public opinion in these countries greatly leaned toward Finland in its David-and-Goliath struggle against the Red Army. However, although British and French leaders rationalized their planning for operations in Scandinavia under the noble guise of defending the principles of freedom against the bondage of communism, the bottom line always remained the need to achieve strategically important gains against Germany; this meant iron ore.[10] To this end, deliberations from December 1939 until early January 1940 centered on two alternatives: either a limited naval action aimed at stopping the ore traffic from Narvik to Germany, possibly by naval patrol vessels or mining of the Leads; or a major land-based expedition designed to secure the Swedish iron ore fields.[11] Working against the latter pro-posal, however, was British determination to avoid becoming embroiled in a conflict with the Soviet Union, and the realization that the success of any Anglo-French expedition was reliant on Norwegian and Swedish acquiescence. Even the limited action proposed for the Norwegian Leads had to be weighed carefully against the damage it would cause to their relations with the Scandinavian neutrals, damage that would undoubtedly make a future land-based operation much more difficult, if not impossible, to carry out. On the other hand, Winston Churchill, First Lord of the Admiralty, felt that action should be taken regardless of the niceties of international law. "Small nations," he asserted on 16 December, "must not tie our hands when we are fighting for their rights and freedom. . . . Humanity, rather than legality, must be our guide." This sentiment found favor in Paris.[12]

During this period, the French were most insistent that operations in Scandinavia be carried out. In fact, they were very taken with the idea of making the Scandinavian Peninsula a major theater of the war by initiating a landing near Petsamo, in northernmost Finland—a move that would sidestep the need to gain Norwegian and Swedish approval. However, the French proposal cut to the very heart of the British cabinet's reluctance to pursue operations in the region: the fear that such action could bring Hitler and Stalin into a closer union, and the appalling prospect of Britain being drawn into direct conflict with the Soviet Union. For example, at the Supreme War Council on 19 December, Edouard Daladier, the French premier—no doubt eager to draw German attention away from the Franco-German border—strongly pressed for action to stop German access to Swedish ores. Neville Chamberlain bluntly countered that his country was not yet ready to declare war on the Soviet Union.[13] Even Churchill, ever an optimist regarding military operations in Norway, and who did not think that operations in Scandinavia would necessarily lead to "general hostilities with Russia," had to admit that he was "most anxious" to avoid such an eventuality.[14]

After mulling over numerous reports weighing the relative efficacy and cost of the two alternatives, the British and French decided to attempt the limited naval action to sever Germany's iron ore supplies, despite the fact that this would require the Royal Navy to operate within Norwegian territorial waters.[15] At the same time, secret preparations were made for a possible occupation of Stavanger, Bergen, and Trondheim. To test diplomatic reaction, the British and French communicated to the Norwegian and Swedish governments their intention to enter Norwegian territorial waters in pursuit of vessels bound for Germany. The predictable outcry that ensued from both Oslo and Stockholm, which clutched their neutrality ever closer to their chests under the shadows of their Communist and fascist neighbors, was so vehement that the Anglo-French leaders were forced to back away from the operation against Narvik traffic on 12 January. In the end, despite the French champing at the bit, and "much to the disgust" of Churchill, the British cabinet refused to commit itself to immediate action, especially after the Chiefs of Staff reported that any attempt to capture the Gällivare fields in the face of Norwegian and Swedish opposition would not be successful.[16] Nevertheless, in the hope that the neutrals could be gently coerced into seeing things the Anglo-French way, they were not advised of the decision to drop the planned violation of Norwegian territorial waters, while in the background, planning for the major land-based expedition continued apace.

Meanwhile, the German Naval Staff carried out Raeder's proposed enlargement of the Wehrmacht's *Studie Nord*. Nearly all the recommendations developed by the navy in this study were repeated in the subsequent planning phases. The naval staff envisaged landings at all the major ports, including Oslo, Kristiansand, Stavanger, Bergen, Trondheim, Narvik, and Tromsö.[17] It also noted that given the relative weakness of the German navy vis-à-vis the Royal Navy, the prerequisite for success would be complete surprise.[18] If this was achieved, Norwegian warships were considered to be of no threat to German forces, while the only British naval vessels they were likely to encounter were weak patrolling units that happened to be in the region at the time of the invasion.[19] The naval staff also felt that the best way to bring in the assault force was in two separate waves. The first of these would arrive by warship once shore batteries had been neutralized. The second wave of soldiers, along with logistical materials, would arrive by merchant vessel. In these deliberations the Luftwaffe was given a relatively limited role because the poor weather conditions of midwinter were unfavorable for conducting large-scale aerial operations.[20]

That the Luftwaffe would have an important role in any Norwegian campaign, however, was recognized early on in the planning process by the less partisan OKW. In the week following Hitler's meeting with Quisling, *Generalmajor* Alfred Jodl, head of the OKW's operations section, met with various Luftwaffe personnel regarding Norway. For instance, on 13 December, and within hours of Hitler's ordering the establishment of a small staff to look into an occupation of Norway, Jodl met with *Hauptmann* von Sternurg, a Luftwaffe staff officer, and on 18 December, he discussed the "Norwegian matter" with Hans Jeschonnek, the Luftwaffe's chief of staff.[21] Two days later, Jodl and *Generaloberst* Wilhelm Keitel, the OKW's chief of staff, discussed deploying elements of the X Fliegerkorps and the Luftwaffe's Strategic Air Reconnaissance Group *"Rowehl"* in reconnaissance over Norway.[22] Indeed, OKW's *Studie Nord* had directed that a Luftwaffe general be appointed head of a special staff created to plan for the campaign and "who would at the same time be entrusted with the execution of any subsequent operation."[23] *Generaloberst* Erhard Milch, the Air Ministry's state secretary and the Luftwaffe's armaments chief, was appointed to head this small staff, called *Oyster (Auster)*, which assembled for the first time on the morning of 14 January 1940. This, however, was also its last meeting, because in late January Hitler recalled *Studie Nord*, dissolved *Oyster*, and placed all the planning for the campaign in the hands of the OKW.[24]

THE KRANKE STAFF

Traditionally, the High Command of the Army (Oberkommando des Heeres, or OKH) had been the primary institution through which the German state had waged war, but in 1938 Hitler established the OKW as a means by which he could gain direct control over all the armed forces. It was as Supreme Commander of the Wehrmacht that Hitler, on 23 January, placed the planning for Norway firmly within the hands of the OKW. As Jodl jotted in his diary, the formulation of plans for the northern theater would now be prepared "only by the OKW."[25] The preamble of the order signed by Keitel noted that it was Hitler's desire that "work on Study 'N' would be continued under his personal and immediate influence." Consequently, a working staff was to be formed within the OKW, creating the nucleus of any subsequent operational planning group.[26] Keitel's closing sentence informed all three service commanders that further operations would be conducted under the code name *Weserübung* (*Weser*-exercise), named after the Weser River, which runs past the German port of Bremerhaven and empties into the North Sea.

The reasons for increasing the pace of the planning and placing it within the hands of the OKW were fourfold. First, the campaign in the west was delayed. Originally Hitler had hoped to carry out his assault on France and the Low Countries before the end of January, but the likelihood of inclement weather in the following months, as well as a major security lapse that resulted in German plans for *Fall Gelb* (Case Yellow) falling into Allied hands on 9 January, forced the Führer to postpone the assault until spring.[27] In the eyes of German planners this delay increased the possibility of Allied operations in Scandinavia, and therefore German preparation of contingency plans for an invasion of Norway needed to be stepped up. Hitler, for his part, was moving gradually closer to Raeder's position, perhaps influenced by spreading rumors and newspaper reports alluding to imminent Anglo-French intervention in Finland.[28] Second, the security breach that delayed *Fall Gelb* led Hitler to believe that secrecy surrounding operations in Norway would be better served by keeping the planning within the OKW. The danger of allowing a wide body of military personnel access to secret material was graphically illustrated by an episode in early January, when, in contravention of standing orders, Hellmuth Reinberger, a Luftwaffe major, had flown to Cologne bearing secret papers concerning *Fall Gelb*. Flying in poor weather, the pilot strayed over Belgium and made a forced landing on Belgian soil when his aircraft suffered engine failure. Although the officer attempted to destroy the documents before capture, he was only partially successful, and the Allies were alerted to German intentions. (The stupidity of the event of course led some Allied commanders to ponder the possibility that it was nothing more than a clever plant by the Germans.) After this event it appears that Hitler hoped that by removing the planning for Norway from the Luftwaffe—an action that created a good measure of ill feeling among its senior officers, including Hermann Göring, the Luftwaffe's commander in chief—and placing it within his personal OKW staff, he could preserve one of the most vital elements of the eventual operation: surprise. Third, never before had the German armed forces undertaken an operation that required the close coordination of naval, air, and army elements over such a great distance. Given this challenge, the Führer evidently believed that the OKW represented the best means of achieving close cooperation. Finally, since the OKW was essentially Hitler's own personal staff—rather than a true joint-operations staff—the campaign would essentially be *his* operation, and would thus fulfill his *Feldherr* (field commander) aspirations. Logically, then, Hitler felt that the OKW, as Germany's military umbrella organization, would be ideally suited to plan and oversee the campaign.

With these factors in mind, the small Norway planning group, under the leadership of *Kapitän* Theodor Kranke, was assembled on 5 February as a distinct section within the OKW's Operations Branch. Within Kranke's staff each armed service was represented by an officer.[29] Aside from the OKW's introductory work, *Studie Nord,* and its subsequent consideration by naval personnel in early January, the Kranke staff had to start from scratch. This was nowhere more apparent than in the area of intelligence.

Even though it was widely assumed after the successful invasion in April that German planners had been gathering intelligence well in advance, this was not the case.[30] In line with Hitler's early determination to keep the Scandinavian nations out of the war, not a single specialist intelligence agent had been assigned to the Scandinavian region, let alone to Norway, before November 1939.[31] Consequently, material had to be assembled in great haste in order to prepare plans. In the first instance, the Germans gleaned general geographic and demographic information from a wide range of sources, including tourist guides and brochures and hydrographic charts.[32] Yet despite the fact that over the years the navy had amassed a considerable amount of material on Norway's long coastline, it lacked photomaps of the ports and bays, which would be essential for disembarking German men and equipment in an invasion. Moreover, the Luftwaffe would require its own accurate photomaps detailing not only Norwegian airfields, which would be targeted for parachute drops followed by airborne landings, but also the disposition of antiaircraft defenses. Despite the efforts of a youthful Luftwaffe attaché, *Hauptmann* Spiller, who had gathered a small amount of useful intelligence since his arrival in Norway in March 1939, the most valuable material came from air reconnaissance, principally the Luftwaffe's Strategic Air Reconnaissance Group, *Rowehl.*[33] Using high-altitude aircraft to avoid overt infringement of Norwegian and Swedish neutrality, *Rowehl* aircrew took photographs of all the important Norwegian navigational channels, significant ports, and serviceable airfields from Oslo in the south to Kirkenes high above the Arctic Circle. To reach the latter far-flung location, the Luftwaffe utilized four-engined Focke-Wulf Fw 200 Condors— converted airliners—flying from East Prussian airfields.[34] *Rowehl* aircraft also made strategic reconnaissance flights over the eastern ports of the British Isles, especially Scapa Flow, with a view to forewarning German planners of Anglo-French preparations for an operation in Norway.[35] Clearly, the information collected by *Rowehl* crews (mostly from late February 1940 onward) was essential to conducting the Norwegian campaign.

Within three weeks and in spite of the intelligence handicaps, Kranke's staff produced a reasonably detailed operational plan. As with *Studie Nord,* the Germans broke Norway into six operational zones: Oslo Fjord and its environs; the region between Langesund and Stavanger; the region around Bergen; Trondheim; Narvik; and, finally, Tromsö and Finnmark. The Kranke staff reasoned that the successful occupation of these relatively isolated and small geographic regions would give German forces control of the entire country.

This prospect was possible because of the physical and climatic conditions that prevail over much of Norway, which is situated on the western portion of the

Scandinavian Peninsula. The coastline and numerous small offshore islands of this nation are bathed in the waters of the relatively sheltered Skagerrak, separating Norway from continental Europe; the North Sea in its western approaches; the Norwegian Sea in the northwest; and the frigid Arctic waters of the Barents Sea in the extreme north.[36] Norway's very long seaboard of 2,600 kilometers (expanding to 20,000 kilometers when offshore islands are included) is made up of steep, narrow fjords punched into the mountainous heart of the country. From the deep waters of these winding fjords rises a rugged and barren mountainous plateau, nine-tenths of which lies at a height of more than 300 meters and one-half at over 600 meters. In addition to this challenging topography, Norway's climate can be severe, particularly in the east, where it shares a 1,600-kilometer border with Sweden, and a lengthy winter season ensures that the region remains covered by snow for much of the year. Although in the west the climate is tempered by the Atlantic Ocean and in the north by the Gulf Stream, which allows harbors to remain open year-round, the rigors of long winter darkness punctuated by blizzards make the northernmost part of Norway particularly inhospitable.

Given these harsh topographic and climatic features, it is not surprising that Norway, although geographically larger than the British Isles, had a population in 1940 that lingered below 3 million, most of whom lived close to the coast in a smattering of urban settlements or in valley farming communities. Of the major cities, only Oslo, the capital and economic heart of Norway, and Bergen boasted of populations over 100,000, while the medieval city of Trondheim, the third-largest urban center and gateway to the north, had approximately 50,000 inhabitants.

The rugged terrain separating these communities also created a formidable barrier to internal communication by rail: in the south a rail network with Oslo at its hub fanned out to Kristiansand and Bergen; the central region was connected by a series of lines focused on Dombaas and Trondheim; and the northern region had only the short line that bore ores from deep within Sweden over a sliver of Norwegian territory to the port of Narvik. Yet no single line covered the whole country; consequently, communication and transportation were more often than not seaborne. Given that these urban centers and other smaller towns dotting the Norwegian coast were relatively isolated, it became clear to the Germans from the beginning of the planning process that they could essentially gain complete control of the nation by the occupation of these modest geographic regions and a handful of strategically important ports (such as Narvik).

The Kranke plan, therefore, envisaged the simultaneous occupation of Oslo, Kristiansand, Arendal, Stavanger, Bergen, Trondheim, and Narvik. Its main point of divergence from the OKW's earlier *Studie Nord* lay with the crucial role assigned to the Luftwaffe. In addition to providing bomber and fighter support, the Luftwaffe would, with the exception of the distant centers of Trondheim and Narvik, be responsible for the delivery of one-half of the occupation forces.[37] On the first day of the invasion alone and in conjunction with the delivery of troops by fast warships, some eight air transport groups would deliver approximately five battalions of paratroops in the first wave. Over the next three days this would be followed by a massive airlift, which would ferry in nearly an entire infantry division. Little Norwegian resistance, either at sea or on land, was expected, and a consolidation of the German position, including the acquisition of naval and air bases in Denmark, would be secured by diplomatic means. This would enable the continuation of the Norwegian government in internal matters, albeit with a reduction in the size of its armed forces. However, this work by the Kranke staff, and all the preceding planning, had been just that: merely planning.

Initially Hitler had been reluctant even to begin contemplating a Norwegian campaign, and once he set the preparations in motion, its progress could best be described as sedate. By mid-February, two months after the setting up of the small staff to look into how one might occupy Norway, the whole project still had a distinctly preliminary air about it. Although Hitler had admitted that German possession of Norway would benefit Raeder's "siege of Britain," and that Germany would be in real difficulties should the Allies take action in Norway, his heart was not really in it. This may be due partially to his concern over the upcoming campaign in the west, but it also appears that he had no real conviction that the British would act first in breach of Norwegian neutrality—that is, not until 16 February 1940, when a spectacular act of piracy inside Norwegian territorial waters snapped Hitler back on his heels.

THE "*ALTMARK* OUTRAGE"

The *Altmark,* an unarmed German supply ship on its homeward journey from the South Atlantic, where it had fueled and provisioned the German raider *Graf Spee* (scuttled in December in the La Plata Delta off Uruguay), slipped into wintry Norwegian territorial waters north of Trondheim on 14 February 1940.[38] In addition to provisioning the doomed pocket battleship, the *Altmark* had taken aboard 303 of its British prisoners. Although Norwegian officials at Bergen were suspicious of the actual nature of the vessel's "cargo," they allowed it to proceed unhindered through the Leads, because under the Hague Rules the *Altmark* as a naval auxiliary flying the colors of the German merchant navy had the right to unhindered use of these waters.[39] Nevertheless, the British were not about to allow the Germans any such generosity and set about to relieve the *Altmark* of its suspected "cargo." By the following day, the Germans realized from intercepts of British signals that "the movement of British light forces in the direction of the north Norwegian coast was probably aimed to intercept the supply ship *Altmark.*" Despite this threat, the German naval staff felt that the "ship seems to run less risk inside territorial waters than outside."[40]

Indeed, British reconnaissance aircraft had already identified the *Altmark,* and by 1500 hours on 16 February, a Royal Navy flotilla of one cruiser and six destroyers was shadowing the supply ship along the coast. Admiralty instructions to the leader of the flotilla, Captain Philip Vian of HMS *Cossack,* ordered that, unless the Norwegians permitted a joint British and Norwegian guard to escort the German supply vessel back to Bergen for a more thorough inspection, he was to board the *Altmark* and release the prisoners.[41] Thus, by midafternoon it was becoming apparent to the German Naval Staff that their belief that the *Altmark* would be "completely safe within Norwegian territorial waters could no longer hold." "In order to preclude an enemy attack in the outer territorial waters," the *Altmark*'s commander, *Kapitän* Heinrich Dau, received instructions at 1612 to make for the nearest Norwegian fjord in the hope that the beleaguered supply ship could shelter there, awaiting the arrival of sufficient German naval vessels to secure safe passage to Germany—an impossibility as it turned out due to the poor operational readiness of German destroyers at the time and navigational difficulties arising from severe ice conditions.[42] Only three hours later, the *Altmark* was forced to seek shelter within Jössing Fjord when the destroyer *Intrepid* tried to come alongside within 200 meters of the shore. By this time the Germans were raining diplomatic censures down upon the heads of the Norwegian government and its officials with respect to breaches of their territorial waters. Meanwhile, at the mouth of the fjord two Norwegian torpedo boats were actually trying to prevent just such a breach, lying in an unenviable position between men-of-war of the Royal Navy and the *Altmark* at anchor in its snow-cloaked sanctuary.

The commander of the *Altmark* was well aware of his vessel's vulnerability and in a bitter message to the British flotilla outside the fjord drew attention to the fact that his ship would be sunk and set on fire "at the moment the first English soldier would cross its rail."[43] However, by the time *Kapitän* Dau dispatched his second communiqué, it had became apparent to him that his unarmed ship had little option but "to yield to force," and he reluctantly declared that he was willing to ferry over the 303 prisoners with his own vessels.[44] Although the British commander of the *Cossack* chose to disregard this offer, he did not ignore Dau's threat that, should a Royal Navy force attempt a boarding action, the men would be repulsed by a "force of arms" wielded by the *Altmark*'s "military body"—a rather grandiose threat, since the crew of the *Altmark* was totally ill equipped to carry out any such action—and this bluff at least goes some way to explaining the tragic events that followed.[45] With a good measure of Royal Navy "derring-do," the *Cossack* breached the Norwegian sentinels' blockade around midnight and burst into the fjord. The British boarding party assaulted the German supply ship, seizing the ship's bridge, and "began firing like maniacs into the German crew," noted the *Altmark*'s own grim after-action report.[46] "The *Cossack* by ruthless means of its weapons," recorded the German Naval Staff war diary, "seized the prisoners and made off with them."[47] Six members of the German crew were killed, and a number were seriously wounded.

For the British, the bold rescue proved to be a propaganda treat back home, and despite howls of protest from the German government regarding violations

of international law and Goebbels's attempt to raise "a hellish choir of indignation" among the international press, they argued adamantly that the Norwegians
were seriously remiss in not searching the vessel and discovering the prisoners in
the first place.[48] In Berlin, however, a completely different assessment of the affair was being made. Circumspectly, Hitler ordered that Norwegian neutrality was
to be strictly observed in the recovery of the *Altmark*—which had run aground
and damaged its propeller—and in continuing naval operations.[49] Underneath,
though, he was seething. His assessment was neatly summed up by the naval staff's
own conclusions: "It is quite clear from Admiralty orders and the steps taken by
the British forces that the operation against the supply ship *Altmark* was carefully
planned and directed with the clear object of using all available means and if necessary violating Norwegian territorial waters, in order to capture the *Altmark* or
to board her and free the prisoners."[50] The "*Altmark* outrage," as Hitler would later
describe it, showed that the British had no intention of observing Norwegian neutrality.[51] Moreover, the apparent ease with which the *Cossack* was able to enter
the fjord despite the presence of two Norwegian torpedo boats, plus the mild diplomatic censures issued against British transgressions by the Norwegians, made
Hitler's blood boil. The whole incident not only suggested that the Norwegians
were all too willing to look the other way in matters of British interest but also
added weight to the reports streaming in from the coconspirators, Quisling and
Hagelin, that secret agreements had been reached between Oslo and London.[52]

In fact, although the British and French had not been able to secure any secret agreement with Norway, they continued their planning and preparations for
a Scandinavian expedition against a background of renewed Soviet assaults on
the Karelian Isthmus in late January and early February, growing popular sympa-
thy for Finland, and the belief that the Germans might attempt to secure their iron
ore supplies in the spring. When the two governments met at the Supreme War
Council on 2 February 1940, they agreed that the preservation of Finland was of
major concern to the Allied cause. Additionally, they generally acknowledged that
aid to Finland—Field Marshal Mannerheim, the Finnish commander in chief, had
requested reinforcements of some 30,000 men—should be coupled with the seizure of Sweden's northern iron ore mines in order to help the Allies accomplish
their main aim: the defeat of Germany. Thus the operation, "ostensibly and nomi-
nally designed for the assistance of Finland," would "kill two birds with one
stone."[53]

To overcome the Nordic neutrals' objections to an advance from the Norwegian coastline through northern Sweden, the Allies proposed moral leverage that
would give them at least some justification for the expedition.[54] Just prior to its
launch, the Allies intended to have Finland deliver an international plea for assistance, with additional diplomatic entreaties to the Norwegians and the Swedes,
appealing for aid to repulse the Soviets from the Scandinavian Peninsula. Originally earmarked for the British Expeditionary Force in France, the 42nd and 44th
Divisions (which Chamberlain proposed could assume the guise of a "volunteer

force") would be held back for Scandinavia. The French prime minister, Daladier, gave his support for the plan, as well as recommending that the earlier Petsamo proposal be kept in mind should they fail to overcome neutral opposition. That the Allies would ever be able to subdue Norwegian and Swedish reluctance, however, always seemed unlikely, particularly after the souring of Anglo-Norwegian relations in the wake of the *Altmark* incident.

The timidity of the Allies was greatly influenced by the fact that Britain had plenty to lose from action in Scandinavia. In addition to British industry's own dependence on considerable amounts of Swedish ore, economic planners also feared jeopardizing the Anglo-Norwegian trade agreement, facilitating the use of Norwegian shipping should these vessels become the target of German U-boats and aircraft. Moreover, the British cabinet desired to act, as much as possible, from the moral high ground as defenders of international law in accordance with the League of Nations. How neutrals worldwide—above all, the United States—would react to an Anglo-French operation that breached Scandinavian neutrality hamstrung Allied planning. Therefore, despite the 5 February agreement, Churchill's continual harping on the subject, and Daladier's desire for swift action (partly resulting from domestic pressure increased by the proximity of French elections), by the end of the month indecision and disagreement over how to proceed were about to rob the Allies of the justification they needed. The Finnish situation had reached the desperation point. Under the onslaught of the Red Army, which had penetrated Finnish defensive lines, and in the face of increasing losses, Finnish morale reached rock bottom.[55]

On 1 March, the Finnish ambassador requested 100 bombers with crews and 50,000 soldiers from Britain, and given the seriousness of Finland's military crisis, he appealed for an answer within twenty-four hours. Britain still hesitated. Its leaders raised numerous technical problems with regard to the delivery of equipment, and the more cynically inclined felt that because of the apparent unreasonableness of the request, the Finns never expected to receive a favorable reply. Rather, the outrageousness of the appeal anticipated a British refusal that would act as a face-saving measure for opening negotiations with the Soviets. Furthermore, many believed that delivery of the aircraft solely by themselves (the most viable option in the short term) would only forestall the inevitable, and once the Finns were defeated, the bombers would be irrecoverably lost. By 5 March, it was all but over, and the Finns entered into negotiations with the Soviets. Despite a flurry of last-minute proposals by the British and the French, which included the possibility of a "semi-peaceable invasion of Norway," the Finno-Soviet peace treaty was signed on 12 March.[56] Over objections from the chief of the Imperial General Staff and the First Lord of the Admiralty, the British decided to disband the units of the expeditionary force.

The British did, however, press on with preparations for one of Churchill's ideas. Code-named *Royal Marine,* the operation involved the aerial dropping of floating mines in the main German waterways, such as the Rhine. Moreover, the

French, under the leadership of Daladier's replacement, Premier Paul Reynaud, wanted a less restrictive interpretation of Scandinavian neutrality. As a note prepared within the French Foreign Ministry stated: "We should not let ourselves be bound . . . by some juridic scruples which our enemies have since thrown to the winds."[57] With this in mind, the French presented a new two-pronged plan to the British on 25 March, which, among other things, called for the cutting of Germany's iron ore supplies via Norway, submarine warfare in the Black Sea, and air attacks on the Caucasus oil fields. This type of economic warfare would strike at German dependence on foreign sources for raw materials, without involving direct offensive action against Germany itself.

On 28 March, at the Supreme War Council, Chamberlain successfully blocked the parts of the French plans that could result in a conflict with the Soviet Union but did agree to the mining operation of Narvik (Operation *Wilfred*) on 5 April. For his part, Reynaud provisionally accepted an early April date for the implementation of *Royal Marine*.[58] The mining of waters off Narvik also opened the possibility of German retaliation in Norway, which would provide the justification for, or even Norwegian consent to, a British and French counteroperation *(Plan R 4)* in southwestern and northern Norway with a view to securing the Swedish iron ore mines. "The moment the Germans set foot on Norwegian soil, or there is clear evidence that they intend to do so," ran an approved report by the Chiefs of Staff,

> our objective should be (a) to dispatch a force to Narvik to secure the port and, subsequently, the railway inland as far as the Norwegian-Swedish frontier, and to pave the way to the Gällivare ore fields; (b) as a defensive measure, to dispatch forces to occupy Stavanger, Bergen and Trondheim, in order to deny their use to the Germans as naval and/or air bases.[59]

Characteristically, and much to the frustration of the British, the French then raised objections to *Royal Marine,* which they wanted delayed by three months in order to prepare defenses around their aircraft and munitions factories so that they would be less vulnerable to retaliatory German air strikes. In the end, despite British exasperation and the admonition of Sir Alexander Cadogan, head of the Foreign Office, that "we really must try to bring them to heel," it was decided to avoid putting further strain on the alliance by simply dropping the *Royal Marine* component from the operation.[60]

Although unaware of the full extent of these Allied considerations and preparations, Hitler was nonetheless infuriated by the "*Altmark* outrage" and the reports reaching Berlin of an Anglo-Norwegian coalition. Hence, on 19 February, he "pressed energetically" for a speeding up of preparations for *Weserübung*.[61] His fears were strengthened over the months of February and March by incautious references made by both Churchill and Reynaud regarding their designs on Norway. For example, on 2 February, the First Lord of the Admiralty dropped a couple of unguarded comments to neutral press attachés at a secret press conference in

London, hinting at an Allied initiative in Norway.[62] He followed this up on 30 March in a BBC broadcast in which he warned Norway that the Allies would continue the fight "wherever it might lead them."[63] On the very same day, German intelligence intercepted a Paris diplomat's report detailing a conversation with Premier Reynaud. Its contents revealed that the Allies would be undertaking action in northern Europe within the next few days. As Hitler relished pointing out after the invasion, British and French security lapses—plus information acquired by Göring's codebreaking *Forschungsamt*—made his decision all the easier to make and greatly hastened the planning process.[64]

Indeed, on 21 February, Hitler received the aristocratic *General die Infanterie* Nikolaus von Falkenhorst, who had been recommended by Jodl to assume overall responsibility for the operation.[65] Jodl's endorsement of Falkenhorst rested largely on the latter's experience gained during Germany's intervention in Finland at the end of the First World War. In reality, Falkenhorst had been only a General Staff officer at the time, and his career since then had been fairly mundane.[66] Consequently, despite being rather grandiosely touted as a Scandinavian expert, he was not considered among the first rank of commanders available, and his nomination reflected the army's relative indifference toward the project. Nevertheless, after introductions, Hitler dramatically impressed upon Falkenhorst the fact that "I cannot and will not begin the offensive in the west before this affair has been settled." After this, Jodl and Keitel detailed the two basic premises of the operation to the general: to forestall Allied action in the region by taking control of the main population centers and ports (in particular Narvik) and to prevent the development of any local resistance or cooperation with British counteroperations.[67] Falkenhorst took his leave of the Führer to purchase a tourist guide in order to determine how Norway could be secured. Although he later admitted that initially he had absolutely "no idea" about how this could be achieved, he worked on the problem in his hotel room, poring over the cheap tourist map until 1700 hours. At that time he returned to the Führer with a favorable assessment and gladly accepted Hitler's offer to command the campaign.[68] By 28 February, Falkenhorst's staff, which included Kranke as the navy's representative, *Oberst* Robert Knauss from the Luftwaffe, *Major* Werner von Tippelskirch from the army, and an *Abwehr* representative, was deliberating in Berlin, and the first fruits of its labor—building heavily on previous investigations—soon came to light.[69]

THE *WESERÜBUNG* DIRECTIVE AND ITS FALLOUT

On 1 March 1940, only thirteen days after the "*Altmark* outrage," Hitler released his "Directive for Case *Weserübung*."[70] In the directive's preamble, he made it clear that the situation in Scandinavia made it necessary to make all preparations for the occupation of Denmark—an innovation introduced by Falkenhorst—and

Norway by formations of the Wehrmacht.[71] Strategically, the occupation would achieve three goals: "It would anticipate English action against Scandinavia and the Baltic, would secure our supplies of ore from Sweden," and would "provide the navy and Luftwaffe with expanded bases for operations against Britain." Although it was Hitler's intention that the campaign be carried out in such a way as to be seen by the peoples of both nations as a *peaceful* occupation, designed to protect the neutrality of the northern nations, any resistance would be broken by force of arms.

The operation was split into two separate and simultaneous undertakings: the occupation of Denmark *(Weserübung Süd)* and the occupation of Norway *(Weserübung Nord)*. The success of *Weserübung Süd* was dependent on the army's ability to secure strategically important points by a lightning thrust through to Skagen and the east coast of Fünen. Meanwhile, once the navy had secured the Nyborg-Korsör route, seized the bridge spanning the Little Belt, and landed troops, it remained responsible for coastal defense. The Luftwaffe was directed to secure northern Danish airfields and subject the Danes to aerial demonstrations of German airpower in flyovers of major urban centers.

Much the larger of the two operations, *Weserübung Nord* was to be a daring surprise occupation of important points along the Norwegian coast by sea and air. The navy was responsible for preparing the transportation by sea of the assault troops and supplies. The Luftwaffe, as well as playing a significant role in the initial assault, was to ensure adequate air defense was provided for the occupying forces and that Norway was fully exploited as a base for the prosecution of the air war against Britain. Although Luftwaffe and naval forces remained subordinated to their respective commanders in chief, an exception was made with regard to one reconnaissance wing and two motorized antiaircraft regiments of the Luftwaffe, which were placed under the immediate command of Falkenhorst until Denmark had been completely occupied.

In carrying out preparations for this campaign, Hitler reminded his commanders that due to the looming threat of Allied operations in Norway, it must be prepared with the "utmost possible speed" because "should the enemy take the initiative in Norway, we must be able to take our own countermeasures at once." He also reiterated the necessity of maintaining total secrecy so that the invasion would be a "complete surprise" to the northern countries and, more important, to "our enemies in the west." To this end all preparations, such as the establishment of supply dumps and embarkation points, should be circumspect, and in order to prevent a slip of the tongue by unwary soldiers and junior officers, troops were to be informed of their true destination only when they had put to sea.

As can be observed from the preceding outline, the directive was typically brief but acted as a framework for the nuts-and-bolts planning that was to follow. Regarding the implementation of these directives, it is important to note that Falkenhorst, as commander of Armee Gruppe XXI (Army Group XXI), remained "immediately subordinated" to Hitler "in all respects."[72] The Führer was obvi-

ously determined to maintain personal control over the project and therefore retained operational command within the OKW. The German military leadership
also hoped that a continuation of the present planning structure would facilitate
Hitler's demand on 3 March to use the "greatest speed" in laying the groundwork
for the Nordic occupation. Hitler's demanding timetable for the OKW and the
respective service commands called for the assembly of forces for *Weserübung*
by 10 March and readiness for the "jump-off" within three days. Thus a landing
in northern Norway would be possible by about 17 March.[73] This schedule proved
too ambitious by about three weeks, in part because residual ice in the Baltic had
yet to thaw, greatly hindering naval preparations in this region. On top of this, the
end of the Soviet-Finnish Winter War on 13 February initially created a degree of
uncertainty about whether the operation was still necessary. Although German
naval planners assessed that the subsequent peace in the Far North deprived the Allies
of their pretext, at least for the "present time," vigilance still needed to be maintained, especially because it appeared likely that the British would not easily give
up their strategic aims in northern Europe.[74] The Führer concurred and ordered that
preparations for *Weserübung* were not to be carried out with "undue haste" but should
continue quietly and with special consideration given to secrecy. This was not, however, a declaration by Hitler that he was intending to abandon his "northern" strategy. Despite reservations by the OKW regarding the likelihood of Allied operations,
the Führer was still convinced that Britain was determined at some point to cut Germany off from its iron ore.[75] This was backed up by reports from the navy that
British warships seemed intent on attacking German iron ore traffic even within
Norwegian territorial waters. Hitler therefore considered that "the execution of
Weserübung is still necessary and [he] insists that preparations for it should be so
far concluded that it will at any time be possible to start the operation at the shortest
notice. *Weserübung* would then be carried out shortly before *Fall Gelb*."[76]

On the whole, Raeder seems to have agreed with his commander in chief because the general consensus of their meeting on 26 March was that "sooner or later
Germany would be faced with the necessity of carrying out the operation," even if
in the short term an Allied assault did not appear on the cards. Thus the German
commanders agreed that the invasion should be carried out as soon as possible,
preferably close to the new moon on 7 April, when the tides would be at their highest, and no later than 15 April, when the nights would be growing too short.[77] Moreover, U-boats positioned for *Weserübung* could not be expected to maintain their
current holding positions past the second week of April, and at present the overall
readiness of naval warships and transports for the campaign was considered good.
In the end, it was not until early April that Hitler reached the final stage in his planning for *Weserübung*. Once he had been informed by Raeder and Göring of the
suitability of the weather for naval and Luftwaffe forces on 2 April, he designated
9 April as *Weser*-day *(Wesertag)* and 0515 as *Weser*-time *(Weserzeit)*.[78]

In some respects, though, the 1 March directive for *Weserübung* came as a
bombshell to the high commands of the army and the Luftwaffe, which took it as

a personal affront that they had been effectively downgraded in the planning process. The army felt, somewhat justifiably, that it had been sidelined in the whole project. As *Generaloberst* Franz Halder, chief of the Army General Staff, scribbled in a parochial marginal note of his war diary on 2 March 1940, Hitler had not "exchanged a single word with the commander of the army on this matter."[79] Moreover, the army was furious not only because troops were being siphoned off by the OKW with scant reference to itself but also because the demands placed on it, especially in light of the army's commitment to the invasion of France and the Low Countries, were too heavy. Jodl was able to placate the OKH somewhat by scaling down the requisition of army forces on 2 March.[80] The Luftwaffe, however, presented an altogether more formidable obstacle in the form of the powerful Hermann Göring, who would plague attempts to establish joint theater commands in Norway (and elsewhere) throughout the war.

The head of the Luftwaffe appeared reluctant to have his forces dissipated by action in Norway from the very inception of the plan. Two reasons may be put forward to explain this. First of all, he disliked the relative demotion of the High Command of the Luftwaffe (Oberkommando der Luftwaffe, or OKL), and hence his own position, when Hitler placed planning for the project in the hands of the OKW. This downgrade rankled with the Luftwaffe's commander in chief and, up until early March, had been expressed by the notable and deliberate absence of the Luftwaffe's representative from the OKW's planning meetings. For example, on 5 February, when the special staff for Norway was assembled to meet Keitel, the chief of the OKW, Jodl noted with a sigh of resignation that the Luftwaffe's representative was "still missing."[81] Second, Göring was afflicted with that most pernicious of military diseases: interservice rivalry. Between the Luftwaffe and the navy, this took the form of competition not only for the Reich's military output but also for control of the naval air arm, which Göring had been coveting for some time—a matter that will be taken up in chapter 5. This, plus his wounded pride at being demoted in the development of the operation, appears to have blinded him to the strategic merits of the proposal and, indeed, to the benefit that bases in Norway would afford air operations. Therefore, Göring was reluctant to commit his prized air resources to an operation he felt was clearly Raeder's hobbyhorse. Consequently, Göring was livid when he discovered that elements of *his* air units were to be taken from *his* command and subordinated to Falkenhorst under the *Weserübung* directive.

Once the directive was released, Göring wasted no time in objecting; after verbally assaulting Keitel, he presented his case to his Führer, resulting in a somewhat reduced demand on the Luftwaffe. On 4 March, Göring again declared his dissatisfaction with the subordination of his aircraft and personnel to Falkenhorst, and the following day all the Luftwaffe units—including the reconnaissance wing and two motorized antiaircraft regiments—were placed within his own X Fliegerkorps for the operation.[82] Nevertheless, these rumblings were merely the calm before the storm.

On 5 March, the heavens burst open at the big *Weserübung* conference attended by all three service commanders and the Führer when Göring threw one of his infamous tantrums. "The *Feldmarschall* vents his spleen," Jodl noted laconically in his diary, "because he was not consulted beforehand." Yes, he could justifiably claim he personally had not been consulted greatly, but, as already noted, Jeschonnek, one of Göring's closest deputies, had been in discussion with Jodl with regard to Norway since at least the third week of December 1939. Moreover, the fact that units of the Luftwaffe's strategic air reconnaissance group, *Rowehl*, had been used extensively in photographic mapping of salient regions of Norway and that the Luftwaffe had overseen the short-lived *Oyster* staff in mid-January demonstrates that Göring was not unaware of the continuing planning process. As Nicolaus von Below, Hitler's Luftwaffe attaché, observed astutely after the outburst, what really stuck in Göring's craw was that he felt downright insulted that "Hitler had not conferred this task on him."[83] Barely concealing his disdain for Göring's petulant display of indignation, Jodl reflected on the overbearing Luftwaffe chief's attempt to dominate proceedings and the lengths to which he went to "demonstrate that all previous planning preparations are all good for nothing." Yet despite Göring's animation and anger, it was, as even Below had to admit, completely "in vain." Hitler, already frustrated with delays to the planning process wrought by the various branches of the armed services, was unimpressed by his air commander's antics and prohibited Göring from attending further meetings with himself for the following month.[84]

The cooperation of the Luftwaffe at the highest level, however, was vital to the success of the undertaking, and on 7 March 1940, Falkenhorst met with Göring at his opulent hunting mansion, Karinhall, to discuss the upcoming campaign and, more important, smooth the *Feldmarschall*'s ruffled feathers. Meanwhile, Milch attempted to impress upon his air chief the strategic significance of Norway by presenting him with a copy of a book by the German naval theorist Wolfgang Wegener.[85] Milch elaborated on this incident after the war by explaining that Wegener, "an admiral in the First World War," had written his book to show the necessity of occupying Norway, "because only once this had been achieved would it be possible for the navy to wage war against England."[86] Milch evidently hoped to impress upon Göring the importance of Norway to the success not only of future naval operations but also of air action in the unfolding war.

OPERATIONAL FINE TUNING

In the face of this Luftwaffe dissatisfaction and interservice squabbling, Hitler was either unable or unwilling to enforce a unified command for the campaign as he had originally hoped. In the short term, surprise and weight of numbers would help pave the way for the eventual victory in Norway, but in the long term the special nature of the war in the Far North was ideally suited to a joint theater command under an officer experienced in at least two of the three services. Early planners had put forward *Generalleutnant* Albert Kesselring, at this stage commander of Luftflotte 2, with his army and Luftwaffe background as an ideal candidate, but Hitler never carried through on this promising initiative.[87] Thus, in the end, Falkenhorst was only really in direct command of the army units, while the OKL and the High Command of the Navy (Oberkommando der Kriegsmarine, or OKM) conducted their own operational planning and maintained separate command of their respective air and naval forces during the campaign. The naval vessels were placed under Naval Groups West and East, and the aircraft of X Fliegerkorps (Tenth Air Corps) were under the sole command of *Generalleutnant* Hans Geisler. Regarding this situation, Halder noted after the success of the invasion that Falkenhorst did not have a single aircraft under his control. In theory at least, this meant that should Falkenhorst require air support at any stage during the invasion, his request made the somewhat tortuous path from Army Gruppe XXI to the OKL, and then on to the X Fliegerkorps, which would subsequently direct the air units. On the other hand, Falkenhorst's position did make him at least first among equals, because any amendments sought by the OKL or the OKM also required his assent. However, because interservice rivalry resulted in a hodgepodge of command and interservice arrangements, the success of *Weserübung* relied to a considerable degree on military professionalism and operational cooperation rather than a rigid, unified command structure.[88]

Aside from Göring's theatrics, 5 March also saw the issuing of the first of many operational orders for the campaign that would be dispatched between early March and early April 1940. Without detailing all the amendments and additions made over this four-week period, it is possible to provide a brief summary of the overall "look" of the operational plans that developed as *Weserübung Nord* and *Weserübung Süd*. *Weserübung Nord* essentially divided the campaign in Norway into two phases: the initial assault on Oslo, Kristiansand, Arandel, Egersund, Bergen, Trondheim, and Narvik, followed by consolidation through reinforcement of men, equipment, and supplies.

"Operational Order No.1 for the Occupation of Norway," issued by Gruppe XXI, placed Falkenhorst's headquarters at Hamburg during the invasion, after which it would be transferred as soon as practicable to Oslo.[89] From these headquarters the *General die Infanterie* had at his disposal the 69th, 163rd, 181st, 196th, and 214th Infantry Divisions and two infantry regiments of the 3rd Mountain Division (the only experienced combat division). Added to this were a tank battalion, four batteries of 10-cm-caliber guns, two batteries of 15-cm-caliber guns, and two companies of railway construction men, plus a communications battalion.[90] An additional three paratrooper companies and three antiaircraft battalions were supplied by the Luftwaffe and remained under the command of X Fliegerkorps. In total, the initial assault force on *Weser*-day numbered some 12,250 men, of whom 8,850 were destined for Norway and 3,400 for Denmark.

The delivery of the majority of these men naturally fell to the German navy. With the Royal Navy lurking in the vicinity, its much weaker opponent needed to achieve surprise because, as Raeder soberly mused in his meeting with Hitler on 9 March:

> This operation runs counter to all the lessons of naval warfare, which indicate that it would only be justified if we possessed the necessary sea power, and this is not the case. On the contrary the operation will have to be carried out in the face of the greatly superior British Fleet. I believe, however, that given complete surprise the dispatch of the troops can and will succeed. History shows many cases of success in operations, which have violated the principles of war, always provided there is the element of surprise.[91]

Therefore, because rapidity of deployment and military precision were required, the initial assault forces would be transported by warship. For the entire occupation of Norway and Denmark, the navy had organized its vessels into eleven groups, of which the first six were dedicated to Norway. These were as follows:

Group 1 (Narvik)	The battle cruisers *Scharnhorst* and *Gneisenau* with 10 destroyers (2,000 troops)
Group 2 (Trondheim)	The cruiser *Hipper* and 4 destroyers (1,700 troops)
Group 3 (Bergen)	The cruisers *Köln* and *Königsberg,* the service ships *Bremse* and *Karl Peters,* 3 torpedo boats, 5 motor torpedo boats (1,900 troops)
Group 4 (Kristiansand-Arendal)	The cruiser *Karlsruhe,* the special service ship *Tsingtau,* 3 torpedo boats, and 7 motor torpedo boats (1,100 troops)
Group 5 (Oslo)	The pocket battleship *Lützow* and cruisers *Blücher* and *Emden,* 3 torpedo boats, 2 armed whaling boats, and 8 minesweepers (2,000 troops)
Group 6 (Egersund)	4 minesweepers (150 troops)[92]

To cover the most vulnerable part of the operation in northern waters, *Scharnhorst* and *Gneisenau* (neither of which carried troops) would act as escort to Groups 1 and 2 as they made their way to Trondheim, and then on *Weser*-day the two battleships would set a northwesterly course to divert the expected arrival of the Royal Navy. There was, however, considerable debate over how long the other warships should remain, particularly at Narvik and Trondheim, after disgorging their human cargo. The navy foresaw that the most dangerous part of its operation would be, as Raeder mentioned to the Führer, the "return voyage which entails breaking through the British naval forces."[93] Raeder planned that once the landings were completed, the warships engaged in the northern landings would combine around the battle cruisers *Scharnhorst* and *Gneisenau* for a breakthrough into southern waters. "At a time when the fate of the German fleet is hanging in the balance," the *Großadmiral* believed, not a single destroyer should be left behind at either Narvik or Trondheim. The army, on the other hand, wanted the warships to remain to provide covering fire for the ground forces, especially because air cover would not be readily available initially in the northern extremities of the campaign. Although Hitler was inclined to agree with the army's position, it was eventually decided that, while two destroyers were to be left at Trondheim, none were to be left behind at Narvik.[94] In the south this was less of a problem because the Luftwaffe would provide air cover for naval operations, and a minefield was to be laid at the entrance of the Skagerrak to protect the western flank of the operations for Oslo and Kristiansand, where considerable British submarine activity could be expected.

All going well, the Germans hoped that there would be little contact with the forces of the Royal Navy and that any major action would be blunted by U-boats under the directives given in Operation *Hartmuth*. To this end, twenty-eight U-boats were deployed off the Norwegian coast and around the Shetlands-Orkney region. Their task was to protect German warships inside Norwegian fjords by stationing themselves (four at Narvik, two at Trondheim, five at Bergen, and two at Stavanger) in such a position that they could intercept British surface vessels attempting to breach the fjords and engage German warships. Additionally, in order to intercept an anticipated Allied counterlanding, a number of U-boats were stationed in groups in open waters (six northeast of the Shetlands, three east of the Orkneys, plus four situated east and west of Pentland Firth). These U-boats (plus two off Stavanger and three west of Naze) were also instructed to prevent British vessels from interrupting maritime communications between Germany and Norway.[95] On 4 March, the German navy began canceling U-boat operations elsewhere, holding the boats in readiness for the invasion. By 11 March, a small number of Dönitz's long-range U-boats were released to cover the major ports along the western Norwegian coast in case of a British operation in the region, and in readiness for their own Nordic invasion.[96]

However, the campaign faced a number of logistical problems that had to be overcome: first, the warships were unable to carry the necessary weapons, munitions, and provisions for the initial assault; second, once the British were alerted to the German invasion, it would be very difficult for supply ships to make their way up the Norwegian coast to deliver the required heavy equipment and reinforcements to consolidate the Germans' Scandinavian foothold; finally, the destroyers of Group 1 and Group 2 would, once they had reached Narvik and Trondheim, need refueling for the lengthy "dash" home.

The first of these problems was overcome by the creation of an "Export Group," so-called because it was intended to appear as normal merchant traffic en route to Murmansk. The seven ships of the "Export Group" would leave Hamburg for Stavanger, Trondheim, and Narvik ahead of the warships. The second problem was solved by the deployment of fifteen vessels of the "1st Naval Transport Group," which would leave Stettin for Copenhagen, Oslo, Kristiansand, Stavanger, and Bergen loaded with the initial reinforcements, including 3,761 men, 672 horses, 1,377 vehicles, and 59,035 tons of army supplies. The last difficulty was resolved by deploying a set of three tankers laden with 21,000 tons of fuel oil. Of these vessels, the *Kattegat* and *Skagerrak* would make for Trondheim and Narvik, respectively, from Wilhelmshaven, while the *Jan Wellen* plied Arctic waters from *Basis Nord,* on the Murmansk coast, to Narvik to refuel the destroyers of Group 1 and Group 2. In addition to these, five smaller tankers would make their way from Hamburg to Oslo, Stavanger, Bergen, and Trondheim. Essentially unprotected, except for monitoring by air reconnaissance, all the vessels involved in the initial reinforcement phase and the refueling of the warships were to travel individually and as inconspicuously as possible with a view to arriving at their respective destinations on the day of the occupation. In the twelve days following the invasion, the "2nd to 8th Naval Transport Groups" would shuttle the remaining reinforcements between German ports and Oslo, totaling approximately 54,500 men, 5,850 horses, 12,600 vehicles, and 48,200 tons of army supplies.[97] Because of the vulnerability of the merchant vessels and the need to maintain absolute secrecy, the OKW ordered that none of these vessels were to leave port more than six days before *Weser*-day. This last demand made it very difficult for the vessels to reach their destinations on time.

The "Operational Order No. 1 for the Occupation of Denmark," *Weserübung Süd,* was issued on 20 March 1940.[98] Command of the Danish campaign was placed in the hands of the XXXI Korps under the leadership of *General der Flieger* Leonhard Kaupisch. At his disposal were the 170th and 198th Infantry Divisions, the 11th Motorized Rifle Brigade, three motorized machine-gun battalions, two batteries of heavy artillery, two tank companies, and three armored trains. From the Luftwaffe a company of parachute troops, a motorcycle company of the "General Göring" Regiment, and two battalions of antiaircraft guns were supplied for the sweep across Jutland. The main objective of *Weserübung Süd* was the capture and securing of Aalborg, at the northern end of the Jutland Peninsula. Aalborg's airfields were to be taken early on *Weser*-day by a parachute platoon and an air-landed battalion. The full weight of the 170th Division and the 11th Motorized Rifle Brigade would then sweep across the entire peninsula from Germany. Considering the bulk of the operation could be carried out by land, and because interference by the Royal Navy was very unlikely, the five groups of naval vessels deployed by the Germans for occupation of the outlying Danish islands and Jutland's west coast were made up of very light units and merchant vessels (the exception being the aptly named First World War battleship *Schleswig-Holstein*):

Group 7 (Korsör and Nyborg)	(1,990 troops)
Group 8 (Copenhagen)	(1,000 troops)
Group 9 (Middelfart)	(400 troops)

Group 10 (Esbjerg)   (none)
Group 11 (Tyborön)   (none)

NORWEGIAN AND DANISH DEFENSES

Neither *Weserübung Nord* nor *Süd* was expected to experience significant resistance from the military forces of either Nordic nation. In fact, the general condition of the Norwegian armed forces was woefully inadequate to meet the looming threat from Germany in the south.[99] In the years following the end of the First World War, and amid the general optimism surrounding the founding of the League of Nations, Norway's defense forces had been allowed to fall into a state of general disrepair. For example, the new defense organization instituted by the Norwegian government in 1933 reduced the number of regular officers and noncommissioned officers from 3,750 to 470 men, and the number of units available for mobilization fell from six divisions to only six brigades. In addition to the forces being relatively small, it was estimated that a total mobilization would take at least 12 to 14 days, especially if a partial mobilization was initiated first and was carried out via the national mail service. Furthermore, although prior to the war the Norwegians increased the duration of compulsory service from 48 to 84 days, it languished well behind those of Denmark and Sweden, which required 190 and 175 days, respectively. With regard to the Norwegian navy, things were not much better. To cover its 2,600-kilometer coastline, Norway had only sixty-three warships, the bulk of which were museum pieces launched between 1874 and 1918, and only five worthy of the description "modern." The Norwegians' overall deployment of these naval vessels was not conducive to defense either, because in order to monitor their territorial waters and uphold their neutrality, they were spread thinly over the entire length of the coast. Thus, should an invasion take place, they could not be deployed in strength quickly. The Norwegian navy also controlled three naval defense districts, which included coastal artillery forts. However, these were manned at only one-third strength because of the navy's belief that the Germans would not attempt an operation in the face of overwhelming British naval superiority, and that the Allies, for their part, had no intention of invading Norway. Although the Germany navy was aware of strong fortifications at Oslo Fjord (including a number of heavy guns of up to 28–cm caliber) and medium defensive installations at Kristiansand, Bergen, and Trondheim (some guns of up to 24-cm caliber), in general the Germans considered the coastal defenses inadequate and antiquated.[100] As for an independent air force, this simply did not exist. Both the Norwegian army and navy had minuscule numbers of aircraft of mainly older design, totaling around 150 planes, of which barely 20 could be considered modern and of any threat to German transport aircraft in the operation.[101] Overall, the Soviet-Finnish War did spur attempts to prepare Norway for a possible conflict, such as the strengthening of the Oslo Fjord fortifications and the placing of orders for fighter aircraft from the United States and Italy. However, it was too little, too late. The Norwegian government simply lacked the "necessary energy and haste" for the major construction of defensive installations, and in the case of the aircraft, events soon overtook the orders.[102]

Similarly, the Danes were ill equipped to meet the German onslaught. Although in late 1932 the Danish government initiated a major rearmament program, Denmark, like Norway, lacked the necessary energy to carry it through, and in any event such efforts were superfluous. The overwhelming scale of the Third Reich's rearmament program, coupled with Denmark's strategic vulnerability on Germany's doorstep, its insignificant size, and the lack of any natural barriers to impede an invading army, all but nullified any Danish preparations. Ironically, it was this very point—Denmark's vulnerability—reasoned Danish leaders, that made any active military action by Hitler against Denmark highly unlikely. What the Danes had not seriously taken into account, however, was the fact that they might be used as a stepping-stone for German forces on the way to Norway. Consequently, in 1940 Denmark's army was small in number, while its navy was essentially a defensive force designed either for coastal operations or for looking after Danish concerns in the Faroes and Greenland as well as its extensive fishing interests. For the most part, its small army and naval air forces (numbering in total around seventy aircraft) were made up of obsolete biplanes, mainly of British or Dutch manufacture, that were ponderous and insufficiently armed to match anything the Luftwaffe could put into the air in 1940.[103]

THE LUFTWAFFE

On 20 March 1940, the covering order for X Fliegerkorps was issued, detailing the wide-ranging part the Luftwaffe would play in the upcoming "lightning occupation":

> The support of the land and sea operations for the seizure of Norway and Denmark through: aerial demonstrations, paratroop operations as well as transportation of airborne army units. It is responsible for breaking any enemy resistance which might arise, providing covering fire for disembarked units against air attack and fighting off an eventual interference attempt by a British airborne operation and/or naval forces.[104]

Given the numerous tasks involved, the eclectic range of aircraft and personnel required, plus the unique nature of the invasion, the flexible organizational structure of the Luftwaffe *Fliegerkorps* was ideally suited to the demands of *Weserübung*. Although in most instances during the war, a *Fliegerkorps* operated under the overall leadership of a *Luftflotte* (air fleet; the largest self-contained air command in the Luftwaffe), at other times it could function autonomously as deemed necessary by the Luftwaffe High Command. Moreover, because the structure of a *Fliegerkorps* was often determined by the immediacy of its given task at any one time, its numbers could vary considerably over relatively short periods and between individual *Fliegerkorps*. Despite this fluidity of size and composition, all *Fliegerkorps* were made up of commonly designated and structured subordinate elements. The smallest of these air units were the *Staffeln* (squadrons), each typically comprising nine aircraft. Next, a force of three squadrons made a *Gruppe* (group), which, when the three aircraft of the group headquarters staff were added, amounted to a total strength of thirty. In turn, three Luftwaffe groups, totaling some ninety aircraft, made up a typical *Geschwader* (wing), which was formed principally around a particular type of aircraft. For example, a wing composed solely of bombers was known as a *Kampfgeschwader* (KG), a wing of dive-bombers as a *Stukageschwader* (StG), a wing of twin-engined fighters as a *Zerstörergeschwader* (ZG), and a wing of single-engined fighters as a *Jagdgeschwader* (JG).

Although prior to *Weserübung* a relatively small entity, X Fliegerkorps would be considerably strengthened with additional air combat units and augmented by increased numbers of reconnaissance and transport aircraft for the invasion of Norway and Denmark. The small but potent core of X Fliegerkorps consisted of the aircraft of KG 26 and KG 30; of these, the former comprised three groups of the sharklike Heinkel He 111 bomber and the latter, three groups of the Luftwaffe's latest and fastest bomber, the Junkers Ju 88.[105] The crews of these twin-engined aircraft were ideally suited to the task at hand because of experience gained over the sea in the economic war waged against Britain since the autumn of 1939. For example, since the outbreak of the war, X Fliegerkorps had been engaged in deep forays against British naval and maritime vessels, reaching as far as the Royal Navy's main base at Scapa Flow.[106] Under the seasoned Geisler, who originally had been head of the Naval Air Command (Führer der Marineluftstreitkräfte) before joining the Luftwaffe, many *Fliegerkorps* personnel had been versed in air and naval cooperation through exposure to a modicum of naval training and joint operations.

Geisler had joined the navy in 1910 and moved steadily up the ranks, often into positions that focused on the German navy's small but vital air arm. Described later in the war as "a most competent officer" by *Generalfeldmarschall* Albert Kesselring, he proved an invaluable asset to the Luftwaffe in air operations over open waters not only off the Norwegian coast but also those surrounding the British Isles and, later in the war, over the Mediterranean.[107] For *Weserübung* his units were supplemented by one group of He 111s from KGr 100 and two groups of He 111s and one group of Ju 88s from KG 4 *(General Wever)*.[108] On the day of the invasion, the bulk of these forces stationed at northern German airfields would, at the highest level of operational readiness, prepare to carry out the Luftwaffe's most important task: the securing of Norway and Denmark against any British attack or landing operation.[109] Over the following days, small individual elements would then be pushed into forward positions at captured Danish and Norwegian airfields to increase air cover as far north and westward as possible. It was conceivable that even in the early stages of the invasion, units of the Royal Navy, which was at least five times as powerful as its German counterpart, could try to penetrate the fjords of Narvik, Trondheim, or Bergen in an attempt to destroy weaker German naval units and ground forces still in the process of consolidating their positions.[110] Even worse, in the eyes of German planners, would be an Allied counterlanding executed under covering fire from the sea against German vanguard troops. Moreover, even if British warships did not attempt such an action, they could very well, just by their presence, trap German ships within the fjords. Although in southern Norway this possibility was remote, given the proximity of German airfields in the region, in western and northern Norway it was a very real danger. Consequently, the Luftwaffe had to ensure vital "flank protection" for the German naval units (*Gneisenau* and *Scharnhorst,* along with ten destroyers) against the might of the Royal Navy in northern Norway, especially on their homeward voyage.[111] Further, in these northern and western extremities it was also hoped that the Luftwaffe's mere presence would frighten off the British Fleet once the German warships had left, in order to facilitate the consolidation of the initial landings, especially the setting up of strong naval batteries at the entrances to the fjords.

Alongside U-boats, the "eyes" of the operation in waters off the Norwegian coast (inclusive of the Orkney-Shetlands region) were the Luftwaffe's long-range reconnaissance aircraft.[112] Most of these were He 111s of X Fliegerkorps' Fernaufklärunggeschwader 122 (Long-Range Reconnaissance Wing 122, (F)/122) and were assigned to observe enemy naval forces and then direct the *Korps'* bomber forces in for the kill.[113] Particularly intensive reconnaissance of the Oslo, Kristiansand, Egersund, Stavanger, and Bergen areas was to be carried out by a squadron of (F)/120 equipped with He 111s and Dornier Do 17s.[114] In addition to these Luftwaffe air units, the naval aircraft of Küstenfliegergruppe 506 (Coastal Reconnaissance and Naval Support Group [KüFlGr] 506) were subordinated to X Fliegerkorps so that its Heinkel He 115 floatplanes could cover inland fjord waters.[115] Overall, though, the numbers of aircraft assigned to this extremely important task would prove to be dangerously inadequate. In total, only about twenty to twenty-five operationally ready long-range reconnaissance aircraft and twenty to twenty-five naval support aircraft were at X Fliegerkorps' disposal for surveillance of the entire region of the North Sea, southern Norway, and the approaches to the lengthy Norwegian and Danish coastlines.[116] In addition to the small numbers involved, although some of these squadrons were designated "long-range," in terms of maritime warfare their range was actually woefully poor—a weakness the British were to exploit at Narvik. Moreover, in the months and years that followed, the lack of significant numbers of long-range aircraft within the Luftwaffe's inventory would be the single most important factor in determining the usefulness or otherwise of Norway as a base for German air operations against Britain and the war at sea as prescribed in Hitler's directive for *Weserübung.*

Of the bomber forces, a handful would engage in aerial demonstrations as part of the Germans' psychological attempt to weaken the will of the Norwegian and Danish governments and frighten them into submission. This was at least partly based on the perceived psychological influence achieved by similar demonstrations of aerial prowess over Czechoslovakia and Austria in March 1939.[117] It was not an unreasonable proposition, as many European countries had been blasted with German propaganda extolling the power of the Luftwaffe in the latter years of peace—propaganda that seemed all too accurate when one considered the terror produced by Luftwaffe dive-bombers on hapless Polish civilians only months earlier.[118] To reinforce this very point, only a few days before the invasion, Curt Bräuer, the German foreign minister to Norway, would show a select Oslo audience *Baptism of Fire,* the official German film of the invasion of Poland, which included footage of the bombing of Warsaw.[119] Hopefully the lessons from this film would not be lost on the audience when, in a show of strength on the day of the invasion, small numbers of Luftwaffe bombers and fighters would attempt to encourage a "friendly occupation." For this purpose, a bomber group escorted by twin-engined fighter-bombers, the long-range Messerschmitt Bf 110, would fly over Copenhagen and Jutland. In Norway, two bomber groups and a few Bf 110s would demonstrate over Oslo, and a further bomber group, also supported by Bf 110s, would parade German aerial supremacy above Kristiansand-Bergen and Stavanger. However, should these aerial exhibitions, accompanied by leaflet drops, fail to cow the two Scandinavian nations into submission, these units would be thrown into the fray against any resistance that should arise.

In addition to escorting demonstration aircraft, two groups of Bf 110s (I./ZG1 and I./ZG76), plus a group of the predatory single-engined Messerschmitt Bf 109 fighters (II./JG77), formed an important component in protection of air transports in the assault on Danish and Norwegian airfields and protection of these bases as forward operation bases from which German bomber aircraft would range against British naval forces.[120] Nevertheless, although combat aircraft such as these fighters are often found at the forefront of airpower analyses, transport aircraft were assigned an equally important role in the campaign by carrying out a massive airlift operation to secure Germany's foothold on Norwegian soil.

THE AIR ASSAULT AND CONSOLIDATION

The German campaign in Norway was the first attempt to utilize transport aircraft in the delivery of paratroops and air-landed forces, followed by light flak units, supplies, and reinforcements into the very forefront of battle. During *Weserübung,* the Luftwaffe's air transport forces had four main tasks.[121] First was the speedy and timely delivery of paratroops and air-landed forces into live combat areas. Only through the application of airpower could the most important airfields be captured quickly enough to enable further use by Luftwaffe units in support of the navy and the army. The unexpectedness of such assaults was deemed the best way of catching defenders off guard. Second, German planners acknowledged that air transport offered the only viable means by which isolated areas could be quickly provisioned and reinforced, especially once the warships and transports had left northern and central Norway for home waters. Third, given the distance between Germany and the widely dispersed objectives, the escorting Bf 110s and Bf 109s (designed for short-range tactical operations) were reliant on the first wave of transports to deliver necessary supplies of aviation fuel, ammunition, servicing equipment, and personnel to enable them to immediately operate from the recently occupied airfields. As the writer of a popular OKW propaganda publication noted after the campaign:

> A fighter wing goes north! A simple thing most people would think. One seats oneself in the machine, travels with the speed of the birds and in an hour travels perhaps 500 kilometers and is there. The reality is different. A fighter unit is organized like a regiment. Numerous teams are essential for the ground organization, for the maintenance of engines, batteries, and the delicate weapons.[122]

Finally, on *Weser*-day and in the days following, this initial work would be augmented by a continued airlift involving not only additional fuel and equipment but also the ferrying in of troops and command staffs to oversee consolidation of German positions. The importance of provisions via airlift in the immediacy of the invasion was doubly important because planners realized that the plundering of local supplies by German forces would be detrimental both to the overall hope of portraying the invasion as a "friendly occupation" and to the local Norwegian economy, which was heavily dependent on overseas supplies of mineral oil, bread grains, foodstuffs, and textiles. Thus, orders declared that local stocks were to be used only in emergencies, and then paid for. Indicating that the Germans intended to stay for a lengthy period, it was further noted that whatever useful supplies were found would be reserved for the OKW or "civilian plenipotentiaries nominated by the Führer."[123]

Administratively, the organization and preparations for the airlift were placed within the command of Geisler's X Fliegerkorps, within which were established the offices of the Air Transport Chief (Land) and the Air Transport Chief (Sea). The latter of these two commands was a relatively minor player in the proceedings because its forces consisted of only twenty-two twin-engined Heinkel He 59 floatplanes and a smattering of Junkers Ju 52s equipped with pontoons. However, *Oberstleutnant* Carl August Freiherr von Gablenz, the Air Transport Chief (Land), was assigned a pivotal role in the proceedings.[124] The directive for the Transport Chief (Land) placed the Air Transport Groups KGzbV (*Kampfgeschwader zur besonderen Verwendung,* bomber wings for special duties) 101, 102, 103, 104, 105, 106, and 107 under Gablenz's command.[125] It should be noted that these transport wings, despite being designated "bomber wings," were composed almost exclusively of ubiquitous triple-engined Ju 52 transports and differed from normal combat wings in that they were made up of only three squadrons, numbering 53 aircraft in total. The sole exception to this organization was KGzbV 105, composed of two squadrons of Ju 52s and a third made up of four-engined Junkers Ju 90 and Focke-Wulf Fw 200 heavy transports, and a single four-engined Junkers G 38. In addition to these units, Gablenz also had the first, second, and third groups and an additional two squadrons of the First Bomber Wing for Special Purposes at his disposal for the most important and possibly most difficult part of the airborne operation. It was the air transport units of this wing, flying some 160 aircraft, that would converge on Aalborg, Oslo, and Stavanger laden with elite German paratroopers. The remaining transports, approximately 340 in all, would deliver the airborne reinforcements, light flak units, supplies, and equipment once the airfields were secured.[126] In total, Gablenz had some 500 transport aircraft, the most that had ever been brought together for a military operation.

Unlike their Anglo-French enemy, the Germans had placed a great deal of importance on the development of a sizable air transport fleet. The Luftwaffe had noted the successful exploitation of transport aircraft by the British during the disturbances in Cyprus in 1931 and the skirmishes in Iraq in 1932. Further displays of the effectiveness of such airlifts occurred in the Chaco War (1932–1934) between Bolivia and Paraguay and later in the Italian Abyssinia campaign of 1935–1936, where troops, supplies, and wounded were all moved by transports. Consequently, astute airpower experts in Germany realized that the possibilities of transport aircraft could, if exploited correctly, change the "essential features of the picture of war."[127]

Aircraft, however, could not continue indefinitely to meet all of the Luftwaffe's requirements in Norway. Consequently, it was apportioned ten sea vessels from the 1st Naval Transport Group to carry supplies, ammunition, and personnel to Oslo, Kristiansand, Stavanger, and Bergen.[128] On top of this, three aircraft tenders would deliver mines, bombs, and high-octane gas to Stavanger and Bergen, and a further four smaller tankers laden solely with octane gas would make their way to Oslo, Stavanger, Bergen, and Trondheim. The single largest delivery of thirty railway trucks loaded with fuel for the Luftwaffe would be made by the 10,397-ton tanker *Friedrich Breme* of the 3rd Naval Transport Group, and in the days following, Luftwaffe supplies would continue to be delivered by the 5th and 8th Naval Transport Groups.

Crucial to achieving surprise and the prompt delivery of paratroopers, airborne units, and supply materials was the tight schedule the transports had to work under. To ensure that Allied suspicions were not aroused, these aircraft were to transfer from their respective home bases to the assembly airfields in northern Germany at Oldenburg, Bremen, Hamburg, and Schleswig-Holstein only three days prior to the invasion. Moreover, to avoid loose lips broadcasting German intentions, the briefing of the transport crews would not commence until the evening prior to *Weser*-day. On *Weser*-day itself, perfect timing was critical. For

instance, the paratroop landings at Fornebu were set at *Weser*-time plus 185 minutes, which gave the paratroopers only 20 minutes to secure the airfields before
the arrival of the transports bearing airborne units at *Weser*-time plus 205 minutes.[129] To facilitate the rapid and frictionless arrival and departure of transports,
the closest liaison between the commander of the transport groups and the officer
in charge of the paratroopers was to be maintained at all times. Contact here, and
throughout the campaign, was to be facilitated by the establishment of a comprehensive Luftwaffe Communication Service (Luftnachtrichten-Truppe) force totaling 51 officers and 3,145 noncommissioned officers and men.[130] To get a better
picture of the careful planning and precision of execution required by the air transport units in cooperation with the combat aircraft, it is at this point germane to
examine in detail each of the proposed Luftwaffe operations.

The ability of the Luftwaffe to carry out its most important task (the interception of British naval forces) was dependent on securing airfields in Norway
and Denmark, thereby removing some 500 to 650 kilometers of flying distance
from sorties against Allied warships and aerial support of isolated ground forces
in the north.[131] This not only would increase the range of the German aircraft but
also would allow for a reduction in the amount of fuel required on any given
mission, which in turn would mean a greater quantity of bombs could be carried.
Realistically, the Germans could only expect to utilize four main airfields initially:
the Danish Aalborg West and East airfields at the northern tip of the Jutland Peninsula, as supporting bases for operations in Norway; the Fornebu airfield, which
would support the army in combat around Oslo; and Stavanger's Sola airfield,
which would act as a central air base in the region for naval support and harassment of British warships.

With regard to logistics and strategic considerations, German planners believed that the northern Danish airfields represented an "exceedingly important"
link in the movement of forces and material between Germany and Norway, as
well as the major staging post for Luftwaffe raids against British sea forces.[132]
Danish defenses here were considered weak at best, and Luftwaffe intelligence
suggested that Jutland was covered by a single squadron of some fifteen obsolete
Hawker Furies based at Okaböl. As for flak defenses, these were almost nonexistent in northern Jutland, since Danish defensive positions, such as they were,
were concentrated in the Zeeland region and southern Jutland.[133] Intelligence therefore concluded that the prerequisites for investment of the Danish airfields appeared "very favorable." Consequently, air transports, under the relatively weak
protection of Bf 110s, would make the first drops of paratroopers at the airfields
of Aalborg West and East within two hours of the German troops' crossing the
Danish frontier. The paratroops were to secure Aalborg West in preparation for
the arrival of transport aircraft bearing army airborne units. To achieve this they
were to gain control of all sectors of the field, especially toward the township of
Aalborg; prevent any aircraft present from taking off; and occupy the airport
buildings to prevent communication with Aalborg East. Any Danish guards were

to be disarmed and nationals of enemy countries detained. All refueling facilities and aviation fuel stocks were to be guarded against intentional destruction. Once the operation was completed, landing crosses were to be laid out and swastika flags erected to show the all clear.

The paratroop drops would then be followed up by air-landed troops. Elements of these would advance on Aalborg East. To make these fields serviceable as early as possible, the next wave of transports would include refueling companies, an air-field command staff, and ground personnel, thus facilitating the rapid turnaround of transport and combat aircraft. Arriving alongside the transports, special purpose signals aircraft would control local air traffic and maintain close radio contact with the *Fliegerkorps'* command post. These signals aircraft were essential for managing the extensive air traffic of German bombers, escort fighters, and transport units expected to hold sway over the whole of Jutland and the western approaches to Danish coastal waters on *Weser*-day. Luftwaffe planners envisaged that, once refueled and rearmed, the escorting Bf 110s would operate out of Aalborg, flying escort for air transports moving between Aalborg, Stavanger, and Oslo. By midday, these would be followed by a small detachment of Stukas ready to do battle with the Royal Navy. What the Aalborg fields had over their Norwegian counterparts—Oslo and Stavanger—aside from this initial airborne arrival of personnel and materials, was that they could be immediately provisioned with aviation fuel, bombs, and munitions by rail from Germany once the region had been secured.[134]

Out of the sprinkling of airfields around Oslo, the Germans selected the commercial Fornebu field for the surprise landing by two parachute companies. Its proximity to the Norwegian capital and the fact that it was nearing completion as Oslo's new commercial airport made Fornebu ideal as an operational base for Luftwaffe support of the army and navy.[135] As at Aalborg West and East, the orders made the parachute companies responsible for gaining the initial foothold and breaking any local resistance. Once captured, the airfield would become the point of entry for a number of regional operations staffs, including those of Falkenhorst, the 69th Infantry Division, and the 193rd Infantry Regiment. Once the field was secured, a bomber squadron of KG 26 that had been demonstrating over Oslo would make a stopover landing, while another KG 26 squadron would make the airfield its operating base.[136]

Although there was little danger of meeting significant aerial opposition in the entire campaign, Luftwaffe planners were aware that of all the possible trouble spots, Oslo was the most likely. Luftwaffe intelligence believed the Norwegians had a squadron of twelve Gloster Gladiators at Oslo's Fornebu airfield, while north of the capital lay the largest military air base in Norway.[137] At the Oslo-Kieller-Lilleströn field the Norwegians had stationed two squadrons of twenty old Fokker CVs and a fighter squadron of about twenty obsolete Hawker Furies. Moreover, the Germans maintained that Oslo had the only flak garrison in Norway, although its weaponry was judged to be "completely unsatisfactory and not modern." The only other area of minor concern was the main Norwegian naval air base situated at Horten near the entrance to Oslo Fjord, where no more than twenty-five aircraft of varying antiquity were believed to reside. While the only relatively modern aircraft were six German He 115 floatplanes, of greater import were the expanded coastal fortifications. Luftwaffe intelligence advised that modern flak in the inner coastal defenses could be reckoned on, while the focus of central fortifications, known as the "Oslo Fortress," was based around the Horten emplacements.[138]

The assault on Stavanger contained most of the essential elements of the Aalborg and Oslo landings. Transported by Ju 52s and escorted by Bf 110s, a platoon of paratroopers were to jump over Stavanger's Sola airfield and secure it for the landing of an infantry company.[139] Deployed troops were warned of resistance, particularly from the western approaches to the airfield, where it was believed that some 150 Norwegian troops were stationed. Lying closest to the British coastline, Sola airfield was expected to bear the brunt of early British air strikes and possibly even an airborne operation. Therefore, it was especially important that flak protection against British air attack be set up quickly at Stavanger. Because the arrival by ship of two flak companies could not be expected until the following day at the earliest, the paratroopers were to establish flak protection against "deep attacks" by British aircraft to bridge this period. Once the airfield was operational, one bomber squadron from KG 26 and one Bf 110 squadron from ZG 76 were to land and prepare for further orders.[140] Planners also hoped to bring in one squadron of Stukas of StG 1 to operate against British naval forces in Norwegian waters and the Skagerrak.[141]

Smaller Luftwaffe operations were envisaged for Kristiansand, Bergen, and Trondheim. At Kristiansand, a small industrial town of some 20,000 inhabitants and a minor naval air base, the attack was to be supported by a special paratroop company (less one platoon), which would be followed up the next day by the air transport of an army battalion.[142] Although the naval base was an insignificant threat to the overall operation, the Germans felt that it represented an important link in tactical operations because the next airfield was some 160 kilometers distant at Sola.[143] The assault on Bergen, the second-largest Norwegian city, with a population of some 100,000, involved the air delivery of a mountain battalion, an infantry regiment (less one company), and a company of engineers. Similarly, these would be followed up on 10 April by the air delivery of reinforcements. In addition to these ground forces, the Luftwaffe would station a multipurpose squadron of KüFlGr 506 at Bergen as an advanced element for aerial reconnaissance and to protect the most important harbor on Norway's central west coast, a logistically valuable point because of its rail link to Oslo.[144] At Trondheim, with a population of 60,000, the navy and army forces were to be supported by two squadrons of KüFlGr 506, which were to make sea landings there once a thorough reconnaissance had been carried out.[145] Trondheim's land-based airfield, Vaernes, was to be taken by troops delivered by naval vessels and made ready for incoming air transports and further aerial operations. Moreover, Vaernes would form the initial aerial link with the most distant forces in the Narvik operation.[146]

KüFlGr 506 gave X Fliegerkorps a considerable degree of tactical flexibility. This was especially true where its seaplanes were able to land in fjords in distant regions where land-based fields were either unsuitable or simply nonexistent close to the point of action. Seaplanes could also greatly increase the operating radius of the Luftwaffe north of Trondheim because, unlike their land-based counterparts, they were not limited by the need to conserve fuel for a return flight when suitable airfields were not available.[147] For all these reasons, the closest coordination of all Luftwaffe activity was considered essential, and therefore KüFlGr 506 was taken from the Naval Air Command West and placed directly under Geisler's air corps.

Naval Air Command West and Naval Air Command East nevertheless were to play their own parts in the upcoming campaign. The former was detailed to work alongside X Fliegerkorps with five flying boat squadrons of KüFlGr 508 and a handful of Dornier Do 26 flying boats from the Transatlantic Squadron in reconnaissance in the North Sea. The Naval Air Command East, on the other hand, was to protect the vulnerable naval transport squadrons from enemy submarine attacks in the Skagerrak.

When the balance of aircraft operated by Naval Air Commands West and East are added to all others, it becomes apparent that the Germans had placed a large number of various aircraft types at the disposal of X Fliegerkorps, with a total over 1,000 machines.[148] How these units would be assembled and deployed alongside naval and ground contingents in the days leading up to 9 April was neatly summarized in the following operational outline:

> The first tanker to put out for Trondheim on *W*-5 day (4 April) will, the next day, be followed by the "export squadron" bound for Trondheim and Narvik. Disembarkation of the Army forces in the landing ports will by this time be completed. On 6 April, the first naval transport squadron will leave Stettin and the naval forces of the Transport Groups, composed of battleships, cruisers and destroyers, some with troops and gear on board, will leave Cuxhaven during the evening of 7 April. Their passage will be assured by the reconnaissance of Naval Air Commander West and X Korps; Naval Air Commander will be on anti-submarine patrol.
>
> On 6 April, the Air Force will assemble the transport Gruppen; on the next day 11 transport Gruppen will assemble in the ports of departure; on 8 April the Paratroop Transport Gruppen will be ready.[149]

THE COUNTDOWN

The success of this initial naval phase was dependent on knowing as accurately as possible the strength and disposition of the British Fleet at all times. Consequently, a number of aircraft from Naval Air Command West and X Fliegerkorps had been deployed in reconnaissance in the days leading up to the invasion in an area stretching from the entrance of the Skagerrak into the North Sea and over the waters of Scapa Flow and its environs. This latter region was home to a considerable portion of the British Fleet and, as such, represented a significant threat to *Weserübung*'s western flank. Nevertheless, the monitoring of these enemy units proved difficult. A number of missions had to be curtailed because of poor weather, such as those made on 28 and 30 March, while others, such as the flight by three long-range He 111s of (F)/122 over the Orkneys on 31 March 1940, met with enemy aircraft and heavy antiaircraft fire from light shore and naval defenses.[150] Despite these obstacles, a rough picture of the Royal Navy's dispositions could be gauged from the results of photoanalysis and radio intercepts. In all, it was estimated that Allied naval strength in the North Sea consisted of approximately five British and two French battleships, fourteen British cruisers (and one French cruiser moving into the region), one or two aircraft carriers, and about six destroyer flotillas, as well as fifteen to twenty-nine submarines.[151]

In the first week of April, the Luftwaffe continued to carry out active reconnaissance over Scapa Flow in conjunction with sorties by aircraft of X Fliegerkorps against convoys plying the waters between the Scandinavian Peninsula and Britain. Whereas the latter operations constituted a continuation of Germany's economic war against Britain, the raids on Scapa were designed not only to gather intelligence but also to follow up the Luftwaffe's successful mid-March raid, which had resulted in the temporary evacuation of Scapa Flow from 19 to 26 March as the Home Fleet took to sea.[152] Because of the proximity of Scapa to the Norwegian coast, it was an ideal operational base from which to patrol the 500-kilometer-wide northern entrance to the North Sea and, as such, offered a significant threat to the German invasion. Although the Germans could not expect subsequent forays to achieve the same glowing results, they hoped to keep the British out of range while preparations for *Weserübung* drew to a close. The results of these raids were, however, often mixed.[153] Although the 2 April attack made by ten planes of KG 30 observed that three light cruisers, plus destroyers and auxiliary vessels, were in Scapa, no hits were made due to a technical problem that hampered the bomb release gear on several of the aircraft, and also because of the light and heavy antiaircraft fire that swept up to meet the German intruders. One of X Fliegerkorps' planes was brought down at Scapa, and a further aircraft was lost over Germany on the return flight. At the same time as this raid on Scapa, eleven planes of KGr 100 attacked British convoys east of the Orkney and Shetland Islands, with similarly dismal results. The next day, reconnaissance aircraft spotted a convoy escorted by one cruiser and six destroyers north of Viking Bank. X Fliegerkorps initially dispatched ten aircraft of KGr 100 and KG 30 and then decided to throw a further seventeen planes of KG 26 into the fray off the Orkneys.[154] The aircraft severely damaged or sunk two patrol boats off Britain's east coast and two patrol boats northwest of the Shetlands. Two steamers also suffered badly at the hands of the Luftwaffe, and one destroyer was hit on its deck. Three more steamers and one further patrol boat were reported damaged, while the German losses amounted to three aircraft.

The following day, the first tanker bound for Trondheim slipped its berth, and on 5 April the "Export Group" of transports left Germany.[155] On the morning of 7 April, the heavy cruiser *Hipper*, fourteen destroyers, and the battle cruisers *Scharnhorst* and *Gneisenau* of Groups 1 and 2 were building up steam on their way to Narvik and Trondheim. Reconnaissance between the Shetlands and Norway for this formation was provided by eighteen Dornier He 18s flying boats and three Heinkel bombers under the Naval Air Command.[156] Similarly, when more warships and supply vessels started out for Kristiansand, Bergen, and Oslo, the Naval Air Commander West put one Do 26 up over the northern Shetland Islands–Norway region, seven Do 17s over the eastern region of the central North Sea, and nine aircraft of X Fliegerkorps' (F)/122 west of these forces.[157]

Aerial reconnaissance, however, could not prevent the first sighting by the British of the German flotilla making its way to Trondheim and Narvik. On 6 April, two high-flying reconnaissance Spitfires had returned to Britain with evidence of a major naval buildup at Wilhelmshaven, which included *Hipper, Scharnhorst,* and *Gneisenau*. The movement of these vessels to the north of Heligoland was recorded by British aircraft that night, and the British attempted to locate them the following day with planes of Coastal Command.[158] In the early hours of daylight, a Coastal Command Hudson successfully spotted *Hipper* and its destroyers. The subsequent air attack by thirty-five Blenheims achieved only a handful of near misses, and twenty-four Wellingtons that followed were thwarted by low cloud. Bf 110s of X Fliegerkorps then fell on the Wellingtons on their return flight, shooting down two aircraft and heavily damaging others for the loss of one German aircraft.[159]

Of greater threat to the German expedition was the decision by Admiral Charles Forbes, commander in chief of the British Home Fleet, to dispatch his forces from Scapa Flow to engage the enemy units. However, the Germans' assessment that the British were not fully aware of their actual intentions proved correct. Based on wireless intercepts, the German Naval Staff concluded that the "Admiralty has not yet drawn conclusions about a large-scale German action within *Weserübung* from the air reconnaissance information, but rather expects a breakthrough into the Atlantic by a pocket battleship."[160] Indeed, despite the unsettling amount of information (including Royal Air Force [RAF] air reconnaissance reports) that showed massive shipping movements taking place in the Baltic and the Heligoland Bight and large numbers of Ju 52 transports amassed around Kiel, it did not dawn on the British Admiralty that the Germans were in the throes of carrying out an invasion of Norway until it was too late.[161] Blinkered by the belief that the Germans could never operate on a large enough scale to carry out such an invasion while Britannia ruled the waves, Forbes was duly informed on 7 April that "all these reports [of German shipping movements] are of doubtful value and may well be only a further move in the war of nerves."[162] Despite this,

Forbes, on his own initiative, set elements of the Home Fleet on a northeasterly course at high speed with a view to intercepting a presumed breakout into the Atlantic. Although this maneuver left the central North Sea and the Norwegian coastline uncovered and arrived too late to intercept Groups 1 and 2, it did place naval vessels at sea with a view to engaging German warships.[163]

Yet vessels of the Home Fleet were not the only threat to the German men-of-war steaming up the Norwegian coastline, as the British also had Royal Navy units in the area secretly laying mines inside Norwegian territorial waters in accordance with Operation *Wilfred*. The Germans only became aware of this development on 8 April, when the British and French governments declared their intention to exclude German shipping from unimpeded use of parts of Norwegian territorial waters by minelaying. They also announced that to prevent Norwegian shipping from falling victim to the fields, British naval units would patrol these areas, at least for the next forty-eight hours. The British claimed to have laid mines in Norwegian waters in the approaches to Vest Fjord north of Bodö, off Bud near Molde, and farther south off Stadland. In reality they had mined only the approaches to Vest Fjord. The "field" off Bud was merely a ruse, and the vessels deployed to lay the Stadland field were recalled before they were able to commence laying mines.[164] This Anglo-French mining venture was both a blessing and a curse to the Germans. Although, as the German Naval Staff war diary pragmatically noted, it was "politically welcome since it gives excellent grounds to the outside world for German actions as a counterblow to the British violation of neutrality," operationally it was unwelcome because the presence of British naval vessels in Norwegian territorial waters threatened the movement of German tankers.[165]

Nevertheless, the British made two crucial decisions that would greatly favor the successful execution of *Weserübung*. First, at 1045 hours on 8 April, the Admiralty ordered the Vest Fjord minelayers and their escort to rejoin the covering force, headed by the battle cruiser *Renown* and light cruiser *Penelope,* and therefore well clear of the Norwegian coastline. This now meant that they were no longer in a position to discover and intercept the German force that was due to pass directly by them. Second, and more important, the Admiralty commanded that, given the strength of the German force at sea, every ship was needed for fleet operations.[166] Originally, the British had recognized that the mining of Norwegian territorial waters could act as a trip wire to German retaliatory action in Norway, which in turn would pave the way for *Plan-R4:* the landing of British and French troops in Norway. Therefore, while the mining was being completed, a number of vessels in Britain remained on standby, laden with troops for just such an eventuality. Quite independently and in spite of the fact that the Home Fleet already greatly outgunned its German adversaries, Churchill ordered these ships to disembark their expeditionary force (originally destined for Stavanger) by 1400 hours and to set a course to join the fleet. Moreover, a light cruiser and six destroyers assembled at Clyde to provide cover for a force intended to bring troops to Trondheim and Narvik were also released to the Home Fleet. Ironically, given his past enthusiasm for such an adventure, Churchill deprived the Allies of the possibility of making timely and perhaps decisive counterlandings when it became clear that the Germans were carrying out a full-scale invasion of Norway.[167]

British efforts were also hampered by misleading German naval maneuvers and poor weather. On 8 April, *Hipper* encountered and, after being rammed, sank the British destroyer *Glowworm,* which had been part of the *Renown*'s minelaying escort group. At the conclusion of this engagement, *Vizeadmiral* Lütjens, the commander of Group 1's covering force—*Scharnhorst* and *Gneisenau*—realized that the action with *Glowworm* would now be known to the Admiralty. Hence, when a report came in that a German Do 26 long-range reconnaissance aircraft had sighted a British force consisting of two battleships, one heavy cruiser, and six destroyers, he decided to complete his operational duties by escorting the ten destroyers en route to Narvik. It was at this point that Groups 1 and 2 separated and made their way to their respective destinations. However, at the conclusion of its confrontation with *Glowworm* and after detaching from the main group of northbound warships, *Hipper* and its four destroyers set a westerly, rather than easterly, course because it was too early to put into Trondheim.[168] At 1530 hours, a British flying boat spotted *Hipper* and its entourage on this deceptive course. Admiral Forbes took up the chase and changed to a northerly and then northwesterly course, thus moving the Home Fleet farther and farther off the Norwegian coast and away from the impending invasion. Aside from this isolated and rather misleading sighting, rain and heavy cloud prevented British Sunderlands and Hudsons from spotting any of the sizable collection of German vessels along the Norwegian coastline making their way to Bergen, Egersund, Kristiansand, Arendal, and Oslo on the day before the invasion.[169]

Meanwhile, nearing the entrance to Vest Fjord on 8 April at 2100 hours, Lütjens broke away from the destroyers bound for Narvik and set *Gneisenau* and *Scharnhorst* on first a westerly and then a northwesterly course into the teeth of a building gale. Thus Lütjens set about fulfilling his other orders: to cover the westward flank of the destroyers operating in Narvik and divert Royal Navy forces in the region. Within eight hours and at 0449 hours on *Weser*-day, *Gneisenau*'s radar detected an enemy ship only twenty kilometers distant. Thirty minutes later, both it and *Scharnhorst* were caught in a running duel in snow squalls and heavy seas with *Renown* and the destroyers of the Vest Fjord minelaying force. Only eighteen minutes into the battle, *Renown* hit *Gneisenau*, destroying the gunnery control in its topmast, while a further hit resulted in a leak in turret A, culminating in a complete electrical failure; *Scharnhorst,* although not hit, had its A turret flooded. Despite commanding newer, faster, and better armored ships, Lütjens appears to have believed that he faced two British battleships, perhaps due to the numerous flashes given off by the supporting destroyers. In order to bring his ships back into battle readiness, he decided to break off the attack, increasing speed and heading northeast, finally shaking off *Renown* at 0730 hours. Lütjens's brush with the enemy had hardly been glorious, but he could, at least for the time being, confidently assume that he had carried out his mission to divert British attention away from the landings that were to follow.

Less dramatically, the six groups of warships with the assault forces for Narvik, Trondheim, Kristiansand, Bergen, Oslo, and Egersund proceeded uneventfully to their operational targets as planned. Additionally, the 1st Sea Transport Division (made up of fifteen steamers carrying the initial reinforcements, supplies, and equipment) was also at sea as planned, and by noon on 8 April, the Bergen and Stavanger groups were making their way through the Skagerrak off the Norwegian coast. The Kristiansand group lay in the vicinity of Skagen, at the tip of the Danish peninsula; and the Oslo group was situated in the Kattegat, off the Danish coast.[170] The overall German situation on the water and the enemy's knowledge of this were neatly summed up in the naval war diary entry of 8 April:

> The enemy is aware that the battleships are included in the Narvik and Trondheim Groups. Our own plans are not yet revealed, but is possible that increased steamer traffic through the entrances to the Baltic may appear a most striking measure both to neutral Scandinavian countries and the enemy in connection with the known concentrations of transports in Hamburg, Stettin, Gdynia which took place some time ago. It can not be ascertained how far the enemy has actually been warned or is acting on supposition.[171]

In fact, the alarm bells within the Admiralty were all but silent. The only real threat posed to German transport forces in transit were the twenty or more submarines positioned off the southwestern and southern coast of Norway and in the shallows of the Skagerrak and Kattegat in order to intercept any counteroperations in response to Operation *Wilfred*. These submarines were ideally situated to attack German transports once they had been positively identified. Of the two transports lost on 8 April, it was the sinking of the *Rio de Janeiro* (of the 1st Transport Group bound for Bergen) off Kristiansand at 1200 hours that caused the Germans a good deal of hand-wringing. When it was sunk by the Polish submarine *Orzel*, German troops in full uniform were rescued by a Norwegian destroyer and local fishing craft. The bedraggled Germans were very forthcoming and confidently informed their rescuers that they were on their way to Bergen "to protect it against the Allies."[172] By 2030 hours, the Reuters news agency broadcast that "the German transport ship *Rio de Janeiro* with 300 men on board had been sunk" off the Norwegian coast. This followed a press release at 1800 hours, which stated that 80 to 100 German naval vessels were proceeding through the Great Belt and Kattegat escorted by auxiliary vessels and trawlers. By late evening on 8 April, German naval staff prematurely concluded that operation "*Weserübung* has left the stage of secrecy and camouflage. . . . our enemies have been warned."[173] Neither Oslo nor London, however, took the matter particularly seriously, and the Allied submarines would not be given the order to sink northbound traffic without positive identification until the afternoon of 9 April. By this time, the juiciest targets had already passed tantalizingly before Allied periscopes and disgorged their deadly cargoes in Norwegian ports.[174]

In London, the Admiralty attached no particular significance to the *Rio de Janeiro* incident, and by the evening of 8 April, its myopic gaze still lingered on the northern gateway to the North Sea and bringing the German warships in this area to battle. Likewise in Oslo, the news of the *Rio de Janeiro* was not taken seriously, and consequently the government did not order a general mobilization or increase the preparedness of Norway's defenses. The failure to recognize the German threat was all the more damning given the large amount of intelligence being relayed to the Norwegians from diplomatic sources in Berlin and Copenhagen.[175] Prime Minister Nygaardsvold and Foreign Minister Koht of Norway failed to give these warnings any credence largely because their concern rested more in the west, with Britain and France. Various declarations made by Churchill, Chamberlain, and Reynaud pointed to the likelihood of some rash action being taken by the Allies rather than Germany.[176] For example, the Supreme War Council's 28 March declaration to Oslo gave notice that the British and French reserved the "right to take such measures as they may think necessary" to hinder or prevent Germany from obtaining Swedish or Norwegian resources "for the purpose of war."[177] As French historian François Kersaudy concluded in his study of the campaign in 1940, "The Norwegians were all but hypnotised by the likelihood of a British operation."[178]

Meanwhile, on the eve of *Weser*-day, as German seaborne assault units prepared to enter Norwegian fjords within a matter of hours, the Luftwaffe made one last throw at Scapa with twenty-four aircraft of X Fliegerkorps. In fading light one battleship was hit amidships and a cruiser was hit astern, while two bombs struck between two cruisers anchored close together, and one bomb fell close to another cruiser.[179] Aside from the shooting down of a single-engined British fighter, no other successes were achieved. However, the report covering the flight revealed that in addition to the vessels mentioned earlier, Scapa Flow was currently home to an aircraft carrier, five or more heavy or light cruisers, and a number of destroyers and auxiliary ships.[180] No doubt the moderate success of the Scapa sortie was received favorably by Geisler at X Fliegerkorps' headquarters in Hamburg's plush Hotel Esplanade. Thus far, German airpower had done all that was required of it. Coupled with a measure of good fortune, bad weather, and the British Admiralty's failure to grasp the full implications of the German naval activity over this period, X Fliegerkorps was able to provide adequate air cover for the Trondheim and Narvik groups and gather valuable information on the strength and disposition of British forces. Yet this was merely the precursor to the campaign. The real test of the Luftwaffe's mettle lay but a few hours away.

3

Norwegian Blitzkrieg

The campaigns in Poland, Holland, Belgium and France, and last, but not least, in Norway had proved unequivocally how important air supremacy is in modern war.

General der Flieger Karl Koller, 1945

At 0615 on 9 April, above the drone of radial engines and the noisy rush of air over the Ju 52s' boxy corrugated fuselage, German paratroopers jumped into the pages of history and the rural landscape of peaceful Denmark. This paratroop assault, the first in the history of warfare, had been hastily arranged only at the last minute. Initial plans drawn up for the deployment of these men had seen them incorporated among troops currently on their way to the Aalborg East and West airfields in northern Jutland, Oslo's Fornebu airfield, and Stavanger's Sola field on Norway's southwestern coast.[1] Yet, only thirty-six hours before *Weser*-time, frantic planners decided to siphon off ninety of the men assigned to Aalborg and deploy them in nine Ju 52s south of Copenhagen, where, under the leadership of *Hauptmann* Walter Gericke, they would capture the three-kilometer-long bridge linking the Gedser ferry terminal in the south to the Danish capital and "hold it until infantry arrived from Gedser."[2] The flight had been uneventful, and the lush Danish countryside and its inhabitants still slumbered as German paratroopers drifted silently groundward. Not a single shout of warning or shot rang out from the fort below, and within minutes of landing, the garrison on the small island of Masnedö was captured.[3] All that was left to do was secure the bridge, and this was achieved just after 0700 with the aid of an advance portion of the army forces pushing through Denmark from Germany. Thus the first paratroop action in the history of warfare had been completed bloodlessly.[4] The invasion of Denmark and Norway had begun.

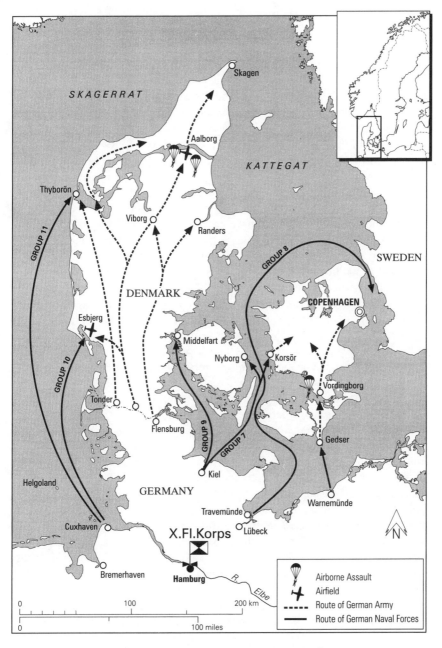

Skagen

SKAGERRAT

Aalborg

KATTEGAT

SWEDEN

Thyborön

GROUP 11

Viborg

Randers

GROUP 8

COPENHAGEN

DENMARK

Esbjerg

GROUP 10

Middelfart

Nyborg

Korsör

Vordingborg

Tonder

Flensburg

GROUP 9

GROUP 7

Gedser

Kiel

GERMANY

Warnemünde

Helgoland

Travemünde

X.Fl.Korps

Lübeck

Cuxhaven

Bremerhaven

Hamburg

R. Elbe

N

Airborne Assault	
Airfield	
Route of German Army	
Route of German Naval Forces	

0   100   200 km

0   100 miles

1. The invasion of Denmark, 9 April 1940.

Meanwhile, at 0535, three more Ju 52 transports laden with paratroops were winging their way from Üntersen toward the Aalborg airfields, which when captured would act as a springboard for aerial operations over Norway.[5] At 0700, the men were dropped over Aalborg East and West. Surprise was again complete, and within only twenty minutes reinforcements were being brought in by 53 Ju 52s. The escorting twin-engined fighters also landed at Aalborg.[6] Before nightfall, the air defenses of the Aalborg bases were in the hands of a Luftwaffe flak unit, and a massive airlift by 139 Ju 52s began the process of ferrying in ground crews, ammunition, and fuel for the Bf 110s, which were to secure the air transport routes running between Aalborg, Stavanger, and Oslo.[7] All in all, transports delivered an impressive amount of personnel, equipment, and supplies on 9 April, including paratroopers, airborne units, radio communications, the forward command staff of the special *Weserübung* Süd Luftgau (for the establishment of the ground organization), service crews, munitions for the fighters, and 170,000 liters of aviation fuel.[8] In addition to the seizure of Aalborg East and West, the Esbjerg airfield, on Denmark's western seaboard, was occupied and Bf 109s stationed there. Defense for this field was the responsibility of a flak unit, which arrived overland from Germany.[9] On 9 April, the only combat experienced by the fighters deployed over Denmark took place at Vaerløse airfield, where Bf 110s escorting bombers of KG 4 shot down a Fokker C-VE as it took to the air. The twin-engined German fighters then swooped on the remaining aircraft on the ground, destroying a substantial number of Danish fighters and reconnaissance aircraft.[10] Other than this one-sided engagement, Bf 110s and Bf 109s lay in wait at Aalborg and Esbjerg airfields, ready to provide defensive cover against possible British air attacks.[11]

The army's advance and the navy's landings were equally trouble-free. At 0515 two motorized brigades and an infantry division swept across the common frontier, shrugging off minor pockets of resistance in North Schleswig.[12] By 0800 all opposition had ceased, and before dusk a motorized rifle brigade had connected with Aalborg and the northernmost tip of Jutland, where soldiers of the Wehrmacht were able to gaze upon the confluence of the Skagerrak and Kattegat. German motorized units had covered the entire 330-kilometer length of Denmark in a day. The naval landings at Korsör, Nyborg, Middelfart, Esbjerg, and Thyborön also went according to plan (aside from the beaching of the First World War battleship *Schleswig-Holstein* in the Great Belt), and beachheads were established without opposition.

In Copenhagen, the Germans were able to take the Danish capital by complete surprise. Although searchlights were brought to bear on the German motorship *Hansestadt Danzig,* flanked by an icebreaker and two picket boats as it entered the port, the guns guarding the harbor's entrance remained silent, unable to fire because of grease in their barrels.[13] The landing was designed to take place simultaneously with aerial demonstrations. On schedule at 0703, aircraft of KG 4 *General Wever,* escorted by twin-engined fighters, buzzed the Danish capital at only 100 meters, raining leaflets on the city's astonished inhabitants. The Heinkels encountered only a minimal amount of ground fire from the southwestern part of the city, to which they replied in kind with their defensive armament. "Other than this," noted the unit history of the *General Wever* bomber wing, "no resistance was given."[14] After being threatened with the bombing of Copenhagen, the Danish government capitulated at 0720.[15] *Weserübung Süd* was a complete success. The Luftwaffe had played its part to perfection by bringing about the swift capture of the strategically important bridge south of Copenhagen, securing the Aalborg airfields for the use of German aircraft, and further weakening the Danes' flagging will to resist through aerial demonstrations. The Germans now held their stepping-stone and staging post for air operations over Norway and its coastline. In Norway, however, a completely different campaign was developing in the face of stiffening resistance and deteriorating weather.

DRAMA AT FORNEBU AND OSLO

On 9 April, 29 transports under the command of *Oberleutnant* Drewes made their way to Oslo's Fornebu airfield filled with paratroopers. The weather, though, did not bode well for the success of the mission. The German meteorologic service was pessimistic about the day's prospects, and as Drewes's aircraft approached the Skagerrak, they appeared even worse than anticipated: fog lay in a dense blanket stretching from sea level to nearly 600 meters, and above this the sky was punctuated with further cloud layers. As the aircraft moved over Oslo Fjord, they became immersed in thick fog, which reduced visibility to a little over 20 meters. While fretting over how to carry out the drop over Fornebu in such atrocious conditions, Drewes was informed that two aircraft were missing. This tipped the scales for the *Oberleutnant,* who radioed Hamburg at 0820: "Turning back due to bad weather. Proceeding to Aalborg."[16]

At the Hotel Esplanade the message was greeted with a great deal of anxiety because events taking place on the water in Oslo Fjord were progressing disastrously. Norwegian resistance was proving a surprising barrier to the might of the German navy attempting to breach the narrows of the fjord leading to the capital. Led by one of Germany's newest men-of-war, the heavy cruiser *Blücher,* Group 5 had left Kiel at 0300 on 8 April and passed into Oslo Fjord around midnight. Its task: secure Oslo, the strategic and political center of the country. Strategically, Oslo was not only Norway's commercial and industrial heart but also the communications hub for all of the southern and central region. Its planned rapid capture by four battalions (two bought in by air via Fornebu and two over water by Group 5) would facilitate the rapid reinforcement and supply by road and rail from Oslo of the relatively weak forces establishing themselves in the other ports. The Germans intended to carry out a coup de main, seizing the king and ministers of government and extracting a capitulation. Hence a failure to capture Oslo quickly could imperil the whole campaign, an outcome that seemed all too possible as

German naval vessels were brought to a grinding halt in the narrows of Oslo Fjord.[17]

Initially, Group 5 had passed the outer entrance without any serious problems. At about the halfway point, a couple of torpedo boats and eight minesweepers broke off to capture the naval air base at Horten and two small forts on the islands of Rauöy and Bolcerne. So far, the dark, moonless night had for the most part cloaked their approach. However, the small German armada still had to pass through the Dröbak narrows, at which lay the main defenses of the fjord. Situated about two-thirds of the way into the fjord, and only 400 meters wide, this narrow channel passes Kaholm Island to the west and the mainland to the east. On the former resided the Oscarsborg fort, armed with three old 28-cm guns manufactured by Krupp in 1905 and an antiquated torpedo battery of Austrian manufacture; the latter boasted a battery of three 15-cm guns and two Bofors, plus a handful of smaller-caliber guns.

In reduced visibility, caused by a heavy haze, *Blücher* reached these defenses at about 0500, and at an almost reckless speed of twenty-five knots proceeded to steam into the Dröbak narrows at the head of Group 5. The Norwegians held their fire until the Germans were at point-blank range, then opened up upon the leading vessels. *Lützow* was struck three times, and heavy shells knocked out the *Blücher*'s bridge while light gunfire ignited the aviation fuel and munitions stacked on its deck, eerily lighting up both sides of the snow-draped fjord. Torpedoes then racked *Blücher*'s hull, and at 0730 the magazine exploded. One of Germany's most modern warships then rolled over and sank in deep water with the loss of about a thousand men. The assault on Oslo was in grave peril. *Lützow* and *Emden* had to withdraw, and the remaining command decided to land men at Sonsbukten on the eastern coast of the fjord for an assault on the narrows by land. Additionally, forces were required to subdue continuing resistance at Horten and at the forts in the outer reaches of the fjord. In short, the naval assault on Oslo would not arrive on time. (In fact, Group 5 was not able to pass through the Dröbak narrows and reach the capital until late in the morning of the following day.) Given this disastrous situation on the water, the dramatic events that were to take place in the air at Fornebu on 9 April were to assume a much greater importance than originally anticipated.

Meanwhile, the success of the defenses in Oslo Fjord had not gone unnoticed in the Norwegian capital. At 0520, Curt Bräuer, the German minister to Norway, delivered to Halvdan Koht, the Norwegian foreign minister, his country's "friendly" ultimatum, which stated in the first instance that "German troops did not set foot on Norwegian soil as enemies," while in the next breath threatening the Norwegian government that "any resistance would . . . be broken up by all possible means . . . and would therefore lead only to absolutely useless bloodshed." The Norwegian reply was swift and to the point: "We will not submit voluntarily; the struggle is already under way."[18] The Oslo Fjord disaster had strengthened the Norwegian hand: the defenses in the Dröbak narrows still held; *Blücher* had been sunk; and the small detachments set ashore below the narrows to clean up and

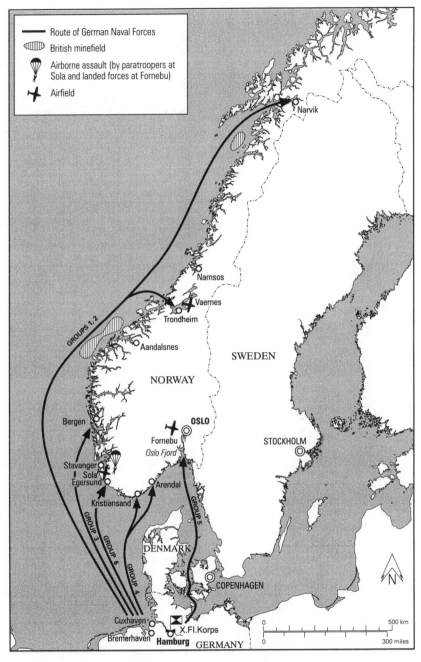

Legend:
- Route of German Naval Forces
- British minefield
- Airborne assault (by paratroopers at Sola and landed forces at Fornebu)
- Airfield

Narvik

Namsos

Vaernes

Trondheim

GROUPS 1, 2

Aandalsnes

SWEDEN

NORWAY

Bergen

OSLO

Fornebu

Oslo Fjord

STOCKHOLM

Stavanger

Sola

Egersund

Arendal

Kristiansand

GROUP 3

GROUP 6

GROUP 4

GROUP 5

DENMARK

COPENHAGEN

N

Cuxhaven

X.Fl.Korps

Bremerhaven

Hamburg

GERMANY

0   500 km

0   300 miles

2. The invasion of Norway, 9 April 1940.

advance on Oslo by foot were still some eighty kilometers from the capital.[19] In short, the Germans' only hope of quickly taking out the key strategic and political center in Norway now lay with the Luftwaffe.

Drewes's determination to turn back with the paratroopers meant hard decisions now had to be made at the Hotel Esplanade over the fate of the second wave of Ju 52s bearing the airborne troops; these aircraft were a mere twenty minutes from Fornebu and, if allowed to continue, would land at an uncaptured airfield perhaps under heavy fire. Aware of the failure of the paratroop drop, *Generalleutnant* Geisler ordered these aircraft also to return, since Göring had made it clear to the commander of X Fliegerkorps that should the air drop not take place, all succeeding echelons were to be recalled.[20] The Transport Chief Land resisted. "They can force a landing even though the airfield has not been secured," exclaimed Gablenz, who promptly refused to recall his units. Geisler, however, was adamant that he would not have the aircraft and the men they carried "shot to pieces," and in his authority as commander of X Fliegerkorps, orders were given by radio for the transports' recall.[21] Amazingly, the officer in charge of the second formation heading for Fornebu, *Hauptmann* Richard Wegner, chose to disregard this directive. His decision seems to have been based, at least partly, on suspicions aroused by the fact that the order was given under the authority of X Fliegerkorps and not, as he would have expected, from the Transport Chief Land. In any case, his resolve appeared justified when the fog near Oslo dissipated and the airfield came into view in the distance. The arrival of the transports over Fornebu coincided with the appearance of Bf 110s under the command of *Oberleutnant* Werner Hansen.

These twin-engined fighters were in an even more desperate situation than the Ju 52s because they were at the limit of their operational range, and therefore returning to Germany was not even an option. Their fuel shortage had been compounded by a couple of skirmishes with up to ten Norwegian Gloster Gladiators just prior to the arrival of the Ju 52s. Although poorly armed, these agile single-engined biplanes proved to be quite a handful and shot down two of the heavy and cumbersome Bf 110s. Eventually the remnants of the defenders were compelled to break off the attack; two planes made forced landings below at the Fornebu airfield and were immediately strafed and set aflame by Hansen's aircraft. They followed this up with further strafing attacks on ground defenses and then resumed their holding positions above the field, praying for the expected arrival of the Ju 52s. Unaware that the first wave of transports was already on its way home, Hansen was amazed when the second wave arrived shortly thereafter at 0905 and began to form into a landing pattern, approaching the runway rather than, as he expected, disgorging paratroopers from above.[22]

On board the leading Ju 52, Wegner had seen the two Gladiators ablaze as his transport banked sharply to line up the runway, and he signaled the pilot to take the aircraft in. As it drew near to touching down, ground fire raked the fuselage of the aircraft, killing Wegner and wounding a number of his men, whereupon the pilot opened up the throttle and the Ju 52 lumbered skyward. Hansen watched wide-eyed from aloft. Based on the fact that the fuel of his six remaining aircraft was perilously low (three were already running on only one engine) and realizing that the transports were in fact intent on landing at the heavily defended airfield, he decided to bring in his Bf 110s and attempt to secure the field. With one aircraft to cover the landings, the remaining fighters landed at 0915. One of these overshot and crashed, while the others taxied to the corners of the airfield, where their rear-firing machine guns could provide some cover for the incoming transports.[23] At the same time, a number of the transports crash-landed due to damage inflicted by ground fire. By this stage, though, the antiaircraft defenses had grown strangely quiet, and when Hansen's crews and airborne infantry "stormed" the defensive positions, they found them empty—the Norwegian forces had withdrawn under orders. Fornebu was in German hands.

The small stream of remaining transports began to land, including stragglers that had become separated from the main formation while navigating the dense fog. Once X Fliegerkorps was informed of the success, the main body of 159 transports began ferrying in significant numbers of troops and Luftwaffe ground staff, aviation supplies, and equipment essential for continued operations.[24] Before nightfall, the infantry units plus paratroopers brought in by air had delivered Oslo into German hands. Two days later the commander of X Fliegerkorps, upon his arrival, shook Hansen's hand, cheerfully confessing: "But for your squadron things might have turned out very differently."[25]

The Luftwaffe's swift action could not, however, prevent the Norwegian king and his government being spirited out of Oslo. The failure to breach Oslo Fjord's defenses meant that the advance on the capital would have to be made from Fornebu, and it was not until 0330 of 9 April that the Germans were able to march on the city with a military brass band and six companies from the airfield. By this time, though, King Haakon and the Parliament had long gone, and subsequent attempts by the Germans to capture them were similarly fruitless, as their prey always remained one step ahead of them. Thus German hopes to bring about a coup de main on 9 April came to nothing, and Norwegian resistance continued.

This was nowhere more evident than in Oslo Fjord, where the Luftwaffe was called upon to clear out the determined Norwegian defenders. The first aerial assault was carried out against the Horten naval base and the Bolcerne fort shortly after the first air units touched down at Fornebu. These were made by twenty-eight Heinkels of KG 26, which had been demonstrating over Oslo but were then directed to immediately attack these pockets of resistance.[26] This was followed by a raid on Holmenkollen and Oslo's other airfield, Kjeller, by twenty-four aircraft of KGr 100, but they were only able to destroy a couple of aircraft on the ground because most had already fled north. Later in the morning, twenty-two Stukas attacked the Oscarsborg fortress. The Norwegians refused to give in, and further air support was requested; He 111s of KG 26 and KG 4 flew a total of some 1,740 sorties in repeatedly bombarding the defenses of Kaholmen,

Oscarsborg, and Dröbak.[27] Finally, at 1705, thirteen hours since the ill-fated *Blücher* attempted to breach the narrows, *Lützow* was informed that "*X Fliegerkorps* is now attacking Dröbak: they consider the time favourable for a breakthrough."[28] Dröbak fell at 1900, but protracted negotiations over the surrender of Kaholmen meant (as already noted) that the German vessels would not pass through the narrows and tie up at Oslo until 1145 the next day. However, thanks to the Luftwaffe, the capital was already in German hands, staving off a crucial delay in securing the key strategic gateway to southern and central Norway.

KRISTIANSAND, STAVANGER, AND BERGEN

Luftwaffe units also proved decisive at Kristiansand. This landing formed the main objective of the navy's Group 4 led by the cruiser *Karlsruhe*, while a minor operation involving the capture of Arendal was carried out successfully around 0900 by a torpedo boat and its small number of troops after being delayed by fog. *Karlsruhe* and its entourage of torpedo boats were also delayed by the thick fog clinging to Kristiansand's coastline, and although they had arrived at the fjord's entrance at 0345, it was not until 0600 that the fog had lifted sufficiently to permit them to navigate the fjord. By this time, though, they could no longer rely on darkness to cloak their movements, and in a short space of time the vessels were spotted by a Norwegian floatplane. The game was up. Originally, the Germans had planned to disembark a reinforced battalion from *Karlsruhe* aboard fast patrol boats and drop it ashore, where it could advance unseen to capture the two island forts guarding the mouth of the fjord. In light of the prevailing situation, *Kapitän zur See* Rieve, *Karlsruhe*'s commander, was forced to abandon this plan and called in the Luftwaffe to bomb the forts, while a much smaller detachment of troops on board two of his torpedo boats were to land directly below the batteries.

The first aerial foray against the fortified positions was delivered by seven Heinkels of KG 4 that were in the vicinity of the fjord carrying out a patrol of the area.[29] However, this small number of bombers, augmented by an Arado floatplane launched from *Karlsruhe*, proved inadequate for the task of subduing the batteries. Nevertheless, a subsequent low-level raid by sixteen Heinkels of KG 26 at 0930 did silence the batteries on both forts and blew up one of their ammunition dumps.[30] Aside from one plane being struck by antiaircraft fire and ditching in the sea, the raid was completely successful. A landing party was able to storm one fortification, and by 1500 the city had been captured. As at Oslo, it was the Luftwaffe that had tipped the scales in the Germans' favor.

The inclement weather experienced at other points along the southern Norwegian coast also affected the landings at Stavanger's Sola airfield. Because of fog and heavy clouds, of the eight Bf 110s dispatched to support the paratroop drop, four were forced to return to Germany and two collided, crashing into the sea. The two remaining twin-engined fighters would provide the sole support for the twenty-four transports laden with over 150 paratroopers. These lumbering aircraft were also finding the conditions difficult. As the squadron commander, *Hauptmann* Günther Capito, commented afterward, "The cloud bank swallowed up the whole squadron," and despite "the closest formation, the nearest aircraft was like a shadow."[31] However, 100 kilometers off the Norwegian coast, the clouds parted and the Ju 52s drew into formation again, dropping from 900 meters to just above the foaming wave crests. When they reached Stavanger's latitude at 0920, they turned inland, hugging the hillsides at a height of just 10 meters to avoid forewarning Sola's ground defenses. They arrived only minutes after the Bf 110s and, after glimpsing the fighters' handiwork—two Norwegian aircraft caught on the ground and now ablaze—climbed to only 120 meters, dropping the paratroopers right over the target. The hail of bullets that rose to meet them was soon subdued by strafing runs made by the fighters and then extinguished by the landed paratroopers. One Norwegian bomber, which along with a handful of other aircraft had managed to flee the German onslaught at Sola, returned to attack but was soon forced off by one of the eight Heinkels of KG 4 which had arrived as part of the supporting exercise. Sola, one of Norway's best airfields, was in German hands. In the following hours a large airlift was carried out by more than a hundred aircraft, bringing in troop reinforcements (part of the special *Luftgau 200* for Norway), flak personnel and equipment, ground crew, and aviation fuel.[32] The airlift was augmented by the men and materials brought in by the 1st Naval Transport Group. By nightfall, the air base was an operational home for twenty-two Stukas, four Bf 110s, and ten He 115s stationed in the harbor.[33] South of Stavanger, a much smaller assault was accomplished with even greater ease when 150 men delivered by four minesweepers of Group 6 took the small coastal town of Egersund.

Group 3, destined for Bergen and led by the light cruisers *Köln* and *Königsberg,* reached the entrance to Kors Fjord at 0430. By this time, *Vizeadmiral* Hubert Schmundt had successfully negotiated the most dangerous leg of the voyage. Because Bergen lay closest to the British coast—only eight to nine hours sailing time from Scapa Flow—Schmundt's force was the most likely group to run into British naval units en route; in addition, Bergen was the most likely target for an Allied counteroperation once the British and French realized what the Germans were up to. (Unbeknownst to Schmundt, his force had already come close to being discovered at 1700 on 8 April, only 110 kilometers from a much larger Royal Navy force; luckily, the latter had been steering northward, away from his units, and had not been sighted.) At the entrance to North By Fjord, troops were disembarked for their assault on the Kvarven batteries. Schmundt, keen to arrive on time at Bergen, decided not to wait for the capture of the batteries and pressed ahead with the force into the fjord. As Group 3 passed first the Kvarven and then the

Sandviken batteries (situated within North By Fjord) at around 0515, the German warships came under fire. The service ships *Bremse* and *Karl Peters* were hit, while *Königsberg* suffered heavy damage, being struck three times. Nevertheless, by 0620 German troops had disembarked and taken over the town. Meanwhile, the batteries at Kvarven and Sandviken still held out, and it was not until the Luftwaffe was called in to dislodge the defenders that the Germans made any progress against the batteries. The bombers of KG 4 arrived over Bergen soon after 0700 and immediately began an aerial assault on the positions; within a short time, German troops were able to seize the fortifications. X Fliegerkorps transports then proceeded to ferry in the troops of the 159th Infantry Regiment with pontoon-equipped Ju 52s.

TRONDHEIM AND NARVIK

Farther up the coast, four destroyers led by the cruiser *Hipper,* under the command of *Kapitän zur See* Hellmuth Heye, cruised into the Frohavet, Trondheim Fjord's outlying waters at 0300 in the morning of 9 April. Despite a minor brush with a Norwegian patrol boat and the outlying batteries at Brettingnes, Hynes, and Agdenes, the German vessels steamed up the fjord at twenty-five knots, soon passing beyond the arc of the sentinels' guns. Three of the destroyers were then detached to land troops to capture the fortifications, while *Hipper* and the fourth destroyer made directly for Trondheim, anchoring there at 0525. Two companies of the 138th Mountain Division went ashore and secured the city without incident. The Germans, however, were unable to subdue resistance within the fortifications before nightfall, and Trondheim's airfield, Vaernes—thirty-two kilometers east of the city—remained in Norwegian hands.

Since Vaernes was unavailable to the Luftwaffe, it became important to carry out the planned deployment of coastal reconnaissance floatplanes of KüFlGr 506 in the harbor waters. Therefore, once Hamburg had heard via radio of the capture of the town, a Condor reconnoitered the harbor to ascertain the overall situation in the region and determine whether it was possible to send in a servicing unit for the anticipated arrival of these floatplanes. The news was favorable, and later in the day personnel and equipment were flown in by five Condors and a single four-engined Junkers G 38.[34] Gablenz's floatplane transports also dropped off mountain troops along the Norwegian coast in small groups. During the remainder of the day, a total of fourteen coastal reconnaissance floatplanes landed in Trondheim's inner waters. The landings were less than smooth, and nearly every aircraft suffered some form of damage. Even worse, the "Export Group" supply ships for Trondheim had not appeared. This made life difficult for Heye (since although *Hipper* had enough fuel for the homeward journey, the destroyers would have to be refueled first), and the newly arrived floatplanes were effectively grounded through a dearth of aviation fuel. Moreover, what fuel they did have Heye preferred to hold back in readiness for the intended return run by the warships, when aerial reconnaissance by KüFlGr 506 would be essential.[35] Consequently, only one reconnaissance flight was made along the outer coast, and that by *Hipper*'s own floatplane.[36]

The failure of the "Export Group" supply ships to turn up at Trondheim was repeated at the most northern point of German operations on 9 April. Nine of the destroyers bound for Narvik (one of the ten had fallen three hours behind in heavy seas) passed into the calmer waters of Ofot Fjord at 0400. Here, at the fjord entrance, one destroyer was left to take up patrolling duties, while at 0440 two destroyers were detached to land troops at the forts of Ramnes and Havnes. As the remaining destroyers moved to the head of the fjord, three broke away to land men thirteen kilometers north of Narvik at the army depot of Elvegaardsmoen in Herjangs Fjord, while the last three headed directly to Norway's most important northern port. This latter triumvirate, under cover of snow flurries, encountered two Norwegian coastal defense ships, the *Norge* and the *Eidsvold*. Though old and considerably outgunned, the Norwegian vessels chose to resist the German destroyers but were quickly dispatched by torpedoes fired from *Wilhelm Heidekamp* and *Bernd von Arnim,* suffering heavy casualties. From the leading destroyer, General Dietl, commander of the mountain forces, was landed and eventually entered into negotiations with the local commander, Colonel Sundlo. In the meantime, while a temporary truce was in force, the Germans moved into the town, setting their own positions to counter the Norwegian defensive placements. Thus, by the time the elderly Sundlo had been advised to repel the Germans, it was too late; he had been outmaneuvered. At 0615, when Dietl pointed out the Germans' superior strength and position, the Norwegian commander was compelled to hand over Narvik to avoid unnecessary bloodshed.[37] Once it was secured, Dietl radioed Falkenhorst at 0800 with the news that Narvik and Elvegaardsmoen were now in German hands.

Dietl's greatest challenge, though, would be to hold Narvik. Originally, the Germans had envisaged utilizing the Norwegian batteries at the fjord entrance to ward off unwelcome British advances. However, after floundering in snow drifts up to six feet deep, the German troops that had been landed earlier to secure these facilities found them to be nonexistent. Moreover, as noted, none of the "Export Group" designated for Narvik arrived, and the limited amount of equipment stowed on the destroyers for the 139th Regiment had been badly knocked around in the heavy seas off the Norwegian coast the day before. The destroyers' situation appeared particularly bleak, since of the three tankers intended for Narvik, only the *Jan Wellen* had arrived, and it could refuel no more than two destroyers at any one time. All in all, the vulnerable warships and the relatively weak and poorly equipped ground forces were ill prepared to meet the challenge the Allies would focus on Narvik in the days ahead.

3. The assault on Narvik, 9 April 1940.

Route of German Naval Forces

SWEDEN
NORWAY

Björnfjell
Hundalen
Elevgaardsmoen
Hartvig Lake
Gjeisvik
Elvenes
Øyjord
RAILWAY
ROMBAKS FJORD
Beisfjord
GRATANGEN
HERJANGS FJORD
Narvik
Ankenes
Haakvik
Emmenes
SKJOMEN
ASTA FJORD
BOGEN
BOGEN
OFOT FJORD
BALLANGEN
Skaanland
Ramnes
Havnes
HINNØY
TJELDSUND

N

20 km
10 miles

WESERÜBUNG OVER THE SEA

The Luftwaffe's success on land on 9 April was repeated at sea. Aside from carrying out the aerial assaults at Aalborg, Fornebu, Kristiansand, and Stavanger, one of the main functions of X Fliegerkorps was the interception of British naval forces. Thus the Luftwaffe was charged with covering the westward flank against both attacks on German vessels on their way to home ports after the invasion and Allied attempts at counterlandings on Norwegian soil. Therefore, throughout the day, forty-nine sorties were flown by the coastal reconnaissance units of the Naval Air Command West.[38] Although these flights were not particularly successful, several sightings were made by reconnaissance aircraft of X Fliegerkorps, and these led German analysts to believe that the British had three flotillas at sea. In reality there were only two: the Home Fleet, consisting of four battleships, three heavy cruisers, seven light cruisers, and fourteen destroyers, under command of Admiral Charles Forbes and lying 150 kilometers off Bergen; and the second flotilla—a detachment of the Home Fleet—made up of four light cruisers and seven destroyers. By midmorning this latter force, under the command of Admiral Layton, was northwest of Forbes's position. Fortunately for the Germans, Forbes's intended assault on their ships within Bergen was countermanded by the Admiralty; had it been carried out, the British would have caught *Köln* steaming alone up the fjord on its way home and the damaged *Königsberg* and *Bremse* vulnerable at their moorings in Bergen. However, instead of surprising the vulnerable German vessels, Forbes and the Admiralty were about to learn that deploying naval units within range of land-based bombers without giving due consideration to adequate antiaircraft defense or fighter cover was a serious oversight. The only carrier in the region was *Furious*. Yet, incredibly, in the Admiralty's rush to do something—anything—to meet the German challenge, *Furious* had been dispatched to rendezvous with the Home Fleet without its fighter squadron and thus proved utterly useless in the immediate operations.

Furious was a veritable sitting duck without fighter cover and operationally useless without its versatile but sluggish Swordfish torpedo-reconnaissance aircraft. It was fortunate for the British that the carrier did not reach Forbes's flotilla in time, since German air crew had been instructed to concentrate on Allied carriers whenever they were sighted.[39] Göring, the principal advocate of sinking aircraft carriers, offered the coveted Knight's Cross and 100,000 reichsmarks to any who succeeded.[40] On the other hand, Britain's failure to have an aircraft carrier in a high state of operational readiness in the region is all the more remarkable since the British had anticipated—even hoped for—German activity in the North Sea in response to the mining of the Leads, Operation *Wilfred*. Indeed, so ill prepared were the British that on 7 April, just one day before the Royal Navy sowed Norwegian territorial waters with mines, *Furious* was docked at least twenty-four hours away at Clyde, on Scotland's west coast.

Meanwhile, the distance German aircraft had to fly to reach potential targets in the North Sea had shortened considerably in the last few hours. For example, at midday on 9 April, although the Home Fleet was still some 650 kilometers away from the Luftwaffe's German bases, the recently acquired Danish and Norwegian airfields considerably reduced the distance between the birds of prey and their waterborne targets: the Aalborg and Sola airfields were now only 520 kilometers and 160 kilometers distant, respectively from Forbes's force. Although both these fields were just in the throes of becoming fully operational, and therefore were unable to directly support the aerial assault about to be made on the Home Fleet, the Sola airfield proved indirectly useful. Nearly two dozen short-range Stukas, sent from Kile-Holtenau to participate in the attack about to take place on the Home Fleet, ran short of fuel before finding the flotilla and were able to land at this field after finding and sinking an isolated Norwegian destroyer.

The main event, however, was taking place farther out to sea and would last for nearly three hours as German bombers attacked the British warships. The initial wave comprising portions of KG 30 reached the Home Fleet at 1530 and soon after was joined by the remaining KG 30 Ju 88s and KG 26 Heinkels—nearly ninety aircraft in total. By early evening it was all over, and X Fliegerkorps claimed a large bag. KG 26 reported that it had made three hits each on a couple of British battleships, and further hits were reported on a battle cruiser (the *Repulse* or *Renown*), a heavy cruiser, and two troop ships. KG 30 was no less confident of its successes, claiming hits on two battleships, a heavy cruiser, and a cruiser. In the tradition of all combat aircrews, the Luftwaffe men had greatly overestimated their successes. In reality, despite the German Naval Staff's confident assertion that these "definite hits can be assumed," only the destroyer *Gurkha* was sunk, while the battleship *Rodney* was hit by a 500-kg bomb that failed to explode, and the cruisers *Devonshire, Glasgow,* and *Southampton* suffered only relatively minor damage from near misses.[41] The mention of troopships was a case of mistaken identity and reflected the Germans' general fears of a swift counterinvasion by the enemy. As for the British, although they had downed four Ju 88s, some of Forbes's warships had shot off up to 40 percent of their antiaircraft ammunition. The Home Fleet commander therefore determined that to remain in the vicinity of German bombers any longer without adequate fighter cover—despite the inconclusive material results of the encounter—was nothing short of suicidal. So, as evening fell on 9 April, Forbes moved his vessels away from the coast.[42] Thus, in one stroke, he made it impossible for the Home Fleet to directly hinder the German warships' dash for home waters in the coming hours, and the Luftwaffe was able to claim to have fended off not only a threat to the German navy's returning warships but also—erroneously—an attempted British landing.[43]

Nevertheless, once Forbes realized that he had to remove his fleet from within the range of German bombers, he also redirected the vulnerable *Furious* farther north for action in the Trondheim region. At 2230, Forbes also proposed that the southern region of the North Sea be relinquished by the Royal Navy to submarines because, owing to the superiority of German airpower, an attempt by surface vessels to restrict enemy sea traffic there would be untenable.[44] The result was an order issued the following evening: "Interference with communications in southern areas must be left mainly to submarines, air and mining, aided by intermittent sweeps when forces allow."[45] The directive was a tacit admission by the British that German airpower was already gaining ascendancy over the Royal Navy in the waters off Norway.

The directive also recognized the notable successes achieved thus far by Royal Navy submarines in the region. Although *Hipper* and *Köln* successfully ran the submarine gauntlet under cover of darkness, other vessels were not so fortunate. During the evening of 9 April, the British submarine *Trident* spotted the cruiser *Karlsruhe* steaming out of Kristiansand headed for Germany, and at 0700 the following morning it struck swiftly; after three agonizing hours of trying to keep afloat, *Karlsruhe* was scuttled. Moreover, when the British cabinet approved attacking shipping on sight, nearly a dozen vessels were sunk in the following week.[46] Thanks to Allied submarines and the threatening presence of Royal Navy surface vessels, not a single vessel of the "Export Groups" had made it to Narvik or Trondheim. In a German navy summary of the successes of the transport steamers for *Weserübung* on 11 April, of the nine steamers and tankers destined for these northern ports seven had been sunk, one had put into Bergen, and one was still at sea.[47] Although twenty-two vessels of the 1st and 2nd Transport Groups did arrive at their central and southern Norwegian destinations, a further five had been lost. Enemy submarines also played a vital part in the heavy damage suffered by *Lützow*. Making its way to Germany from Oslo on what was supposed to be one of the shortest and safest routes, *Lützow* was unexpectedly hit astern by a torpedo from the submarine *Spearfish*. With a mangled rudder and smashed propellers, the pocket battleship was barely able to prevent beaching on the Danish coast; it limped into Kiel three days later, so badly mauled that a year would pass before it was again seaworthy. More important, the Allied submarines wreaked havoc with vital German supply and reinforcement plans. British submarine successes, however, could not continue. The ever shorter summer nights and the diminishing influence of Royal Navy surface vessels, coupled with a correspondingly increased German presence, made operations increasingly hazardous. This was due in no small measure to the decision on 10 April to place X Fliegerkorps in sole charge of antisubmarine operations for a limited period. Consequently, bombers were deployed in escorting naval transports between Germany and Norway and on active antishipping sorties.[48] In addition, the OKW made the transports a much more difficult target to hit by employing lighter and faster vessels to dash between northern Denmark and southern Norway rather than the larger, more ponderous merchant ships. By 16 April these "fast convoys" were under way, and aided by the increased air activity, they proved very successful.[49] In the following weeks, Allied submarine activity gradually fell away with the loss of four submarines. Yet, in the short term, the damage had been done, and the German supply ships loaded with reinforcements and supplies destined for Bergen, Trondheim, and Narvik were decimated.

On the whole, though, 9 April belonged to the Wehrmacht. All military objectives had been achieved, and as the Naval Staff realistically concluded, "Losses which have been incurred, especially that of the newest heavy cruiser *Blücher,* are grievous; they are, however, in proportion to the risk run and anticipated, and cannot be called excessively high."[50] Regarding the cost to the Luftwaffe, of its combat aircraft three Heinkels, four Ju 88s, and two Bf 110s were lost, while of the transports eight aircraft were either shot down or crashed.[51] Nonetheless, the achievements of the Luftwaffe were decisive to the success of the German invasion on 9 April. Through reconnaissance, bomber, and transport operations, the units of X Fliegerkorps tipped the scales in the early hours of *Weserübung,* when a rapid German victory looked far from assured. The Luftwaffe's part in the proceedings was, nevertheless, merely beginning because the Norwegian centers of Oslo, Kristiansand, Stavanger, Bergen, Trondheim, and Narvik were still held only by weak German forces, and the loss of sea transports would place even greater pressure on X Fliegerkorps to reinforce and supply the central and northern regions in the days ahead. Moreover, in the wake of the invasion and the failure to achieve a coup de main, the Norwegian government, king, and army had withdrawn from the capital and were preparing to continue the fight in the heart of Norway.

NORWEGIAN RESISTANCE

In Berlin on 9 April, Hitler was jubilant. Beaming, he exclaimed to Rosenberg: "Now Quisling can set up his government in Oslo."[52] Aside from the failure to capture the Norwegian government and king—which may well have brought about a quick and relatively bloodless capitulation similar to that which had brought an end to Danish resistance—the German insistence that the Norwegians accept a new government under the unpopular Quisling was a political mistake that had important military consequences and would allow the conflict to drag on into May and June. Once in Oslo, the German leadership's main task was to broker a peaceful settlement with the current Norwegian administration, which in the first instance resided in Hamar, and then in Elverum, only eighty kilometers from the Swedish border. Further muddying the political waters, Quisling opportunistically stepped into the momentary political vacuum in Oslo and assembled his own cabinet. Up until this point, Curt Bräuer, the German foreign minister to Norway, was certain that the legitimate Norwegian government had a strong desire to reach a settlement with the invaders. However, once Quisling was inserted into the equation and, at the prompting of Hitler, essentially became the touchstone of German demands, Norwegian resistance crystallized, and in the afternoon of 9 April the king refused to acquiesce to Quisling forming a government. When Bräuer finally realized five days later that he had to drop the unpopular Quisling, it was too late. The Norwegian government would not now enter into negotiations at all, since it believed a successful Allied counterattack was imminent.[53] As for Quisling, his political ambitions remained stillborn as the pariah's puppet government failed to get off the ground. Hitler replaced him on 19 April with Joseph Terboven, a faithful National Socialist official, as *Reichskommissar* for the Occupied Norwegian Territories. Nevertheless, the damage had already been done.

The resulting resistance in central Norway was of crucial importance to the German positions in northern Norway, since Norwegian soldiers still held the rail and road communications linking Oslo with Trondheim, which in turn was the gateway to Narvik. This prevented reinforcement overland of Trondheim in the immediate future. Additionally, because German airpower could not be deployed in any significant strength in the latter region, the Royal Navy held a firm grasp on sea lanes in waters off northern Norway. With land routes blocked by the Norwegians and the sea lanes controlled by the British, the Luftwaffe remained the sole protector and supplier to German forces in the Far North around Narvik. However, X Fliegerkorps was not yet fully prepared to meet this challenge. As already noted, the floatplanes based at Trondheim were hamstrung by a lack of aviation fuel and could not perform reconnaissance over Narvik and North Sea waters. Moreover, the ten or so He 115s of KüFlGr 106 assigned to Stavanger's Sola field were over 500 kilometers from Trondheim and more than 1,000 from Narvik. Furthermore, the short-range Ju 87s at Sola were clearly incapable of covering this huge airpower gap. Only the Aalborg East and West airfields in Denmark offered a jumping-off base for the longer range bombers of X Fliegerkorps. Yet the distance between these Danish fields and any potential threat to German naval forces and isolated ground units holed up in northern Norwegian fjords militated against their ability to operate effectively in this region. The Germans did not have to wait long for the British to exploit this weak link in their defenses.

THE FIRST BATTLE OF NARVIK AND THE POWERLESS LUFTWAFFE

Konteradmiral Friedrich Bonte, the German naval commander at Narvik, was in an unenviable position: cut off over 1,500 kilometers from Germany, lacking air cover and adequate reconnaissance, and aware that the Royal Navy was prowling the waters outside Ofot Fjord. Moreover, before Bonte could even consider making a dash for home, his destroyers needed refueling. This was frustratingly slow, since *Jan Wellen,* the only tanker to reach Narvik, could refuel only two destroyers at a time, and this took seven to eight hours. Bonte's early warning system was based around U-boats patrolling the entrance to the fjord, which he also hoped would at least damage any British vessels attempting to penetrate it. On the evening of 9 April, he deployed three destroyers in the northern Herjangs Fjord and two in the southern Ballangen Fjord, while another guarded Narvik Bay. The four remaining destroyers lay within the bay itself. The port, however, was in the grips of winter, and Captain B. A. Warburton-Lee, the commander of the British 2nd Destroyer Flotilla, which had been part of the force laying mines for Operation *Wilfred*, was able to slip his five destroyers undetected into the Ofot Fjord at 1600 on 9 April. At dawn, amid snow flurries, his destroyers burst into crowded Narvik Bay. An after-action narrative detailing the ensuing events described the situation on Bonte's bridge:

> On the destroyer leader the watch hears a shot, nothing is to be seen, but immediately clamorous bells shrill through the decks: "Alarrrrrm." The commander, sleeping fully clothed in the chart-house bursts out on to the bridge. When he sees the driving snow he only says: "Are you crazy? Are you seeing white mice?" The signalman's mate on watch is just going to raise his binoculars in order to determine what the cause of this alarm is in the driving snow when a hellish din breaks loose—the British are here![54]

Just how difficult it would be to retain a foothold in northern Norway was becoming all too clear back in Berlin when, at 0832, the German destroyer *Berndt von Arnim* radioed Germany with the ominous news that a fierce destroyer action was taking place off Narvik. In the ensuing melee, the British sank two German destroyers and damaged the remaining three. Warburton-Lee's withdrawal was not so successful as the German destroyers deployed in the flanking fjords fell upon him. First, those in Harjangs Fjord struck from 7,000 to 9,000 meters; then, as the British ships attempted to steam out of range, those of Ballangen Fjord emerged from the fog south of fleeing vessels. The more powerful German destroyers sunk one British vessel and damaged another. Warburton's own vessel, *Hardy*, was in the thick of the battle, and its fate was chronicled by one of the survivors:

> First they shot wide, then they got us on target. Things got hot. The Germans got a direct hit on us. It was then that Captain Warburton-Lee was hit. . . . The skipper's secretary, Lieutenant Stanning, took command. By this time we were in a worse condition than anybody else. . . . Soon the steering wouldn't work. We ran into shallow water and grounded on the rocks about 300 to 400 yards from shore.[55]

Three of the British destroyers escaped, though, since the Germans were reluctant to give chase with such low fuel supplies. Nevertheless, the Germans were the losers in the First Battle of Narvik: two ships were destroyed, two more were seriously damaged, and three further destroyers were moderately damaged. The British, on the other hand, had acquitted themselves extremely well, especially considering that the German vessels were significantly larger. Only two British destroyers were lost, and one was seriously damaged. Adding insult to injury, the British caught the *Rauenfels*—a large German transport laden with artillery, flak batteries, and ammunition bound for Narvik—while withdrawing and promptly set the defenseless vessel ablaze. Surprise had given the British vessels an important initial advantage over their superior foes. The failure at Narvik was the failure to provide adequate aerial reconnaissance and support for the destroyers—not that the Luftwaffe was unwilling to assist.

The news that German destroyers were under attack at Narvik brought about a flurry of activity at X Fliegerkorps' headquarters. But the officers there had few options. Using the seaplanes at Trondheim and Stavanger would mean that they would have to land at Narvik, where there was even less aviation fuel than at their fuel-strapped Norwegian home bases. The Luftwaffe's final desperate option was to dispatch an entire bomber group of Heinkels on a one-way trip, and as the battle raged, it requested a situation briefing from the navy. Although too late to influence the outcome of the events of 10 April, X Fliegerkorps offered a bomber wing for the following day when the Luftwaffe considered a "fresh British attack there to wipe out their destroyers and capture the town is probable."[56] However, while the German Naval Staff concurred that a "British naval attempt to force Narvik early on the morning of 11 April" appeared "possible, even probable," "an all-out use of a whole bomber group" was judged too high a risk. Using a few long-range bombers (five to six) that could return was held to constitute a better solution.[57] Yet even five to six long-range bombers were hard to come by in the entire Luftwaffe, let alone X Fliegerkorps. The only plane in the Luftwaffe's armory suitable for such a task was the converted long-range passenger aircraft, the Condor. Designed to fly the North Atlantic commercial route, the four-engined Condor was a stopgap measure to cover the German decision to concentrate on tactical medium-range twin-engined bombers in the interwar period, a decision ultimately detrimental to strategic bomber and ocean reconnaissance aircraft development (a matter discussed at greater length in chapter 5). Aside from the eight unarmed Condors used as transports by Gablenz, the only operational armed Condors were those of KG 40's Long-Range Reconnaissance Squadron (Fernaufklärungsstaffel). Given the small number of Condors flying with the Luftwaffe and the unavailability of northern Norwegian bases for twin-engined Heinkels and Ju 88s, X Fliegerkorps was able to dispatch only a single Condor carrying a paltry four 250-kg bombs northward from Aalborg to provide air support for the destroyers on 10 April.[58] The aircraft failed to sight enemy forces and returned to northern Denmark.[59]

OKW deemed the situation in Narvik to be very serious and realized that any solution to the problem would be dependent on X Fliegerkorps' ability to project itself farther north and on the use of available U-boats to guard the entrance to Ofot Fjord. To achieve this, every effort was made to get the Trondheim and Stavanger airfields fully functional. At Trondheim, the Vaernes airfield was captured on 10 April, and the Germans immediately began the process of making it operational. Moreover, to alleviate the fuel shortage at Trondheim, an investigation was to be carried out into the feasibility of using U-boats to ferry aviation fuel and supplies northward. In an attempt to prevent further breaches of Narvik's Ofot Fjord and similar forays at Trondheim, the German navy increased the number of U-boats to eight and four outside the respective fjords.[60] This last measure seemed at the time to be of crucial importance, because although two of the remaining German destroyers were ready to break out that night after refueling, it soon became clear—based on a U-boat report—that this would not be possible; British destroyers lay in wait inside Bronte Fjord, and these were further covered by cruisers in the rear. These enemy units prevented a dash for German-controlled waters over the night of 10–11 April, particularly because there was little cloud cover to mask their escape. In fact, these forces would never leave Narvik. Over the next two days, patrolling British vessels and clear weather conditions would have made any attempted flight south suicidal.

The situation in northern Norway was the Luftwaffe's top priority, and its "main task" *(schwerpünkt Aufgabe)* reflected this: the support of Dietl's Narvik force.[61] The Luftwaffe hoped that a squadron of He 115 floatplanes could be directed to Narvik and a group of He 111s could be positioned at Stavanger for operations against an eventual enemy. In addition to antisubmarine operations in the Skagerrak and reconnaissance between Bergen and Stavanger, the Luftwaffe's orders for 11 April deployed KG 40's long-range squadron of Condors to operate from Aalborg to cover the coast off Narvik.[62] In compliance with the last directive, an active reconnaissance mission was carried out by three Condors, and on 11 April the first report was received:

> Examined Narvik at 1945 and 2040. Harbour appeared quiet: 11 steamers sunk, 4 German destroyers, one with steam up, three at the pier, and 1 U-boat. Two merchant ships apparently beached. One steamer in the dockyard. Dropped 4 SC 500 kg. bombs on the transmitting station at Tromsoe, without success. All quiet in Harstad. No naval forces of any kind sighted off Vestfiord.[63]

While for the most part the Condors were engaged in active reconnaissance missions over this northern Norwegian port, the Luftwaffe bolstered its long-range supply efforts by bringing in a handful of four-engined Junkers Ju 90s. Originally designed as part of Germany's anticipated strategic bomber force, Junkers subsequently adapted this aircraft as a transport for Lufthansa after the abandonment of the four-engined bomber program in 1937.[64] Added to this small number of Ju 90s was another excellent long-range machine that was never brought into quantity production: the Dornier Do 26 flying boat. Designed to carry mail nonstop from Lisbon to New York, only six of these aircraft were ever made, four of which were already flying with the Luftwaffe when war broke out in September 1939. Given the growing demands of *Weserübung,* the remaining two aircraft were soon pressed into transportation and reconnaissance duties along the Norwegian coast.[65] As the war diary of the General of the Luftwaffe attached to the Navy Supreme Command (General der Luftwaffe beim Oberbefehlshaber der Marine) records, it was the Führer himself who ordered that all the operationally ready Do 26s of the navy's Transoceanic Squadron were to be subordinated under X Fliegerkorps and deployed in "supplying Narvik."[66] The Ju 90s would deliver all material that could be dropped in by air, such as provisions and munitions, while the handful of Do 26s would fly in, among other things, fuel.[67] Accordingly, on 12 April, Dietl's mountain forces received a morale-boosting air drop from a single Ju 90 and supplies from a Do 26.[68] In conjunction with Luftwaffe efforts, Hitler ordered the German navy to begin the process of supplying Narvik by U-boat. On 12 April, Dönitz directed additional U-boats to join *U 43,* the first vessel already on its way north. The manifest of this vessel making its way north reflected Dietl's most pressing needs; of the total thirty-five tons of cargo, fifteen tons were 2-cm ammunition, thirteen tons infantry ammunition, and seven tons mortar ammunition.[69] Despite these efforts, time was rapidly running out both for the surviving destroyers and for Dietl's mountain forces holed up in Narvik.

BRITISH AIRPOWER ATTEMPTS TO HIT BACK

In the meantime, the British made air raids against German coastal positions in Norway, with mixed results. Aside from a foray by a single Blenheim over Stavanger, which destroyed three German aircraft, the first significant enemy aerial attack was made by the Fleet Air Arm rather than the RAF. On 12 April, fifteen British Blackburn Skuas—a single-engined fighter–dive-bomber—operating at maximum range, raided Bergen at 0805. The Germans were caught completely unawares as the first Skua tipped into sixty-degree dive toward *Königsberg,* its bombs heaving the light cruiser almost out of the water as they barely missed the vessel's hull. The following Skuas hit *Königsberg* three times, while other bombs fell close enough to cause further damage. The direct hits reduced the ship to a blazing wreck; once the fire reached its magazines, the resulting explosion tore it in half, and *Königsberg* capsized.[70] In minutes, the Skuas had become the first aircraft to sink a major warship. The next aerial assault was made by Swordfish biplanes that had finally been loaded upon *Furious.* After rendezvousing with *Warspite* near the Shetlands, both the carrier and the battleship joined Admiral Forbes's Home Fleet en route to Trondheim. The total complement of this force was now formidable and included three battleships, one aircraft carrier, three heavy cruisers, and eighteen destroyers. At Trondheim, Forbes hoped to use *Furious*'s torpedo bombers to attack the German naval vessels he believed to be sheltering there. *Hipper* and one destroyer had, however, already left Trondheim on the evening of 10 April, narrowly missing the Home Fleet steaming northward. Thus when the eighteen Swordfish were launched at 0400 on 11 April, the larger prey had slipped through Forbes's net, and only three destroyers were found within the harbor. Moreover, the first air strike by carrier-borne aircraft was a failure for the British because not a single hit was made on either the destroyers or the

U-boat within Trondheim Fjord. Although Coastal Command continued its attacks throughout 11 April on coastal targets using London flying boats, while Blenheims struck at Hardanger Fjord, Stavanger, and Bergen, the results were limited. The first raid by Bomber Command was also made on 11 April, by six Wellingtons and two Blenheims on Vaernes. Little damage was inflicted on German aircraft, but the runway did suffer some damage that—together with a period of heavy rainfall—limited the airfield's serviceability.[71]

The British failure to achieve any kind of success was due to the very changeable late winter weather over the North Sea, including persistent low cloud and very low temperatures. Heavy icing on the wings and tailplanes of the aircraft made them very difficult to control and resulted in several losses. Add to this a lack of navigational experience over the open sea, the difficulty in finding targets along the lengthy Norwegian coastline, and, once a vessel was located, a dearth of expertise in bombing ships at sea—a weakness that would also become evident among German aircrew—and it is hardly surprising that in the three days Bomber Command spent trying to harry German warships and supply ships, only one ammunition ship was sunk.[72] The most concerning feature of raids throughout the campaign, though, was the British failure to make any significant impression on those Norwegian airfields in German hands. Indeed, since the German success in Norway from the outset was reliant on airpower, the inability of the British to combat this in the initial stages did not augur well for future operations.[73] For the most part this was due to the fact that, excluding the southwestern extremities of Norway, the greater portion of the country simply fell beyond the range of Bomber Command's "heavy" bombers; its Hampdens and Wellingtons could barely make Stavanger, and only the greater endurance of the Whitley allowed it to reach as far as Oslo's Fornebu field or Trondheim's Vaernes airfield. Moreover, the number of aircraft available was insufficient for the task at hand.

In all, Bomber Command possessed a meager total of 216 operational aircraft at the time of the invasion, including those dispatched to the Striking Force in France.[74] This represented barely one-quarter of the number of bombers the Germans had at their disposal at this time. Yet even the deployment of a larger proportion of Bomber Command's aircraft was impractical, due to the scarcity of adequate airfields in Scotland and the lack of a long-range fighter for escort duty. This last deficiency was exacerbated in central Norway because British bombers could only expect to fly under cover of darkness for a very short period; at other times they remained exposed to Luftwaffe fighters, and targets were very difficult to find. Consequently, although Sola developed as the primary objective of British aerial assaults, only an average of six aircraft raided the field each day for most of the campaign.[75] Unless the British could secure Norwegian airfields for themselves, these obstacles ensured that the bulk of air operations would fall to Coastal Command's squadrons based in Scotland and northern England. Yet these units were a mixed bag of obsolete and more modern aircraft types—ranging from

London and Stranraer flying boats to Hudsons and Bristol Beauforts—which already struggled to carry out duties ranging from escorting Allied shipping to antisubmarine warfare and, in the case of Hudson-equipped squadrons, search-and-destroy missions against German shipping. The Fleet Air Arm was also poorly situated to operate for any sustained time against the German armada or the landings that followed. Southern Norway was at the extreme range of the Skuas based in the Orkneys, and the only aircraft carrier in the neighborhood was *Furious*. Thus the British lacked the requisite airpower resources to make any impression on the northbound invasion force or to sustain prolonged air operations against German positions once the latter were established in Norway.

Compounding the lack of suitable aircraft available to hit the Germans where it really mattered—on the captured Norwegian airfields—was the uneven nature of British intelligence. On the positive side, the British were furnished with a "fairly accurate" picture of the German units involved in the campaign by the cryptanalysts who were breaking Luftwaffe Enigma signals in Hut Six at Bletchley Park, Britain's famous codebreaking center, which was euphemistically titled the Government Code and Cipher School (GCCS).[76] Until recently, historians have had great difficulty in determining the value of Ultra material received during the Norwegian campaign. For instance, in his 1978 work on Ultra, Ronald Lewin suggested that during the Norwegian campaign "the decrypts were insignificant, providing, for example, commonplace details about postings of Luftwaffe personal and some Army traffic."[77] Little had changed by 1994, when Ralph Bennett admitted some uncertainty regarding how useful the April to May 1940 material might have been "because neither decrypts nor translations are open to inspection."[78] Nevertheless, since the 1996 release of the GCCS histories, it is now clear that the unprecedented volume of intercepts contained invaluable information. Written by the codebreakers themselves at the end of the war, these previously withheld histories reveal not only the sheer quantity but also the quality of the material made available to the British during the campaign. In the only major campaign prior to Norway, the invasion of Poland, the Luftwaffe had strongly favored the use of landline telephone and teleprinter communications over that of wireless, resulting in a dearth of intercepts from which to piece together even a basic intelligence picture of the Luftwaffe's overall operational structure. Hence, when Germany invaded Norway on 9 April, the British Air Ministry still had a very incomplete picture of the Luftwaffe order of battle—so much so that the GCCS history of the invasion confessed that "*Fliegerkorps* and *Fliegerführer* (Air Leader) were new terms, the significance of which became apparent only gradually."[79] However, given the poor communications that existed throughout Norway and the extreme distances involved, the Germans were forced to use wireless signals even for high-level operational purposes. Consequently, when on 10 April the Germans introduced their new *Yellow* Enigma key for the Luftwaffe and army, Bletchley Park's Hut Six was awash with signals traffic—which was often decrypted within hours—until the traffic ceased on 14 May.[80]

As early as 12 April, thanks to these decoded signals, the British—despite drastically underestimating the number of bombers and transport aircraft involved—did have a rough picture of X Fliegerkorps' mix of aircraft types, which they believed consisted of "at least three bomber Staffeln, a fighter Gruppe, a Stuka Gruppe, two Gruppen of heavy fighters, two transport Staffeln, two long-range reconnaissance units, and one coastal unit."[81] As the campaign continued, decrypts started to appear detailing aircraft strengths, the state of airfield serviceability, the results of British attacks, and German ammunition and fuel stock levels. By way of illustration, from 17 April the German airfields at Stavanger, Trondheim, and Oslo would report every few days to X Fliegerkorps' headquarters their respective aircraft strengths; from early May, Sola reported its strength daily and sometimes twice a day with a report of anticipated strength for the following day.[82] With regard to signals containing information on troop and supply transportation plus the delivery of paratroops, none of the decrypts took longer than one to two days, and a good number were completed prior to the operations themselves. The type of information contained in these signals can be gauged from a small sample from April that included information about the reinforcement of Trondheim and Bergen on 15 April, the expected transfer of the 138th Rifle Regiment to Narvik on 16 April, and the headquarters of the 181st Division and the headquarters of the 1st and 2nd Battalions of 334 Infantry Regiment, which were awaiting transport under the orders of Gruppe XXI at Stade airfield.[83]

A number of factors, however, militated against the productive use of this wealth of intelligence. Initially, the tidal wave of material that followed the breaking of the Norwegian Enigma caught Bletchley Park unawares and lacking the necessary numbers of staff with adequate military experience to evaluate the decrypts. On top of this, in order to conceal the true source of the information, when it was sent to service commanders (who were unaccustomed to dealing with such material), invariably they were informed that it had been obtained through less sensitive, more common sources such as "information from our own forces."[84] At the other end of the spectrum, many of those in the War Office or the Air Ministry who were aware of the true nature of the intelligence remained suspicious and unwilling to place too much trust in such an untested source, especially amid the confusion that followed the German invasion.[85] Either way, the result was the same: commanders gave the intelligence received via Ultra less credence than, with the benefit of hindsight, we can see it merited. Moreover, once the Allied expedition landed on Norwegian soil on 14 April, even those disposed to make use of such valuable data near the front lines would be unable to do so because as yet no secure system of communicating such sensitive material had been established, and the British simply lacked enough trained personnel in the field to handle Ultra material.[86]

One of British intelligence's most significant costly sins of omission in this early period would be the failure to recognize the importance of the Aalborg East and West airfields to the Luftwaffe buildup in Norway. The main linking point in the logistical and operational network bridging northern Germany and Norway, these fields were invaluable to the Luftwaffe's effort. Yet despite the fields' relative proximity to the British Isles and their obvious importance to the Germans, British intelligence was extremely slow in appreciating the role they played in the consolidation phase of *Weserübung*. Even after a 17 April reconnoiter of the area by two Hampdens revealed some fifty aircraft jammed "wingtip to wingtip" on one of the fields, it was not until the night of 20 April that Bomber Command actually sent a handful of planes to target them.[87] Although attacks increased in the days that followed, the damage had already been done because the Luftwaffe had had nearly two vital weeks of uninterrupted use of these Danish fields.

The full value of such a rich seam of intelligence was, of course, reduced for the Air Ministry anyway, since it did not have the aircraft—in quantity or quality—to make full use of Ultra even if it wanted to. Moreover, the operational employment of the meager numbers of aircraft on their way to Norway, directed by commanders who *did* take note of their new signals intelligence, was greatly hindered by a lack of topographic intelligence. In events reminiscent of the hasty German planning two months earlier, the British scrambled to amass sufficient tourist guides and maps to direct aerial assaults. While British intelligence agencies had collected some data after the outbreak of war, when Allied planning examined possible operations in Norway, the German attack, of course, followed a completely different plan. This left the British short of full topographic intelligence for the areas now in German hands. Incredibly, the pilots of Bomber Command were forced to make do with Baedeker's *Scandinavia* (revised 1912 edition) for their raids on German-controlled airfields in southern Norway, and the early raids on Narvik by naval aircraft from *Furious* would be dependent on Admiralty charts that lacked contour markings to guide them in poor weather through steep-sided fjords to their German targets.[88]

The most significant contribution to the British effort by the RAF was made indirectly under the innocuous code name *Gardening* and involved the sowing of mines (nicknamed "vegetables") in areas of the Norwegian coast known to have a high concentration of German naval traffic. The brainchild of Arthur Harris, the future commander of Bomber Command, the magnetic mines were delivered to the target area after lengthy flights by Hampdens—which were of little use for anything else. Here they were "sown" from a height of no more than 180 meters and at a speed not exceeding 320 kilometers per hour to prevent the 680-kg mines from disintegrating on contact with the water. On the night of 13 April, the first mines were dropped in Danish and Norwegian waters.[89] The results for the British were pleasing, and twelve German ships were sunk over the period of the German offensive. Yet the destructive crop resulting from *Gardening* missions proved to be too little, too late to arrest the German tide sweeping Norway, and the only real hope lay with operations against airfields.

LUFTWAFFE CONSOLIDATION AND THE ARRIVAL OF MILCH

Increasing the difficulties confronting British airmen when attacking German positions on Norwegian soil were X Fliegerkorps' moves to consolidate control of central and southern Norwegian airfields. On 10 April, Stavanger (the Ju 87 base) received nine KG 26 Heinkel bombers and additional Bf 110s of ZG 76 from Aalborg. On the following day, more of ZG 76's Bf 110s arrived along with some Junkers Ju 88Cs—a heavy fighter variant of the Ju 88 bomber—of KG 30 and three reconnaissance "Flying Pencils," the Dornier Do 17, of 1(F)/120.[90] The capture of the small airfield at Kristiansand provided a much needed staging point for short-range aircraft flying between Germany and Norway; on 11 April the field became the operational base for Bf 109s of JG 77, which were to transfer from Denmark's Esbjerg airfield. At Oslo, Fornebu was reinforced and the newly captured Kjeller airfield occupied. In addition to these aircraft transfers, *Oberstleutnant* Gablenz continued the airlift of large amounts of personnel, equipment, and supplies throughout 10 and 11 April. At Stavanger, for example, on 10 April, eighteen He 59s of KGrzbV 108 and additional Ju 52s delivered the personnel of the 33rd Flak Regiment, 193rd Infantry Regiment, and the ground staff and personnel for ZG 76 and KG 26, while on 11 April Ju 52s brought in elements of the 3rd Signals Regiment.[91] This was followed by 235 transport sorties between Germany and Oslo on 12 and 13 April.[92] Yet the arrival of flak personnel for Stavanger did not mean that the Luftwaffe was in a position to deter potential British raids once they had breached the Germans' outer aerial patrols.[93] In fact, flak defenses remained weak for a considerable time, despite an entry in *Generaloberst* Erhard Milch's notebook for 12 April suggesting otherwise.[94]

Milch's sudden interest in Luftwaffe activity over Norway was, as he boldly scrawled in his notebook on 11 April, based on Göring's decision to place X Fliegerkorps "under my command."[95] The creation of the Luftflotte 5 (Air Fleet 5) command, with Milch in the cockpit, was a reflection of the growing operational and administrative demands being placed on the Luftwaffe in Norway. The establishment of a *Luftflotte* for Norway has been criticized, at least by one commentator, as the "first major instance of over-organisation" that was later to become so characteristic of the Luftwaffe, particularly when in following years the number of aircraft deployed in Norway declined rapidly as they were siphoned off into other theaters.[96] It should, however, be remembered that although Luftflotte 5 had only one *Fliegerkorps* as opposed to the usual two, X Fliegerkorps numbered over 1,000 aircraft (and these were being supplemented all the time) at the height of the campaign in 1940. In fact, Luftflotte 5 exceeded the size of an "average" *Luftflotte* by over 200 aircraft, thanks to the large number of transports and naval aircraft subordinated to X Fliegerkorps. Consequently, the establishment of the highest operational entity within the Luftwaffe was not unwarranted, at least in the short term, given the number and variety of aircraft deployed at the time and the vastness of the Norwegian theater.

The growing importance of the campaign was also emphasized by the appointment of Göring's second-in-command to head Luftflotte 5. Erhard Milch, who had commanded a fighter squadron late in the First World War and was director of Lufthansa, Germany's civil aviation company, from 1925 to 1933, astutely caught the winds of change sweeping Germany in 1933 and promptly joined the National Socialist Party. Overlooking Milch's paternal "Jewishness," Göring appreciated his abilities as a planner and administrator, appointing him state secretary for aviation *(Staatssekretär im Reichsluftfahrtministerium)* in 1933, a position he would hold until 1944, and general inspector of the Luftwaffe *(Generalinsspekteur der Luftwaffe)* in 1939.[97] Although often caustic and egocentric—personal characteristics that did not endear him to a good number of his Luftwaffe contemporaries—Milch did have a way of cutting through red tape and getting to the heart of seemingly intractable Luftwaffe problems, such as the one now developing in northern Norway. Acknowledging the need to have *Weserübung* sewn up before the campaign in the west began, and perhaps requiring a potential scapegoat should the Luftwaffe fail in Norway, Göring selected his deputy.[98] Nevertheless, given how jealously Milch guarded his position of power in Berlin—where he had direct access to his commander's ear—Göring's decision to send him out to the fringes in Hamburg and subsequently Oslo must have been somewhat heartrending for Milch. Yet the separation was tempered by Göring's assurances that his deputy would retain his rights as state secretary for aviation and would return as Göring's representative in Berlin before the invasion in the west. Above all, the "posting" would gain him the coveted *Feldherr* experience he lacked and, if all went well, put him on a par, at least in his own eyes, with other senior Luftwaffe officers who tended to look down on his lack of operational exposure. As one airpower historian rather ungraciously observed, Norway provided Milch with the opportunity to "punch his ticket."[99] Yet a careful examination of Milch's notebook and diary for this period—neither of which has previously been applied to an appraisal of his role in the campaign—reveals that he applied his customary industry to the job at hand.[100]

Meanwhile, the continuing consolidation of Luftwaffe positions in Norway bore fruit on 12 April. The first German success was achieved by the Bf 109s newly installed at Kristiansand, when a Hudson shadowing *Scharnhorst, Gneisenau,* and *Hipper* as they steamed toward Germany was shot down. Then twenty-four Hampdens dispatched to attack the southward-bound German warships failed to find them and made for Kristiansand, aiming to strike naval vessels deployed there instead. The nimble Bf 109s shot down six of the Hampdens, severely mauling many of the remainder. Not that the Hampdens were defenseless. In fact, in what should have been a one-sided affair, the overconfident Germans lost five of their own single-engined fighters by straying too close to the rear gunners of the fleeing bombers.[101] Meanwhile, further attacks were attempted by forty-four of Coastal Command's Hampdens and Wellingtons on Stavanger, by nineteen Fleet Air Arm Skuas on Bergen, and by a dozen of *Furious*'s Swordfish on Narvik. While the Skuas achieved little at Bergen and escaped with only minor damage, Coastal

Command's raid on Stavanger met stiff resistance from the newly arrived Luftwaffe heavy fighters, which cut a swath through the bombers. For the loss of only one plane, the Bf 110s and Ju 88Cs shot down seven British aircraft and seriously damaged many more. At Narvik, the Swordfish slightly damaged a German destroyer and severely damaged a Norwegian fishing vessel while losing two of their number to antiaircraft fire. In all, the Germans destroyed seventeen enemy aircraft on 12 April. The lesson was not lost on the British and brought about one of the most significant turning points in Bomber Command's operational history: an end to daylight raids. For the next four years British bombers, with few exceptions, would fly only by night and eventually to terrifying effect over the cities of Germany.[102]

While the Luftwaffe attempted to close the aerial gap in northern Norway and consolidate its position elsewhere on land, further X Fliegerkorps and Naval Air Command West aircraft were engaged in reconnaissance and attacks in the North Sea region. The first big sweep took place at 1500 on 10 April, when ten Heinkel 111s of KGr 100 led an armed reconnaissance mission into the region between the Shetlands and the Norwegian coastline. These "point" aircraft were followed by a thirty-five-strong strike force of KG 26 Heinkels. Although they sighted vessels, "bad weather" and enemy harassment were enough to prevent any hits on British ships.[103] The sighting of a British formation southwest of Shetland, however, spurred German efforts, and a force of nineteen Heinkels from KG 26 and nineteen Ju 88s from KG 30 took off simultaneously at 1700 to attack these ships and bomb the naval oil supplies at Scapa Flow. Yet in the face of defending Hurricanes, antiaircraft fire, and poor visibility, no successes were achieved, and five aircraft were lost.[104]

A potentially devastating assault, however, was made the next day by ten Heinkels of KG 26 while on an armed reconnaissance mission. Flying in the direction of Narvik, the Heinkels spotted the Home Fleet steaming northward, about sixty-five kilometers off the Trondheim coast.[105] The British formation was reported to include battleships, one aircraft carrier, two cruisers, and fourteen destroyers. At 1700 the bombers attacked the British warships through a wall of intense antiaircraft fire. The German pilots claimed hits on a cruiser with two 50-kg bombs and the aircraft carrier with a single 250-kg bomb.[106] In reality, only one hit had been made on the destroyer *Eclipse,* which was forced to retire to Scapa. In spite of the limited results, the Germans—with less than a dozen aircraft—had shot another warning salvo across the bow of the Royal Navy by once again showing the danger posed to large naval units lacking adequate fighter protection when they strayed too close to land-based aircraft.

In addition to these operations, the Luftwaffe provided aerial support for the German army against Norwegian armed resistance from 10 to 12 April. For example, as well as providing the bulk of forces in the southern region, KG 4 bombed opposing ground forces to the north of Kristiansand and traffic around Oslo on 11 April.[107] Because the Germans believed that the Norwegian General Staff was holed up at Nybergund, close to the Swedish border, KG 26 Heinkels attacked the town.[108]

The destruction caused by these attacks in pursuit of the king and the government was witnessed by an American, Captain Robert Losey, who had been directed by Washington to collect intelligence in the days after the German invasion. On 15 April, after slipping into Norway from Sweden, he was shown the results of a German raid on Elverum. He noted in his confidential report that although the church and hospital at one end of the town were untouched, "about a ten square block had been razed completely with not an intact wall left in the area," and "this had been done in a series of attacks over a four hour period, by never more than six planes."[109] The king, who barely survived the raid on Nybergund on 11 April, decided to move with his son and the government to the Norwegian army's headquarters at Lillehammer to the north.

It was here that General Otto Ruge, the army's newly appointed commander in chief, was endeavoring, as he put it, to "spend miles rather than men" in anticipation of British assistance.[110] His forces were a motley lot, made up of raw recruits and veterans, many of whom, he noted, had "never been under fire of artillery, planes and tanks."[111] The men under Ruge's command throughout Norway did not "exceed 30,000," estimated Losey, and "ammunition was very short," since all the arsenals were in German hands.[112] Moreover, although the Norwegian troops were getting over their "almost irrational fear of German troops," they still feared the Luftwaffe, "which has been constantly conducting observational flights and attacking with bombs and machine gunfire." With regard to Norwegian airpower, Losey ascertained that the Norwegians had only nine aircraft at the beginning of hostilities, and "all of these have been lost." While this last estimation was overly pessimistic because a handful of Norwegian aircraft had survived the initial onslaught, their influence on the unfolding campaign was almost nil as they flew from one place of refuge to another. Ruge summed up the grim situation in his first telegraphed plea for help to the British prime minister on 12 April:

> We began this war in the belief that the British government would act at once. We were surprised before we had time to mobilise and lost all our aircraft, supplies and stores. I am now rallying a [?few] infantry battalions and two or three batteries, who have had to fight during mobilisation. We are prepared to receive troops at once and act immediately from our side. My King, Crown Prince and government are being hunted by German bombers and were bombed last night. The people are all for fighting but they cannot fight without assistance.[113]

THE SECOND BATTLE OF NARVIK

British assistance, however, was already bound for Narvik, where the beleaguered German mountain troops still lacked adequate supplies and the trapped German destroyers adequate air cover. X Fliegerkorps had been working feverishly to overcome these twin problems but with only limited success. Although in the days following the invasion the Vaernes aerodrome at Trondheim had been captured and brought up to operational readiness, its limited capacity meant that by 12 April only four Stukas had been stationed there.[114] At Stavanger the situation was only marginally better because Allied bombers had damaged the airfield, thereby reducing Sola's operational readiness. At Narvik itself, though, the situation on 12 April looked a little more hopeful when Dietl advised that Hartvig, a frozen lake north of Narvik, would be ready to receive landplanes on 13 April.

To utilize Hartvig, the Germans assembled sixteen Ju 52 transports at Oslo's Fornebu field. Of these, twelve would bear the officers and men of a detachment of the 112th Mountain Battalion, along with four of their 75-cm mountain artillery and as much ammunition as possible.[115] The importance of the mission was underlined with the inclusion of a communications Ju 52, and the main body would be followed by three further Ju 52s laden with fuel to allow the transports to make the return journey. At 0845 on 13 April, the aircraft carrying the troops and artillery headed northward, unaware of the fireworks that awaited their arrival.

In the meantime, the British decided that Narvik needed to be cleared of enemy naval units. To ensure success of the operation, the battleship *Warspite* (a 30,000-ton Great War veteran), under Admiral William Whitworth's flag, provided the nucleus of a detachment including nine destroyers.[116] This force breached the outer reaches of Ofot Fjord on its way to Narvik at about 1100 on 13 April, undetected either by German aerial reconnaissance or by any of the four U-boats deployed in that area.[117] *Warspite*'s floatplane not only spotted two German destroyers tucked into Hamnesholm, one-third of the way into Ofot Fjord, but also sank *U 64* at the head of Harjangs Fjord. As the Royal Navy vessels came into view, *Hermann Künne* broke away, steaming deeper into the fjord toward Narvik at twenty-four knots and loosing off a number of ineffectual salvos at 20,000 meters. Meanwhile, the remaining destroyer, *Erich Koellner,* which had been damaged two days previously, made a dash for Djupvik Bay on the southern side of the fjord from where it could launch torpedo attacks against the incoming British warships. Forewarned by the scouting aircraft, the British used the covering destroyers to overwhelm the isolated German vessel with torpedo and gunfire before *Warspite* opened up its big guns and finished it off.

Outnumbered and heavily outgunned, four German destroyers *(Luedemann, Zenker, Arnim,* and *Künne)* under the command of Bonte's successor, *Fregattenkapitän* Erich Bey, moved into a blocking position before the port with a view to sinking the leading British vessels or, if possible, dispatching *Warspite* with torpedoes.[118] To the Germans, *Warspite* suddenly loomed incredibly large. In moments, Bey's destroyers were engaged in a running battle with the British capital ship, which was firing its 38-cm guns over the top of its escorts. A narrative produced after the battle described the scene: "The first British shells fall in the water of the harbour on the wharf installations and the buildings of the city. . . . It's the first very heavy ordnance experienced by the destroyer crews. The discharges roar with terrific crashes, the thunder of the heavy guns rumble, echoing from the mountain slopes and gorges around the harbour."[119] A lone German Condor soaring above the stranded German naval units sent back the following alarming report: "Six German destroyers fighting a delaying action in Narvik harbour. One British cruiser and six destroyers approaching the harbour. Narvik in the hands of German troops. Weather very bad. Supplies dropped according to plan."[120] X Fliegerkorps was not totally unprepared for this eventuality, but despite a frantic Göring repeatedly ringing Milch throughout the day, ordering him to launch large-scale attacks in support of Dietl, Luftflotte 5's options remained very limited.[121] The *Fliegerkorps* had been ordered the previous day to make available a bomber group to provide air cover for Narvik, and indeed twenty-two Heinkels of KG 26, under the command of *Oberst* Fuchs, took off early on 13 April for the port. However, at 1105, about 100 kilometers north of Bergen, bad weather hit the flight. Low clouds reduced Fuchs's visibility, and he was forced to abandon the mission. The sole aerial support came during the afternoon with the arrival of four He 115s of KüFlGr 106 from Stavanger.[122] The slow floatplanes, however, were in no position to threaten the British warships and were driven off by the heavy antiaircraft fire of the enemy destroyers around Narvik. The only other aircraft to put in an appearance were the Ju 52s carrying mountain artillery and men; these flew in low over the fjord into a hail of fire from the British vessels in and around Narvik.[123] Five of the transports were struck by antiaircraft fire, and two crashed. The remaining aircraft landed on the frozen lake, eight sustaining considerable damage due to the onset of the spring thaw. The signals aircraft reported that only two aircraft could be considered ready for a return flight, but since the three Ju 52s bearing fuel had not yet arrived, this was unlikely to occur.[124]

Nearing 1400, the German destroyers were still undamaged, but stocks of ammunition were nearly exhausted. Bey ordered his vessels to retire, and the British took up the chase. Aided by aircraft from *Furious,* the Royal Navy warships hunted down the German destroyers among the narrow fjords. *Furious*'s Swordfish, however, again proved inadequate to the task at hand; the ten that arrived failed to score a single hit, and two were shot down in the process. The first German casualty, though, was *Künne,* which beached itself, only to be struck by a British torpedo. Then two damaged destroyers, *Giese* and *Roeder,* were dispatched. "It's a sight," recorded a Royal Navy petty officer from his lofty perch on board *Warspite,* "burning and sinking enemy ships all around us, and our own destroyers search every corner that might hide something."[125] The remaining resisting destroyers—*Zenker, Arnim, Thiele,* and *Luedemann*—were holed up in the Rombaks Fjord, which at its narrowest point was a mere 500 meters across. Although this precluded *Warspite* from bringing its guns to bear on the trapped German vessels, the enemy destroyers moved in. The British destroyer *Eskimo* was damaged by a torpedo, and *Thiele* was run onto the rocks. This last action allowed time for the crews of *Zenker, Arnim,* and *Luedemann* to escape to shore.[126]

The one-sided battle had ended. *Warspite* and its dutiful entourage had annihilated the entire German force at the cost of a heavy mauling for *Cossack* and *Eskimo*. The battleship took up position off Narvik, while Whitworth signaled the Admiralty with the news of the destruction of the destroyers plus a U-boat and a favorable situation for the "landing of a party to occupy the town as the opposition had apparently been silenced." Yet he was not so unrealistic as to consider putting a party ashore against an enemy that some sources estimated stood at 2,000 highly trained men, already dug in for just such an eventuality.[127] What was needed was a fully equipped force ready to take on Dietl's isolated mountain troops. Unfortunately, none were immediately available. Had Churchill not been so keen on 8 April to cast ashore the troops that had already embarked for *Plan R4,* the British would have been in a good position to take advantage of this promising tactical situation.[128] As it was, a landing did not take place until 15 April, and then eighty kilometers to the north at Harstad on the island of Hinnöy.

For the Germans, the losses were disheartening. "This evening a serious and depressed mood marks the Naval Staff's impression of events," recorded the German navy's war diary. "Ten of our modern destroyers, half of our powerful and most urgently required destroyer arm, lie shot to pieces, damaged or sunk in Ofot and Rombaks Fjords."[129] However, the loss of the destroyers was Dietl's gain, because nearly 2,500 men were rescued and immediately incorporated into his existing forces, doubling his manpower for the defense of the town. Thus as evening drew on, Dietl's Narvik Group was able to report that no landing had occurred, although enemy destroyers lay off Narvik, and made an "urgent request . . . for submarines to attack destroyers off Tranoy and Rombaken."[130]

TORPEDO FAILURES

Ironically, little did Dietl know that U-boat actions in northern waters had proved an abject failure, particularly against those British forces that he himself had seen shattering German destroyers in Narvik during the last four days. As noted in the previous chapter, the Germans planned to use U-boats under Operation *Hartmuth* to provide a protective screen for surface vessels engaged in the invasion, strike at attempted enemy landings, and secure German sea communications from Oslo in the south to Narvik in the north. Lying in clusters off the Norwegian coast on 9 April, Dönitz's forces were in a position to intercept British vessels as they approached the fjords within which German ships were operating. Compared with the difficulties of finding targets in the open sea, the expected Royal Navy responses to *Weserübung* should have provided the U-boats with relatively easy pickings. The results could not have been more different.

The initial warning bells indicating that something was amiss followed the First Battle of Narvik. Under cover of a blizzard, the Royal Navy's 2nd Destroyer Flotilla slipped unnoticed between *U 25, U 46, U 51,* and *U 64.* After creating mayhem within Narvik, the British vessels prepared to exit the fjord as visibility was improving. Both *U 25* and *U 51* were then able to fire a number of torpedoes at the escaping destroyers—but with no success. The torpedoes detonated prematurely, and a wireless report from *U 51* noted two failures: "One detonated at safety distance, one after 30 seconds, 100 meters off a large destroyer."[131] These and other unsettling wireless messages were beginning to paint a disturbing picture for the navy. Out of twelve torpedoes fired on 10 April, six to eight (50 to 75 percent) had self-detonated, and this was only the beginning of an unprecedented debacle that could have cost the Germans northern Norway.[132] The next day, Dönitz ordered four more U-boats—*U 38*, *U 47*, *U 48*, and *U 49*—to the waters around Vest Fjord because signals intelligence was revealing the movement of heavy British forces northward.[133] *Kapitänleutnant* Herbert Schultz, commander of *U 48*, made two attacks on a light cruiser en route, on both occasions firing a "fan" of three torpedoes that all detonated harmlessly before reaching their target.[134] Dönitz concluded that these reports were nothing short of "calamitous."[135] On 13 April, the U-boats were equally ineffectual. They not only failed to prevent the penetration into Ofot Fjord below Narvik but also, because of poor weather, did not even spot the arrival of *Warspite* and its destroyers. When the British ships finally attempted to leave Narvik early the following day, even the Führer's personal order that the "attack be beaten off by all means" could not inspire the torpedoes to perform.[136] Once again, *U 48* sent Dönitz the depressing news: "Torpedo failures against *Warspite* and two destroyers."[137] In the German destroyers' most desperate hour, the U-boats had been unable, largely because of equipment failure, to carry out their primary function: the protection of surface vessels engaged in landing troops. They also failed to prevent Allied landings.

The next day *U 47* (under *Kapitänleutnant* Günter Prien, the man who sank *Royal Oak* in Scapa Flow) sighted transports disembarking troops, protected by two cruisers northwest of Narvik in Bygden Fjord. An exasperated Prien sent in the following report detailing the events of 15 April: "2242, fired four torpedoes. Shortest range 750 yards, longest range 1,500 yards. Depth setting for the torpedoes 12 and 15 feet. Ships stretched in a solid wall in front of me. Result nil. Enemy not alerted. Reloaded. Delivered second attack, on surface at midnight. . . . No success. One torpedo off course exploded against the cliff."[138] The British could not fail to be alerted by the second attack in the narrows of the fjord, and Prien barely escaped after running aground while being pursued with depth charges. Dönitz tried systematically to determine the cause of the problem bedeviling the torpedoes by making adjustments to the firing methods used, but to no avail. It would not be until after the Norwegian campaign had ended that the Germans would determine that their problems lay in a multitude of factors: defective action of the striker within the contact pistol, which occurred at certain angles of incidence; excess pressure in the balance chambers, which caused many torpedoes to run below their targets; and the susceptibility of magnetic pistols to the strong magnetic fields around northern Scandinavia, resulting in irregular behavior of launched torpedoes.[139] All the more damning is the fact that both OKM and Dönitz had been aware of the defective nature of their torpedoes for a considerable time and yet chose to use them in this vital campaign. Inadequate attention to the procurement of effective torpedoes prior to the war plus, as Dönitz later pontificated, testing coupled with an uncritical "attitude by the Torpedo Experimental Establishment towards its own achievements" hamstrung the effectiveness of the U-boat arm well after its scandalous performance during the invasion of Norway.[140] In the immediate wake of the torpedo failure, and in his postwar memoirs, Dönitz freely lambasted the developers of the poor-performing torpedoes, claiming that in "all of history I doubt whether men have ever had to rely on such a useless weapon." It should not, however, be forgotten that numerous problems associated with the current batch of torpedoes had been cataloged well before Norway. Surely a good deal of blame for the affair rested with Dönitz, who had commanded the U-boat arm since September 1935.[141]

In the meantime, continued attempts by U-boats to attack enemy vessels achieved nothing other than to put them in danger of discovery—much to the despair of their crews. "How the hell do they expect us to fight with dummy rifles," exclaimed Prien.[142] Dönitz concurred. On 17 April, he decided that enough was enough and ordered the withdrawal of his U-boats from the Norwegian campaign. The boats had been singularly unsuccessful, and the German U-boat Command was left to rue what might have been; a later analysis showed that excluding minor attacks under less than favorable conditions, U-boats made no fewer than four torpedo attacks on *Warspite,* up to sixteen on cruisers, ten to twelve on destroyers, and more than ten on transports.[143] The grand total sunk after more than forty attacks: one merchant vessel. Having read Prien's after-action report, Dönitz summed up his thoughts on the whole fiasco: "The case of *U 47* is a clear example of many attacks which have failed because of defective torpedoes, and have prevented the U-boats from contributing more effectively to the occupation of Norway. Had these failures not occurred, the role of the U-boats could have been far-reaching, since all other conditions were in their favour."[144]

The failure of the U-boats left a considerable gap in the German ability to throw off the Allied landing that followed the clearing out of Narvik. As soon as fighting began, the British war cabinet decided that its best option lay with an attack on Narvik, and on 11 April the first ships laden with troops and equipment slipped their berths. By 13 April, under the influence of Churchill, the cabinet began to consider the possibility of deploying some of these troops against Trondheim—dramatically dubbed Operation *Hammer*—supported by flanking operations at Namsos and Aandalsnes. In the end, only flanking assaults were undertaken on 14 and 17 April in central Norway, while the Allied landings (as observed by Prien) began northwest of Narvik on 15 April. The landings had two immediate consequences for their opponents: a crisis in command, and a redoubling of the Luftwaffe's efforts to shore up the German position.

CHAOS IN COMMAND

Hitler received news of the destroyers' destruction badly because he assumed, naturally enough, that the British were about to make a direct assault on his beleaguered troops in Narvik. Initially, when it became apparent that Dietl's forces would come under increasing pressure, the Führer had sent a special communiqué to the mountain troop commander ordering him to "defend Narvik area against attack under all circumstances." However, within twenty-four hours he was already beginning to have doubts and discussed with OKW the possibility of abandoning the Germans' northernmost outpost.[145] So began a period that Alfred Jodl, Hitler's closest military adviser, laconically described as "chaos in command" *(Führungschaos).*[146] "Terribly agitated," Hitler saw no alternative for the isolated and poorly equipped forces in Narvik but to evacuate the town and make for Trondheim. He promptly promoted Dietl on 14 April to *Generalleutnant* and dictated a withdrawal order to Keitel.[147]

For the first time during the war, Hitler came under real command pressure and was found wanting. The whole raison d'être for the campaign flowed from the need to secure this port to ensure continued iron ore supplies for the Reich, and now he was prepared to hand it to the Allies on a plate. Verging on a serious nervous breakdown, the German leader leaped from one impossible scheme to another as he sought a way to withdraw Dietl's men: a march south to Trondheim; flying them out; and, should all else fail, a retreat into Sweden, from where they (along with the Swedes) could defend the iron ore fields.[148] Halder wrote scathingly in his diary that Hitler's lame comment after discussing the serious situation with Walter von Brauchitsch, commander in chief OKH, was simply "We have had bad luck."[149] Hitler seems to have swung in the following days from periods of great agitation to deep depression. On one occasion during the *"Führungschaos,"* Walter Warlimont—deputy chief of OKW operations staff—visited Jodl in the Reich Chancellery, only to find "Hitler hunched in a chair in a corner, unnoticed and staring in front of him, a picture of brooding gloom."[150]

Out of earshot, however, members of the Führer's inner circle balked at his withdrawal order. No doubt many concurred with the naval assessment that, contingent on adequate food and equipment, Dietl's force—now numbering over 4,000—could be expected to hold out for a considerable period in terrain favoring defensive operations. Moreover, there was a certain conviction demanding that, given the great sacrifice of the destroyers, the force should hold on for as long as supplies permitted.[151] *Oberst* Bernard von Lossberg, Jodl's army staff officer, refused to send the withdrawal order as it stood.[152] Tearing up Keitel's handwritten note, he persuaded Brauchitsch to sign a hastily scrawled message to Dietl congratulating the latter on his recent promotion, adding a valediction: "I am sure you will defend your position, which is vital to Germany, to the last man."[153] With that, the first day of the battle in Berlin over the battle in Narvik came to an end.

During the next few days, matters remained unresolved. The atmosphere around Hitler was electric, with stormy outbursts and gloomy depression as the Führer bordered on a mental breakdown.[154] In the midst of it all, Jodl alternated between offering soothing assurances and firm resistance, gradually bringing Hitler to see reason over the situation at Narvik. On 17 April, Jodl took the matter in hand and explained yet again some basic hard truths to his Führer, who in a "temperamental" sort of way was reiterating that Dietl would have to march south or be evacuated by air. Jodl simply stated the obvious: a march south was impossible; and even an air transport could evacuate only very small units, with the loss of many aircraft in treacherous weather conditions, not to mention the effect of the evacuation on the morale of the Dietl Group. "A thing should be considered lost only when it is actually lost," reasoned Jodl.[155] Even a professor specializing in things Norwegian was dragged from Innsbruck to Berlin to explain the sheer lunacy of expecting Dietl's forces to traverse the mountainous terrain laying between Narvik and Fauske some 200 kilometers to the south. That evening, beaten down by Jodl's dogged persistence, Hitler signed the order for Dietl "to hold out as long as possible."[156] The die was cast, and Jodl began the next day's diary entry with "Führer is calm again."[157]

4

Air Control of Central
and Northern Norway

*The possibility of landing more troops or maintaining the troops then ashore
depended entirely on our being able to obtain control of the situation in the air.*
Lieutenant General H. R. S. Massy, May 1946

While Hitler panicked, Milch set about the task of bringing Luftflotte 5 up to
full operational readiness. The Second Battle of Narvik and the inability of X
Fliegerkorps to aid the destroyers rankled with Milch. At 1900 on 13 April, he
rushed to Karinhall—Göring's opulent hunting estate north of Berlin—where,
along with the Supreme Commander of the Luftwaffe and Jeschonnek, he drew
up plans for extending the Luftwaffe's operational reach farther north. Burning
the midnight oil, the three Luftwaffe leaders discussed the future tasks of Luftflotte
5. By the end of the meeting, Milch's notebook was full to overflowing with plans
centered on reconnaissance around the Lofoten Islands, directives for attacks on
any enemy naval transports, and the reinforcement of Trondheim.[1] German air
transportation of troops to Oslo and Aalborg was to cease for a period so attention could be concentrated on Trondheim and Narvik.

Despite criticism in later years from his rivals, it is clear from the details he
scrawled into his diary and notebook throughout this period that Milch rapidly
became immersed in Luftflotte 5's campaign.[2] Although it is true that there is little
indication that Milch was a great field commander, he was an excellent organizer
and administrator, and these skills were essential to laying the foundation for the
success of airpower in Norway. In part, Milch's initial reluctance to shift the headquarters of the *Luftflotte* to Oslo reflected the poor communication links that
existed within Norway, especially between Oslo, the main airfield at Stavanger,
and the most northern base of operations, Trondheim. However, Milch not only
attacked this weakness in communications with vigor but also encouraged the de-

velopment of new airfields and the consolidation of fields already in use by the Luftwaffe. To carry out this latter task, on 16 April he appealed for authorization to establish three "repair and construction columns" *(Reparaturkolonnen)* from the civilian population.[3] Ten days later, aided by claims of resistance among the local populace and even sabotage, he was granted approval to set up Air Depot Oslo (Luftpark Oslo), augmented by some 200 specialists and tradesmen from Luftflotten 1 and 4.[4] Thus Milch initiated the process of establishing the infrastructure required to support the operations of Luftflotte 5. Although these behind-the-scenes efforts were hardly the stuff extolled in contemporary and later narratives, they were Milch's greatest legacy to the campaign, and ones from which the frontline commanders of 1940 and subsequent years reaped the benefits.

In the meantime, the focus of air operations was about to shift south from Narvik as Allied forces landed above and below Trondheim in an attempt to take the city through advancing northern and southern pincers. Initially, as per Milch's meeting with Göring and Jeschonnek, X Fliegerkorps was directed to give priority to the relief and supply of Narvik, with the most weight given to the development of landing facilities at Vaernes, to which aviation fuel and ammunition were to being delivered. Milch hoped that Trondheim's airfield would soon be the base for a group of KG 26 Heinkel bombers and Ju 88C fighter-bombers of KG 30 to operate against Narvik. In addition, further groups from these bomber wings were to be shifted north to Stavanger and Aalborg. Interestingly, in addition to reconnaissance around the Lofoten Islands, KüFlGr 506's remaining squadron was directed to patrol the sea off Namsos and Aandalsnes, and in his diary, but not in the subsequent directive, Milch made reference to the possibility of "French transports" appearing in this zone of operations.[5]

THE SECOND PHASE: ALLIED LANDINGS

Milch's concern regarding possible enemy action in these areas was doubtless derived from the excellent intelligence being provided by the German Beobachtung-Dienst (Observation Service), the section of naval intelligence dedicated to the interception and decryption of foreign wireless traffic.[6] B-Dienst, which was reading the Royal Navy's most secret cipher prior to the war, provided the German commanders in Norway with accurate information throughout the campaign, enabling the bulk of the larger surface vessels to escape the clutches of the Royal Navy immediately following the invasion. It now provided detailed information regarding the likely sites for an Allied landing.[7] Thus, on 12 April, B-Dienst intercepted a message which revealed that an attack on Narvik would probably take place on the afternoon of 13 April.[8] Naval intelligence then correctly predicted, based on further intercepted messages and the departure of Royal Navy vessels from Scapa, that a landing would occur in the vicinity of Harstad on 15 April.

Regarding the Trondheim region, on 12 April B-Dienst intercepted a message detailing a reconnaissance mission by a British destroyer with the purpose of assessing the suitability of Namsos for an Allied landing. By the next day, although the situation on land was "assured in southern Norway," the Naval Staff war diary warned that the "Trondheim-Narvik area" was "threatened with imminent large-scale enemy landings," in particular, at Narvik, Namsos, and Aandalsnes.[9] Of these landings, those north and south of Trondheim, where the Germans had only a relatively small number of troops, were to be regarded as the most dangerous from a strategic point of view. Should the city be lost, so would Narvik. However, if Trondheim was held and strengthened, it would open the way for effective aid to Narvik at a future date. Since both Namsos and Aandalsnes were unoccupied by German ground forces, the only impediments to successful Allied landings and subsequent advances on Trondheim were U-boats and the Luftwaffe. Yet, in an admission of breathtaking brevity and understatement, the German Naval Staff was forced to shamefacedly note that its U-boats had "so far not come up to expectations"; the weight of the operations would fall on the Luftwaffe.[10] The Luftwaffe's immediate tasks were laid out in an order issued by the Führer on 14 April: "Destroy the British which have landed near Aandalsnes, prevent further landings. Attack enemy forces north of Aalesund. Occupy Dombaas with paratroops and take steps to protect it. Use every endeavor to bring reinforcements to Trondheim by air."[11]

The initial landing near Aandalsnes actually took place in Molde Fjord, situated at the entrance to a series of fjords that reach some 50 kilometers inland to Aandalsnes, and was little more than an advance party of some 700 men. Unlike Milch's work with the Luftwaffe, the Allied operation was a halfhearted, ill-organized effort, and the main landings would not occur for two days. Unaware of this, concerned German planners, under Hitler's orders, hastily assembled a paratroop drop over the strategically situated town of Dombaas. Located 80 kilometers southeast of Aandalsnes, Dombaas was the junction of one of the only two communications routes, the Gudbrandsdal and Osterdal valleys, linking Oslo to Trondheim. The town, 350 kilometers northwest of Oslo by road and 200 kilometers south of Trondheim, appeared to Hitler, the promulgator of the airdrop, as an ideal point for the Germans to secure the Oslo-Trondheim railway and slow down the southern pincer directed at Trondheim, while at the same time delaying a linkup between Allied and Norwegian forces in central Norway. Nevertheless, despite the strategic advantages, the Dombaas drop was a complete disaster.[12] Although in a postwar assessment *Generalmajor* Fritz Morzik, the Wehrmacht's chief of air transport, felt that the operation should be considered "a complete success," in reality rushed preparations and hasty execution doomed it from the outset.

A paratroop detachment of 160 men was brought together quickly by *Generalmajor* Süssmann, commanding general of Luftgaukommando Norwegen, under the command of *Oberleutnant* Schmidt, and flown to Dombaas in fifteen Ju 52s. The weather was extremely poor, forcing the transports to circle above in search of the target area, and hereafter the situation deteriorated further. Ground fire fatally struck one aircraft, resulting in a crash landing that left only eight alive, while seven planes returned home, where at least four were written off, and one was interned in Sweden. As for the remaining paratroops, some were dropped too low and killed; others, including Schmidt, were lost in the first engagement against Norwegian forces. Only forty-five men survived the flight, the drop, and ensuing small-arms fire. The Germans had originally hoped to keep these men supplied by air. However, atrocious weather during subsequent days thwarted the implementation of this plan. For a time, these cold, isolated troops were able to block the road between Oslo and Trondheim and do considerable damage to the communications and rail center there, yet within the space of six days they were surrounded and forced to surrender on 19 April.[13] Süssmann was court-martialed for the fiasco but escaped with an acquittal.[14]

BRITISH AIR RAIDS AND *SUFFOLK*

The Luftwaffe, meanwhile, was making heavy work of fulfilling another of the Führer's orders: to destroy British vessels and prevent further landings. Indeed, by 19 April, the British had some 6,000 men on either side of Trondheim at Namsos and Aandalsnes, in a position to isolate and eventually advance on the German defenders occupying the old Norwegian city. The failure of German aircraft to prevent the landings was due in part to British air support operations. To hamper Luftwaffe efforts against the landings, the British initiated a number of raids (amounting to nearly 200 sorties) against German-held airfields between 14 and 21 April. These operations delayed the detection of the landings and meant the Germans were unable to make immediate strikes in strength to arrest the Allied consolidation. The brunt of these British raids naturally fell on Sola, where Milch had arrived at midday on 16 April to get a firsthand look at the front. It was not a pretty sight. The field had been badly damaged overnight by a British raid, and although only two aircraft had been destroyed, the landing strip was so badly damaged, and the field so crowded with transports, that when a wing of Ju 88s tried to put down on the field, no fewer than nine were damaged.[15] In spite of the fact that only relatively small numbers of British bombers were reaching Stavanger on each occasion, it was all too obvious to Milch that they could still do considerable damage, particularly to the airfield's landing strip, because the field lacked adequate antiaircraft defenses. In his diary he bluntly wrote: "Flak."[16]

Milch had to reconsider rapidly his initial assessment of the situation at Sola. Four days earlier, he had written in his notebook under the heading *"Flak Norwegen"* that the Germans, only four days into the campaign, either had, or were looking to have, six heavy and four light flak batteries at Stavanger, the center of aerial operations; three heavy and one light battery at Bergen, the closest operational point to the British Isles; three heavy and two light batteries at both

Oslo and Trondheim; and three heavy and one light battery at Narvik. Whether this entry of 12 April was a statement of intent or what Milch actually believed was already in the field is unclear from his customary abbreviated entry. In any case, it bore little semblance to the reality he now faced. Indeed, a report of 15 April reveals that Stavanger possessed only a single heavy and light battery; Bergen could boast of an additional light battery; while both Oslo and Trondheim had one heavy and two light, and one heavy and one light battery, respectively, with which to defend their airfields.[17] Jodl, who was watching events in the north with a great deal of interest, pointed to the cause of this shortage of flak defenses in his diary entry of 14 April: "Another three Luftwaffe antiaircraft batteries onboard ship torpedoed by submarine."[18]

As a result of the damage caused by the British bombing raids and the large numbers of aircraft jammed into Sola, the Germans were forced to close it to incoming traffic for a short period, and aircraft that could be moved were flown to Oslo to ease overcrowding. Ironically, though, the raids had a somewhat beneficial outcome for Luftflotte 5 because Sola was fairly empty—only thirty-seven aircraft remained, and the majority of these were from ZG 76, KG 26, and Z./KG 30—when the British made another desperate attempt to shut the airfield down overnight, this time by means of a heavy cruiser.[19] At 0630, Milch's breakfast was disturbed by the sounds of heavy shelling.[20] *Suffolk* had crept in close to Stavanger overnight and, guided by flares released from a Hudson, subjected the seaplane base to heavy bombardment for three-quarters of an hour.[21] Although the land-based airfield suffered no damage, the seaplane headquarters were soon set ablaze, with four reconnaissance floatplanes destroyed and two others damaged.[22] Having awakened the German defenders, *Suffolk* ran for Scapa at thirty knots with a handful of escorting destroyers.[23] The Luftwaffe was not far behind.

The ten Heinkels of KG 26 that took off from Sola at 0815 were the first to lash *Suffolk*. They struck the heavy cruiser twice at about 0825 but were unable to slow it. These were followed by Dornier flying boats from Bergen and Ju 88s from Westerland in northern Germany. Although the Luftwaffe made almost continuous attacks against *Suffolk*—more than eighty sorties over a seven-hour period—the cruiser escaped sinking by a hairsbreadth, limping into Scapa with its "quarter-deck awash."[24] The German inability to sink the heavily damaged warship, even after it was reduced to eighteen knots, can be attributed to the vicissitudes of fortune and *Suffolk*'s antiaircraft defenses, coupled with the difficulties associated with high-level bombing runs against vessels taking evasive action under full steam.

Initially, the British had planned on covering the retreat of *Suffolk* with a fighter escort; however, these aircraft failed to meet up with the heavy cruiser, and it was perhaps only the arrival of twelve Blenheims that prevented further damage being done. *Suffolk* had only just received a hit to its "X" turret during its dash for home when, "acting like fighters," the Blenheims, en route to bomb Sola, dove upon the Ju 88s that were swarming over the fleeing vessel.[25] They broke up the German attack, saving the wounded *Suffolk* from being sent to the bottom of the North Sea. Thereafter, the Blenheims continued on to Sola, where they added to the general difficulties of the Germans in keeping the base operational. The attack was particularly disturbing for Milch, who observed at close hand the inadequacies of the defenses at Sola when a noncommissioned officer was struck and killed by flying splinters barely ten meters from where Milch stood.[26]

The survival of the heavy cruiser was also aided by its antiaircraft defenses of sixteen 101-mm guns augmented by two quadruple 40-mm guns.[27] These defensive batteries were suited to deterring the main mode of attack employed by the Germans and the British against naval vessels early in the war—that of high-level bombing. Although not a single German aircraft was knocked out, the combined defensive fire made it extremely difficult for bombers such as the Heinkel to achieve hits against an enemy vessel maneuvering in the open sea. Of the thirty-three separate attacks made on *Suffolk,* twenty-one were of the high-level variety, while the most successful—including the hit on the "X" turret—were those made by Ju 88s in diving assaults.[28] The accuracy of aerial attacks increased immensely when aircraft capable of diving on a target were available, as already demonstrated by the success of Skuas when they sank *Königsberg* in Bergen. At this stage of the war, however, the Germans lacked sufficient numbers of Ju 88s to make a significant impression off the coast of Norway, while the Stuka dive-bombers based on Norwegian soil were too few and lacked the requisite legs to operate over longer distances.

The lack of bombers capable of accurate dive-bombing was compounded by a dearth of torpedo bombers. While Germany was one of the first countries to investigate the development of an airborne torpedo, establishing its first torpedo squadron in 1916, little was done to follow up this groundwork in the interwar period. By the end of the First World War, 36,000 tons of merchant shipping and a Russian destroyer had been sunk by aerial-delivered torpedoes, but a lack of development after the cessation of hostilities meant that by September 1939 not a single German airborne torpedo was in production, let alone a purpose-built aircraft capable of delivering it.[29] Additionally, the Luftwaffe lacked adequate aiming and release gear that could be coupled to existing aircraft types deemed suitable for low-level torpedo runs. Consequently, when war broke out, the only available torpedo in the Luftwaffe inventory was, ironically, an improved Norwegian "Horten" torpedo. Yet it would not be until after the Norwegian campaign had concluded that German aircraft such as the He 115 seaplane, the Heinkel and Ju 88 bombers, and the Condor would be adapted to carry torpedoes.[30] Even then, it was not until ten obsolete Swordfish torpedo bombers had knocked out three Italian battleships in Taranto harbor in November 1940—not only altering the balance of power in the Mediterranean but also heralding the twilight of the battleship era—that Göring seriously spurred on Germany's development of its own torpedo bomber force.[31] Had the Luftwaffe possessed more Ju 88s and even a few torpedo squadrons during the Norwegian invasion, *Suffolk* and its entourage would have suffered far greater losses than they did at the hands of X Fliegerkorps.

THE LUFTWAFFE AND THE CANCELLATION OF *HAMMER*

The primary significance of the almost continual Luftwaffe assaults on *Suffolk* was that they confirmed in the minds of many in Britain and the Admiralty the threat land-based aircraft posed to warships that lacked adequate air cover. The immediate result was the cancellation of Operation *Hammer,* a direct assault by the Allies on Trondheim. The strategic significance of Trondheim, the main port and city in central Norway, was immediately appreciated by the Germans and Allies alike. The Allies, for their part, realized that a successful operation against the German force of some 2,000 men at Trondheim would effectively cut the Germans off from the entire northern part of Norway. Geographically, the port is located at a point where the country is pinched at the waist, a mere ninety-five kilometers overland from the Norwegian-Swedish border. Moreover, situated at the northwestern end of Norway's central communication axis, linked by both road and rail along the Gudbrandsdal and Osterdal valleys all the way to Oslo, Trondheim, once secured, would provide the logical base from which an established Allied force could drive south on the Norwegian capital.

First considered by the Military Co-ordination Committee on 13 April, *Hammer* envisaged no difficulties in silencing the defensive batteries guarding the entrance of Trondheim Fjord. Air cover would be provided by the two aircraft carriers *Ark Royal* and *Glorious,* the latter recently transferred into the region from the Mediterranean to aid the ailing Allied airpower situation. Having breached the outreaches of the fjord, the Allies' main assault would take place near Vaernes airfield, while supporting operations above and below Trondheim at Namsos and Aandalsnes would converge on the city and the Dombaas junction, respectively, thereby covering the operation's northern and southern flanks. On 17 April, the attack was laid down to take place in five days' time. However, the pounding *Suffolk* received at the hands of the Luftwaffe on the same date highlighted Allied concerns for the safety of the considerable naval resources required for the expedition—three battleships with supporting cruisers and destroyers and the two aircraft carriers.[32] As the Joint Chiefs of Staff reluctantly pointed out to the Military Co-ordination Committee, there were at least six reasons for abandoning the proposed direct assault on Trondheim in favor of the converging Namsos and Aandalsnes pincers alone: both Namsos and Aandalsnes were already secured and ready for further landings; the German defensive positions were continually being strengthened at Trondheim; the Germans were probably aware of the likelihood of a landing at Trondheim and would be prepared; it would be difficult to make adequate preparations in the short time available; it was not possible to obtain satisfactory aerial reconnaissance of the proposed landing sites; and finally there was an increasing threat of aerial assaults on naval vessels. Of these, the last was the overriding concern, since *Hammer* required the "concentration of almost the whole of the Home Fleet in an area where it could be subjected to heavy air attack."[33] Much to the chagrin of Churchill, this assessment resulted in the cancellation of *Hammer* on 18 April. German airpower—or, more accurately, the threat of German airpower—had once again played an important part in the direction that the Allied effort was taking.

It is worth noting that in marked contrast to the German invasion of 9 April, the British counteroperations lacked not only the benefit of surprise but also the other salient feature of *Weserübung:* the ability to carry out airborne transportation of reinforcements to follow up seaborne landings. Unlike the Germans, the British had failed to develop a cheap and reliable transport like the Ju 52 in the period prior to the outbreak of the Second World War. On successive occasions in the 1920s and early 1930s, the British were able to deploy a small number of Vickers Victorias and other miscellaneous aircraft as troop carriers: in the evacuation of Kabul in 1929, the disturbances in Cyprus in 1931, and during the fighting in Iraq in 1932, where twenty-five troop-carrying aircraft transferred a complete battalion from Egypt to Baghdad in six days. However, when these aircraft passed into obsolescence, the Air Staff neglected to procure a specific transport aircraft type in the 1930s.[34] Influenced by Hugh Trenchard's insistence that the RAF steer clear of aircraft designed purely as ancillaries to British land and sea forces, plus fiscal restraints and the lack of a decent civilian aviation industry centered on landplanes (as opposed to seaplanes), the RAF did not bother to seek out a replacement.[35] In this period, only the Bristol Bombay, which first flew in June 1935 and was capable of carrying twenty-four fully equipped men, offered the British a true transport aircraft. Yet they failed to appreciate the potential of such a machine, and only fifty were built in the years leading up to the war. If the RAF had had anything like the same number of efficient transports as the Germans deployed during this campaign, they would have proved ideal for supporting both *Hammer* and operations elsewhere.[36]

Apart from a minor attempt to revive the direct assault a few days later, the Allies' main focus now lay on building up forces at Aandalsnes and Namsos. The effectiveness of these plans was, however, hamstrung by appalling British preparations, which were, to quote the frank official report on the landings, "well nigh disastrous."[37] Artillery pieces were loaded without their corresponding detachments and with little or no ammunition, and the small number of vehicles involved in the expedition were embarked without their drivers.[38] On top of this, German airpower once again was about to play a decisive role not only directly by bringing its aircraft to bear in the field but also indirectly by influencing decisions being made in London.

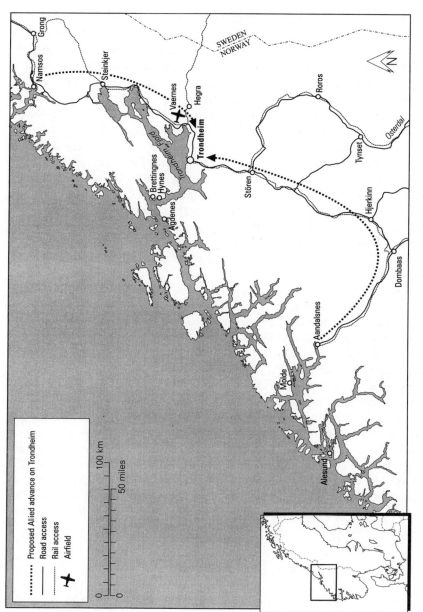

4. Planned route of the Allied advance on Trondheim.

Meanwhile, the Germans were unable to fully carry out Hitler's order to "use every endeavor to bring up reinforcements to Trondheim by air" because on the very day that this directive was given, 14 April, the spring thaw rendered the Vaernes airfield unusable. Vaernes had been serviceable on 12 April because of frosty weather, but the odd warmer day had the potential to reduce the airfield to a muddy quagmire.[39] These difficulties were highlighted by the very low levels of supplies on hand for aircraft at Trondheim on 14 April: eight 500-kg bombs, ten 50-kg bombs, 4,000 liters of fuel, and 2,600 liters of oil.[40] Although this problem was somewhat alleviated by the establishment of an auxiliary airfield at Jonsvatnetsee, southeast of Trondheim, which could be used for the arrival of transports, it could not bring about a rapid improvement of X Fliegerkorps' logistical position nearer the city. On 16 April, the German Naval Staff war diary noted that although the "seaplane base and the [Vaernes] aerodrome are serviceable," the "operational readiness of the planes so far brought up, however, is very slight owing to the lack of ground staff and the great demands on personnel and material."[41] Thus the U-boats were called upon once again to take up the slack by an increasingly worried OKW.

Indicative of the changing focus of the campaign, *U 43* was redirected from its mission to Narvik in the north to Trondheim in central Norway on 14 April.[42] The other U-boats intended for Narvik were similarly trained on the main point of effort and were followed in the days ahead by a second wave of converted U-boats bearing vital supplies, including bombs and 130 tons of aviation fuel stored in specially designed tanks.[43] In all, seven U-boats were deployed in this manner and proved far more effective than their fellow U-boats had been in actual combat. Nevertheless, the number of U-boats available was limited, and only the Luftwaffe had the capacity to shore up the German position in Trondheim. The Luftwaffe commenced the undertaking on 20 April, when over ninety aircraft were finally able to bring in the 359th Regiment Staff with equipment, 208 men and four guns, and 146 mountain troops.[44] This operation was followed up over 23–24 April by a further 120 Ju 52 sorties that brought in more reinforcements, including elements of the 33rd Flak Regiment.[45] The arrival of these forces coincided with a redoubled effort by the Luftwaffe against the Allied landings north and south of Trondheim.

AIRPOWER THE KEY IN CENTRAL NORWAY

Up until this point, reconnaissance and attacks against Allied forces put ashore had been either relatively minor or abandoned because of poor weather.[46] On 19 April, the Führer personally stepped in again, ordering as follows:

> On 20 April the main point of effort *[Schwerpunkt]* of Luftflotte 5 is to be attacks on the disembarkation at Namsos. Likewise similar operations are to be urgently undertaken against the landings at Aandalsnes. By order of the

Führer the towns and rail junctions of Namsos and Aandalsnes are to be destroyed without consideration for the civilian population, the rail line and roads near these junctions are to be interrupted for a considerable duration.[47]

This order would unleash a veritable hail of fire on Allied positions in both these areas. In atrocious weather on 20 April, about 120 aircraft of KGr 100, KG 26, and KG 30 attacked the enemy. Although clouds lay as low as 200 meters in the fjords, the aircraft struck heavily in accordance with Hitler's orders. Namsos was on the receiving end of the greater part of the Luftwaffe's attention. The town itself, the harbor, the railway station, and the rail line all received extensive damage from the bombers of KGr 100 and KG 26.[48] Around Aandalsnes, despite claiming to have hit a cruiser with a 1,000-kg bomb and making two hits on a transport, the Luftwaffe was denied any successes as a result of the poor flying conditions.[49] General Carton de Wiart, commander of the Allied forces at Namsos, was despondent; the wooden wharves had been smashed to matchwood, while all the rolling stock was destroyed. In addition, nearly all the French ammunition and equipment had been torched in the ensuing blaze. De Wiart radioed London the same day to advise his superiors not to send any more ships because there no longer were port facilities to accommodate them; the next day he prophetically signaled the War Office: "I see little chance of carrying out decisive, or indeed any operations, unless enemy air activity is considerably restricted."[50]

At first, X Fliegerkorps concentrated its efforts against de Wiart's northern pincer of British and French troops as it pushed toward Steinkjer. The latter were almost immediately threatened by the arrival of German troops on the western flank of de Wiart's positions, by German destroyers still in Trondheim Fjord, and by Luftwaffe attacks on Steinkjer and its connecting roads on 21 April. At the same time, German forces advanced from Trondheim, pushing Norwegian units lying in the heart of the country backward toward the Allied positions. The Luftwaffe flattened the British communications center in Steinkjer, and both the brigade and battalion headquarters were forced to evacuate.[51] On 22 April, the German destroyers bombarded de Wiart's western flank, and Luftwaffe bombers resumed aerial attacks on Namsos and targets in the harbor. In all, KG 4 dropped some twenty-two tons of bombs around Namsos with relative impunity. Harassed incessantly by the Luftwaffe and without antiaircraft defenses, the Allied position north of Trondheim was particularly grim. The situation in the south was little better. For example, on 22 April, the Allied vessels gathered in Molde and Romsdal Fjords. Their disembarked men and the roads leading out of Aandalsnes were attacked by thirty-four Heinkel bombers from KG 4, KG 26, and KGr 100 and eighteen Ju 88s from KG 30 and LG 1, which dropped thirty-seven tons of incendiaries and high explosives.[52]

The appearance of a new bomber wing, LG 1 (*Lehrgeschwader,* or training wing), in these attacks was the result of a general reinforcement of the Luftwaffe's strength in Norway in the last two weeks of April, designed to shut down the Allied landings as soon as possible. In recognition of the growing intensity of the campaign, Geisler's *Fliegerkorps* was reinforced on 21 April by two groups of Ju 88s from LG 1, two groups from KG 45, and a squadron of new Condors from KG 40.[53] In total, this represented an increase of the fighting strength of Luftflotte 5 by some 140 aircraft. The transport arm of X Fliegerkorps also received a boost with the allocation of a number of prototype long-range seaplanes to KGzbV 108, including three Blohm and Voss Ha 139A floatplanes, two BV 138s, and five Do 26 flying boats, while KGzbV 105 received two four-engined Blohm and Voss BV 142 prototype airliners.[54]

The most significant operational change was the establishment of a forward command to more effectively pursue the elimination of the Allied positions. Fliegerführer Stavanger (Air Leader Stavanger), under the determined and resourceful command of *Oberst* Robert Fuchs, was created, comprising KG 30 bombers, ZG 76 and JG 77 fighters, and various land-based and coastal reconnaissance units.[55] This eclectic assemblage of aircraft at the Germans' most effective forward base allowed Fuchs to carry out everything from coastal reconnaissance and assaults on naval craft to battlefield interdiction and the interception of Allied raiders. This latter task was aided—albeit unpredictably—by a newly installed *Würzburg* radar installation. In one of the first successful German radar-assisted interceptions of the war, six Blenheims were picked up forty kilometers out from Stavanger. Consequently, by the time they swooped in low over Sola, Bf 110s were already airborne and diving on their unsuspecting prey. One Blenheim was shot down, while the rest broke for home. From 15 April to 3 May, 115 sorties were flown against Stavanger with fourteen attackers dispatched by the Germans.[56] These victories were at the expense of seventeen Luftwaffe aircraft, eight of them transports, over the period 10 to 30 April. At Oslo, the results of British raids were similarly inconclusive. Up until 5 May, the Allies destroyed twelve German aircraft and damaged another thirty-one at Fornebu. These raids were blunted by interceptions made by II/JG 77 Bf 109s based at Kristiansand, which for the loss of five of their own aircraft shot down ten British raiders.

The only relief for the Allies was that German airpower was not yet sufficiently proficient in attacking naval units to inflict higher casualties in the campaign for central Norway. In total, only three trawlers and a sloop were sunk at Namsos up until 30 April, while at Aandalsnes seven trawlers were lost because of Luftwaffe attacks. As for vessels badly damaged in the same period, *Suffolk* had been pounded off Stavanger on 17 April; the French cruiser *Emile Bertin* and the sloop *Bittern* were damaged on 19 April and 30 April; at Aandalsnes the sloop *Pelican,* the flak cruiser *Curaçao,* and the sloop *Black Swan* were badly damaged on 22, 24, and 28 April, respectively.[57] Nevertheless, the Luftwaffe's meager catch—considering the bountiful targets available and the number of raids undertaken—provided little solace to Allied ground personnel in snow-covered positions, trying to avoid the attention of German aircraft.

In order to quell de Wiart's concerns and blunt the aerial bombardment of Allied troops, London dispatched eighteen Gladiator biplanes of 263 Squadron to Norway.[58] Symbolic of the Allies' disjointed and shambolic response to the German invasion, the deployment of these obsolete aircraft proved a disaster from the start. While German aircraft continued their sorties against Allied positions, the Gladiators flew from the aircraft carrier *Glorious* onto the frozen lake of Lesjaskog near Aandalsnes on 24 April. These were soon joined by four Skuas. Under normal circumstances, a squadron would be supported by a large number of men trained in aircraft maintenance, transportation, administration, and even catering, but here the pilots had to rely completely on what local labor could be scraped together.[59] Totally exposed on the frozen lake, they found no shelter from either the elements or the enemy. Because there were no fuel trucks, aviation fuel had to be carried on sleighs in four-gallon drums. The Gladiator crews soon realized they would be carrying out not only the refueling but also the rearming, since they had only one armorer to service all seventy-two of the squadron's machine guns.[60] These difficulties were merely a prelude to what was to follow.

Having spotted the arrival of the British aircraft the night before, the Luftwaffe set about raiding the frozen base at dawn on 25 April, then continued to bomb and strafe the aircraft and crews at regular intervals over the following eight hours.[61] Between 0900 and 1000, a handful of German bombers raided the airfield, destroying four Gladiators on the ground, damaging others, and wounding three pilots.[62] The RAF crews faced extreme difficulties in getting the Gladiators airborne because the starter batteries were flat and the carburetors had frozen. Some of the biplanes did, however, manage to take off and carry out tasks, which included some reconnaissance and spotting for the Allied ground forces, in addition to a number of successful air battles with German bombers. Considering the performance of the Gladiators and the unfavorable conditions under which they were forced to operate, the RAF pilots claimed a remarkable fourteen confirmed victories during the nearly forty-eight hours they resided in central Norway.[63] Nevertheless, by noon, ten of their aircraft had been destroyed either by direct hits or, more often than not, by near misses setting the aircraft ablaze. By the end of the day, only five aircraft were still flyable, and these were transferred to another hastily prepared site just before midnight. It was all over by the late afternoon of 26 April. Even the handful of aircraft in a semiserviceable state were unable to take part in operations, since all fuel reserves had been exhausted; in the end, the aircraft had to be torched.

The destruction of these aircraft was a great blow to the Allied effort and proved the turning point in the campaign in central Norway. As Lieutenant General H. R. C. Massy, commander of Allied expeditionary forces on either side of Trondheim, later elaborated, the fate of the whole campaign here hinged on airpower:

On the 25th April, I was directed by the Chiefs of Staff to submit an appreciation on the situation in Norway. As it appeared to me then, the possibility of landing further troops or of maintaining the troops then ashore depended entirely on our being able to obtain control of the situation in the air. In my appreciation I stated this fact and gave it as my opinion that should adequate air support be available I had no reason to suppose that we could not hold our existing positions against the Germans, and at a later date eject them from Trondheim. Without it I had little doubt that any further operations would become impossible and that we should be compelled to evacuate our forces from . . . central Norway.[64]

With the loss of the only land-based aerial support in the region, Massy threw in the towel. His assessment of 25 April had been written without any prior knowledge of the decision to attempt to secure some airpower support on land at Lesjaskog. On the following day, when he heard of its failure, he realized that any hope of competing with the "German air menace" had disappeared and reluctantly concluded that "evacuation would therefore be necessary."[65]

Massy was all too aware of the impossibility of continuing operations from Namsos and Aandalsnes, and of the advance being made by the Germans up through Gudbrandsdal, threatening a linkup between the Germans in the southern part of the country and their Trondheim-based comrades-in-arms. Although the main focus of the Luftwaffe in this period naturally was directed against the Namsos and Aandalsnes pincers, support for the German army forces pushing northward was not completely ignored. Initially, though, the Luftwaffe's effort was not great. For instance, KG 4, which provided the bulk of battlefield interdiction for the army, made only about sixty sorties against enemy positions in three main raids on 11, 20, and 21 April.[66] Aside from the occasional strafing runs provided by the twin-engined Bf 110s of ZG 76, the German ground forces had to rely on short-range army cooperation reconnaissance units equipped with small numbers of Henschel Hs 126s—a lightweight, single-engined, low-flying aircraft that was the mainstay of the German army's tactical reconnaissance force until late 1942.

The difficulties of operating in the narrow, steep-sided valleys where much of the fighting occurred made the use of Luftwaffe aircraft in close air support nearly impossible on occasions. Typical of the type of aerial support rendered, and the difficulties experienced by aircraft flying in the valleys, was an ill-fated flight by an Hs 126 on 30 April. While the aircraft was able to support the German ground forces successfully as they advanced on Dombaas by dropping bombs and flares on likely targets, its low altitude coupled with its relatively slow speed made it vulnerable to ground fire, which shot it down.[67] Consequently, the progress of the army up through central Norway from Oslo had been slow because of the astute tactics employed by Ruge. He took full advantage of the mountainous terrain, which lent itself to defense, and the deep snow cover, which restricted German movements to the roads. In these conditions the Norwegian commander in chief invariably employed roadblocks and shelled the advancing Germans from elevated flanking positions.[68]

The Germans realized, however, that the key to finishing the campaign lay with securing the Gudbrandsdal and Osterdal valleys and, to this end, began strengthening their forces for a final twin-pronged thrust through the heart of Norway. Already by 24 April, German forces had reached the halfway point between Lillehammer and Dombaas. Two forces were created the same day to carry out the final advance: *Generalleutnant* Richard Pellengahr's "Group Pellengahr," consisting of seven infantry battalions, one motorized machine-gun battalion (less one company), two artillery battalions, a company of engineers, and a platoon of tanks, would advance up Gudbrandsdal; *Oberst* Hermann Fischer's "Group Fischer," made up of three infantry battalions, two artillery battalions, one engineer battalion, two motorized companies of the General Göring Regiment, one motorized machine-gun company, and a few platoons of tanks, would push through Osterdal.[69] The Luftwaffe aided these forces when required. For example, on 25 April, Group Pellengahr struck determined opposition at Kvam. Milch's diary picks up the story on 27 April: "Morning, Falkenhorst here: very downcast. 'Without strong air activity progress is impossible!' Agreed. Midday, Kvam and Bagn taken. Gruppe XXI holds its head up again."[70]

Aerial assaults, along with German artillery, had successfully dislodged Norwegian and Allied defenders. On 27 April, when Group Fischer came up against stiff resistance at Naaverdalen, this was also crushed by the Luftwaffe. Consequently, Naaverdalen, a mere fifty kilometers from Trondheim, was taken on 28 April, and two days later Group Fischer linked up with German forces advancing southward from Trondheim. Hitler was delighted and extravagantly proclaimed to Rosenberg that this was more than simply the matter of "a battle won"; it represented the winning of the whole campaign. More pragmatically, he proceeded to direct the deployment of pioneers and flak for the consolidation of Vaernes's airfield.[71] Group Pellengahr, on the western arm of the northward advance, reached Otta on 28 April, only forty kilometers from Dombaas.

Despite the relatively small number of casualties caused by the air attacks—in total the Namsos and Aandalsnes pincers lost only 1,402 and 157 men, respectively, to all causes, including capture—the Luftwaffe effectively shut down reinforcement and delivery of supplies into the region.[72] Moreover, continual aerial attacks on the Allied communication centers forced the expedition's headquarters to remain constantly on the move. Thus the Luftwaffe also acted as an intimidatory factor, greatly demoralizing the Allied forces.[73] The German advance in central Norway and the failure of the Allies to provide adequate air cover for their own operations left the British with no alternative but to abandon the region. On 28 April, the Admiralty informed Admiral Forbes that the forces landed at Namsos and Aandalsnes were to "re-embark . . . as soon as possible."[74] This decision, of course, coincided with the Luftwaffe's main effort against the Aandalsnes and

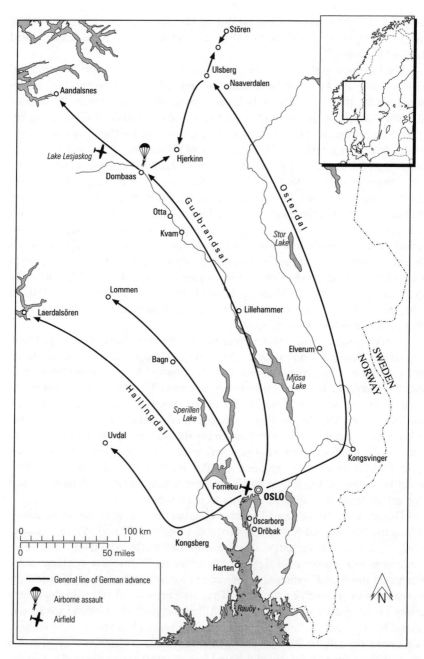

Stören

Ulsberg
Naaverdalen

Aandalsnes

Lake Lesjaskog ✈

Hjerkinn

Dombaas

Otta

Kvam

Stor Lake

G u d b r a n d s a l

O s t e r d a l

Lommen

Laerdalsören

Lillehammer

Bagn

Elverum

Mjösa Lake

H a l l i n g d a l

Sperillen Lake

Uvdal

Kongsvinger

S W E D E N

N O R W A Y

Fornebu ✈

OSLO

0   100 km
|—|—|—|—|—|—|—|—|—|—|
0   50 miles

Oscarborg
Dröbak

Kongsberg

——— General line of German advance

🪂 Airborne assault

✈ Airfield

Harten

Rauöy

N

5. The German advance in southern and central Norway, 9 April–2 May 1940.

Namsos bridgeheads and the subsequent bombardment of the withdrawing Allied forces—despite the fact that the Germans did not fully realize that an evacuation was occurring until relatively late in the withdrawal.

In fact, although X Fliegerkorps' field commanders (in particular, *Major* Martin Harlinghausen, the outstanding commander of Fliegerführer Drontheim, who regularly led reconnaissance missions himself over enemy coastal operations) reported that the Allies were in the process of abandoning the areas north and south of Trondheim, the German Naval Staff remained skeptical.[75] Initially, the naval planners assumed that the arrival of significant numbers of Allied vessels in the region was merely a prelude to an assault on Trondheim itself; even as late as 1 May, they speculated that although the troops south of Trondheim were clearly to be reembarked, it was possible the Allied units might be transferred to Narvik given the unsustainability of the southern pincer.[76]

ALLIED EVACUATION

Nevertheless, with Group Pellengahr and Group Fischer hard on their heels in central Norway, the Allies were hastening to their Aandalsnes and Namsos embarkation points. The British tried to cover the evacuations, which took place on the nights of 30 April–2 May and 1–3 May, respectively, with attacks on German airfields in the region. Operating from *Ark Royal,* the Fleet Air Arm struck at Vaernes, while the RAF raided Sola, Fornebu, and Aalborg.[77] Although these efforts destroyed a handful of aircraft, tore up the Vaernes runway, and so badly damaged Sola that landings there were possible only in cases of "extreme necessity"—hinting once again at what British airpower could have achieved if it had had sufficient numbers of either carrier-borne aircraft or long-range bombers—they only slightly blunted the Luftwaffe's ability to attack the embarking forces and the vessels gathering to ferry them to Britain.[78] On 28 April, the full weight of Geisler's bomber units—KG 30, KG 26, StkG 1, LG 40, and KG 40 (some ninety aircraft in all)—was brought to bear on the enemy.[79] Aerial reconnaissance and naval intelligence had located two Allied convoys heading for Namsos and Aandalsnes, and it was on these units that X Fliegerkorps fell.[80]

During the days that followed, the air corps repeatedly struck at the retreating forces, as the aircraft carriers vainly attempted to cover the withdrawal. By way of illustration, the air situation reports contained in the German Naval Staff diary's entry of 28 April note that about eighty aircraft were involved in the attacks on Allied vessels, sinking two freighters and causing damage to a further five and a couple of light cruisers in the vicinity of Namsos. Elsewhere around Aandalsnes in Molde Fjord and Aalesund, a tanker and transport were sunk and four freighters damaged.[81] Alongside these raids, OKL stipulated that over the "next few days the urgent assignment is the attack on the enemy aircraft carriers . . . lying off Namsos-Aandalsnes."[82] To effect this, a KG 26 bomber group at Stavanger and a group from KG 30 at Westerland were to remain on standby, prepared to act swiftly once the two carriers were located. Overall responsibility for the operation was placed in the hands of Fliegerführer Stavanger, Fuchs, and the *Commodore* of KG 30. On top of this, OKL directed that, as soon as possible, a group of Stukas be transferred to Harlinghausen's Fliegerführer Trondheim, where these accurate dive-bombers could be brought to bear on the enemy warships. The ability of Vaernes to accommodate additional aircraft was due in good part to Milch's organizational efforts, which bore fruit with the completion of the airfield's 790-meter-long wooden runway on 30 April.[83] Nevertheless, despite the carefully laid plans and a number of determined sorties, mostly by KG 26 and KG 30, and at least one near miss on 1 May, both *Ark Royal* and *Glorious* survived the onslaught.[84] Once again, the difficulties associated with aerial attacks on vessels at sea, even against those of "barn door" proportions, had been highlighted. The threat to the carriers, however, was too much for the anxious Admiralty, and both were ordered home, leaving the escaping land forces without air cover.

Despite the earlier bombing of Aandalsnes and Namsos, the actual British embarkations went off relatively unmolested due to the efforts of the Royal Navy, which carried out the loading of the vessels during the small number of hours of darkness available each night.[85] As de Wiart later observed: "In the course of the last endless day I got a message from the Navy to say that they would evacuate the whole of my force that night. I thought it was impossible, but learned a few hours later that the Navy did not know the word."[86] Having failed to disrupt the evacuation completely, X Fliegerkorps set about intercepting the retreating convoy laden with Allied troops, and on 3 May a reconnaissance flight by KüFlGr 506 floatplanes spotted four cruisers and nine destroyers about 110 kilometers off Folda Fjord at 0550, steaming at high speed on a westerly course.[87] This was followed at 0614 by sightings of a battleship, a heavy and light cruiser, and up to ten destroyers 30 kilometers off Vikten Island. It now became clear, even to the German Naval Staff, that an evacuation had been carried out. The Luftwaffe, however, was already swinging into action.

The majority of the aircraft that struck these British units were the newly arrived Stukas at Vaernes. Since these aircraft lacked adequate navigational aids with which to find their prey in the expanse of the North Sea, each successive wave of Stukas—totaling around fifty aircraft—was guided to the convoy by coastal reconnaissance floatplanes in the first systematic use of dive-bombers over the sea.[88] The first wave, made up of six Stukas, accompanied by seven Heinkels of KGr 100—also a recent arrival at Vaernes—attacked at 0900 without success. The following wave of fourteen additional Stukas arrived above the convoy an hour later and began to dive upon the British vessels. The results, at least according to the Luftwaffe aircrew, were substantial. A hit by a 250-kg bomb was reported between the forward turrets of a battleship; half a minute later it was followed by a strong explosion and a 500-meter-high tongue of fire. Other aircraft saw the conflagration and confirmed that either *Hood* or *Repulse* had been sunk. On top of this alleged masterstroke, further hits were made on a destroyer and a transport, and significantly on a cruiser, parts of which were seen to "fly into the air."[89] In reality, the force the air corps was attacking was Vice-Admiral Cunningham's Battle Group, which did not include any battleships—let alone the illustrious *Hood* or *Repulse*—but rather eight cruisers and ten destroyers. It was one of these latter vessels (the French destroyer *Bision,* whose magazine was hit) that was the source of the observed fire, subsequently going down with the loss of 108 crew members. The fourth wave of Stukas hit the convoy again and submitted the following report on its return: "The attack was renewed at 1400 and achieved two hits by 500-kg bombs on a heavy cruiser of the York class. One bomb hit on the forward third and one on the aft third of the ship. 100 meter-high explosion, dense smoke and after 30 minutes the ship sank. The success was confirmed by several eye witnesses."[90] In spite of the "eyewitness" account provided by the German pilots, the Naval Staff was rightly cautious and guessed correctly that the Luftwaffe might well have sunk a destroyer rather than a heavy cruiser.[91] Indeed, the destroyer concerned turned out to be *Afridi,* which went down with the loss of sixty-three lives. On top of these actual losses, three antisubmarine vessels were damaged by near misses.[92] By the next day, the Germans were still unable to confirm whether X Fliegerkorps' reports were accurate, but they pointed out that if "in fact a British battleship was sunk, then 3 May must be claimed as the day in which the Luftwaffe achieved its greatest success over the sea." The announcement of the "sinking" awakened a lively debate on the theme of "battleship versus plane," and even the German News Bureau (Deutsches Nachrichten-Büro) excitedly trumpeted that "this great success of the Luftwaffe has clearly demonstrated that in this age of air war the ascendancy of even so powerful a fleet can be broken anywhere."[93] Although the German navy was quick to pour cold water on rather premature and extravagant conjecture suggesting that the Royal Navy, which was built around a core of battleships, was now obsolete, it nevertheless concluded that even if a battleship had not been sunk by a Stuka, "It is at least clear that operations by heavy forces in enemy coastal waters—even when there is no enemy fleet of equal strength—expose the ships to extreme danger, particularly when carried out within dive-bomber range, and constitute a risk which Britain will hardly undertake in the future."[94]

THE ROLE OF AIRPOWER IN SOUTHERN AND CENTRAL NORWAY

The significance of events here and earlier in the campaign not only was appreciated at the time but also has become a feature of the growing body of literature examining the invasion, highlighting *Weserübung*'s importance to the continuing evolution of the role of airpower in maritime warfare and a corresponding decline in that of the battleship. "It is the first real conclusive proof we have," concurred General Sir Alan Brooke on 2 May 1940, "of the undermining of sea power by air power."[95] T. K. Derry's official history of the campaign, published in 1952, also hit upon this theme, concluding that "no degree of foresight could at the time have prevented us from suffering the full effects of German air superiority."[96] One of the lessons to be learned from Norway, observed S. W. Roskill in his official history *The War at Sea* (1954), centered on "the effect of air power on the control of the sea." "It can no longer be doubted," he continued, "that, if effective air cover was lacking, warships could not operate protractedly and the Army could not be maintained overseas."[97] As Hubatsch pointed out in his 1960 campaign analysis, it was during *Weserübung* that the impression originated that a strong air force could "reduce or nullify" naval superiority in coastal regions.[98] Writing in the comprehensive *Das Deutsche Reich und der Zweite Weltkrieg*, Bernd Stegemann echoed Jodl's comments of thirty-five years earlier when he observed that the "Royal Navy had been the first to learn that even a vastly superior fleet could not operate successfully in waters dominated by the enemy air force."[99] Gerhard Weinberg agreed in his *A World at Arms* that the "control of the airports in Norway, secured in the first two days by the Germans, allowed them to demonstrate dramatically and quickly early in the war the critical importance of land-based air power as dominant over seapower and the landing forces without their own land-based air force."[100]

Numerically, though, X Fliegerkorps' record throughout *Weserübung* of one cruiser, six destroyers and sloops, a dozen smaller vessels, and twenty-one merchantmen could not be considered overwhelming—especially against the warships—considering the effort devoted to aerial assaults on naval units. As the Norwegian historian Olav Riste has pointed out, the Luftwaffe's relatively meager success has led to somewhat divergent conclusions being drawn by others.[101] In 1966 Major General J. L. Moulton felt that the British failure could not be laid simply at the feet of German aerial superiority—as influential as this was—but with the British inability to appreciate the demands of three-dimensional land, sea, and air strategy.[102] Riste also points to Liddell Hart's comments, which indicate that although airpower was the "most decisive factor in German success," its effects were chiefly psychological and "paralysed the Allies countermoves."[103] Riste, for his part, favors the Moulton–Liddell Hart thesis, adding that the overall requirements of British strategy at sea figured prominently: "The range of defensive commitments binding the Royal Navy in 1940 made preservation of the fleet an aim overriding even the comparatively minor danger which the Luftwaffe constituted at the time of the Norwegian campaign."[104] Yet the claim that the Luftwaffe constituted a "comparatively minor danger" rests on the fact that the British never attempted to test the thesis by carrying out their proposed incursion into Bergen or the direct assault on Trondheim.

Furthermore, whether or not the impact of German airpower in southern and central Norway was decisive in *real* terms misses the point. The fact is, large surface vessels were far more expensive and time-consuming to build, equip, and outfit than a good number of aircraft. In light of this, and because of its large overseas commitment, Britain was not prepared to put the matter of "sea power versus airpower" to the decisive test in a peripheral theater, when these vessels may very well have been needed elsewhere at a later date. Therefore, while the Luftwaffe was prepared to throw any amount of its aircraft at the Royal Navy, the British acted on their real or imagined fears and relinquished supremacy in Norwegian waters to the Luftwaffe. In this sense, the Luftwaffe did play a decisive role during the campaign in severely curtailing Britannia's command of the waves. Its effectiveness against warships operating without sufficient air cover would be more than adequately demonstrated a year later at Crete, where the Royal Navy would suffer an even worse ordeal at the hands of German dive-bombers while endeavoring to evacuate Allied troops from the island. Nevertheless, Luftflotte 5's parting shots in May 1940 highlighted the overriding reason for German success in central Norway: air superiority. As undisputed ruler of the air, the Luftwaffe had reduced the Namsos and Aandalsnes bases to matchwood, harassed cold and weary Allied troops at will, threatened to completely shut down the sea approaches, and regularly cut the lines of communication to forward units.[105] In short, the Luftwaffe had made the whole British operation untenable.

THE THIRD PHASE: NARVIK

Since the main concern of OKW from the third week of April until early May lay in ejecting the Allies from the Trondheim region, the number of German aircraft carrying out sorties around Narvik had been negligible. The most encouraging action in the Far North prior to this period had been a near miss on *Furious* on 18 April, forcing the carrier to retire from the theater. Nevertheless, in the wake of Hitler's order of 20 April directing the Luftwaffe to concentrate its efforts on central Norway, support for Dietl's isolated group arrived intermittently in the form of single Condors making overflights of the port, where they dropped small amounts of supplies, attacked ground targets, and generally gathered reconnaissance information.[106] This amount of support was totally insufficient to meet the demands of even Dietl's small force of only 4,600 men, of which 2,600 were survivors of the beached German destroyers, armed with weapons taken from captured Norwegian stocks held at Elvegaardsmoen. Two of the three mountain battalions were deployed twenty-five kilometers north of Narvik, while the remaining battalion was positioned in Narvik itself. The naval personnel had been dispersed over three areas: on the eastern shore of Herjangs Fjord; along the rail line linking Narvik with Sweden; and in support of the mountain troops in the town. By the time the Germans had ejected the Allies from Namsos and Aandalsnes, the position of Dietl's meager and ill-equipped troops in and around Narvik was growing increasingly tenuous, especially as the Allied expeditionary troops began to tighten their noose around the port.

Since the first landing on 15 April, the Allies had built up a considerable force attempting to encircle Dietl's position. The Allies, however, were hampered by the failure of the war cabinet and Chiefs of Staff to establish a clear chain of command in northern Norway, where both the navy and army commanders were independent and responsible only to their respective service chiefs.[107] Hence, to achieve anything, a high level of personal cooperation was required from the commanders on the spot, and this never occurred. The energetic and determined Admiral Lord Cork, commander of the naval effort, pushed immediately for a direct assault on Narvik from the sea, while the thorough and methodical Major General P. J. Mackesy, commanding the land forces, favored a more cautious approach that would allow for a slow buildup, followed by an overland advance.[108] Even though Cork outranked the general, he had no authority over Mackesy, and because of the lack of landing craft and suitable sites elsewhere for an amphibious assault, the quay itself was the only feasible point of attack. Mackesy argued that such a frontal assault would be impossible unless a naval bombardment destroyed the concealed machine-gun posts. Under considerable pressure from London for action—and from Cork, who in turn was being chastised by Churchill for inaction—Mackesy acquiesced to the direct attempt on 24 April. Despite a three-hour naval bombardment of the town, led by Lord Cork in the cruiser *Effingham* and including *Warspite,* it was impossible to ascertain its effectiveness on the defenders thanks in part to bad weather conditions, including high winds and snowfalls, which greatly cut down visibility. Reluctantly, and probably fortunately for the troops assigned to the landing, the operation was called off. Nevertheless, the Allies were now compelled to find an indirect route.

If the shelling of the town on 24 April apparently made little impression on the defenders, it did illustrate the freedom of movement afforded the Royal Navy in northern Norway and was followed by the landing of British and French troops to the north and south of the town on the night of 28–29 April. Although the Allied advances were slowed by heavy snowdrifts and a lack of trucks and coastal steamers to support the forward units, Dietl became increasingly agitated about his own lack of supplies and his weak forward force, Group Windisch, at Elvegaard (some twenty kilometers north of Narvik by road), which was attempting to cover the German northern flank. On 4 May, he made his feelings known to OKW in a pointed communiqué:

Request support for the following: (1) In spite of repeated and urgent requests, I have received neither snow-shoes nor snow-glasses. Detachment is as a result at a great disadvantage *vis-à-vis* the Norwegians, who are splendidly equipped and extremely mobile in the snow. (2) In spite of urgent requests, we have had no supplies dropped by air for five days. The serious position of Group Windisch regarding ammunition and provisions can only be remedied by the air since, owing to the difficult terrain, German forces cannot bring up a sufficient supply. Group Windisch cannot hold out unless supplied soon, particularly with ammunition.[109]

Under these conditions, the Luftwaffe had four main tasks: to supply and reinforce Narvik; to hinder the advance of the British, French, Polish, and Norwegian troops converging on the town; to attack Allied shipping supporting the advancing forces; and to support a German overland advance on Narvik.

To fulfill these tasks, Geisler's air corps was reorganized, partly to deal with the situation in Narvik but also in preparation for the major German offensive in the west, *Fall Gelb* (Operation Yellow). On 4 May, Milch received Göring's summons for the coming French campaign and, along with Geisler, was awarded the coveted Knight's Cross for his efforts in Norway.[110] Milch was replaced by *Generaloberst* Hans-Jürgen Stumpff, a grenadier officer in the First World War, who had became a General Staff officer in the Reichwehr during the interwar years. In 1933, Stumpff transferred to the Luftwaffe as head of the Reich's Air Ministry Personnel Office, and from June 1937 to January 1939, he served as chief of the Luftwaffe General Staff. Subsequently, he took up the reins of Luftflotte 1 prior to his Norwegian posting. Like a good number of military commanders in the early part of the war, Stumpff had little operational aviation command experience. Moreover, like his predecessor, he excelled in administrative matters. In the short term, this forced him to rely on his previous army experience, which, as we shall see, did not always greatly impress his subordinates, but over time he became a more than competent commander in Norway under very demanding circumstances.

Milch's departure also heralded the withdrawal of a substantial number of aircraft from the theater for the invasion of France and the Low Countries. Bomber units of KG 4, KG 30, KG 54, and LG 1 and twin-engined fighters of ZG 1 were transferred south along with nearly all the transport aircraft, excluding those of KGzbV 107 and KGzbV 108. Only slightly offsetting these withdrawals was the arrival of a squadron of (J)/LG 2 and a group of Me 110s of ZG 76, while a squadron of JG 77's fighters was deployed at Vaernes.[111] In addition to these, 177 aircraft of Geisler's X Fliegerkorps (including the remaining Ju 52s) remained in support of Luftflotte 5.[112] Organizationally, Harlinghausen—who, for his earlier efforts along with *Hauptmann* Paul-Werner Hozzel, the commander of the Stuka group at Vaernes, was awarded the Knight's Cross—was now placed in command of Fliegerführer Stavanger.[113] His complement of aircraft numbered around 80 fighters and reconnaissance aircraft, while farther north Fuchs took over Fliegerführer Drontheim, which had been strengthened to 190 aircraft, including most of the bombers in Norway.[114] From Trondheim the Heinkels and Ju 88s could reach Narvik, but as yet, without an intermediate airfield, the feared Stukas of Fliegerführer Drontheim were restricted to operations in support of an overland advance north from Trondheim by the army. Additionally, conditions at this latter field were less than ideal, and the number of aircraft now crowded onto Vaernes stretched the ground crews and the base facilities to the limit. Given these trying circumstances, it was not surprising that on occasions they got the better of aircrew and ground staff. For example, with the transfer of KG 26 to Trondheim on 6 May, the time appeared ripe for decisive action against the Allied positions around Narvik. These good intentions, however, were dampened when a flight of eighteen aircraft planned for the following day had to be abandoned when water was discovered in the fuel lines.[115] Apparently the aviation fuel had become contaminated on its journey via U-boat to Trondheim, much to the frustration of all concerned.

AIR SUPPORT OF THE ADVANCE ON NARVIK

In spite of fuel problems and cramped conditions at Vaernes, the Luftwaffe began its support of the advance from Trondheim to Narvik of the 2nd Mountain Division and the 181st Infantry Division under the command of *Generalleutnant* Valentin Feuerstein. The Luftwaffe was to work in close cooperation with Feuerstein's force, providing reconnaissance information and supplies via parachute drops and seaplanes. The ground forces, as well as pushing northward, would be on the lookout for an "intermediate landing field between Trondheim and Narvik" suitable for the use of Stukas. Such a field would enable the relatively short-range dive-bombers to take part in aerial bombardments of naval and land targets at Narvik and then stop over at the intermediate field for refueling on the return leg to Trondheim. In a straight line, the distance between Narvik and Trondheim is 480 kilometers, and the terrain is mountainous and frequently cut by steep-sided, snow-covered fjords. On top of this, the roads were of extremely poor quality and for at least a quarter of the distance simply did not exist. So rugged is the terrain that the Allies considered it impassable; instead of withdrawing their Namsos force overland toward Narvik in a delaying action, they decided to establish points of resistance by naval landings along the projected German advance at Mosjöen and Bodö. To this end, two Allied companies were landed at Mosjöen and three at Bodö, while a further company was landed at Mo.[116] Norwegians in the area totaled no more than a reserve battalion and another battalion retreating north from Namsos in the wake of the Allied evacuation.

Group Feuerstein's progress over the "impassable" terrain to the north was impressive; within four days, it had covered nearly 145 kilometers, taking Mosjöen on 11 May. The next day, the Germans launched Operation *Wildente* (Wild Duck), a sea- and airborne advance from Trondheim to the Hemnesöy Peninsula in the fjord at Mo. In all, a company and a half were delivered by coastal steamer and seaplanes just behind the Allied front. Their position remained precarious until eased by forty-four Stuka raids undertaken by the Luftwaffe in "very unfavorable weather" on 12 May and the advance of the main body of German troops.[117]

Nevertheless, Feuerstein's progress was held up a few days later when he met the first real British resistance in the region at Els Fjord, forty kilometers north of Mosjöen, and Fliegerführer Drondheim was quickly reminded that "Division Feuerstein will be supported by reconnaissance, by supplies and by Stuka attacks."[118] It was also reported on 16 May that ground forces had located an intermediate airfield suitable for Stukas at Hattfjeildal, and the Germans hoped that the dive-bombers could be using this base in the near future to bring relief to the situation at Narvik.[119] In addition to these duties, a minor paratroop landing of fourteen men was carried out on 17 May around a pocket of determined resistance at Stien. Dropped on the westward flank of British positions by four Ju 52s in support of a flanking move by ground forces to the east, these paratroops played a part—albeit minor—in forcing the British units to fall back north of Mo, allowing the Germans to occupy Stien and then Mo on 18 May.[120]

By now, the Allied forces numbered some 4,500 men deployed north of Mo and in the region of Bodö; arrayed against these units, Feuerstein's force, which had been growing all the time, now numbered at least 6,000.[121] Given the difficulties of the terrain, however, the numerical difference was not substantial, in spite of the fact that Germans were supported by a small number of tanks, artillery, and of course the Luftwaffe. Rather, the overriding Allied weakness lay in its poor dispostion of forces, which were deployed not at the main point of effort above Mo but at Bodö, and these reinforcements were slow to filter south. Furthermore, the assembly of British troops at Bodö also suffered a setback with the sinking of a transport and the grounding of a cruiser carrying troops on 18 May. The cruiser *Effingham* had struck an uncharted rock, and Fliegerführer Drondheim's Stukas were dispatched to sink the stranded vessel. By the time they arrived, however, it had already capsized, and they instead proceeded to attack and sink a nearby transport.[122] By 28 May, the Germans were within sight of the main Allied position at Fauske, only forty-five kilometers east of Bodö.

Events in another theater now came into play. On 24 May, based on the rapid German successes in France, the Allies decided that the expedition in northern Norway would be wound up. This being the case, there was no longer any reason for continuing the delaying action south of Narvik. The evacuation of the Allied troops via Bodö was carried out uneventfully on 31 May with one prong of Group Feuerstein close on their heels, while a second pushed northward toward Narvik through the trackless and inhospitable wilderness.

Of importance to the Luftwaffe, though, was the appearance of three Gloster Gladiators operating from Bodö in the last few days of Allied resistance because it heralded a renewed attempt by the British to provide something close to adequate aerial support and erase the disaster of Lesjaskog. On 26 May, the Gladiators were sent to Bodö, and from here they were to provide air cover for the retreating troops. Bodö's airfield, however, was not up to the task, as the pilots found to their great displeasure when they landed on muddy ground. Nevertheless, with German aircraft flying over the field at regular intervals, two of the

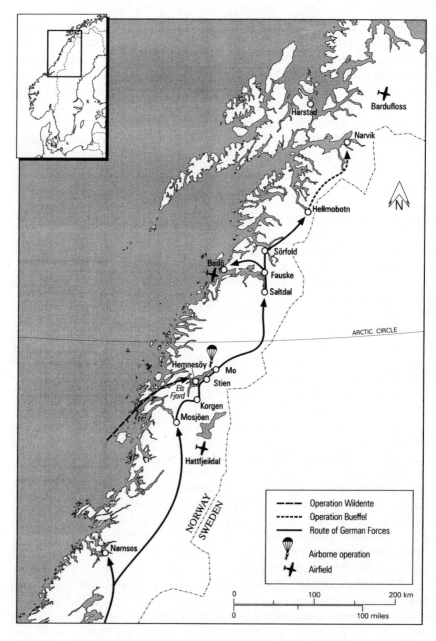

Harstad

Bardufloss

Narvik

Hellmobotn

Sörfold

Bodö

Fauske

Saltdal

ARCTIC CIRCLE

Hemnesöy

Mo

Els
Fjord

Stien

Korgen

Mosjöen

Hattfjeildal

NORWAY

SWEDEN

Namsos

N

	Operation Wildente
	Operation Bueffel
	Route of German Forces
	Airborne operation
	Airfield

0	100	200 km
0		100 miles

6. From Trondheim to Narvik, 2 May to 13 June 1940.

refueled Gladiators managed to extricate themselves from the quagmire and claimed to have shot down four German aircraft.[123] The British proposed to supplement these Gladiators with a dozen Hurricanes from *Glorious,* but the soft field caused two of the seven that did touch down to nose over; the last five aircraft flew on to the main British airfield north of Narvik at Bardufloss. Of course the Luftwaffe, which by now was only too well aware of the presence of the base and the retreating Allied soldiers, made plans overnight for its destruction and for that of the Bodö township. The Luftwaffe's attack was recorded in the diary of one of the Gladiator pilots: "Suddenly at 0800 hours, the balloon went up. There were 110s and Ju 87s all around us, and the 87s started dive-bombing a jetty about 300 yards from the aerodrome. . . . we watched the dive-bombing in terror."[124] Stukas and Heinkels reduced the town to a fiery wreck and destroyed the runway, but not before a good number of the undamaged RAF aircraft had taken to the air, where they shot down at least one Stuka before departing for Bardufloss.[125]

BARDUFLOSS AND LUFTWAFFE LIMITATIONS

The best equipped and best prepared British airfield in Norway, Bardufloss was to demonstrate how dangerous a well-established enemy airfield on Norwegian soil could have been to the Luftwaffe, because while it remained operational it enabled the Allies to gain at least some air parity in northern Norway.[126] With the assistance of some 600 locals, the one-and-a-half-meter-deep snow cover had been removed at Bardufloss airfield, the landing strip extended, and an antiblast screen constructed to prevent the destruction of aircraft from anything other than a direct hit. Drainage trenches followed, to prevent the field being reduced to a muddy bog when the thaw set in, and serviceable air-raid shelters and base headquarters were built. Antiaircraft defenses were provided by a single heavy battery and a light battery, which, along with all supplies and equipment, had to be brought up to Bardufloss by a narrow twenty-seven-kilometer track from the nearest port at Sörresia. By 21 May, all was ready for the first arrivals, and within two days, fourteen Gladiators of 263 Squadron had arrived. These were detailed to run cover patrols over Bardufloss itself, the Allied expedition's headquarters at Harstad, and the fleet in Vaags Fjord.[127] A Heinkel straying over the airfield became the base's first victim on 24 May and was soon followed by other victories when a patrolling aircraft shot down a Condor and two Blohm and Voss floatplanes. Bad weather then set in, restricting the Luftwaffe's offensive operations around Narvik to almost nil on 26 May and 27 May and giving the British more time to consolidate their Bardufloss position. On 26 May, 46 Squadron (equipped with Hurricanes) arrived. Thus the base would be ready for the most important part of the Allies' ill-fated expedition: the capture of Narvik and subsequent withdrawal from the region.

Prior to this, the Luftwaffe made strenuous efforts to fulfill its three other roles: attacking Allied shipping and ground forces, and supplying Dietl's units. Despite the poor weather prevailing in the region and the noted fuel problems, Fuchs's aircraft began the task of harrying Allied surface vessels in the Narvik area. Making 205 bomber sorties between 1 and 10 May, they sank the Polish destroyer *Grom* and damaged the Royal Navy cruiser *Aurora;* on 18 May the battleship *Resolution* was so badly damaged that it was forced to retire to Scapa.[128] At the forefront of these attacks around Narvik were KG 26, KGr 100, LG 1, and, after mid-May, recently returned units from KG 30. In the last half of May, these aircraft—aided by the arrival at Trondheim of over a dozen steamers laden with sorely needed bombs and aviation fuel—repeatedly attacked Allied vessels operating in support of the expedition to Narvik. The bombers destroyed and damaged more than a dozen warships, transports, and storeships, including, on 26 May, the cruiser *Curlew.*[129]

In addition to these sorties, the Luftwaffe examined the possibility of mining the fjords around Narvik, in particular Rombaks Fjord, where Royal Navy vessels operated with relative impunity. British cruisers and destroyers had already bombarded German positions along the rail line, and to restrict Royal Navy vessels from further shelling this area, Dietl requested that Rombaks Fjord be closed at its narrowest point, the Straum Strait, by mining carried out by U-boats or aircraft. Given British naval ascendancy, though, U-boats were precluded from the equation by OKW, thus leaving the Luftwaffe to attempt sowing the waters with TMAs (noncontact moored mines) along the lines of the RAF's successful *Gardening* campaign in the Kattegat and Skagerrak. Although both the British and proposed Luftwaffe operations centered on aerial mining, the similarities between the two operations end there.[130] For a start, the British *Gardening* campaign was carried out by dropping the mines at low altitude, whereas the TMAs were placed after an aircraft actually touched down on the water. This meant that the Luftwaffe would be forced to divert some of its limited number of floatplanes, currently engaged in valuable reconnaissance missions, to carry out mining missions whose efficacy had yet to be proved. Moreover, due to the limited range of the most suitable aircraft, Dietl's proposal was simply beyond the range of the majority of German float planes and seaplanes flying from Trondheim. Only after Group Feuerstein secured Mosjöen in the second week of May was the Luftwaffe in a position to even contemplate attempting the operation.

It was from Mosjöen that Naval Air Commander East, who oversaw the proposed mining, reported on 23 May that a *Kette* (a formation of three aircraft) of He 59 floatplanes had sown a single mine each off the southern shoreline of Straum Strait.[131] With the successful deployment of these three mines, Luftflotte 5 proposed an enlarged minelaying campaign in these waters and put in a request for additional mines. The only problem was that only nine TMAs existed in the entire Wehrmacht inventory. It also appears that the mines were inadequate for the task because those sown in Rombaks Fjord did not prevent British warships

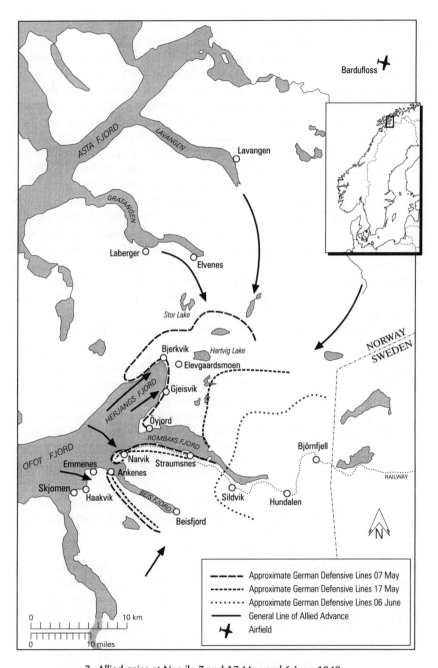

Map labels:

Barduffloss

ASTA FJORD

LAVANGEN

Lavangen

GRATANGEN

Laberger

Elvenes

Stor Lake

Bjerkvik   Hartvig Lake

Elevgaardsmoen

HERJANGS FJORD   Gjeisvik

Öyjord

ROMBAKS FJORD

NORWAY

SWEDEN

Björnfjell

OFOT FJORD

Emmenes   Narvik   Straumsnes

Ankenes

Skjomen   Haakvik   BEIS FJORD

Beisfjord   Sildvik   Hundalen

RAILWAY

N

0   10 km

0   10 miles

– – – – – Approximate German Defensive Lines 07 May
· · · · · · · Approximate German Defensive Lines 17 May
∙ ∙ ∙ ∙ ∙ ∙ ∙ Approximate German Defensive Lines 06 June
————— General Line of Allied Advance
✈ Airfield

7. Allied gains at Narvik, 7 and 17 May and 6 June 1940.

advancing into the fjord, nor did those sown elsewhere achieve any result.[132] Later mining operations in early June were similarly unsuccessful.

As the Luftwaffe gamely struggled to hamper the Royal Navy's freedom of movement around Narvik, it also hoped to shore up Dietl's defensive positions within the town, along the rail line, and to the north (Group Windisch). While the Swedes had reluctantly acquiesced to rail transportation of rations, medical supplies, clothing, ski equipment, and some specialists via Sweden (the first men and material arriving on 26 April), they would not allow ammunition and troops to be carried on this route to Dietl's supply depot, established just within Norwegian territory at Björnfjell. The bulk of ammunition and supplies, therefore, had to be brought in by air, and some 260 long-distance transport sorties by Blohm and Voss and Dornier flying boats, Condors, and a small number of Ju 52s were undertaken between mid-April and the first week of May. In addition to this, they successfully delivered two mountain battalions and artillery.[133] Although a good many transports had been transferred to Germany in preparation for the blitzkrieg in the west, most of these were Ju 52s that, in any case, could not participate fully in the flights to Narvik, since no suitable airfield existed around the town. Thus airdrops became the predominant means of supporting Dietl's forces. The types and amounts of materials that were delivered in this period can be seen in the following signal sent by the *Luftflotte* to Göring on 18 May, detailing a successful aerial drop:

> For the supply of Groups Windisch and Dietl, there were dropped in Narvik: 16 heavy machine guns, 2 81-mm mortars, 31 cases heavy grenade thrower [81-mm mortar] ammunition, 6 cases mortar ammunition, 12 anti-tank rifles, 14 cases AT rifle ammunition, 12 pieces MG receivers, 6 cases infantry ammunition, 10 cases SS, SMK, and SMKL, 6 aerial delivery units with infantry ammunition, . . . 2 cases MG-belts, 285 kg mail, 2 packages with Swastika flags, 1 case of films, 3 cases dry fuel, 34 cargo chutes were used. Total weight 5,872 kg.[134]

One of the first attempts to bring supplementary mountain troops to Dietl took place on 8 May, when six Dornier 26 flying boats made their way to Narvik, escorted by bombers that would keep British vessels in the vicinity of the town occupied while the naval aircraft landed, disembarked their human cargo, and then took off. Poor weather prevented four of the aircraft reaching their destination, while the two that did so were forced to carry out their mission largely unaided, since most of the accompanying bombers had also turned back because of the conditions. Ultimately, one of the flying boats crash-landed after being attacked by three British fighters. The loss of the flying boat highlighted the vulnerability of these cumbersome aircraft when faced with single-engined British types. Orders were drawn up advising that, from now on, Do 26s were to be employed only "under the protection of bomber and long-range fighter *(Zerstörer)* aircraft."[135]

Despite these measures, this type of operation was clearly too risky because it was dependent on several variables. The most important of these was the need for both the transports and the bombers to arrive over the region at the same time so that the latter could divert British attention away from the flying boats, which, after touching down, were dangerously exposed to enemy fire, including gunfire from naval vessels. Although a number of other similar flights were still undertaken to deliver items such as artillery and radio equipment, the bulk of the men were brought in by Ju 52s in paratroop drops near Narvik, once a suitable drop zone had been located by reconnaissance aircraft. In all, around 650 men were flown in in this manner between 23 and 30 May.[136] Yet, as time passed, the Luftwaffe's capabilities became noticeably stretched. This was no more evident than in the paratroop drop of 23 May. With the opening of the campaign in the west, Norway became a sideshow in the eyes of many German commanders and as such could no longer draw on the resources it once had under Milch's leadership. Consequently, having exhausted nearly all of its fully trained paratroopers in earlier drops over Narvik, Stumpff could gather up only sixty-six men aboard seven aircraft for the operation; moreover, the only training these intrepid souls were given for the mission was a hastily arranged ten-day course in parachuting.[137] Jodl, who still kept one eye on the Norwegian campaign, was relieved to note that despite receiving such an inadequate grounding, there were "no losses" among the men.[138]

Despite this valiant and energetic attempt to bolster Group Dietl's position and restrict the movement of Allied ships in and around Narvik, the Luftwaffe, along with poor weather, could only slow rather than halt the approach of the British, French, Polish, and Norwegian ground forces closing in on the port. Since late April, the 27,000 Allied soldiers had heavily outnumbered Dietl's beleaguered force of 6,000 men. Moreover, the Allies were ably supported by an artillery force of twenty-four guns and an antiaircraft component of one heavy and four light batteries.[139] These units, now under the command of Lieutenant General Claude Auchinleck, who had replaced Mackesy, moved on Narvik in the third week of May, aiming to capture the town and destroy the iron ore handling facilities before withdrawing to Britain.

DIETL'S WITHDRAWAL FROM NARVIK

On 27 May, reconnaissance aircraft reported that enemy naval units lying off Narvik and within Rombaks Fjord were subjecting the town and the rail line to heavy bombardment. The shelling was intense, and the daily Luftwaffe report noted tersely that "Narvik was burning."[140] The next report, in the early hours of the following day, revealed that no fewer than ten warships were bombarding the town, and at 0130 German positions at Hestafjell were under attack. Group Narvik urgently signaled for air support and, on account of the heavy shelling by naval units, also pointed out ominously that an enemy landing near the town had been achieved with the support of Allied airpower.[141] All available aircraft were scrambled to aid Dietl, including—for the first time—Stukas now operating from the intermediary airfield near Mosjöen. Initially, the war in the air went the Luftwaffe's way on 28 May because dense fog cloaked Bardufloss, allowing the Germans free rein against naval vessels supporting the assault on Narvik. The Stukas struck Lord Cork's flagship twice, so badly damaging *Cairo* (an antiaircraft cruiser) that it could no longer provide air defense fire, while near misses on the cruiser *Coventry* delayed the insertion of a French battalion.[142] Luftwaffe aircraft, including Ju 88s and Heinkel bombers from KG 30, KG 26, and KGr 100, plus some Bf 110s, bombed and strafed Allied ground positions, as witnessed by the following account from a soldier in the Polish contingent as it captured Ankenes south of Narvik: "Fat Dorniers [*sic*], having a clear run, were whirling like angry eagles low over the ground, almost touching the tree tops, and sweeping the grey thicket with murderous machine-gun fire. The fall of bombs was short and heavy, like that of ripe apples from an apple tree."[143] Once the fog lifted from Bardufloss, however, the British fighters picked up where they had left off a couple of days earlier. In ninety-five sorties they downed two German bombers and destroyed two Do 26 flying boats on the water as they frantically attempted to unload artillery pieces for the defense of Narvik.[144] The Fleet Air Arm also chimed in, with Gladiators from *Glorious* shooting down a Heinkel He 115 floatplane. Two further bombers were claimed by antiaircraft fire. While the air battle raged, Dietl's situation grew more desperate. Heavily outnumbered, he could do little to prevent the Polish Highland Brigade attack on Ankenes, the French *Chasseurs Alpins* thrust along the southern shore of Rombaks Fjord, the Foreign Legion and Norwegian direct push eastward into Narvik, and the British navy's landings on the waterfront.[145] Dietl was forced to abandon Narvik. Skillfully avoiding encirclement within the township, he guided his troops along the rail line, leaving behind most of their heavy equipment.

With the destruction of futher Luftwaffe aircraft at the hands of the Bardufloss fighters, it is remarkable that the first German raid on the airfield—a halfhearted one at that—did not occur until the next day, particularly since the Luftwaffe's attempt to counter the successes of Allied fighters by transferring increasing numbers of Bf 110s to support the bombers had failed. The twin-engined fighters had proved no match for the faster and more nimble Hurricanes, especially because many of the German aircraft were fitted with the "Dachshund's belly" *(Dackelbauch),* a long-range fuel tank that allowed them to reach Narvik with enough fuel for a twenty- to thirty-minute action but also proved to be an additional handicap for the slower aircraft.[146] Although other attempts were made to utilize the Stukas' intermediary field near Mosjöen for the Bf 110s, this could not be achieved prior to the Allied withdrawal. Consequently, given the German inability to provide adequate fighter protection in the face of climbing losses at RAF hands, it would appear, at least on the surface, that a concerted effort should have been made to shut down the Bardufloss airfield.

CONTROVERSY OVER THE USE OF AIRPOWER

A divergence of opinion among the leading German commanders in Norway prevented attacks on Bardufloss from being carried out. It would appear that, on the one hand, Falkenhorst and Stumpff advocated using airpower primarily in direct support of Dietl's forces, while on the other hand, Geisler and his chief of staff, *General der Flieger* Ulrich Kessler, and nearly all the officers leading the operations in the air favored the reestablishment of air superiority as the number one priority, followed by attacks on Allied shipping. That Stumpff, as head of Luftflotte 5, supported Falkenhorst's position was seen by contemporary airmen in Norway as purely misguided loyalty, since Stumpff had been the latter's junior in the Reichwehr. Kessler wrote scathingly after the war that Stumpff's "fawning" over Falkenhorst meant that the Luftwaffe effort was shifted more and more toward close air support of ground troops at Narvik and Feuerstein's northward advance from Trondheim, neglecting far more important targets. "At a distance of 800 kilometres bombers were committed to bomb machine gun nests," remarked Kessler, "and the twin-engine fighters to strafing attacks against enemy infantrymen they could hardly recognise."[147] In many respects, this argument holds a good deal of weight, since there is little evidence to suggest that the aerial attacks on Allied forces converging on the town significantly impeded or even slowed their progress. The situation in northern Norway was not like the attacks on Allied ground forces in central Norway, which had played a significant role in demoralizing enemy troops and destroying their communication lines. For example, while attacks on the Namsos and Aandalsnes bridgeheads and advancing forces could be undertaken by a greater number of aircraft from nearly all the other airfields involved in the operation—Aalborg, Fornebu, and Sola—the attacks on Narvik could be made only from the cramped and undersupplied Vaernes field. On top of this, the northern region was subject to far worse weather in this period than had been the case over central Norway a month earlier, and this made the sighting and targeting of enemy positions all the more difficult, even when sorties could be made. With the addition of British fighters into the equation, the Luftwaffe's ability to greatly influence matters in northern Norway was gradually eroded. Therefore, it does appear that the air units should have been deployed more aggressively in the first instance against the threat to German aerial superiority (the Bardufloss airfield) and then against targets more easily seen and effectively attacked (the warships and transports in and around Narvik) rather than in close support of the army.

Hard-and-fast rules of this nature, however, ignore the vagaries of any campaign, and it does seem clear—despite Kessler's oversimplification—that the employment of the Luftwaffe's resources in support of Feuerstein's northward thrust was justified. In short, Kessler's argument ignored the fact that the most accurate aircraft in the Luftwaffe's armory, the Stuka, could not reach Narvik—let alone Bardufloss—for much of May and, therefore, was logically employed in support of Feuerstein's ground forces. This not only hastened the withdrawal of the Allies from between Trondheim and Bodö but also provided—albeit belatedly—the intermediary base near Mosjöen. Without the latter, the Stukas would never have been able to strike at Allied shipping in and around Narvik in the closing days of the campaign.

Moreover, in defense of Falkenhorst and Stumpff, it might also be noted that their emphasis on attacking the Allied ground forces pushing Dietl back toward Sweden was based on an appreciation of the larger picture and the Führer's direct involvement. The commanders of Gruppe XXI and Luftflotte 5 were only too keenly aware that while a desperate defensive struggle was being waged by Dietl, back in Berlin a flurry of proposals were being put together in an effort to stave off defeat in northern Norway. With this planning going on behind the scenes, it is clear that the main objective was to make every effort to help Dietl hang on, even if this meant an overconcentration on ground targets, which, although not as rewarding, comparatively speaking, as warships, could make the difference between losing or holding on in time for a relief operation to be undertaken. Behind this planning was Hitler himself.

The Germans, right up until the Allies' evacuation, believed that their combined enemies were going to make a final lunge and drive Dietl's force out of the theater for good. This would then facilitate the establishment of a permanent Allied base of operations in northern Norway, cutting the Reich off from its Swedish iron ore supplies routed through Narvik. (How the Germans expected the Allies to maintain this position with the bulk of the country in German control and so far from Britain was never elaborated.) In Hitler's eyes, this was anathema, since the whole raison d'être for *Weserübung* revolved around holding the iron ore port. On 30 May, clearly recovered from his earlier nervous breakdown and buoyed by the success achieved in the west, Hitler instructed Gruppe XXI to notify Dietl that his force was to be supported by all possible means.[148] Dietl's task was to fight a defensive action for up to five or six days, by which time a relief operation could be undertaken. During this period, Stumpff's air fleet was ordered to aid Dietl directly. Thus, the role of the Luftwaffe in the final couple of weeks was simply to help stave off defeat for the ground forces, while relief operations swung into action.

Numerous fanciful initiatives were examined and discarded in the rush to do something, anything, to prevent Dietl's defeat and the loss of the port. A good many of these proposals never got beyond the planning stage, either through impracticality or because they were simply overtaken by events. One of these, the brainchild of the Führer himself, involved large numbers of gliders in the transportation of mountain troops to Narvik.[149] Mountain troops were readied for the operation, and on 29 May, OKL assembled the glider force at Aalborg. Numerous delays followed, however, and Hitler was forced to reduce the number of available gliders to only six. In the end, even these were never used. Instead, on 4 June, planners decided on reinforcing Dietl with two parachute battalions, totaling over 1,800 men. However, as with the Fuhrer's glider plan, this was overly optimistic given the shortage of troops trained for paradrops and Vaernes's crowded state and overstretched resources. Consequently, paratroopers and mountain troops were dropped only in small numbers.

Another overly ambitious scheme, code-named *Naumburg,* was developed in the first few days of June by OKW.[150] The operation would see a strong force of 6,000 men and a dozen tanks landed by the fast passenger liners *Bremen* and *Europa* 145 kilometers north of Narvik at Lyngen Fjord. From here, this force would drive south to attack the enemy's rear while the Luftwaffe undertook a daring aerial assault on Bardufloss, from which it would subsequently operate in support of the advancing ground units.[151] OKW planned to execute the operation in the third week of June and, to cover this sally north, proposed using the recently repaired German warships damaged in the first days of *Weserübung.* Since the Allied evacuation was executed before this date, the mission was never undertaken. This was probably a good thing for the Luftwaffe because the earlier successful aerial assaults had been made under favorable conditions, which did not exist at the RAF's well-defended Bardufloss airfield.

That German warships would be in the region to protect the passage of the liners was all part of the navy's own operation planned to assist Group Narvik, code-named *Juno.* Under the reasonable, but false, impression that the war in Europe was drawing to a close, Raeder and the Naval Staff proposed an aggressive use of their warships in a bid to assure future support from Hitler for the navy's development in the decades ahead.[152] The main thrust of *Juno* was to be made by the battle cruisers *Scharnhorst* and *Gneisenau* and the cruiser *Hipper,* supported by four of Germany's remaining destroyers. Originally, operations were to be undertaken "in the sea between Norway and Shetland," indirectly supporting Group Narvik by disrupting supply lines; yet with the deterioration of Dietl's position, and with Hitler's encouragement, these plans were gradually overturned in favor of giving direct relief to Dietl.[153] Overriding concerns from Naval Group West and Fleet Command with Hitler's dictum "No great success without great effort," Raeder issued a directive on 29 May.[154] "The first and principal task," ordered the *Großadmiral,* was the penetration of Vaags Fjord and the destruction of enemy warships and transports there, followed by the shelling of Harstad.[155] If, however, aerial reconnaissance indicated that penetration into Ofot Fjord, even as far as Narvik, "would be more promising, then this would become the main task." The secondary objective involved protecting the army supply route running from Trondheim to Saltdal-Bodö-Mo and was tied into the final proposal in support of Dietl, Operation *Bueffel.*

By the end of May, a handpicked force of some 2,500 had been assembled near Sörfold. Under *Bueffel,* these units were to make the last leg of the advance on Narvik along the coast from the Bodö region. The daunting terrain, plus the harsh weather, which fluctuated between rain, snow, and fog, excluded the use of trucks or even pack animals. Supplies could be brought in only by airdrops, and when the force arrived within sight of Narvik some ten days later, further airdrops would be made of ammunition and heavy weapons in preparation for an assault on the Allies positioned below Narvik.

Yet all these operations were dependent on one factor alone: Dietl holding out long enough for their planning and execution to be effective. Should he fail to do this, all the work and resources being committed to *Naumburg, Bueffel,* and *Juno* would be wasted and Narvik effectively lost. With this in mind, Falkenhorst and Stumpff's decision to place the greater emphasis on close air support does not seem at all out of place. Although it did not make the ground targets any easier to hit at the time, the reason for attempting to do so is easier to understand. As the commander of Group Narvik wrote after the Allied evacuation: "We had no artillery, so the Luftwaffe had to substitute as artillery for us. Low flying bombers again and again attacked the troop concentrations opposite us and the traffic on the roads, and thus to a certain degree replaced the artillery we lacked."[156] The Swedish, who were naturally watching the unfolding drama across their common border with Norway, concurred. On 5 June, in Stockholm's major daily, *Aftonbladet,* it was noted: "The Luftwaffe has succeeded in keeping the positions of the Western Powers in and around Narvik under intensive fire. In Narvik itself they were able to destroy the post office building and thus telephone communications with the position of the Western Powers north of Narvik, among other things."[157] All of this goes some way to challenging what appeared in the eyes of Kessler to be a blatant misuse of airpower. It should also be mentioned that during the eleven-day period, 28 May to 7 June, adverse weather prevented the Luftwaffe from undertaking major bombing missions over Narvik on all except four of these days (28 and 29 May, and 2 and 7 June). Thus, given the small window of opportunity available for the bombers of Luftflotte 5, operations against Bardufloss may have been considered a luxury that at the time could be ill afforded.

It may also be argued that, even had the Germans been able to destroy the RAF's Bardufloss base, it would not have significantly altered the Luftwaffe's ability to operate in the region anyway. Not only did inclement weather militate against effective airpower support, but overall losses to RAF fighters were not crucial to the campaign in northern Norway, with at least one analysis showing that the sixty-three aircraft lost by the *Luftflotte* at the hands of Bardufloss's Gladiators and Hurricanes were not at all decisive.[158] British military historian Maurice Harvey points out that such was the scale of the Luftwaffe campaign, compared with that of the RAF, that if the German losses were equally distributed, each Luftwaffe squadron would have lost only three of its reserve aircraft; overall, therefore, the number of sorties undertaken would not have diminished at all.[159] As one RAF participant bemoaned when comparing the RAF's own position vis-à-vis the Luftwaffe:

> As for us, the RAF, they were asking that from makeshift stations, supplied over laborious and faulty lines of communication, we should match ourselves against the greatly outnumbering Luftwaffe—which was operating from bases decently equipped . . . and big enough for twenty times the concentration of planes that we could make. With two squadrons at Bardufloss we had come to saturation point.[160]

Bearing this in mind, and the need to keep Dietl's force in action long enough for the relief plans to be implemented, plus the relatively few days available in which bombing sorties could be undertaken, the case for largely ignoring the Bardufloss airfield and focusing on ground support is not unreasonable.

This does not mean, of course, that attacks were not made on Bardufloss, but merely that, when carried out, they were of relatively minor importance compared with those made against Allied shipping and ground targets. Indeed, the first attack on 29 May was by three KG 26 Heinkels that were looking for an aircraft carrier in the vicinity and, after failing to locate the vessel, diverted their attention to the RAF field. At only 600 meters, the bombers roared over Bardufloss. The base's sleeping quarters suffered a direct hit from one aircraft, but the other two planes dropped their bombs clear of the field, causing no damage.[161] A scrambled Gladiator shot down one of the Heinkels over Narvik. A further twenty-six bombers on this day also made their way to Narvik, escorted by Bf 110s specifically to attack shipping in the port. Two of their number were shot down by patrolling Hurricanes. Bad weather stepped in again, and although Allied ground forces bore the brunt of limited Luftwaffe activity on 30 May, this was followed by a three-day spell of bad weather that prevented any significant missions being flown. By 2 June, conditions had improved sufficiently to allow a major operation by Luftflotte 5.

It was on this day that the "clash between *Luftlotte* and X Fliegerkorps" came to a head. Initially, it would appear that a large number of aircraft were dispatched early in the morning of 2 June for Bardufloss, much to the joy of most crews, which were naturally looking for an opportunity to strike at the airfield that was responsible for the loss of a number of their fellows. Nevertheless, the *Luftflotte* determined that these aircraft should return for use, alongside other air units, in close air support of Dietl. This, of course, rankled with both aircrews and X Fliegerkorps' hierarchy who not only were deprived of the opportunity to hit back at the RAF at Bardufloss but also lost a full eight hours in the process of wastefully dropping their bombs on the return flight to Vaernes and being rearmed and refueled before taking to the air again. Kessler resigned on the spot. In the end, Stumpff's force made forty-seven bomber and dive-bomber sorties in attacks against shipping and Allied ground positions. While sweeps of the area were made by Bf 110s, continuous waves of bombers raided the Allied base and shipping at Harstad in and around Narvik.[162] The center of Narvik itself also came under bomber attack, and the mostly wooden buildings became engulfed in flames. "At times the bombs fell in such rapid succession that it sounded like heavy automatic gun-fire," noted an English observer.[163] "Bombs began to fall," recorded a Polish soldier. "Fires broke out, spreading from one wooden house to another, and in minutes Narvik was a roaring sea of flame."[164] In no time at all, the center of the town had been gutted. Although the Vadsoe radio-transmitting station at Kirkenes was attacked and the hut destroyed, no other notable successes were achieved at a total cost of four aircraft.[165] Naturally, these losses and the *Luftflotte*'s counterorder demoralized some aircrews, while others were outraged that they had not been able to "get even with the British fighters." In reality, despite Kessler's understandable frustration and Luftflotte 5's bungling of the original mission plan, it is evident that Stumpff's decisions here and elsewhere were based on the need to help Dietl hang on until help appeared.

The action on 2 June, though, was the exception to the rule, since over the period 3–6 June poor weather once again grounded the bulk of the air fleet's bombers, much to the consternation of all concerned. "Unfavorable flying weather (rain and snowstorms) prevented an operation in support of the Group Narvik," ran the Luftwaffe's daily situation report of 3 June.[166] "The Luftwaffe cannot help us again today," declared Dietl's adjutant on 4 June, because "the weather remains terrible."[167] On top of this, the mountain and naval troops' remaining supplies fell to an almost negligible level as a result of the prevailing weather. "Group Windisch in a difficult position north of Rombaken Fjord," lamented the Naval Staff war diary: Superior forces are attacking. Our forces' powers of resistance are greatly diminished by long-drawn-out bad weather and lack of ammunition supplies. It is not possible at present to bring up reinforcements by parachute troops because of the unfavorable weather. A strong enemy attack is expected."[168] Despite the belief in an imminent final assault and a halfhearted Swedish-inspired diplomatic proposal revolving around the possibility of neutralizing Narvik, the Allies, under the cover of the abysmal weather, began their long-planned evacuation of northern Norway.[169]

ANOTHER BRITISH EVACUATION AND *GLORIOUS*

The British, who had proved very proficient at carrying out evacuations—at Namsos and Aandalsnes a month earlier, Bodö only days before, and currently in the final throes of the Dunkirk miracle—commenced embarking Allied troops from Narvik on 4 June. The first 15,000 men around Narvik were loaded aboard troopships between 4 and 6 June, while the remainder embarked on 7 and 8 June. At 0900 on 8 June, the operation's rear guard left Harstad aboard the cruiser *Southampton*. Covered by an array of escorting vessels and the aircraft of *Ark*

Royal, the evacuations were a complete success. In addition to getting all their men safely off Norwegian soil, the Allies were able to load the bulk of the remaining stores and equipment without mishap. Inclement weather covered much of the embarkation, and the Germans were of the firm opinion that the enemy was in the throes of preparing for a final assault to finish off Group Narvik. Even when a flight was possible on 7 June and a large evacuation fleet was spotted by German reconnaissance, no real thought was given to the possibility of an Allied evacuation until 8 June.[170]

By the morning of 8 June, it had become apparent to all that the "remarkably lively" convoy traffic between Great Britain and northern Norway, noted the day before, signified not a buildup of Allied forces but rather a withdrawal.[171] Dietl concurred, reporting that he believed the British were evacuating Narvik and it would soon be possible to regain Straum Strait.[172] Aerial reconnaissance reports came in thick and fast, informing Luftwaffe and naval commanders that the enemy was "already in the process of evacuating northern Norway."[173] X Fliegerkorps' aircraft spotted a heavy cruiser, eight destroyers, and sixteen merchant vessels steaming away from the Norwegian coastline in an area west of Andoe Island. At the same time, an aircraft carrier was sighted in the region. This was *Glorious,* which had just received Bardufloss's ten Gladiators and seven Hurricanes. Although by midafternoon the distance between Trondheim and the fleet was considerable, the Luftwaffe sent a squadron each of Ju 88s and Heinkels, plus floatplanes, in search of the enemy at sea; their main target was the carrier, but aside from damaging a steamer forty-eight kilometers off Andoe Island, little else was achieved. Nevertheless, where the Luftwaffe had failed, the German navy stepped in.

In accordance with Operation *Juno,* the German fleet departed Kiel on 4 June, steaming through the Great Belt, then up the Norwegian coast toward its target area in and around Harstad and Narvik. Yet by the time the vessels had closed in on northern Norway, it became apparent through aerial reports and B-Dienst intelligence that major elements of British naval forces in the area were now at sea rather than within the fjords.[174] This led Admiral Wilhelm Marschall, the commander of the fleet, to conclude: "It occurs to me that the noticeable westward movement may indicate a British evacuation of Norway, and that the westward-bound convoys will now offer valuable targets."[175] He therefore, somewhat controversially, abandoned the proposed operations within the fjords for the time being—preventing, he felt, his vessels from suffering the indignity of falling foul of Allied nets, mines, and gun and torpedo batteries deployed at the entrance of the fjords—and informed the Naval Staff of his intention to attack the convoys.[176] Although by the early hours of 8 June, the German fleet prowling these waters had been able to pick off only a few stragglers—a tanker, an escort trawler, and the troopship *Orama*—bigger pickings were just around the corner in the form of the aircraft carrier *Glorious.*

Accompanied by only two destroyers, *Glorious* was spotted at 1645. Although the heavy cruiser *Hipper* and its destroyers were bound for Trondheim in support of the Germany army's northward *Bueffel* advance overland to Narvik, the remaining German battle cruisers, *Scharnhorst* and *Gneisenau,* were more than capable of dispatching the vulnerable aircraft carrier. Despite Ultra indicating the movement of German vessels into the southern North Sea, and Harry Hinsley at Bletchley Park warning the British Operational Intelligence Centre that German warships might take "offensive action," the Admiralty chose not to alert its forces at sea.[177] Amazingly, given the proximity of *Glorious* to the Norwegian coast, Captain Guy D'Oyly-Hughes, the carrier's skipper, had not put up any patrolling aircraft, nor were any ready for immediate action. The German battle cruisers opened up at a range of 25,000 meters. The destroyers gallantly attempted to shroud the zigzagging *Glorious* with a smokescreen and force off *Scharnhorst* and *Gneisenau* by using their torpedoes. The destroyer *Ardent,* though, was the first to succumb to the barrage of heavy-caliber shells. In the meantime, *Glorious*'s deck had been opened up "like a lid of a box" by the German battleships, observed Marschall.[178] Once the ammunition and fuel stocks caught fire, it was all over. "Slowly the giant began to turn on her side," ran a German report, pouring "out flames and smoke. . . . a moment later she sank."[179] The remaining destroyer, *Acasta,* in its final desperate throw, struck *Scharnhorst* with a torpedo near its after turret, only to go down a short time later. Believing that the torpedo had been fired by a submarine in the area and with *Scharnhorst*'s speed reduced to twenty knots, Marschall called off further action and put into Trondheim. This decision, forced on Marschall by the limping *Scharnhorst,* and for which he would be vigorously attacked by Raeder, doubtless saved a troop convoy less than 160 kilometers distant as it made its way to Britain.[180] Adding insult to injury, when *Gneisenau,* under Marschall's replacement, *Vizeadmiral* Günther Lütjens, put to sea on 20 June to cover *Scharnhorst*'s return to Germany, it was also struck by a torpedo that actually was fired by a British submarine. Neither *Scharnhorst* nor *Gneisenau* would be fit again for operations until December 1940.

VICTORY

On land that evening, Dietl, the commander of Narvik Group, proudly reported that Narvik was "again occupied by our troops."[181] Apparently, the enemy had completely evacuated northern Norway, and the Norwegian king and government were at sea bound for Britain. At 1600 the next day, the commanding officer of the Norwegian army in the Narvik region capitulated.[182] The Germans occupied Bardufloss on 12 June; by the following day, Tromsö was in German hands.

Although the German success in northern Norway had been brought about chiefly by the Allied decision to withdraw from the region, the Germans still had much to congratulate themselves for. Falkenhorst, the commander in chief of the German forces in Norway, waxed lyrical when congratulating Dietl and his men:

On 9 April you were landed in Norway at the command of your Führer and from that day onward defended and held this area with exemplary tenacity under great privations and despite all the inclement weather against all the assaults of a greatly superior adversary. . . . Soldiers! The adversary has abandoned the conflict[,] laid down his weapons[,] and capitulated. You have remained victors and have won imperishable laurels.[183]

Hitler likewise was exuberant in his 13 June 1940 order of the day to his victorious troops in Norway:

I transmit the expressions of the proud admiration of the German people to the fighters of Narvik. All you who stood together there in the Far North, soldiers of the Austrian mountains, crews of our warships, paratroops, combat fliers, and transport pilots, will go down in history as the best representatives of the highest German soldiership. To *Generalleutnant* Dietl I express the thanks of the German people for the honorable page he has added to the book of German history.[184]

Undoubtedly, the German achievement had been considerable, and in terms of men and material lost, the ledger was remarkably even. Official figures released during the war showed German losses in the invasion of Denmark and Norway stood at 1,317 dead, 1,604 wounded, and 2,375 missing; Allied losses numbered some 1,896 British personnel, 530 French and Poles, and 1,335 Norwegians. Similarly, the naval losses on both sides were reasonably close. The Germans, for their part, lost one heavy and two light cruisers, ten destroyers, one torpedo boat, one gunnery training ship, one R-boat, and four U-boats. All up, the German navy lost, excluding auxiliary vessels, eighteen ships totaling 88,604 tons prior to 22 May. Allied naval losses—which would unquestionably have been much greater but for the torpedo debacle—included one aircraft carrier, two light cruisers, nine destroyers, six submarines, and a large number of auxiliary vessels. On top of this, the British lost some 2,500 men at sea. Despite this parity in naval losses, the Germans were no position to absorb theirs as easily as the British, and at the completion of the campaign, the Germans could put only one heavy cruiser, two light cruisers, and four destroyers to sea for immediate action.[185]

The Luftwaffe rightly received a prominent place on the victors' rostrum. As Hitler declared in his famous speech of 19 July 1940:

The Luftwaffe, which was often the only real means of transport and communication in this enormous area, surpassed itself in every respect. The daring attacks on the enemy, on ships, and on disembarked troops can hardly be more highly praised than the tenacity and courage displayed by those transport pilots who, in spite of foul weather, kept flying in the Land of the Midnight Sun in order to land soldiers and throw down supplies, often in blinding snowstorms.[186]

Luftwaffe commanders and their aircrews had proved themselves in the field of combat. Hitler was generous in his praise and acknowledged their achievements with promotions and awards. Gablenz was rewarded for his exceptional airlift effort with rapid promotion in following years to *Generalmajor,* while Geisler was awarded a Knight's Cross for his sterling work with X Fliegerkorps and promoted to *General die Flieger*.[187] For his planning and operations role in *Weserübung,* Knauss was promoted to *Generalleutnant* and at the end of 1940 was placed in command of the Luftwaffe's General Staff Academy. Of the two aggressive *Fliegerführers,* Harlinghausen tended to outshine Fuchs for his hands-on approach to operational command, often flying reconnaissance missions in person over central Norway. As already noted, Harlinghausen and *Hauptmann* Paul-Werner Hozzel, the commander of StG 1, received the Knight's Cross for their unflagging pursuit of the Allies from north and south of Trondheim. For his determined efforts in bringing the communication network together and airfields up to speed, Milch also was awarded the Knight's Cross and, with further success in the west, was one of three Luftwaffe officers to be promoted to *Generalfeldmarschall*. To appease Göring in the round of promotions and awards in the wake of Norway and the fall of France, Hitler created a new rank, *Reichsmarschall,* and an award befitting Göring's massive ego, the Grand Cross of the Iron Cross (Großkreuz des Eisernen Kreuzes).[188] To Hitler's credit, after *Weserübung* came to an end, he also "acknowledged and praised Jodl's achievement" and, for Jodl's efforts here and in the west, promoted him to *General der Artillerie*.[189]

Yet the overall success of the campaign and the round of backslapping that followed blinded Göring and Hitler to a number of disturbing weaknesses evident in the Luftwaffe effort. The Luftwaffe's inability to intervene in the First and Second Battles of Narvik and the extreme difficulties it faced when attempting to support Dietl's far-flung mountain troops did not augur well for the future of air warfare from Norway against Britain in the months and years ahead.

Ein Volk, ein Reich, ein Führer!

1. Once Norway was within his grasp, Adolf Hitler was eager to incorporate it into his expanded "one Reich." An investigation of Hitler's role in the invasion and subsequent occupation of Norway opens a valuable window of understanding on the Führer's leadership and his appreciation of airpower and joint- service operations.

2. Flanked by subordinates, *Großadmiral* Erich Raeder, the commander in chief of the German navy, plans the invasion of Norway, code-named *Weserübung*. With the assistance of Alfred Rosenberg and Vidkun Quisling, Raeder convinced Hitler of the need to preempt a potential British initiative and secure Germany's supply of Scandinavian iron ore, and of the long-term strategic advantages arising from a German-occupied Norway.

3. *General der Flieger* Robert Knauss was an influential airpower strategist prior to the Second World War and served as the Luftwaffe chief of operations for *Weserübung*. Luftwaffe involvement in the planning and implementation of the invasion was essential given its pivotal role in the risky undertaking.

4. As well as fending off the Royal Navy, Luftwaffe aircraft were deployed as cover for German seaborne forces, as illustrated by this Heinkel He 111 overflight of a troop-laden transport. In addition, the role of the Luftwaffe in delivering paratroops and ground units and supplying and reinforcing forward positions was a significant factor in the overall success of the invasion.

5. The mountainous terrain of much of Norway remained an obstacle to the rapid reinforcement of vanguard units and hindered the movement of the supporting firepower usually delivered by artillery or tanks. Therefore, for much of the campaign these twin tasks fell to airpower.

6. Photographs showing Junkers Ju 52s against the backdrop of burning enemy aircraft at Oslo's Fornebu airfield became the staple of German postinvasion accounts of *Weserübung*. The assault on this strategic airfield was the task of the Luftwaffe, whose success here enabled the swift occupation of the Norwegian capital.

7. Not all landings in the invasion went as smoothly as planned. A significant number of German aircraft, including bombers and transports, came to grief at Oslo's Fornebu airfield during *Weserübung*.

8. Air-landed troops unload supplies as part of the first large-scale airborne invasion in history. The ubiquitous Ju 52 was the backbone of the Luftwaffe's transport operation.

9. Where land-based airfields did not exist, the Germans were forced to rely on floatplanes such as the antiquated Heinkel He 59 to support forward operations.

10. Lacking long-range four-engined bombers, the Luftwaffe was powerless to stop the destruction of German destroyers by British warships in the First and Second Battles of Narvik. The seriousness of this deficiency was never fully appreciated at the time.

11. Disliked by a number of contemporaries for his sometimes caustic manner, *Generalfeldmarschall* Erhard Milch was a brilliant administrator whose organizational skills were in great demand throughout the war. The secondment of Milch (Göring's second-in-command) to Norway underlined the importance placed on the whole campaign in the north. With characteristic determination and vigor, he rose to the considerable challenges faced in Norway.

12. "By order of the Führer the towns and rail junctions of Namsos and Aandalsnes are to be destroyed [by the Luftwaffe] without consideration for the civilian population; the rail line and the roads near these junctions are to be interrupted for a considerable duration." The results of this 19 April 1940 order can be seen in this grim aerial shot of Namsos Harbor.

13. The destruction of the Namsos rail system (foreground) prevented Allied reinforcement of forward units struggling toward Trondheim from the north.

14. Aandalsnes burns after another Luftwaffe raid, further weakening the southern pincer of the abortive Allied advance on Trondheim.

15. A destroyed aircraft testifies to German aerial supremacy over southern and central Norway in the weeks following the invasion.

16. While the Junkers Ju 87 Stuka had proved an indispensable asset in the invasion of Poland, its limited range proved a serious handicap (even for the longer-range aircraft carrier variant employed in Norway) because of the operational distances involved. Nevertheless, on those occasions when it could be used, its dive-bombing accuracy proved deadly against shipping.

17. *Generaloberst* Erhard Milch, the first commander of Luftflotte 5, encourages Stuka crews at Trondheim. Milch's upgrading of Trondheim's Vaernes airfield and establishment of a Luftwaffe infrastructure laid the groundwork for operations in the years that followed.

18. Despite their usefulness in a country with only rudimentary land-based airfields, seaplanes like this Dornier Do 24 were extremely vulnerable to even light enemy fire when landing supplies for isolated units in northern Norway.

19. *Generaloberst* Hans-Jürgen Stumpff replaced Milch as commander of Germany's most northern air fleet in early May 1940, a position he would hold for over three years. Originally an army officer, Stumpff soon adapted to the peculiarities of airpower and the difficulties associated with ever-increasing demands and dwindling resources afflicting all theaters after the invasion of Russia in 1941.

20. The Messerschmitt Bf 110 was used in support of bombers over Narvik and in the only major raid made by Luftflotte 5 from Norway during the Battle of Britain. On both occasions it was found seriously wanting.

21. Cut off from maritime and land-based support by the British naval supremacy and the tortuous terrain of the Far North, *General* Eduard Dietl's beleaguered mountain troops in and around Narvik could only be supplied with additional men and material by airpower.

22. The arrival of hastily trained paratroops at Narvik was insufficient to counter the weight of Allied arms bearing down on the town. Nevertheless, the occupation of Narvik on 28 May 1940 was short-lived because the Allies were soon forced to evacuate the theater as events in France demanded a readjustment in strategic priorities.

23. At the invasion's end, German warships and floatplanes made themselves at home in Norwegian harbors. Nevertheless, in the years ahead, the high cost of *Weserübung* to the navy, and the limited range of available Luftwaffe aircraft, made Norway less of a strategic asset than Hitler had initially imagined.

24. *Reichsmarschall* Hermann Göring, as commander in chief of the Luftwaffe, must assume some of the responsibility for the four-engined bomber fiasco and even more for preventing the establishment of a unified command in the German northern theater of operations. As a First World War ace Göring had been a rather dashing and widely admired pilot, but fortunately for the Allies, during the Third Reich's darkest hours his ferocious Luftwaffe parochialism and lack of strategic vision would prove costly to the German war effort.

25. The tug-of-war between Raeder and the Luftwaffe over control of the navy's air arm, of which this Heinkel He 60 seaplane unit was a part in 1937, was a protracted and messy affair heavily weighted in Göring's favor. The result was an underresourced maritime air force that could never completely satisfy naval demands in Norway or elsewhere.

26. The Heinkel He 115 floatplane, although slow, cumbersome, and lightly armed, served with distinction in supporting forward forces during *Weserübung;* harassing enemy shipping in the North Sea from occupied Norway in 1941; and, in the following year, attacking Arctic convoys. Nevertheless, German reliance on this sluggish machine highlighted the dearth of modern long-range aircraft available for cooperation with naval forces.

27. Dubbed the *Piratenflugzeuge*, the maritime variant of the Heinkel He 177 had the potential to provide Germany with a long-range aircraft capable of sweeping from Norway and France out into the Atlantic in antishipping and U-boat support missions. Plagued by delays and often conflicting design requirements, it eventually arrived too late and in too few numbers to make a difference to the war effort. This captured example was probably used in RAF evaluation testing.

28. During the invasion of Norway, the graceful Focke-Wulf Fw 200 Condor's long range meant that it was one of the few aircraft in the Luftwaffe inventory capable of making the round trip from Denmark to Narvik on reconnaissance and supply missions with relative ease. In later years, Condors, despite their small numbers, showed in operations over the Atlantic what might have been, had Germany possessed sufficient numbers of long-range four-engined maritime aircraft with which to use alongside the navy's U-boat arm in a blockade of Britain.

29. Stumpff enjoys a cigarette and drink with the commander of the Finnish air force. In June 1941, Luftflotte 5 was able to contribute only a meager sixty aircraft to the German and Finnish attack in the Far North.

30. In the face of PQ 17's concentrated defensive fire, Ju 88s were unable to press home their attacks. Once the convoy scattered, however, these twin-engined bombers, along with He 111s, were able to pick off individual vessels fleeing to Murmansk and Archangel.

31. An He 111 launches a torpedo attack on an Arctic convoy in 1942. Without a modern purpose-built torpedo aircraft, the Luftwaffe quickly adapted the He 111 and Ju 88 to the task.

32. A freighter is hit in Arctic waters. Hitler's fear of an Allied operation in Norway and the importance of cutting off Stalin from Anglo-American war materials led him to boost the number of aircraft in the region in 1942.

33. Heavy flak does not prevent a successful Luftwaffe hit on a cruiser in the Arctic convoy battles. As important as these warships were, it was the appearance of escort carriers that decisively tipped the scales against the Germans.

34. Since most flights from Norway took place over the North Sea or freezing Arctic waters, an efficient and well-equipped Air Sea Rescue Service, working closely with the navy, was essential to recover downed flyers and maintain morale. Anxious Luftwaffe personnel surround a recovered crewman as he is maneuvered off an Air Sea Rescue floatplane.

35. Later in the war, fighter defenses were strengthened by the appearance of the Focke-Wulf Fw 190. The relatively small numbers of this single-engined fighter, however, failed to stem the tide of raids by Bomber Command and the Eighth Air Force on strategic industries and *Tirpitz* hiding in northern Norway.

36. This German Würzburg-Riese radar formed part of the defensive line that had been established along the Norwegian coast by 1944. In theory this was a well-designed system, but in reality the small numbers of Luftwaffe fighters actually available to intercept incoming enemy aircraft made it little more than window dressing.

5

The Battle and Siege of Britain

Here is the most tragic chapter of all. When I think of it, gentlemen, it is enough to make me scream. I do not possess a single long-range bomber.

Hermann Göring, 13 September 1942

In terms of the broad goals of Hitler's war directive of 1 March 1940, the Germans won the race for Norway, securing iron ore supplies from Sweden and providing expanded bases for the navy and Luftwaffe for future operations against Britain.[1] Economically, although the campaign guaranteed Germany access to the rich iron ores of Sweden via Narvik, this proved to be less important than had been originally anticipated (and some historians later argued), since Germany had overrun the large Lorraine ore fields in its western blitzkrieg.[2] Despite this, Norway was destined to become part of Hitler's New Order. Unlike France, which was to be milked heavily until the war ended, Norway would enter the German "greater economic sphere" *(Großraumwitschaft)*.[3] Germany planned to boost Norway's agricultural production to decrease its dependence on food imports; use its fishing industry to alleviate the Third Reich's protein deficiency; harness its large hydroelectrical power capacity in the production of aluminum, high-grade nitrogenous fertilizer, ferric alloys, and zinc; and increase its mining capacity in other important metals such as copper, nickel, rutile, and molybdenum.[4] In addition to the procurement of minerals, Hitler, in the months and years ahead, laid out grandiose plans that included turning Norway into a major supplier of electricity for the Reich. "One day Norway will have to become an electrical center of northern Europe," proclaimed Hitler one evening in August 1941. "Then the Norwegians will have finally found a European mission to fulfill."[5] To this end, a German-Norwegian body was established in 1941 to oversee a 10-million-kilowatt increase in output, of which the greater part was to be transported by cable to the Continent.[6]

Norway, along with other occupied countries, was also drawn into a vast plan to utilize its workforce for the Luftwaffe. Thus, considering the Luftwaffe's potential airpower presence in Norway, plans were also quickly drawn up for the exploitation of skilled labor in the Norwegian aviation industry. By early May, Hitler was already giving orders for the future direction of the relatively small Norwegian and Danish aviation industries and the part they would play in meeting Luftwaffe requirements. Whereas the Führer stipulated that enlistment of the Danish armaments economy was to be undertaken on a "friendly basis" *(freundschaftlichster Grundlage)*, Norway, due to ongoing resistance in early May, was to be considered an "enemy territory" *(Feindesland)* in which the economy would be exploited.[7] By late May, as the fight for Norway was drawing to a close, Göring was already drafting documents and sending them to *Luftflotten* and their respective *Luftgau,* including Luftflotte 5 and Luftgaukommando Norwegen, concerning the payments to gangs of skilled workers in the aviation industries lying outside the Reich.[8] In a September 1940 report, *Generaloberst* Ernst Udet, chief of the Luftwaffe's Technical Office, noted that the Luftwaffe was, with regard to Norway (now seen in a more favorable light with the cessation of hostilities), Denmark, the Netherlands, and Belgium, to proceed with payments to the air industries concerned, according to an agreed exchange rate. In particular, immediate payment was to be arranged for Belgium and Norway through credit provided by the state banks.[9] By 10 January 1941, Luftgaukommando Norwegen in Oslo had local engineers repairing Junkers aircraft at Kambo near Moss.[10] By the end of the war, Norwegian skilled labor at over fifty locations up and down the country was involved in the repair, servicing, and testing of aircraft engines, the production of duralumin sheets and spares for patching up damaged aircraft, work on both landplanes and seaplanes, and the dismantling and salvaging of parts from wrecked planes.[11]

Strategically, however, the centerpiece of the Führer's northern empire would be a huge naval base at Trondheim, which he described as a "super-Singapore" that, he proclaimed, would make Britain's Far East namesake look like "child's play" *("Kinderspiel")* in comparison.[12] Hitler dreamed of building a "beautiful German city" on Trondheim Fjord (separate from the existing town), which, noted Albert Speer in August 1940, would become Germany's northernmost cultural center, boasting not only an opera house, library, theater, and art gallery of German masters but also a stadium and swimming pools.[13] More important, Hitler's architect recalled after the war, Trondheim would be Germany's largest naval base; alongside "shipyards and docks a city of a quarter of a million Germans would be built and incorporated into the German Third Reich."[14] In a conference with Raeder on 11 July 1940, Hitler made clear his wish that Trondheim—linked directly to Germany by a magnificent four-lane autobahn running via Lübeck and huge bridges crossing into Sweden—would form the fulcrum of the German navy's presence in northern waters.[15] Not surprisingly, the plan received the full support of the *Großadmiral* because, as early Naval Staff considerations had demonstrated, the port offered the navy numerous advantages in a war with Britain: it was sufficiently sheltered to prevent bombardment from the sea; the depth of water made enemy mining activities extremely difficult; several entry and exit routes existed; its central position shortened the lines of communication with Germany and offered a shorter route into the Atlantic; the fjord contained many basins suitable for U-boats; and, finally, the city already had a good deal of industrial and supply facilities suitable for supporting large-scale maritime operations.[16] Further augmentation would occur with the construction of massive shipbuilding yards, capable of handling vessels of even the largest draft. In all, the proposed new naval facilities alone would be able to accommodate some 55,000 crew and worker families and enable the annual construction of one battleship and the servicing and repair of up to two battleships, six cruisers, and twenty-four U-boats at any one time.[17] This massive project was worked on until 1943, when labor and material shortages curtailed Hitler's grand plan.[18] Overall, though, the basic premise behind the development of Trondheim was primarily as a base from which to wage war against Britain, as had been envisaged as far back as Wegener's First World War memorandums and as recently as March 1940 in the directive for *Weserübung*.

THE DISTANT-DISTANT BLOCKADE THWARTS NAVAL PLANS

Yet while these future grandiose plans were being formulated for Trondheim, in reality Norway became less important in terms of actual naval operations than originally planned. In addition to the dearth of available surface vessels and warships to utilize Hitler's latest acquisition, the Germans now occupied more favorably sited naval bases on the French Atlantic coast. As already noted, as a result of the losses suffered during the invasion, Raeder could call on only one heavy cruiser, two light cruisers, and four destroyers, while the damaged *Scharnhorst* and *Gneisenau* would not be able to put to sea until late December 1940. The U-boat arm was no better off and on 1 July had only fifteen U-boats at sea.[19] Even as late as December 1941, Assmann, in an otherwise upbeat assessment entitled the "Improvement of the Strategical Situation Through the Norwegian Occupation" *(Verbesserung der strategischen Lage durch Norwegenbesetzung)*, had to admit the navy still lacked first-line vessels that would permit larger scale operations from Norway than had been undertaken to date.[20] Therefore, although Germany had achieved Wegener's prerequisites for a successful war against Britain with the acquisition of bases in Norway and France, it lacked enough vessels to push home its greatly improved strategic position in open waters. As Wegener had realized twenty years earlier, bases alone were of little use without the requisite forces available to utilize them. Moreover, what naval vessels were available could be better used in operations from Brest bases, which provided an even shorter route into the Atlantic, cutting over 800 kilometers off the distance to the main U-boat operational area west of the British Isles.[21] On top of this, the usefulness of Norway was further reduced by the British occupation of Iceland.

In the First World War, the establishment of a distant blockade had thwarted German naval plans. The blockade had shut the navy within the North Sea by closing the Straits of Dover with the Channel Fleet, and the northern gateway with the Grand Fleet based at Scapa Flow. The establishment of minefields in both approaches further restricted German freedom of movement. Although to a great degree the Second World War had seen the reimplementation of a similar distant blockade, the German occupation of Norway and the fall of France turned the tables on the British, threatening to outflank them to both the north and the south. "To keep Germany in the watery triangle of the German Bight" had been the British plan of naval warfare from 1914 to 1918, proclaimed Karl Silex, editor of *Deutsche Allgemeine Zeitung,* in the paper's 15 April 1940 edition, but now "Germany was out of its watery corner."[22] Nevertheless, in many respects Germany's northern corner had only been enlarged rather than truly liberated, since Britain, beaten to the prize of Norway and under the belief that Iceland would soon be gobbled up by Hitler as well, swooped on the latter in a preemptive occupation in May 1940.

Even before the invasion of Norway, Hitler had apparently been gazing farther afield. As Walter Warlimont, the head of OKW's Operations Division, recalled after the war, the Führer was interested in occupying Iceland—along with plans for the Canary and Cape Verde Islands—because, in "the first place, he wanted to prevent 'anyone else' from coming [*sic*] there; and, in the second place, he also wanted to use Iceland as an air base for the protection of our submarines operating in that area."[23] Despite the Führer's pre-*Weserübung* interest in Iceland, it was not until it had fallen into Allied hands that he belatedly pushed for a German counterinvasion—dubbed *Fall Ikarus*—to capture the strategically important island. When *Juno,* the planned relief of Dietl by the converted liners *Europa* and *Bremen,* was no longer needed, Hitler leaped at the opportunity to utilize these and additional vessels in an invasion of Iceland. The German Naval Staff was aghast and dismayed when told by OKW of Hitler's plans on 12 June 1940. "An occupation of Iceland," argued the staff, "will not entail any improvement of the strategic situation at present, since the sea area around Iceland and between Iceland and the Faroes is not controlled by German forces, and utilization of Iceland as a base for German forces is out of the question."[24] The Luftwaffe concurred, and Göring could support such an undertaking only if it was "possible to create landing and taking off facilities for the fighters and bombers on the island."[25] Of course, since these did not exist in 1940, the Luftwaffe was not about to lend its support to such a risky operation.[26]

Yet Hitler pressed ahead and on 20 June met with Raeder to thrash out *Ikarus.*[27] Although Raeder dutifully answered all the Führer's concerns regarding preparations, he bluntly warned Hitler of the "impossibility of continuous resupply" and that *Ikarus* would demand the "full employment of the navy."[28] Not that Raeder did not favor an eventual occupation of the island, since it was agreed by all that the "British blockade in the Iceland area on a line with the Shetlands presents a continuous and unbearable threat to German safety [which] must be broken *once and for all.*"[29] But what the *Großadmiral* and his staff also realized was that such an operation could not be realistically undertaken in the short to medium term. As Raeder pointed out after the conference: "The task consists of transferring large numbers of men and quantities of material to remote waters for the most part controlled by the enemy. Here, in contrast to the northern Norwegian area, we are dealing with a sea area constantly occupied by enemy forces (cruisers and auxiliary cruisers) in the course of the enemy's long-range blockade."[30] Against these considerable forces the Germans were able to deploy only a single heavy cruiser and, thanks to the First and Second Battles of Narvik, a mere four destroyers for escort duties. In addition to these overwhelming odds, the anticipated slow speed of the task force and lack of air cover would make just getting to Iceland an extremely risky, if not foolhardy, exercise. Moreover, should a successful landing take place, it was concluded that "it will be impossible to keep our invasion forces supplied regularly." In the end, *Fall Ikarus* died a natural death, since it was clearly beyond the capabilities of the German navy in the wake of *Weserübung;* as Hitler himself became more and more preoccupied with *Seelöwe* and later *Barbarossa,* the Iceland project was quietly forgotten.[31]

Therefore, although the Germans had greatly improved their strategic position with the acquisition of bases in Norway, the gloss of victory had been tarnished somewhat with the British occupation of Iceland. As the German historian Walther Hubatsch observed, this action meant the blockade line Scapa-Bergen "only needed to be turned through 90 degrees to establish a new blockade line," Shetlands-Iceland-Greenland.[32] Wegener had foreseen that a German occupation of Norway would result in the British falling back to a "line Shetlands-Faroes-Iceland," but in *Die Seestrategie des Weltkrieges* he expressed a belief that they would have great difficulty in maintaining such a blockade given the distances involved. Initially it did seem as though this would be the case, since at first the forces stationed at Iceland were relatively ineffective and could not prevent large German surface warships passing between Greenland and Iceland into the Atlantic, where they set about raiding Allied convoys in late 1940 and early 1941. Nevertheless, even from a purely naval point of view, Wegener had been of the opinion that for the strategic offensive to be brought to a conclusion and perfected, Germany would have to "jump across the North Sea" with a view to "conquering a geographical position—for example the Shetlands—and taking root there."[33] In the final analysis, Norway itself was in his eyes really only a stepping-stone to the Shetlands-Faroes-Iceland island chain.[34] In time, this was borne out as Iceland developed into an excellent escort base and, in April 1941, a factor Wegener had not taken into account came into play: airpower.[35] The establishment of an air base on Iceland gradually closed the air cover gap on the Allied convoy route running between Newfoundland and Britain, further highlighting its strategic importance in the region. Therefore, despite German hopes, it became clear that the islands between Scotland and Greenland, not Norway alone, represented the key to controlling the North Atlantic and the naval exits from northern Europe into the Atlantic.[36]

GEOSTRATEGY AND GERMAN AIRPOWER

Initially, the pundits waxed lyrical about the advantages now open to Germany's air units. Even before the battle was over, the *Deutsche Luftwacht* (German Air Sentinel) magazine of the Nationalsozialistisches Flieger-Korps (National Socialist Fliers' Corps) proclaimed that with "the occupation, Germany has won great possibilities for further attacking operations in the air."[37] "From the Norwegian west coast—which is far closer than the German Bight," continued the magazine article, "the German Luftwaffe can carry out attacks against Britain and especially Scapa Flow." While an operation from an airfield in Germany against Scapa covered nearly 980 kilometers in the outward flight, the same operation from Bergen would involve only 370 kilometers. Despite the occupation of the French coast, Norway was still seen as an important base from which to outflank Britain. "There are no longer any islands," proclaimed a German propaganda leaflet, which graphically showed that "the operational range of the Luftwaffe casts threatening shadows over Britain."[38] On the map, the operational range of Luftwaffe bombers was demonstrated by concentric circles marking the flying time *(Flugzeit)* to targets within the British Isles from France, Belgium, Holland, and Norway, which, the author pointed out, had been intended to "keep the war away from Britain's shores" but now were "taking-off grounds from which the German Luftwaffe with its superior strength can attack Britain from all sides." For example, an aircraft taking off from Sola could threaten not only Scapa Flow but also the Scottish cities of Aberdeen and Edinburgh and England's Newcastle in flights of no more than eighty minutes. This theme was also picked up in a popular Luftwaffe history, *Luftwaffe von Sieg zu Sieg* (Luftwaffe from victory to victory) (1941), in which the author supported his favorable conclusions by quoting an OKW statement: "The campaign in Norway has broken the English blockade front. Greater Germany now holds a strategically important flanking position against England's East Coast."[39]

Nevertheless, despite what propagandists grandly proclaimed and planners had initially hoped for, the advantages to be gained from possessing air bases in Norway were not as great as had been anticipated, and, in many ways, the benefits predicted to accrue from possessing Norway were never fully realized. Blinded by success in Norway and western Europe, the Germans failed to appreciate the extent of the dilemma they now faced. Prior to the Scandinavian invasion, the directive for *Weserübung* had clearly laid out that an occupation of Norway would provide the "Luftwaffe with the expanded bases for operations against Britain."[40] Yet, as the navy was discovering, merely possessing Norwegian bases did little to improve Luftwaffe operational possibilities if it lacked the wherewithal to exploit them. One of *Weserübung*'s leading commanders, Hans Geisler, had foreseen this situation as early as August 1939, when he pointed out that after taking into account the limitations of the He 111 and the Ju 88, and the lack of unit training for such an operation, "an air war against Britain in 1940 can only result in partial, though important, success, which could not have an effect, and threaten the British conduct of the war, before the second year of the war"; even this could be achieved only "with the most rigorous concentration of all forces, and provided their operations could be sustained for a longer period leading to the breakdown of the enemy defence and gradual expansion of the German squadrons."[41]

Tragically for the Germans, this assessment was to prove all too accurate. Although in October 1939 naval planners recognized that "a speedy and large-scale expansion" had to be made of aircraft types suitable for warfare against Britain from Norway, the Luftwaffe did not have a single purpose-built long-range maritime aircraft or strategic bomber available for deployment in Norway.[42] The consequences of this deficiency would be far-reaching. The failure to speed up the development and production of a long-range aircraft was important not only because it meant that Luftflotte 5 would have to withdraw from the Battle of Britain after a single day of campaigning in August 1940 but also because Norway could never fulfill its role in supporting a U-boat-led siege of Britain as originally anticipated in the directive for *Weserübung*. To explain how this situation arose, much of the remainder of this chapter will be devoted to examining two key underlying, interrelated factors: the lack of a coherent maritime strategy within the German armed forces and the presence of a pernicious interservice rivalry that had developed between the navy and the Luftwaffe over the control and use of aircraft in naval warfare. Thereafter will follow a detailed discussion of the subsequent impact these shortcomings had on both the air battle over Britain and the war at sea.

THE BATTLE FOR CONTROL OF NAVAL AIR UNITS

As soon as the National Socialists began their rearmament program in 1933, the navy had sought to establish its own independent air force, an air arm whose strength, training, organization, and operational use would be determined by the navy, for the navy.[43] This naturally flowed from the experience of the Imperial Navy during the First World War when, along with the army, it had possessed its own air arm. Possession of this arm was jealously guarded. When the army suggested in 1915 that all air units be brought under a single command, the navy refused, arguing that it alone knew how best to develop and build naval aircraft and dirigibles and to train crews for operations at sea.[44] Over the next twenty years, in contravention of the Treaty of Versailles, the navy, like the army, worked quietly to reinvigorate its air arm. However, with the advent of the Third Reich a new path for German airpower was proposed: an air force independent of both the army and the navy. In a reiteration of its 1915 arguments, the navy attempted to thwart this development but without success, and Hermann Göring was appointed by Hitler to establish the Luftwaffe. In this man, the navy found a resourceful and determined opponent who believed that everything that flew should be under his command. Clearly, Raeder had his work cut out for him, since, unlike himself, Hitler really liked his "Iron Man," who not only was the second most powerful man in the Reich but also controlled the German economy.[45]

Although Göring never understood either airpower theory or grand strategy, he thoroughly understood ideas of patronage. Consequently, he was only too willing to place less emphasis on naval matters simply because his master's focus rested elsewhere. In doing so, he was merely reflecting a long-standing divergence of opinion over where Germany's real interests lay: either over water in the Atlantic and Mediterranean in the west and south, as emphasized by the navy, or on land in the east, as demanded by army officers.[46] This, of course, would become apparent in 1940 with Hitler's decision, supported by the army, for an operation in the east rather than the navy's Mediterranean initiative, which wanted to make North Africa, Gibraltar, and the Atlantic islands the fulcrum of German strategy.[47] Given the Führer's hatred of Slavs and his quest for Caucasus oil, as well as Göring's desire to please Hitler with a view to increasing his own air empire, it is clear that Raeder would be engaged in an uphill battle to retain a naval air arm.

Nevertheless, whereas Göring was determined to have all air units brought under his own command, Raeder passionately argued the case for control of his own air force in reconnaissance, attack, and defense in the war at sea. The contemporary documents dealing with this struggle reveal the Naval Staff belief that a single command for all naval forces, including air units, was the most effective means of conducting maritime warfare. They argue that the success of any aerial operation over the sea was dependent on those involved being trained and fully experienced under such flying conditions, and that since airpower could carry out reconnaissance over a wide area and deliver swift defensive and offensive attacks, it could no longer be considered a mere ancillary but an integral part of naval warfare.[48] As Horst Boog, a leading Luftwaffe historian, has pointed out, to Raeder "the aircraft was an integral sea-weapon like the mine, the torpedo and the artillery of men-of-war, and belonged to the fleet organically."[49] No doubt Göring would have retorted by arguing that the emerging Luftwaffe was quite capable of becoming competent in operations over land and sea, making a separate air arm for the navy both redundant and a wasteful duplication of resources that the Reich could ill afford.

Initially, the issue of control of aircraft to be used in naval operations was left in abeyance, although the Air Ministry did agree to pursue the development and production of suitable naval types. Nevertheless, the divergence of opinion was always simmering just below the surface. It finally boiled over in the mid-1930s, just as the first cycle of aircraft production had been completed and increased numbers of trained aircrew were becoming available.[50] The catalyst for the conflagration that followed was a letter signed by Kesselring, dated 21 December 1936, from Göring's Air Ministry to Raeder. Bold to the point of rudeness, the letter declared that the navy's two land-based long-range reconnaissance squadrons and six land-based long-range fighter squadrons would be "taken over by the Luftwaffe."[51] In reply, the naval recipient reacted by scrawling in the margin: "It is not fit to do this!" However, Göring believed that long-range reconnaissance over the sea and against hostile coasts and harbors was "decidedly the task of the Luftwaffe." "Due to the special needs which may arise in the course of war," concluded Kesselring, the overall conduct "required the concentration of all fighting forces under the command of the commander in chief of the Luftwaffe." Raeder, of course, was not about to "freely agree" to these proposals, as Kesselring had optimistically hoped, and a conference was held between the Air Ministry and the navy to thrash out the problem. Although the navy prepared extensively for the meeting held on 11 March 1937, little was settled. At its conclusion, a relaxed Göring stated rather offhandedly that he would "study the memorandum" that summarized Raeder's arguments.

At this point, the OKW stepped forward, offering a compromise. On 31 March, it issued a directive establishing naval and air zones of operation: "The Coastal Defence District of the Navy is part of the theatre of war which borders the open sea. It includes territorial waters, fortified areas, naval garrisons and bases. In the Coastal Defence District the Commanding admiral is responsible for the defence against attacks from the sea as well as from the air."[52]

Yet the exact borders between the navy's "Defence District" and the Luftwaffe's "Reich Air Defence District" were never clearly defined. A further conference was organized for 11 May 1937, at which the navy was determined that the Luftwaffe accept its 11 March memorandum: "This is vital for a successful conduct of the war at sea, command at sea can be only in one hand, that of the Commander in Chief, Navy. All arms which serve naval aims in time of war must be united under his command. During peace, Commander in Chief, Navy must therefore have far-reaching influence over the Naval Air Forces."[53] As with the previous conferences, nothing concrete came of this exchange of views, and a protracted standoff between the two services characterized the period from mid-1937 to early 1939. Meanwhile, alongside this disagreement over the actual control of forces to be used in maritime operations, considerable disagreement had arisen over the number of aircraft to be developed specifically for the naval effort. In 1935 the navy put forward its first estimate, totaling twenty-five squadrons.[54] By the following year, however, it became clear to the naval planners that twenty-five squadrons would be totally insufficient to meet their needs, especially if a war with Britain ever developed. Moreover, since it was likely that the Luftwaffe's main area of operations would be continental rather than maritime, in a future European war the navy would be left without adequate air units to wage a war at sea. Thus between 1936 and 1938, just as it was becoming more and more likely that Germany would have to face off with Britain, the navy pressed for a sixty-two-squadron program.[55]

The Luftwaffe and Göring's Air Ministry were having none of this. In a meeting of 24 November 1938 between the two services, *Generalmajor* Hans-Jürgen Stumpff, then a Luftwaffe General Staff officer, pointed out that the projected Concentrated Aircraft Program (Konzentriertes Flugzeugmuster-Programm) set for completion in the spring of 1942 called for the establishment of fifty-eight bomber wings; of these, thirteen were earmarked for air-sea warfare.[56] Stumpff went on to state that the "simultaneous expansion of the Naval Air Force from 25 to 62 squadrons is impossible and unnecessary since the Luftwaffe is prepared to take over all offensive tasks and part of the reconnaissance duties with its 13 bomber wings detailed for air-sea warfare."[57] In accordance with this plan, the Luftwaffe intended to assign a large number of the four wings of Heinkel He 177 reconnaissance and bomber aircraft to the navy. In other words, Raeder would get more aircraft for maritime operations than requested, but they would be owned, crewed, and commanded by the Luftwaffe. The introduction of the He 177 into the equation was significant. Postwar commentators often do not realize that this four-engined aircraft was to be developed not only as a strategic bomber but also as a land-based long-range reconnaissance aircraft suitable for maritime work, as indicated by one of its nicknames: the *Piratenflugzeuge* (pirate aircraft).[58] The story of the failure to develop this aircraft, also known as the *Griffon,* was "destined to provide the most dismal chapter in the wartime record of the German aircraft industry."[59] It would bear directly on Luftflotte 5's inability to strike effectively at Britain from Norway in 1940 and to operate in combination with naval forces over great distances in the years that followed.

THE FAILURE TO DEVELOP THE *PIRATENFLUGZEUGE*

Even before the Nazis came to power in 1933, German military planners had grappled with the problem of producing a four-engined strategic bomber with a long-range, high-altitude, and heavy bomb-load capability. Contrary to the conclusions of various scholars, professional air strategists in Germany in the late 1920s and early 1930s were zealous followers of the credo of strategic bombing espoused by the influential Italian aviation theorist Giulio Douhet.[60] Douhet passionately believed in the primacy of airpower in determining future wars. He declared that the main burden of effort would be borne not by the army and navy, as in past wars, but by the air force, which would wage war against the enemy's sources of power, such as its air force, and industrial and population centers.[61] The publication of Douhet's classic *Il Dominio Dell' Aria* (Command of the air) as *Luftherrschaft* in 1929, coupled with the appearance in 1933 of articles by an equally colorful American, Billy Mitchell, made a significant impression on air aviation strategists in Germany.[62]

To create an aircraft that could meet the ideals of both theorists and strategists required the development of powerful new engines, pressurized cabins, adequate high-altitude bombing systems and aiming devices, and better long-range navigational equipment.[63] Moreover, ease of serviceability and reliability for constant operational use were essential. Bearing in mind these considerable technical difficulties, Reichswehr planners concluded it would not be possible to produce such a bomber in large numbers until the late 1930s. Therefore, both *Oberstleutnant* Wilhelm Wimmer, of the Ordnance Office, and *Major* Hellmuth Felmy, of the Air Operations and Training Office, strongly pushed for long-term planning that would include strategic bombers in Germany's future air force. With the easing of French watchfulness in the wake of the economic crisis of the late 1920s, German planners in the Reichswehr made tentative plans for the inclusion of a large strike force. In February 1932, Wimmer wrote to his section commander, commenting that he had "not the least doubt that in the future, the only nations to have anything to say will be those that possess powerful air fleets around an air plane that can day or night strike fear in the hearts of their opponent's population."[64] At the same time, Felmy put forward a blueprint for an eighty-squadron-strong air force of 1,056 aircraft for 1938, including forty-two bomber squadrons.[65]

When the Nazis came to power, the reorganization of Germany's air force slightly delayed plans to develop the strategic bomber, although a number of factors encouraged the continuation of these earlier ideas in military circles from 1933 until the outbreak of war in 1939. These influential factors included memories of the stalemate that had developed in the Great War, the *Dolchstoßtheorie* (which had heightened the importance of the home front in modern warfare), and the vulnerable military and political position in which the fledgling Nazi state found itself in 1933.[66] In light of these factors, the leaders of the new Reich began planning for an air force with which it could attack the morale of the enemy by striking at its very heart with strategic bombers. Not unlike their contemporaries in the RAF and the United States Army Air Corps (USAAC), Luftwaffe planning personnel saw substantial potential for strategic bombing. For example, Robert Knauss, at that time an airpower expert with Lufthansa, persuasively argued in 1933 for the establishment of a 400-strong bomber force with which to pursue any future war to the very core of the enemy's resistance. He suggested that "the terrorisation of the main cities and industrial regions of the enemy by bombing would lead that much more quickly to a collapse of morale."[67]

Moreover, the War Ministry's prestigious journal, the *Militärwissenschaftliche Rundschau* (Military Science Magazine), published a number of important articles dealing with airpower. Nearly all of these stressed the use of aircraft as a strategic weapon. In one article on this subject a *Major* Bartz wrote that, considering the latest generation of bombers, it was apparent that "already in today's circumstances the bomber offensive would be as unstoppable as the flight of a shell."[68] In addition to these aspirations, the Luftwaffe was blessed with one of the Reichswehr's most outstanding officers. Early in the Nazi period, Walter Wever was selected as chief of the Air Command Office over another shining aspirant, Erich von Manstein. Wever, an intensely nationalistic man and a keen air strategist, fully supported the Führer's plans for the rearmament of Germany and, by 1934, was a fervent advocate of an independent air arm spearheaded by a fleet of heavy strategic bombers. As an indication of the potential of these machines, Wever informally referred to them as *Uralbombers*.[69]

The very day after Hitler took power, the Ordinance Office released the rewritten specification for the strategic bomber, and by May 1934 the heavy bomber had first priority in the Luftwaffe's developmental program. The timetable called for a mock-up by mid-1935, the production of prototypes by July 1936, a preproduction series by the winter of 1937, and full-scale production from 1938 onward.[70] Göring had been advised of these plans but made no comment at the time. However, the self-important Luftwaffe chief flew into a rage when he viewed the mock-up of the Junkers Ju 89 four-engined bomber in early June 1935. He made it clear that he, and he alone, had the authority to decide such matters, and that the Technical Office had gone beyond its brief in commissioning models from Junkers and Dornier.[71] The reaction of *General* Werner von Blomberg, the war minister, could not have been more different.[72] Having seen the mock-up of the other contender for the Luftwaffe's heavy bomber fleet, the Dornier Do 19, he asked *Oberst* Wilhelm Wimmer when it would be ready for production. In response to Wimmer's answer of, "about 1939 or 1940," the war minister paused for a moment, looked skyward, and remarked prophetically, "That is about right."[73]

Unfortunately for the Germans, from this point on the development of their *Uralbomber-Piratenflugzeuge* was plagued by delays and technical difficulties. Although both prototypes were ready for their flight tests by late 1936, Luftwaffe planners were having second thoughts. Principally, these doubts centered on new specifications issued on 17 April 1936 that effectively killed the Dornier and Junker prototypes, because the range and speed required were nearly double that of models currently under consideration. Consequently, by October 1936 the preproduction run of the Do 19 and the Ju 89 was listed as "undetermined" and unlikely to be taken up in the near future.[74] Although the rather underpowered and cumbersome Do 19 progressively appeared inadequate for the task at hand, the large Ju 89 showed much promise, and the decision to cancel it would fatally set back the German development of a four-engined bomber.[75] The potential of the Ju 89 was ably demonstrated by its commercial derivative, the Ju 90, which set a number of load and altitude records in 1938 and was one of the few aircraft available that could be swung into action in support of Dietl's mountain troops in Norway in 1940.[76]

In many respects, though, the termination of both models reflected hard-nosed realism and changes within the Luftwaffe's hierarchy. Sadly for the future of the

Luftwaffe, Wever had been killed in an air accident on 3 June 1936. Albert Kesselring took up his position, while Wimmer was replaced by Ernest Udet. It would appear that these men decided, in light of the inability of this first generation of bombers to meet the new specifications personally endorsed by Wever, that it was not worthwhile to persevere with their development. Göring ordered work on these machines to be stopped on 27 July 1937—a decision that he himself would later have cause to regret.

When discussing the decision to cancel the first generation of long-range bombers and the subsequent shambolic attempt to pursue it later, many historians parade a number of "enemies of the four-engined bomber," such as Göring, Udet, and Milch, in a regular rogues' gallery, while lamenting the death of its die-hard supporter, Wever.[77] While, as we shall see, there is some merit to this contention—especially where Göring and Udet are concerned—it should not be forgotten that the strategic thinking of the Luftwaffe was severely tempered by a number of geographic and resource-based factors. Such a view also plays down the Luftwaffe's unique practical experience gained in the second half of the 1930s.[78] First, Luftwaffe strategic planning was, on the whole, made on the basis of a war restricted to continental Europe, which accordingly failed to take into account the possibility of war with Britain until it was too late. Unlike their American and British counterparts, German military strategists were forced to accept the likelihood of a land battle immediately after war broke out. It was not considered realistic for the Germans solely to develop large numbers of strategic bombers when Germany, situated in the middle of continental Europe, had to win the land war first if it was to pursue victory in a protracted conflict. It was pointless to talk of attacking strategic targets such as factories and population centers when the loss of Silesia and the Rhineland would prove catastrophic.[79] If these initial land battles were lost, the result could be fatal. Both the British and the Americans, on the other hand, had the natural advantage of a sea barrier, which allowed them to absorb any loss on mainland Europe without irrevocably losing the war. It is therefore of little surprise that German air policy in the interwar period reflected a more diversified approach than that of the exclusive "strategic dogma" of the RAF and USAAC.[80]

Second, the German resource base prohibited the development of a massive strategic bomber fleet comparable to those assembled by the British and Americans during the war. The geopolitical reality of Germany's Continental position was coupled with a serious shortage of resources. Unlike Britain and, in particular, the United States, Germany possessed very limited reserves of natural resources. It relied on imports for nearly all of those raw materials vital to the development of a significant war economy.[81] Although the Reich could have purchased a greater amount of raw materials in the postdepression era, a decline in its own exports brought about a shortage of foreign exchange in Germany. This was exacerbated by rising prices of industrial goods on the international market from the mid-1930s onward. Even as late as May 1939, Milch was urgently warning Göring that the serious lack of iron, steel, and other materials might lead to a reduction of overall aircraft production of up to 30 or 40 percent.[82] Shortages in iron, steel, aluminum, and magnesium, coupled with a shortage of electrical power in the Reich, proved to be the Achilles' heel of the Führer's ambitious rearmament plans and, rightly or wrongly, impinged on Göring's 1937 decision. The latter's rationale is neatly illustrated in a prewar discussion of the four-engined bomber program in which he inquired, "How many twin-engined aircraft can we make for each four-engined one?" To this, the reply was "about two and a half." "The Führer," concluded Göring, "does not ask me how big my bombers are, but how many there are."[83] Nevertheless, despite the snappy answer (which has often been quoted), we shall see that Germany did, in fact, have enough materials to produce a genuine strategic bomber, although it appeared too late to affect the outcome of the war. Germany's main aviation problem was a failure to focus on the quantity production of effective designs, rather than a shortage of materials.

Third, the experiences of the German Condor Legion in the Spanish civil war spurred the development of close air support and dive-bombing. The Condor Legion experience was to play a significant long-term role in the declining ability of the Germans to develop and produce four-engined bombers, particularly in light of the abysmal results recorded in contemporary high-altitude horizontal bombing tests. The best figures the training wing of the Luftwaffe could get with the Goerz-Visier 219 bombsight were only 1 to 2 percent hit rates from 4,000 meters. In stark contrast to this, reports from the Condor Legion in Spain pointed to the far better results that could be achieved by dive-bombers and low-level attacks with high-speed bombers. In turn, this was confirmed by the training wing of the Luftwaffe, which in low-level attacks scored a 12 to 25 percent success rate, while its dive-bombers were consistently able to drop their bombs within 50 meters of the target.[84] Due to these factors, Ernst Udet, chief of the Reich Air Ministry's Technical Office, was keen at every opportunity to ensure that Germany's new generation of bombers, no matter how big, could dive, although as he once lamely confessed to Heinkel, he did not actually "understand production" and knew even "less about big aeroplanes."[85] Consequently, in the period immediately preceding the war, the Germans tended to limit themselves to medium and light bombers, which offered the greatest degree of accuracy.[86]

And the medium bomber most Germans had in mind as the "wonder" aircraft was the Ju 88. This was especially true during the plane's early development, when it seemed likely that this new twin-engined bomber would ably fulfill both tactical and strategic demands. Even as late as April 1939, Count Galeazzo Ciano, the Italian foreign minister, recalled Göring telling him that because of its "long range" the Ju 88 "would be used to attack not only Britain herself, but also could branch out towards the West, to bombard the ships approaching Britain from the Atlantic."[87] Touted, among other things, as a long-range bomber able to sweep even beyond Ireland, the Ju 88 was oversold from its inception. Moreover, thanks to a plethora of major and minor structural changes foisted upon the so-called fast bomber by Udet, who demanded that it be capable of diving, the Ju 88 never lived up to prewar expectations, with its limitations revealed in dramatic fashion during the Battle of Britain and the Blitz.

Notwithstanding these strong arguments suggesting that the Germans were neither in the position to, nor did not need to, create a *massive* fleet of heavy four-engined bombers (comparable to the British and American bomber fleets that attacked the Reich's heartland from 1943 to 1944), the capacity and the need existed to develop a *medium*-sized fleet of such aircraft. A force such as this, numbering some 200 to 300, would have proved useful not only in strategic bombing operations but also in more important maritime work prior to 1942.[88] That it was possible to produce such a force (contrary to prewar misgivings) was demonstrated in the eventual production of some 1,146 He 177s during the war. Although nearly 85 percent of these rolled off the production lines after the beginning of 1943, and consequently arrived too late to influence the outcome of the Second World War, the number built do demonstrate that, given the will, Germany certainly had the means to enter the war prepared for an all-encompassing aerial campaign against Britain.[89]

THE HEINKEL HE 177

With the failure to develop fully the Do 19 and Ju 89 designs to meet the new 1936 specifications, the concept of a strategic bomber may well have been laid to rest but for growing fears of an Anglo-German confrontation that created renewed interest in the heavy bomber among the General Staff in the last quarter of the 1930s. Although Göring had always hoped to avoid a war with the British, in February 1938 he cautiously advised Hellmuth Felmy, one of his tactical commanders, to draw up plans for an assault on Britain. After the Anschluß, Anglo-German relations worsened, and consequently the likelihood of a war with Britain became a "probability" rather than a mere "possibility." Felmy pointed out that, unless the Germans secured bases from beyond their borders, such as in Holland and Belgium, their existing bombers would not be able to penetrate any farther than 690 kilometers with a half-ton bomb load.[90] Accordingly, Göring belatedly realized that the four-engined bombers ordered by Wever would be needed not only for strategic raids on Britain but also for the thirteen wings of *Piratenflugzeuge* earmarked for Germany's maritime operations. However, as the Germans once again took up the development of a genuine heavy bomber, the growing influence of the dive-bomber concept began to severely curtail any significant progress.

In 1938, Udet approached the Ernst Heinkel Flugzeugwerke for a four-engined bomber capable of reaching Britain with a sizable payload. The result was the potentially brilliant Siegfried Günter–designed He 177, which first flew in November 1939. The aircraft was designed to meet a required top speed of 600 kilometers per hour, a cruising speed of 500 kilometers per hour, and a range of 3,600 kilometers with a two-ton load and 6,000 kilometers with a one-ton load.[91] Based on the results achieved with dive-bombing and the need for precision bombing against shipping in the advent of a war with Britain, Udet, who had no technical expertise, demanded that the He 177 be able to perform sixty-degree diving attacks rather than the medium-angle dive required by the Technical Office specifications.[92] This amazing requirement came in the middle of the model's development and proved to be its undoing, even more so than the promising Ju 88. Major structural changes to enable the He 177 to withstand the steep sixty-degree dive and subsequent pullout maneuver substantially increased the weight of the aircraft and resulted in a sharp decline in performance.[93] Moreover, to reduce stress on the wings in a dive, a tandem-engine arrangement was devised.[94] Günter originally wanted to employ two 2,000-hp engines, but, due to the lack of high-octane fuel in the Reich, he resorted to coupling together two 1,000-hp Daimler-Benz DB 601 units.[95] On its maiden flight on 19 November 1939, the aircraft was able to stay aloft for only twelve minutes because of overheating. The propensity of the coupled He 177 engines to overcook and catch fire was to be a recurring problem that would never be completely solved.

With Britain's continued resistance following the German successes in Norway and France, Udet, who had been promoted to inspector general of the Luftwaffe and was responsible for aircraft procurement, attempted to rush the aircraft into production in October 1940. But, as Ernst Heinkel recalled, this was not as easily achieved as the Luftwaffe's inept inspector general hoped:

> Production had to be stopped until the plants had had time to retool for the large aircraft. All this was bound to take months. . . . The long-range, heavily-armed bomber seemed to be the only hope. Yet, it was precisely in this respect that catastrophe struck. Now produced for the first time in quantity and subject to thorough testing, the He 177 with its parallel-coupled engines did not measure up to the military requirements for which it had been designed. Many of them went down in flames when their engines caught fire, or crashed when their wings cracked for apparently inexplicable reasons. Thus, as suddenly as it had been released for production, the He 177 had to be withdrawn once more.[96]

These problems would still be evident well into the war and were highlighted in an address given by the *Reichsmarschall* to representatives of the German aircraft industry on 13 September 1942. Although he had thirty-six He 177s in his inventory by this time, only two were ready for action, thanks to a spate of so-called fire-and-crash epidemics. Göring regaled the audience:

> Now to deal with the long-range bombers. Here is the most tragic chapter of all. When I think of it, gentlemen, it is enough to make me scream. I do not possess a single long-range bomber. When I think of all the lies I was told about the Ju 88! It was supposed to fly anywhere; it could fly for about an

hour beyond Ireland. We calculated accurately how we were going to wipe out convoys everywhere. And then I had to count myself lucky if anything ever got beyond London. . . . It is with terrific envy that I regard the four-engined British and American aircraft. They are far, far in advance of us. The only thing which remains is the He 177. It is there but I dare not use it. . . . I was told that there would be two engines, built one behind the other, and then suddenly I find myself confronted by an abortion of an engine, made up of two engines welded together; no one can get at it and maintenance is made extremely difficult. This engine is put into the He 177 and then the exhaust flame damper is so badly arranged that the undercarriage has to be divided into two parts so as not to interfere with the arrangement of the exhaust pipes; and . . . such things mean that it may go up in flames at any moment. . . . Can anyone conceive how such an engine is to be serviced at the front? I do not think the plugs can be taken out without dismantling the entire engine![97]

Heinkel responded to Göring's attack by stating that his firm had nearly overcome the fire problem but was still working on reinforcing the airframe to allow the bomber to be able to dive. Göring curtly shot back: "It does not need to dive." "I should make it quite clear what we expect of the He 177," continued the exasperated *Reichsmarschall.*

First of all, it should be able to carry torpedoes for long distances. It does not need to be able to dive to do that. . . . In addition, it must be able to carry special bombs to attack shipping at great distances. And if we want to raid Swerdlowsk or somewhere like that, it must be able to fly at a suitable height. . . . But do see to it that the thing is at last a really long-range bomber which can carry a decent load over long distances, and which is above all reliable and safe in every detail of construction (the engines particularly), so that it can be used to fly long distances over the sea to attack convoys at places where they are not very well protected.

In the end, though, despite Göring's belated foot-stamping speech, it was too late, and the whole project remained continually dogged by technical difficulties well into 1942. Ironically, it was not until 1943, after the tide had well and truly turned against Germany and after Allied four-engined bombers began in earnest their strategic offensive against the Reich, that He 177 production shot up from only 166 machines in 1942 to 415 aircraft in 1943 and a peak of 565 in 1944.[98] As impressive as this rate of production was given the shortages within the industry, it was simply too late, and with declining fuel stocks and crews, the He 177 program was eventually brought to an end in October 1944 due to the demands of the Jäger-Notprogramm (Emergency Fighter Program).[99] Thus it had been impossible to fulfill the hopes of either the navy or Göring for their own long-range bomber when it was most urgently required, in the first three years of the war.

RAEDER'S CAPITULATION TO GÖRING

Even as early as 1938, however, it had become clear that the Luftwaffe would not be able to assign anywhere near the thirteen wings previously promised for minelaying, torpedo missions, and general naval duties. And those aircraft that could be made available for maritime tasks would not be placed under the command of the navy. In the end, Raeder simply gave in. He may have been placated by the thought that at least some of the thirteen wings could yet eventuate, or he may have decided to cut his losses, since approval would soon be forthcoming for a huge battle fleet (the Z-Plan). Whatever the case, in a conference with the Luftwaffe on 27 January, Raeder effectively ended any prospect of an independent Naval Air Force.[100] In the final agreement between the two services, Göring got nearly everything he wanted: in a future war the operational area of the Luftwaffe would be Britain and sea areas in which naval forces were unable to operate; in naval actions, tactical intervention by the Luftwaffe would take place only when agreed on by both parties; and for minelaying, the Luftwaffe had complete freedom of action beyond the reach of Raeder's forces.[101] Moreover, although the Naval Air Force was to be increased, control of these new units fell to the newly established General of the Luftwaffe with the commander in chief of the navy, who was directly subordinate to Göring himself.[102] In time of war, the former would be responsible for all air units deployed with the navy.[103] The relationship of the navy and the Luftwaffe when war did arrive can be summarized by the following partition of responsibility: "(a) The Luftwaffe was responsible for the procurement, training and equipment of all German air units; (b) The Navy was responsible for air operations at sea and in defence of coastal areas; (c) The Luftwaffe was to provide the Navy with sufficient air strength to carry out the objective under (b)."[104]

The fruits of Göring's failure to make sufficient material preparations for a war that required operations over the sea against Britain began to appear only months before the Second World War broke out. In the second week of May 1939, Luftflotte 2 conducted a war game designed to ascertain the Luftwaffe's operational readiness, and a number of sobering conclusions were reached regarding the command, communications, and supply procedures in a war with Britain in 1942. The resultant study, entitled "Operational Targets for the Luftwaffe in the Event of War Against Britain in 1939," observed that the air fleet lacked the requisite strength, training, and aircraft of extended operational range to bring about a quick decision against Britain.[105] The range of most of the aircraft in Luftflotte 2's inventory was insufficient to reach the ports of Britain's western and southwestern coast, and aircrew were inexperienced at flying over such distances in bad weather. The only success for the air fleet that could be expected was against the British aircraft industry because damage inflicted here would be harder to mend in the short term,and even small formations of bombers would be able to attack the widely dispersed targets.[106] The definition of aircraft industry was soon enlarged to encompass all industry and supply facilities. This was approved by Göring on 19 June and would form the basis for the decision to attack the British air industry and airfields rather than coastal targets in 1940. Thus, even before the war had begun, the Luftwaffe was decidedly uneasy about its ability to lay siege to Britain anytime before 1942.

When war with Britain did arrive, the Luftwaffe and the Naval Air Force were unprepared. The latter, stripped of most of its strength, could muster only fourteen coastal squadrons, consisting mostly of Heinkel He 59 floatplanes and Dornier Do 18 flying boats.[107] A number of types were undergoing trials, including the He 115 floatplane and triple-engined BV 138 flying boat. Slow, poorly armed, and confronted with the impossibility of escort fighters being employed to protect them, all these aircraft were slipping into obsolescence even before the war began. But with low priority assigned to research and development by the Germans in maritime aircraft, the crews and field commanders had little choice but to make the best of a bad situation. In all, around 130 seaplanes were available for action in early September, and not a single He 177 was to be seen.[108]

In 1938, the Luftwaffe had promised thirty-two wings of bombers for maritime work. But bottlenecks in the armaments industry, the sheer impossibility of meeting the unrealistic goals of the Concentrated Program, and the early arrival of war meant that in total the Luftwaffe had only thirty wings for all tasks, let alone what could be spared for deployment with the navy.[109] Nevertheless, Göring— after years of ignoring the need for a strong force of bombers and reconnaissance aircraft with crew trained for operations over the sea and able to work in close cooperation with the navy—ordered the formation of X Fliegerdivision on 3 September 1939 under the hand of Geisler. Consisting of four groups from KG 26 and KG 30, this newly formed force totaled no more than fifty to sixty serviceable He 111s and ten to fifteen serviceable Ju 88s.[110] This was not the 1,100 bombers originally promised, but it was a start.

EARLY AIR AND SEA COOPERATION

In the months ahead, combined navy-Luftwaffe actions were at best poor, and on occasions appallingly bad. Operations in October and November 1939 and February 1940 clearly exposed the poor preparation and attention to the demands of air and sea cooperation. An attack on the British Home Fleet on 9 October by Geisler's force (recently upgraded from a *Fliegerdivision* to a *Fliegerkorps* and augmented with aircraft of LG 1, totaling 127 He 111s, 21 Ju 88s, plus sundry naval air units) was singly unsuccessful.[111] Planned to coincide with operations by a potent German naval force against enemy shipping, "strong winds, poor visibility and low cloud" wreaked havoc on the vital interplay of "reconnaissance, shadowing, leading in and attack."[112] Geisler was forced to confess that his crews were still poorly versed in flying in such miserable weather over the sea, and Göring prohibited future large-scale undertakings in such "unfavorable weather"; the prospect of success simply was not proportional to the dangers involved.[113] Although two hits were claimed, six aircraft were lost (a Ju 88, 3 He 111s, a He 59, and a Do 18).[114] This was followed up by a poorly coordinated Luftwaffe-navy air operation against a convoy off Cromer on 21 October.[115] The plan for the mission called for 10 slower He 115s of KüFlGr 406 to attack first, when the defenders were less ready for such an assault, which would then be followed up by 3 Ju 88s. Unfortunately for the naval pilots, the Ju 88s arrived first, encountering defenses of only "medium strength," while the "the ten He 115s met with very heavy British defense which was forewarned."[116] The premature arrival of the Luftwaffe bombers had alerted the RAF, which was at a high state of readiness by the time the lumbering He 115s arrived on the scene; the latter were quickly cut to pieces. Four of the He 115 floatplanes were shot down, and another was heavily damaged. Operations in November were less costly in aircraft but similarly miserable in results.

The low point of interservice relations came on 22 February 1940 when the Luftwaffe sank two German destroyers. These vessels, *Maass* and *Schultz,* were part of a six-strong destroyer force taking part in Operation *Wikinger,* designed to put an end to British fishing off Dogger Bank.[117] However, on the same day, eight bombers of X Fliegerkorps were dispatched to attack shipping between the Thames and the Firth of Forth, and it was these aircraft that, between 1945 and 2000, spotted an armed vessel thirty kilometers off Tershelling Lightship.[118] The bombers promptly attacked the vessel in the face of light flak and machine-gun fire, hitting it twice amidships. The crew later reported that the ship had caught fire and finally sunk.[119] By 2030, the commander of the destroyers signaled that he had lost two of his warships and sought permission to abandon the mission. The inquiry into the debacle found that the Luftwaffe had sunk *Maass* and *Schultz,* and although X Fliegerkorps had informed the navy of its upcoming sortie, the Naval Staff had not informed the Luftwaffe of the destroyer operations in time to brief the aircrews before they took off.[120] Furthermore, upon learning of the naval mission, X Fliegerkorps failed to signal the first wave of bombers of the presence of German destroyers in the area, on the grounds that doing so would endanger their own operation.[121] Raeder was livid and declared:

> Irrespective of the results of further inquiries by the special commission, I wish to state that the 1st Destroyer Flotilla should have been informed about the mission to be undertaken by KG 26, and X Fliegerkorps should have been informed earlier about the destroyer operations. In future each arm must be adequately briefed on the other's operations, and this exchange of information is to take place well beforehand.[122]

This costly loss of ships and lives graphically showed the dangers involved with two separate commands operating in the same area. This failure logically offered two practical solutions: either the remaining naval forces be placed under the operational control of the Luftwaffe through X Fliegerkorps or the air corps be placed under the direct control of the navy through Naval Group West (which controlled all naval operations along western Europe's coastline). But Raeder did not have a chance in his mismatched struggle with Göring.[123] By the end of 1939, the navy was left with only fifteen squadrons, since Göring had seen fit to withdraw twelve multipurpose squadrons from naval tactical command.[124] Not yet satisfied with control of air units, Göring grasped for other weapons of value in the navy's armory. Consequently, a bitter wrangle developed over ownership of mines and, later, torpedoes, both of which eventually came under Luftwaffe authority in 1940. Control of the former weapon gave rise to the establishment of IX Fliegerdivision, the second Luftwaffe force designated for naval operations.[125] Under the command of *Generalmajor* Coeler, IX Fliegerdivision was created on 1 February 1940 and attached administratively to Luftflotte 2, while operationally it was controlled directly through Göring. In many ways, the achievements of his maritime units up until the end of the first quarter of 1940 could hardly be described as impressive. But Göring was able to gain a certain amount of solace that he was at least on the right track—and that the Luftwaffe, not the navy, was best suited to control maritime air operations—when reports of X Fliegerkorps' sterling performance during the April invasion of Norway came to hand.

THE SIGNIFICANCE OF *WESERÜBUNG*

As already noted, on the surface the campaign in Norway did support Göring's belief that the Luftwaffe could carry out maritime operations and that Raeder's concerns were therefore ill founded. Certainly, the overall Luftwaffe effort had been successful and, alongside the naval aircraft, played an influential role in the rapid victory in the southern parts of the country, while in the second phase it had demonstrated the influence of air superiority in the battlefield with the ejection of the Allies from central Norway. Yet with the rapid victory in Norway and the glory heaped upon him after the fall of France, Göring was in no mood to consider the fact that the Norwegian campaign, although successful, had revealed a number of weaknesses in the Luftwaffe—and that these directly reduced its ability to wage war at sea or over longer distances than those normally flown in support of the army in Continental campaigns. Even early on, it became clear that the distances involved were beyond the operational radius of nearly all Luftwaffe and naval aircraft, when the few available Condors had to be brought in to carry out routine reconnaissance over Narvik. Indeed, X Fliegerkorps' offer to send a whole bomber group on a one-way mission to attack British warships after the First Battle of Narvik on 10 April was a depressing admission of the inadequacy of either service's aircraft for the task at hand. Moreover, although a good number of Allied vessels had been sunk or badly damaged, it had not been a spectacular affirmation of "aircraft over warship" given the plethora of targets available. In fact, aerial recognition was so bad that enemy destroyers were often erroneously identified as battleships and, on occasion, even aircraft carriers, demonstrating that X Fliegerkorps' aircrews were still learning the trade of maritime work.

With the ejection of the Allies from central Norway, the Germans had been able to secure Trondheim's Vaernes airfield. Nevertheless, even with this forward field, the Ju 88s and He 111s were not really suited to this type of long-range antishipping mission. Likewise, the Bf 110 was equally unsuited to escorting the bombers on their way to Narvik, with its cumbersome handling abilities further eroded by the fitting of an external fuel tank for long-distance flight. What Göring failed to ask himself was: "If my premier maritime air units are having difficulties of this sort over Norway, how suited are they to operations over Britain, where instead of facing merely a couple of hastily thrown together fighter squadrons, they would meet not only the full weight of Fighter Command's considerable firepower but also a carefully designed defensive system?" The inability to recognize the problem and the cumulative effect of years of neglect, indifference, and interservice infighting over developing a genuine long-range bomber suitable for maritime and strategic bombing operations would be tragically exposed by Luftflotte 5's ill-fated first and last major raid of the Battle of Britain on 15 August 1940.

AIR WAR OVER BRITAIN

As both *Weserübung* and the battle for France drew to a close in June 1940, the victorious Führer pondered two possible courses of action. He could arrange a compromise peace with Britain or, should these peace overtures fail, instruct his staff to make preparations for an invasion of the British Isles. Flush from his French success, Hitler felt confident that Britain would accept a peace that allowed it to retain its empire and participate in the sharing out of French colonial properties. Britain, however, rejected Germany's clandestine and public offers. Therefore, on 2 July, Hitler made it known that a "landing in England is possible."[126] Within two weeks he issued Directive 16, "Preparations for the Invasion of England," code-named Operation *Seelöwe (Sealion)*. In this directive Hitler stated: "As England, in spite of the hopelessness of her military position, has so far shown herself unwilling to come to any compromise, I have therefore decided to begin preparations for, and if necessary to carry out, an invasion of England."[127] This invasion would take place "on a broad front extending approximately from Ramsgate" to Lyme Regis, some 430 kilometers in length.[128] Ninety thousand seaborne troops would assault the British coastal defenses on the first day, and within three days a beachhead of up to 260,000 men was envisaged.[129] This would be followed by second and third waves containing armored and infantry divisions, respectively. In all, the Germans planned to disembark thirty-one divisions within four weeks, and the defeat of Britain would be all but completed shortly thereafter.

The most important role was assigned to the Luftwaffe. Directive 16 stated that, to make a landing possible, "The British Air Force must be eliminated to such an extent that it will be incapable of putting up any opposition to a German crossing."[130] This harked back to Hitler's order of 2 July, which stipulated to the planners of Operation *Seelöwe* "that a landing in England is possible, providing that air superiority can be attained."[131] The Luftwaffe's leadership planned to strike British airfields, aircraft factories, and auxiliary facilities in southeast England, and thereby eventually wear the RAF down until aerial superiority had been achieved.[132] In spite of the fact that Germany's air force leaders realized that their operation was seen only as the preliminary part of *Seelöwe,* unofficially they "hoped that air action alone would force Britain to sue for peace."[133]

The Luftwaffe's preparatory operations for *Seelöwe* were relatively limited. On 10 July, while the Germans were still assembling aircraft and preparing air-field facilities in northwest France, the Luftwaffe engaged in probing assaults on British ports and convoys. This resulted in the loss of some 150 British fighters and 286 German aircraft. By 5 August, the German Air Staff had prepared plans for the air assault proper. *Generalfeldmarschall* Albert Kesselring's Luftflotte 2 and *Generalfeldmarschall* Hugo Sperrle's Luftflotte 3 were assigned targets in southwest England, while Stumpff's smaller Luftflotte 5 would assault targets farther north from its bases in Norway.[134]

Indeed, Luftflotte 5's sphere of operations was markedly smaller than those allotted to the *Luftflotten* based in France. It encompassed a rather diminutive area bordered by the Humber estuary in the south and the Scottish border in the north and stretching inland, almost reaching the city of Lancaster on the west coast. The limited zone of operations given to Stumpff's air fleet was indicative of its size and the fact that most of the Luftwaffe's important targets lay farther south, be-yond the reach of German aircraft based in Norway. While it was ostensibly di-rected to make attacks on the enemy's air force and air industries, Göring revealed in a speech of 21 August that Luftflotte 5 had also been deployed to "tie up enemy fighter units on central England's east coast."[135]

Since the conclusion of the Norwegian campaign, Luftflotte 5 had seen a large portion of its bomber strike force siphoned off to the southern air fleets. Conse-quently, by the beginning of August, Stumpff's air fleet was decidedly the poor relation of its two French cousins. Gone were the glory days of May when Luftflotte 5 boasted over 700 combat aircraft. Now a shadow of its former self, the air fleet was reduced to four bomber groups belonging to X Fliegerkorps' KG 26 and KG 30. These Heinkel and Ju 88 bombers were augmented by limited numbers of ZG 76 Bf 110s and JG 77 Bf 109s; the latter, of course, were only capable of defen-sive operations over Norway by reason of their limited range.[136] For coastal re-connaissance and minelaying operations, Luftlotte 5 still retained KüFlGr 506 and its He 115 floatplanes, and for long-range reconnaissance the He 111s and Ju 88s of a handful of so-called long-range reconnaissance squadrons.[137] Of these air-craft, Stumpff was able to bring only 175 to bear on Britain (138 He 111s and Ju

88s, and 37 Bf 110s), compared with the 1,232 aircraft Luftlotten 2 and 3 were able to field.[138] Clearly, though, in total the Germans were able to deploy a significant aerial armada for the upcoming battle. For example, the Luftwaffe had about 2,350 serviceable frontline aircraft of all types, and the RAF had 1,150.[139] The difference in fighter strength was not so marked, since the British had nearly 690 serviceable fighters compared with the Germans' 960.

Notwithstanding a number of postponements, *Adlertag* (Eagle Day) was eventually set for 13 August 1940. The ensuing battle itself went through four main stages.[140] Between 13 and 23 August, the Luftwaffe attacked British airfields and radar stations in southeast England. From 24 August to 6 September, the Luftwaffe went farther afield to RAF and other military facilities around London, and, toward the end of this phase, to British aircraft factories and related industries. On 7 September, in an attempt to bring the RAF to battle more directly, the Luftwaffe began making day and night raids on targets in London, up until 19 September. From this point on, the Germans switched to indiscriminate night raids on London in order to bring about conditions suitable for *Seelöwe*. Although the Blitz continued into the spring of 1941, it did not seriously affect Britain's industry or its will to fight. Within these four phases of the conflict, the part played by Luftflotte 5 seemed so embarrassingly brief that hitherto it has warranted little more than a cursory paragraph or two in many histories of the Battle of Britain. However, given the serious deficiencies it exposed and the importance of these to future aerial activity from Norway, it deserves greater consideration.

LUFTFLOTTE 5'S CONTRIBUTION TO THE BATTLE OF BRITAIN

Stumpff's air fleet was to swing into action soon after the two larger *Luftflotten* had dealt the first blow on 13 August. This they did two days later, when all three *Luftflotten* converged on Britain in the largest raid of the battle so far. Their task: to attack British airfields and radar along a wide front, and thereby bring as many RAF aircraft to battle as possible. Of the nearly 2,000 German aircraft taking part, Luftflotte 5 contributed only 154. These were divided into two attacking groups— one based in Sola and the other at the Danish field of Aalborg.[141]

The more southern thrust from Aalborg consisted of fifty of KG 30's Ju 88s, which were to hit the airfield at Driffield, East Yorkshire. The northern Sola thrust was composed of sixty-three KG 30 Heinkels whose primary targets were the Dishforth and Linton-on-Ouse airfields, with Newcastle, Sunderland, and Middlesbrough as secondary objectives. Escorting the He 111s were twenty-one Bf 110s of Sola's ZG 76—the twin-engined fighter wing that had covered itself in glory in the capture of the Oslo airfield on the opening day of *Weserübung*. Reaching their targets would, however, be no easy matter given the distances involved. For many of KG 30, KG 26, and ZG 76, the operation brought back unpleasant memories of the extremely difficult conditions they had only recently experienced during the Norwegian campaign in flights from Sola and Trondheim in support of Dietl's far-flung forces in northern Norway. The outward and return flights of both prongs of the attack measured roughly 1,500 kilometers alone, to which 20 percent had to be added to the flying time to cover takeoff and landing, navigational errors, and the all-important attack—over 1,800 kilometers in all.[142] This put the bombers at the extreme end of their operational range and forced a reduction in bomb loads of the Heinkels to only 1,360 kilograms per aircraft, including incendiaries and 500- and 250-kg high explosives.[143] In a repeat of their operations in support of the bombers flying over Narvik in June, the escorting Bf 110s were fitted with the *Dackelbauch,* a belly-drop fuel tank holding over 800 liters of additional fuel to increase the fighter's operational range.[144] The Ju 88s were given no true fighter escort. This is perhaps due to their higher speed compared with the lumbering Heinkel and the fact that some of these were the Ju 88C fighter-bomber. These aircraft were to provide a degree of cover for the other Ju 88s and as such did not carry any bombs.

Nevertheless, the raid was extremely risky and to a great degree was based on the erroneous belief that previous assaults on southern England by Luftflotten 2 and 3 had led to a transfer of the RAF's northern-based fighters to the south.[145] The inspiration for the northern raid seems to have originated with *Oberst* Josef Schmid, Göring's chief of intelligence. Schmid, though, had not reckoned on the stubbornness of Air Chief Marshal Sir Hugh Dowding, commander in chief of Britain's Fighter Command, who refused demands by the southern 11 and 12 Groups for a general strengthening of their own units with aircraft from the quiet northern 13 Group.[146] Just as he had wisely refused to send more fighter squadrons into the black hole of the French campaign months earlier, Dowding now refused to stop the rotation of tired units to the relatively peaceful north.[147] Consequently, just when Stumpff's aircraft were about to raid northern England, 13 Group boasted six fighter squadrons, some of which were made up of seasoned pilots. Yet even if Dowding had seen fit to send some of 13 Group's fighters to southern groups, leaving a smaller number of squadrons to meet the incoming aircraft of Luftfotte 5, these still would have presented a considerable threat to the German bombers and twin-engined fighters, as illustrated in late May and early June 1940 over Narvik, when a handful of Gladiators and Hurricanes claimed to have successfully shot down sixty-three German aircraft in a very short time. Clearly the lesson from Norway—that German medium bombers and twin-engined fighters operating at the edge of operational range were easy pickings for nimble enemy fighters—had not been learned.

On top of this, the Luftwaffe was to be taught another lesson because the British, on their home soil, had the invaluable benefit of radar. The advantage of radar—never fully appreciated by the Germans at the time—was intensified in northern England simply because the distances involved meant that aircraft flying from Norway and northern Denmark were often picked up well off the English coastline, giving the defenders ample time to get their aircraft airborne and into an attacking position from which to intercept the intruders. Moreover, if the Germans had hoped that the northern radar system would be less vigilant than its southern counterparts, they were sorely mistaken; an important convoy was sailing north from Hull around midday on 15 August, and all radar stations in the region had been ordered to maintain a high degree of alertness throughout its voyage.[148] The combination of these two factors—ample numbers of single-engined fighters directed by alert radar operators—was to exact a terrible toll on Luftflotte 5's crews and aircraft.

The Heinkel bombers of KG 26 left a windswept Sola at 1000 hours (GMT). These were followed in quick succession by the twenty-one Bf 110s. Although reasonably confident that the defenses in northern England presented less of a threat than those in the south, Luftwaffe planners did attempt to deceive and avoid enemy interception as much as possible by putting up a decoy flight of twenty He 115 floatplanes. And the leading Bf 110, piloted by *Hauptmann* Werner Restemeyer, was fitted with special wireless monitoring equipment, operated by *Hauptmann* Hartwich, X Fliegerkorps' chief signals officer, designed to intercept the enemy's ground control communications.[149] This attempt to sidestep defending fighters was to fail completely, while the floatplane feint actually worked against German success because KG 26 navigation was awry. As the twenty floatplanes (having taken to the air thirty minutes before the main force) made for the Firth of Forth, well north of the bomber targets at Dishforth and Linton-on-Ouse, a three-degree error in the flight path of the bomber force and its escorting fighters brought them toward the English coast 125 kilometers off course, almost to the point where the floatplanes would have made landfall.[150] "Thanks to this error," noted *Kapitän* Arno Kleyenstüber, a staff officer at X Fliegerkorps headquarters, "the mock attack achieved the opposite of what we intended. The British fighter defense force was not only alerted in good time, but made contact with the genuine attacking force."[151]

British radar operators picked up the floatplanes—which they accurately estimated to be twenty strong—at just after 1200 hours, and at 1215, 72 Squadron Spitfires at Acklington were scrambled to patrol over the field. By this time, the Heinkel crews had become aware of their navigational error, and the aircraft were swung south, while the floatplanes had already turned back sixty-five kilometers off the Scottish coast. Over the following ten minutes, it soon became apparent to the British that there were now more than the twenty to thirty aircraft originally estimated by radar operators, and two flights of Hurricanes from 605 Squadron were scrambled from Drem to join those from 607 already on course to intercept the intruders. Spitfires of 79 and 41 Squadrons were also put into the air, although only the former was directly situated along the route flown by the German aircraft. The Spitfires were first to spot the German attackers, which were cruising at approximately 4,270 meters off the Farne Islands. To the RAF pilots' surprise, the incoming Germans numbered not thirty but nearly a hundred strong. With a

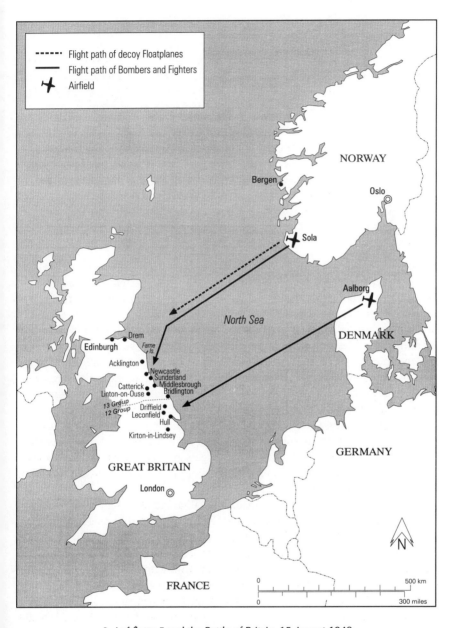

Legend:
- - - - - Flight path of decoy Floatplanes
───── Flight path of Bombers and Fighters
✈ Airfield

NORWAY

Bergen

Oslo

Sola

Aalborg

North Sea

DENMARK

Drem
Edinburgh
Farne Is.
Acklington
Newcastle
Sunderland
Catterick
Middlesbrough
Linton-on-Ouse
Bridlington
13 Group
Driffield
12 Group
Leconfield
Hull
Kirton-in-Lindsey

GERMANY

GREAT BRITAIN

London

N

FRANCE

0   500 km
0   300 miles

8. Luftflotte 5 and the Battle of Britain, 15 August 1940.

910-meter height advantage, the Spitfires dove out of the sun upon the unsuspecting fighters and bombers of X Fliegerkorps.

In minutes the first two German Bf 110s, one of which was Restemeyer's aircraft, had been shot down in flames. The bombers were scattered, and the RAF fighters forced the twin-engined fighters into defensive circles. One of the fighter pilots, *Oberleutnant* Hans Kettling, described his own experience:

> I heard *Obergefreiter* Volk, my radio-operator and rear-gunner, fire his machine guns and on looking back I stared into the flaming guns of four Spitfires in splendid formation. The plane was hit—not severely, but the right-hand motor was dead. . . . I tried to reach the protection of the bombers which were overhead, but without success. . . . as Spitfires came in for the kill, I sent out my Mayday. This time the RAF fighter got the left-hand motor and knocked out the rear gunner (who was wounded in the knee) and the front screen. The bullets missed my head by inches.[152]

Kettling survived the crash landing, but others of ZG 76 were less fortunate. The Bf 110s were unable to fend off the British single-engined fighters without heavy losses and escaped only after losing seven aircraft—a third of their force. Despite claiming to have shot down eleven enemy Spitfires, in reality the Bf 110s failed to destroy a single RAF fighter in the melee. As for the bombers, while the Luftwaffe after-action report stated that "because of strong fighter defense and deep clouds, success was not individually observed," and the 8th Abteilung's 1943 history of the Battle of Britain confidently stated that "extensive fires were observed in the hangars at Whitby airfield," the actual results were less than spectacular.[153] It appears that a good number of the Heinkels simply jettisoned their bombs harmlessly into coastal waters and turned tail for Norway, but not before eight of their number were shot down. None of those that pressed ahead along the coast successfully reached the designated targets, but some sprinkled their bombs over county Durham. By 1335, the failed operation was over, and the surviving bombers limped back over the North Sea.

Farther south, the fifty Ju 88s made landfall at Flamborough Head and, having been picked up by radar, were engaged by Spitfires of 616 Squadron and Hurricanes of 73 Squadron, which had been scrambled at 1307. The ensuing air battle forced the German force to disperse into eight smaller formations. Of these, some bombed houses and an ammunition dump in Bridlington, while the bulk of the remaining aircraft flew on to Driffield, a 4 Group bomber station, where they successfully destroyed ten Whitleys and damaged four hangars in one of the day's most successful raids.[154] Nevertheless, heavy antiaircraft fire at the field brought down one of the bombers, for a total loss to KG 30 of six of its Ju 88s, that is, nearly a 10 percent loss rate.[155]

The overall losses to Luftflotte 5 were unacceptably high, and of its total complement of 154 aircraft, Stumpff's air fleet had lost 20 planes, with many more damaged. Although as late as 6 September the OKL war diary indicated that

Luftflotte 5 would again be used to "tie down sizable defensive forces" while attacking the "enemy air industry," suggestions were being made to have X Fliegerkorps assigned to Kesselring's Luftflotte 2 at the end of August. In the first week of September, units of the air corps were transferred.[156] The campaign proper had only just begun, and Luftflotte 5 was already out of the action. Indeed, 15 August proved to be the first and last time Stumpff's aircraft would sally forth in any significant daylight raid on Britain.[157] As Dowding astutely noted after the raid: "The sustained resistance which [the Luftwaffe] was meeting in southeast England probably led them to believe that fighter squadrons had been withdrawn, wholly or in part, from the north in order to meet the attack. The contrary was soon apparent, and the bombers received such a drubbing that the experiment was not repeated."[158] Within weeks of the raid, the northern air fleet was stripped of its most potent strike force, the bombers of KG 26 and KG 30 and some of the Bf 110s.[159] Having shown that these aircraft lacked the range to operate effectively over Britain from Norway, the Luftwaffe had little choice but to transfer them to Luftflotte 2.

In many ways, Luftflotte 5's 15 August disaster revealed glaring weaknesses in German airpower ability, first hinted at during *Weserübung,* that would doom not only its attempt to achieve aerial superiority in the skies above England but also Germany's "siege of Britain." Principally, the Germans had embarked on a war against Britain without a long-range four-engined aircraft capable of either bombing at high altitudes with heavy payloads or undertaking reconnaissance over great distances in support of the U-boat war. To show how effective this may have been, one needs to consider what a four-engined bomber flying from Norway and France could have achieved in raids on British airfields and industry and, more important, in implementing a "siege of Britain."

FOUR-ENGINED BOMBERS AND THE WAR AGAINST BRITAIN

It can be argued that the turning point with regard to the likelihood of an invasion of Britain was 15 September, when the Luftwaffe launched an even bigger raid than its 15 August predecessor and lost 65 aircraft (some press claims at the time stated 185) as against only 26 RAF machines.[160] From this point on, the threat of a seaborne invasion began to recede. It was clear that the Germans had not achieved the air supremacy they needed to launch *Seelöwe.* Therefore, by early September, discussions regarding the invasion began to reflect the likelihood of it being postponed until the following year. For example, in an order of 1 September, Keitel revealed that preparations for Operation *Seelöwe* could not be completed before 15 September and that "the Führer will decide whether the invasion will take place this year or not; his decision will depend largely on the outcome of the air offensive."[161] On 12 October, Hitler made the inevitable order to call off the invasion for 1940, stating that "until the Spring [of 1941], preparations for *Seelöwe* shall be continued solely for the purpose of maintaining political and military pressure on England."[162] In the autumn of 1940, Hitler turned his attention eastward to the Soviet Union.

Of the four main phases of the Battle of Britain, it is the second phase—from 24 August until 6 September 1940—that this study will use as a framework from which to discuss the significance of the German failure to produce sufficient numbers of four-engined bombers. It was arguably in this period that the Luftwaffe came closest to achieving air superiority over the RAF, as is ably demonstrated by an examination of Fighter Command's crisis in aircraft supply. Although by 2 September the daily losses for each side were about equal, the RAF's position was worse because of its rapidly falling stocks of aircraft. On 10 August, the RAF had 129 Spitfires and 160 Hurricanes available to replace the 64 lost in battles or accidents over the preceding week.[163] Nevertheless, in the following four-week period, losses reached an average of 240 aircraft per week, reaching a peak in the last two weeks, when 297 Hurricanes and 209 Spitfires were destroyed in combat or were written off because of pilot error. On 7 September, therefore, only 39 Spitfires and 86 Hurricanes were available for immediate issue: Fighter Command had reached a crisis in supply. Thus, as American historian Robin Higham has noted, if "the Germans continued their attacks at the time, they would have run Fighter Command out of aircraft."[164] Yet as serious as this was, the loss of experienced pilots was far graver. Not only had losses in aircraft been 200 in excess of the number produced in the final two weeks of August, but the loss of 300 pilots over the whole month left a shortfall of 40 trained replacements. Of the original 1,000 pilots who had started the war with the RAF, barely a quarter were still in action. Although the situation was never quite as bad as Churchill and earlier commentators asserted, if the raids on airfields, industry, and supporting facilities had continued, the deficit, which grew to a peak of 181 at the end of August, would most certainly have accumulated to reach near-critical proportions.[165]

Fortunately for the British, the Luftwaffe's own considerable losses—which had reduced its fighter strength to below that of the RAF—for what appeared, at the time, to be little decisive result, led to a change in strategy in early September. The Luftwaffe's attacks on the air defense system of the British Isles gave no indication that the RAF's position had been considerably weakened. Furthermore, Hitler, in response to Bomber Command's raids on Berlin, now sanctioned retaliatory raids on London.[166] On 4 September, he raged: "When they declare that they will attack our cities in great measure, we will erase their cities. . . . The hour will come when one of us will crack, and it will not be National Socialist Germany!"[167] Certainly, the subsequent raid of 7 September, which heralded this new approach, did look spectacular. Members of the British Air Council stood on the roof of the Air Ministry and watched (before seeking shelter below) the impressive sight of 600 bombers and 300 fighters flying above the Thames.[168] In the ensuing raid the London docks were set alight. The city's firemen fought nine fires, requiring over 100 pumps, and one intense inferno that required over 300 pumps to bring it under control.[169] However, the Luftwaffe's change in strategy had given the British Isles' defensive system, particularly Fighter Command, the breathing space it so badly needed.

If, during this decisive period, the Germans had had a four-engined bomber capable of flying from Scandinavian airfields at Sola and Aalborg as well as France, Holland, and Denmark, it may have tipped the scales in the Luftwaffe's favor. Accordingly, when attempting to explain the failure of the Luftwaffe to gain mastery over the RAF, historians and military commentators often cite the lack of true four-engined bombers as a significant factor.[170] This view was also held by many of the participants who, with the benefit of hindsight, agreed with Kesselring's postwar lamentation regarding the Battle of Britain: "We needed four-engined bombers with great range of action, climbing power, speed, load capacity and armament."[171] With regard to Kesselring's observation, and bearing in mind the RAF's aircraft and personnel crisis in the period 24 August to 6 September, it is possible to enumerate three reasons that significant numbers of four-engined bombers would have enabled the Luftwaffe to achieve air superiority over the RAF. First, due to their long range, the planes would have stretched the defensive resources of the RAF to the breaking point.[172] Second, the much greater weight of bombs dropped might have struck a decisive blow against Britain's air defense system. Third, the high altitude attainable by a four-engined bomber would have placed the defending fighters at an extreme disadvantage.[173]

As Richard Suchenwirth notes in his postwar study of the battle, "Long-range bombers could have created an entirely different situation, due to their ability to appear anywhere over the British Isles," and British defenses, "admirably developed for use against the German medium bombers, would have been so thoroughly dissipated by long-range bombers that defeat would have been inevitable."[174] Although the "inevitability" of defeat is doubtful, it is clear that a strategic bomber would have enabled the German air force to strike not only from northwest France against southeast England and London but also from Norway to the farthest corners of the British Isles. After 15 August, instead of having to transfer its bomber forces from Norway to France because of the limited operational radius of its twin-engined bombers, Luftflotte 5, with a handful of squadrons of long-range bombers, could have continued the fight against Britain from its Scandinavian bases.[175] Bombers such as the He 111 and the Ju 88 had a relatively limited operational range of some 2,000 and 2,500 kilometers, respectively.[176] If the Germans had been able to deploy an aircraft with a 5,500- to 6,000-kilometer range, as envisaged in the He 177, flying from bases encompassing Norway in the north to France in the south, they would have forced the RAF to spread its defensive net farther afield. Bearing in mind the RAF's critical situation in August and early September, if it had dispersed some of its squadrons away from southeast England to combat long-range bombers, it may have been forced to surrender ascendancy in the air.

Moreover, the production of a heavy bomber fleet would have significantly increased the punching power of the Luftwaffe. The proposed He 177 would have been able to deliver 7,000 kilograms, not far below the load carried by two of the most successful Allied bombers, the British Lancaster and the American B-17 Flying Fortress (at 10,000 and 8,000 kilograms, respectively).[177] The mainstays of the German aerial assault, the He 111 and the early Ju 88s, could carry only between 1,000 and 2,000 kilograms.[178] Consequently, the overemphasis on the twin-engined bomber severely limited the Luftwaffe's potential for destructiveness. In light of what the Germans accomplished in August and early September against the British aircraft industry and air facilities with twin-engined bombers, it is apparent that significant numbers of four-engined bombers would have wrought even greater damage. The potential that existed can be seen in an incident of August 1942 in which, during operational trials from Bordeaux-Mérignac, an He 177 dropped a single 250-kg bomb on Bristol's Broad Wier district, killing forty-five civilians and injuring an additional sixty-six. This was the most destructive single bombing raid to occur in Bristol during the entire war.[179]

These operational trials also highlighted the advantage of altitude. In 1940, the available British fighters would have been at an extreme disadvantage against a bomber like the He 177, which could enter their airspace at an altitude of up to 8,000 meters. Moreover, the He 277, which differed from the He 177 by having the customary and practical layout of four separate engines, was able to operate at an incredible 15,000 meters.[180] Although only eight He 277s were ever made in 1943–1944, they did demonstrate what the Luftwaffe could have achieved but for decisions made during the prewar period. The He 111 and Ju 88, on the other hand, operated at altitudes ideally suited to Britain's defending fighters. Consequently, they needed fighter escort, which both the Bf 109 and the Bf 110 were ill equipped to provide when flying from France and Norway, respectively. The low speed of the twin-engined bombers meant that once over England the Bf 110 had only twenty minutes' combat time, not enough to provide adequate cover, especially since the RAF often held off until the fighter cover had turned for home before attacking. The unsuitability of the Bf 110 had been demonstrated graphically on 15 August, and subsequently the Bf 110 itself required an escort in missions over Britain.[181] A high-altitude bomber in 1940 would have put RAF defenses at a disadvantage because of the time required to reach the height of the incoming bombers. This was particularly true of the Hurricane and early Spitfire models— the very aircraft that had severely cut up Luftflotte 5's bomber and twin-engined fighter force on 15 August—whose performance declined considerably at higher altitudes.

To appreciate the difficulties required to meet high-altitude bombers, a cursory examination of what took place with regard to twin-engined bomber raids from France clearly shows the constraints the defenders faced. A bomber traveling from Pas de Calais to London, a distance of 145 kilometers, at 300 kilometers per hour, took 28½ minutes.[182] The British fighters needed approximately 6½ minutes to climb to 4,600 meters, 10 minutes to reach 6,000 meters, and additional time to maneuver into a suitable attack position. When the inevitable delays between radar, filter room, and assessment by the controller are added to the time needed to reach the incoming bomber, the margin between a successful interception and arriving too late was very narrow indeed.[183] If the RAF had had to contend with a high-altitude bomber traveling at over 6,000 meters, interception would have been even more difficult because the performance of both British single-engined fighters fell off markedly above 3,600 to 4,600 meters.[184] Even with the earlier warning given by radar of incoming raiders over the North Sea from Sola and Aalborg, the RAF still would have been hamstrung by the attacking altitude of high-flying four-engined bombers. This point is further attested to by the fact that it was not until 21 January 1944 that an He 177 was shot down over Britain, significantly by a high-altitude Mosquito.[185] In 1940, the RAF simply did not possess the defensive fighters required to combat adequately any German high-altitude bomber.

The potential of a four-engined bomber flying at great altitude was demonstrated in the east as late as 1944. Although the ninety He 177s deployed on the eastern front in the spring of 1944 could have struck at strategic targets, they were deployed in support of the army against Soviet troop concentrations and supply lines. Attacking in daylight at about 6,000 meters, only a small number were lost because few Soviet fighters were able to reach an attacking altitude, and those that did rarely pressed home the attack against the heavy defensive armament the He 177 then boasted.[186]

Of course, a cheaper and perhaps less time-consuming alternative to the production of a four-engined bomber might have been the development of a long-range escort fighter. Given the short range of the Bf 109 and the poor performance of the Bf 110, a specially designed fighter capable of flying over long distances— along the lines of the celebrated Anglo-American Mustang P-51—would have provided cover to Luftflotten 1 and 2's bombers and also directly challenged the aerial supremacy of RAF fighters over Britain. Moreover, it not only would have solved the escort problem for medium bombers operating from French bases but also would have certainly allowed Luftflotte 5 to operate from Norway with adequate fighter protection for KG 26 and KG 30 bombers. Although this line of reasoning has much merit, it fails to take into account the fact that while the He 177 was designed as a long-range bomber, it also, as already noted, had been earmarked for a task that no single-engined fighter could accomplish: long-range maritime reconnaissance and antishipping duties.

NORWAY, THE "SIEGE OF BRITAIN," AND THE CONDOR

It is worth noting that the four-engined bomber may well have fulfilled Jodl's belief, expressed on 30 June 1940, that a blockade would have brought the British to their senses without an invasion: "In conjunction with propaganda and terror raids from time to time—announced as 'reprisals'—a cumulative depletion of Britain's food stocks will paralyse the will of the people to resist, and then break it altogether, forcing the capitulation of their government."[187] As Adolf Galland, the famous German fighter ace noted, had the Luftwaffe concentrated all its efforts on ports and coastal convoys, it "might well have brought Britain to her knees since Britain's endurance without imports was only about six weeks."[188] Notwithstanding Galland's highly speculative estimation, it is true that Britain was heavily reliant on imports to feed its people, maintain its industry, and keep its armed forces equipped and supplied in the field. At the beginning of the war, it was estimated that Britain needed some 55 million tons of goods by sea, including all of its domestic oil requirements and about half of its food needs.[189] Severing Britain from these essential imports via an investment of its ports and shipping lanes could be achieved only by a combination of U-boats and four-engined long-range reconnaissance bombers.

That such aircraft operating from Norway and France could have gained much was demonstrated by Luftflotte 5 before and after the decision to cancel Seelöwe had been finalized, when impressive results were achieved with miserly numbers of barely adequate aircraft. In July 1940, Stumpff's forces participated in the antishipping campaign by sending X Fliegerkorps bombers, and the naval units of KüFlGr 506, in numerous successful attacks on convoys plying the waters off Scotland's east coast. Sorties were undertaken in the Orkney area on 6 July, south of Iceland on 12 July, and on Britain's east coast on 18 July. In these operations two destroyers and one patrol vessel were sunk, and a cruiser and seventeen steamers were damaged.[190] Stumpff's air units were also engaged in mining operations off Aberdeen, the Firth of Forth, Berwick-on-Tweed, Hartlepool, and Middlesbrough. As Walter Gaul has noted, regarding the whole effort by all the Luftflotten involved:

> The period from the end of June up to the middle of August thus demonstrates the capacity of an air force efficiently controlled and given one objective, in this case the destruction of enemy shipping. As a result of the reciprocal use of mines and bombs, of alternation between day and night operations, of the appearance of bombers with torpedoes and bombs at scattered points on the coast and the extension of aerial minelaying operations to the west coast of Britain as far as Belfast, the enemy was faced by colossal tasks.[191]

In this period, between 500 and 600 mines were laid during fifty to sixty bomber sorties flown against British shipping. Although this had given a taste of what could have been achieved in a proper "siege of Britain," the campaign against shipping and ports was relegated to secondary importance with the issuing of Directive 17, when the main effort was switched to land-based targets. Despite Luftflotte 5's continued involvement in these coastal operations throughout the Battle of Britain, concentrated attacks against shipping targets were not resumed until November 1940, when the real impetus had already gone out of the air war against Britain.

In spite of the fact that attacks against coastal targets were important, to complete the economic strangulation of Britain, the Germans required aircraft capable of engaging in longer range antishipping and maritime reconnaissance in close cooperation with the U-boat arm from bases in Norway and France. The advantages of having suitable aircraft available for U-boat operations were readily understood by all those involved in maritime warfare. First and foremost, in submarine operations the target has to be located, and with the decline in its own air arm and the dearth of long-range aircraft available for maritime operations, the navy was forced to use U-boats for reconnaissance. This was a task for which they were most ill suited, since their very low conning tower allowed a maximum visual range of only thirty kilometers, which in turn could be greatly reduced in poor weather and heavy swells. Nevertheless, without suitable aircraft the navy was forced to use these vessels in the "reconnaissance line abreast" formation, which consisted of up to four or five U-boats—but often rose as high as thirty boats later in the war—moving on a parallel course and close enough for their range of vision to overlap.[192] This strip formation, however, was very inefficient because inaccurate navigation, coupled with fog, rain, or heavy seas, easily broke up the line of vessels and made it possible for convoys to slip through the line unsighted. Moreover, given the expanse of the Atlantic Ocean, the convoy could easily pass on either side of the U-boat's relatively small reconnaissance strip without mishap, even without the aid of poor weather. In addition, once a convoy was found, U-boats experienced great difficulty in shadowing it, especially because the convoy would make a change of course of up to twenty degrees at three- to fifteen-minute intervals.[193] Following this zigzagging convoy during daylight hours necessitated U-boats maintaining visual contact with the convoy without being spotted themselves. This usually involved traveling on the surface, since a submerged U-boat was reduced to a snail's pace of four knots, and that only briefly, before falling well behind the merchant vessels. Thus, only after a convoy had been spotted and successfully shadowed were U-boats directed into the path of oncoming merchantmen to achieve their primary task, the attack. Clearly this method of reconnaissance was a fairly hit-and-miss affair and, with the limited boats available, an extremely inefficient method of waging warfare against enemy shipping.

Unlike the poor view afforded the U-boat, aircraft were able to reconnoiter a huge expanse of water in a single sweep, which even an extremely large formation of U-boats traveling abreast could never hope to cover. Having spotted a convoy, the aircraft could then shadow it and report course changes. This information allowed U-Boat Command to bring its forces together into a favorable position ahead of the convoy for a massed attack. Dönitz, as U-boat commander, was only too fully aware of the potential of air reconnaissance, since his own boats were of little value in this area because, as he admitted, their "radius of vision is too small." "Air reconnaissance on the other hand can obtain for us clear and accurate information with regard to the position and movement of enemy shipping at sea," he continued in a December 1940 summary of demands submitted to OKM, "and thus give us the data upon which we can group our U-boats to the greatest advantage." On top of this, he stated that air attacks should be encouraged, since the "more the air arm attacks, damages and sinks ships, the more it harasses and distracts the enemy and throws him into confusion, the better pleased the U-boat arm will be." Nevertheless, although as early as 8 June 1940 Dönitz had seen the potential to use the newly won bases in northern France "to carry out air reconnaissance, aimed at discovering the presence of the enemy convoys," it soon became clear that they lacked aircraft of necessary range, and it was only occasionally that "one solitary plane" was available to fly "one solitary sortie."[194] Consequently, in the second half of 1940, Raeder was unable to coordinate a single combined operation that resulted in any significant success. The following entry for 14 December 1940 in the U-Boat Command diary summarized the frustrating situation:

Close cooperation has so far been carried out with the following units:
1. Coastal Air Group 406, Brest, which is tactically subordinate to Group Command West. Their long-range aircraft type BV 138 are however grounded for about two months because of technical defects.
2. KG 40 Bordeaux—in war independent [in other words, officially no contact]. Cooperation by personal agreement. Type FW 200. At present generally only one aircraft out by day.
3. Luftflotte 5 flies reconnaissance of a certain area on special request in each case. So far only carried out once. Recently requested again but refused because of lack of forces.[195]

As in the Battle of Britain, Norway was simply unable to rise to the high pre-*Weserübung* expectations as a base for Luftwaffe operations in the "siege of Britain." Luftflotte 5's cupboard was bare of long-range maritime aircraft, and its so-called Long-Range Reconnaissance Group (Aufklarungs Gruppe) was really made up of medium-range machines such as He 111s, Ju 88s, and Do 17 flying boats.

As in the invasion of Norway, when true long-distance machines had been required, the most suitable aircraft available to support Dönitz's U-boats were the Condors, now stationed in France. An economic strangulation via the investment of its ports and shipping lanes by combining the U-boat and aircraft like the Condor may have precipitated a negotiated settlement with Britain, especially if enough of them had been available for deployment in both France and Norway. This sleek civilian airliner was adopted by the Luftwaffe for use in long-range reconnaissance and antishipping activities. It was never a true strategic bomber structurally stressed for heavy military use, as testified to by the number that littered Luftwaffe airfields with broken backs. But as it had shown during *Weserübung*, where it was deployed in sorties no other German aircraft could reasonably be expected to cover, it proved to be a most useful aircraft for the role to which it was adapted. Flying from Bordeaux-Mérignac in June 1940, I./KG 40 Condors began dropping 1,000-kg experimental mines in port entrances on England's east coast.[196] However, the Condors' real worth became apparent during August and September 1940 when, operating as antishipping aircraft, they sank no less than 90,000 tons of shipping and became widely feared after bombing the 42,000-ton liner *Empress of Britain* on 26 October.[197] During 1940, the Condors—which Churchill dramatically dubbed the "scourge of the Atlantic"—sank over 580,000 tons of Allied shipping.[198] Whether long-range aircraft like the Condor—or a more suitable aircraft like the He 177—flying from France and Norway could have tipped the scales in Germany's favor in the Battle of the Atlantic we might never have known, were it not for Göring taking a hunting trip in early 1941.

GÖRING GOES HUNTING AND DÖNITZ GETS HIS PLANES

On 2 January, Dönitz had once again taken his complaints to Raeder, who on this occasion sent him to see Jodl in Berlin. Dönitz explained his predicament and his desperate long-range reconnaissance requirements to the OKW chief of staff. Seeing that Jodl was sympathetic to his plight, the U-boat commander requested the use of the Luftwaffe's longest ranged planes, the Condors of I./KG 40. Fortunately for Dönitz and Raeder, the *Reichsmarschall* was out of town on a shooting trip, and when the matter came to the attention of Hitler, he simply placed the twelve Condors of I./KG 40 under the tactical command of the U-boat commander.[199] Hitler, although more concerned with plans for the invasion of the Soviet Union, had already been pestered on this subject by Raeder at a number of December meetings, at which the *Großadmiral* had impressed upon his Führer that support of U-boats "by air reconnaissance, working together in closest possible cooperation in the operational area, is of decisive importance for increasing the effectiveness of submarine warfare."[200] Thus Hitler, who had been primed by Raeder, was prepared to accede to this reasonable request. Göring, on the other hand, upon hearing of the loss of his aircraft, promptly demanded their return—a demand Dönitz flatly refused. More than a little miffed, Göring spat out that the U-boat commander need not expect any future cooperation from the Luftwaffe. Nevertheless, since the commander of I./KG 40 was none other than the former naval officer *Oberstleutnant* Harlinghausen, who had covered himself in glory during the operations in Norway, Dönitz had little to worry about with regard to tactical deployment.[201] Upon receipt of the Condors, Dönitz realistically commented: "This order marks a decisive advance in U-boat warfare. It is only the first step in this direction and in view of the few aircraft available and the various technical difficulties still to be resolved, the immediate effect will not be great. However, I intend to gain the best results from the cooperation."[202]

Ironically, the first successful joint operation came about by a U-boat leading the Condors into the kill rather than the other way around, when, on 8 February 1941, a boat sighted a homeward-bound Gibraltar Convoy (HG 53).[203] The

U-boat was ordered to shadow the estimated twenty vessels (eighteen steamers, one destroyer, and a gunboat) in order to guide the aircraft in. After the U-boat had sunk two of the convoy's merchant ships, six Condors then sank a further five. *Hipper*, which was in the region, then chimed in, sinking a straggler. Dönitz's staff were rightly pleased: "Great importance is attached to this first success of an operation by aircraft brought to the enemy by a U-boat, not only because of the tonnage damaged, but because it proves for the first time that even at this early stage cooperation between U-boats and the Luftwaffe can lead to considerable success."[204] The combined operation was the first of its kind for the Germans, and it tantalizingly showed what could be achieved, given the resources and forward planning. Nevertheless, success was more often the exception than the rule, because the navy and the Luftwaffe simply lacked enough aircraft for such missions, and the very success of the combined operation led to the British spreading their convoys farther afield, particularly along northern routes as far as Iceland.[205] U-boats were similarly sent into these waters, but providing adequate aerial reconnaissance was another matter. As promised, Göring refused to transfer I./KG 40 to Stavanger in support of the U-boats. Being unable to fly directly from Stavanger—the ideal base, in conjunction with those in France, from which to completely encircle the British Isles—greatly reduced the effective range of the Condors in the war against Britain. To overcome these difficulties, the Condors, from the third week of February 1941, would fly east of the British Isles from Bordeaux, reconnoiter the North Channel, land at Sola, and return via the same route the following day.

The success of this and later operations, alongside concerted lobbying by Raeder and Dönitz, brought about a change in emphasis in the war against Britain. In his supplement to Directive 9, "Instructions for Warfare Against the Economy of the Enemy" (26 May 1940), and in Directive 17, "For the Conduct of the Air and Sea War Against Britain" (1 August 1940), Hitler had demanded that Luftwaffe attention be placed on the source of Britain's airpower—the RAF and its supporting infrastructure—while operations against shipping were of secondary importance. But in Directive 23 of 6 February 1941, "Guidelines for the Warfare Against the British War Economy," Hitler now asserted that "contrary to our former view, the greatest effect of our operations on the British war economy was caused by the high losses in shipping inflicted by sea and air warfare."[206] Rescinding Directives 9 and 17, he stipulated in the freshly drafted directive that it would be "desirable in the future to concentrate air attacks more closely and to deliver them primarily against targets whose destruction supplements the naval war."

Certainly, Göring was moved enough by the directive and, no doubt, the loss of the Condors, to initiate the Luftwaffe's first genuine attempt at coordinating operations with the navy in a systematic manner. A number of Luftwaffe air commands designed to engage in maritime operations were formed: Fliegerführer Atlantic, which, as the name implies, covered the Atlantic; Führer der Seeluftstreitkräfte (F.d.Luft), designated as providing air reconnaissance in the North Sea (between fifty-two and fifty-eight degrees) and the entrance to the Baltic, plus providing air cover to U-boats as far as Cherbourg; and Fliegerführer Nord, charged with supplying reconnaissance for U-boats, protection for German warships, and shipping and antishipping duties north of fifty-eight degrees, that is, above Scotland.[207] Other smaller areas were covered by elements of Luftflotten 2 and 3. Despite the establishment of these new commands, the Luftwaffe's main emphasis still rested firmly on the Continent. Even though Directive 23 stressed that these duties were to be undertaken, Hitler cautioned in the directive that "a large portion of the Luftwaffe and a smaller proportion of naval forces" assigned for these duties may well be "withdrawn in the course of the year for employment in other theaters."[208]

Even at their inception, the commands were painfully small, and they would be further reduced as the war drew on. While Fliegerführer Atlantic was the largest force, it boasted only two bomber groups of He 111s, a small number of Condors, and a coastal air command group with eight squadrons, typically equipped with He 115 floatplanes, Ar 196 seaplanes, and BV 138 flying boats.[209] A squadron of Ju 88s was to supplement the force. F.d.Luft was made up of only two coastal air staffs with six squadrons. Fliegerführer Nord was equipped with two so-called long-range Ju 88 squadrons and three Do 18 flying boat squadrons. Aside from the numerical inadequacy of these forces, considering the sheer enormity of ocean they were supposed to cover, none of the forces, particularly those of Fliegerführer Atlantic and Fliegerführer Nord, had any significant numbers of true long-range aircraft.

Meanwhile, notwithstanding the poor weather over Norway during February and March 1941, the Condors proved the worth of long-distance aircraft to the war at sea by making a number of important sightings that led to major U-boat operations.[210] A Condor making its way to Sola on 19 February made the first sighting of a convoy, numbering some forty-five ships, 130 kilometers northwest of Cape Wrath.[211] Based on this report, all available U-boats were directed southward from their waiting point near Iceland to set a contact line across the path of the westbound convoy (OB 287).[212] Two more aircraft picked up the vessels the next day. Nevertheless, the Condor crews' reports were so inexact that the boats failed to make contact with the vessels, and the operation was called off on the third day.[213] On 22 February, an aircraft flying the return route from Stavanger sighted westbound convoy OB 288, 66 kilometers off Lousy Bank.[214] Although a further machine was detailed to reconnoiter the next day, this was not possible because at that stage the convoy was judged to be at the extreme perimeter of the Condors' range.[215] Nevertheless, contact was made on 23 February by a single U-boat, and then four boats were able to attack the convoy overnight, sinking nine ships, with only torpedo failures preventing a larger haul for the Germans. A simultaneous action against OB 284 netted two more ships.

This success was followed by a U-boat chancing on OB 290 between 25 and 27 April. The sighting was made by Günther Prien, who shadowed the convoy until Condors could make contact; when they did, nine vessels were sunk. When added to Prien's hits, this meant that the convoy lost no fewer than twelve ships. Dönitz's diary noted that, according to "U-boat reports I./KG 40 attacked with considerable success at midday with one and in the evening with five aircraft."[216] This operation was followed on 2 May by another large, but this time unsuccessful, undertaking. After a I./KG 40 aircraft spotted OB 292 west of North Channel, numerous U-boats were diverted to the area and by the following day were arrayed in a patrol line to intercept the oncoming ships. On 3 May, though, the convoy was lost despite three Condors scouring the area; it was not picked up again until the next day, when it was 250 kilometers north of the original sighting.[217] Although a new line was established, continued contact proved impossible, and when the convoy passed beyond the range of the Condors, the operation was abandoned. The close cooperation by U-boats and aircraft did not go unnoticed by the British. In his 6 March directive for "The Battle of the Atlantic," Churchill, fearing the imminent success of Germany's attempt to cut off Britain from its food supplies and the United States, declared the British must "take the offensive against the U-boat and the Focke-Wulf wherever we can and whenever we can."[218]

Notwithstanding the British warlord's concerns and the early promise of these Condor–U-boat undertakings, combined operations from January to May revealed that there were simply not enough aircraft to meet the demands of the navy. On the whole, there were too few machines available to pull the noose tightly around Britain. Over this period, on average only two sorties could be flown daily due to the handful of operational aircraft. Moreover, despite the Condor's reputation as a long-distance aircraft, the plane's range was still below that really required for work in a vast ocean. Even though the Condor was capable of up to a 3,370-kilometer flight—nearly 1,000 kilometers farther than the twin-engined Ju 88 bomber—this fell well short of He 177's 5,500-kilometer range.[219] Thus, despite the fact that Condors were able to reach the main area of reconnaissance in this period, west of the North Channel they were unable to do little more than sight and report convoy positions. In other words, it was simply not possible for them to shadow the convoy for any length of time so that U-boats could follow homing signals onto the ships.[220] Certainly, once a convoy had spotted the Condor and observed the aircraft abandon its shadowing position, the ships were then diverted along another route, greatly impeding the U-boats' subsequent attempts to make contact.[221] That the Germans did not have enough of these aircraft to base a squadron or two in Norway undoubtedly compounded this problem, since the Condors were forced to take the route from France around the west coast of Ireland and then on to Stavanger, rather than direct operations over the North Channel from Norway.

Added to this deficiency, errors in navigation, caused by the difficulties of making precise measurements over extremely long flights—a good portion of which were undertaken at night buffeted by strong winds—meant that at times the position of a convoy as reported by a Condor was over 100 kilometers off.[222]

Under these circumstances, flight reports detailing the position of sighted vessels could often lead U-boats astray, and at least two of the operations undertaken by U-boats in February and early March were failures because of poor Luftwaffe plotting of the convoy's location.

Generally, though, even with these teething problems and taking into account the shift of convoy routes to colder climes, which meant the Germans were unable to put effective reconnaissance into the air from Norway, the air effort had shown that it was worth persevering. In May, the Luftwaffe sent 48 ships (totaling nearly 158,000 tons) to the bottom of the ocean. By June, the delivery rate of U-boats reached fifteen per month, and Britain was starting to feel the impact of the war at sea as the U-boats dispatched 284,000 tons and the Luftwaffe 195,193.[223] In total, and including losses from all causes, May saw 585,400 tons of shipping (140 ships) sunk—the worst month of the war so far for the British.[224] Winston Churchill had calculated that his country needed 31 million tons of imports a year (excluding fuel stocks) to maintain its war footing. But under the present rate of losses, the nation could expect only 28 million tons. With a handful of U-boats and even fewer aircraft, Dönitz had indicated what could have been done had he been given the requisite forces. In 1941, the Condor alone sunk over 1 million tons.[225]

Unfortunately for the Germans, the small number of these four-engined machines produced (twenty-six in 1940 and fifty-eight in 1941) precluded extensive deployment.[226] Coupled with the small number of U-boats available—until the spring of 1941, Dönitz rarely had more than a dozen boats at sea at any one time—this situation prevented the introduction of true wolf-pack tactics until 1942. This meant that the German attack evolved slowly enough for the enemy to implement effective countermeasures.[227] However, the results attained by such a small number of aircraft and U-boats revealed the potential of such operations, especially if the Luftwaffe had been able to deploy significant numbers of four-engined bombers purpose-built for antishipping and maritime reconnaissance duties. In his postmortem of the Battle of Britain, Adolf Galland bemoaned the failure of the Luftwaffe command to concentrate on the enemy's weakest and most vulnerable points, which were "without doubt, his supply routes from overseas":

> Outstanding successes against them could have been scored in the initial stages, for the range of British fighters was not great enough to enable them effectively to protect merchant shipping. It is almost certain that if all the forces of the Luftwaffe had been concentrated to operate in conjunction with the U-boats and warships, a decisive blow could have been delivered to British supply lines.[228]

As a British historian, Richard Overy, wrote: "Only Göring's refusal to divert more aircraft to the war at sea and the failure to produce a satisfactory long-range bomber built for the purpose prevented aircraft from achieving an even higher degree of destruction."[229] In this sense, therefore, the lack of a four-engined bomber was a most significant factor because, coupled with the use of U-boats and twin-engined bomber raids on Britain's eastern ports, it may have starved Britain into surrender.[230] That the Germans sank 6 million tons of shipping up until the summer of 1941 suggests that a greater emphasis on the production of U-boats and long-range maritime aircraft could well have turned the tide of war in their favor.

By at least one assessment, in its daily operations Germany probably needed 40 to 50 Condors for Britain to be effectively blockaded—that is, after taking into account servicing and losses, a full complement of up to 150 aircraft. With a sizable force of *Piratenflugzeuge* flying from France and Norway, which were able to effectively reconnoiter an area covering 40°N to 65°N and up to 30° west (that is, a square area of sea encompassing the British Isles, with Lisbon at its southeastern corner, stretching into the Atlantic as far as the Azores on its southwestern point, then climbing northward as far as Iceland and then westward toward Trondheim), it is difficult to see how British shipping could have escaped observation.[231]

TOO LITTLE, TOO LATE

Ironically, one of the Allies' most effective U-boat countermeasures was the deployment of their own long-range aircraft. Unlike the Germans, who on any one day during the Battle of the Atlantic had on average only 3 aircraft actually in the air by 1942, the Allies had devoted roughly 500 aircraft to the battle, which by at least one estimate was equal to perhaps ten times the Luftwaffe's effort.[232] Even without the very long-range (VLR) planes it would boast in the latter half of the war, as early as 1941, Coastal Command's flying boats, the Sunderland and the Catalina (which could patrol for two hours at a distance of 960 kilometers and 1,280 kilometers, respectively), were pushing U-boats to operate beyond the range of their only aerial support, the Condors. In particular, the Sunderlands based in Iceland were doing an admirable job in beginning to close the gap through which Allied convoys had to pass without air cover in the North Atlantic.[233]

To counter the effectiveness of Allied aircraft and aid his U-boats in 1942, Dönitz recalled:

> We had for a long time been eagerly awaiting the advent of the He 177, which was said to have a radius of action of some 2,400 kilometres which therefore would operate in those sea areas in which the U-boat arm can still attack convoys, provided that it is supported by the German Air Force in operations against enemy air cover.
>
> The Naval Commander in Chief strongly urged Luftwaffe headquarters to accede to this request for the employment of the He 177s in the war at sea, and there seemed to be every prospect of their being so used within a few months. In any event they were destined never to become operational.[234]

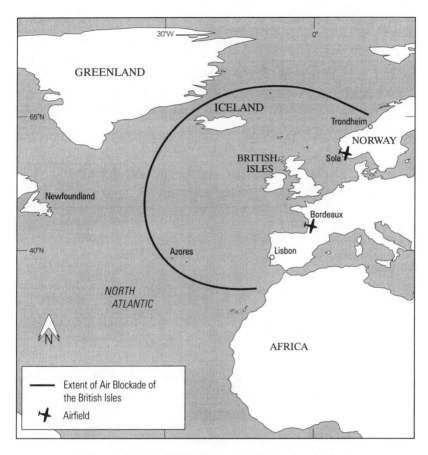

9. Proposed siege of Britain by long-range aircraft and U-boats.

By September 1942 the situation had become so bad, and Allied aircraft so effective against both U-boats and the small number of lightly armed Condors, that the navy felt that it now needed a more heavily armed aircraft that could reach areas even beyond the range that the long-awaited He 177 was supposed to deliver. As the Luftwaffe replied on 3 October 1942, the request

> for the production of an aircraft capable of giving cover in the more distant areas of the Atlantic cannot at the moment be met. For this purpose even a type similar to the American bomber would be required. Desirable as the possession of such an aircraft undoubtedly is, we have not, at present, the necessary technical data, from which it could be developed.[235]

Behind the scenes, however, even Göring was fuming. In a heated exchange with Jeschonnek over the range of the He 177, he blasted:

That is all nonsense. The enemy has aircraft with an operational radius of between 3,000 and 4,000 kilometres, and here we are slipping back by a tenth. I am not trying to be funny, but I really wonder whether it would not be a good thing for someone here to go out and procure the best of the enemy's four-engine aircraft and halfwittedly copy it, then present the copy to our aircraft engineers saying "You are too dull to find anything better, so copy this junk."[236]

After the disaster at Stalingrad in the winter of 1942–1943 and, with it, his Continental plan of conquest, even Hitler was forced to place greater emphasis on maritime strategy. On 23 March 1943, he met with senior aviation industry representatives to consider the long-range aircraft situation.[237] From his audience Hitler demanded a bomber not only capable of attacking London by day and night at an altitude beyond the reach of defending fighters but also able to attack Allied convoys far into the Atlantic.[238] The aircraft selected to meet the Führer's demands was the He 177's natural successor, the He 277. Impractical to the last, Göring felt Hitler's pipe dreams could actually be realized even at this late juncture. In May 1944, just before the landings at Normandy in the west and as the Soviets prepared to enter Poland in the east on their way to Berlin, the *Reichsmarschall* revealed that he had absolutely no comprehension of the situation at hand when he set the monthly delivery rate for the He 277 at no fewer than 200 aircraft. Of the 8 that were actually produced, only two or three ever tested their systems in flight.[239]

Meanwhile, German chances of U-boat success in the Battle of the Atlantic had rapidly declined by 1942, and during 1943 any chance of winning the war at sea disappeared. The final nail in the coffin of the German effort arrived in March 1943, when the long-range American-built B-24 Liberator entered the fray, effectively closing the gap by providing convoys with air cover all the way across the Atlantic.[240] Successfully converted from a high-altitude bomber to a VLR, low-altitude, antisubmarine role, the Liberator could spend three hours on patrol at 1,760 kilometers from base.[241] Using radar, this aircraft and others effectively brought an end to German wolf-pack operations, since they forced the U-boats to remain submerged for longer periods.[242] In addition, by 1943 the British had drastically reduced their need for imports through rationing from 60 million tons to 26 million tons per year, while better port management had resulted in a reduction in port congestion and a rationalization of Britain's shipping schedules and imports, producing a savings of 3 million tons in 1941 alone. Moreover, the Allies' ability to build vessels faster than the Germans could sink them, thanks to the entry of the United States into the war in late 1941, meant that by mid-1943 they had more than enough shipping to meet Britain's needs.[243] As Dönitz confessed in the summer of 1943, the only argument for continuing the U-boat war was that it produced a cost-effective means of diverting Allied attention away from areas of greater strategic importance to the Germans.[244] Consequently, by the end of May 1943, Dönitz was forced to throw in the towel. As he noted in his war diary, his own losses had now reached an intolerable level in relation to the tonnage of merchant vessels being sunk; and, he added, the "enemy air force played a decisive role in inflicting these high losses."[245] Although in the autumn of 1943 he was promised He 177s, some newly converted Ju 290 transports—a very-long-range successor to the Ju 90—and the leviathan of floatplanes, the six-engined BV 222, to augment his overworked Condors, by mid-November he was forced to admit that the "enemy has all the trumps in his hand. . . . On our side, as yet no air reconnaissance; the U-boat its own scout, with minimum of scouting range."[246]

That the Germans had entered the war without a long-range aircraft suitable for maritime work was the single most important factor in preventing the Luftwaffe from making use of Norway as originally planned. Certainly, had either the navy or the Luftwaffe been equipped with such aircraft in significant numbers, Norway would have served as a genuine northern arm of a deadly embrace of the British Isles. Through a combination of U-boats and long-range reconnaissance, antishipping *Piratenflugzeuge,* Germany might well have forced a British capitulation in 1942. As it was, neither the navy nor the Luftwaffe had sufficient numbers suitable for maritime operations, and once the war spread from northern and western Europe to the Mediterranean and then the Soviet Union, the Luftwaffe was increasingly unable to devote even its medium-range twin-engined bombers to the likes of Fliegerführer Atlantic, let alone Fliegerführer Nord in Norway. Although it is true that the war came earlier than anticipated, and thus stymied the grand rearmament plans of both services, it is clear that aircraft for maritime deployment was never high on the Reich's shopping list. Whether a 200-strong force of four-engined aircraft suitable for naval warfare was under the direct control of the navy or the Luftwaffe is somewhat irrelevant; what is significant is that no such force was ever created.

The single biggest impediment to developing such a maritime air arm was Hermann Göring. His struggle with Raeder was long and bitter, and although he was determined to command everything that flew, he never really understood the demands of naval warfare and the benefits to be gained from the effective utilization of airpower at sea, whether the planes were based in Norway or elsewhere. Consequently, his efforts in this area were lethargic and stingy. His inability to grasp his culpability in failing to develop a four-engined, long-range aircraft suitable for maritime operations was revealed in February 1943:

> This entire issue suffers from a complete lack of planning, which had prevailed in previous years. Also from the smug complacency which surrounded the Director General of Luftwaffe Equipment at the time, and the general reluctance to point out defects at the right time. . . . I must apportion to myself a little of the blame, insomuch as my confidence was sadly misplaced. Anyway we are here and now to formulate a definite plan for our bombers.[247]

Definite plan or not, the time had already passed in which a reliable and effective four-engined bomber could have turned the war for the Germans at sea, and despite Göring's magnanimous acceptance of "a little of the blame," it is clear that the decision to cancel the earlier heavy bomber types was his alone. Moreover, once the He 177 project was set in motion, his attention to it was woefully inadequate, to the point of outright negligence. Nowhere is this attitude more neatly illustrated than on the occasion of his failure to attend a meeting with Heinkel regarding a replacement for the He 177, simply because he decided to spend the day at a well-known Viennese jewelry shop.[248] Alongside the baneful influence of Udet's dive-bombing obsession, Göring's slapdash attitude prevented Germany from producing the *Piratenflugzeuge* it so desperately needed. Nevertheless, Göring may well have placed more stress on naval aircraft had his leader not been so sure that a war with Britain could be easily avoided and placed a greater emphasis on maritime strategy rather than that of a Continental nature. And yet it was Hitler's Continental strategy that would invigorate, if ever so briefly, Luftflotte 5's role in the war when, with the fate of the Third Reich hanging in the balance on the eastern front, the Führer ordered Germany's northernmost air fleet to strike against Anglo-American convoys plying Arctic waters.

6

Luftflotte 5 Versus Arctic Convoys

Herr Reichmarschall! I beg to report the destruction of Convoy PQ 17.
Generaloberst Hans-Jürgen Stumpff, 12 July 1942

At 0315 on 22 June 1941, Hitler launched the greatest assault in the history of warfare. German armies, totaling around 3.6 million German and allied troops, 3,350 tanks, and 2,700 aircraft, supported by more than 7,000 artillery pieces, drove deep wedges into a front stretching from Arctic waters to the Black Sea. It is little wonder that Hitler boasted, "When Operation *Barbarossa* is launched the world will hold its breath."[1]

The detailed planning for the invasion of the Soviet Union had taken shape under Hitler's Directive 21, dated 18 December 1940, which stipulated that the general aim of *Barbarossa* was "to crush Soviet Russia in a lightning campaign," with the final goal the erection of "a barrier against Asiatic Russia on the general line Volga-Archangel."[2] To achieve this, the bulk of the Red Army stationed in western Russia was to be destroyed in a series of daring operations spearheaded by armored thrusts, which would prevent the organized withdrawal of intact units. While by far the greater part of the invasion would be undertaken by Army Groups North, Center, and South along a front stretching from the Baltic to the Black Sea, a further sector would be established in the Far North, the Karelian Front. Decidedly the smaller arm in the invasion, *General der Infanterie* Nikolaus von Falkenhorst's Gruppe XXI was mainly intended to protect Norway, including the Petsamo area's nickel mines and the Arctic highway running across the top of the Scandinavian Peninsula. Once this was accomplished, his forces were to advance with their Finnish "brothers-in-arms" against the Murmansk railway to prevent the passage of supplies south from Russia's Arctic ports to Leningrad and Moscow.

187

According to *Barbarossa,* the Luftwaffe's role was to make available "supporting forces of such strength that the army will be able to bring land operations to a rapid conclusion." Yet the ever-increasing demands on Göring's air units made this more than a little difficult. Of a total frontline strength of 3,340 combat planes in 1941, the defense of the Reich accounted for 190 machines, the Mediterranean was fitted out with some 370 (Fliegerkorps X and Fliegerführer Afrika), while those deployed in the western theater accounted for 780, of which 680 were deployed with Luftflotte 3. Where the northernmost front was concerned, of Stumpff's total complement of 180 aircraft, Luftflotte 5 was forced to make do with 120 aircraft for its duties in western Norway.[3] In sum, then, this left the eastern front with only 1,945 planes, no more than 50 percent of the Luftwaffe's total complement.

As with the war against Britain in 1940, Luftflotte 5 found itself at the periphery of the main event at hand. By the time the invasion of the Soviet Union was about to begin, the air fleet had been reorganized, with Luftgau Norwegen's headquarters situated in Oslo; Fliegerführer Stavanger covering the central and northern parts of the country; Jagdfliegerführer Norwegen controlling the air fleet's fighter units; and Fliegerführer Kirkenes established at the very top of the country with airfields at Kirkenes and Banak.[4] Of Luftflotte 5's 180 aircraft, 60 would be dedicated to operations on the Karelian Front, which was anticipated to extend up to 350 kilometers in length and nearly 900 kilometers in depth from Fliegerführer Kirkenes's main base of operations at Banak to the farthest target, Archangel.[5] Under the command of *Oberst* Andreas Nielsen, Fliegerführer Kirkenes was by far the weakest force involved in *Barbarossa,* constituting only 10 Ju 88 bombers of KG 30, 30 dive-bombers, 10 JG 77 Bf 109 fighters, a *Schwarm* (five aircraft) of ZG 76 Bf 110s, 10 reconnaissance planes, and an antiaircraft artillery battalion.[6] In comparison, Luftflotten 1, 2, and 4 numbered 430, 910, and 600 aircraft, respectively.[7] In addition to raiding the ports of Murmansk and Archangel, Germany's northernmost air fleet was charged with attacking Soviet shipping, providing close air support for the army, interdicting troop movements on the Murmansk railroad, bringing about the destruction of Soviet air facilities, and destroying the lock controlling the Baltic–White Sea Canal.[8]

It is clear that these 60 aircraft were totally inadequate to the task at hand. Quite apart from their small numbers, the region's climate, the terrain, and the emphasis placed on resources for more important sectors along the front meant that Germans were never able to achieve their offensive goals in this theater. In general, the land war in the Far North was a dismal affair, carried out in some of the harshest conditions of the entire war on any front. "There is no favourable season for operations," noted Earl Ziemke in a standard work on the land war in the Far North, and climate and "terrain are always enemies, particularly to offensive operations."[9] Although winter provided the best time for advances, since hard snow at least provided some sure footing for soldiers, the perpetual darkness made large-scale actions impossible. The only really favorable time was in late winter, when daylight hours were on the increase and underfoot conditions still relatively firm. Nevertheless, the period available for advance was very short, and once the spring thaw set in, operations were not possible. The ground forces employed along the Karelian Front were, like their aerial counterparts, never large enough to make any great gains in the Far North, and at no time did they break the northern stretch of the Murmansk rail line.[10] Although the main weight of aerial operations was, as we shall see, directed at closing the Arctic Sea route running from Iceland to Murmansk, the main land-based effort was designed to close the second and subsequent leg for supplies dispatched by the Anglo-American powers: the rail link between Murmansk and Moscow. Indeed, this line not only was important as the main artery through which war materials were pumped to the heart of the Soviet military machine but also was one of the main means by which the Red Army was able to fend off the German and Finnish advance in the Far North.[11] Unlike their German and Finnish opponents, who labored under a transportation system that at best could be described as second-rate in comparison, the Soviets were able to assemble, mobilize, and deploy troops along the entire length of the Murmansk railway to points of main effort whenever required.[12]

With the failure of Operation *Silberfuchs (Silver Fox),* whose main objectives included an attempt to overrun the rail line and occupy Murmansk in 1941, and the abandonment of *Lachsfang (Salmon Catch)*—another bid to sever the rail line in the following year—the Germans attempted to break the main north-south artery by other means.[13] The Luftwaffe bombed the line and its bridges and made numerous attacks on the port of Murmansk and other railroad stations. But these attempts, and those made by commando-style units dropped in to attack the line, were only partially successful, and the line was quickly repaired. In short, the terrain and climate, plus the limited ground and air resources dedicated to the region, prevented any great gains. In fact, the only significant reinforcement of German resources would be dictated not by a growing demand for ground support but rather by the defense of Norway against an anticipated Allied expedition, followed by operations against the Arctic convoys. Stumpff's air fleet, which had proved its mettle during *Weserübung,* would get a chance to recapture some of its past glory in attacks on Anglo-American convoys on their way to the Soviet Union's northern ports.

HITLER'S INVASION PARANOIA

Although Hitler would later proudly claim that he had always planned to utilize Norway for U-boat and Luftwaffe operations against Allied convoys to northern Russia, in reality the strengthening of naval and air defenses in the region in late 1941 and early 1942 was initially undertaken for defensive rather than offensive purposes. The groundwork, paving the way for the subsequent attacks on the Arctic convoys, was based on Hitler's fear of an Allied attack on Norway.[14] The Führer's concern was fueled by a British raid in the Lofotens area in early March 1941, which resulted in industrial plants being destroyed, vessels sunk and damaged, a number of Norwegian collaborators ("Quislings") being taken prisoner, and the British gathering valuable intelligence. The incursion revealed the palpable weaknesses of the German defenses and poor organizational structure in Norway. On 8 March, the British raid was the first item on the German strategic agenda, and the OKW chief delivered a report to Hitler detailing the current status of the coastal defenses and what measures could be taken to reinforce them.[15] Although by the end of the year only marginal improvements had been implemented, on 25 December 1941, on the basis of clandestine information received that indicated a possible Anglo-American initiative, OKW called for an up-to-date assessment of the Germans' ability to thwart such an attempt.[16] Falkenhorst's subsequent report said his forces would be too weak to repel an incursion and requested 12,000 reinforcements to bring his units up to full strength and provide reserves for defensive positions in depth.

As if to highlight again the vulnerability of the German situation, the British launched their second Lofotens raid on 27 December.[17] In the foray, a cruiser and destroyer force shelled and landed troops on the Lofotens and two other locations along the coast. Although the assault was brief, a jittery OKW was somewhat alarmed by the attack, feeling that it was perhaps an indication of things to come and part of an Allied probing action designed to ascertain likely weak points along the Norwegian coastline for a subsequent invasion.[18] As an examination of the Naval Staff's war diary reveals, whispers of an impending operation were widespread:

> 30 December 1941: British rumors, spread intentionally, spoke of a larger action in the next few days in order to occupy permanently the Lofoten Islands, the Vester Aalen Islands, and Bodö. Eighty U.S. transports would be used for this operation.
>
> 2 January 1942: According to an allegedly very reliable report from an agent, Swedish military circles believe that a British landing attempt in Scandinavia would most likely take place in the following areas: Alta Fjord, Tana Fjord, Varanger Fjord, Honningvaag. . . . To this would be added the political effect on the Scandinavian countries. The period between the beginning of March and the beginning of May is a likely time for such a British operation.
>
> 3 January 1942: According to a reliable agent report, Great Britain and Russia have agreed to launch a joint offensive against Finland.
>
> 6 January 1942: The naval attaché, Stockholm, quotes an unidentified source to the effect that there is talk at the British embassy in Stockholm about an impending action against Narvik and the ore railroad.[19]

Hitler was clearly shaken by the prospect. As the year came to an end, he warned Keitel and Raeder: "If the British go about things properly they will attack northern Norway at several points. In an all-out attack by their fleet and landing troops, they will try to displace us there, take Narvik if possible, and thus exert pressure on Sweden and Finland."[20] So desperate was Hitler to prevent such a possibility that he ordered *Scharnhorst, Gneisenau,* and the cruiser *Prinz Eugen,* languishing in Brest, to make a dramatic dash through the Channel for deployment in the defense of Norway.[21] The Germans envisaged that they could also be used in operations against Arctic convoys, though how suited to this task they would be was as yet unknown. Nevertheless, should it not be possible to make a surprise breakout, Hitler contemplated decommissioning the ships so that their guns and crews could be used in reinforcing Norwegian defenses.

By early 1942, Hitler's concern had become a fixation. In a conference with Raeder on 12 January, he now asserted "that if a strong task force of battleships and cruisers, practically the entire German fleet, were stationed along the Norwegian coast, it could, in conjunction with the Luftwaffe, make a decisive contribution toward the defense of the area of Norway."[22] Ten days later, at his next meeting with Raeder, Hitler grandly proclaimed that Norway was "the decisive theater of the war." "On the basis of latest reports," noted the Naval Staff diary, "the Führer is absolutely sure that Great Britain and the U.S. are bent on attacking northern Norway in order to bring about a decisive turn in the outcome of the course of the war."[23] He demanded that both the army and the Luftwaffe strengthen their forces in Norway, while the navy was instructed to "exert the utmost effort to nip the British plans in the bud," ordering "all available U-boats" to proceed there immediately. Only when told of the considerable successes being achieved by a very small number of boats in American waters the next day did he back away from placing "all available U-boats" in northern Norway. Nevertheless, on 24 January, OKM ordered an extremely reluctant Dönitz to send eight boats into the Iceland-Faroes-Scotland area for the protection of Norway, and by 15 February twenty U-boats were expected to be stationed in the region (with six in Norwegian waters, two in a state of operational readiness in Narvik or Tromsö, two at Trondheim, and a further couple at Bergen).[24] For the land-based defenses, Falkenhorst was promised his 12,000 men plus twenty so-called fortress battalions of older men wielding captured weapons and numbering 18,000 in all. In addition, he would receive the 3rd Mountain Division by the spring of 1942 and a Panzer division formed along with a strengthening of German coastal defenses.[25] In scenes reminiscent of March 1940, Hitler even thought of establishing a single command for operations in Norway under the same candidate for the position prior to *Weserübung,* Kesselring.[26] Unfortunately for the Germans, however, this would never be carried out. Operations in the region, though successful to a limited degree against the convoys, would have been far more efficiently executed had a joint staff with a single theater commander been established, especially under the able leadership of Kesselring.

CHURCHILL'S NORDIC MANIA

There can be little doubt that, given the opportunity, Churchill would have jumped at the chance to have another go at Norway.[27] His interest in Norwegian operations began before the German invasion of April 1940 and would continue to occupy a special place within his fertile imagination until at least 1944. Following the German invasion of the Soviet Union in June 1941, Churchill received a telegram from Stalin urging the establishment of two fronts in the west, one on the French coast and the other in the Arctic region. Such a campaign in the Far North would not only relieve some of the pressure on the Red Army in the east but also, with the beginning of the Arctic convoys, secure their safe passage. From this point on, Churchill's mania for Nordic operations increased. Under the general code name *Jupiter,* the British prime minister hatched a number of schemes centered on the Far North. For example, in October 1941 *Ajax* was born, entailing the capture of Trondheim with the aid of an imaginary Norwegian underground army, followed by an advance on the Swedish border. In November 1941, *Ajax* was followed by *Marrow,* which called for an assault on Petsamo and Kirkenes. For this operation the bulk of the forces would be drawn from the Red Army and the Norwegian forces based in Britain, with support provided by the Royal Navy and a significant number of British aircraft.

Other plans followed, based on his opinion that "we could begin to roll the map of Hitler's Europe down from the top!" But Churchill found little support from the Americans, who, like many others, felt there was little to be gained from an operation in such a peripheral area and plenty to lose in men and material. At best, *Jupiter* would have been on a par with the Italian campaign, essentially an advance going nowhere, but at worst it had all the hallmarks of Churchill's ill-conceived Gallipoli disaster of the Great War.[28] A Chiefs of Staff report of 7 August 1942 realistically concluded that *Jupiter* "is an extremely hazardous operation . . . and the result might be a military disaster of the first magnitude. . . . [Its] risks would only be acceptable if politically the results to be achieved were judged to be of the highest importance."[29] Therefore, in 1942 *Jupiter* as an independent operation gradually fell further into disfavor among sensible men. Although in subsequent years it was revived briefly as a possible alternative to, or deception for, *Torch* and *Overlord,* it never looked like taking off because the Allies were heavily committed elsewhere.[30]

Nevertheless, the fear of such an Allied undertaking was very real in Hitler's mind, and the buildup of forces in Norway went ahead at a great pace. On land by the end of April 1942, Falkenhorst was pleased to see that nearly all his requests for additional manpower had been met and coastal defenses were well on the way to being substantially strengthened. The transfer of naval vessels was also carried out with considerable haste. The first major surface ship to arrive was *Tirpitz,* docking at Trondheim on 16 January, and over the next few months a significant proportion of the German surface fleet made its way into Norwegian waters. By

May, the total Norwegian-based force included one battleship, three heavy cruisers, eight destroyers, four torpedo boats, and twenty U-boats positioned along the Norwegian coast from Trondheim to Kirkenes.[31] Although these forces did not include *Scharnhorst* and *Gneisenau,* which in their famous run through the Channel had been damaged by British mines, the German naval presence in Norway was formidable.[32]

The German naval commanders were, however, fully aware that this force not only represented a potential threat to any Allied landing or naval operation in the region but also remained particularly vulnerable to air attack. It was in this context that the navy pushed strenuously for a buildup of Luftwaffe strength in northern Norway. Even before *Tirpitz* had docked in Trondheim, the navy was adamant that adequate "air reconnaissance as well as a readily available force of bombers" be on hand, since the big battleship would be vulnerable should a convoy escorted by "several heavy cruisers and destroyers appear."[33] As Hubert Schmundt, *Admiral Nordmeer,* observed unhappily on 22 December 1941, the number of aircraft available for distant reconnaissance in his region was so small that between 1 and 15 December only two operations could be carried out by a couple of Ju 88s.[34] However, soon after the second Lofotens raid, calls were being made by the navy for the focus of Luftflotte 5's effort to be shifted northward. On 30 December, the *Admiral Nordmeer* requested Stumpff to reinforce his units in northwestern Norway with pursuit planes and bombers. Luftflotte 5's commander was, however, reluctant to make such transfers, which would further dilute his already thinly spread defensive line in the west of the country; he pointed out that even though his air fleet would operate "with all means at its disposal from Banak and Stavanger, this depended on the situation, including the prevailing weather conditions."[35] Actual transfers of his precious units to Bardufloss, even temporarily, would rest on the prevailing demands in eastern and western areas.

Nevertheless, in accordance with Hitler's wishes and the navy's concerns, a slow buildup of airpower in the region began with the transfer of the catapult ship *Schwabenland* to northern Norway, to expand the reconnaissance radius available to the navy, and the transfer to Sola of the torpedo-equipped He 115 floatplanes of KüFlGr 1./406.[36] This navy squadron was subordinated to Stumpff's command and, as the Naval Staff noted with an air of resignation, signified another depletion of their own airpower resources, since "the possibility of ever reassigning the squadron to the Commander Naval Air may be considered practically nonexistent once such a step has been taken."[37] More significantly, by the end of December 1941, the third bomber group of KG 30 had been transferred to Norway from Holland, and early in the New Year Stumpff received a welcome addition to his overworked and underequipped units with the transfer to Trondheim from Bordeaux of another squadron of KG 40's long-range Condors.[38]

Still, Luftflotte 5 was hardly a great force to be reckoned with. As the chief of Naval Staff pointed out on 24 January 1942, regarding the air defense of Norway, the "most important prerequisite for an effective defense against enemy landing operations is the possession of a strong airpower. In this respect the present shortage of German air forces is particularly deplorable."[39] The relatively slow and meager consolidation of air units in the Far North was to be expected, explained Göring to Hitler on 22 January, given the overall shortage of aircraft and the difficulties associated with the fact that the landing grounds in the Far North were relatively small and few in number.[40] Nevertheless, at the end of the month Göring was prepared to order the establishment of an aerial torpedo wing. According to the plan, Luftflotte 5 would receive one bomber group with three squadrons of He 111s equipped with torpedoes, and two further groups would be deployed with Luftflotte 4 and the commanding general, Armed Forces South.[41]

ARCTIC CONVOYS

Up until this point, little attention had been paid to the eleven convoys that had already successfully made the journey from Britain to Russia, since the main focus of the buildup remained defensive and the convoys prior to March 1942 had been relatively small (averaging a mere eight vessels per convoy) and therefore were of only peripheral interest to the German forces gathering in the region.[42] Moreover, even the Luftwaffe's limited resources were essentially hamstrung over Arctic waters, since the uninterrupted darkness of the winter months made antishipping operations particularly troublesome. Thus, before March 1942, Stumpff's air units were better employed in attacking Murmansk and the rail line.

While the Arctic route had not been overburdened with vessels carrying supplies for Stalin's armed forces in 1941, the numbers in each individual convoy steadily rose in 1942 and would eventually peak in November with PQ 18's forty ships (Russia-bound convoys were prefixed "PQ," while the return convoys were designated "QP"). This increase in volume certainly had an impact on Hitler, who was now faced with the realization that, after the failure to take Moscow in 1941, the war on the eastern front would not be concluded in the near future. Naturally enough, his long-term planning increasingly began to focus on the Soviet Union's primary and most direct source of Allied aid, the Arctic supply corridor. By at least one German estimate, the Arctic route accounted for more than half of the Soviets' incoming supplies in 1942. Of a total of 2.3 million tons of supplies shipped into the Soviet Union, those entering the White Sea ports of Murmansk and Archangel equaled 1.2 million tons, while the Persian ports took in 600,000 tons, and the Soviet Union's Far Eastern conduit points handled 500,000 tons. Of the supplies coming in through the northern waters, 49 percent was made up of industrial raw materials, 20 percent was food, 18 percent was war materials, and the remaining 13 percent was mineral oil. Of the all-important war material this included 1,880 aircraft, 2,350 tanks, 8,300 trucks, 6,400 other vehicles, and 2,250 field guns.[43] With this volume of material being brought into the region for use against his forces, Hitler decided that he might as well use those naval and air units he had amassed for defensive operations against the convoys. Thus in northern Norway, Hitler's Continental strategy meshed with his Scandinavian fears as he became increasingly conscious of the importance of seaborne supplies to the Soviet war effort.

That the newly arrived forces were still finding their feet in the Far North in March 1942 was demonstrated by the potentially disastrous sortie against PQ 12. To demonstrate the danger posed by the presence of *Tirpitz* in the region, the Germans decided to send the battleship and a handful of destroyers against the British convoy. On 5 March, PQ 12—consisting of fifteen merchantmen, escorted by a cruiser, two destroyers, and two other vessels—was spotted near Jan Mayen by a Condor flying from Sola.[44] *Tirpitz* slipped its Trondheim moorings the next day, supported by three destroyers. Over the following three days, as a result of inadequate aerial reconnaissance, the battleship and its escorts floundered blindly around the region between Jan Mayen and Bear Island, unable to make contact with PQ 12 or with QP 8, which was also in the area.[45] Distressingly, the pride of the German navy was subjected to a frightening attack on 8 April by obsolete Albacore torpedo bombers flying from *Victorious,* part of a strong covering force including two battleships, *King George V* and *Duke of York,* and the battle cruiser *Renown.* While some of these vessels lingered at the edge of the action, the greater number cruised some 80 to 160 kilometers southward of the convoy, in a position to bring *Tirpitz* to battle. Fortunately for the Germans, all the aerial torpedoes missed their target, and a potentially disastrous turning point in the war at sea had been averted. Had the British planes been successful, the whole naval balance would have been completely altered, since the mere presence of the battleship in northern waters tied down considerable Royal Navy strength.[46] In general, the failure of the *Tirpitz* sortie would lead to a reluctance to sally forth with the battleship in future actions against convoys, especially since its primary task, reasoned Raeder, was defensive. This, in turn, led to a greater emphasis than had originally been intended on the navy's U-boat arm and the air units of Luftflotte 5 in the offensive operations that were to follow.

Just as bad weather probably saved the *Tirpitz* from an unfavorable battle with the Home Fleet, an absence of German reconnaissance aircraft prevented the battleship from striking at the convoy. Luftwaffe participation had been particularly dismal all around, even in the defense of *Tirpitz.* The sole attack on *Victorious* was made by three Ju 88s on 9 March, after a BV floatplane had sighted and shadowed the aircraft carrier from 1015 onward. The weak bomber attack at 1545 was, unsurprisingly, a complete failure, and after dropping their bombs wide of the target, the Ju 88s were sent packing by *Victorious*'s antiaircraft fire and defensive fighters. A force of nine Stukas was also dispatched, but unfavorable weather forced them to break off their mission.[47]

The difficulties experienced by the dive-bombers would be repeated throughout the attacks on convoys and reflected the extremely harsh climatic conditions

10. The Arctic convoys.

prevailing in the Arctic and sub-Arctic regions where Stumpff's aircraft would have to fly.[48] At the western end of the convoy route between Greenland and Norway lies one of the world's most turbulent stretches of water. Over this 1,440-kilometer expanse, high winds laden with snow, sleet, and hail push the heavy seas around the North Cape into the Barents Sea, where waters seldom exceed four degrees centigrade. The chances of survival for the hunter or the hunted, once sunk or downed in Arctic waters, were very low unless rescue occurred within a very short time. For a convoy, the cold waters and frigid air temperatures combined to produce a potentially deadly layer of ice over the surface of vessels as they plowed their way through heavy seas. Unless it was chipped off immediately, ice from sea spray accumulated so rapidly that smaller ships could quickly become unstable and vulnerable to capsizing in rough weather.

Added to these icy Arctic waters are the much warmer waters generated in the Gulf of Mexico, known as the Gulf Stream but rechristened the North Atlantic Drift as they slip northeast past the Florida Keys into the Atlantic. After bathing Britain's southwestern coast, the North Atlantic Drift sweeps between Scotland and Iceland, still bearing a residue of its subtropical origins. At the top of Norway it splits into two flows, one pushing north above Bear Island and then over the western coast of Spitzbergen, while the southern stream follows the Murman coast before entering the Barents Sea. The mixing of these two currents, one very cold and the other somewhat warmer and more saline, results in great swaths of fog swirling across the region. This unique phenomenon produced conditions both beneficial and restrictive for the German forces in the north. Although the fog would certainly hinder Luftwaffe pilots in their search for convoys, the blending of colder and warmer streams would make it almost impossible for the escorting vessels to effectively use sound detection apparatus in antisubmarine activities, since U-boat captains were able to hide their boats among the varying thermal layers and waters of differing densities.

In addition to these Arctic peculiarities, the region's northern boundary advances and contracts with the seasons. In the winter months, the ice shelf can expand southward from the Arctic Cap to within 80 kilometers of North Cape, while milder summer temperatures and the North Atlantic Drift can eat away at the ice shelf, until for a limited period it recedes so far north that ships can pass north of Spitzbergen. On top of this, for long periods the region is cloaked in either perpetual darkness or unbroken daylight during winter and summer, respectively, because of the area's high latitude. During winter this meant that despite shipping being forced to travel closer to the Norwegian coastline—and, therefore, to German air and naval bases—the long winter darkness provided shelter, making it particularly difficult for the Luftwaffe to locate convoys. Meanwhile, for periods on either side of these four months, the small number of hours of daylight severely restricted flying time.[49] However, although the summer months allowed Allied vessels to ply more distant waters, the pack ice still stretched far enough south to force the convoys within 480 kilometers of German air bases.[50] This, coupled with the lengthening hours of daylight, would be greatly exploited by the Luftwaffe in the months ahead, when around-the-clock operations would be possible.[51]

Notwithstanding the advantages of the Far North's long summer days, the Arctic was "from the flying standpoint extremely difficult," noted the Luftwaffe's own detailed guide to the region published in 1941.[52] Although the climatic conditions in Norway's most northern region vary from place to place, often dependent on the topography or latitude, on the whole they present considerable challenges to year-round aerial operations. On top of the fog, the unsettled and cloudy weather that predominates in all seasons can greatly restrict visibility. Low cloud above all the airfields was a determining factor in their usefulness at any given time and could make flying over the coastal regions nothing short of treacherous. Moreover, noted Werner Baumbach, the famous German bomber pilot who flew in Norway against the convoys, takeoffs and landings on cement and wooden runways in narrow valleys enclosed by hills and ridges over a thousand meters high—often lashed by extremely hazardous crosswinds—would "normally be regarded as lunacy."[53] Ironically, it was this poor weather, including the prevailing snow and leaden skies in the transition from winter to spring in March 1942, that not only grounded the Luftwaffe's forces but also probably helped save *Tirpitz* from meeting the Home Fleet and suffering the same fate as its sister ship, *Bismarck.*

Despite the late winter weather, Raeder was livid over the Luftwaffe's poor performance and concluded that only skillful "defensive maneuvers, coupled with good luck, were responsible for the *Tirpitz*'s escape." In his meeting of 12 March with Hitler, the *Großadmiral* pointed out that the extreme weakness of the German coastal defenses in northern waters was evidenced by the fact that the enemy dared to advance in these waters "without being smashed by the Luftwaffe." To improve the defensive situation, he made a number of recommendations to the Führer regarding airpower:

> Strong support from all our air units in the Norwegian area is, in the absence of aircraft carriers, an absolute prerequisite to the successful operation in the Arctic Ocean. (Air reconnaissance is needed, even if it should be at the expense of Fliegerführer Atlantic. Torpedo aircraft must be thrown into the fight.) . . . Therefore, our own naval forces should be held back at first, in order to ensure their availability for repulsing enemy landing attempts. They should be committed only after the enemy's exact position and strength have been accurately and unequivocally ascertained by air reconnaissance, and when there is sufficient support by the Luftwaffe. . . . The Luftwaffe must be ordered to wage relentless warfare against the enemy carriers.[54]

Aside from the Führer agreeing to inform Göring that Luftflotte 5 was to be reinforced and advised of the Luftwaffe's revised purpose and aims in the Far North, he also pushed for an acceleration of work on the never-to-be completed aircraft carrier *Graf Zeppelin.*[55]

The threat of carrier-borne aircraft to his precious battleship had not been lost on Hitler, who requested that work be stepped up on the sole surviving carrier of the four originally envisaged under the ambitious Z-Plan. How useful such vessels would have been to the German effort in the Battle of the Atlantic is a matter of some debate, but it is clear that with the premature arrival of war they could not all be completed, given the pressing needs for valuable war materials.[56] Although Eberhard Weichold, former director of the German Naval Academy, argued after the war that Germany would have benefited greatly from the possession of such vessels, it is clear, given the difficulty of supporting individual surface raiders at sea in 1939–1940, that it would have been beyond Germany's abilities to supply and provision a task force large enough to protect them. Thus, as soon as the Allies departed from Narvik in June 1940, the German leadership decided to cancel the development of *Zeppelin* and send its heavy armaments to Norway as part of the buildup of coastal defenses. Nevertheless, the reemergence of the idea of an aircraft carrier in 1942 reflected German appreciation of the Allied escort carriers in convoy work and the effectiveness of Japanese carriers in the Pacific.

Wishing to emulate such successes, Hitler pressed for the completion of the half-finished *Zeppelin* languishing at Gotenhafen. Nonetheless, the navy was realistic and, despite Hitler's enthusiasm, realized that even with an injection of additional resources the vessel would not be ready until late 1943 at the earliest.[57] In addition, naval estimates calculated that even then there would be only ten converted fighters and twenty-two converted bombers and reconnaissance planes ready to fly from the carrier once completed, while the adaptation of torpedo bombers was still some way off. A more practical option, the creation of a series of auxiliary carriers in the mold of Allied escort carriers, was also put forward in 1943, in which the liners *Europa* and *Potsdam* and the warships *Seydlitz* and *Gneisenau* would be converted to carriers that could accommodate eighteen to forty-two aircraft.[58] Despite these grand proposals, in actuality the whole scheme was plagued by manpower problems as increasing numbers of shipyard workers were siphoned off for frontline duties, while other more important projects always pushed the completion of *Zeppelin* and the auxiliary carriers into the background. Moreover, even if these vessels had been ready to put to sea in 1944, they, like the He 177, would have arrived too late to influence the outcome of the war at sea.

GEARING UP FOR THE ASSAULT

Meanwhile, in mid-March 1942, Hitler took up Raeder's concerns by issuing a directive for the intensification of the war against Arctic convoys. This order was based on the need to weaken the Soviet Union's powers of resistance and prevent a possible buildup of Allied forces in northern Russia that could facilitate an enemy landing on Norway's Arctic coast. To this end, an expansion of Luftwaffe and navy strength was called for in order to "bring to a stop the enemy's until now undisturbed merchant traffic between the Anglo-American states and Russia in the Arctic Sea" and the elimination of the enemy's naval threat in the region.[59] Göring obediently fell in behind Hitler's wishes and issued an order to Stumpff instructing that the battle against the convoy route to Russia was to be at the "foreground" of Luftflotte 5 efforts, and to carry out this task the air fleet was to work in the "closest" cooperation with the navy.[60] For the "frictionless" achievement of this goal, Luftflotte 5 was made responsible for maintaining a tightly uniform command and was to guarantee faultless signals communication with the responsible naval commanders in the area. In addition, a simplification of the command structures and the reporting systems between both staffs was to be established. To ensure that both the Luftwaffe and the navy were fully cognizant of their obligations, a conference was to be held and binding agreements formed.[61] The ideal solution, and one favored by the navy, was the establishment of a combined command, but with little enthusiasm for this from within the Luftwaffe, it had to settle for swapping liaison officers.[62]

Alongside these command considerations, more aircraft were to be transferred into the region. To increase the air fleet's striking power, 2/KG 30 was to be prepared for their shift to the region, and the general staff officer (*General-quartiermeister*) of KG 30 was ordered to accelerate the operational readiness of his force. The scouting forces were to be strengthened by the arrival of one of Aufkl.Fl.Gr 125's reconnaissance squadrons, and for long-range reconnaissance, further Condors of KG 40 were to fly north from France. A corresponding strengthening of the ground organization was demanded "without delay."[63]

By late March, Luftflotte 5 had been divided into three main forces: Fliegerführer Nord (Ost) based at Kirkenes, Fliegerführer Lofotens sited at Bardufloss, and Fliegerführer Nord (West) at Sola. The largest of these local tactical commands was *Oberst* Alexander Holle's Fliegerführer Nord (Ost). Containing the bulk of Luftflotte 5's units, this air command was assigned the dual role of supporting the army on land and attacks on convoys at sea. In addition, Fliegerführer Nord (Ost) would, as conditions and forces allowed, raid the Murmansk and Archangel ports. Although the Kirkenes base was home to the greater part of Holle's forces (2/JG 5, 10/ZG 5, 1/StG 5, 1./(F)124), other units were dispersed to Petsamo (5 and 6./JG 5, 3/KG 26), Banak (2 and 3/KG 30, 1./(F)22), and Billefjord (1./KüKlGr 125). Fliegerführer Lofotens, under the command of *Oberst* Hans Roth, did not have any permanent forces under its control. Rather, units would be assigned as the situation demanded and at the beginning of the campaign against shipping included only two coastal patrol squadrons, one based at Trondheim (3./KüFlGr 906) and the other at Tromsö (1./KüFlGr 123). At Stavanger, Fliegerführer Nord (West) was assigned the all-important early reconnaissance role and attacks on convoys south of a line stretching from Trondheim westward to the Shetlands and Iceland. To carry out these tasks, the force was allocated a reconnaissance squadron and group (1./(F) 22 and 1/KG 40), the latter being made up of Condors, two coastal patrol squadrons (1 and 2./KüFlGr 406), and a weather reconnaissance squadron. The gradual buildup had seen Stumpff's air fleet grow from a paltry 152 aircraft in January 1942 to 175 in February; now, one month later, it rested at 221 combat planes.[64]

The part each of these commands would play in the upcoming attacks was fairly straightforward. Fliegerführer Nord (West), upon being informed by intelligence reports that a convoy was being assembled, would put up its long-distance reconnaissance aircraft in order to scour the ports of northern Scotland and Iceland and the entry points into Arctic waters. Once vessels were sighted, these aircraft and those of the other two air commands were expected to keep constant contact with the convoy. Due to the extremely difficult weather conditions in the region this was not always possible, but should contact be lost, a probable course for the convoy was to be plotted based on the last aerial sighting; from this, intensive overlapping reconnaissance flights would be made until it was relocated. Once an assembling convoy had been sighted, all aircraft in the region were themselves assembled for the assault on the Allied vessels as they made their way eastward. The initial attacks would be undertaken by Fliegerführer Lofotens until the convoy crossed a line reaching from the North Cape to Spitzbergen Island. From this point the convoy fell into the range of Fliegerführer Nord (Ost) bombers. Fliegerführer Nord (Ost)'s sole objective was the destruction of the convoy, and without express orders from Stumpff himself, not a single aircraft was to be used in support of ground forces along the Finno-Russian front while this task remained uncompleted. At this juncture of the operation, and in order to maximize effort, the forces under Fliegerführer Lofotens now came under Fliegerführer Nord (Ost)'s command, and aircraft based at Bardufloss would fly successively to Kirkenes or Petsamo so that they could take advantage of the closer proximity of these fields to the action as the convoy moved farther eastward. The general idea was to hit the convoy continuously from the time it first came within range of the bombers based in the Far North until it docked at Murmansk or Archangel.

Stumpff's efforts to bring the greater part of these forces to bear from the third week of March until the end of May against the Murmansk-bound convoys (PQ 13, 14, 15, and 16) and those making the return run (QP 9, 10, 11, and 12) were largely ineffectual, thanks to the weather prevailing over the region in this period. Of the 16 merchant ships sunk en route to the Soviet Union, the Luftwaffe accounted for a dozen, while only 5 of the outward-sailing vessels were sunk, and of these only 2 were directly attributable to Luftwaffe action. In all, the Germans had succeeded in sinking no more than 21 out of a total of 166 merchantmen that sailed from Britain and Russia during these months. Indeed, German anticonvoy activity was only marginally more successful in preventing Allied ships reaching their destinations than bad weather, which alone forced 16 of PQ 14's ships to abandon their voyage.

Attacks on shipping in early April 1942 were thwarted by the spring thaw, which wreaked havoc on the northern airfields, while those undertaken in May had to contend with abysmal weather. For example, in accordance with Göring's 15 March order, the Luftwaffe attempted not only to maintain contact with PQ 13 but also to lead the U-boats to the convoy via a wireless-direction frequency, only to have bad weather force contact to be broken off. These difficulties were also compounded by the fact that gales forced the convoy to scatter, making it impossible to locate in the long hours of darkness, at a time when German surface vessels were only just putting to sea and too far from the main area of action. Weather conditions of this sort greatly frustrated Stumpff's efforts and meant that attacks on any given convoy had a decidedly halfhearted appearance. Assaults often were undertaken by niggardly formations seldom numbering more than a dozen planes and usually many fewer. This, of course, presented the defending escorts with the opportunity to concentrate their fire on only a handful of attacking aircraft, which resulted in the shooting down of a number of Luftflotte 5 planes during April and May.

The situation was not altogether gloomy, since in these two months the navy and the Luftwaffe had ample opportunity to iron out a number of interservice problems that would lay a good cooperative framework for action against PQ 17 and 18. By way of illustration, although the navy's after-action report for operations against PQ 14 noted that "low cloud cover" had "prevented sustained attacks" by the Luftwaffe, overall cooperation had been "frictionless," especially between U-boats and aircraft with regard to direction-finding work.[65] Likewise, during the action against PQ 15 and QP 11, *Admiral Nordmeer* was quick to note that despite the Luftwaffe's excellent reconnaissance having to be curtailed at times because of the terrible weather, "no difficulties were encountered in the cooperation of the Luftwaffe with the U-boats and also with the destroyers."[66] It does appear from these entries that local *Fliegerführer* commanders and their U-boat counterparts had developed an effective cooperative arrangement at a tactical level in the Far North. As we shall see, however, at a higher level, a yawning gulf still existed between how the navy and Luftwaffe top brass approached larger actions involving surface vessels in the region.

On top of these achievements, the German attacks on PQ 16 (which accounted for half of the ships sunk by the Luftwaffe from April to late May) showed that the gradual buildup of strength and improving weather were increasingly tipping the scales against the Allies. The convoy of thirty-five ships (totaling 200,000 tons) was first sighted on the morning of 25 May about 195 kilometers east of Jan Mayen Island, steaming in an easterly direction. The escort initially consisted of a cruiser, five destroyers, and eight other vessels, but this was soon supplemented by four cruisers. The first success was made by a U-boat the following day, while the Luftwaffe's main effort would take place on 27 April, just as Hitler, in another fit of Norwegian paranoia, made it known that he expected an immediate attack on Norway and accordingly ordered as many ships as possible "be sent to the bottom, so as to forestall any intended landing."[67] In obedience to his Führer, Stumpff put the largest formation of German aircraft so far seen in the Far North into the air against the PQ 16, now situated southeast of Bear Island. Flying from the northern Norwegian airfields were not only bombers and Stukas but also the freshly arrived torpedo bombers.

As noted earlier, the Germans had only taken an interest in utilizing aircraft as torpedo carriers in December 1941, when the establishment of such a force was begun with elements of KG 26. In January 1942, squadrons from this bomber wing were sent to Grosseto in central Italy for training, and by May the first units were beginning to arrive in northern Norway.[68] Junkers 88s and He 111s had been found suitable for the low-flying delivery of torpedos, and twelve trained crews had arrived at Bardufloss on 1 May to fly KG 26 torpedo-adapted He 111s, along with sixty more standard Ju 88 bombers as part of the general strengthening of Stumpff's air fleet.[69]

Supplemented by these new forces, a total of 101 Ju 88s and 7 torpedo-carrying He 111s fell on the convoy in a series of well-executed waves.[70] While the Germans suffered relatively light losses (3 Ju 88s), the Luftwaffe crews reported inflicting heavy damage on the convoy. Nine merchant ships, totaling 62,000 tons, were said to have been definitely sunk, while a further six merchant ships, totaling 99,500 tons, were claimed to have suffered so badly at the hands of Luftflotte 5 that they were probably sunk. In addition, sixteen more merchantmen were claimed damaged. "Thus supplies to Russia from Britain and America have been dealt a severe blow," crowed the air fleet's diary.[71] Likewise, the Naval Staff were rapt with the results, concluding that the "enemy has learned unmistakably what risks he takes by bringing strong expeditionary forces into the range of the Luftwaffe."[72] All in all, there was some reason to believe that the whole convoy had been sent to the icy depths of the Arctic Ocean. Yet the blow, although grievous, was not as severe as the Luftwaffe suggested, since in reality only six ships had been sunk by aircraft (five by bombs and one by torpedo) and one merchantman forced to return home due to damage sustained.

Notwithstanding these exaggerated claims and the mistaken belief that PQ 17 was part of an expeditionary force, of the convoy's thirty-five ships, only twenty-seven made it to Murmansk and Archangel, that is, a loss of one-fifth of the convoy. U-boat participation had been slight; because of good visibility and constant daylight, they had been driven off by the escorting warships—and on one occasion by a German dive-bomber—before they could get close enough to attack.[73] Added to the Luftwaffe successes, though, were the valuable lessons learned in the attacks by bombers and torpedo-bearing He 111s, the latter of which had already sunk three vessels in their first outing against PQ 15 and one more against PQ 16. As a writer of the war diary of Luftflotte 5 concluded on 1 June 1942, the fight against PQ 16 had demonstrated that the "correct combination of torpedo and diving attacks could bring about special success at the cost of modest losses."[74] The general idea was to assault the clustered vessels in integrated high-level dive-bombing attacks and low-level torpedo runs in order to dissipate the firepower of the defending escorts.[75] The torpedo attacks by the He 111s were made by a formation in wide line abreast, and the "tin fish" would be simultaneously launched from all aircraft at a distance of some 100 meters from the merchant ships. Known as the *Goldene Zange* (Golden Comb), this method of attack was designed to take place at twilight, when the targets would be silhouetted against the sky.

AIR-SEA RESCUE

On the negative side, the operations had highlighted for Stumpff the weakness of his air-sea rescue force. Often ignored in airpower histories, but very much in the air fleet commander's thoughts in the days following the final assault on PQ 16, the sea rescue units were an integral and essential component of Luftflotte 5. Working alongside the navy, local lifeboat societies dotted along the coastline, and ships moving along the coast at any given time, the Luftwaffe's Seenotdienst (Sea Rescue Service) was charged with the task of recovering ship and aircraft crew from offshore waters. The Luftwaffe's sea rescue regions in Norway were broken into two commands: Seenotbereichs VIII (Stavanger), incorporating Stavanger, Bergen, and Trondheim; and Seenotbereichs IX (Kirkenes), which covered Tromsö, Bille Fjord, and Kirkenes.[76] Just as close cooperation with the navy was required for combat operations, the rescue of either naval or air personnel was dependent on the rapid transmission of information and timely deployment of either naval vessels or, more often than not, the Luftwaffe's sea rescue service, if the survivors were to be recovered before being claimed by the region's harsh natural elements. Luftflotte 5's sea rescue units, flying He 59 floatplanes and Do 18 and Do 24 seaplanes, rescued a considerable number of both German and Allied airmen and sailors.[77] From the beginning of the war until 1944, these air units rescued many Germans and an estimated 492 Allied aircrew, of whom 252 were picked up in 1943 alone.[78]

Despite the increase in aerial activity in the region, OKL, due to the general shortage of available crews everywhere, was not able to allocate more crews for sea rescue forces in Norway. Stumpff, however, tried to force the issue. In a handwritten note to Jeschonnek, the Luftwaffe's chief of General Staff pointed out that the continual deployment of his combat forces against convoys represented a considerable risk, since a forced landing in these waters demanded rapid recovery if the men were not to perish in the extremely low temperatures.[79] His crews "must be given a chance of rescue" if morale was to be maintained. Moreover, attacks on "PQ 16 have shown to our great regret," noted the air fleet's war diary on 30 May, "that the air sea rescue service available is inadequate for the vast amount of sea area and for major operations."[80] Yet when it became clear that Jeschonnek was unable to assign more resources to Norway for this purpose, Stumpff took the matter into his own hands by reorganizing his coastal reconnaissance units so that during the heat of battle they would be on standby to carry out emergency rescue operations. Certainly, this was a good compromise, since once the convoy came under assault by Stumpff's main fighting force, the reconnaissance He 115 floatplanes would play little part in the actual combat phase of the operation. This reorganization soon paid off not only for those Germans who were forced to ditch in the Arctic Ocean but also for their opponents. During the operations against PQ 17, the rescue aircraft of Seenotbereichs IX (Kirkenes) would recover thirty-four Allied survivors.[81]

Another problem facing the Luftwaffe in its Arctic endeavors was the growing strength of Soviet airpower in the region, resulting in increasingly stiff resistance at the eastern end of the convoys' passage and in repeated attacks on German airfields. For example, attacks on PQ 16 fell off after 27 May not only because Soviet destroyers joined the escort force in the final run to Murmansk but also because Soviet bombers were put above the convoy for added defense and fighters began to appear over the convoy on 29 May.[82] The increasing numbers of enemy planes in the region can be seen from the German claims for May, which ran to 162 aircraft, of which 113 were British-supplied Hurricanes.[83] On 28 May alone, Luftflotte 5 maintained having shot down 22 aircraft, apparently without any loss of its own.[84] Although these assertions were invariably too high, the growing numbers of Soviet aircraft were a worrying trend for Stumpff, who saw his airfields at Petsamo, Kirkenes, and Banak regularly coming under attack from enemy bombers and fighters. Forays of this nature were often timed to prevent German aircraft getting off the ground to attack the convoys. For instance, on 29 May, alongside attempts to jam the contact and tactical radio frequencies being used by Luftflotte 5, the Soviets launched raids with fairly small formations and single aircraft against Kirkenes.[85] These hit-and-run sorties were, as yet, not hugely destructive, but they taxed Stumpff's defensive reserves and made raids on Murmansk increasingly costly.

RÖSSELSPRUNG

During June, the air fleet's war diary records that not a single convoy was sighted, which was fortunate for pilots and their crews, since the weather over this four-week period was particularly unfavorable for operations. Attacks against harbor facilities continued for much of June in the face of an increasing Soviet airpower presence. In the background, training and familiarization with the integrated high dive-bomber and torpedo attack, the *Goldene Zange,* continued unabated in preparation for the next convoy. And all the while the German forces were slowly being built up. By the end of May, Stumpff had a 264-strong force at his disposal. The most potent weapon in the air fleet's armory was its strike arm of 103 Ju 88 bombers, 42 He 111 torpedo bombers, and 30 Stuka dive-bombers. For long-range reconnaissance, he could call on 8 Condors and 22 Ju 88s. In addition to these

Luftwaffe resources, he had at his disposal a further 44 BV 138 seaplanes for reconnaissance and 15 multipurpose floatplanes.[86]

For the navy, the situation in the Far North was particularly frustrating. Ever since the ill-fated deployment of *Tirpitz* against PQ 12, Raeder had been decidedly reluctant to chance his arm with the bulk of the German navy's surface force, and especially its prize battleship, until he felt air cover could be assured. Paralyzed by this uncertainty and the lack of fuel oil, the German fleet had failed to put to sea at all during the assault on PQ 16, while previous dashes from the fjords had been restricted to destroyer forces in relatively fleeting tip-and-run raids. Despite, or perhaps more because of, this dismal performance, the navy began planning a major operation utilizing the force now dispersed through Norway's northern fjords, just as a new allocation of 15,000 tons of fuel came through in June.[87] Since *Admiral* Rolf Carls, the commanding officer of Navy Group North, considered the pocket battleships decidedly unsuited to operating independently because of their inferior main armament, poor antiaircraft defenses, and relatively slow speed, which made them particularly vulnerable to either air attack or a major engagement with the Home Fleet, decisive results could be obtained only by bringing all German warships, including *Tirpitz*, to bear in a future thrust from their Nordic hiding places.[88]

Raeder agreed, and planning was initiated for just such an undertaking, codenamed Operation *Rösselsprung (Knight's Move)*. A plan for the operation was prepared by the Naval Staff on 9 June which divided the German surface fleet in Norway into two forces, the Drontheim-Gruppe, composed of *Tirpitz, Hipper,* and six destroyers; and the Narvik-Gruppe, made up of *Lützow, Scheer,* and another half dozen destroyers.[89] The main task of the surface fleet was nothing less than the rapid "destruction of the enemy merchant ships." Certainly, the forces proposed and eventually gathered together for *Rösselsprung* were formidable; *Tirpitz,* flying *Admiral* Otto Schniewind's flag as the fleet commander, displacing some 42,000 tons, and bearing eight 38-cm guns (supplemented by *Hipper*'s 20-cm guns) was more than a match for any vessel the British could put to sea, while both *Scheer* and *Lützow* were well able to dispatch the convoy merchantmen with their 28-cm armament. An engagement, though, with a superior enemy fleet was to be avoided at all costs, and the operation was to be completed before the enemy could intervene with its strong covering force lying in the Faroe-Iceland region.

Three U-boats were to be stationed northeast of Iceland and were to act as a trip wire for locating the convoy, while up to four further U-boats were to lie in wait between Jan Mayen and Bear Island. These boats, however, were to shadow rather than attack the convoy, in order to avoid mistakenly torpedoing German warships.[90] Dönitz would, of course, rather have had his boats all in the Atlantic, where targets were more plentiful and away from the continuous daylight in the Arctic that made U-boat action particularly nerve-racking for his crews. To his mind, the "Luftwaffe was more suited to combat convoys in the North during the summer," and he felt it an extravagant waste to use his boats in mere shadowing operations.[91] The Naval Staff disagreed and wanted at least six to eight U-boats at sea in the vicinity of the convoys at any one time.[92]

As with the U-boats, the Luftwaffe was to play the role of support force to the operation by maintaining continuous contact with the convoy and determining the strength of its escorting force, and through long-range reconnaissance, locating the anticipated distant heavy covering force in the Shetlands–Faroe–Iceland–Jan Mayen area. As for attacking the enemy directly, the plan stipulated in no uncertain terms that the Luftwaffe was only to assault aircraft carriers and merchant shipping once the surface forces had engaged the enemy. This placed Stumpff's air fleet in a decidedly secondary role. Because all the senior naval officers from the *Großadmiral* downward felt that the Luftwaffe's primary function was reconnaissance, not combat, Stumpff's scouting machines were to enable the surface force to attack and destroy the convoy and return to their Scandinavian bolt-holes without interference from British carrier aircraft or battleships of the Home Fleet. The navy was certain that it was more than well enough equipped to deal with the convoy on its own; moreover, it will be "almost impossible," reasoned the navy's Group North, for Luftflotte 5, "even in good weather, to make adequate reconnaissance flights in addition to carrying out combat missions." "The sea area is too great," continued Carls: "Such reconnaissance is necessary for accurately determining the position of the probable remote escort consisting of heavy forces, including aircraft carriers, and proper employment of pocket battleships is dependent on this knowledge."[93]

The Navy informed the Luftwaffe's Operations Staff of its improved fuel oil situation and that this would probably result in an intensification of action against the Murmansk convoys, but—and here was the crux of the message—this would require greater reconnaissance than had hitherto been afforded the navy. The Naval Staff was aware, however, that this would not sit well with either Göring or Stumpff. It wrote a honeyed communiqué couched very carefully to play up Luftflotte 5's success against PQ 16—though it already knew full well that most of the convoy had actually made it to Russia's Arctic ports—and stressed the soundness of its request for the sake of Germany's war effort in the Far North:

> The Naval Staff is aware of the fact that increased reconnaissance will inevitably result in a withdrawal of bomber planes, the action of which brought such gratifying results against convoy PQ 16. It feels, however, that such a step is in the common interest and that the increased prospect of success on the part of the naval forces will compensate for the withdrawal of the planes.[94]

To this end, on 8 April the navy requested that the Luftwaffe hierarchy make it clear to the commander of Luftflotte 5 that he was required to meet all the requests of the local naval commanders as much as reasonably possible, even if this meant utilizing the air fleet's bombers in a reconnaissance role.

INTERSERVICE INFIGHTING AND CONVOLUTED COMMUNICATIONS

Placing the Luftwaffe in this decidedly secondary role, and at the whim of the navy, did not sit well with either Göring's Operations Staff in Berlin or Stumpff in Norway, no matter how sweetly presented. The request was promptly refused. "Additional reconnaissance forces cannot be furnished and under no circumstances are bombers to be used for reconnaissance tasks only," replied the Luftwaffe's Operations Staff on 10 June 1942.[95] Why should the Luftwaffe be forced to play second fiddle by diverting its bombers to reconnaissance missions just to support a naval action, especially when, in the past few months, the navy had hardly set the Arctic ablaze with forceful actions, while the Luftwaffe had been at the forefront of anti-convoy operations such as the recently completed attack on PQ 16? If Luftflotte 5 was to repeat such a success, concluded the Operations Staff, Stumpff's already weak bomber force had to remain untouched. Thus the Luftwaffe refused to comply.

The festering resentment and frustration harbored by the navy toward the Luftwaffe is clearly revealed in the bitter, sarcastic war diary entries that followed the refusal. It seemed obvious, at least to naval officers, that the Luftwaffe believed that bombers were all that was needed for operations against convoys. Scathingly, they pointed out that this one-sided point of view "cannot go unchallenged" because, although the success of Stumpff's force against PQ 16 had been "gratifying," it needed to be acknowledged that about twenty-five ships "did reach the port of destination." "On the other hand," the entry continued, "an operation such as *Rösselsprung* harbors the possibility of *completely destroying an entire convoy* if circumstances are at all favorable."

To further put the airmen in their place, the Naval Staff pointed to Luftflotte 5's admission that ten enemy aircraft had been able to reconnoiter the berths of German vessels in Narvik on 26, 27, and 28 May unimpeded, in order to ascertain the likely dispositions of surface vessels in Norway. While the enemy was able to do this with impunity, mocked the navy, the Luftwaffe, in contrast, would not even permit consideration of the request for increased naval reconnaissance. This remarkable diatribe in a normally austere and functionary war diary was an outpouring of the navy's long-held frustration at its inability to retain control of its own aircraft or get effective Luftwaffe support in maritime work. The underlying resentment was evident in the concluding remarks of 9 June:

> As a result, the Luftwaffe will simply have to acknowledge once more that the RAF is numerically better able to cope with the more or less self-evident fundamental requirements of any sort of naval warfare. This example [of 26, 27, and 28 May] shows with striking clarity a discrepancy that can never be sufficiently regretted, namely, the absence of a naval air force or even a certain amount of authority of naval commanders over air forces.[96]

Raeder's staff, totally unimpressed—and having tried the nice approach, only to be rudely rebuffed—proposed that the "attitude of the Luftwaffe's Operation Staff be mentioned to the Führer," since the success of *Rösselsprung* was dependent on good reconnaissance.

This rather pathetic cry for "intervention by the highest authority" was an indictment not only against the failure to adequately equip naval forces with suitable aircraft in significant numbers but also against the German military system that fostered such corrosive interservice rivalry. Blotting out this sort of self-defeating infighting would have been very difficult in prewar Germany, given the long-held parochialism of the army, navy, and latterly the Luftwaffe, and impossible in the white-hot heat of war. Nevertheless, its most pernicious tendencies could have been ameliorated here and elsewhere by the establishment of a single theater commander. Hitler's brief flirtation with the idea of placing someone of the caliber of Kesselring as Supreme Commander, Norway, would have been equally beneficial in 1942 as when it was first mooted in 1940.

The Führer's failure to bring this squabbling to an end by establishing a combined navy-Luftwaffe command structure in Norway was repeated in other theaters and was one of his greatest failures as head of the Wehrmacht. In some ways, though, the disunited command structure that existed in all German theaters of war suited Hitler's predilection for meddling as the final arbiter of important and less important decisions that were made daily. In this sense, it meant that he was truly the warlord that Churchill and Roosevelt could never be; on the other hand, it also meant, as the war progressed and spread like a cancerous growth over central and then western and northern Europe, the Mediterranean, and finally the Soviet Union, that his attention was necessarily diluted over far too many regions and often fell only on areas of increasing importance such as the eastern front for any significant period of the time. In the end, it took Hitler's intervention to bring the Luftwaffe to heel.

On 10 June, the Luftwaffe advised the navy that it would be able to support the warships with only three squadrons of Condors, four squadrons of BV 138s, and a relatively small number of reconnaissance flights equipped with a *Kette* of Ju 88s each.[97] The navy did not hold out much hope that the Luftwaffe could be coerced into withdrawing bombers for reconnaissance purposes "without intervention by the highest authority." This was achieved when Raeder met with Hitler on 15 June to discuss *Rösselsprung*. The Führer agreed with most of its proposals but was very uneasy about the possible appearance of British aircraft carriers, since he considered them to be a "great threat to the large vessels."[98] Consequently, he was prepared to approve *Rösselsprung* only on condition that enemy carriers be located before Raeder's warships left their lairs and subsequently "rendered harmless by our Ju 88 planes before the attack gets under way." Moreover, even if any carriers lay beyond the range of Stumpff's units, the attack remained "subject to the Führer's approval." These caveats on the intended enterprise as envisaged by the navy would prove to be the operation's death knell because they tied the hands of every flag officer in the long and tortuous chain of command that ran from Otto Schniewind aboard *Tirpitz* in Trondheim, up to Schmundt as *Admiral Nordmeer* in Narvik, through Carls in Wilhelmshaven, and finally on to Raeder at the apex of power in Berlin.[99]

Compounding the lengthy channels of communication present within the navy were the rather convoluted and disjointed communication links between the two services in the region. As observed earlier, at a tactical level the local Luftwaffe officers had developed a good rapport with their naval counterparts, but when it came to larger scale operations the pressures brought about by interservice rivalry were further strained by the nature of the communications system prevailing over the whole country.[100] Since the Germans were fully aware that their wireless traffic could be intercepted by the enemy, they were compelled to use incredibly long landlines stretching the entire length of Norway for the much slower coded teleprinter signals.

The difficulties of this method can be readily appreciated by examining the Luftwaffe's position. For example, a reconnaissance report from Fliegerführer Nord (West) at Stavanger had to be sent to forward headquarters at Kemi, and thence over thousands of kilometers of rough terrain to the main headquarters in Oslo. The data received would be analyzed and prioritized before eventual dispatch by teleprinter signal back up the center of the country to *Admiral Nordmeer,* Hubert Schmundt in Narvik, from where the relevant material had to be dispersed through the navy's own meandering communication channels. Consequently, it is unsurprising that a good number of important signals would only reach the respective naval commander's desk long after it was possible to make use of the material, no more so than in the case of PQ 17. Although the navy played with the idea of transferring *Admiral Nordmeer* and a small staff from Narvik to Banak to shortcut the system, the move was deemed impractical.[101] It should be mentioned that *Admiral Nordmeer* had been transferred to Narvik recently in order to improve the situation, only to make matters worse by creating yet another link in the communication chain.[102] What was needed was the establishment of a combined-services center under the leadership of a single theater commander—this would have made it possible for the Germans to get the best out of their forces in Norway.

Nevertheless, the navy had won a rare victory over the Luftwaffe, and Göring was compelled to have his forces comply fully with naval requests. As the Naval Staff gloated, the order issued by the Luftwaffe's Operations Staff now actually exceeded its initial demands and, if weather permitted, "should suffice to prevent any surprises."[103] The solution was somewhat of a compromise, since Stumpff's bomber forces would still not be used for reconnaissance, but OKL was forced to transfer in additional suitable types for naval demands on 23 June.[104] Luftlotte 5's operational orders for *Rösselsprung* directed Stumpff's scouting units to reconnoiter an area extending some 480 kilometers north from the Norwegian coast or as far as the ice barrier, as thoroughly as possible.[105] The organization of the flights was to be made in such a way as to ensure that any given area was flown over every four hours. In addition, the movement of the two German surface forces into the area of battle was to be overseen by escorting fighters as a precautionary move should Allied aircraft threaten the safe passage of these irreplaceable ships.

While this interservice wrangling had been taking place backstage, German intelligence was pointing to a slow accumulation of escort and convoy vessels at the western end of the convoy route. In addition to photoreconnaissance during the last few days of May, which identified a large contingent of British and American warships at anchor in Scapa Flow (including three battleships, three heavy cruisers, four light cruisers, and twenty-two destroyers), agent reports buttressed by Luftwaffe reconnaissance revealed that more warships, including an aircraft carrier, were lying in wait off Iceland. These reports were soon followed in early June by others revealing the gathering of merchantmen on Iceland's southwest coast.[106] With what looked like the gradual formation of a convoy, Schmundt ordered his first three U-boats (U 251, U 376, and U 408), designated *Eisteufel* (Ice Devil), into the Denmark Strait to sweep the region in anticipation of PQ 17.[107]

In the end, *Eisteufel* would have to wait longer than expected for the convoy to breach its observation zone. It was not until 27 June that PQ 17 began filing out of Iceland's Hval Fjord ("like so many dirty ducks," observed a crew member aboard one of the escorts, "they waddled out past the nets and out to sea").[108] Beneath their unkempt and bedraggled appearance, however, the thirty-five ships were packed to overflowing with weapons of war for Stalin: 297 aircraft, 594 tanks, 4,246 trucks and gun carriers, and over 156,000 tons of general cargo. Should this precious material ever reach Russia's Arctic ports, it could equip an army of 50,000 men.[109]

The Allies, though, had been informed by their intelligence services of German plans for a heavy surface forces attack east of Bear Island, an area in which *Tirpitz* and escorts could wreak havoc under the protective umbrella of around-the-clock air cover. The only hope the British had of thwarting such an enterprise was to lure the German fleet westward into the vicinity of the powerful Home Fleet. Under the command of Admiral Sir John Tovey, the fleet was positioned as a distant cover force northeast of Jan Mayen Island in the rather forlorn hope that Allied submarines off the Norwegian coast would intercept the German warships as they moved in to attack. Medium-range support for PQ 17 would be provided by a covering force of four cruisers and three destroyers under the control of Rear Admiral Louis Hamilton, operating from a position north of the convoy route until PQ 17 passed what was considered the danger zone for an enemy surface attack, whereupon it would then turn for home. The British envisaged that Hamilton's cruiser force would not proceed beyond Bear Island or, at the farthest, the meridian of twenty-five degrees east.[110] Close support for the convoy against Luftwaffe and U-boat attacks all the way to Russia was provided by Commander Jack Broome's force of six destroyers, four corvettes, three minesweepers, two antiaircraft ships, and four trawlers. Clandestine support came in the form of two submarines that were to remain hidden until such time as an attack was made by German warships, at which point they were to counterattack the enemy vessels.[111]

Certainly the whole situation looked as though it were designed as a trap with PQ 17 the unfortunate live bait. Yet the plan, which if successful would have brought the two powerful protagonists together in a major naval showdown, was contingent on Raeder's forces attacking the convoy west of, or very near to, Bear Island. Should an attack by German surface forces occur here, the Allies' extremely strong distant and cruiser covering forces would do their best to ambush the *Tirpitz*-led raid. However, should an assault take place once the cruiser force had departed and the convoy was well beyond the range of the Home Fleet, the Admiralty's instructions ominously directed that "circumstances may arise in which the best thing would be for [the] convoy to disperse with orders to proceed to Russian ports."[112]

THE ASSAULT BEGINS

Although British naval forces were sighted off Iceland on 28 June, bad weather and poor visibility prevented another sighting until 1 July, when a high-flying Condor spotted the convoy. *Eisteufel* soon picked up the convoy ninety-five kilometers east of Jan Mayen Island and was joined subsequently by other U-boats, which took up shadowing positions behind the convoy. On 2 July, the first probing Luftwaffe attack was made by seven He 115s carrying torpedoes, but one of the floatplanes was shot down, and, due to the ferocity of the antiaircraft barrage put up by the escort, the rest were eventually forced to retire without hitting a single ship. Late the next day, another seven He 115s took off to assault the convoy, and on this occasion a quick attack by one of these aircraft caught the defenders napping. The Liberty ship *Christopher Newport* was hit in the early hours of 4 July; the crew failed to scuttle the ship, which had to be left behind for the prowling U-boats to finish off.[113]

Reconnaissance once again picked up PQ 17 on 4 July, and a much larger attack by Stumpff's forces was mustered against the convoy. Since by this stage the navy was still uncertain of the exact location of the Allies' aircraft carrier, but thanks to aerial reconnaissance had been made aware of Hamilton's northern covering force (which was reported incorrectly to include a battleship), it was as yet reluctant to chance its arm.[114] Therefore, Stumpff decided to launch his bombers against the convoy while it remained within effective range of his bases. The initial strike by torpedo-carrying floatplanes was thwarted by 300- to 400-meter-high cloud cover cloaking the convoy and after an hour-long search was abandoned in the face of the escorts' heavy defenses. By now, the Germans were aware that the formation adopted by the convoy consisted of thirty-eight ships arrayed in column in line abreast, protected from frontal and flanking attacking attacks by PQ 17 destroyers and light escort vessels, and they planned their next major raid accordingly.[115] To distract the defensive fire, a small force of Ju 88s was to dive on the convoy moments before KG 30's twenty-three He 111 torpedo bombers split into two groups, one making a low-level beam attack while the other undertook a run from the stern quarter against the convoy. The Ju 88's diversionary flight failed to materialize in the face of intensive defensive fire, however, and the assault was left to the twenty-three Heinkels. At 0820 the low-level run began. The first wave of ten bombers was met by a murderous hail of antiaircraft fire at a height of about only twenty meters as it pressed on to the bow of the convoy. One aircraft was quickly dispatched, and many of the others panicked, releasing their torpedoes while well outside optimum range before turning tail. The second wave approached the convoy's stern, and nine bombers were able to launch their torpedoes within range. While five of these then pulled away, four continued to hurtle toward the core of the merchantmen, passing through the outer protective screen. Everything the escorts and merchantmen had in the way of defense was thrown against the intruders in a cacophony of rockets, 10-cm guns, and machine guns of various calibers.[116] Led by *Leutnant* Hennemann, the Heinkels struck three ships, two fatally, and within five minutes the attack was over. The German assault had cost them three He 111s, one of them belonging to Hennemann, who was posthumously awarded the Knight's Cross for his gallantry.

The defensive fire of the convoy had proved more than a match for Stumpff's air units now limping back to Banak. Although the convoy had to abandon the Liberty ship *William Hooper* and British merchantman *Navarino* thanks to two crippling torpedo hits—at the time Luftflotte 5 claimed five vessels sunk and five heavily damaged—it had shown that if vessels joined together behind a cordon of escorting warships, they stood a more than even chance of fending off the Luftwaffe's best.[117] To Broome, as well as to Hamilton, whose cruiser force had moved into view when the aerial attack began, it appeared that if the convoy kept together it should be able to repel Luftwaffe attacks without incurring substantial losses. Decisions in London, though, were about to change all this, turning the situation decidedly in Stumpff's favor.

CONVOY IS TO SCATTER AND COLD FEET FOR *RÖSSELSPRUNG*

The Admiralty, already fretting about the possibility of a major German attack on the convoy, was uncertain of the whereabouts of enemy ships. Decoded signals remained inconclusive, and at 0830 on 4 July, just as Hennemann's aircraft plowed into icy Arctic waters, Admiral Sir Dudley Pound, First Sea Lord, called together his senior officers to examine the situation and decide whether the convoy should continue on its present course or scatter. Already ill with a brain tumor that would claim his life the following year, Pound personally drafted the order for the convoy to scatter. Broome received the order with dismay but duly passed it on, since he was sure that it meant an imminent attack by the German surface fleet. As if to confirm this, Hamilton's cruiser force withdrew heading southwest in accordance with his earlier orders, but for all intents and purposes looking as though it was en route to engage the enemy. With the convoy scattering, Broome decided to follow Hamilton in anticipation of tackling the German battle group.

In fact, the Germans were as uncertain as to what was happening as were the British. On 4 July, the German Naval Staff was still under the impression that Hamilton's cruiser force might include a battleship and that the sighting of two torpedo bombers meant that there was a carrier in the vicinity.[118] Although the two "torpedo bombers" were in reality only a couple of catapult-launched floatplanes, the jittery Naval Staff concluded that the presence of a "heavy force in the vicinity of the convoy makes it impossible to carry out operation *Rösselsprung*" until such time as dispatched Luftwaffe and U-boat forces had achieved their desired effect on the enemy's heavy vessels.[119] However, on the following day the navy learned that the British fleet was withdrawing. With this news, the go-ahead was finally given for the big ships to proceed with *Rösselsprung*. Eager for battle, the warships set a course for the convoy. Expectancy soon turned to doubt, however, when they were spotted by a Russian submarine and a British aircraft. Raeder was racked with unease; could the Home Fleet and a carrier still be in the area and this plane and submarine merely part of their scouting force? In the end, tied by Hitler's express order that "the fleet should not venture a thrust unless the enemy carrier has been *located* and *eliminated*," he got cold feet and ordered his ships to return. It was a bitter blow to the naval officers and crew, and Schniewind could not help but take a swipe at the Luftwaffe, repeating the navy's old complaint:

> I see the reasons for this as being a certain degree of understandable hesitancy in the Luftwaffe to divide their own limited forces available, and to detach reconnaissance planes to shadow enemy heavy forces, particularly when there is a carrier in the vicinity. Once again we see the great disadvantages we labour under, lacking as we do our own Fleet Air Arm.[120]

Naval gripes could not, however, cover up the fact that Raeder was strongly wedded to the idea of a "fleet-in-being" and was not about to risk his remaining precious ships unless he was absolutely certain of success; this was a certainty the Luftwaffe could never guarantee, no matter how many aircraft it devoted to the task, given the barrier weather posed to spotting ships at sea and even in getting airborne from fogbound northern Norwegian airfields.

On the whole, though, in spite of dreadful weather conditions the Luftwaffe had done a more than adequate job of securing information about enemy dispositions. On the day that the decision was made to recall the big ships, Fliegerführer Lofotens had reported that as of 1004 no enemy was sighted under "good visibility conditions between 14° and 26° E up to the ice barrier"—in other words, revealing that Hamilton's northern covering force had departed.[121] Göring, never one to miss an opportunity to stick the boot in, appeared incredulous of the reason for the navy's hastily aborted sortie and made rumblings about putting the Führer into the picture regarding Raeder's excessive cautiousness.[122] If Schniewind had been a little unfair regarding Stumpff's efforts, he was prepared to concede that the Luftwaffe and U-boats had worked well together and that during their brief sortie the heavy surface forces did get adequate air cover. Still, he would have preferred that the two tactical headquarters of the respective services be closer together—an admirable aim, though still short of the single theater commander really needed. Notwithstanding these grumblings, with the abandonment of *Rösselsprung* it was left to Stumpff's air units and the U-boats to pick off the now practically defenseless ships scurrying toward Russia.[123]

On 5 July, Luftflotte 5 found the convoy scattered, with individual ships sailing on the edge of the northern ice belt and faster vessels heading directly for the cover of severe weather to the east. Naturally, but wrongly, Stumpff concluded that the breaking up of the convoy had been caused by his bombers' efforts the preceding day, and he was determined to complete the task. Aerial reconnaissance and U-boat reports determined that the bulk of PQ 17 still lay within a 60-square-kilometer area stretching up to 200 kilometers from north to south, and it was upon these hapless vessels that Luftflotte 5 and the U-boats fell. Although the air fleet would eventually claim the bulk of the sinkings, in fact a good many of the ships sent to the bottom were victims of combined efforts.

THE MAIN EVENT

Early on 5 July, *U 334* dispatched the abandoned *Navarino* and *William Hooper*, both of which had sustained fatal damage the previous day at the hands of the Luftwaffe. These actions were soon followed by *U 706* sending *Empire Byron* to the bottom with a load of Churchill tanks destined for the Red Army. *U 88* hit the American freighter *Carlton* at 0945; after abandoning ship, most of its crew were recovered by German aircraft of the *Seenotdienst*.[124] *U 88* then found *Daniel Morgan* and *Fairfield City* at the same time as KG 30 Ju 88s were making attacks on these vessels at about 1500.[125] *Fairfield City* was bombed and sunk, while five further Ju 88s soon caught up with *Daniel Morgan* about midafternoon and brought it to a halt with a near miss. The stricken ship was finished off by *U 88*, which then joined in an attack on *Honomu*, sinking it after the crew had abandoned ship. The 7,000-ton *Earlston* was found by more of Stumpff's bombers, which, with another near miss alongside the engine room, forced the crew to abandon the explosive-laden merchantman. To the crew members' amazement, as soon as they left their vessel, three U-boats surfaced to sink it. Among these boats, *U 334* suffered the indignity shortly thereafter of being attacked by a Ju 88, which apparently mistook it for an Allied submarine. Fortunately, the bomber had only enough bombs for a single run before completing the attack with a relatively harmless strafing run.[126]

Nevertheless, the initial damage sustained by *U 334* was considerable, and Schmundt ordered *U 456* to escort the stricken boat—with its steering damaged and unable to submerge—back to Kirkenes.[127] The Naval Staff was far from impressed, and Luftflotte 5 later carried out an investigation into the incident. Stumpff failed to find the culprit, and the Luftwaffe even went so far as to suggest that the attack might well have been made by a Russian aircraft resembling a Ju 88. The navy, though, strongly dismissed this notion, since the U-boat had observed the attack by Stumpff's aircraft on *Earlston* only twenty minutes before its own close call, and not a single Russian aircraft had been sighted in the region.[128]

Having completed their rescue recovery duties as devised by Stumpff, the aircraft of KüFlGr 906 resumed the attack with torpedo runs against *Peter Kerr.* Although over a two-hour period this American ship successfully evaded nearly a dozen torpedoes launched against it by the slow He 115 floatplanes, Ju 88s led by *Hauptmann* Willi Flechner's KG 30 unit appeared at 1700 and scored three direct hits amid a string of near misses.[129] At about the same time as *Peter Kerr* went down, Ju 88s attacked *Washington,* which was part of a trio of ships (including *Bolton Castle* and *Paulus Potter*) that had stuck together following the order to scatter. Near misses added to damage sustained earlier, but *Washington* was not sunk until 1730, when several more of the Junkers bombers appeared to conclude the matter and then dealt with *Bolton Castle* and *Paulus Potter.*

Following this cluster of three doomed ships was the slower *Olopana,* which had avoided attack by an ingenious ruse incorporating a fake abandonment and onboard fire. When *Olopana* finally steamed into view, the bedraggled survivors of *Washington, Paulus Potter,* and *Bolton Castle* were decidedly unwilling to be rescued, preferring days adrift in the safety of their lifeboats over the risk of boarding another unarmed merchant ship in these conditions. As the captain of *Olopana* reported afterward: "The *Olopana* headed in the direction of the vessels burning on the horizon, to pick up survivors. The *Washington*'s boats were the first encountered; but the crew were so badly shaken up that another session of dive-bombing was the last thing they desired."[130]

The massed attack on the trio had been made possible by the lifting of fog over northern Norway's airfields, which meant that all three of KG 30's squadrons, totaling sixty-nine Ju 88s, were now able to prowl the entire area, remorselessly hunting down the convoy's remnants.[131] At 1730, four of these Ju 88s came across a cluster of vessels making for Novaya Zemlya in search of refuge. They included the convoy's oiler *Aldersdale,* the Royal Navy minesweeper *Salamander,* a British merchantman, *Ocean Freedom,* and one of the two rescue ships, *Zamalek.* Demonstrating the effectiveness of even this motley group when combined defenses were put into play, the first three bombers broke off their attacking dives, dropping their loads harmlessly wide of the defiant ships. Only the fourth aircraft pressed home its attack, scoring a near miss on *Aldersdale*'s engine room; the buckled hull plates soon split with a rush of water amidships, forcing an evacuation.[132] At the same time as these eastern sorties were being undertaken, a more northern sweep spotted *Pankraft.* Loaded with aircraft parts and a deck full of bombers, the American freighter was edging its way along the ice barrier when, at 1700, a Condor guided three Ju 88s into an attack. Stacked with over 5,000 tons of TNT, it was soon left to the ice by the crew after a high-level bombing attack. Following a strafing run, *Pankraft* was eventually set alight by incendiary shells.[133] At 2230, the day's final success was claimed by *U 703,* which sank *River Afton,* also skirting as close to the ice shelf as possible in the hope of hiding in the prevalent fog banks.

In spite of the fact that the next few days saw less frenzied sorties, Stumpff's air fleet, along with Schmundt's U-boats, continued to wreak havoc on the dwindling convoy in a manner similar to 5 July's spectacular successes. Significantly, Stumpff found that the torpedo bombers were less useful in attack on widely dispersed individual vessels than against clustered ships in convoy station, and because of bad weather, combined bomber and torpedo bomber operations were not continued after the abortive 4 July attempt. Thus most of the damage was inflicted by the ubiquitous Ju 88. By the evening of 6 July even the German Naval Staff had put its complaints aside, confessing:

> This is the biggest success ever achieved against the enemy with one blow—a blow executed with the exemplary collaboration between Luftwaffe and submarine units. . . . In a three-day operation, fought under the most favorable conditions, the submarines and the Luftwaffe have achieved what had been the intention of the operation *Rösselsprung,* the attack of our surface units on the convoy's merchant ships.[134]

Poor weather over the three days from 6 July to 9 July limited the Luftwaffe's contribution to a single hit on *Pan Atlantic* that sent the ship, laden with tanks, steel, nickel, aluminum, foodstuffs, two oil stills, and cordite, sky high. Most of the kills in this period were made by U-boats.[135] Nevertheless, Stumpff's air fleet still had one throw left, and when perfect flying weather reappeared on 10 April, his aircraft brought the operation against PQ 17 to a glorious end for the airmen in the Far North.

A small surviving group of four merchantmen—escorted by a couple of PQ 17 antiaircraft ships, three minesweepers, and three trawlers—found their way into the Kara Sea barred by ice and thus set a course south for Iokanka on the Kola Peninsula. Approaching midnight on 9 July, an ice barrier had forced the convoy southwest toward German airfields. The ships were soon under surveillance by two BV 138 seaplanes, which kept well out of the range of the antiaircraft escorts but duly sent out homing signals to draw in the U-boats and Stumpff's bomber units.[136] The conditions were ideal for aerial action. As one of the commanders of the U-boats signaled in, even at this late hour there was plenty of daylight available, with the sun just above the horizon, very little wind, and at least 30-kilometer visibility.[137] For those manning the ships, this was one last desperate lunge for the Russian coast only 95 kilometers away, with Murmansk a further 130 kilometers distant.

At Banak, thirty-eight Ju 88s were scrambled and fell upon these unfortunates just before midnight. The first casualty was an American freighter, *Hossier.*

Near misses had opened up some of its seams, and the chief engineer determined that the ship could not continue, leaving the captain no alternative but to order it abandoned. The German pilots continued to bomb *Hossier,* still on an even keel, until eventually a U-boat finished it off.[138] Meanwhile, the Ju 88s continued their attacks on the departing convoy as it steamed south. Flying out of a low sun, the aircraft were particularly difficult to spot, while the antiaircraft ships had nearly expended their complement of ammunition. Over four hours, the Luftwaffe sank one freighter and scored a number of near misses on *El Capitán* and the rescue ship *Zamalek.* The final knockout blow for *El Capitán* was not delivered until about 0600 the next morning, when three bombs from a lone Ju 88 struck near the engine, forcing the abandonment of the crippled vessel. Of the returning aircraft, the second squadron was able to return to Banak, but the first was forced to land at Petsamo as fog shut down the former airfield.[139]

By this stage, the Luftwaffe was convinced that the "surviving ships of the convoy trying to reach Iokanko were annihilated" and was surprised to receive reconnaissance information that 190 kilometers east of Murmansk were two merchant ships. Without hesitation, sixteen more Ju 88s from KG 30 and its experimental squadron took to the air from Banak. Hits were claimed by these aircraft, and another mission was undertaken by eighteen Ju 88s from KG 30's second group, again from Banak. By this time, however, the Soviets were prepared to meet the bombers with Petlykov Pe-3 twin-engined fighters and Hurricanes, and the German planes were fought off. Notwithstanding this setback, crew reports boasted that those ships "not sunk have been so badly damaged that their destruction can be claimed for certain." "According to available figures, it is correct to assume that not one ship of PQ 17 reached a port," concluded the entry in Luftflotte 5's diary for 10 July.[140] With this, the air fleet's operations against PQ 17 were brought to an end. Two days later, Stumpff reported to Göring by teleprinter:

> *Herr Reichsmarschall!* I beg to report the destruction of Convoy PQ 17. During reconnaissance made on July 10, 1942, in the White Sea, the western passage, the Kola coast, and the sea area north of the coast, not a single merchant ship was observed. Photographic reconnaissance of Jokanga showed that no ship belonging to PQ 17 has reached that harbor. I report the sinking by Luftflotte 5 of: one cruiser, one destroyer, two escorts, totaling 4,000 tons, and 22 merchant ships, totaling 142,216 tons.[141]

Although Stumpff's claims were typically exaggerated, his air fleet had indeed played a significant part in the destruction of two-thirds of PQ 17. Of the twenty-four merchant ships lost, eight vessels (totaling 40,376 tons) were sunk by aircraft, and a further eight (totaling 54,093 tons) were damaged by aircraft and finished off by U-boats.[142] The remaining eight (48,218 tons) fell solely to U-boat action. In achieving its considerable and exceptional success, the Luftwaffe had expended 210 kilograms of high explosives and sixty-one aerial torpedoes in over 200 sorties and had lost up to a dozen aircraft.[143] Thanks to the combined aerial and U-boat effort, Stalin's forces would never see the 210 aircraft, 430 tanks, 3,350 vehicles, and a little over 100,000 tons of munitions, explosives, and raw materials that now lay strewn across the bed of the Barents Sea.[144]

PQ 18 AND THE END OF LUFTWAFFE ASCENDANCY

The battle against PQ 17 was the high point of Luftwaffe operations against the Arctic convoys. It was not until mid-September that another convoy sailed, and, severely chastened by the PQ 17 debacle, the British were determined not to repeat their mistakes. The forty-strong convoy (PQ 18) was accompanied all the way to Russia by a so-called Fighting Destroyer Escort made up of nineteen destroyers plus additional corvettes, minesweepers, trawlers, antiaircraft ships, submarines, and a Carrier Force comprising the escort carrier *Avenger* with a complement of twelve Sea Hurricane fighters, three Swordfish antisubmarine aircraft, and two dedicated destroyers. Additional air cover would be provided by the transfer of some of Coastal Command's seek-and-strike planes and crews to northern Russia.[145] The Fighting Escort Force would provide escort for PQ 18 right into the Barents Sea, at which point it would link up with the returning convoy QP 14 on its way west. With this kind of protection, Stumpff's forces were in for a torrid time, even with the recent arrival of more aircraft, including Ju 88 torpedo bombers.

Because of poor weather, the convoy was not picked up by Luftwaffe surveillance until 12 September.[146] The first of four Luftwaffe raids was made the following day in which the *Goldene Zange* was used successfully for the first time.[147] KG 30 and KG 26 bombers and torpedo bombers flying from Fliegerführer Lofoten and Fliegerführer Nord (Ost)'s airfields sunk eight ships in attacks from 1500 to 2035, and, after some less than dramatic halfhearted attempts, He 115 floatplanes delivered a couple of torpedo runs.[148] Although four Hurricanes were lost, new defensive measures adopted by the British were successful in bringing about the loss of five of Stumpff's aircraft. Further attacks on 14, 15, and 18 September followed, directed—at Göring's behest—against the carrier. Although a further five ships were sunk, the establishment of a continual aerial patrol over the convoy and determined escort defensive fire started to cut deep into Luftflotte 5's forces. Over the two days 13 and 14 September alone, KG 26 lost twenty aircraft and fourteen crews.[149] Despite Göring's demand on 17 September that "the battle against PQ 18 is to be continued with all available means until entered port" and that the destruction of the "ships in this convoy is of decisive importance," by the next day KG 26 was able to put only a dozen of its original ninety-two torpedo bombers into the air, such was the savage mauling received at the hands of antiaircraft fire and the Hurricanes.[150] Finally, deteriorating weather and the arrival of Pe3 fighters over the convoy brought an end to the Luftwaffe's participation against the convoy.

At the conclusion of the operation, the Luftwaffe, in over 330 sorties, had contributed to the sinking of thirteen ships, of which ten were direct victims of air action.[151] The cost had been extremely high. During the entire operation against PQ 18, Luftlotte 5 lost forty-four aircraft, of which thirty-eight were torpedo bombers. As the RAF's postwar analysis of the operation concluded, the British escorts had proved more than a match for the Luftwaffe: "It was found that not only was it impossible to approach the carrier to launch an effective attack—on account of fighters—but that a wide screen of warships made the launching of torpedoes against the inner merchant vessels an extremely hazardous undertaking."[152] Nevertheless, despite these losses, the experiences of KG 26 in Norway had confirmed the effectiveness of aerial torpedos in maritime warfare. Ten of the thirteen ships destroyed were the victims of torpedoes delivered by KG 26. Of the 860 sorties flown by Stumpff's aircraft against PQs 16, 17, and 18, over 340 were made by torpedo bombers. German assessments of these operations confirmed that the torpedo bomber was the most efficient means of knocking out enemy merchantmen. The Luftwaffe's 8th Abteilung calculated that while only one vessel was sunk for every 19 bombing sorties undertaken, torpedo missions sank an Allied vessel every 8 sorties; that is, they were on average twice as effective as high-level or dive-bombing attacks, and one-quarter of all the torpedoes launched struck home.[153]

In many ways convoys PQ 17 and PQ 18 represented the changing fortunes of the German effort at sea and the role of airpower in this environment. PQ 17, for its part, represented "what might have been" in the siege of Britain much earlier in the war, when heavily escorted convoys were far from the norm and very little air cover was available. Prior to 1942, the Germans had their best chance through using bases in France and Norway to combine U-boats and long-range maritime aircraft in achieving a stranglehold over the British Isles. Even though the Germans now—in 1942—finally had some torpedo bombers, they had needed them in 1940–1941, well in advance of the establishment of a complete interlocking convoy system, a Mid-ocean Escort Force, and the increasing use of specialized long-range aircraft and more effective antisubmarine measures. As PQ 18 had demonstrated, by September 1942 the opportunity for the Germans to bring about the capitulation of Britain had well and truly passed. How further operations against the convoys would have gone we will never know for certain because events in another theater were about to turn Norway once again into an operational backwater.

7
Slow Death, 1943–1945

The navy could really never count on operational support by trained and sizeable air units in Norway.

Vizeadmiral Otto Schniewind, 1945

Operation *Torch,* the Allied landings in North Africa in November 1942, saw four wings of bombers and torpedo bombers transferred from northern Norway to the Mediterranean.[1] As in early 1941 with the assignment of Geisler's X Fliegerkorps to this southern theater, Luftflotte 5 was once again gutted of its strike force; the remaining dregs included the slow He 115, which proved entirely unsuited to anticonvoy work, and Stukas, which were notoriously vulnerable to the Allies' single-engined fighters. In the months and years that followed, the northernmost air fleet would receive some reinforcements but never on a level commensurate with Allied activity in the region.

Not that the navy's effort in the following years was particularly glowing either. Having somewhat mollified Stalin with earlier efforts and the proposed North Africa landings, Churchill suspended the Arctic convoys until the end of the year, when the first in a newly titled JW eastbound and RA westbound series began, starting with JW 51A in the second week of December 1942. This group of merchantmen passed unseen by the Germans—an indication of the declining abilities of Luftflotte 5—but the next voyage would bring about the demise of the navy's commander in chief. *Lützow, Hipper,* and five destroyers left Alta Fjord on 30 December in search of JW 51B but were able to bring their guns to bear on the ships only briefly before being forced to disengage upon the appearance of British cruisers, which damaged *Hipper* with their very first salvo. For Hitler, who was hoping for a victory in Arctic waters to counter the disasters looming at Stalingrad and in North Africa, this was the last straw. In a heated diatribe, he detailed to Raeder the dismal performance of the German navy since 1866; when he declared his intention to scrap the big ships, Raeder felt compelled to resign in favor of Dönitz. As the navy's new leader, the ex-submariner Dönitz was able to get the Führer to rescind his order to have all vessels larger than destroyers scrapped, at least as far as the ships in Norway were concerned; those spared included not only the battleship *Tirpitz* and the pocket battleship *Lützow* but also the battle cruiser *Scharnhorst,* which arrived in March 1943.[2]

In many ways, the decision not to break up the big ships was a vindication of Raeder's belief in the "fleet in being," which, although never materially threatening the convoys, weighed heavily on the British Admiralty. The mere presence of these warships in northern Norway posed enough of a menace in the minds of the Royal Navy to constrain it to retain a disproportionately strong force at Scapa Flow centered on battleships and, when possible, a fleet carrier. Only with a Home Fleet of this strength did the British feel they could counter any moves, such as an unexpected strike at a passing convoy or a breakout into the Atlantic made by the German ships, especially *Tirpitz.*[3] In turn, this limited the amount of forces available to the British in arguably more important regions, including the Atlantic proper, the Mediterranean, and the Pacific. For Dönitz, though, his warships still had unfinished business in the Far North.

Prior to taking up the navy reins, Dönitz had not been favorably disposed to a further employment of the big ships in Norway, but he had slowly come around to the view that given the right conditions they still could be committed to battle.[4] Soon after his appointment, he laid down the conditions for such an action in a directive to the respective officers in command of the surface forces:

> The conditions required for successful operations by surface ships against traffic in the Arctic will occur very seldom, since the enemy, to judge from past experience, will deploy for the protection—immediate and indirect—of his convoys, forces of such strength as will undoubtedly be superior to that of our own forces. Nevertheless, there may occur opportunities for attacking unescorted or lightly-escorted ships or small groups sailing independently. Whenever such an opportunity occurs it must be seized with determination, but with due observance of tactical principles.[5]

By March 1943, Dönitz had *Tirpitz* and *Scharnhorst,* with their respective destroyer flotillas, in northern Norway. In the meantime, the British had suspended convoy sailings over the summer months in order to prevent a repeat of the disasters of 1942, and also because the tide of battle on the eastern front had well and truly turned against the Germans with the destruction of the German Sixth Army at Stalingrad. Consequently, it was no longer imperative to push supplies through to the Soviets regardless of cost. With no opportunity to attack convoys, the German vessels took part in a morale-boosting foray against enemy port installations, coal mines, and weather stations on Spitzbergen. This operation, undertaken on

6 September 1943, rekindled British concerns about the presence of *Tirpitz* and hastened a Royal Navy operation to send six midget submarines into the big ship's lair later that month. Two of these managed to sneak past the defensive nets and lay mines that successfully damaged *Tirpitz*'s steering and propeller shafts, effectively putting the ship out of action for at least six months. Despite the loss of *Tirpitz,* Dönitz was determined to attack at the first sign of renewed Arctic convoys.

RECONNAISSANCE

To support a *Scharnhorst*-led incursion into northern waters, the navy was only all too well aware of the Luftwaffe's declining ability to provide even the most perfunctory of reconnaissance sorties, let alone air cover for the duration of any major operation undertaken. Although *Vizeadmiral* Schniewind's postwar assessment of Luftflotte 5's performance from 1942 was typically, and somewhat unfairly, critical of the Luftwaffe's inability to adequately support the navy, his assessment neatly summed up the situation in Norway *after* the removal of most of Luftflotte 5's force in November of that year:

> From 1942 on, air support, both reconnaissance and fighter protection for the naval bases was inadequate in the area of Norway. Air reconnaissance of Murmansk convoys was always weak and often late, while air cover at times didn't appear at all, or lost contact with the convoy. The Navy could really never count on operational support by trained and sizeable air units in Norway. Difficulties arose in regard to the determination of the focal point of attack. Inadequate fighter cover made full use of naval bases at Trondheim and Bergen impossible, and finally resulted in endangering the ships in the northernmost bases (the *Tirpitz,* for instance).[6]

The head of the Naval Staff, *Vizeadmiral* Wilhelm Meisel, was also painfully aware of the Luftwaffe's shortcomings in the post-1942 era. In a memorandum of 3 November 1943 on aerial reconnaissance over the North Sea and Arctic waters, he pointed out a number of instances that highlighted Luftlotte 5's inability to achieve anything of significance in the previous twelve months. At the top of his list was the attack by an Anglo-American task force headed by *Duke of York* and the United States carrier *Ranger* on German shipping plying Norwegian coastal waters off Bodö in October 1943. Taking advantage of *Tirpitz*'s poor condition, and right under the nose of the Luftwaffe, this force ventured to within 250 kilometers of the coast, at which point the carrier's Dauntless dive-bombers and Avenger torpedo bombers "sunk as well as damaged seven of our tankers," noted Meisel indignantly.[7] In fact, up to 23,000 tons of German shipping had been sent to an icy grave or damaged by *Ranger*'s aircraft.[8] This intimidatory attack graphically demonstrated how far Stumpff's forces had fallen. In 1940 the Royal Navy received a mauling all along the Norwegian coast at the hands of the Luftwaffe, but three years later there was barely a snarl.[9]

Despite continuing naval remonstrations, little had been done to remedy the reconnaissance situation because the Luftwaffe was simply too stretched on all fronts to consider the reinforcement of Norway seriously. For Meisel, it was clear that a continuation of this situation would sooner or later spell disaster, since the enemy could potentially advance almost unobserved into any number of fjords along the coast. Yet he had to admit in his memorandum of late 1943 that although the prospects for improving this situation were not encouraging, with the forces presently available to the Luftwaffe and their allotted fuel quota insufficient for extended tasks, the oncoming winter and darkness would make wide-ranging reconnaissance at best incomplete anyway.[10] His only hope, and a forlorn one at that, was to alert the Luftwaffe to the dangerous situation.

Previously, in the summer of 1943, the navy had asked the Luftwaffe to reconsider its earlier request for bomber units in Norway to be employed in reconnaissance duties. In a memorandum to Luftflotte 5's headquarters in Oslo, Schniewind enumerated his concerns regarding the present situation:

1. The air reconnaissance requested by Naval Group North, which is supposed to serve as a basis for the operations of the command, cannot be nearly fulfilled, even under favorable weather conditions, with forces available.
2. The bomber forces available can under no circumstances be used for reconnaissance because such use of bomber forces is in opposition to strict orders from C.-in-C. Luftwaffe.
3. It is impossible to rely on other reconnaissance forces being brought in. Even if other special bomber formations should be brought in, they can under no circumstances be used for reconnaissance tasks.[11]

Given the weakened state of the northern air fleet, Schniewind was careful to point out that he in no way intended to hold Luftflotte 5 responsible for the lack of offensive operations. But since it seemed highly unlikely that a reinforcement of the air fleet was in the offing, he proposed that the ban on the use of bombers for reconnaissance purposes be lifted. Moreover, he hastened to add, this was not a demand for a separate air arm, since he felt that even if the navy had such a force, it would be able to achieve "no more than Luftflotte 5 is achieving now." The Naval Staff concurred and forwarded the correspondence between the air fleet and the Maringruppenord on this subject to the head of the Luftwaffe General Staff, along with its own recommendation that "in cases of emergency, freedom of decision should be given to Luftflottenkommando 5 as to whether bomber aircraft should be brought in for reconnaissance."[12] This reasonable naval initiative, though, ignored one important fact: Luftflotte 5 did not currently possess any bombers for bombing missions, let alone reconnaissance tasks.

Even as the navy passed on its concerns to OKL, Stumpff in Norway was only too well aware of how ill equipped his so-called air fleet was to support any operation by *Scharnhorst*. If he had had difficulties in providing adequate air cover for *Rösselsprung* in July 1942, when his inventory had stood at nearly 270 aircraft, by mid-1943 he was considerably worse off with no more than 170 combat aircraft.[13] Of the 100-odd aircraft lost by Stumpff to the Mediterranean, most had been the offensive heart of his air fleet—the Ju 88 and He 111 bombers and torpedo bombers of KG 30 and KG 26. Thus his strike force was now nonexistent. Of the remaining planes, 70 were fighters and 100 were coastal and long-range reconnaissance types. Adding to Stumpff's woes was the fact that while numbers of the latter types had not fallen, they were now facing an increasingly heavy workload all along the coastline and, as the *Ranger* incident had demonstrated, could not cover every nook and cranny along Norway's 2,600-kilometer length. Moreover, the fact that only 30 of these 100 reconnaissance aircraft were designated long-range and that, of these, only 13 were the true long-range Condors of KG 30 was also of increasing concern.

METEOROLOGIC DUTIES

The Condors not only were engaged in reconnaissance duties, however, but also often found themselves taking part in clandestine relief missions to manned weather stations dotted around the Arctic region. Since the meteorologic conditions of Norway and all of western Europe are greatly influenced by the weather moving from west to east, the Germans engaged in a relentless struggle from early in the war to obtain the most up-to-date information on weather patterns in this region.[14] They did this initially by using weather-reporting ships in the North Atlantic, before the loss of a number of these in 1941 led to the establishment of land-based weather stations from 1942 until the end of the war. Although aircraft could be used for weather-monitoring work, and in fact during this period Norway had a couple of meteorologic squadrons *(Wetterkundungsstaffelen)*, Westa 3 and 4, based at Trondheim, and a *Wetterkette* (weather detachments numbering three aircraft) situated at both Stavanger and Banak, the aircraft typically engaged in this work were able to venture only as far as the southern tip of Spitzbergen in the north and as far west as Jan Mayen and the Faroe Islands.[15] Known to British intelligence as *Zenit* forces—so named because of the "Zenith code" used by the Germans to encipher visual observations—these Luftwaffe units, usually equipped with Ju 88s and BV 138s and on occasion supplemented by Condors, regularly undertook weather-monitoring flights.[16] In this capacity the *Zenit* planes acted almost as freelance agents of the Luftwaffe, providing accurate and recent meteorologic information.[17]

On top of this, Luftwaffe reconnaissance aircraft were at various times co-opted into supporting the land-based meteorologic stations established on

Spitzbergen and Greenland. Of the two types of weather stations in common use, the automatic transmitter and the permanent meteorologic and wireless station, the latter clearly needed greater regular provisioning and support. While U-boats were employed periodically for this purpose, more flexible operations could be undertaken by aircraft—in this case the Condor, although BV 138s were also used, and later in the war, the BV 222. For example, when the *Holzauge* station on Sabine Island, off Greenland's barren east coast, was bombed by American aircraft in the latter part of May 1943, Condors from Norway were dispatched on relief missions to the isolated scientists. Over the 1943–1944 winter, these flights continued, with Ultra intercepts revealing that they were undertaken with the purpose of dropping supplies.[18] By way of illustration, decrypts show that on 16 November a flight was scheduled to take off from the Lofoten Islands to supply the isolated Germans, and this was followed on 11 January 1944 by a Condor operation from Norway "in connection with the Greenland meteorological station." During February, a specially equipped and manned He 111 was dispatched from the Fatherland to Banak to meet the supply needs of the large numbers of men stationed in Greenland and elsewhere, and on 14 March another Condor relief flight was completed.[19] In the end, though, pressure from Allied forces trying to locate and close down the facilities forced their evacuation by BV 138s and U-boats in that same year.[20]

The mention of BV 138s in these operations is intriguing, since their rather limited range would normally have precluded their use over such long distances. It does seem likely, however, that the Luftwaffe, in an attempt to utilize greater numbers of aircraft in long-range sorties, was forced to devise ways of ingeniously refueling these aircraft by U-boats. One of the best-known of such missions was undertaken in the latter part of the summer of 1943, when two BV 138s, with the aid of U-boats for refueling, carried out sorties from the Soviet Novaya Zemlya Islands over a period of twenty-one days in an attempt to monitor shipping in the Kara Sea.[21] As clever as this was, the complex refueling and oiling process was time-consuming and potentially dangerous for both U-boat and plane as they sat as helpless as ducks on a pond. This method of extending the range of the BV 138s was, however, really only a stopgap measure that could never come close to satisfying the Luftwaffe's and navy's need for a genuine long-distance reconnaissance aircraft.[22] That this type of operation was embarked on at all was indicative of the lack of long-range planes in the Luftwaffe in general and in Norway in particular.

A snapshot revealing the small number of reconnaissance flights of all types being undertaken from Norway, and the extent to which weather sorties cut into aircraft availability, is revealed in a recently declassified British intelligence report from the period. Derived from Luftwaffe Enigma decrypts detailing bomber, reconnaissance, and coastal operations in the areas of Luftflotte 3 and 5, the lengthy summary looks at the week of 22–28 August 1943.[23] Although, unsurprisingly, there were no offensive bomber operations recorded in this period for the Norwegian-based air fleet, there were a number of reconnaissance and weather flights. For instance, Fliegerführer Nord (West) had two aircraft regularly reconnoitering the Scottish east coast, and at least one operation around the north and northwest coast of Scotland was undertaken. Interestingly, the signals data also point to the arrival of a long-range photoreconnaissance Bf 109 for a flight over Scapa, while from Stavanger irregular morning reconnaissance missions were flown by He 115s to supplement the regular evening sorties. From Trondheim, routine reconnaissance was carried out daily by two Condors between Iceland and Jan Mayen, but no sightings were reported, and Westa 5 (based here and at Banak) engaged in its usual *Zenit* flights. Fliegerführer Lofoten was strangely quiet, and flights were not recorded until 28 August, when four BV 138s undertook a special but unknown mission. In the far northeastern reaches of the country, Fliegerführer Nord (Ost)'s routine morning observational excursions were made by two Ju 88s. In all, about 85 sorties were flown during this one week (compared with the over 400 flown by Luftflotte 3)—that is, only 12 reconnaissance sorties a day for the whole of the Norwegian coast and its environs, plus the reconnaissance missions reaching farther afield.

Luftflotte 5's shortage of reconnaissance aircraft was highlighted in a teletype message sent by Dönitz to the Führer in mid-December 1943 regarding the "burning question of long-range reconnaissance for submarine warfare," in which he noted that the enemy's increasing use of radar had forced his U-boats "more and more below the surface." "Surface tactics by submarines are a thing of the past," he lamented, for although finding convoys on the surface had been difficult at the best of times, Dönitz estimated that now being forced to operate submerged reduced by half the possibility of locating convoys. Therefore, the problem being felt in the Atlantic, as well as in Norway, was the lack of long-distance aircraft available for maritime work. Dönitz's concerns were elaborated upon in the Naval Staff war diary:

> Even now operations without air reconnaissance hold no promise of success. The past two months, however, clearly confirm that the extremely weak forces at the disposal of the Fliegerführer Atlantik cannot carry out the minimum reconnaissance requirements necessary for a submarine operation, even when strained to the utmost. Nine of the 14 joint operations already carried out were failures because the reconnaissance forces were so weak they could not detect the convoy sailing close by the submarine patrol line.[24]

Dönitz pushed for an acceleration of the Ju 290 program. Hitler concurred, but Göring revealed that at this stage of production it was just not possible because the building capacity of the Luftwaffe was already overburdened. If once again the lack of four-engined long-range bombers was having a detrimental effect on the war in the Atlantic, its impact was soon to be sharply brought into focus in the Arctic, where the dearth of long-range aircraft and an inefficient divided command structure would spell the death knell of *Scharnhorst*.

Even at this late stage of the war, some officers in the field still felt that a consolidation of the respective operation staffs under a single command for Norway was required. In the second week of December 1943, *Vizeadmiral* Otto Ciliax, Naval Command Norway, who was at the forefront of these recommendations, suggested, in accordance with the Führer's aim of saving personnel, that a joint Armed Forces Operations Staff in Norway be established. He laid out to the Naval Staff the advantages such a reorganization offered:

1. Concentration of all military forces in Norway in one hand, thereby achieving an intensified defensive and offensive force.
2. Simplifying of the project for reinforcement of the defense of the whole area and its execution.
3. Stronger representation of the armed forces with civilian authorities and better utilization of the forces employed by the latter.
4. The previous occurrence of discord and doubling up of work among the three branches of the armed forces all working along their own lines would cease.
5. Considerable saving of personnel in command and administration.[25]

The Naval Staff's response was typically parochial. It rejected the proposal, feeling that it not only would increase the requirements of the naval personnel if one of its own was put in charge but also would weaken its own hold over the naval forces in Norway because the new commander would be more dependent on OKW than the Naval Staff.[26] What the navy had not fully appreciated yet was the fact that the vessels it still had parked in the north had well passed their use-by date and, without coordinated air cover in future strikes, were increasingly a threat to the safety of their crews when at sea. With the Naval Staff unable or unwilling to establish a single regional command and transfer in more aircraft, the stage was set for a tragic German naval blunder.

THE DEATH OF *SCHARNHORST*

On 22 December 1943, a Luftwaffe aircraft sighted a convoy that would become the focus of Germany's next attempt to bring its Norway-based surface force to bear on the Arctic traffic. The aircrew's report stated that this convoy, 670 kilometers west of Tromsö bearing northeast, consisted of about seventeen merchantmen and three tankers, with an escorting force of three or four cruisers and nine destroyers and corvettes.[27] Significantly, a covering force had not been sighted but was presumed to be up to 780 kilometers distant in accordance with previous procedures and was unlikely to be spotted at this stage because of the thinner cover provided by the Luftwaffe farther north of Norway's Arctic coast.

The actual composition of JW 55B included nineteen merchantmen, accompanied by ten destroyers. Although the British did not have a three- to four-strong cruiser escort attached directly to the convoy, as mentioned in the reconnaissance report, they did have such a force made up of *Norfolk, Belfast,* and *Sheffield* under the command of Rear Admiral Robert Burnett on hand in the Barents Sea, protecting a convoy of empty vessels making its way back toward the British Isles. The usual distant covering force trailing some way behind JW 55B was Admiral Sir Bruce Fraser's Home Fleet, made up of the battleship *Duke of York,* the cruiser *Jamaica,* and four destroyers. Neither of these forces had been spotted by German reconnaissance, and hence they were unknown to the Naval Staff.

Meanwhile, Göring had refused point-blank to transfer any forces to Norway to operate against the convoy.[28] On top of this, Stumpff was reticent about expending his limited resources. On 22 December 1943, he stressed that he had no suitable combat forces available to participate in the proposed operation and thought that any further reconnaissance over the convoy area, on a scale to which the navy had hitherto become accustomed, was "an unnecessary waste of personnel and material unless the navy actually intended to take action."[29] This was not an unreasonable position, given the surface forces' halfhearted attempts to date. Stumpff asked Group North for information regarding its intentions, and in his reply, *Vizeadmiral* Schniewind, the fleet commander, was to the point. Without adequate reconnaissance, the operation simply could not be carried out effectively. In quick-fire fashion, he listed three important reasons: continuous reconnoitering by air units was the only way to effectively lead surface vessels in for the kill; even after the convoy was picked up by U-boats, aircraft were indispensable for shadowing the convoy; and last, but not least, the Luftwaffe was desperately needed to sight a possible covering force. Nevertheless, Schniewind concluded that if there were "prospects for success, naval forces will operate against the convoy even if the *Luftflotte* does not carry out combat operations, which is only to be expected in view of the strained situation and nonarrival of reinforcements."[30]

Notwithstanding the conciliatory ending to the *Vizeadmiral*'s assessment, the arguments were compelling. With a dire need to do as much as possible to shore up the desperate German position on the eastern front, Stumpff agreed to support the navy-inspired effort, under operation orders aptly entitled *Ostfront.* The next day, he informed the Naval Staff that his air fleet would do all that it could with the limited resources on hand, "not only because it is demanded by the navy, but in the clear knowledge of what is at stake."[31] He promised continuous reconnaissance and maintenance of contact with the convoy and constant, but not complete, contact with the covering group up to a distance of one day's run around the convoy. Stumpff's long-range aircraft would undertake probing reconnaissance as far as the east coast of Scotland and the region between the Shetlands and Jan Mayen. For the attacking surface forces, he could provide close air support as weather permitted, but no bomber sorties could be undertaken. In other words, Stumpff would do what he could, but gaps were bound to appear.[32] True to his word, Luftflotte 5 had two Ju 88s and four Condors dispatched to monitor contact with the convoy; in all, thirty-six planes were sent up on reconnaissance sorties throughout 24 December.[33] Nevertheless, JW 55B's covering forces still remained undetected, since even with a large portion of its reconnaissance force in the air, Luftflotte 5 had to cover an area that was simply beyond its capacity by late 1943. *Konteradmiral* Erich Bey, commander of the *Scharnhorst*-led Task Force, exclaimed on Christmas Day that "the present reconnaissance over the convoy was completely inadequate and that it was absolutely necessary to extend it in search of the heavy enemy forces."[34] Prospects, however, were not good, since deteriorating weather conditions were forecast for the day laid down for the operation, 26 December.

The predicted strong winds (force 6 to 8), heavy southwest seas, dense clouds, intermittent rain, and declining visibility (expected to fall to five to seven kilometers) not only would make air operations impossible, warned Fliegerführer Lofoten, but also would almost certainly force the U-boats to abandon their positions ahead of the convoy. In this situation, the *Admiral Nordmeer, Kapitän* Rudolf Peters in Narvik, recommended that the operation be broken off. The Naval Staff, however, pushed ahead, explaining that the critical situation facing the German army on the eastern front demanded action, and, since a covering force had yet to be detected by aerial reconnaissance, a quick attack on the convoy was warranted. Nevertheless, the operation was certainly risky, a fact fully appreciated by many, as indicated by *Kapitän zur See* Hans Düwel (the first operations officer, *Admiral Nordmeer*) in the early hours of 24 December:

> The Luftwaffe commanders are doing their utmost with the strength available to locate the supposed enemy squadron. . . . They will not, however, be in a position to give us an absolutely clear picture. . . . The British unit located yesterday by its [wireless] transmissions may well be the cover force closing. . . . Even if it is not reported today by air reconnaissance, we should still suppose it to exist, not only outside the 300-mile limit of air reconnaissance, but even *inside* this, having regard to the weather and intermittent failure of the equipment.[35]

In spite of these concerns, Dönitz—as he later wrote in his memoirs—deemed the situation ripe for action: "Our reconnaissance had not discovered the presence of any heavy enemy formation, though that, of course, did not mean that no such force was at sea. But if it were, it must have been a long way from the convoy, and the *Scharnhorst* seemed to have every chance of delivering a rapid and successful attack."[36] Should heavy seas prohibit the use of destroyers, *Scharnhorst* was instructed to carry out the attack alone in "cruiser warfare style." The Task Force left Alta Fjord at 1900 hours on Christmas Day.

By 0730 on 26 December, Bey calculated that this force was now situated northwest of the convoy and sent his destroyers south in extremely heavy seas to reconnoiter its likely path. Unbeknownst to Bey, though, Admiral Fraser, in anticipation of an attack, had sent the convoy on a northbound course farther away from German Arctic naval bases and Luftwaffe airfields. At the same time, he directed Burnett to close up his three cruisers with the convoy. The situation was rapidly turning against the Germans, and, separated from its destroyers, *Scharnhorst* came under fire at 0926 from the cruisers. Bey, however, could not determine where the fire was coming from because his ship was shrouded in a snowstorm. It was not long before shells began falling with alarming accuracy all around the battle cruiser, and within moments a hit knocked out the ship's radar room. Under the abysmal prevailing weather conditions, it did not take long for Bey to conclude that the enemy ships had initially located *Scharnhorst* (and were now tracking its movements) with the assistance of radar. While his own equipment had been turned off to avoid detection, for the last fifty minutes the Royal Navy cruisers had been able to follow his every move, setting up an ambush. Although on paper the cruisers lacked the pure muscle for a stand-up fight with a battle cruiser, their radar-directed salvos were extremely accurate and were more than a match for the heavier firepower of *Scharnhorst,* which could only be directed very imprecisely by the muzzle flashes of the enemy. This put the big ship at a decided disadvantage, especially because both *Belfast* and *Sheffield* were using a new nonflash powder.[37] Under the impression that he had been engaged by a battleship, Bey, in obedience to his strict instructions not to engage heavy forces, disengaged and ordered the German destroyers south of the battle to withdraw from the field. As *Scharnhorst* fled southeast, slowly pulling away from the trailing British cruisers and the convoy's destroyers, Fraser's force began to close in on its quarry.

Not that the Germans were totally unaware of *Duke of York* drawing the noose around *Scharnhorst.* Since 0943, the naval signals intercept service, B-Dienst, had been picking up a constant flow of messages that were obviously originating from Burnett, detailing the movements of the *Scharnhorst.* The recipient of these messages, under the call sign "DGO," was more of a mystery, although intelligence personnel assumed ominously that it was another surface force.[38] At 1113, Marinekommandonord/Flotte postulated that the "reporting from one British unit to another could have been addressed to the convoy from a cruiser, but may well equally have been a direction of the supposed heavy cover force towards the target."[39] These reports, however, were not forwarded to Bey, who remained oblivious to this unpleasant possibility.

Confirmation of naval suspicions was being gathered by the Luftwaffe. Although Fliegerführer Nord (West) reported that it would not be able to carry out its scheduled flights until 2100, and in spite of Fliegerführer Lofoten's earlier indications that it would not even be able to get aircraft into the air because of the turbulent snowstorms buffeting the area, the gravity of unfolding events led to the latter air commander getting aloft at least three BV 138s loaded with the latest *Hohentwiel* radar sets.[40] Indeed, these were the only aircraft that would have made any difference to the outcome of what was to shortly take place, since their effectiveness was based not on optical visibility, close to nil by this time, but rather on technical efficiency. At 1012, contact was made with Fraser's force and a brief report sent in.[41] For the next hour and a half, contact was maintained with the enemy vessels, and at 1140 a more detailed second signal stated that "apparently one large and several small vessels" had been located and were believed to be traveling south at high speed.[42]

Incredibly, this vital information, collected by aircrews at great personal risk, languished at Fliegerführer Lofoten's headquarters for a full three hours before even the first brief signal was passed on to the navy at 1306. The second detailed message was withheld even longer, apparently because the air commander, *Oberst* Roth, doubted that such a detailed picture of the fast-moving force could be accurate given the weather situation.[43] Only after the aircrews had returned and verbally corroborated the assessment did Roth forward the latter report, but by then it was too late. The enemy group picked up by the airborne Luftwaffe radar was, of course, the force led by *Duke of York,* but since only the initial cursory report was relayed to the navy, Bey was just informed that several vessels had been located. At 1530, after receiving the news via *Admiral Nordmeer,* the crew was informed: "Signal from the Luftwaffe. Reconnaissance plane reports enemy fleet detachment 250 kilometres west. Keep sharp lookout."[44] The report had taken over five hours to reach Bey and, unlike the second report, made no mention of the possibility of a capital ship being present. Poor interservice communication and the twin command structures in Norway were once again having an adverse effect on the war in the Far North.

Meanwhile, time was rapidly running out for the German battle cruiser because, at 1617, the mysterious "DGO" signaled that it had made contact with a target only thirty-eight kilometers distant. The conclusion was obvious. "As 'DGO' later sent out tactical orders to the rest of the formation she was most probably in command of the covering group," deduced the Naval Staff in Berlin. By 1643, the British battleship, using its radar in pitch darkness, had reduced the distance to its unsuspecting prey to barely thirteen kilometers. Within minutes, *Scharnhorst* was engaged in a life-and-death running battle with *Duke of York* and Burnett's cruisers. It was a decidedly mismatched struggle, and the following signals from Bey chronicled the demise of his warship:

1656   Engagement with a heavy battleship.

1724   I am encircled by heavy forces.

1819   Enemy firing by radar at range of more than 18 kilometers.

1825   To Führer! We will fight on until last shell is fired.[45]

Through a number of direct hits, the 36-cm guns of the British battleship slowed the ailing *Scharnhorst;* these were soon followed by a series of torpedo strikes delivered by the destroyers, further reducing its speed.[46] Although the Naval Staff made a desperate and impossible plea to the Luftwaffe at 1935 for a torpedo attack, it was already too late. Once *Scharnhorst*'s heavy armament was knocked out, *Jamaica* and *Belfast* were sent in to finish off the stricken vessel with torpedoes. The ship capsized at 1945, and nearly 2,000 men were killed.

The soul-searching aftermath of the ill-fated *Ostfront* operation identified two critical flaws. The first centered on the enemy's ability to locate, track, and attack the German ship even in the most appalling conditions, thanks to its accurate radar system. In theory, *Scharnhorst* had the upper hand against the cruisers that struck early on in the battle, but enjoying the benefits of modern technology, the Royal Navy easily nullified the German ship's superior armament. The Führer was naturally unhappy with the outcome of *Ostfront* and in particular with Bey's decision to break off his fight with the cruisers when clearly—on paper—his ship was superior to them with regard to both fighting power and armament. An exasperated Dönitz countered: "Surface ships are no longer able to fight without effective radar equipment." On top of this, the British radar prevented the *Scharnhorst* quietly slipping from the battlefield because its movements could be monitored at all times. This allowed the cruisers to maintain contact with the fleeing ship and guide in Fraser's battleship.

Naturally enough, the second deficiency isolated in the inevitable postmortem of the sinking focused on the lack of air reconnaissance. In his assessment, Schniewind stressed not only the importance of British radar but also the "inadequacy of our air reconnaissance" as causes for the loss of the big ship.[47] The Naval Staff concurred, pointing out that "weak German air reconnaissance was unable to detect the position of the enemy forces in time, so the latter were able to cut the *Scharnhorst* off from its base, encircle and destroy her."[48] Perhaps more remarkable was the fact that given the appalling weather conditions, Luftflotte 5 was able to get *any* aircraft into the air and that the new airborne radar actually worked. Nevertheless, this, and poor interservice communications, aside, the loss of *Scharnhorst* had demonstrated what everyone already knew: the Luftwaffe in the Far North simply did not have enough aircraft to satisfactorily perform even the most rudimentary of reconnaissance tasks.

Luftflotte 5's strength did not substantially increase in the New Year. Although the new commander, *General der Flieger* Josef Kammhuber (the former head of night fighters), could call on about fifteen Condors, he was unable to do anything to impede the progress of the Murmansk-bound convoys, since the air fleet still lacked a strike force. In early January, Stumpff had been appointed commander of Luftwaffe Befehlshaber Mitte, which was soon to be upgraded to Luftflotte Reich—an unenviable posting and, despite greater numbers of aircraft at his disposal than in Norway, even more difficult.[49] Meanwhile, the unavailability of a strike force was compounded by the Allies' increasing use of escort carriers over the 1943–1944 winter and the resurgence of Soviet airpower at the eastern end of the Arctic route. For Luftflotte 5, the continued appearance of escort carriers was particularly disconcerting, and in March 1944 Allied aircraft from these carriers dealt the air fleet's reconnaissance forces a heavy blow when they shot down six German machines. This was the last straw. On 2 April, Kammhuber advised the navy that he would no longer authorize maritime reconnaissance in its support.

This effectively ended the Luftwaffe's threat to convoys.[50] The cost had simply become too high to justify the meager results achieved.

As if the *Scharnhorst* tragedy and the admission that it was unable to undertake further daylight reconnaissance were not enough, the Luftwaffe in the Far North had one other reminder that revealed how far the mighty had fallen. As a stark testimony to Germany's flawed strategy (or rather lack of strategy) that saw it begin a war without long-range maritime aircraft, the He 177 finally arrived in Norway in February 1944—over three years too late. Intended to replace the faithful Condors, more often than not these ill-omened behemoths simply sat on Trondheim's bleak, windswept Vaernes airfield as the Allies' own four-engined bombers struck at the Third Reich's fuel supplies.[51] With the "fuel famine" biting deep into Luftwaffe fuel reserves, planners determined that Germany simply could not afford to have many of these fuel-hungry planes in use, especially in Norway, when the main effort now firmly rested with the defense of the Reich. It has been calculated that a single medium-range attack by a wing of He 177s would consume at least 480 tons of fuel, that is, an average day's output from the Reich's entire fuel production in August 1944.[52] Although, as we shall see, the Luftwaffe in Norway was remarkably well off compared with the Fatherland with regard to aviation fuel stocks in the latter part of the war, in early 1944 these four-engined machines were more of a burden than an asset because of their high fuel consumption. Göring had prophetically foreseen this eventuality in February 1943, when at a major conference focusing on the He 177 he stated: "I am of the opinion that the building of our aircraft should not depend in any way on the fuel program. I would rather have a mass of aircraft standing around unable to fly owing to lack of petrol, than not have them at all."[53] His bizarre preference was fulfilled with the He 177 in Norway, where these giants were forced to languish while less thirsty aircraft took to the air.[54] Realistically, though, even if the Luftwaffe could have utilized this handful of aircraft, they were unequal to the now insurmountable tasks that faced the Germans in Norway and elsewhere. The planes had been needed in 1940, in Luftflotte 5's attempt to stretch the defenses of Fighter Command during the Battle of Britain, while from 1940 until 1942 they would have been invaluable flying from Norwegian and French airfields in establishing a "siege of Britain" in cooperation with the navy's U-boats. It was at these times and places that the possession of significant numbers of He 177s might well have swung the conflict in Germany's favor, but not in early 1944, when for all intents and purposes the outcome of the war had been decided.

FIGHTER DEFENSE

As if the ignominious and avoidable loss of *Scharnhorst* was not a bitter enough pill for Luftflotte 5 to swallow, the weakness of the Luftwaffe's fighter forces was also laid bare by an increasing number of air raids being made by Allied bombers on Hitler's northern empire. Throughout 1941 and 1942, Bomber Command had undertaken barely 100 sorties to Norway, and many of these were for minelaying operations; but by 1943, major raids were possible and included a significant contribution by the Americans.[55] Stumpff's fighter defenses in Norway came principally under the control of Jagdfliegerführer Norwegen, consisting loosely of four single-engined fighter groups *(Jagdgruppen)*, a twin-engined squadron of Bf 110s *(Zerstörstaffel)*, and a fighter-bomber squadron of Ju 88s *(Jabostaffel)*, whose main force was JG 5 *Eismeer*, under the command of *Oberleutnant* Gotthardt Handrick.[56] Of the seventy to eighty single-engined Bf 109s and Focke Wulf Fw 190 fighters operating in Norway in mid-1943, at least half (I/JG 5) were at any one time based above the Arctic Circle, protecting the vital German supply ships plying northern Norwegian coastal waters from Soviet-based aircraft; the balance (IV/JG 5) were deployed below the Arctic Circle to fend off bomber raids launched from Britain.[57] Although the former were able to successfully prevent even a single coastal vessel from being sunk between June and October 1943, the latter units had to cover too great an area with too few machines. Thus, against the increasing numbers of high-flying Anglo-American foes appearing over Norway in 1943–1944, they were unable to do little more than niggle at the attackers. Incredibly, given its already weakened state, the Luftwaffe began transferring units away from Luftfotte 5 at least as early as October 1943, and by December fully half of JG 5 was based in Germany for home defense.[58]

The last major success of the defensive fighters of JG 5 against British aircraft had come in the closing days of 1941 when they shot down eight out of twenty-nine Bomber Command aircraft sent to support the raids at Lofotens and elsewhere that had fueled Hitler's Norway paranoia. In 1942 and in the years that followed, successes such as these would be few and far between. For the most part, the Anglo-American raids were directed either at the industrial facilities forming the heart of Hitler's economic plans for Norway or at the U-boat pens under construction at Bergen and Trondheim, destined to become his Nordic Singapore. Of these raids, the major missions (excluding the minelaying of coastal waters) were undertaken by the United States' Eighth Air Force and RAF's Bomber Command. An examination of the mission folders of the American effort reveals with startling clarity the weakness of German defenses.

From their fields in East Anglia, the Eighth Air Force took off for Norway for the first time on 24 July 1943, its target: the newly constructed aluminum, magnesium, and nitrate factories at Heroya, lying between Kristiansand and Oslo on Norway's southeastern shores, and the U-boat and harbor installations at Trondheim and Bergen. The main target was the light metals works at Heroya, and since only light defenses were anticipated, the 167 B-17 bombers would fly in at a very low operational altitude of 4,900 meters and without the protection of long-range fighters. In the end, they may as well have flown much lower because defensive measures were completely lacking; as the report detailing the mission noted, enemy "opposition was weak."[59] At 1158, the American aircraft were picked up eighty-three kilometers southwest of Stavanger by the extensive German radar system running along the coast. Jagdfliegerführer Norwegen immediately put up an estimated five *Rotten* of fighters to patrol between Stavanger and Lister, and further aircraft were sent north as soon as operations personnel realized that bombers were also making their way toward northern targets.[60] The encounters of the American 1st Wing while dropping over 400 tons of bombs on Heroya were described in the after-action report: "The three forces of 1st Wing experienced a total of 21 encounters, 14 from Fw 190s and 7 from Bf 109s. The attacks started at about 1330, after the first force had bombed and begun on the return journey, lasting until about 1500. Encounters were sporadic and by single enemy aircraft, and varied from weak attacks to aggressive attacks pressed home."[61] Farther north, the raid on Bergen and Trondheim was being carried out by 4th Wing, whose aircraft had been specially equipped with long-range fuel tanks, allowing them to undertake the Eighth Air Force's longest round-trip mission thus far in the war. Although, in the face of impenetrable cloud cover, the Bergen component had to be aborted because of the American policy of avoiding indiscriminate bombing over occupied territories, 41 bombers did make it to Trondheim, where seventy-nine tons of bombs were dropped on harbor installations. Aerial defenses over Trondheim were even lighter than those over Heroya, and only twelve encounters were recorded, beginning at 1415 and ending at 1435. The lack of adequate protection gave the B-17s plenty of opportunity to hit targets with few distractions, and at Heroya the ensuing damage brought work at the nitrate plant to a halt for three and a half months, while the Germans were forced to completely abandon the partially completed aluminum and magnesium installations.[62] At Trondheim, although one eyewitness felt that the bombing had been carried out with "impressive accuracy" and that a good deal of the harbor had been badly damaged, the U-boat pens' thick concrete construction prevented any significant impression being made on these facilities.[63] Overall, Luftwaffe opposition was at best slight, and only a single bomber of the 309 sent to Norway failed to return—and that machine, which landed safely in Sweden, had been damaged by flak, not fighters. That the German defenses here were markedly inferior to their homeland counterparts was glaringly apparent to the Americans, who in the period 24 to 30 July 1943 had lost 88 aircraft in six costly raids on the heart of the Third Reich.[64]

Two subsequent Norwegian attacks were made by the Americans on 16 and 18 November 1943, with similar results. The targets of the first raid were all based in southwestern Norway at the Vemork power station and electrolysis plant at Rjukan, the molybdenum mines at Knaben, and the Oslo-Kjeller Aircraft Repair Depot and aerodrome. Once again, the B-17s and B-24s were forced to rely on their own substantial defensive armament, since no fighter escort was possible, and a belief that flak defenses would be weak meant the attacks would be made at no more than 3,700 meters. By now, the number of aircraft on call to the Jagdfliegerführer had fallen further as fighters were siphoned off for home defense. The Americans correctly calculated that the German fighter commander had no more than 50 single-engined fighters at his disposal in southern Norway and another 30 night fighters in northern Denmark. As Eighth Air Force records show, once the enemy bombers were picked up by radar the Luftwaffe put up its meager clutch of fighters with the same depressing results:

> When the enemy realized that the bombers were about to cross the Norwegian coast, he sent single engine fighters to meet the bombers both from bases north of the entry, and from bases south of their entry in Denmark. . . . The attacks by both these formations lacked aggressiveness and skill, and only a few of the enemy even made any attacks.[65]

Cloud cover over Oslo prevented an attack there, but the flak and fighter defenses were so weak at both Rjukan and Knaben that the bombers were permitted to make on average two runs over both targets, wreaking havoc on the power station, the electrolysis plant, and the mines. Of the 388 aircraft dispatched, only 2 bombers suffered injury.

The failure to attack the Luftwaffe's supply and maintenance depot at Oslo's Kjeller airfield led to a renewed effort two days later by seventy-eight Liberators. To intercept this force, aircraft from the Norwegian airfields of Lister, Stavanger, and Bergen were scrambled, as well as twin-engined fighters from Grove and Aalborg in Denmark. Wireless intercepts of Jagdfliegerführer Norwegen's local controllers graphically reveal the piecemeal effort the Germans were able to muster in response to the incoming bombers:

1045	4 Fw 190s landed in Sola from Herdla
1126	2 Fw 190s landed in Herdla from Vaernes
1218	1 Fw 190 started from Sola
12—	4 Me 109s started from Sola
1220	2 Me 109s started from Sola
1243	2 Fw 190s started from Sola
1547–49	4 Fw 190s landed at Sola
1546	2 Me 109s landed at Sola[66]

Once again, a majority of pilots failed to press home their attacks in a total of 50 to 60 sorties, although the few that did were rewarded for their efforts and, along with flak, hit nine Liberators—some of which made their way to Sweden and internment. In general, though, the small number of aircraft available was in no way equal to the task at hand and proved of only minor nuisance value. Overall, of the 775 sorties carried out by the Eighth Air Force in these three missions, only twelve aircraft were lost.

The Luftwaffe in Norway was also spectacularly ineffectual against British operations. Excluding the regular mine-laying sorties in Norwegian coastal waters, Bomber Command from 1943 until only a few days before the end of the war carried out numerous missions over Norway, more often than not by Mosquito-supported Lancasters. These ranged in scope from the relatively small 10-plane raid on the molybdenum mine at Knaben in March 1943 to the large 237-strong bomber attack on the U-boat pens at Bergen in October 1944. This latter target became increasingly important after D-Day when, once the Germans lost their French U-boat bases, they were forced to shift the bulk of their U-boat effort to Norway. It was at Bergen that Allied bombing over Norway would inflict the heaviest civilian losses. Unlike the Americans, the British were less circumspect about where their bombs fell, and in two big raids on 4 and 28 October 1944, over 150 people were killed—that is, one-fifth of all civilian casualties (752) suffered throughout the war in Norway as a result of Allied bombing.[67] Nevertheless, in figures closely paralleling the American offensive, Bomber Command in some 780 sorties lost only about 12 aircraft—and a good proportion of these were accounted for by flak rather than defensive fighters.[68]

Jagdfliegerführer Norwegen, like the other *Fliegerführeren* in Norway, simply lacked the requisite forces to threaten seriously, let alone prevent, Allied bombers from flying over Norway and leaving a trail of carnage in their wake. As an examination of the Luftwaffe effort reveals, because of a dearth of available fighter units, the Germans were often only able to put machines into the air in twos and threes, and these, of course, were often unwilling to press home attacks against a large number of Allied bombers fairly bristling with defensive armament and flying in close formation. The only saving grace for the German defenses was that the Anglo-American bomber fleets had richer and more important targets to hit over continental Europe, and therefore Norwegian facilities escaped the full brunt of the Allies' considerable might. The depths to which the Luftwaffe in Norway had sunk were highlighted by the shameful antics surrounding the sinking of *Tirpitz*.

THE LOSS OF *TIRPITZ*

Alongside the U-boat pens, *Tirpitz* remained the only consistently attacked target in Norway. Although for most of the war the battleship had remained tucked safely in its Nordic hideaway, to the British its mere presence represented a threat to any passing convoy. The damage caused by the midget submarines in September was not repaired until the spring of 1944, by which time, of course, the RAF had well and truly found its feet in aerial operations over Norway. Numerous strikes were made against the battleship up until September 1944, when in a particularly heavy raid thirty-nine Lancasters caught the 45,000-ton battleship in Alta Fjord and damaged it so badly that it had to be towed to Tromsö to operate as a stationary floating battery. In none of these strikes were German defensive aircraft even a minor hazard, let alone a significant deterrent. In fact, a disturbing decline in Luftflotte

5's fighter operations had begun to set in by the second half of the year. From January to June 1944, the air fleet's fighter forces had averaged 497 sorties per month, but for the next five months this figure fell dramatically to only 31 per month.[69] Coupled with this was the Luftwaffe's continued refusal to provide permanent air cover for the battleship now residing once again in Alta Fjord, since it reasoned that JG 5 was only eighty kilometers away by air at Banak.[70] With British determination to dispose of the battleship once and for all and the concurrent sharp decline in fighter capabilities, the scene was set for a disaster of titanic proportions.

On 12 November 1944, thirty Lancasters took off from Lossiemouth in northern Scotland to attack *Tirpitz*. Enjoying perfect weather, the bombers approached the ship from the east, hitting it with at least two six-ton *Tallboys*. Violent explosions racked the hull, causing the ship to capsize, and despite attempts to rescue as many as possible of the trapped crew by cutting holes in the upturned hull, 1,000 of the 1,900 men on board were lost. "Our own fighters," noted the OKW war diary, were ineffectual and "arrived too late" on the scene to be of any use.[71] Yet again, the Luftwaffe had not even shown its face, despite the fact that radar had given ample warning of the incoming intruders. Numerous explanations were given for the failure of JG 5's fighters to intercept the bombers. The most innocuous suggested that an interservice communication failure had prevented contact, but more sinister rumors abounded. For instance, a Luftwaffe Field Workshop *Obergefreiter* at Bardfloss reported under interrogation that when *Tirpitz* was sunk, the pilots were having a drinking party; when the alarm went off, "they were drunk and flew in the wrong direction."[72] Although this report may well have a degree of truth to it, in fact it does appear that *Major* Heinrich Ehrler, JG 5's *Kommodore,* was on unofficial leave with his girlfriend in Oslo at the time, and in the resulting furor Dönitz had him successfully court-martialed. Only Ehrler's exemplary record and status as an ace, with some 200 victories claimed, saved him from execution. He was transferred to home defense, where he flew Messerschmitt Me 262s until his death at the controls of one of these jets on 4 April 1945.[73] In many ways, even if the drinking stories were true and the *Major*'s dereliction of duty is taken into account, it does seem likely that *Tirpitz* was on borrowed time. This was especially so when one considers that even with sober pilots and JG 5's *Kommodore* on site, the British had already hit the battleship on numerous occasions without Luftwaffe opposition.

The loss of *Tirpitz* changed the face of the war in the Far North overnight. As Stephen Roskill noted in his multivolume official work *The War at Sea,* "One may doubt whether a single ship 'in being' had ever exerted such great influence on maritime strategy."[74] Though the ship had only once fired its guns in anger, and that against land-based targets on Spitzbergen, *Tirpitz's* sheer size, speed, and firepower had made Germany's last true battleship a threat right to the end. Its presence in the Far North forced the British to maintain at all times a strong fleet combining battleships, carriers, and supporting vessels just in case it was aroused to intercept a convoy or, worse yet, attempt a breakout into the Atlantic. With its death, the Royal Navy's global deployment benefited greatly. Resources no longer were tied up on the chance that *Tirpitz* might do something but instead could be distributed to areas of greater need. For the Germans, their surface fleet was reduced to the two pocket battleships *Scheer* and *Lützow,* a handful of cruisers, and some destroyers. Of these, the bulk were committed to supporting the hapless German retreat in the Baltic. Once again, Allied bombers had been able to act with impunity over German-occupied Norway.

FRESH FEARS OF INVASION AND THE PAPER AIR FORCE

The sinking of *Scharnhorst* and the poor performance of the Luftwaffe may well have helped rekindle Hitler's "Norway paranoia." From late 1943, the Führer's concern for his most northern possession began to burn brightly once more, fed by Allied deception plans for the Normandy landings and dubious unsubstantiated intelligence reports surrounding the possibility of an Allied landing somewhere on the northern flank in 1944 and 1945. Despite the disasters of Stalingrad and Kursk, Hitler felt that the greatest danger to the Reich lay in the west. "The danger in the east remains," he cautioned in November 1943, "but a greater danger now appears in the west: an Anglo-American landing!"[75] He reasoned that the huge territory in the east made it possible to lose ground there on a very large scale without Germany suffering a fatal blow to its "nervous system." On the other hand, an invasion in western Europe along a broad front would prove to be too great a threat to German conduct of the war, and Hitler ominously warned that its "immediate consequence would be unforeseeable." His solution was a reinforcement of forces, and although Norway did not get a specific mention in these plans, he pointedly stressed that a "pinning down and diversionary attack" could be expected on other fronts, including a possible major assault on Denmark. Norway, however, was too close to the Führer's heart to be ignored for long, and in 1944 the "zone of fate" assumed ever-increasing importance in his mind.

The Allies, for their part, had no serious intention of operating in Norway, despite Churchill's own Nordic obsession. The only major operation they had planned for Norway was of the deceptive variety. Under the umbrella deception action known as *Bodyguard,* Operations *Fortitude North* (Norway) and *Fortitude South* (Pas de Calais) were designed to fool the Germans into believing that the Allies planned not one but a series of invasions along the shores of occupied western Europe. This would lead them to divert their defenses farther afield and away from the intended landing site at Normandy. To create a believable impression that such operations actually were being prepared, a gradual buildup of radio traffic was generated in Britain at the imaginary headquarters responsible for the two false expeditions. The illusory Norwegian operation was to be accomplished by the notional Fourth British Army based in Scotland and Northern Ireland.[76]

These deception measures were also reinforced by reports sent to Germany from a number of controlled and uncontrolled sources in Britain, of which the supposedly pro-German Swedish naval and air attachés in London were the most influential. In the first half of 1944, via these attachés, collectively known as *Josephine,* the German *Abwehr* officer in Stockholm received information alleging that large numbers of troops were being assembled in Scotland for an Allied expedition to Scandinavia.[77] Although scholarship remains divided over the effectiveness of *Fortitude North* (the Pas de Calais deception, on the other hand, was indisputably successful), there can be little doubt that both Hitler and the navy were still convinced of the strategic importance of Norway to the German war effort.[78] Therefore, these deceptions preyed on the preexisting German preoccupation with Nordic security, and consequently troop numbers there increased from 359,233 men on 1 March to 372,063 men on 1 July 1944, while coastal defenses were further reinforced.[79] Although this was a considerable figure, it should not be forgotten that overall it did not represent Germany's fighting elite; aside from the force withdrawn from the northern sector of the eastern front, it included a significant proportion of elderly men who were poorly trained and equipped.

The Luftwaffe was not to be left out of Hitler's schemes, and even though it was not possible to carry out a large reinforcement of Luftflotte 5 at the time, Göring issued a major contingency plan for the Northern Flank on 6 January 1944 that would remain in force until the end of the war. Going under the ponderous code name *Drohende Gefahr Nord (Impending Threat North),* the plan noted that despite increasing signs that a landing was imminent in the west, the Germans could also reckon with the "possibility of an enemy landing attempt in Norway or Denmark, or even a simultaneous operation including southern Norway and Jutland."[80] Unwittingly echoing Churchill's suggestion that the Allies roll up Europe from the top, Göring pointed out that such an enemy action could be attempted either as a "decisive operation to roll up our northern front" or as a diversionary undertaking for a major landing in western Europe. "In any case," he continued, "warding off this landing attempt would be decisive for the conclusion of the war."

In the following plans, contingencies were examined and geographic operational areas assigned. For instance, should an Allied expedition attempt an operation in Norway, the command of all resources of Luftwaffe Befehlshaber Mitte (Gen.d.Lw.Dänemark), an adjunct of the soon-to-be-established Luftflotte Reich, would fall to Luftlotte 5's command, whose operational and reconnaissance area stretched north from a line running out to Newcastle on England's northeastern coast from the northern tip of Jutland.[81] The units in Europe to be made available for "immediate reinforcement" of Luftflotte 5 in the advent of a major Allied operation included reconnaissance units and bombers from Luftflotte 3, comprising five groups from KGs 26, 100, and 54 and a single group of He 177s from KG 40's Bordeaux base. Five fighter (Bf 109) and two Bf 110 groups also would be surrendered from Luftwaffe Befehlshaber Mitte. On top of these, ground attack units of Fw 190s from

Luftflotten 2 and 3 and night fighter units from Luftwaffe Befehlshaber Mitte would be included in the force. Should the Norwegian invasion take place without a corresponding landing in the west, the Luftwaffe in Norway could reckon on being supplied with further fighter wings of Bf 109s, a further bomber wing of Ju 88s in strength up to three groups, and a long-range squadron of Junkers Ju 188s from Luftwaffe Befehlshaber Mitte (Gen.d.Lw.Dänemark).[82] In theory, then, the air fleet could have approximately 500 additional aircraft at its disposal in the advent of an invasion of Norway.

Certainly on paper this looked impressive, and if carried through it would have brought the air fleet in Norway close to its combat strength of April–June 1940. In other words, Luftflotte 5 would have been more than an air fleet in name only. Whether this grand scheme would have worked we will never know, but what the plans do demonstrate is that Hitler was still obsessed with Norway and only too willing to prepare schemes against the day the Allies did show up at Norway's front door. The strategy also had one other important ramification that was not widely appreciated: it diverted a large amount of aviation fuel to Norway.

Contrary to popular belief, Norway did not suffer an aviation fuel shortage during the closing months of the Second World War. While vital defensive operations being flown over the Reich in the final stages of the war were severely hampered on occasion by petrol shortages, the planes stationed in Norway, though few in number, never had to worry about running short of aviation fuel. The documents surviving the war tend to suggest that this resulted from the stockpiling of aviation fuel for Drohende Gefahr Nord. Luftwaffe planners were only too well aware that the arrival of large numbers of aircraft in Norway as envisaged in this plan would require equally large stocks of fuel on hand for subsequent missions. Consequently, over 1944 the Germans began to assemble considerable petrol stocks in Norway in case Drohende Gefahr Nord was ever activated.

The Germans had begun the war with a stock of 492,000 tons of aviation fuel, capable of supporting three months of campaigning. Although this was two-thirds below the amount the Luftwaffe had hoped to enter a war with, it was ample to meet the demands of blitzkrieg assaults launched on Poland, Norway, France, and the Low Countries. It was only after the invasion of the Soviet Union that the Luftwaffe, and the other two services, began to feel the pinch of inadequate supplies. Up until then, Germany had been a big importer of Soviet oil, but of course this ceased with *Barbarossa,* forcing it to rely increasingly on domestic synthetic production and Romanian imports. Despite a couple of serious dips in Luftwaffe reserves in the intervening years—falling as low as 160,000 tons in mid-1942— by April 1944 stocks had risen to 580,000.[83] In the very next month, however, the German synthetic oil industry was sent reeling by the bomber strikes of the Eighth Air Force. Flying mostly by day, the American aircraft in May were so effective that at least 90 percent of the aviation fuel industry was hit.[84] Production fell immediately from 188,000 tons to barely 9,000 tons per month. Although some 200,000 workers were brought in to restore the industry to its previous capacity, monthly production slumped to an amazing low in September of only 3,500 tons after renewed air attacks, and by December 1944 it had recovered to just 25,000.[85]

Such a dramatic fall in production was naturally followed by a rapid decline in Luftwaffe and OKW reserves, with stocks plunging from the high-water mark of 580,000 tons to 180,000 in September 1944. The usual curtailing of aircraft testing and training programs was insufficient to stem the decline, and the Luftwaffe was forced to reduce air reconnaissance, while the number of night fighter sorties was pared back, and close air support for the army was permitted only in "decisive situations."[86] Despite occasional surges in activity, a renewed Allied bombing effort against the synthetic fuel plants in early 1945, as well as an overall decline in the availability of pilots and munitions, meant that the bulk of aircraft in Germany would never see action again as they sat out the final months of war in large air parks.[87] Notwithstanding this general decline in aerial activity over Germany, in Norway the fear of an Allied invasion even so late in the war prompted not only the transfer in of a small bomber strike force but also an expansion of existing operations.

Despite the fact that Norway was not directly involved in the main event taking place on the Continent, this northern arm of Hitler's shrinking empire was more important than ever because from mid-1944 it remained the Reich's sole strategically significant naval center. This was especially true because the Führer believed that, like their rocket and jet wonder-weapon cousins, Dönitz's new and improved U-boat types equipped with *Schnorchel* (which enabled U-boats to recharge their batteries while at periscope depth) were destined to bring about a revival of Germany's fortunes. Or so Hitler vainly imagined. For the navy, besides providing invaluable bases for U-boats, control of southern Norway and Jutland was indispensable for maintaining the free movement of its vessels in and around the Baltic approaches.[88] Heightening German concern was the Swedish government's decision in August and September to withhold insuring Swedish ships bound for German ports and the closure of Sweden's ports to Axis shipping. The former move deprived Germany of one-quarter of the shipping available for imports, while the latter forced it to rely solely on Narvik for iron ore. These Swedish initiatives deepened German mistrust and, combined with Finland's departure from the Axis cause in August, made Norway more important than ever in Hitler's eyes. Added to these concerns were, of course, the ubiquitous reports making their way to the German Naval Staff in October and November, warning of imminent invasion all along the Norwegian coast and Denmark.[89]

Although there were plenty who doubted that such an operation was possible or was even being considered by the Allies, Hitler was not about to take any chances, since he felt that the deteriorating relationship between Britain and the Soviet Union was just the catalyst to spark an occupation of Narvik by the former in order to thwart a Red Army advance down Norway's western coast. Hitler's fears were fueled by the dubious reports submitted from the likes of *Josephine* and by a large Soviet push in the Far North supported by a Soviet landing on the

Barents Sea coastline in behind the German northernmost flank.[90] The Soviet assault was successful. On 15 October, the port of Petsamo was occupied, and by 25 October, Kirkenes was captured and the Germans pursued as far as Tana Fjord. Although the Soviets made no further advances and even pulled back slightly, the occupation of this small segment of northern Norway and the loss of *Tirpitz* in December meant (in Hitler's mind at least) that the possibility of a British operation could not be ignored.

REAL REINFORCEMENTS, BUT LITTLE CHANGE

In addition to strengthening and improving coastal defenses, increasing the strength of land-based forces, and shuffling around the navy's embarrassingly small resources, it was at this time that the Luftwaffe also got a shot in the arm.[91] To protect German shipping plying Norwegian coastal waters with supplies for the northern-based soldiers and to resume attacks on Arctic traffic, the Luftwaffe received a strike force once more. By late October 1944, two groups of KG 26 Ju 88 torpedo bombers had arrived—the first to be stationed there in nearly two years.[92] In anticipation of the arrival of these forces, reconnaissance, which as already noted had been canceled since April 1944, was recommenced in September. With the increasingly tenuous coastal supply line to northern Norway being subjected to Allied naval and air interference, JG 5's III and IV Groups received an extra squadron each from Reich defense, and by mid-December even night fighters were brought in to combat antishipping sweeps by Coastal Command— making the fighter defense in Norway stronger than at any time since 1940.[93] In addition, 1944 saw a reorganization of the air fleet's structure with the establishment of Fliegerführer 3, which covered some of the northern fields of its predecessor, Fliegerführer Nord (Ost), including Petsamo, Kirkenes, and Bille Fjord; Fliegerführer 5, based mostly at Tromsö and Vaernes; and Fliegerführer 4, covering the southern administrative and industrial heart of Norway with airfields stretching from Stavanger's Sola field to Kjevik at Oslo. Jagdfliegerführer Norwegen retained its old designation and had its fighters dispersed over Forus, Lista, Sola, Herdla, and Gossen.[94] The results of this shuffling of resources and the transfer in of new units were, however, less than spectacular. Emulating the failure to make a dent in the Anglo-American bomber raids over Norway and prevent the *Tirpitz* debacle, attacking enemy convoys and protecting German shipping in the winter of 1944–1945 proved beyond the capabilities of these units.

The ability of the strengthened fighter units to protect their own vessels engaged in the provisioning and transfer of forces around Norway was particularly poor. Indeed, in November, twenty-two German ships were sunk and nineteen damaged, and in the following month a further thirteen ships were lost and thirteen damaged.[95] This greatly affected not only the movement of forces and their supply but also the ore shipments from Narvik. It was estimated at the time that these fell from 40,000 tons in October 1943 to 27,000 tons in October 1944, and in November of that same year they totaled an inadequate 12,000 tons.[96] As *Vizeadmiral* Ciliax noted after the war: "At one time the situation along the open stretch of coastline between Kristiansand and Stavanger . . . was extremely critical."[97] Because of "constant heavy attacks . . . off the Norwegian coast," explained Dönitz to Hitler on the first day of December 1944, "the time is not far off when ship movements in this region will come to a complete standstill."[98] Even in Oslo Fjord, the nerve center of German rule in Norway, Coastal Command increasingly frustrated German efforts by dropping mines and attacking harbor facilities. For instance, on 2 March 1945, the Naval Staff war diary records that recent minelaying activities had incapacitated "50 percent of the minesweepers," while air attacks had destroyed important docks, which in turn greatly hindered shipping in the fjord.[99]

More important, Hitler wanted the most battle-worthy force in Norway, the 20th Mountain Division, moved south for an eventual transfer across the Skagerrak to aid in the defense of the Fatherland. This did not mean that Hitler was about to abandon northern Norway; rather, it constituted a belated recognition that the final battle would be fought out in the heart of Germany, not in Norway.[100] That he still found it difficult to reconcile his Norway obsession with the demands at his very own door can be seen in his contradictory response to the 11 March 1945 recommendation by Jodl (who had played such a big role in *Weserübung* in April 1940) that the northern region be abandoned:

> The Führer believes that if we vacated Narvik we might be providing Sweden with an opportunity to enter the war against us, since she would then have excellent connections with the Anglo-Americans. The Lofotens are also one of the most valuable Norwegian fishing areas, and they are important for our food supply. The Führer does not permit an evacuation of this area. However, he asks for suggestions how might troops be withdrawn from there so as to release troops for the home theater of war.[101]

Coastal Command's activities were, however, a threat not only to the movement of this fighting force but also to shipping carrying coal to Norway for use on the overburdened rail system, which was needed to carry a good portion of the 20th Mountain Division's 170,000 men overland to Oslo.[102] Although the Germans had ample oil reserves, they lacked a good supply of coal. Therefore, in addition to the difficulties presented by the hemorrhaging infrastructure of the Reich, the Germans also had to consider obstacles presented by Coastal Command's direct aerial attacks and indirect mining operations to the likely success of the operation. In the end, these factors proved insurmountable, and the slow transfer ground to a halt in April.[103]

Notwithstanding this depressing situation, there was at least one Luftwaffe defensive action worthy of mention, since it was one of the few occasions in the latter months of the war that the Luftwaffe secured a notable victory over the RAF, and in which the fighting spirit of the German fighter pilots rose above impossible odds. The German destroyer Z 33 had been making its way south along the Norwegian coast from Trondheim to Bergen when it entered Forde Fjord on 9 February 1945. Like all of the Germans' remaining warships, Z 33 (a destroyer of the famous Narvik class) was a prime candidate for Coastal Command's attention. Once the destroyer was spotted on the morning of 9 April, a relatively large strike force, including three Beaufighter and two Mustang squadrons, was dispatched to attack the vessel and other ships sheltering in the fjord. The latter long-range machines were to provide much-needed cover for the slower and somewhat more cumbersome Beaufighters. Realizing that his ship had been sighted, the commander of Z 33 sought shelter deeper in the fjord, and it was here that the enemy's air units found it around 1600. Meanwhile, apparently warned by radar at 1550, twelve Fw 190s of JG 5 based at Herdla were scrambled to intercept the intruders. These squadrons led by *Feldweber* Rudolf Artner, with seventeen victories to his credit, and *Leutnant* Rudolf Linz—a genuine ace who had amassed seventy successes in the Far North—fell on the enemy soon after 1605. Artner described the first few moments of the battle in his after-action report:

> At 1608 we made contact with approximately 30 Beaufighters and ten escort planes of the Mustang type. The squadron went to attack in formation. I was successful in getting behind and above one of the Beaufighters, and fired a long round. He began to burn at once and came down vertically approximately ten kilometres north-west of Forde at 1610. The pilot stayed in his plane.[104]

The melee soon spread over a considerable area, and in minutes Artner scored his nineteenth victory of the war. As he recalled, "I followed a Beaufighter at low altitude and fired two short rounds. The plane swerved a little off course and then after another round the plane went straight down and began to burn at once. This was approximately five kilometres north-east of Naustdal and the time was 1613."[105] By 1630 the battle was over. In some fifteen minutes, the Luftwaffe pilots had shot down one Mustang and nine Beaufighters, and fourteen Allied airmen had lost their lives. But the fight had not been without its cost. Of the four German fighters shot down, two pilots had been killed; one of these was Linz, the Luftwaffe's highest scoring ace in Norway. In spite of this loss, the operation had restored some pride to the Luftwaffe's effort and was greatly welcomed by the navy, which not only appreciated the successful defense of one of its few remaining ships but also, like everyone else, was grasping for any ray of light in the dark pit into which the Third Reich had descended. Dönitz wired Göring: "I am pleased with the great success of the Luftwaffe in Norway as it fended off aerial attacks against Destroyer Z 33 and the attack on the PQ convoy. I wish the successful fliers the best of luck in future fighting."[106]

Luck, however, could not turn back the clock, nor could it change the increasingly impossible odds the Luftwaffe faced, even though success here restored some pride to the beleaguered fighter units, and Z 33 was able to continue its journey in one piece. Nevertheless, the Luftwaffe's experience in Norway in the latter stages of the war was dismal overall. For example, despite the low numbers of aircraft in the region, on 26 March the Kommandierender der Deutschen Luftwaffe in Norwegen (the air fleet had finally been downgraded to a mere Luftwaffe General in February) had to turn down the transfer in of a coastal reconnaissance unit (KüFlGr 2/196), "since the air situation is characterized by almost daily intrusions by Mosquitos and Beaufighter units with fighter protection," and under these circumstances the slow German aircraft would be more of a liability than an asset.[107] This decline in defensive abilities was equaled in the offensive achievements of the newly arrived bomber force.

ARCTIC CONVOYS AND THE END IN NORWAY

The arrival in October 1944 of KG 26's torpedo bombers was intended primarily to enable Luftwaffe General Norwegen to resume attacks on Arctic traffic. Obviously, though, this was little more than wishful thinking, since the small number of bombers available could do little to discourage the well-defended Allied ships from traversing the Arctic route in the last quarter of 1944. The attacks on Anglo-American convoys closely matched the disappointment of the fighters; of the 159 Russia-bound vessels, not a single one was lost in the second half of 1944, while of the 100 returning westward, only 2 were sunk.[108] The failure of the nearly seventy Ju 88 torpedo bombers and the loss of nine U-boats during these operations can be attributed to the very strong escort forces fielded, in particular the now ubiquitous presence of escort carriers.[109] Nevertheless, the fact that they were able to operate at all given the squeeze on reserves was mostly due to the fact that although the Germans lacked sufficient quantities of coal in Norway, aviation fuel stocks, set aside for Drohende Gefahr Nord, were relatively plentiful. In the grand scheme of things, the reserves were trifling, but in the context of the final months of the war, they were highly contested.

The exact amount of stocks available in early 1945 is unclear. Based on what is known of the levels in March 1945 and the rate of consumption of the air units in Norway at the time, however, they could not have totaled much more than 6,000 to 7,000 tons—about one-fifth of the Luftwaffe's entire reserve pool of 25,000 tons.[110] Since the beginning of January, OKW had been greedily eyeing this cache for use in the defense of the Reich. OKL's war diary notes that the Armed Forces High Command made its play for the stocks (from which it had already successfully siphoned off an unknown quantity) on 13 February by first stating enviously that the establishment of Drohende Gefahr Nord had resulted in "considerable fuel stocks being laid down in Norway."[111] The general quartermaster *(Generalquartiermeister)* of OKW then called for a further transfer of fuel from Norway. Two days later the issue was revisited, and "by reason of the strained fuel situation in the Reich," the general quartermaster proposed that "out of the stored fuel stocks in Norway for Drohende Nord 2,000 tons be drawn off."[112] After an examination of the present situation, the chief of the Luftwaffe's Operations Staff determined that based on the current demands of the aircraft in Norway and because Drohende Gefahr Nord required a certain level of readiness at all times, he could not support further depletion of the stocks. The Luftwaffe's own first operations officer was, however, more pragmatic. He suggested that the best way around the current impasse would be to simply "do away with" some of Drohende Gefahr Nord's demands, since the fuel situation in the Reich simply did not permit unused stocks to remain outside Germany's borders. "Furthermore, the intended transfer of reinforcement units to Norway [as per Drohende Gefahr Nord] would itself demand high fuel consumption," argued the officer, "and in all probability during a real enemy landing would only arrive after the first decisive day."[113]

Whether or not the fuel was transferred is uncertain, but a footnote in a Luftwaffe breakdown of the aviation fuel situation on 10 April suggests that it probably was not, since it points out that of OKW's total 6,985-ton reserve, 2,000 still resided in Norway, perhaps prevented from being transported to the Reich because of the considerable difficulties and risks now facing shipping in the region.[114] By the end of March 1945, Luftwaffe General Norwegen still had 4,400 tons of the total 25,000 tons of Luftwaffe stocks on hand.[115] This was far better than the reserves available to Luftflotte Reich, which virtually lived from hand to mouth. Aiding the favorable fuel situation in the Far-North, of course, was the fact that with only three bomber groups flying at marginal strength due to declining serviceability, consumption rested at a low 12 tons per day. Although by 26 April consumption had reached 40 tons per day, there was no danger of the remaining 4,090 tons being exhausted before the likely end of the war.[116]

In the meantime, the New Year and having ample fuel on hand brought no improvement to the Luftwaffe's actual combat fortunes in Norway. Two attacks of note were made on the inward-bound JW 64 and its homeward-bound partner, RA 64, in February, but they only served to highlight the impotence of the Luftwaffe in the region. The first assault was attempted on 7 February by forty-eight aircraft, including reconnaissance planes and KG 26 torpedo bombers.[117] Thanks to a radar failure on the shadowing aircraft, however, the strike force completely failed to make contact with the twenty-four-strong convoy but lost six aircraft in the process.[118] In spite of the navy crowing that the whole day's work had been a "special occasion" because it represented the "first successful combat for a long time with a convoy in which the Luftwaffe also participated," it really demonstrated that the Luftwaffe's days as an effective force were long gone.[119] Three days later, this abortive assault was followed by a thirty-strong torpedo bomber attack, which took place in two waves. The antiaircraft and fighter defenses were too strong, and despite the overoptimistic reports—claiming that one Liberty ship and one destroyer had been "positively sunk," another Liberty ship "probably sunk," and a further cruiser, destroyer, and merchant ship "damaged"—not a single ship had actually received a scratch.[120] In spite of the fact that this demonstrated Luftwaffe crews had not lost any of their ability to greatly exaggerate their successes, it also highlighted, rather depressingly for the Germans, the hopelessness of the situation. Neither the eight U-boats placed ahead of the convoy nor the Luftwaffe could effectively counter the strong escort force, which consisted of two escort carriers, a cruiser, and seventeen flotilla vessels.[121]

Further poor returns followed in subsequent missions undertaken by the small torpedo bomber strike force in February and March. Luftwaffe operations against RA 64's thirty-four returning ships by thirty-five Ju 88s on 20 and 23 February were characteristically unspectacular despite even grander claims. Overall, during the double convoy assaults in the third week of February, the Germans had lost up to fourteen aircraft with only a single straggler, the Liberty ship *Henry Bacon,* to their credit—the last ship to be sunk by the Luftwaffe during the war.[122] Further Arctic convoys continued, and the Luftwaffe in Norway even got approval from the *Reichsmarschall* for KG 26 to attack enemy traffic on Britain's east coast. But air reconnaissance, such as it was, only made a belated sighting of the Second World War's last eastbound Arctic convoy on 1 May.[123]

Yet the Luftwaffe was to suffer one final indignity before all was over. On the first day of May, after a couple of failed previous attempts, the Home Fleet sailed from Scapa toward the Norwegian coast to attack the Arctic U-boat flotilla supply ship and any other vessels present in Vest Fjord. The operation by a force made up of two cruisers, three escort carriers, and seven destroyers was a great success: the carriers' Avengers and Wildcats laid waste the German base facilities, sunk the supply ship and a small merchantman, and destroyed a U-boat.[124] It was the last major sweep by the Home Fleet in the war and showed just how far the Luftwaffe had fallen. In 1940, the Royal Navy had been so knocked about by the Luftwaffe that it dared not venture into the waters off Norway for the next two years. Times had certainly changed. In May 1945, the Royal Navy and its aircraft demonstrated once and for all that Britannia had reclaimed the waves off Norway from the Luftwaffe.

Conclusion

When he came to power in 1933, Hitler had been relatively indifferent to including Norway in any future conflict, and even at the outbreak of the Second World War, he had been keen to make known that Germany would respect all the Scandinavian nations' "integrity in so far as they maintain strict neutrality." However, with the specter of an Anglo-French Scandinavian operation in the offing, Hitler grew increasingly determined to "safeguard" German interests, and plans slowly advanced between December 1939 and March 1940 for an invasion of Norway. Notwithstanding some early reluctance, once the planning reached the final stage of development, Hitler had become deeply interested in the project, and after the campaign started he kept a close eye on events as they unfolded on his northern flank. Once Norway was firmly in his grasp, Hitler became increasingly obsessed with both protecting it from imaginary Allied attempts to wrest it from his control and incorporating it within Germany's postwar economic empire (supplying the victorious Reich with everything from iron ore and aluminum to fish and electricity). In addition to these economic and political aims, his *Weserübung* directive had foreseen that, strategically, Norway would not only provide the navy with deepwater naval bases such as Trondheim (Hitler's future Nordic Singapore) but also offer the opportunity to expand the available bases from which the Luftwaffe could operate against Britain. Certainly, the invasion of Norway on 9 April gave every indication that these designs would be realized.

WESERÜBUNG'S FIRST AND SECOND PHASES: THE LUFTWAFFE TRIUMPHANT

Although the performance of the Luftwaffe over Norway in latter years proved particularly dismal, in 1940—when Hitler launched *Weserübung*—it constituted a vital element in the German triumph, and there was a good deal of truth in Jodl's boast at the time that the "Luftwaffe proved to be the decisive factor in the success of the operation."[1] Perhaps the most striking feature of Luftwaffe participation was the unprecedented airlift. On 9 April, the rapid deployment of paratroops and forces air landed by transports enabled the Germans to capture in quick succession the widely scattered airfields of Aalborg East and West, Fornebu, and Sola. At Oslo this was doubly important because it permitted the Germans to march on the capital from Fornebu even though the planned naval-bound occupation was delayed by the sinking of *Blücher* and Norwegian resistance along the fjord leading into Oslo. The continuing airlift enabled airfields to be brought up to operational readiness within a very short time—in some cases within hours—and became the main means by which the relatively weak German vanguard positions in central and northern Norway received reinforcements and supplies while overland communication links were slowly secured with Oslo. This was nowhere more vital than at Bergen, Trondheim, and Narvik, where naval supply ships had been decimated en route. In April alone, Gablenz's 582 transports made a phenomenal 3,000 flights, of which 1,800 carried troops and 1,200 additional material.[2] A breakdown of these flights reveals that a total of 2,370 tons of supplies, 29,280 men, and 1,178,100 liters of fuel were delivered for the loss of 150 aircraft.[3]

From these secured bases, in the second phase of Luftwaffe operations, X Fliegerkorps set about carrying out its main role: threatening the Royal Navy and thwarting Allied counterlandings. A good number of bombers had already participated in aerial displays over Danish and Norwegian cities and had crucially assisted the navy on *Weser*-day by repeatedly bombing defenses within the Dröbak narrows, hastening the eventual arrival of German vessels in Oslo and at Kristiansand, where their support proved instrumental in the capture of the city. Within a short time, the bulk of X Fliegerkorps' bombers had concentrated on either northern German airfields or newly captured Danish and Norwegian fields in anticipation of Allied attempts to trap weaker German ships inside Norwegian fjords or undertake counterlandings. On the whole, the Luftwaffe was able to prevent either of these eventualities occurring in waters off southern and central Norway, and the fright Admiral Forbes received at the hands of German bombers on 9 April and the lashing of *Suffolk* on 17 April had important repercussions. In the short term, the former event led to the cancellation of an attempt to eject the Germans from Bergen and an abandonment of the southern North Sea to submarines, while the latter led to the decision not to attempt a direct assault on Trondheim. In other words, for the first time in history, airpower had gained a clear ascendancy over sea power. At the time, many contemporaries observed as Jodl did: "The Luftwaffe has provided a proof, decisive for the future developments, that no fleet (however strong it may be) can operate in the long run within the close effective range of an enemy aircraft."[4]

Materially, though, the Luftwaffe's tally for the entire campaign of one cruiser, six destroyers and sloops, a dozen smaller vessels, and twenty-one merchantmen was hardly spectacular. Nevertheless, whether or not the threat posed by the

Luftwaffe was more psychological than real, the British were unwilling to test the waters by carrying out their proposed incursion into Bergen or the direct assault on Trondheim. Had they done so, the Luftwaffe's tally of warships would almost certainly have been higher, especially if it had been able to deploy greater numbers of more accurate Ju 88s and, especially, the dive-bombing Stukas. It had been Stukas that inflicted most of the damage on *Suffolk* and, on 3 May, sunk two of the destroyers escorting the British evacuation from central Norway. The fact that they did not increase their tally rested on their small numbers and, in the last phase of the campaign, the distance between Vaernes and Narvik.

Their effectiveness against warships operating without adequate air cover would be more than adequately demonstrated one year later off Crete,where Allied naval losses soared to three cruisers and six destroyers sunk, curtailing evacuation of the island. Moreover, had the Germans been able to put torpedo bombers into the air, the Luftwaffe might well have presented a still greater threat to the Royal Navy. As Taranto in November 1940 and the attack on Pearl Harbor and the sinking of *Prince of Wales* and *Repulse* in December 1941 all graphically revealed, torpedo bombers—whether carrier-based or land-based—had brought the age of the invincible battleship to an end. In 1942, the effectiveness of the torpedo bomber was further underlined in the attacks on Arctic convoys PQs 16, 17, and 18, in which torpedo-carrying He 111s and Ju 88s were shown to be on average twice as deadly as high-level and dive-bombing aircraft. As part of this transitional process, the Norwegian campaign writes an early and significant chapter in the gradual appreciation of airpower as a foil to sea power in modern warfare.

Moreover, there can be little doubt that German aerial superiority over central Norway was instrumental in bringing the Allied counteroperation to an end. Although, as at sea, casualties suffered at the hands of German aircraft on land were light, the Luftwaffe's destruction of the Namsos and Aandalsnes bridgeheads, constant harassment of Allied ground troops, and regular attacks on communication centers made the whole operation untenable. With their enemy lacking anti-aircraft defenses of any note, the Luftwaffe delivered the final indignity to the Allied expedition in central Norway when at Lesjaskog airfield it crushed the RAF's woeful, short-lived attempt to achieve some sort of airpower parity.

WESERÜBUNG'S THIRD PHASE: A GRIM PORTENT

Given the crucial role played by the Luftwaffe during the first and second phases of the air war over Norway, it is perhaps not surprising to find that nearly all studies of the campaign have ignored the fact that the Luftwaffe's contribution during the third and final phase—running for a full month from early May until early June—was nowhere near as important as is generally assumed. Unlike in southern and central Norway, Luftwaffe participation in the Far North could not be described—as Matthew Cooper did in his 1981 study of the German air force—as "the decisive factor in the German victory."[5] At least four factors hampered Luftwaffe operations against the Allied forces facing Dietl's beleaguered units. First, the Luftwaffe was limited to a single air base from which to launch the bulk of its missions. In marked contrast, during both the initial invasion and consolidation stages of the campaign, the Luftwaffe had enjoyed the continuous use of numerous well-serviced airfields within close proximity, encompassing Germany itself and subsequently occupied Denmark and Norway. This, of course, enabled a far greater number of aircraft to be brought to bear on any given target, affording the bombers the advantage of being able to substitute fuel capacity for increased payloads. Second, although Vaernes was the most northern Luftwaffe base, it still lay a considerable distance (some 650 kilometers) from Narvik. Consequently, the short-range but highly accurate Stukas remained unable to make any contribution to the action over Narvik until late in the battle. This meant that Dietl's forces received less effective close air support than they might have otherwise expected, and that enemy naval vessels largely escaped the terrifying prospect of accurate dive-bombing attacks. Additionally, because of the distances involved, the longer range but less accurate Heinkel and Ju 88 bombers were forced to make their sorties with only limited escort. Therefore, despite the presence of small numbers of Bf 110s, this left them at the mercy of British fighters at Bardufloss.

Third, the presence of the RAF at Bardufloss brought a measure of parity to the situation in the air over northern Norway, at least in the latter part of the campaign. Unchallenged for much of *Weserübung,* the Luftwaffe had destroyed 93 of the 169 British aircraft lost thus far during the campaign. Of these, 43 were downed in aerial combat, 24 by flak, and the remainder were either destroyed on the ground or would be lost with *Glorious.* Yet prior to the loss of these latter carrier-delivered aircraft, the two RAF fighter squadrons at Bardufloss rapidly turned the tables on the Luftwaffe, and the contest for air superiority was renewed. Fourth, compounding these difficulties, and nearly always overlooked by later commentators, was the impact of atrocious weather on Luftflotte 5 operations. Over northern Norway in this period, low cloud, rainstorms, and snowstorms prevented the Luftwaffe making anywhere near the number of sorties it had in the previous month. During the crucial last twelve days of the campaign, the Luftwaffe could bring its bomber forces to bear on the enemy in the north on only a miserly four occasions. This hardly qualifies as a significant contribution, and since the Allies had already decided to leave the region on 24 May, it is clear that the Luftwaffe had very little influence on bringing about the eventual evacuation, despite what was believed at the time and glossed over later.

The Luftwaffe's only real claim to fame in the Far North during *Weserübung* must lie with the tenuous lifeline it provided for the isolated German forces, and at times a limited degree of what might loosely be termed close air support but more accurately battlefield air interdiction.[6] As part of the German attempt to enable Group Narvik to hang on long enough for relief operations to be undertaken, the Luftwaffe gamely flew in supplies for Dietl's forces whenever it could by aerial drops or by flying boats. Yet once again rain and snow hampered any attempts to meet all Dietl's demands for supplies or close air support, while the sporadic parachute drops of additional men were in reality a drop in the bucket compared with the Allied forces closing on the town. Consequently, Dietl's claim that the "Luftwaffe proved the decisive factor in the success of the operation" is not as applicable to the final month of the campaign as it is for April. In the final analysis, the loss of France and Dunkirk in the west had much more of a say in the outcome of events in the Far North than the Luftwaffe.

NO *PIRATENFLUGZUEGE* FOR WEGENER'S SIEGE OF BRITAIN

Both this third phase and earlier incidents in the campaign should really have set alarm bells ringing in the offices of the Luftwaffe hierarchy. Alongside the need to secure the safe and unimpeded transportation of Swedish iron ore via Narvik, the Norwegian campaign was touted by the Germans as providing much-needed operational bases for the navy's warships and the Luftwaffe's aircraft against Britain. This grand design never eventuated. For the navy, the loss of a good part of its fighting power during *Weserübung* meant that it would never have the requisite forces with which to fully utilize its newly acquired Nordic bases. Moreover, the British occupation of Iceland effectively reinstated the traditional scheme of a distant blockade, albeit running from the Shetlands through Iceland to Greenland (as distinct from its Great War predecessor, which ran across the top of the North Sea to the southern Norwegian coast). *Weserübung* revealed that the Luftwaffe did not possess the necessary types of aircraft with which to utilize Norwegian airfields fully in the years ahead.

In order to exploit Norway as an advanced air and naval base, the Germans needed not only torpedo bombers but also, and more important, long-range aircraft for maritime warfare. From the very onset of *Weserübung,* it rapidly became clear that neither the Luftwaffe nor the navy possessed machines capable of covering the distances involved when Condors had to be hastily brought in specifically to provide a modicum of support for warships and men isolated in and around Narvik. Although the Royal Navy had been driven from southern and central waters by the Luftwaffe, it was quick to seize the upper hand in the First and Second Battles of Narvik, comfortable in the knowledge that its warships were beyond the range of the Luftwaffe's bomber force. Surely nothing reveals more the inadequacy of the German aircraft on hand than X Fliegerkorps' desperate offer to send an entire bomber wing on a one-way flight to hit the British warships in the area. Even later, when Milch's efforts in upgrading Trondheim's Vaernes airfield were finally realized, the He 111 and Ju 88 simply were not suited to such missions without adequate air cover, which the Bf 110s were equally poorly equipped to provide. Hastily assembled Hurricanes and Gladiators operating from a ramshackle field north of Narvik were more than a match for these machines.

With the withdrawal of the Allied force from Narvik, though, the inadequacies of the Luftwaffe were soon forgotten in the euphoria of victory here and in the west. But the problems remained. The directive for *Weserübung* had clearly stated that the invasion of Norway would provide the Luftwaffe with expanded bases for "operations against Britain." The impossibility of ever achieving this goal was tragically laid bare only four months after Norway had been secured,when, for the first and last time, the Germans attempted to utilize bases in Norway as Hitler had originally conceived in his directive by participating in the Battle of Britain. Paralleling missions undertaken from Vaernes to Narvik, the distances from Sola and Aalborg to northern England were at the outer limit of He 111 and Ju 88 range and precluded adequate escort. Here, though, the similarities end. Unlike over northern Norway, where German aircrew had difficulty contending with only one small RAF base precariously situated on foreign soil, over Britain they were up against Fighter Command's large and carefully organized defensive system centered on radar and well-equipped fighter units. Such was the subsequent bloodbath suffered in the course of this single mission that never again would Luftflotte 5 sally forth in daylight raids against Britain.

As soon as it became apparent that Norway could not be used as a major Luftwaffe base for aerial assaults on the British Isles, Luftflotte 5 was stripped of its bombers, and from a peak of approximately 650 combat planes in May 1940, Stumpff could call on barely 50 such aircraft by December. Without a true long-range heavy bomber, which could have comfortably operated from Norway in conjunction with the raids taking place on southern England from France, the Germans were unable to snap the back of Fighter Command's defensive network, which in August 1940 reached a breaking point with regard to the availability of machines and pilots. Had the Germans possessed an aircraft able to appear anywhere over the British Isles at high altitude, it might well have dealt a fatal blow to British resistance.

Norway and the four-engined bomber were potentially even more important to the naval war. Wolfgang Wegener had originally believed that Norway was a vital component in a maritime "siege of Britain." Yet, like many of his contemporaries, he mistakenly assumed that the surface warship would prove the means to achieve this. In reality, it is now clear that the U-boat supported by aircraft offered the Germans their best opportunity to win the war at sea. Working together against the sea lanes supplying Britain's war industry, the U-boat and the long-range aircraft operating from France and Norway would have afforded the most efficient means of locking the British Isles within a deadly embrace. As it was, with a small number of U-boats and even fewer Condors in 1940 and 1941, the Germans showed what would have been possible with much greater numbers of each. In particular, the potential of a fleet of 200 to 300 purpose-built *Piratenflugzeuge* was demonstrated clearly when, with a small number of converted airliners, the Luftwaffe sank no less than 500,000 tons of shipping in 1940 and a further 1 million tons in 1941.

Much of the blame for entering the war without such an aircraft must be laid at the feet of one man: Hermann Göring. Vain, boastful, and covetous, the head of the Luftwaffe, and the second most powerful man in the Reich, was the four-engined bomber's nemesis. His decision to stop production on both the Do 19 and the more promising Ju 89 in 1937 put German development in this area back at least four years. The potential of the Ju 89, in particular, was ably demonstrated when its air transport derivative, the Ju 90, worked alongside the Condor in sup-port of Dietl's mountain troops in Narvik. The demise of the Do 19 and the Ju 89, however, did not spell the end of the development of an aircraft capable of mari-time work, as the four-engined long-range bomber baton was passed on to the ill-fated He 177. Although Udet must take a good deal of the blame for the He 177's shortcomings, Göring's incredulous cry in 1942 that "it need not be able to dive" came years after the ludicrous decision first had been made. Whether, as this implies, he truly was unaware of this situation or failed to reverse it at the time because of inattention, his patent and continued negligence meant that Germany entered the war poorly equipped to establish a blockade of Britain.

Göring's failure to develop such an aircraft, his fighting with Raeder over the Naval Air Arm, and his inability to adequately address the needs of maritime warfare all reveal that he was generally strategically illiterate and particularly ignorant of matters nautical. This was appreciated early in the war by Milch when, in an effort to explain to Göring the importance of Norway to Germany's future world position, he was compelled to present his commander with a copy of Wegener's *Die Seestrategie des Weltkrieges*. Nevertheless, despite his stra-tegic deficiencies, Göring was all too aware that his position and that of the Luftwaffe were dependent on the patronage of the Führer, and for the most part it was from Hitler that he took his lead.

Ultimately, it was with the Supreme Commander of the Wehrmacht that the shaky foundation for the war at sea rested. Because of Hitler's overemphasis on a Continental strategy, bolstered by his mistaken belief that a war with Britain could be avoided, Germany never pushed forward with any great energy the develop-ment of a substantial surface fleet or—more important—a strong U-boat arm. Likewise, Hitler's land-based focus meant not only that the navy was ill prepared for the ensuing war at sea but also that the Luftwaffe was caught short. The over-all strategic focus of the Luftwaffe followed a Continental bent as an ancillary of the army in any future conflict within Europe. In light of this, the Luftwaffe for the most part developed aircraft suitable to this task, namely, dive-bombers and twin-engined medium bombers. However, with the likelihood of a war with Britain more in the cards than ever in the wake of the Czechoslovak crisis of May 1938, reports produced from Luftwaffe maneuvers designed to ascertain Germany's technical and tactical shortcomings in an aerial campaign against Britain made sobering reading.

In part, they indicated that without forward bases in Holland and Belgium, the Luftwaffe would not be ready to hit at Britain until 1942, by which time four-engined bombers should be available.

While Göring scrambled to rectify his ill-considered ditching of the four-engined bomber program by pursing the He 177, Hitler remained totally oblivious to the larger implications of these findings to his proposed invasion of Norway in 1940 and subsequent operations from there. Although in October 1939 Raeder had stressed that to best utilize Norway the Luftwaffe still needed "suitable types" of aircraft, Hitler showed little cognizance of this in his *Weserübung* directive. In determining that Norway would "provide the navy and the Luftwaffe with expanded bases for operations against Britain," the Führer failed to appreciate that captured bases, no matter how good, were essentially redundant without the long-range aircraft to fly from them. Thus, in April 1940, the failure of Hitler and Göring to adequately address the needs of maritime warfare in their long-term prewar strategic planning fatally hamstrung Germany's efforts in the war at sea and in particular the exploitation of Norway as a base for long-range aircraft working in close cooperation with U-boats. Yet Hitler did not simply fail in his tasks here. After having embarked on the conquest of Norway, he was unwilling to set in place a command structure that would facilitate the optimum use of what Luftwaffe and naval resources were deployed in the area, namely, the establishment of a joint operations staff under a single theater commander.

THE COST OF DIVIDED COMMAND

Even without the long-range aircraft that could have operated from Norway in conjunction with U-boats to seal off the northwestern approaches to the British Isles in the Battle of the Atlantic, the Germans did have medium bombers suitable for operations in the less expansive waters of the Far North. Nevertheless, Germany's inability to effectively coordinate its resources in this region against Arctic convoys stems not only from the atrocious weather conditions prevailing in this bleak area but also from the failure to establish a unified command prior to the invasion of Norway and in the years that followed—because beneath the success of *Weserübung* dwelled the insidious canker of interservice rivalry. Although the invasion of Norway had shown that blitzkrieg warfare could more than compensate for a poor command structure, once the element of surprise had diminished and Germany's military machine began to stretch visibly over several fronts after the invasion of the Soviet Union in mid-1941, a major restructuring of the organization was needed to coordinate the declining capacity of the German armed services in the face of a corresponding improvement in the Allied ability to wage war.

In many ways, the German command structure for the invasion of Norway resembled the Allies' chaotic Norwegian expeditionary model of 1940: it lacked a unified joint operations staff with a single head responsible for directing the battle in the field. Before and during the campaign, the fierce interservice rivalry that existed between the three German armed forces meant that at the highest level cooperation was given only grudgingly at any one time.[7] This was revealed in Gruppe XXI's after-action report for *Weserübung,* which stressed that any future operation involving the three armed services must be undertaken with a single leader who, along with his personal staff, operates "without restrictions" to ensure a frictionless and uniform command. Of course this never occurred, and strident interservice rivalry continued to bedevil German operations throughout the war. This was certainly true in Norway after the successful completion of the campaign, as Falkenhorst declared at his war crime trial:

> In the inter-relation of commands no change was made; until my recall [in December 1944], the system that I was to collaborate with the respective Commanders-in-Chief regarding Navy and Luftwaffe questions remained in force. . . . I was in fact, however, only *primus inter pares,* since the Navy and the Luftwaffe remained under Raeder and Göring . . . and always took great care that their position as independent parts of the Armed Forces *(Wehrmacht)* should not be assailed.[8]

Yet in spite of this hostile climate, success here and elsewhere occurred because spats between Göring, Keitel, and Raeder and their immediate minions were greatly ameliorated in the field at a lower level, where, more often than not, service parochialism was set aside in order to get the job done. Gruppe XXI's report reflected on the remarkable degree to which this had been achieved in *Weserübung:*

> That the commands and troop contingents of the three armed forces branches worked together almost without friction cannot be credited to purposeful organisation of the commanding staff. It was, instead, entirely an achievement of the personalities involved who knew how to cooperate closely in order to overcome the inadequacies of the organisation.[9]

In this regard, the Luftwaffe was particularly blessed with a number of resourceful and competent personalities who not only were able to function alongside their army and navy counterparts but also carried out their Luftwaffe duties with a great deal of skill. Both Geisler and Gablenz worked together extremely well to facilitate the close cooperation of their combat and transport aircraft in a campaign in which operational and logistical requirements were closely intertwined. In the front lines, the Luftwaffe was ably served by the two aggressive *Fliegerführers* in the persons of Harlinghausen and Fuchs. Harlinghausen in particular had a hands-on approach to operational command and in central Norway often flew reconnaissance missions himself. Lower ranks also exhibited a great degree of initiative and an ability to improvise to achieve the required results. Confronted with appalling weather and the sinking of *Blücher,* it was only *Hauptmann* Richard Wegner's determination to press on to Fornebu with his Ju 52s—in contravention of an order to return to Germany—and the quick thinking of *Oberleutnant* Werner Hansen, who, with a handful of his Bf 110s, secured the airfield for the incoming transports, that enabled the Germans to occupy Oslo on 9 April. The resourcefulness of junior Luftwaffe commanders was demonstrated on a number of occasions, perhaps no more so than in the first systematic use of Stukas over the open sea against fleeing Allied warships and troopladen transports on 3 May. Lacking adequate navigational instruments and training to locate the Allied fleet, the *Fliegerkorps* hit on the idea of deploying coastal reconnaissance floatplanes as guides for the Stukas, resulting in the sinking of two destroyers.

Milch and Stumpff, as successive leaders of Luftflotte 5, have come in for a good deal of criticism from contemporaries and postwar critics, yet each proved capable commanders in his own way. Milch, in particular, during his brief stint as the air fleet's commander, has been described as the "half-Jewish Nazi" who "wanted his command time, but . . . did not want to actually leave Germany" and as a commander who failed to make any significant contribution to the "operational direction of the campaign."[10] This stems from unfavorable opinions held by his contemporaries but also from the fact that he did not appear to play a great part in the actual tactical deployment of the aircraft under his command. Nevertheless, oversimplified analyses of Milch's performance fail to take into account his contribution in other areas that were vitally important to the Luftwaffe's fight over Norway.

Although he was clearly reluctant to leave Göring's side, this should not be taken—as many historians have asserted—as indicating Milch's lack of enthusiasm for the task at hand. On the contrary, during his sojourn in northern climes, Milch attacked organizational and administrative problems with his customary vigor: between 16 April and 1 May, he made fifteen flights to airfields in Denmark and southern and central Norway, clocking up over 4,500 kilometers in the process. While commander of Luftflotte 5, Milch visited Oslo's Kjeller and Fornebu fields five times, Sola and Vaernes twice each, and Kristiansand and Aalborg East and West once each. Given the distances involved, it is no wonder that after a particularly hectic day he could refer to a one-hour trip from Sola to the capital as merely the "Stavanger-Oslo hop!"[11] Milch's diary reveals that during these visits—lasting on occasions only a few hours, but more often than not requiring at least an overnight stay—he went through the whole gamut of frontline experiences. In this respect he was no different from a good number of field commanders: Milch had the opportunity to sample some of Norway's finest hotels; had at least one big fight with a belligerent frontline *Fliegerführer;* was forced to dodge bombs at Sola; and received more than his fair share of harassment in the form of late night telephone calls and the odd "idiotic telegram" from Göring.[12] During an admittedly brief spell in Norway, he dramatically improved the communications network and set in place the groundwork for the creation of new fields and the upgrading of current fields, such as Vaernes, as well as the necessary infrastructure to achieve this. Clearly, Milch was more than just "punching his ticket," and at least for his administrative and organizational effort he deserved his Knight's Cross as much as Harlinghausen did for his frontline leadership. Later in 1942, Hitler reminisced with Speer and a handful of officers about how, when the situation was at its darkest in Norway in 1940 and all appeared lost, Milch had stepped into the breach: "And why? Because here was a man like me, who just did not know the word 'impossible.'"[13]

Milch's replacement, Stumpff, was faced with the very difficult task of supporting Dietl's isolated forces in and around Narvik. Although his army background did not win him any great support from his subordinates and his decision not to place greater weight on attacking Bardufloss was understandably unpopular among airmen, what can be said with some assurance is that Stumpff did have a greater appreciation of the overall situation than some of X Fliegerkorps' commanders at the time. An examination of the evidence has shown that Stumpff's decision to attempt to directly support Dietl, as opposed to Kessler's demand that they strike at Bardufloss airfield, was—given the importance of buying time for the relief projects—the right decision at the time, even if the results were less than impressive and it went against the conventional wisdom of aviation purists. That Stumpff was an ex-army officer who could not grasp the essentials of air warfare not only was untrue in May 1940 but also would be fully disproved by his astute leadership of the *Luftflotte* in the years ahead.

Subsequently, in particularly grueling and frustrating circumstances, Stumpff weathered the siphoning off of his forces at the end of *Weserübung* and the stripping of its remaining bomber force after the bloodbath of August 1940, only to see the force he had built up for attacks against PQ convoys in 1942 once again plundered for the Mediterranean and thereafter slip into relative oblivion. His courage and ingenious use of limited resources were epitomized in his determination to bring all his forces to bear on Arctic convoys. The various *Fliegerführer* were organized in such a manner that at any one time the largest possible attack force in the region could be brought into action, while coastal scouting squadrons performed an important dual role as sea-rescue units after they had fulfilled their reconnaissance tasks. Stumpff was also strongly parochial and, given the forces available, was prepared to back his units whenever he felt they offered the best means of crushing enemy forces, and on the whole his cooperation with local U-boat commanders appears to have been well received. His achievements in working with negligible forces in extremely difficult circumstances were obviously appreciated in Berlin and doubtless influenced the decision to transfer him out of Norway in 1943 for an equally unenviable task: the air defense of the Reich. Nevertheless, his strong Luftwaffe parochialism (which won over many previously antagonistic airmen and was characteristic of so many officers of all services), although in itself not unhealthy, illustrated one of the major hindrances to Germany utilizing Norway efficiently. While speed, surprise, and weight of numbers all helped to carry the day during *Weserübung,* this type of attitude resulted in the failure to appoint a desperately needed single Norwegian-theater commander in the years that followed.

The biggest impediment to establishing a combined command in this region, and other theaters, was the man who had canceled the four-engined bomber program in 1937 and was determined to control everything that flew: Hermann Göring. With regard to the invasion of Norway, he pompously proclaimed to the International Military Tribunal at his trial in 1946: "I could only take a very definite stand against this undertaking."[14] He frankly admitted expressing his opposition in an "unmistakable and unfriendly fashion" for no other reason than he had been informed too late of the impending campaign and rather lamely that the "plans did not seem quite right to me." In reality, though, Göring had not even wanted his air units deployed in Norway, especially after Hitler took the planning for the campaign away from the Luftwaffe and initially placed them under the command of Falkenhorst. Göring's petulance and overriding Luftwaffe bias, which effectively spelled the death knell for any hope of a unified command in the invasion, must be considered his second greatest failing regarding *Weserübung* and Norway in following years.

Yet Hitler, who had a propensity for interfering at every turn, was unprepared to intervene on the one issue that could have made a difference to the fighting in Norway: he was unwilling to rein in his second-in-command. The continual squabbling between the Luftwaffe and the navy in Norway could easily have been settled but for Hitler's unwillingness to put the *Reichsmarschall* in his place. As Hitler pointed out to Erich von Manstein, who after the tragedy of Stalingrad suggested the establishment of a chief of staff with authority over all three branches in Russia, Göring, as Germany's only *Reichsmarschall,* would never submit to anyone's authority but the Führer's.[15] Unable, or perhaps more accurately unwilling, to rein in his recalcitrant Luftwaffe chief, Hitler simply let the inefficient and often corrosive dual command structure remain in Norway as he did in other theaters. In many ways, the fragmented command structure pervading the German military machine suited Hitler's predilection for meddling and, when necessary, allowed him to step in as the final arbiter when particularly bitter feuds broke out.

HITLER THE MEDDLER

The Führer's penchant for playing the omniscient warlord was more evident in the invasion of Norway than is usually recognized, with the campaign revealing a number of disturbing tendencies in Hitler's leadership that would ultimately prove fatal. He not only had collapsed at the very first crisis but also, throughout *Weserübung,* had revealed a propensity to meddle persistently with even the smallest of operational details. Potentially the most important incident occurred after the Second Battle of Narvik, when it appeared that the British were about to land and take the town itself. Only Jodl's firm hand, despite a flurry of unrealistic demands made by Hitler, prevented the premature loss of the northern iron ore port. If anyone in high command deserved praise, it was Alfred Jodl, who—despite his postwar image as a Hitler sycophant—prevented the campaign going badly awry when Hitler cracked under the strain of command.[16] As Nicolaus von Below, Hitler's Luftwaffe adjutant, observed, Jodl openly made his opinions known to the Führer and to a large degree carried Hitler through the campaign's most difficult periods.[17]

Nevertheless, had Dietl's force been ordered over the Swedish border—as Hitler frantically demanded—prior to the invasion of the Low Countries and France, it is possible that the Allies could have secured an extremely strong foothold in the two months prior to Dunkirk, a foothold they might have decided to retain once firmly established there. From here, they could have continued the fight, since the Germans would have had great difficulty dislodging them, given the distances involved, the terrain, and the Royal Navy's relative mastery of the Far North. Persuaded not to make a premature withdrawal from Narvik, Hitler nevertheless continued to leave his personal mark everywhere—at least until he was distracted by the even greater excitement of his invasion in the west. Seemingly, no matter was too small for the Führer's personal attention, as demonstrated by his transfer of the Transatlantic Squadron to the theater and a pioneer detachment to Trondheim in late April. While many of these decisions were fairly innocuous and often beneficial to the overall effort, when combined with a little pressure, Hitler's propensity to interfere could produce tragic results. Nowhere was this more evident than in the ill-fated Dombaas drop in mid-April. Overreacting to the Allied landings at Aandalsnes and Namsos, Hitler once again panicked and, without giving due consideration to meteorologic and logistical factors, demanded that the Dombaas rail junction be secured. In addition to completely failing to fulfill their mission, 115 of the 160 men deployed were lost. Although these cracks in the facade of the German warlord's abilities were papered over by the eventual success of the campaign, they would be tragically exposed on the Russian front, where the stakes were much higher.

Hitler's habitual meddling tendencies, coupled with his unwillingness to bring the *Reichsmarschall* to heel, go some way to explaining his unwillingness to establish a unified command to facilitate the most effective use of resources on hand because it would have impinged on his own freedom of action and meant ruffling the feathers of his most volatile subordinate. Thus Hitler never went any further than toying with the idea of assigning a supreme commander for the Norwegian theater, even though this made a lot of sense at the time. And while Germany was engaged in limited blitzkrieg campaigns in the early stages of the war, the prevailing flawed structure never significantly impeded success. However, as the war gradually began to take on the form of a multitheater conflict engulfing not only western and northern Europe but also the Mediterranean and ultimately the vast Soviet Union, Hitler's ability to personally oversee operations in all these areas rapidly declined. Without a single command to direct and coordinate the Luftwaffe and the navy in Norway, coupled with a dissipation of strength and focus over many fronts, it is not surprising that tragic consequences followed.

This was nowhere more evident than in raids against the 1942 Arctic convoys. With the element of surprise well spent and the Allies rapidly regrouping under a united banner, the Germans needed to bring their forces together under one commander to sever the flow of valuable war materials over this northern sea route to the Soviet Union. It was at this point that Kesselring's name was thrown into the ring a second time as a possible supreme commander, and once again this proposal was never implemented. Even though, on the surface, Kesselring appeared an admirable candidate for such a position, doubtless resistance from the navy, which was unwilling to place its remaining precious big ships (squirreled away in Norwegian fjords) in the hands of an airman, stymied this initiative. Despite the fact that Kesselring was one of his own men, Göring also was unlikely to support such an appointment inasmuch as he probably foresaw himself being sidelined by such a move, which would give OKW the upper hand in controlling his precious air units in the region. This very same reasoning thwarted an effort by senior naval officers in Norway to have a single commander appointed to the region in 1943. Although the proposal envisaged a navy man filling the post, the Naval Staff also balked at the prospect of losing any say over its naval units to OKW.

Of course, even if Hitler at this point had been inclined to bang a few heads together to bring about a unified command, his own leadership style would have made any such commander's life extremely difficult. This was ably demonstrated by the experience of the twice-mooted leader for Norway, Kesselring, who came closest to becoming a true active combat theater commander when he was appointed Commander in Chief South in December 1941 and landed with the task of achieving air and sea superiority in the Mediterranean. Nonetheless, although this ostensibly placed him in charge of all Axis forces in the region, he had to contend not just with the Italian High Command but also with Rommel in Africa and the great meddler himself, Hitler. Therefore, even if Kesselring had been appointed Commander in Chief North, with control over Luftwaffe, navy, and army forces in Norway, he still probably would have had to deal with Germany's Supreme Commander of the Armed Services and a number of bellicose senior airmen and sailors.

The hopelessness of the situation was illustrated by the acrimonious argument that broke out between Luftwaffe and Naval Staffs over the use of bombers for reconnaissance duties during *Rösselsprung*. In planning for the attack on PQ 17, the navy was desperate to avoid a repeat performance of the March 1942 debacle, which nearly saw *Tirpitz* lost in conditions depressingly similar to those that claimed its sister ship, *Bismarck,* in May 1941. Therefore, it made a point of requesting that the Luftwaffe divert strike aircraft to scouting duties during the big ship's operation. Aside from once again revealing the inadequacy of the numbers and types of aircraft available for reconnaissance duties, the squabbling that resulted showed neither the navy nor the Luftwaffe was able to work harmoniously for a common good. Although, as during *Weserübung,* officers at the lower level achieved a degree of successful cooperation between U-boats and aircraft, at the highest level, where the operations where planned and directed, the lack of cooperation was painfully evident.

In the pre-*Rösselsprung* preparations, the navy had argued vociferously for the Luftwaffe to take a backseat in the operation and use its bombers in lieu of dedicated reconnaissance aircraft, while Stumpff was equally adamant that he did not want his limited air units expended on such a secondary role when they could, and should, be at the forefront of the battle. Only the intervention of Hitler brought the argument to an end in favor of the navy, though even with total Luftwaffe support, the insufficient number of aircraft available to the task at hand never provided Raeder with enough confidence to implement *Rösselsprung.* Thus Stumpff got his way in the end anyway, and, after the British Admiralty unwisely ordered the convoy to scatter, his air units (working in tandem with U-boats) were able to pick off the hapless vessels one at a time. Notwithstanding the eventual success of the attack on PQ 17, the fracas surrounding the convoy assault highlighted the serious inadequacies of the German command structure.

THE TURNING POINT IN THE FAR NORTH

Operationally, PQ 17 and subsequently PQ 18 represented turning points in the drama playing itself out in the air and at sea in the northern theater. Until this time, Germany, even with its declining resources, had held, if not the actual advantage, a psychological ascendancy over the British due to the pasting they had suffered during *Weserübung.* Even though the falling strength of the Luftwaffe in the region, the navy's unwillingness to risk remaining big ships, and the flawed dual command structure all ensured that the actual offensive potential was never fully realized, the aura of the Luftwaffe, coupled with the presence of these vessels, had been enough to safeguard the defensive integrity of Germany's position in Norway. Superficially, the attack on PQ 17 suggested that this British fear of German airpower was justified. In cooperation with U-boats, Stumpff's air fleet had played a significant part in the destruction of two-thirds of an Arctic convoy. In many ways PQ 17 represented what "might have been" in a genuine "siege of Britain" had the Luftwaffe been able to deploy a sufficient number of aircraft to the Battle of the Atlantic. For it was in the years before 1942, well in advance of the introduction of heavily escorted convoys and when enemy air cover was almost nonexistent, that long-range antishipping aircraft operating from both Norway and France, and working hand in glove with Dönitz's U-boats, could have achieved a stranglehold over the British Isles.

That success in the war at sea was in the process of passing out of Germany's grasp was demonstrated in the following assault on PQ 18. Just as the establishment of an interlocking convoy system, a Mid-ocean Escort Force group, and the increasing use of long-range aircraft and more effective antisubmarine technology were turning the tide against the Germans in the Battle of the Atlantic, the heavily escorted PQ 18 broke the spell of Luftwaffe ascendancy in the Far North. Even though the Luftwaffe increased its torpedo strength in Norway in anticipation of PQ 18, the Allies pulled out all the stops to prevent another tragedy on the scale of PQ 17 by providing the convoy with an extremely strong destroyer force and air cover from a dedicated escort carrier. This latter factor proved decisive in the end, and although Luftflotte 5 was able to sink thirteen ships during a number of attacks, the escort carrier's Sea Hurricane fighters, coupled with the destroyers' heavy defensive fire, led to the loss of forty-four German bombers—nearly one-sixth of the air fleet's strength. Whether the Luftwaffe would be able to counter these Allied measures in subsequent anticonvoy operations we shall never know because with the Anglo-American landings in North Africa, Luftflotte 5 lost nearly all its strike force to the Mediterranean, and convoys were suspended until the New Year.

The poor relations between the two staffs and problems associated with communications, plus the operational strength of the air fleet in Norway, reached their nadir when *Scharnhorst* put to sea in December 1943 to attack another convoy. Göring had been unwilling to transfer in aircraft from other hard-pressed fronts, and Stumpff was forced to provide reconnaissance support from the meager forces available, although he had to confess that he could not guarantee coverage. Remarkably, despite particularly foul weather the Luftwaffe got planes airborne and actually picked up on radar what appeared to be an enemy fleet detachment in the area, including a possible capital ship. It was at this juncture that the twin command structure and the poor communications network that snaked its way up and down the country effectively brought about the demise of *Scharnhorst*. The report of a possible capital ship never made it to the battle cruiser, and once the trap was sprung, the radar-equipped British ships, including *Duke of York,* detected, tracked, and eventually sank the ship. Notwithstanding the Royal Navy's prowess and technological advances, the loss of *Scharnhorst* was the direct result of insufficient numbers of aircraft suited to maritime reconnaissance and the lack of a joint staff under a single commander in the region to coordinate combined operations. As if in complete acknowledgment of its failure, by April 1944 Luftflotte 5 abandoned even the pretense of a limited reconnaissance capability by refusing to authorize any support for the navy. Aside from a brief period of activity in the final months of the war, the air fleet's war against convoys was over.

Overall, even when the hammering inflicted on PQ 17 is taken into account, the Allies could claim that the Arctic convoys had proved remarkably successful. Between December 1942 and May 1945, these convoys delivered a massive 4,964,231 tons of equipment and materials, including 5,218 tanks, 7,411 aircraft, and 4,932 antitank guns.[18] Although of the global total sent to the Soviet Union of 16,366,474 tons the Persian route accounted for the largest share, the Arctic route accounted for nearly 23 percent, and early on in the war was by far the most important because it was the most direct and quickest path through which urgent supplies could be sent to bolster the hard-pressed Soviets until post-Stalingrad. Of the 811 merchant ships dispatched with this valuable war material, 720 reached Russian ports, while 33 were forced to turn back for various reasons, and 58 were lost. Of those 715 making the return trip, only 29 were lost.[19] Taken together, these figures not only reveal the success of the convoys and the huge amount of material delivered but also point to a serious failure in German efforts to stop them.

The main reason for the termination of aerial reconnaissance from Norwegian airfields was not a lack of fighting spirit among the German aircrews but simply an ongoing decline in operational strength, which had begun as soon as *Weserübung* came to an end. In May 1940, the air fleet had boasted 700 aircraft, but within three months most of its strike force had been sent south due to their limited range for operations against Britain; with 175 combat machines on hand, it ceased to be a *Luftflotte* in all but name. Furthermore, after the heavy losses of 15 August, Luftflotte 5 was soon stripped of its remaining four bomber groups. Although the air fleet was bolstered for attacks on Arctic convoys to 264 aircraft in May 1942, the losses suffered against PQ 18 and the subsequent transfer of many bomber units to the Mediterranean meant that, by mid-1943, Stumpff once again had only 170 combat aircraft at his disposal. By this time, the Germans did not have sufficient reconnaissance aircraft to cover Norway's 2,600-kilometer coast and bombers to hit at passing convoys, let alone an adequate fighter force. A rapid decline in fighter numbers in the latter half of 1943 as they were transferred to Germany for home defense or the eastern front meant Luftflotte 5 would find itself completely unable to stem the tide of Allied bombers that appeared increasingly over Norway.

The Anglo-American bomber raids during 1943–1944 both hit directly at Hitler's economic dreams for Norway and shamed the defensive fighter force based there. For example, the American raids on 24 July and on 16 and 18 December 1943 were undertaken at low altitude without long-range fighter support, conditions that would have been suicidal over the Continent. The results of raids against newly constructed aluminum, magnesium, and nitrate factories at Heroya, the Trondheim U-boat pens, the Vermork power station, the electrolysis plant at Rjukan, the molybdenum mines at Knaben, and the Olso-Kjeller aircraft factory were mixed. At Heroya, for example, the bombers effectively shut down the plants for the rest of the war, while the thick concrete of the U-boat pens remained impervious to repeated Allied bombing. The 60 to 70 fighters on hand in mid-1943 to meet raids of up to 100 bombers at a time, and on one occasion over 300 machines, faced a well-nigh impossible task, especially when the effects of servicing and repairs on the operational strength of the defenders and the size of the theater are taken into account. Often intercepting bomber formations in ones and twos, the German fighters seldom pushed home their attacks. The results make sorry reading for the Germans. When Bomber Command's considerable effort (excluding minelaying missions) is added to that of the Eighth Air Force, the Allies flew more than 1,500 sorties over Norway for the loss of fewer than 30 machines. And of even this small number of casualties, most fell to flak rather than fighters. By 1943, the Germans simply could not justify transferring in further fighters for Norway when home defense was crying out for greater resources. In the end, this crushed Hitler's economic hopes for Norway within the Reich's expanding economic sphere and, as a final blow, brought about the loss of some 1,000 lives with the sinking of *Tirpitz* in 1944.

Despite this appalling showing in later years and the fact that should an actual Allied expedition take place, the air defense of Norway rested with a "paper air force," Hitler's determination to retain Norway did not wane, even in the twilight of the war. Although the approximately 300,000 troops stationed there in the latter months of the war would have been far better deployed on German soil in defense of the Reich, he was not prepared to give up his Nordic base, reasoning, as the Red Army bore down on Berlin, that it should be retained not only to prevent the Swedes from entering the war on the Allied side but also because of its importance as an invaluable source of fish. In general, though, Norway failed to live up to its billing as a base for aerial operations against Britain almost as soon as the Germans secured the country. In April 1942 Hitler declared that the invasion of Norway had been one of the two most decisive events so far in the entire war—the other being the defensive battle outside Moscow during December 1941—because control of the Norwegian coastline enabled his forces to launch attacks on northern Britain and Arctic convoys to the Soviet Union, but in reality the results were far from spectacular. Despite Luftflotte 5's brief period of glory against PQ 17, Norway very quickly reverted to a strategic backwater, the retention of which reflected more the Führer's obsession than pressing military reality. In the end, where the Luftwaffe and the navy are concerned, not only were the strategic opportunities offered by the Norwegian invasion never realized, but later, as tactical efficiency was beset by shrinking forces, bitter interservice feuding, and high command interference, they never received the priority they deserved in what was one of the Second World War's most demanding theaters.

Notes

1. BLOOD AND IRON, AND THE SPIRIT OF THE ATLANTIC

1. H. Picker, ed., *Hitlers Tischgespräche im Führerhauptquartier* (Berlin: Ullstein, 1993), 238–39.

2. U.S. Department of State, *Documents on German Foreign Policy, 1918–1945* Series D, Vol. 7, Doc. 525 [hereafter *DGFP* D/7/525] (Washington, D.C.: Government Printing Office, 1956), 502–3.

3. M. Domarus, *Hitler: Reden und Proklamationen 1932 bis 1945. Teil II Untergang,* vol. 2 (Leonberg: Pamminger and Partner, 1988), 1385. However, it should be remembered that the Danes had signed a nonaggression pact with Germany on 31 May 1939.

4. E. F. Ziemke, "The German Decision to Invade Norway and Denmark," in *Command Decisions,* ed. K. R. Greenfield (Washington, D.C.: Office of the Chief of Military History, United States Army, 1960), 50.

5. V. E. Tarrant, *The U-Boat Offensive, 1914–1918* (London: Arms and Armour, 1989), 45.

6. E. F. Ziemke, *The German Northern Theater of Operations, 1940–1945,* Pamphlet No. 20–271 (Washington, D.C.: Department of the Army, 1959), 2; T. K. Derry, *The Campaign in Norway* (London: HMSO, 1952), 5.

7. M. Curtis, ed., *Documents on International Affairs: Norway and the War, September 1939–December 1940* (London: Oxford University Press, 1941), 27; Ziemke, *German Northern Theater,* 518.

8. D. Irving, *Hitler's War* (1976; London: Focal Point, 1991), 227.

9. *Fuehrer Conferences on Matters Dealing with the German Navy* [hereafter *Fuehrer Conferences*] (Wilmington, Del.: Scholarly Resources in cooperation with the U.S. Naval Historical Center, 1983), 23 September 1939, emphasis in the original. In many documents from this period "England" is synonymous with "Britain." Therefore, for clarity and consistency I have changed these where applicable to "Britain." Likewise, nearly all references to the "German Air Force," or "GAF" in English translations of primary documents and secondary works have been replaced with "Luftwaffe" throughout.

10. *Kriegstagebuch der Seekriegsleitung, 1. Abteilung* [hereafter *KTB Skl*] (Wilmington, Del.: Scholarly Resources in cooperation with the U.S. Naval Historical Center, 1984), 2 October 1939.

11. Ibid., 3 October 1939.

12. The best discussion of the strategic significance of Scandinavia to German planners in the late nineteenth and early twentieth centuries is provided by C. Gemzell in two meticulously documented works: *Raeder, Hitler und Skandinavien: Der Kampf für einen maritimen Operationsplan* (Lund: CWK Gleerup, 1965); and *Organization, Conflict, and Innovation: A Study of German Naval Strategic Planning, 1888–1940* (Lund: Esselte Studium, 1973). The former addresses the more immediate military and political factors influencing German naval thought, and the latter looks at the more long-term maritime antecedents of the Norwegian campaign in 1940. See also M. Salewski's three-volume standard work on the German navy in this period, *Die deutsche Seekriegsleitung 1935–45*, vol. 1, *1935–1941* (Frankfurt am Main: Bernard & Graefe, 1970), in which the author neatly places the Norwegian campaign within the context of the war at sea; and H.-M. Ottmer's recent addition to historiography, *"Weserübung." Der deutsche Angriff auf Dänemark und Norwegen im April 1940* (Munich: R. Oldenbourg 1994). For the kaiser's imperial interest in Norway, see Gemzell, *Organization, Conflict and Innovation*, 65.

13. Ibid., 216.

14. Ibid.

15. Ibid., 221.

16. Ibid., 271; Derry, *Campaign in Norway*, 16.

17. W. Wegener, *The Naval Strategy of the World War*, ed. and trans. H. H. Herwig (Annapolis, Md.: Naval Institute, 1989), 73–74.

18. Ibid., 75.

19. Herwig, "Introduction: Wolfgang Wegener and German Naval Strategy from Tirpitz to Raeder," in ibid., xlii.

20. Ibid., xliii.

21. Whether Raeder was a true "convert" to Wegener's ideas or even understood them is discussed in H. H. Herwig, "The Failure of German Sea Power, 1914–1945: Mahan, Tirpitz, and Raeder Reconsidered," *International History Review* 10 (February 1988): 68–105; and Herwig, "Introduction: Wolfgang Wegener," xliii–xlviii. See also Salewski, *Seekriegsleitung 1935–45*, 1:177; and Salewski, "Germany and North Norway: Strategy and Ideology," in *Narvik 1940: Five-Nation War in the High North*, ed. K. Rommetveit (Oslo: Institutt for Forvarsstudier, 1991), 40–41.

22. In fact, although Raeder gave no credit to the retired *Vizeadmiral* in his talk, a comparison of the speech and the text of *Seestrategie des Weltkrieges* reveals that he blatantly "lifted" material from the latter's work. Gemzell shows this "cribbing" of Wegener's work by Raeder neatly by comparing excerpts from each side by side. Gemzell, *Raeder, Hitler und Skandinavien*, 54–56.

23. *Fuehrer Conferences*, 10 October 1939.

24. United States Air Force Historical Research Agency [hereafter USAFHRA] K113.305/K1027V: *Luftkrieg im Norden: Die Entwicklung der militär-politischen Lage bis zum Frühjahr 1940. Befehlshaber der U-Boote (Großadmiral Dönitz) an das Oberkommando der Kriegsmarine als "Geheime Kommandosache" betr. "Stützpunkt in Norwegen": 9.10.1939.*

25. Unsigned memorandum from Hitler to Brauchitsch, Raeder, Göring, Keitel, 9 October 1939, in *Trial of Major War Criminals by the International Military Tribunal Sitting at Nuremberg, Germany,* vol. 37, Doc. 052–L [hereafter *IMT* 37/052–L] (Nuremberg: International Military Tribunal, 1947–1949), 466–86.

26. "Gespräch mit dem Führer am 2,11,34 bei Meldung des Kommandanten der *Emden,*" *IMT* 34/190–C, 775–76.

27. The exact date in 1936 for the composition of this important document is not known. However, it was given to Albert Speer personally by Hitler in 1944. For the complete text and Speer's covering note explaining the circumstances by which it came into his possession, see *DGFP* C/5/490, 853–62; T. Wilhelm, "Hitlers Denkschrift zum Vierjahresplan," *Vierteljahrshefte für Zeitgeschichte* 3 (April 1955): 184–210; R. Overy, *War and Economy in the Third Reich* (Oxford: Clarendon Press, 1994), 233–56; D. Irving, *Göring: A Biography* (London: Macmillan, 1989), 166–67.

28. For a discussion of the importance of oil in Germany's strategic planning see J. S. A. Hayward, "Hitler's Quest for Oil: The Impact of Economic Considerations on Military Strategy, 1941–42," *Journal of Strategic Studies* 18, no. 4 (December 1995): 94–135.

29. *DGFP* C/5/490, 862.

30. For the postwar debate over the importance of iron ore, see R. Karlbom, "Sweden's Iron Ore Exports to Germany, 1933–1944," *Scandinavian Economic History Review* 13 (1965): 65–93; A. S. Milward, "Could Sweden Have Stopped the Second World War?" *Scandinavian Economic History Review* 15 (1967): 127–38; J. Jäger, "Sweden's Iron Ore Exports to Germany, 1933–1944: A Reply to Rolf Karlbom's Article on the Same Subject," *Scandinavian Economic History Review* 15 (1967): 139–47.

31. M. Fritz, *German Steel and Swedish Iron Ore, 1939–1945* (Göteborg: Publications of the Institute of Economic History of the Göteborg University, 1974), 30–31.

32. Ibid., 31.

33. *United States Strategic Bombing Survey: The Effects of Strategic Bombing on the German War Economy* (n. p.: Overall Economic Effects Division, 1945), 99.

34. National Archives, Washington, D.C. [hereafter NA] T84/195: *Die Eisenerzversorgung Großdeutschlands während der gegenwärtigen kriegerischen Verwicklungen, Bearbeitet im Institut für Weltwirtschaft, Dezember 1939.*

35. For a contemporary assessment of the iron and steel situation under the Four-Year Plan until 1940, see NA T71/135: *Die Eisen- u. Stahlversorgung des Vierjahresplanes, Stand v.1.1.38. Zusammengestellt von Abt. III/H Amtes für Deutsche Roh- u. Werkstoffe jetzt: Abt. P Reichsstelle für Wirtschaftsausbau Sachbearbeiter: Dr. Dittebrand.*

36. Fritz, *German Steel and Swedish Iron Ore,* 33 n. 9; in addition to this mine the other sources of importance were the so-called *Doggererzreviere* (Dogger ore mines) of southern Germany and the *Wesergebirge;* see NA T77/214: *Dr. F. Friedensburg, Regierungspräsident a.D., Die deutsche Roh - und Treibstofflage, 3.10.1940.*

37. Fritz, *German Steel and Swedish Iron Ore,* 33.

38. Ibid.

39. *United States Strategic Bombing Survey,* 247.

40. NA T84/195: *Die Eisenerzversorgung Großdeutschlands während der gegenwärtigen kriegerischen Verwicklungen, Bearbeitet im Institut für Weltwirtschaft, Dezember 1939.*

41. NA T77/214: *Dr. F. Friedensburg, Regierungspräsident a.D., Die deutsche Roh - und Treibstofflage, 3.10.1940.*

42. Fritz, *German Steel and Swedish Iron Ore,* 34.

43. NA T77/701: *W Stb W Wi VI Nr. 340/39 gK II.Ang., 29.4.1939. Die Eisenerz- versorgung Deutschlands im Kriege unter besonderer Berücksichtigung der schwedischen Einfuhr, abgestellt auf die Versorgungslage in den Jahren 1939 und 1940.*

44. How war could impact German ore supplies was demonstrated graphically by the falling level of Spanish ore imports due to the outbreak of the Spanish civil war; NA T84/134–35: *OKW WiRüAmt, Die Wirtschaftstruktur Spaniens, März 1941.*

45. Declining mobilization requirements were due to projected increases in domes- tic production. Additionally, the assessment also took into account the fact that the iron content of central Swedish mines was about 5 to 10 percent lower than those of northern Sweden. NA T77/701: *W Stb W Wi VI Nr. 340/39 gK II.Ang., 29.4.1939. Die Eisenerzver- sorgung Deutschlands im Kriege unter besonderer Berücksichtigung der schwedischen Einfuhr, abgestellt auf die Versorgungslage in den Jahren 1939 und 1940.*

46. NA T77/701: *W Wi VI a, Anlage zu 4238/38 g.K., 22.12.1938: Übersicht über die Untersuchung der Erzversorgungslage Deutschlands im Krieg.* Although the 29.4.39 document is fuller in content, both reports follow basically the same format, and their as- sessments come to essentially the same conclusions.

47. NA T22/701: *Oberkommando der Wehrmacht Wehrwirtschaftstab Az. W Stb W Wi Id/VIb Nr. 101/38 g.K. An R d L u. Ob d L Gen.St.d.Lw. Betr.: Deutsche Erzeinfuhr aus Schweden. Berlin, den 14.1.1939.*

48. NA T22/701: *Der Reichsminister der Luftfahrt und Oberbefehlshaber der Luft- waffe, Generalstab 5.Abtlg. Az.: 8 h 32, Nr. 74/39 g.Kdos.(IV). An Oberkommando der Wehrmacht Wehrwirtschaftsstab, Berlin. Bezug: OKW - Wehrwirtschaftsstab- Az.W Stb W Wi Id/IVb Nr.101/39g.K.vom 14.1.1939. Betr.: Deutsche Erzeinfuhr aus Schweden. Berlin, den 24.1.1939.*

49. Cf. NA T77/701: *Anlagen 3. Gefährdung der nordschwedischen Erzgruben durch russische Luftstreitkräfte,* in *Die Eisenerzversorgung Deutschlands im Kriege unter besonderer Berücksichtigung der schwedischen Einfuhr, abgestellt auf die Versorgungslage in den Jahren 1939 und 1940.*

50. Domarus, *Hitler: Reden und Proklamationen,* vol. 3, 1251–52.

51. Ibid., 1371–73.

52. *DGFP* D/8/162, 167–68.

53. *KTB Skl,* 17, 30 October 1939.

54. NA RG457: *G.C. & C.S. Naval History,* vol. 23, *Northern Waters* (part of the British Government Code and Cipher School histories prepared immediately after the war by Ultra staff at Bletchley Park and only recently declassified by the U.S. National Security Agency), 6–8; M. Salewski, "Basis Nord: Eine fast vergessene Episode aus dem Zweiten Weltkrieg," *Schiff und Zeit* 3 (1976): 13–14. Salewski's study of *Basis Nord* has now been supplemented by T. R. Philbin, *The Lure of Neptune: German- Soviet Naval Collaboration and Ambitions, 1919–1941* (Columbia: University of South Carolina, 1994).

55. K. A. Maier, "Die Sicherung der europäischen Nordflanke: I. Die deutsche Strategie," in *Das Deutsche Reich und der Zweite Weltkrieg,* vol. 2, *Die Errichtung der Hegemonie auf dem europäischen Kontinent,* ed. K. A. Maier et al. (Stuttgart: Deutsche

Verlags-Anstalt, 1979), 195; see also NA T77/214: *W Wi VI a Anlage zu 4238/38 g.K. Übersicht über die Untersuchung der Erzversorgungslage Deutschlands im Krieg.*

56. For a breakdown of ore imports by German ports, see NA T71/14: *Wirtschaftsgruppe Eisen schaffende Industrie nur für das Reichswirtschaftsministerium, "Der Bezug der deutschen Hochofen- und Stahlwerks an Eisen und Manganerzen (ohne Schwefelkiesabbrände) unter Berücksichtigung der Verkehrswege im Jahr 1938."*

57. The best concise discussion of Allied plans in this period is D. Dilks, "Great Britain and Scandinavia in the 'Phony War,'" *Scandinavian Journal of History* 2 (1977): 29–51.

58. C. J. M. Goulter, *A Forgotten Offensive: Royal Air Force Coastal Command's Anti-shipping Campaign, 1940–1945* (London: Frank Cass, 1995), 116.

59. Dilks, "Great Britain and Scandinavia," 31–32.

60. Ibid., 34.

61. *KTB Skl,* 13 October 1939. For one of the most detailed reports, see the summary of the chief of the Naval Intelligence Division, *KTB Skl,* 4 December 1939.

62. Ibid., 10 November 1939.

63. Ibid., 15 November 1939.

64. Ibid., 27 November 1939.

65. *Fuehrer Conferences,* 8 December 1939.

66. NA 1546PS: *E. Raeder, Die Besetzung von Norwegen 9.IV.1940.* Memorandum prepared on 10 July 1945 by Raeder for the Office of U.S. Chief of Counsel for the Prosecution of Axis Criminality on the occupation of Norway on 9 April 1940; see also similar reflections by Raeder, *KTB Skl,* 25 November 1939.

67. The best discussion on the ideological component of the decision to invade Norway is still H.-D. Loock, *Quisling, Rosenberg und Terboven. Zur Vorgeschichte und Geschichte der nationalsozialistischen Revolution in Norwegen* (Stuttgart: Deutsche Verlags-Anstalt, 1970).

68. A. Rosenberg, *Der Mythus des 20 Jahrhunderts* (Munich: Hoheneichen, 1933), 642.

69. Ibid., 676.

70. A. Rosenberg, "Kurzer Tätigkeitsbericht des Außenpolitschen Amtes der NSDAP von 1933–1943," in *IMT* D/25/007-PS, 34–35; Loock, *Quisling, Rosenberg und Terboven,* 161–86.

71. Rosenberg, "Kurzer Tätigkeitsbericht des Außenpolitschen Amtes," 35.

72. A. S. Milward, *The Fascist Economy in Norway* (Oxford: Clarendon Press 1972), 6.

73. NA T454/79: *Programm der Reichstagung der Nordischen Gesellschaft vom 23. bis 30. Juni 1935 in Lübeck.* This document was found in a *Kanzlie Rosenberg* folder containing the activities of the *Nordische Gesellschaft.*

74. NA T454/79: *Aus "Dagbladet, Oslo," 28.6.35. "Die Leiter der deutschen Tscheka im Vorstand der Nordischen Gesellschaft."*

75. Of these, forty came from Sweden, fifteen from Norway, thirty-five from Denmark, and six from Finland; H. Jacobsen, *National-sozialistische Außenpolitik, 1933–1938* (Frankfurt am Main: Alfred Metzner, 1968), 489; H.-D. Loock, "Nordeuropa zwischen Außenpolitik und 'großermanisher' Innenpolitik," in *Hitler, Deutschland und die Mächte: Materialien zur Außenpolitik des Dritten Reiches,* ed. M. Funke (Kronberg: Athenäum 1978), 690.

76. H.-G. Seraphim, ed., *Das politisches Tagebuch Alfred Rosenbergs, 1934/35 und 1939/40* (Munich: Deutscher Taschenbuch, 1964), 37.

77. Loock, *Quisling, Rosenberg und Terboven,* 187.

78. H.-D. Loock, "*Weserübung:* A Step Towards the Greater German Reich," *Scandinavian Journal of History* 2 (1977): 88.

79. Loock, "*Weserübung,*" 49.

80. Rosenberg, "Kurzer Tätigkeitsbericht des Außenpolitschen Amtes," 35.

81. V. Quisling, *Russia and Ourselves* (London: Hodder and Stoughton, 1931), 27, 181–82; Rosenberg, *Mythus des 20 Jahrhunderts,* 112–13, 152.

82. Quisling, *Russia and Ourselves,* 147–48.

83. Ibid., 275–76.

84. Milward, *Fascist Economy in Norway,* 5.

85. Ibid., 9–10.

86. Rosenberg, "Anlagen I zum kurzen Tätigkeitsbericht des Außenpolitischen Amtes der NSDAP von 1933–1943: Die politische Vorbereitung der militärischen Besetzung Norwegens in den Kriegsjahren 1939/1940," *IMT* 25/007–PS, 40. That Quisling and Rosenberg were not in significant contact with each other until the last quarter of 1939 (despite Rosenberg's later suggestions to the contrary) can be observed from the fact that neither the entries for the period 1934–1935 and June to December 1939 in Seraphim, *Das politisches Tagebuch Alfred Rosenbergs,* nor the "Kurzer Tätigkeitsbericht des Außenpolitischen Amtes" (*IMT* 25/003–PS, 15–25), prepared by Rosenberg in October 1935, make any mention of either Quisling or Nasjonal Samling. This fact is also supported by the relatively extensive surviving records of Außenpolitisches Amt and Rosenberg material for this period held at the National Archives, Washington, D.C.; see Record Group T454, which contains records of the Reichsministerium für die besetzten Ostgebiete.

87. *KTB Skl,* "Report of the Commander in Chief, Navy to the Fuehrer on 12 December 1939 at 1200."

88. The exact date of this first meeting is uncertain; Jodl's diary indicates 13 December, while Raeder, in a note on a letter from Rosenberg, states 14 December, which in turn is in disagreement with Rosenberg's Außenpolitisches Amt report of June 1940, which gives 16 December 1939 as the date. *The Jodl Diaries with Annotations by General der Artillerie Walter Warlimont, 1937–1945. Reel DJ 84* [hereafter *Jodl, Tagebuch*] (Wakefield, England: Microform, 1973), 13 December 1939; Ziemke, *German Northern Theater,* 9 n. 20; A. Rosenberg, "Die politische Vorbereitung der Norwegen-Aktion," *IMT* 25/004–PS, 28–29.

89. Rosenberg, "Die politische Vorbereitung der Norwegen-Aktion," 29; cf. USAFHRA K113/305: *Luftkrieg im Norden: Die Entwicklung der militär-politischen Lage bis zum Frühjahr 1940. Hitler nach einer Unterredung mit Quisling am 18.12.1939.*

90. *Jodl, Tagebuch,* 13 December 1939.

91. A. Hitler, *Mein Kampf* (Munich: Franz Eher Nachfolger, 1933), 313.

92. Ibid., 357, 732.

93. Ibid., 735.

94. G. Weinberg, ed., *Hitlers zweites Buch: Ein Dockument aus dem Jahr 1928* (Stuttgart: Deutsche, 1961).

95. Ibid., 156. This is almost identical wording to Rosenberg, *Mythus des 20 Jahrhunderts,* 112–13.

96. Weinberg, *Hitlers zweites Buch,* 157.

97. Ibid., 125.

98. Ibid., 127, 132.

99. Ibid., 124.

100. Cf. Loock, *"Weserübung,"* 87–88; Irving, *Hitler's War,* 264. For a brief discussion on the concept and importance of Nordic superiority in Hitler's thinking, see J. Hiden and J. Farquharson, *Explaining Hitler's Germany: Historians and the Third Reich* (London: Batsford Academic and Educational, 1983), 14–15.

101. *DGFP* D/7/525, 502–3.

102. The glaring omission of Finland from this clause was clearly deliberate, and in line with the conditions of the secret protocols of the German-Soviet pact of August.

103. W. Hubatsch, *Hitlers Weisungen für die Kriegführung 1939–1945: Dokumente des Oberkommandos der Wehrmacht* (Koblenz: Bernard & Graefe, 1983), 47–50.

2. PLANNING FOR *WESERÜBUNG*

1. D. Irving, *Hitler's War* (London: Focal Point, 1991), 271.

2. M. Domarus, *Hitler: Reden und Proklamationen 1932 bis 1945. Teil II Untergang,* vol. 3 (Leonberg: Pamminger and Partner, 1988), 1523.

3. Rosenberg, "Die politische Vorbereitung der Norwegen-Aktion," *IMT* 25/004-PS, 29.

4. Ibid.

5. Ibid., 30.

6. Rosenberg, "Anlage I zum Tätigkeitsbericht des Außenpolitischen Amtes," *IMT* 25/007-PS, 41–42.

7. *Fuehrer Conferences,* 30 December 1939.

8. The memorandum had been completed in late December 1939, but Hitler had it withheld for two weeks before releasing it. F. Halder, *Halder, Kriegstagebuch: Tägliche Aufzeichungen des Chefs des Generalstabes des Heeres 1939–1945,* vol. 1 [hereafter *Halder, Kriegstagebuch*] (Stuttgart: Kohlhammer, 1962), 1 January 1940.

9. *KTB Skl,* 13 January 1940; NA T022/1818: *Lagebetrachtung zur Studie "Nord."*

10. K. A. Maier, "Die Sicherung der europäischen Nordflanke: II. Die alliierte Strategie," in *Das Deutsche Reich und der Zweite Weltkrieg,* vol. 2, *Die Errichtung der Hegemonie auf dem europäischen Kontinent,* ed. K. A. Maier et al. (Stuttgart: Deutsche Verlags-Anstalt, 1979), 204; F. Bédarida, "France, Britain and the Nordic Countries," *Scandinavian Journal of History* 2 (1997): 13–14.

11. J. R. M. Butler, *Grand Strategy,* vol. 2, *September 1939–June 1941* (London: HMSO, 1957), 101.

12. M. Gilbert, *The Churchill War Papers,* vol. 1, *At the Admiralty, September 1939–May 1940* (London: Norton, 1993), 524; D. Dilks, "Great Britain and Scandinavia in the 'Phony War,'" *Scandinavian Journal of History* 2 (1977): 35.

13. Dilks, "Great Britain and Scandinavia," 35.

14. Ibid.

15. Butler, *Grand Strategy,* 2:103–4.

16. R. Macleod, ed., *The Ironside Diaries, 1937–1940* (London: Constable, 1962), 196; Dilks, "Great Britain and Scandinavia," 37.

17. C. Gemzell, *Organization, Conflict, and Innovation: A Study of German Naval Strategic Planning, 1888–1940* (Lund: Esselte Studium, 1973), 404.

18. Cf. NA T1022/1818: *Lagebetrachtung zur Studie "Nord,"* 11.

19. This examination of the German navy's *Überlegungen Studie Nord* is based on E. F. Ziemke's discussion of the document, *The German Northern Theater of Operations, 1940–1945,* Pamphlet No. 20-271 (Washington, D.C.: Department of the Army, 1959), 12–13; and NA T1022/1818: *Lagebetrachtung zur Studie "Nord,"* 1–23.

20. NA T1022/1818: *Lagebetrachtung zur Studie "Nord,"* 9–10.

21. *Jodl, Tagebuch,* 13, 18 December 1939.

22. Ibid., 20 December 1939.

23. *KTB Skl,* 13 December.

24. *Documents relating to Gfm. Erhard Milch. Reel DJ 59: Transcripts of Diaries and Notebooks* [hereafter *Milch, Tagebuch* or *Milch, Merkbuch* as applicable] (Wakefield, England: Microform, 1978), 14 January; D. Irving, *The Rise and Fall of the Luftwaffe: The Life of Luftwaffe Marshal Erhard Milch* (London: Futura, 1976), 85–86; *Jodl, Tagebuch,* 21 January 1940.

25. *Jodl, Tagebuch,* 23 January 1940.

26. *Nazi Conspiracy and Aggression,* vol. 6, Doc. C-63 (Washington, D.C.: U.S. Government Printing Office, 1946), 883.

27. See annotations by W. Warlimont in *Jodl, Tagebuch,* 23 January; cf. H. Greiner, "The Campaigns in Western and Northern Europe, 1940," in *World War II German Military Studies,* vol. 7, pt. 4, *The OKW War Diary Series* (London: Garland, 1979), 14–15.

28. Ziemke, *German Northern Theater,* 12.

29. Ziemke (ibid., 14–16) provides the basis for this discussion of the Kranke staff; see also H. M. Ottmer, "Das Unternahmen *Weserübung.* Die Besetzung Dänemarks und Norwegens durch die deutsche Wehrmacht im April 1940. Vorgeschichte, Vorbereitung und Durchführung der Landeunternehmungen in Norwegen," in *Ideen und Strategien 1940. Ausgewählte Operationen und deren militärgeschichtliche Aufarbeitung,* ed. Militärgeschichtlichen Forschungsamt (Herford: E. S. Mittler & Sohn, 1991), 74–75; "Herrn Admiral Assman zur eigenen Unterrichtung, b. Weserübung. Vom Raeder, 10.1.44," *IMT* 34/C-66, 281–82.

30. USAF Historical Support Office, Bolling Air Force Base, Washington, D.C. [hereafter USAFHSO] K113.107-171: *A. L. Nielsen, "The collection and evaluation of intelligence for the German Air Force High Command" (1955),* 113.

31. Ibid.

32. Ziemke, *German Northern Theater,* 15; for lack of military maps, see W. Hubatsch, *"Weserübung." Die deutsche Besetzung von Dänemark und Norwegen 1940* (Göttingen: Musterschmidt Verlag, 1960), 40.

33. USAFHSO K113.107-171: *Nielsen,* 11.

34. D. Kahn, *Hitler's Spies: German Military Intelligence in World War II* (New York: Macmillan, 1978), 119.

35. USAFHSO K113.107–171: *Nielsen,* 115.

36. Physical description prepared from S. P. Parker, ed., *World Geographical Encyclopedia,* vol. 4, *Europe* (New York: McGraw-Hill, 1995), 137–40; T. K. Derry, *The Campaign in Norway* (London: HMSO, 1952), 1–3; "Topography and Communications," in USAFHSO 512.277B: *List of Airfields, Landing Grounds, and Seaplane Bases: Norway* (British Air Ministry, 1943); Royal Institute of International Affairs, *The Scandina-*

vian States and Finland: A Political and Economic Survey (Hertfordshire: Broadwater, 1951), 151.

37. Ziemke, *German Northern Theater*, 15.

38. NA T1022/2188 PG/33487: *1/Skl.II/47 gKdos, Band 1 betr. "Übersee - Etappenschiffe" Beiheft 1: Tabu - Schiffe. Bereicht über Tätigkeit der "Altmark" in der Zeit vom 19.8.1939 bis 7.3.1940,* 14; for earlier *Altmark* activity, see also NA T1022/2998 PG/48001: *Operationen und Taktik. Auswertung wichtiger Ereignisse des Seekrieges, Heft . . . Die Operation des Panzerschiffes "Admiral Graf Spee" (Kapitän zur See Langadorff) und des Troßschiffes "Altmark" (Kapitänleutnant d.R. Dau). Oberkommando der Kriegsmarine,* Berlin 1945.

39. *KTB Skl,* 14 February 1940.

40. Ibid., 15 February 1940.

41. Butler, *Grand Strategy,* 2:111.

42. *KTB Skl,* 16 February 1940.

43. NA T1022/2188 PG/33487: *Anlagen 2: An den Befehlshaber der vor dem Jösingfjord liegenden englishen Seestreitkräfte (M.S.T. Altmark, Jösingfjord, den 16.2.1940),* in *1/Skl.II/47 gKdos, Band 1 betr. "Übersee - Etappenschiffe" Beiheft 1: Tabu - Schiffe. Bereicht über Tätigkeit der "Altmark" in der Zeit vom 19.8.1939 bis 7.3.1940.*

44. NA T1022/2188 PG/33487: *Anlagen 4: An den Kommanten des englishen Kriegsschiffes,* in *1/Skl.II/47 gKdos, Band 1 betr. "Übersee - Etappenschiffe" Beiheft 1: Tabu - Schiffe. Bereicht über Tätigkeit der "Altmark" in der Zeit vom 19.8.1939 bis 7.3.1940.*

45. For whether or not the crew was armed, see G. Weinberg, *A World at Arms: A Global History of World War II* (Cambridge: Cambridge University Press, 1994), 953 n. 77.

46. Irving, *Hitler's War,* 264.

47. *KTB Skl,* 17 February 1940.

48. R. G. Reuth, ed., *Joseph Goebbels Tagebücher,* vol. 4, *1940–1942* (Munich: Piper, 1992), 19 February.

49. *KTB Skl,* 17, 18 February 1940; NA T1022/1756 PG 32305: *Skl, KTB, Teil D 1 d, Luftlagemeldungen,* 18 February 1940.

50. *KTB Skl,* 16 February 1940.

51. H. Picker, ed., *Hitlers Tischgespräche im Führerhauptquartier* (Berlin: Ullstein, 1993), 16 August 1942; T. Kranke, "Wahrheit über die Operation 'Weserübung,'" *Deutsche Soldaten-Zeitung* 4 (April 1956): 5.

52. N. Below, *Als Hitlers Adjutant, 1937–45* (Mainz: Hase & Koehler, 1980), 221; Rosenberg, "Anlage I zum Tätigkeitsbericht des Außenpolitischen Amtes," 41–42; for a German assessment of the Norwegian role in the *Altmark* incident, see *Notiz betr. "Altmark," den 19.2.1940,* inserted within NA T1022/3438: *Abschrift. Geheim! Gefechtsbericht des Zerstörers "Georg Thiele" über den Bombenangriff feindlicher Trägerflugzeuge auf den Zerstörerverband im Narvik am 12.4.1940 (Anlage zu T.B.K. B.Nr. 3515/40 Prüf-Nr. 8).*

53. Butler, *Grand Strategy,* 2:106–7.

54. Ibid., 107.

55. N. I. Baryshnikov, "The Soviet-Finnish War of 1939–1940," *Soviet Studies in History* (winter 1990–1991): 56–57.

56. Butler, *Grand Strategy,* 2:113–14; Macleod, *Ironside Diaries,* 228–30; *KTB Skl,* 10 March 1940.

57. Quoted in Bédarida, "France, Britain, and the Nordic Countries," 23 n. 58.

58. Gilbert, *Churchill War Papers*, 929–31.

59. Butler, *Grand Strategy*, 2:122–23.

60. Dilks, "Great Britain and Scandinavia," 50.

61. For naval concerns, see *KTB Skl*, 10 March 1940.

62. Irving, *Hitler's War*, 270–71; *KTB Skl*, 30 March 1940.

63. Gilbert, *Churchill War Papers*, 935–38; D. Irving, *Göring: A Biography* (London: Macmillan, 1989), 285.

64. Domarus, *Hitler: Reden und Proklamationen*, 3:1544–45; J. H. Waller, *The Unseen War in Europe: Espionage and Conspiracy in the Second World War* (New York: Random House, 1996), 21.

65. Halder, *Kriegstagebuch*, 21 February 1940.

66. H.-M. Ottmer, *"Weserübung." Der deutsche Angriff auf Dänemark und Norwegen im April 1940* (Munich: R. Oldenbourg, 1994), 42; Hubatsch; *"Weserübung,"* 39.

67. H.-D. Loock, *"Weserübung:* A Step Towards the Greater German Reich," *Scandinavian Journal of History* 2 (1977): 83; USAFHRA K113.305: *Norwegen Feldzug 1940. Auszüge aus dem Kriegstagebuch der Gruppe XXI (278/1)* [hereafter *Kriegstagebuch der Gruppe XXI*], 21 February 1940. The original diary of *Gruppe XXI* was destroyed in a fire, and these extracts are taken from the Germany army archives.

68. Domarus, *Hitler: Reden und Proklamationen*, 3:1463; Below, *Als Hitlers Adjutant*, 221.

69. USAFHRA K113.305: *Kriegstagebuch der Gruppe XXI*, 26 February 1940.

70. W. Hubatsch, *Hitlers Weisungen für die Kriegführung 1939–1945: Dokumente des Oberkommandos der Wehrmacht* (Koblenz: Bernard & Graefe, 1983), 47–50.

71. For earlier considerations regarding the inclusion of Denmark, see *Halder, Kriegstagebuch*, 10 January 1940.

72. Hubatsch, *Hitlers Weisungen*, 47; The term *Gruppe* is used to define a unit that falls in size and composition between a corps and an army.

73. Jodl, *Tagebuch*, 3 March 1940; *Halder, Kriegstagebuch*, 3 March 1940.

74. *KTB Skl*, 13 March 1940.

75. For doubts about the continued necessity of *Weserübung* in the light of the ending of the Winter War, see *Jodl, Tagebuch*, 28 March 1940.

76. *KTB Skl*, 15 March 1940.

77. *Fuehrer Conferences*, 26 March 1940.

78. USAFHRA K113.305: *Kriegstagebuch der Gruppe XXI*, 2 April 1940; *KTB Skl*, 2 April 1940. For the influence of ice in the Baltic in slowing preparations in late February and early March, see *KTB Skl*, 14 March 1940.

79. *Halder, Kriegstagebuch*, 21 February 1940. It would appear that on 2 March Halder went back to this 21 February entry to add the marginal note; cf. Halder's comments in USAFHRA K113.305: *Norwegen (Aus einer Bearbeitung des Nachkriegsprojekts von Rohden. Europaeische Beitraege zur Geschichte des Weltkrieges II.1939/ 194. Luftkrieg, Heft 14, Seite 114–171). "Das Ringen um Norwegen."*

80. Jodl, *Tagebuch*, 2 March 1940.

81. Ibid., 5 March 1940.

82. E. H. Stevens, ed., *Trial of Nikolaus von Falkenhorst* (London: William Hodge, 1949), 256.

83. Below, *Als Hitlers Adjutant*, 225.

84. Irving, *Göring*, 284–85. For Hitler's disapproval of delays caused by the armed services, see *Jodl, Tagebuch*, 3 March 1940.

85. *Milch, Merkbuch*, 13 March 1940.

86. Ibid., editor's interview.

87. R. Knauss, *Der Feldzug in Norwegen 1940* (unpublished after-action narrative and analysis from the collection of Professor J. Corum, SAAS, Air University, Alabama, n.d.), 27.

88. For a brief description of how this was supposed to work on the first day of the invasion, see USAFHRA K113.305: *Generalkommando, X.Fl.K., Ia B.Nr.10053/40 gKdos. Gefechtsstand, den 20.3.40. Anlage zu X.Fl.K., Ia Nr. 10053/40 gKdos. Auszug au "Der Führer und Oberster Befehlshaber der Wehrmacht" WFA/Abt. L Nr. 22094/40 gKdos Chefs.;* Ziemke, *The German Northern Theater*, 31–32.

89. "Betr.: 'Weserübung Nord': Operationsbefehl für die Besetzung Norwaegens Nr 1," in Hubatsch, *"Weserübung,"* appendix H, 441–45.

90. K. Assman, *The German Campaign in Norway* (London: Naval Staff Admiralty, 1948), 14; Ziemke, *German Northern Theater*, 32–33.

91. *KTB Skl*, 9 March 1940.

92. Assman, *German Campaign in Norway*, 10–11.

93. *Fuehrer Conferences*, 9 March 1940.

94. *KTB Skl*, 29 March, 2 April 1940.

95. K. Doenitz, *Memoirs: Ten Years and Twenty Days* (1959; Annapolis, Md.: Naval Institute, 1990), 76–77.

96. *KTB Skl*, 4 March 1940.

97. Assman, *German Campaign in Norway*, 12–13.

98. Hubatsch, *"Weserübung,"* 464–73; Ziemke, *German Northern Theater*, 35–36.

99. O. U. Munthe-Kaas, "The Campaign in Norway in 1940 and the Norwegian and the British War Direction Machineries," *Revue Internationale d'Histoire Militaire* 47 (1980): 37–39.

100. Assman, *German Campaign in Norway*, 19.

101. Knauss, *Der Feldzug in Norwegen 1940*, 18.

102. Ibid.

103. R. L. Tarnstrom, *The Sword of Scandinavia* (Lindsborg, Kans.: Trogen Books, 1996), 74–77.

104. NA T971/20: *Generalkommando X.Fl.K., Ia B.Nr.10053/40 gKdos. Operationalbefehl für das X.Fliegerkorps am Wesertag. Gefechtsstand, den 20.3.1940;* USAFHRA K133.305: *Die deutsche Luftwaffe bei der Besetzung Daenemarks und Norwegens (Auszug aus einer Studie der 8 Abteilung des Generalstabs "Ueberblick ueber die deutsche Luftkriegsfuehrung vom 21.9.44).*

105. For air units, see NA T971/20: *Generalkommando X.Fl.K., Ia B.Nr.10053/40 gKdos. Operationalbefehl für das X.Fliegerkorps am Wesertag. Gefechtsstand, den 20.3.1940;* and U. O. E. Kessler, "The Role of the Luftwaffe in the Campaign in Norway 1940," in *World War II German Military Studies*, vol. 23, pt. 10, *Special Topics*, 5–6.

106. See W. Gaul, "The German Naval Air Force: The Development of the Naval Air Force up to the Outbreak of the 1939–1945 War and Its Activity During the First Seven Months of the War," in *Essays by German Officers and Officials About World War II* (Wilmington, Del.: Scholarly Resources in cooperation with the U.S. Naval Historical Center, n.d.), 12.

107. Quoted in R. Brett-Smith, *Hitler's Generals* (San Rafael, Calif.: Presidio, 1985), 133; K. F. Hildebrand, *Die Generale der deutschen Luftwaffe 1935–1945, Bd. 2* (Osnabrück: Biblio, 1991), 351–52.

108. NA T971/16: *Geschichte der I./KG General Wever 4 vom 1.9.1939 bis 15.7.1944 und Geschichte der III.KG General Wever 4 vom 1941 bis Oktober 1943.*

109. NA T971/20: *Generalkommando X.Fl.K., Ia B.Nr.10053/40 gKdos. Operationalbefehl für das X.Fliegerkorps am Wesertag. Gefechtsstand, den 20.3.1940.*

110. Knauss, *Der Feldzug in Norwegen 1940,* 21.

111. USAFHRA K113:305: *Der "Norwegen-Feldzug" 1940. (Gesamtueberblick) (Quellen: Akten des X. Flieger-Korps ueber Weseruebung (Norwegen u. Daenemark) Vorarbeiten der 8. Abteilung des Generalstabes der Lw. ueber den Norwegenfeldzug. Notizen des Lw. Fuehrungstabes ueber die Luftlandungen der I/Z.G.76 (Vorarbeiten der 8. Abteilung) Die Luftnachtrichtentruppe im Norwegen Feldzug (8. Abteilung 1944) Angagen ueber Luftransportleistungen. General Morzik 1945. Kriegstagebuch der Kriegsmarine vom 1.-11.6.1940).* This document was prepared from work by the Luftwaffe's *8 Abteilung* on the Norwegian campaign.

112. NA T971/20: *Generalkommando X.Fl.K., Ia B.Nr.10053/40 gKdos. Operationalbefehl für das X.Fliegerkorps am Wesertag. Gefechtsstand, den 20.3.1940.*

113. USAFHRA K113.305: *Generalkommando X. Fl. Korps, Ia op Nr.10072/40 gKdos. Befehl fuer Einsatz der Auflaerungsstaffel (F)1.122 waehrend der Weseruebung. Gefechtsstand, d. 20.3.40.*

114. W. Gaul, "The Part Played by the German Air Force and the Naval Air Force in the Invasion of Norway," in *Essays by German Officers and Officials About World War II* (Wilmington, Del.: Scholarly Resources in cooperation with the U.S. Naval Historical Center, n.d.), 12; USAFHRA K113.305: *Generalkommando X. Fl. Korps, Ia op Nr.10071/40 gKdos. Befehl fuer den Einsatz der 1./F120 am Wesertag. Gefechtstand, d. 20.3.40.*

115. USAFHRA K113.305: *Generalkommando X.Fliegerkorps, Ia op Nr.10077/40, Befehl fuer den Einsatz der Küstenfliegergruppe 506 waehrend der Weseruebung. Gefechtstand, den 20.3.40.*

116. USAFHRA K133.305: *Norwegen (Aus einer Bearbeitung des Nachkriegsprojekts von Rohden. "Europaeische Beitrage zur Geschichte des Weltkrieges" II.1939/194. Luftkrieg, Heft 14, Seite 114–171),* 8.

117. Ibid., 9.

118. Air Ministry, British [hereafter AMB], *The Rise and Fall of the German Air Force, 1933–1945* (London: Arms and Armour, 1983), 58–59.

119. J. L. Moulton, *The Norwegian Campaign of 1940: A Study of Warfare in Three Dimensions* (London: Eyre and Spottiswoode, 1966), 68; Hubatsch, *"Weserübung,"* 140.

120. USAFHRA K113.305: *Generalkommando X.Fl.K. Ia op Nr.10145/40 gKdos. Befehl fuer den Einsatz der I./Z.G.1 am Wesertag. Gefechtsstand, den 3.4.40;* USAFHRA K113.305: *Generalkommando X.Fl.K. Ia op Br.B.Nr.10052/40 gKdos 2.Ang. Befehl für den Einsatz der I./Z.G.76 am Wesertag. Gefechtsstand: d.3.4.40.*

121. F. Morzik, *German Air Force Airlift Operations,* USAF Historical Studies No. 167 (New York: Arno Press, 1961), 90.

122. Oberkommando der Wehrmacht, *Kampf um Norwegen* (Berlin: Zeitgeschichte-Verlag Wilhelm Andermann, 1940), 66; see also Moulton, *Norwegian Campaign of 1940,* 67.

123. NA T971/20: *Generalkommando des X.Fliegerkorps. Ia op.Br.B.Nr.10066/40 gKdos. Weisungen für den Transportchef (Land) für die Weserübung. Gefechtsstand, 20.3.40.*

124. Morzik, *German Air Force Airlift Operations,* 91.

125. NA T971/20: *Generalkommando des X.Fliegerkorps. Ia op.Br.B.Nr.10066/40 gKdos. Weisungen für den Transportchef (Land) für die Weserübung. Gefechtsstand, 20.3.40;* USAFHRA K113.305: *Der Oberbefehlshaber der Luftwaffe. Fuehrungsstab I c. Nr.3343/40 gKdos (III). Einsatz der Fallschrim-und Luftransportverbande bei der Besetzung von Daenemark und Norwegen am 9.4.1940. H. Qu., den 10.4.1940.*

126. AMB, *Rise and Fall of the German Air Force,* 60.

127. USAFHRA 512.621: *The Use of Transport Aircraft in the Present War. A Study Prepared by the German Air Historical Branch (8th Abteilung), dated 25th March, 1944 (Air Historical Branch, Translation No. VII/69, 30th April, 1948),* 1.

128. Gaul, "Part Played by the German Air Force," 6; Assman, *German Campaign in Norway,* 12–13; Ziemke, *German Northern Theater,* 28–29.

129. NA T971/20: *Generalkommando des X.Fliegerkorps. Ia op.Br.B.Nr.10066/40 gKdos. Weisungen für den Transportchef (Land) für die Weserübung. Gefechtsstand, 20.3.40;* C. Bekker, *Angriffshöhe 4000: Ein Kriegstagebuch der deutschen Luftwaffe 1939– 1945* (Gräfelfing vor München: Urbes Verlag Hans Jürgen Hansen, 1964), 92.

130. NA T971/3: *Sonderheft 5 der Truppenschriften. Teil: Die Luftnachtrichten-Truppe im Norwegen-Feldzug. Bearb.: Oberst Dürr. Karlsbad, den 13.8.1944.*

131. A. Lee, *The German Air Force* (London: Duckworth, 1946), 50.

132. NA T971/20: *Generalkommando X.Fl.K. Ia op Nr.10074/40 gKdos. Befehl für den Einsatz der 4./Fallsch.Jäg Regt.1 am Wesertag. Gefechtsstand, den 20.3.40.*

133. NA T971/20: *Abschrift. anlage 1 zu X.Fl.K.Ia Nr.10033/40 gKdos. Geheime Kommandosache! Feinddschrichtenblatt. Jutland.*

134. Knauss, *Der Feldzug in Norwegen,* 32.

135. USAFHSO 512.277B: *List of Airfields, Landing Grounds, and Seaplane Bases: Norway,* unnumbered pages.

136. Gaul, "Part Played by the German Air Force," 11.

137. NA T971/20: *Anlage 3 zu Generalkommando des X.Fliegerk., Ia Br.B.Nr.10053/ 40 gKdos. Feindnachrichtenblatt Oslo und Oslofjord.*

138. Ibid.

139. NA T971/20: *Generalkommando X.Fl.K. Ia op.Nr10058/40 gKdos. Befehl für den Einsatz der 3./Fallsch.Jäg.Regt.1 am Wesertag. Gefechtstand, den 20.3.40.*

140. USAFHRA K113.305: *Generalkommando X.Fl.K. Ta op Br.B.Nr.10064 gKdos. Befehl für den Einsatz des Kampfgeschwaders 26 am Wesertag. Gefechtsstand, 28.3.1940;* NA T971/20: *Generalkommando X.Fl.K. Ia op Br.B.Nr.10052/40 gKdos 2,Ang. Befehl für den Einsatz der I./Z.G.76 am Wesertag. Gefechtsstand, d.3.4.40.*

141. Gaul, "The Part Played by the German Air Force," 11; USAFHRA K113.305: *Generalkommando X.Fl.Korps, Ia op Nr.10055/40 gKdos. Befehl für den Einsatz der I./ Stukageschwader 1 am Wesertag. Gefechtsstand, den 3.4.1940.*

142. Gaul, "Part Played by the German Air Force," 11–12; NA T971/20: *Anlage 4 zu Generalkommando des X.Fliegerkorps Ia Br.B.Nr.10053/40 gKdos. Feindnachrichtenblatt Kristiansand.*

143. NA T971/20: *Anlage 4 zu Generalkommando des X.Fliegerkorps Ia Br.B.Nr.10053/ 40 gKdos. Feindnachrichtenblatt Kristiansand.*

144. NA T971/20: *Anlage 6 zu X.Fl.K. Ia Nr. 10053 gKdos. Feindnachrichtenblatt Bergen.*

145. Gaul, "Part Played by the German Air Force," 12.

146. NA T971/20: *Generalkommando des X.Fliegerkorps. Ia op.Br.B.Nr.10066/40 gKdos. Weisungen für den Transportchef (Land) für die Weserübung. Gefechtsstand, 20.3.40.*

147. Gaul, "Part Played by the German Air Force," 11.

148. C. Shores, *Fledgling Eagles: The Complete Account of Air Operations During the Phoney War and the Norwegian Campaign, 1940* (London: Grub Street, 1991), 59; USAFHRA K113.305: *Oberst a.D. i.G. Torsten G. E. Christ, Die deutsche Luftwaffe im Kampf um Norwegen* (n.d.), 3–4.

149. Quoted in Gaul, "Part Played by the German Air Force," 7.

150. *KTB Skl,* 28, 30, 31 March 1940.

151. Ibid., 30 March 1940; Gaul, "Part Played by the German Air Force," 7–8.

152. S. Roskill, *The War at Sea,* vol. 1, *The Defensive* (London: HMSO, 1954), 155.

153. NA T1022/1756: *Oberkommando der Kriegsmarine. 1 Skl-Teil D: Luftlage, 1. März bis 31. Juli 1940. Abschrift. Generalstab der Luftwaffe meldet am 3.4.40 7.45 Uhr.* Although dated 3.4.40, the report concerned the previous day's activities.

154. *KTB Skl,* 3 April 1940.

155. A brief but useful chronological breakdown of events pertinent to aerial preparations and activities in the seven days prior to 9 April can be found in USAFHRA K113:305: *Kriegstagebuch der Gruppe XXI.*

156. Gaul, "Part Played by the German Air Force," 8–9.

157. Ibid.

158. USAFHRA K113.305: *Kriegstagebuch der Gruppe XXI,* 4 April 1940.

159. Shores, *Fledgling Eagles,* 217–18; *KTB Skl,* 7 April 1940.

160. KTB Skl, 7 April 1940; Roskill, *War at Sea,* 1:158.

161. Shores, *Fledgling Eagles,* 217.

162. Quoted in N. Miller, *War at Sea: A Naval History of World War II* (London: Scribner, 1995); Moulton, *Norwegian Campaign of 1940,* 70.

163. Roskill, *War at Sea,* 1:159.

164. Derry, *Campaign in Norway,* 26.

165. *KTB Skl,* 8 April 1940.

166. Derry, *Campaign in Norway,* 26.

167. Ibid.

168. B. Stegemann, "Die Sicherung der europäischen Nordflanke: III. Das Unternehmen 'Weserübung,'" in *Das Deutsche Reich und der Zweite Weltkrieg,* vol. 2, 212; Hubatsch, *"Weserübung,"* 65–67.

169. Shores, *Fledgling Eagles,* 224–25.

170. *KTB Skl,* 8 April 1940.

171. Ibid.

172. Roskill, *War at Sea,* 1:164.

173. *KTB Skl,* 8 April 1940.

174. Moulton, *Norwegian Campaign of 1940,* 72.

175. For a brief discussion of some of the diplomatic warnings flowing into Norway, see F. Kersaudy, *Norway 1940* (London: Collins, 1990), 60–61.

176. *KTB Skl,* 3 April 1940.

177. Kersaudy, *Norway 1940,* 61–62.

178. Ibid., 61.

179. *KTB Skl,* 8 April 1940.

180. NA T1022/1756: *Oberkommando der Kriegsmarine, 1 Skl-Teil D Luftlage 1. März bis 31. Juli 1940. Meldungen Genst. Luftwaffe 9.4.40) 7.30 Uhr.*

3. NORWEGIAN BLITZKRIEG

1. NA T971/20: *Generalkommando X.Fl.K. Ia op Nr.10074/40 gKdos. Befehl für den Einsatz der 4./FallschJäg Regt.1 am Wesertag. Gefechtsstand, den 20.3.40.*

2. USAFHRA K113.305: *Gen.Kdo. X.Fl. Korps. /22.00. An Ob.d.L Fueh.Stab Ia z. H. Herrn Oberst i.G.v. Waldau;* C. Bekker, *Angriffhöhe 4000: Ein Kriegstagebuch der deutschen Luftwaffe 1939–1945* (Gräfelfing vor München: Urbes Verlag Hans Jürgen Hansen, 1964), 92.

3. V. Kühn, *Deutsche Fallschrimjäger im Zweiten Weltkrieg* (Stuttgart: Motorbuch, 1977), 29–30.

4. Bekker, *Angriffhöhe 4000,* 93.

5. NA T1022/1756: *Oberkommando der Kriegsmarine, 1 Skl-Teil D Luftlage 1. März bis 31. Juli 1940. Meldungen Genst. Luftwaffe 9.4.40, 7.30 Uhr;* USAFHRA K113.305: *Der "Norwegen-Feldzug" 1940,* 17.

6. C. Shores, *Fledgling Eagles: The Complete Account of Air Operations During the Phoney War and the Norwegian Campaign, 1940* (London: Grub Street, 1991), 227. Alongside primary documents, Shores and two others have proved invaluable in charting the events and details surrounding the activity of the Luftwaffe over Norway during *Weserübung.* Shores's chronology is detailed and, from my familiarity with the primary material, must be considered accurate overall. The second solid narrative of the Norwegian campaign utilized here is E. R. Hooton's *Phoenix Triumphant: The Rise and Rise of the Luftwaffe* (London: Arms and Armour, 1994). Last, but certainly not least, is W. Gaul's unpublished work, "The Part Played by the German Air Force and the Naval Air Force in the Invasion of Norway," in *Essays by German Officers and Officials About World War II* (Wilmington, Del.: Scholarly Resources in cooperation with the U. S. Naval Historical Center, n.d.). Originally drafted as *Die Beteiligung der Luftwaffe und der Seeluftstreitkraefte an der Norwegenoperation,* this excellent translated narrative is based on Gaul's extensive firsthand knowledge of the campaign and access to surviving naval documents. Neither Gaul's German work nor the English version has been widely used previously.

7. Shores, *Fledgling Eagles,* 227; J. Vasco and P. D. Cornwell, *Zerstörer: The Messerschmitt 110 and Its Units in 1940* (Norfolk, Va.: JAC Publications, 1995), 13; NA T971/6: *Erfahrungen aus Einsatz der I./Z.G.76 in Norwegenfeldzug* (n.d. for this specific document, but it appears with a number of separate reports under *Bericht von April 1940 ueber Einsatz der Luftwaffe bei der Besetzung von Denmark und Norwegen am 9 Apirl 1940).*

8. USAFHRA K113.305: *Der Oberbefehlshaber der Luftwaffe, Fuehrungsstab Ic Nr. 3343/40 gKdos (III). Einsatz der Fallschrim-und Lufttransportverbaende bei der Besetzung von Daenemark und Norwegen am 9.4.1940. H. Qu., den 10.4.1940.*

9. Shores, *Fledgling Eagles,* 227.

10. Ibid.

11. USAFHRA K113:305: *Der "Norwegen-Feldzug" 1940*, 9.

12. E. F. Ziemke, *The German Northern Theater of Operations, 1940–1945*, Pamphlet No. 20-271 (Washington, D.C.: Department of the Army, 1959), 59–62.

13. Ibid., 60.

14. NA T971/16: *Geschichte der I./K.G. General Wever 4 vom 1.9.1939 bis 15.7.1944 und Geschichte der III./K.G. General Wever 4 vom January 1941 bis Oktober 1943.*

15. Ibid.

16. Bekker, *Angriffhöhe 4000*, 94.

17. J. L. Moulton, *The Norwegian Campaign of 1940: A Study of Warfare in Three Dimensions* (London: Eyre and Spottiswoode, 1966), 93.

18. *DGFP* D/9/65, 102.

19. Moulton, *Norwegian Campaign of 1940*, 96–97.

20. Bekker, *Angriffhöhe 4000*, 94.

21. Ibid., 94–96.

22. Vasco and Cornwell, *Zerstörer*, 13.

23. Shores, *Fledgling Eagles*, 227.

24. Ibid., 236–37.

25. Bekker, *Angriffhöhe 4000*, 101; Vasco and Cornwell, *Zerstörer*, 15.

26. NA T1022/1756: *Oberkommando der Kriegsmarine, 1 Skl-Teil D Luftlage 1. März bis 31. Juli 1940. Meldungen Genst. Luftwaffe 9.4.40., 8.11 Uhr.*

27. Shores, *Fledgling Eagles*, 236; NA 971/16: *Geschichte der I./K.G. General Wever 4 vom 1.9.1939 bis 15.7.1944 und Geschichte der III./K.G. General Wever 4 vom January 1941 bis Oktober 1943.*

28. Gaul, "Part Played by the German Air Force," 13.

29. W. Hubatsch, *"Weserübung." Die deutsche Besetzung von Dänemark und Norwegen 1940* (Gottingen: Musterschmidt Verlag, 1960), 82.

30. E. Loewenstern, *Luftwaffe über dem Feind* (Berlin: Wjlhelm Limpert, 1941), 60.

31. Bekker, *Angriffhöhe 4000*, 101.

32. USAFHRA K113.305: *Gen.d.Lw. I.Abt. NR. 5695/40. Weseruebung. Befehle des X.Fl.K Kriegstagebuch, eingeg. 30.3.40*, entry for 9 April 1940; USAFHRA K113:305: *Der Oberbefehlshaber der Luftwaffe, Fuehrungsstab Ic Nr. 3343/40 gKdos (III). Einsatz der Fallschrim-und Lufttransportverbaende bei der Besetzung von Daenemark und Norwegen am 9.4.1940. H. Qu., den 10.4.1940.*

33. Shores, *Fledgling Eagles*, 239.

34. Ibid., 229.

35. Gaul, "Part Played by the German Air Force," 16; *KTB Skl*, 9 April 1940.

36. Moulton, *Norwegian Campaign of 1940*, 86.

37. F. Kurowski, *Generaloberst Dietl. Deutscher Heerführer am Polarkreis* (Berg am Starnberger See: Verlagsgemeinschaft Berg, 1990), 62–63.

38. Hooton, *Phoenix Triumphant*, 226.

39. Moulton, *Norwegian Campaign of 1940*, 107.

40. U. O. E. Kessler, "The Role of the Luftwaffe in the Campaign in Norway 1940," in *World War II German Military Studies*, vol. 23, pt. 10, *Special Topics* (London: Garland, 1979), 17.

41. *KTB Skl*, 9 April 1940; S. Roskill, *The War at Sea*, vol. 1, *The Defensive* (London: HMSO, 1954), 171; Hubatsch, *"Weserübung,"* 97.

42. N. Miller, *War at Sea: A Naval History of World War II* (London: Scribner, 1995), 66.

43. *KTB Skl,* 9 April 1940.

44. Roskill, *War at Sea,* 1:171–72.

45. T. K. Derry, *The Campaign in Norway* (London: HMSO, 1952), 34.

46. Ibid.

47. *KTB Skl,* 11 April 1940.

48. Gaul, "Part Played by the German Air Force," 16.

49. J. S. Corum, "The German Campaign in Norway 1940 as a Joint Operation" (paper presented at the conference of the Society for Military History, Montgomery, Alabama, April 1997); *KTB Skl,* 11, 14, 16 April 1940.

50. *KTB Skl,* 9 April 1940.

51. Total figures vary between accounts. I have chosen to accept the totals in Gaul, "Part Played by the German Air Force," 15; and USAFHRA K113.305: *Der Oberbefehlshaber der Luftwaffe, Fuehrungsstab Ic Nr. 3343/40 gKdos (III). Einsatz der Fallschrim-und Lufttransportverbaende bei der Besetzung von Daenemark und Norwegen am 9.4.1940. H. Qu., den 10.4.1940.*

52. D. Irving, *Hitler's War* (London: Focal Point, 1991), 273.

53. Ziemke, *German Northern Theater,* 57.

54. F. O. Busch, "Narvik: The Story of the Heroic Battle of the German Destroyers," in *Essays by German Officers and Officials About World War II* (Wilmington, Del.: Scholarly Resources in cooperation with the U.S. Naval Historical Center, n.d.), 123.

55. J. Winton, ed., *The War at Sea, 1939–45* (London: Pimlico, 1997), 31–32.

56. *KTB Skl,* 10 April 1940.

57. Ibid.

58. Gaul, "Part Played by the German Air Force," 15; regarding the Germans' difficulties experienced throughout the invasion in long-distance operations, I am indebted to Nils Naastad, a lecturer at the Norwegian Air Force Academy, who, in personal correspondence, highlighted this aspect of the campaign.

59. NA T1022/1756: *Oberkommando der Kriegsmarine, 1 Skl-Teil D Luftlage 1. März bis 31. Juli 1940. Tagesverlauf Luftwaffe 10.4.40.*

60. *KTB Skl,* 10 April 1940; *War Diaries of the German Submarine Command (BdU, KTB)* [hereafter *BdU, KTB*], 1939–1945 (Wilmington, Del.: Scholarly Resources in cooperation with the U.S. Naval Historical Center, 1984), 10 April 1940.

61. NA T1022/1756: *Oberkommando der Kriegsmarine, 1 Skl-Teil D Luftlage 1. März bis 31. Juli 1940. Tagesverlauf Luftwaffe 10.4.40.*

62. Ibid.

63. Gaul, "Part Played by the German Air Force," 15.

64. J. R. Smith and A. L. Kay, *German Aircraft of the Second World War* (London: Putnam, 1989), 418.

65. Ibid., 125.

66. NA T1022/3349: *Kriegstagebuch, General der Luftwaffe beim Oberbefehlshaber der Marine,* 11.4.40; *KTB Skl,* 10 April 1940; for a description of the *G.d.Luft b. Ober d.M.*'s liaison role, see USAFHRA 519.681 B-4: *Air Staff Post Hostilities Intelligence Requirements on German Air Force (Headquarters United States Air Forces in Europe, 7 September 1945),* 6–7.

67. *KTB Skl,* 10 April 1940.

68. Gaul, "Part Played by the German Air Force," 15.

69. *BdU, KTB,* 12 April 1940; *KTB Skl,* 10 April 1940.

70. Winton, *War at Sea,* 27–29.

71. Gaul, "Part Played by the German Air Force," 21.

72. D. Richards, *The Hardest Victory: RAF Bomber Command in the Second World War* (London: Hodder and Stoughton, 1994), 34.

73. The greater part of this assessment of British airpower in northern Britain is drawn from Shores's concise discussion of the subject (*Fledgling Eagles,* 218–19).

74. Derry, *Campaign in Norway,* 53.

75. Ibid.

76. NA RG457/94–99: *G.C. & C.S. Air and Military History,* vol. 2, *The Air War in the West, 1940–1941,* 15.

77. R. Lewin, *Ultra Goes to War: The Secret Story* (London: Hutchinson, 1978), 61.

78. R. Bennett, *Behind the Battle: Intelligence in the War with Germany, 1939–45* (London: Sinclear-Stevenson, 1994), 43.

79. NA RG457/94–99: *G.C. & C.S. Air and Military History,* 2:14.

80. F. H. Hinsley, *British Intelligence in the Second World War: Its Influence on Strategy and Operations,* vol. 1 (London: HMSO, 1979), 137.

81. NA RG457/94–99: *G.C. & C.S. Air and Military History,* 2:15.

82. Ibid.

83. Ibid.

84. Hinsley, *British Intelligence,* 1:140.

85. Bennett, *Behind the Battle,* 41.

86. Ibid., 43.

87. Shores, *Fledgling Eagles,* 277; M. Middlebrook and C. Everitt, *The Bomber Command War Diaries: An Operational Reference Book, 1939–1945* (New York: Viking, 1985), 35.

88. Hinsley, *British Intelligence,* 1:140.

89. Richards, *Hardest Victory,* 36.

90. Shores, *Fledgling Eagles,* 244; Smith and Kay, *German Aircraft of the Second World War,* 402.

91. Shores, *Fledgling Eagles,* 250; a full breakdown of the large number of flights made by the transport formations can be found in NA T1022/1756: *Oberkommando der Kriegsmarine, 1 Skl-Teil D Luftlage 1. März bis 31. Juli 1940. Tagesverlauf Luftwaffe 10.4.40.*

92. Hooton, *Phoenix Triumphant,* 227.

93. Shores, *Fledgling Eagles,* 244.

94. *Milch, Merkbuch,* 12 April 1940; H.-A. Koch, *Flak: Die Geschichte der Deutschen Flakartillerie 1935–1945* (Bad Nauheim: Hans-Henning Podzun, 1954), 37.

95. *Milch, Merkbuch,* 11 April.

96. Kessler, "Role of the Luftwaffe," 10.

97. F. Hildebrand, *Die General der deutschen Luftwaffe 1935–1945,* vol. 2, (Osnabrück Biblio, 1991), 394–95.

98. D. Irving, *The Rise and Fall of the Luftwaffe: The Life of Luftwaffe Marshal Erhard Milch* (London: Futura, 1976), 86.

99. Hooton, *Phoenix Triumphant,* 227.

100. The only exception to this is, of course, Irving's Milch biography. Yet even here, Irving devotes only three pages to Milch's involvement in the Norwegian campaign; see *Rise and Fall of the Luftwaffe*, 85–88.

101. Shores, *Fledgling Eagles*, 257.

102. Middlebrook and Everitt, *Bomber Command War Diaries*, 31.

103. NA T1022/1756: *Oberkommando der Kriegsmarine, 1 Skl-Teil D Luftlage 1. März bis 31. Juli 1940. Tagesverlauf Luftwaffe 10.4.40.*

104. Ibid.; Hooton, *Phoenix Triumphant*, 227.

105. *KTB Skl*, 11 April 1940; Gaul, "Part Played by the German Air Force," 20.

106. Gaul, "Part Played by the German Air Force," 20.

107. NA T971/16: *Geschichte der I./K.G. General Wever 4 vom 1.9.1939 bis 15.7.1944 und Geschichte der III./K.G. General Wever 4 vom January 1941 bis Oktober 1943.*

108. Shores, *Fledgling Eagles*, 255.

109. USAFHRA 248.50 1-71: *Confidential. Norway (Combat). Subject: Military Operations—General. 6–4 2016–1297, 93. Stockholm, Sweden. April 19, 1940*, 1.

110. Ibid.

111. F. Kersaudy, *Norway 1940* (London: Collins, 1990), 109.

112. USAFHRA 248.50 1-71: *Confidential. Norway (Combat)*, 3.

113. Kersaudy, *Norway 1940*, 110.

114. Gaul, "Part Played by the German Air Force," 21.

115. Shores, *Fledgling Eagles*, 262.

116. The narrative detailing the exploits of the Royal Navy in the Second Battle of Narvik has been drawn principally from Derry, *Campaign in Norway*, 49–51.

117. A contemporary German account of the unfolding battle can be found in NA1022/3438: *Abscrift. Gefechtsbericht des Zerstörers "George Thiele" über das Seegefecht vor Narvik am 13.4.1940. Anlagen zu T.B.K. G 3515/40 Pef.Nr. 8.*

118. Moulton, *Norwegian Campaign of 1940*, 114.

119. Busch, "Narvik," 171.

120. Gaul, "Part Played by the German Air Force," 21.

121. *Milch, Tagebuch*, 13 April; Irving, *Rise and Fall of the Luftwaffe*, 87.

122. *KTB Skl*, 13 April 1940.

123. *Jodl, Tagebuch*, 13 April 1940.

124. Shores, *Fledgling Eagles*, 262; F. Morzik, *German Air Force Airlift Operations*, USAF Historical Studies No. 167 (New York: Arno Press, 1968), 104.

125. Miller, *War at Sea*, 70.

126. K. Assmann, *The German Campaign in Norway* (London: Naval Staff Admiralty, 1948), 43–44.

127. Roskill, *War at Sea*, 1:178.

128. Ibid.

129. *KTB Skl*, 13 April 1940.

130. Ibid.

131. *BdU, KTB*, 1 to 14 April 1940. Dönitz's growing concern about the torpedo situation is covered in "Address Excerpt from Enquiry into Torpedo Failures (M 83 S/42 Most Secret)"; C. Bekker, *Hitler's Naval War* (New York: Kensington, 1978), 130–31.

132. *BdU, KTB*, 1 to 14 April 1940; "Address Excerpt from Enquiry into Torpedo Failures (M 83 S/42 Most Secret)."

133. *BdU, KTB,* 12 April 1940.

134. Bekker, *Hitler's Naval War,* 130–31.

135. K. Doenitz, *Memoirs: Ten Years and Twenty Days* (Annapolis, Md.: Naval Institute, 1990), 84.

136. *BdU, KTB,* Appendix I, 12 April 1940.

137. Doenitz, *Memoirs,* 84.

138. Ibid., 85.

139. J. Terraine, *Business in Great Waters: The U-Boat Wars, 1916–1945* (London: Leo Cooper, 1989), 237–38; G. Hessler, *The German U-Boat War in the Atlantic,* vol. 1, *1939–1941* (London: HMSO, 1989), 26.

140. G. Till, "The Battle of the Atlantic as History," in *The Battle of the Atlantic, 1939–1945,* ed. S. Howarth and D. Law (Annapolis, Md.: Naval Institute, 1994), 589; Doenitz, *Memoirs,* 84–90.

141. Hessler, *German U-Boat War in the Atlantic,* 1:26. For details on the problems experienced prior to Norway, see Bekker, *Hitler's Naval War,* 121–28; and Terraine, *Business in Great Waters,* 238–40.

142. Bekker, *Hitler's Naval War,* 133.

143. Hessler, *German U-Boat War in the Atlantic,* 1:25.

144. Ibid., 26.

145. *KTB Skl,* 13 April 1940.

146. *Jodl, Tagebuch,* 18 April 1940; W. Görlitz, *The German General Staff* (London: Hollis and Carter, 1953), 373.

147. *Jodl, Tagebuch,* 14 April 1940.

148. H. Greiner, "The Campaigns in Western and Northern Europe, 1940," in *World War II German Military Studies,* vol. 7, pt. 4, *The OKW War Diary Series* (London: Garland, 1979), 24–25.

149. *Halder, Tagebuch,* 14 April 1940.

150. W. Warlimont, *Inside Hitler's Headquarters, 1939–45* (London: Weidenfeld and Nicolson, 1964), 79–80.

151. *KTB Skl,* 15 April 1940.

152. Greiner, "Campaigns in Western and Northern Europe," 25.

153. Irving, *Hitler's War,* 275.

154. Greiner, "Campaigns in Western and Northern Europe," 25.

155. *Jodl, Tagebuch,* 17 April 1940.

156. Ibid.

157. Ibid., 18 April 1940.

4. AIR CONTROL OF CENTRAL AND NORTHERN NORWAY

1. *Milch, Merkbuch,* 13 April 1940.

2. D. Irving, *The Rise and Fall of the Luftwaffe: The Life of Luftwaffe Marshal Erhard Milch* (London: Futura, 1976), 85–88.

3. NA T971/39: *Abschrift. Fernschreibstelle Fl. Korps X. Betr.: "Reparaturkolonnen Norwegen." 16.4.1940.*

4. *KTB Skl,* 14 April 1940; *Milch, Merkbuch,* 13 April 1940; NA T971/39: *Abschrift. Fernschreibstelle: Fl.Korps X. Oberstlt. v. Gablenz üb. Fl. Korps X - Lfl. Kdo. 5.*

Geheime Kommandosache, Sofort verlegen. 26.4.1940; NA T971/39: *Abschrift Geheime-Kommandosache. Der Reichsminister der Luftfahrt und Oberbefehlshaber der Luftwaffe, Generalluftzeugmeister LN. Berlin, den 26.April 1940;* E. R. Hooton, *Phoenix Triumphant: The Rise and Rise of the Luftwaffe* (London: Arms and Armour, 1994), 227; for Allied knowledge of *Luftpark Oslo* near the end of the war, see USAFHRA 512.651D-4: *Aircraft and Aero-Engine Factories in Norway, A.I.2(a) Report No.C.125/45 dated 20th February, 1945,* 5.

5. *Milch, Merkbuch,* 13 April.

6. NA RG457/94–99: *G.C. & C.S. Naval History,* vol. 23, *Northern Waters,* 183.

7. D. Kahn, *Hitler's Spies: German Military Intelligence in World War II* (New York: Macmillan, 1978), 215–17; USAFHRA K113.107-191: *Colonel Kurt Gottschling, German Air Signal Corps (Retired), Radio Intercept Service of the German Air Force,* 143.

8. *KTB Skl,* 12 April 1940.

9. Ibid., 13 April 1940.

10. Ibid.

11. Ibid., 14 April 1940.

12. F. Morzik, *German Air Force Airlift Operations,* USAF Historical Studies No. 167 (New York: Arno Press, 1968), 103.

13. Hooton, *Phoenix Triumphant,* 228; USAFHRA 248.50 1-71: *Confidential. Norway (Combat),* 4; P. Gupf, *Luftwaffe von Sieg zu Sieg, von Norwegen bis Kreta* (Berlin: Deutschen, 1941), 57–59.

14. U. O. E. Kessler, "The Role of the Luftwaffe in the Campaign in Norway 1940," in *World War II German Military Studies,* vol. 23, pt. 10, *Special Topics* (London: Garland, 1979), 12.

15. W. Gaul, "The Part Played by the German Air Force and the Naval Air Force in the Invasion of Norway," in *Essays by German Officers and Officials About World War II* (Wilmington, Del.: Scholarly Resources in cooperation with the U. S. Naval Historical Center, n.d.), 26.

16. *Milch, Tagebuch,* 16 April 1940.

17. Gaul, "Part Played by the German Air Force," 26–27; of course, German planners had prepared for greater numbers of flak batteries than actually made it onto Norwegian soil in the first few days; for Narvik, see USAFHRA K113.305: *Generalkommando X. Fliegerkorps, Ia Nr.10089/40 gKdos (handschriftlich). Befehl fuer Vorkommando der I./Flak-Regiment 32 (zu oeffnen nach Auslaufen des Kriegsschiffes), 10.Maerz 1940;* for Trondheim, USAFHRA K113.305: *Generalkommando X. Fliegerkorps, Ia op Nr.10090/40 gKdos (handschriftlich). Befehl fuer I./Flak-Regt. 611 (zu oeffnen nach Auslaufen des Kriegsschiffes). 10.Maerz 1940;* and for Bergen, Stavanger, Kristiansand, and Oslo, USAFHRA K113.305: *Generalkommando X. Fliegerkorps, Ia Nr.10091/40 gKdos (handschriftlich). Einsatz fuer II./Flak-Regt. 33 (zu oeffnen nach Auslaufen mit 1 Seetransport). Geheime Kommandosache!* For a later report on flak in Norway, see NA T971/60: *Lfl. 5, Lg. Norwegen. FS Lg. Norwegen (Iaop2), Bnr. 2071/40 geh., 3.10.40.*

18. *Jodl, Tagebuch,* 14 April 1940.

19. Hooton, *Phoenix Triumphant,* 230.

20. *Milch, Tagebuch,* 17 April 1940.

21. NA T1022/1756: *Oberkommando der Kriegsmarine, 1 Skl-Teil D Luftlage 1. März bis 31. Juli 1940. Tagesverlauf Luftwaffe 17.4.40.*

22. Ibid.

23. Hooton, *Phoenix Triumphant*, 230.

24. S. Roskill, *The War at Sea*, vol. 1, *The Defensive* (London: HMSO, 1954), 186.

25. C. Shores, *Fledgling Eagles: The Complete Account of Air Operations During the Phoney War and the Norwegian Campaign, 1940* (London: Grub Street, 1991), 271.

26. Milch, *Tagebuch*, 17 April 1940; NA T1022/1756: *Oberkommando der Kriegsmarine, 1 Skl-Teil D Luftlage 1. März bis 31. Juli 1940. Tagesverlauf Luftwaffe 17.4.40;* Shores, 271.

27. Hooton, *Phoenix Triumphant*, 230.

28. D. MacIntyre, *Narvik* (London: Evans Brothers, 1959), 119–20.

29. W. Baumbach, *The Life and Death of the Luftwaffe* (Newport Beach, Calif.: Noontide Press, 1991), 93.

30. Ibid., 93–94.

31. B. Stegemann, "Die zweite Phase der Seekriegführung bis zum Frühjahr 1941: II. Die Zusammenarbeit mit der Luftwaffe," *Das Deutsche Reich und der Zweite Weltkrieg*, vol. 2, *Die Errichtung der Hegemonie auf dem europäischen Kontinent*, ed. K. A. Maier et al. (Stuttgart: Deutsche Verlags-Anstalt, 1979), 350; for the Taranto story, see A. J. Smithers, *Taranto 1940* (London: Leo Cooper, 1995).

32. J. L. Moulton, *The Norwegian Campaign of 1940: A Study of Warfare in Three Dimensions* (London: Eyre and Spottiswode, 1966), 155.

33. T. K. Derry, *The Campaign in Norway* (London: HMSO, 1952), 76.

34. M. Dean, *The Royal Air Force and Two World Wars* (London: Cassell, 1979), 80; USAFHRA 512.621: *The Use of Transport Aircraft in the Present War;* P. Duff, "R.A.F. Operations Overseas," in *Wonders of World Aviation*, vol. 2, ed. C. Winchester (London: Fleetway House, c. 1938), 742.

35. Dean, *Royal Air Force and Two World Wars*, 80.

36. G. V. Orange, "The Good, the Bad and the Ugly: Building the Royal Air Force, 1938–1940" (paper presented to the Royal Aeronautical Society, Wellington Branch, New Zealand, December 1997), 17; M. Harvey, *Scandinavian Misadventure: The Campaign in Norway, 1940* (Tunbridge Wells, Kent: Spellmount, 1990), 191.

37. USAFHRA 512.952A-3: *Supplement to the London Gazette, 28 May 1946.*

38. Ibid.

39. *KTB Skl*, 12 April 1940.

40. Gaul, "Part Played by the German Air Force," 24.

41. *KTB Skl*, 16 April 1940.

42. *BdU, KTB*, 14 April 1940.

43. G. Hessler, *The German U-Boat War in the Atlantic*, vol. 1, *1939–1945* (London: HMSO, 1989), 24.

44. *KTB Skl*, 20 April 1940; Gaul, "Part Played by the German Air Force," 32.

45. See Shores, *Fledgling Eagles*, 283, for 24 April 1940.

46. *KTB Skl*, 19 April 1940.

47. NA T1022/1756: *Oberkommando der Kriegsmarine, 1 Skl-Teil D Luftlage 1. März bis 31. Juli 1940. Tagesverlauf Luftwaffe 19.4.40.*

48. Ibid., 20.4.40

49. Ibid.

50. J. Adams, *The Doomed Expedition: The Campaign in Norway, 1940* (London: Leo Cooper, 1989), 97.

51. Ibid., 99.

52. Shores, *Fledgling Eagles,* 279.

53. NA T1022/1756: *Oberkommando der Kriegsmarine, 1 Skl-Teil D Luftlage 1. März bis 31. Juli 1940. Tagesverlauf Luftwaffe 20, 22–24.4.40;* Hooton, *Phoenix Triumphant,* 228; Shores, *Fledgling Eagles,* 279.

54. Hooton, *Phoenix Triumphant,* 228.

55. Fuchs's force was composed of 2. and Z./KG 30, I/ZG 76, II/Jg 77, 1 and 3.(F)/ObdL, 1.(F)/120, 1.(F)/122, and 1./KüFlGr 106; Hooton, *Phoenix Triumphant,* 230; Shores, *Fledgling Eagles,* 282.

56. This summary of Allied raids on Sola and Fornebu is based on Hooton's concise discussion of the events (*Phoenix Triumphant,* 229).

57. K. Assmann, *The German Campaign in Norway* (London: Naval Staff Admiralty, 1948), 57.

58. USAFHRA 512.952A-3: *Supplement to the London Gazette, 28 May 1946. Appendix A.*

59. V. MacClure, *Gladiators over Norway* (London: Allen, 1942), 11.

60. Ibid.

61. NA T1022/1756: *Oberkommando der Kriegsmarine, 1 Skl-Teil D Luftlage 1. März bis 31. Juli 1940. Tagesverlauf Luftwaffe 25.4.40.*

62. Ibid.; MacClure, *Gladiators over Norway,* 12; Shores, *Fledgling Eagles,* 286.

63. MacClure, *Gladiators over Norway,* 19.

64. USAFHRA 512.952A-3: *Supplement to the London Gazette, 28 May 1946.*

65. Ibid.

66. Hooton, *Phoenix Triumphant,* 228.

67. USAFHRA 512.952A-3: *Supplement to the London Gazette, 28 May 1946.*

68. E. F. Ziemke, *The German Northern Theater of Operations, 1940–1945,* Pamphlet No. 20-271 (Washington, D.C.: Department of the Army, 1959), 72.

69. Ibid., 75.

70. *Milch, Tagebuch,* 27 April; Irving, *Rise and Fall of the Luftwaffe,* 376 n. 38.

71. H.-G. Serephim, ed., *Das politische Tagebuch Alfred Rosenbergs, 1934/35 und 1939/40* (Munich: Deutscher Taschenbuch, 1964), 133.

72. Derry, *Campaign in Norway,* 143.

73. Adams, *Doomed Expedition,* 172–73.

74. Roskill, *War at Sea,* 1:188.

75. *KTB Skl,* 29 April 1940.

76. Ibid., 28 April, 1 May 1940.

77. *Milch, Tagebuch,* 30 April, 1 and 2 May 1940.

78. D. Richards, *Royal Air Force, 1939–1945,* vol. 1, *The Fight at Odds* (London: HMSO, 1953), 95; NA RG 457: *G.C. & C.S. Air and Military History,* vol. 2, 22.

79. NA T1022/1756: *Oberkommando der Kriegsmarine, 1 Skl-Teil D Luftlage 1. März bis 31. Juli 1940. Tagesverlauf Luftwaffe 28.4.40.*

80. *KTB Skl,* 27 April 1940; NA T1022/1756: *Oberkommando der Kriegsmarine, 1 Skl-Teil D Luftlage 1. März bis 31. Juli 1940. Tagesverlauf Luftwaffe 27.4.40.*

81. Ibid., 28.4.40.

82. Ibid., 29.4.40.

83. *Milch, Tagebuch,* 30 April 1940.

84. NA T1022/1756: *Oberkommando der Kriegsmarine, 1 Skl-Teil D Luftlage 1. März bis 31. Juli 1940. Tagesverlauf Luftwaffe 28.4.40.*

85. USAFHRA 512.952A-3: *Supplement to the London Gazette, 28 May 1946.*

86. N. Miller, *War at Sea: A Naval History of World War II* (London: Scribner, 1995), 72–73.

87. NA T1022/1756: *Oberkommando der Kriegsmarine, 1 Skl-Teil D Luftlage 1. März bis 31. Juli 1940. Tagesverlauf Luftwaffe 3.5.40.*

88. Derry, *Campaign in Norway,* 142.

89. NA T1022/1756: *Oberkommando der Kriegsmarine, 1 Skl-Teil D Luftlage 1. März bis 31. Juli 1940. Tagesverlauf Luftwaffe 4.5.40.* Although the attack took place on 3 April, the full details did not appear until the next day in the Naval Staff War Diary Air Situation reports.

90. Ibid.

91. *KTB Skl,* 3 May 1940.

92. Shores, *Fledgling Eagles,* 304.

93. *Deutsches Nachrichten-Büro,* 4 May 1940, quoted in F. O. Busch, "Narvik: The Story of the Heroic Battle of the German Destroyers," in *Essays by German Officers and Officials About World War II* (Wilmington, Del.: Scholarly Resources in cooperation with the U. S. Naval Historical Center, n.d.), 288.

94. *KTB Skl,* 4 April 1940.

95. A. Bryant, *The Turn of the Tide: A Study Based on the Diaries and Autobiographical Notes of Field Marshal the Viscount Alanbrooke* (London: Collins, 1957), 88.

96. Derry, *Campaign in Norway,* 233–34.

97. Roskill, *War at Sea,* 1:199.

98. W. Hubatsch, *"Weserübung." Die deutsche Besetzung von Dänemark und Norwegen 1940* (Göttingen: Musterschmidt Verlag, 1960), 222.

99. Stegemann, "Die Sicherung der europäischen Nordflanke: III. Das Unternahmen 'Weserübung,'" in *Das Deutsche Reich und der Zweite Weltkrieg,* vol. 2, 225.

100. G. L. Weinberg, *A World at Arms: A Global History of World War II* (Cambridge: Cambridge University Press, 1994), 117.

101. O. Riste, "Sea Power, Air Power, and Weserübung" (paper presented to the International Commission for Military History, Washington, D.C., August 1975, ACTA No. 2, 125–27.

102. Ibid., 125; Moulton, *Norwegian Campaign of 1940,* 12.

103. Riste, "Sea Power, Air Power," 125; B. Liddell Hart, *History of the Second World War* (London: Cassell, 1970), 59.

104. Riste, "Sea Power, Air Power," 127; Riste's thoughts were picked up and elaborated at length by Adams, *Doomed Expedition,* 171–74.

105. Derry, *Campaign in Norway,* 142–43.

106. Gaul, "Part Played by the German Air Force," 43.

107. The best analysis of the entire leadership problem and one upon which this discussion is based is to be found in Harvey, *Scandinavian Misadventure,* 201–23, 252–62.

108. Ibid., 201–23.

109. Gaul, "Part Played by the German Air Force," 44.

110. *Milch, Tagebuch,* 4 May, 1940.

111. Hooton, *Phoenix Triumphant,* 231.

112. Ibid., 232.

113. *Milch, Tagebuch,* 4 May, 1940.

114. Hooton, *Phoenix Triumphant,* 231–32.

115. NA T1022/1756: *Oberkommando der Kriegsmarine, 1 Skl-Teil D Luftlage 1. März bis 31. Juli 1940. Tagesverlauf Luftwaffe 7.5.40.*

116. Ziemke, *German Northern Theater*, 95.

117. NA T1022/1756: *Oberkommando der Kriegsmarine, 1 Skl-Teil D Luftlage 1. März bis 31. Juli 1940. Eingegangene Meldungen Luftwaffe, 12.5.40;* USAFHRA 519.601B-2: *Air Staff Post Hostilities Intelligence Requirements on German Air Force; Records and Report Systems, Statistical Controls and Planning Methods (Section II). Appendix IV: A Series of Daily Tactical Reports on the Norwegian Campaign (Narvik Sector),* 3.

118. Ibid., 6.

119. *KTB Skl,* 15, 16 May 1940.

120. NA T1022/1756: *Oberkommando der Kriegsmarine, 1 Skl-Teil D Luftlage 1. März bis 31. Juli 1940. Eingegangene Meldungen Generalstab Luftwaffe während des 19.5.40.*

121. Ziemke, *German Northern Theater*, 98.

122. NA T1022/1756: *Oberkommando der Kriegsmarine, 1 Skl-Teil D Luftlage 1. März bis 31. Juli 1940. Eingegangene Meldungen Generalstab Luftwaffe während des 19.5.40.*

123. Shores, *Fledgling Eagles,* 331–32.

124. MacClure, *Gladiators over Norway,* 40–41.

125. NA T1022/1756: *Oberkommando der Kriegsmarine, 1 Skl-Teil D Luftlage 1. März bis 31. Juli 1940. Eingegangene Meldungen Generalstab Luftwaffe während des 27.5.40.*

126. Harvey, *Scandinavian Misadventure,* 279.

127. Ibid.

128. Hooton, *Phoenix Triumphant,* 233.

129. Gaul, "Part Played by the German Air Force," 50; *KTB Skl,* 25 May 1940.

130. *KTB Skl,* 16 May 1940.

131. Gaul, "Part Played by the German Air Force," 49.

132. Ibid.

133. Hooton, *Phoenix Triumphant,* 232–33.

134. USAFHRA 519.601B-2: *Air Staff Post Hostilities Intelligence Requirements on German Air Force (Section II). Appendix IV: A Series of Daily Tactical Reports on the Norwegian Campaign (Narvik Sector),* 8.

135. Ibid., 1.

136. Shores, *Fledgling Eagles,* 326–36.

137. Hooton, *Phoenix Triumphant,* 233; NA T1022/1756: *Oberkommando der Kriegsmarine, 1 Skl-Teil D Luftlage 1. März bis 31. Juli 1940. Eingegangene Meldungen Generalstab Luftwaffe während des 23.5.40.*

138. Jodl, *Tagebuch,* 25 May.

139. Harvey, *Scandinavian Misadventure,* 255.

140. NA T1022/1756: *Oberkommando der Kriegsmarine, 1 Skl-Teil D Luftlage 1. März bis 31. Juli 1940. Eingegangene Meldungen Generalstab Luftwaffe während des 27.5.40.*

141. *KTB Skl,* 27 May 1940.

142. Hooton, *Phoenix Triumphant,* 234.

143. K. Zbyszewski and J. Natanson, *The Fight for Narvik: Impressions of the Polish Campaign in Norway* (London: Lindsay Drummond, 1941), 21.

144. Shores, *Fledgling Eagles*, 333–35; Hooton, *Phoenix Triumphant*, 234.

145. Zbyszewski and Natanson, *Fight for Narvik*, 27.

146. Kessler, "Role of the Luftwaffe," 21.

147. Ibid., 22.

148. Ziemke, *German Northern Theater*, 101.

149. Jodl, *Tagebuch*, 16 May; Ziemke, *German Northern Theater*, 102.

150. *KTB Skl*, 6 June 1940; *Fuehrer Conferences*, 4 June 1940; Hubatsch, *"Weserübung,"* 479–80.

151. Hubatsch, *"Weserübung,"* 477–79.

152. Ziemke, *German Northern Theater*, 104–5; *KTB Skl*, 18 May 1940.

153. *KTB Skl*, 16 May 1940.

154. Ibid., 22 May 1940.

155. Assmann, *German Campaign in Norway*, 70.

156. Busch, "Narvik," 249; for the psychological impact of bombing on troops around Narvik, see P. O. Lapie, *With the Foreign Legion at Narvik* (London: John Murray, 1941), 55–56.

157. *Aftonbladet*, 5 June, quoted in Busch, "Narvik," 298.

158. Harvey, *Scandinavian Misadventure*, 279–80.

159. Ibid., 279.

160. MacClure, *Gladiators over Norway*, 44.

161. Ibid., 41–42.

162. Shores, *Fledgling Eagles*, 337–40; Hooton, *Phoenix Triumphant*, 235.

163. P. Dalzel-Job, *From Arctic Snow to the Dust of Normandy* (Ross-shire: Nead-an-Eoin, 1992), 41.

164. Zbyszewski and Natanson, *Fight for Narvik*, 28.

165. NA T1022/1756: *Oberkommando der Kriegsmarine, 1 Skl-Teil D Luftlage 1. März bis 31. Juli 1940. Eingegangene Meldungen Generalstab Luftwaffe während des 2.6.40.*

166. NA T1022/1756: *Oberkommando der Kriegsmarine, 1 Skl-Teil D Luftlage 1. März bis 31. Juli 1940. Eingegangene Meldungen Generalstab Luftwaffe während des 3.6.40; KTB Skl*, 3 June 1940.

167. F. Kurowski, *Generaloberst Dietl. Deutscher Heerführer am Polarkreis* (Berg am Starnberger See: Verlagsgemeinschaft Berg, 1990), 129.

168. *KTB Skl*, 2 June 1940.

169. For German considerations of the Swedish proposal for the neutralization of Narvik, see *KTB Skl*, 3 June 1940; Ziemke, *German Northern Theater of Operations*, 103.

170. *KTB Skl*, 7 June 1940.

171. Ibid., 7, 8 June 1940.

172. Gaul, "Part Played by the German Air Force," 52.

173. *KTB Skl*, 8 June 1940; NA T1022/1756: *Oberkommando der Kriegsmarine, 1 Skl-Teil D Luftlage 1. März bis 31. Juli 1940. Eingegangene Meldungen Generalstab Luftwaffe während des 8.6.40.*

174. C. Bekker, *Hitler's Naval War* (New York: Kensington, 1978), 46–47.

175. Assman, *German Campaign in Norway*, 72.

176. For the controversy over Marschall's decision to attack the convoys rather than enter the fjords, see ibid., 68–76; Stegemann, "Das Unternehmen 'Weserübung,'" 222–24; J. Winton, *Carrier Glorious: The Life and Death of an Aircraft Carrier* (London: Leo Cooper, 1986), 162; *KTB Skl*, 8 June 1940.

177. F. H. Hinsley, *British Intelligence in the Second World War: Its Influence on Strategy and Operations,* vol. 1 (London: HMSO, 1979), 141–43; D. Kahn, *Seizing the Enigma: The Race to Break the U-Boat Codes, 1939–1943* (Boston: Houghton Mifflin, 1991), 121–23.

178. Winton, *Carrier Glorious,* 168; Miller, *War at Sea,* 75. For an eyewitness account onboard *Glorious,* see K. Cross with G. V. Orange, *Straight and Level* (London: Grub Street, 1993), 101–4.

179. Miller, *War at Sea,* 75.

180. Roskill, *War at Sea,* 1:196.

181. *KTB Skl,* 8 June 1940.

182. NA T1022/1756: *Oberkommando der Kriegsmarine, 1 Skl-Teil D Luftlage 1. März bis 31. Juli 1940. Eingegangene Meldungen Generalstab Luftwaffe während des 9.6.40.*

183. Busch, "Narvik," 301.

184. M. Domarus, *Hitler, Reden und Proklamation, 1932 bis 1945. Teil II Untergang,* vol. 3 (Leonberg: Pamminger and Partner, 1988), 1523.

185. Stegemann, "Das Unternehmen 'Weserübung,'" 224.

186. Domarus, *Hitler, Reden und Proklamationen,* 3:1545.

187. Ibid., 1553.

188. Ibid., 1551.

189. Ibid., 1553.

5. THE BATTLE AND SIEGE OF BRITAIN

1. W. Hubatsch, *Hitlers Weisungen für die Kriegführung 1939–1945: Dokumente des Oberkommandos der Wehrmacht* (Koblenz: Bernard & Graefe, 1983), 47–50.

2. *Fuehrer Conferences,* 11 July 1940.

3. A. S. Milward, *The Fascist Economy in Norway* (Oxford: Clarendon Press, 1972), 67.

4. Ibid., 38–39, 67–94.

5. H. Picker, ed., *Hitlers Tischgespräche im Führerhauptquartier* (Berlin: Ullstein, 1993), 66.

6. The William Donovan Papers Box 54C: *"8" Norway and Sweden Misc, 1942–1943* (OSS Records on Norway, held at the U.S. Army Center for Military History, Carlisle Barracks, Pa., c. 1943).

7. NA T971/4: *Der Generalluftzeugmeister. GL 2 Nr. 1750/40 g. Betr.: Inanspruchnahme Dänemarks und Norwegens für Zwecke der Luftwaffenrüstung. Berlin, den 9. Mai 1940.*

8. Ibid.; NA T971/47: *Abschrift. Der Reichsminister der Luftfahrt und Oberbefehlshaber der Luftwaffe. Betrifft. Zahlung an Monteurkolonnen der Luftfahrtindustrie, die außerhalb der Reichsgrenzen eingesetzt werden. Berlin, den. 30 Mai 1940.*

9. NA T971/47: *Abschrift. Der Reichsminister der Luftfahrt und Oberbefehlshaber der Luftwaffe. Der Generalluftzeugmeister, Az.:66.p. Nr.25043/40 (LF 3 III). Richtlinien über die Einschaltung der Firmen der Luftfahrtindustrie in den besetzten Gebieten (ohne Generalgouvernment). Berlin, den 27 Sept 1940.*

10. NA T971/47: *Abschrift. Der Reichsminister der Luftfahrt und Oberbefehlshaber der Luftwaffe. Az.66p. Nr. 27154/40 (III A). Betrifft: Abfindung der in besetztes Gebiet*

einzeln oder im Rahmen von Monteurkolonnen entsandten Fachkräfte der Luftfahrt-industrie. Berlin, den 10 Januar 1941. The rates of pay for the various groups of workers in Norway and other occupied territories in 1941 can be found in NA T971/47: *Abschrift. Der Reichsminister der Luftfahrt und Oberbefehlshaber der Luftwaffe. Az. 66 r 28 Nr. 23521 (LF 3 III A). Betrifft: Regelung des Arbeitsverhältnisses für Angehörige der deutschen Luftfahrtindustrie, die im Auftrag des Generalluftzeugmeisters ausserhalb des Reichgebietes bezw. im Operationsgebiet unmittelbar für die Truppe tätig sind. Berlin, den 24 Mai 1941.*

11. USAFHRA 512.651D-4: *Aircraft and Aero-Engine Factories in Norway, A.I.2(a) Report No.C.125/45 dated 20th February, 1945.* This short but useful document details the location, the specific firm, and its activities with regard to Norwegian factories involved in support of the German air war after occupation.

12. R. G. Reuth, ed., *Joseph Goebbels Tagebücher,* vol. 4, *1940–1942* (Munich: Piper, 1992), 21 September 1940; H.-G. Serephim, *Das politische Tagebuch Alfred Rosenbergs 1934/35 und 1939/40* (Munich: Deutscher Taschenbuch, 1964), 133.

13. *Fuehrer Conferences,* 11 July 1940; H.-D. Loock, *Quisling, Rosenberg und Terboven. Zur Vorgeschichte und Geschichte der nationalsozialistischen Revolution in Norwegen* (Stuttgart: Deutsche Verlags-Anstalt, 1970), 457; Picker, *Hitlers Tischgespräche,* 109; *Joseph Goebbels Tagebücher,* 9 July 1940.

14. A. Speer, *Inside the Third Reich* (London: Weidenfeld and Nicolson, 1970), 181–82; N. Below, *Als Hitlers Adjutant* (Mainz: Hase & Koehler, 1980), 227.

15. J. Thies, *Architekt der Weltherrschaft: Die "Endziele" Hitlers* (Düsseldorf: Droste, 1976), 131.

16. USAFHRA K113.305: *Luftkrieg im Norden: Die Entwicklung der militärpolitischen Lage bis zum Frühjahr 1940. Befehlshaber der U-Boote (Großadmiral Dönitz) an das Oberkommando der Kriegsmarine als "Geheime Kommandosache" betr. "Stützpunkt in Norwegen": 9.10.1939; IMT* 34/005–C, 159–61; *KTB, Skl,* 12, 15 May 1940; M. Salewski, *Die deutsche Seekriegsleitung 1935–1945,* vol. 1, *1935–1941* (Frankfurt am Main: Bernard & Graefe, 1970), 194.

17. G. L. Weinberg, *A World at Arms: A Global History of World War II* (Cambridge: Cambridge University Press, 1994), 983 n. 235.

18. G. Weinberg, *Germany, Hitler and World War II: Essays in Modern German and World History* (Cambridge: Cambridge University Press, 1995), 198.

19. *BdU, KTB,* 1 July 1940; further figures on the small number of U-boats available in the wake of *Weserübung* and *Fall Gelb* can be found in B. Stegemann, "Die zweite Phase der Seekriegführung bis zum Frühjahr 1941: I. Der U-boot-Krieg" in *Das Deutsche Reich und der Zweite Weltkrieg,* vol. 2, *Die Errichtung der Hegemonie auf dem europäischen Kontinent,* ed. K. A. Maier et al. (Stuttgart: Deutsche Verlags-Anstalt 1979), 345.

20. NA RG 457 PG14261: *Vortrag des Korvettenkapitän Assman (1.Abt.Seekriegsleitung) über "Aufgaben und Probleme der deutschen Seekriegsführung" gehalten am 8. November 1941 OKM bei der Tagung der Kommandeure, Chefs und Kommandanten,* 6.

21. For the use of French bases see, J. Kessler, "U-boat Bases in the Bay of Biscay," in *The Battle of the Atlantic, 1939–1945,* ed. S. Howarth and D. Law (Annapolis, Md.: Naval Institute, 1994), 252–65; Stegemann, "Der U-boot-Krieg," 345.

22. *Deutsche Allgemeine Zeitung,* 15 April 1940, quoted in F. O. Busch, "Narvik: The Story of the Heroic Battle of the German Destroyers," in *Essays by German Officers*

and Officials About World War II (Wilmington, Del.: Scholarly Resources in cooperation with U.S. Navel Historical Centers, n.d.), 0229.

23. "An interview with Gen Art Walter Warlimont," in *World War II German Military Studies,* vol. 2, pt. 2, *The Ethint Series,* (London: Garland, 1979), 2; D. F. Bittner, *The Lion and the White Falcon: Britain and Iceland in the World War II Era* (Hamden, Conn.: Archon, 1983), 50.

24. *KTB, Skl,* 12 June 1940.

25. Bittner, *The Lion and the White Falcon,* 51–52.

26. *KTB, Skl,* 18 June 1940.

27. Ibid., 20 June 1940.

28. *Fuehrer Conferences,* 20 June 1940.

29. Ibid., Annex 2, 20 June 1940.

30. Ibid., 20 June 1940.

31. Bittner, *The Lion and the White Falcon,* 53.

32. W. Hubatsch, "Problems of the Norwegian Campaign, 1940," *RUSI Journal* 103 (1958): 340; cf. E. Weichold, "German Surface Ships: Policy and Operations in World War II," in *Essays by German Officers and Officials About World War II,* 39–40.

33. W. Wegener, *The Naval Strategy of the World War,* ed. and trans. H. H. Herwig (Annapolis, Md.: Naval Institute, 1989), 33; C. Gemzell, *Raeder, Hitler und Skandinavien: Der Kampf für einen maritimen Operationsplan* (Lund: CWK Gleerup, 1965), 140; Gemzell, *Organization, Conflict, and Innovation: A Study of German Naval Strategic Planning, 1888–1940* (Lund: Esselte Studium, 1973), 320–21; H.-M. Ottmer, "Skandinavien in den marinestrategischen Planungen der Reichs- bzw. Kriegsmarine," in *Neutralität und totalitäre Aggression: Nordeuropa und die Großmächte im Zweiten Weltkrieg,* eds. R. Bohn et al. (Stuttgart: Franz Steiner, 1991), 53.

34. Wegener, *Naval Strategy of the World War,* 33; Gemzell, *Raeder, Hitler und Skandinavien,* 140; Gemzell, *Organization, Conflict, and Innovation,* 320–21.

35. K. Doentiz, *Memoirs: Ten Years and Twenty Days* (Annapolis, Md.: Naval Institute, 1990), 144.

36. Cf. NA RG 457 PG14261: *Vortrag des Korvettenkapitän Assman (1.Abt.Seekriegsleitung) über "Aufgaben und Probleme der deutschen Seekriegführung" gehalten am 8. November 1941 OKM bei der Tagung der Kommandeure, Chefs und Kommandanten,* 6.

37. *Deutsche Luftwacht,* 1 May 1940, 161.

38. K. A. Maier, "Direkte Strategie Gegen England: III. Die Luftschlacht um England," in *Das Deutsche Reich und der Zweite Weltkrieg,* vol. 2, *Die Errichtung der Hegemonie auf dem europäischen Kontinent,* ed. K. A. Maier et al. (Stuttgart: Deutsche Verlags-Anstalt, 1979) 376.

39. P. Gupf, *Luftwaffe von Sieg zu Sieg, von Norwegen bis Kreta. Mit Unterstützung des Oberbefehlshabers der Luftwaffe* (Berlin: Deutschen, 1941), 73; cf. USAFHRA K113.305: *Oberst a.D. i.G. Torsten G. E. Christ, Die deutsche Luftwaffe im Kampf um Norwegen,* 20–21.

40. Hubatsch, *Hitlers Weisungen,* 47.

41. Quoted in H. Boog, "German Air Intelligence in the Second World War," in *Intelligence and Military Operations,* ed. M. I. Handel (London: Frank Cass, 1990), 358.

42. *KTB, Skl,* 2 October 1940.

43. USAFHRA 519.601B-4: *Air Staff Post Hostilities Intelligence Requirements on the German Air Force. Appendix V: "Attitude Towards an Independent Naval Air Force—*

Admiral Schniewind C of S German Navy." AAF Sta. 379, APO 633, U.S. Army, 7 Sep-tember 1945.

44. H. Boog, "Luftwaffe Support of the German Navy," in *The Battle of the Atlantic,* 303.

45. Ibid., 302.

46. Ibid.

47. H. H. Herwig, *Politics of Frustration: The United States in German Naval Planning, 1889–1941* (Boston: Little, Brown, 1976), 253; Boog, "Luftwaffe Support of the German Navy," 302.

48. Adapted from Gaul, "The Development of the Naval Air Force," 1.

49. Boog, "Luftwaffe Support of the German Navy," 303.

50. NA RG 457/743: *German Naval Air 1933 to 1945. A Report Based on German Naval Staff Documents (Washington, D.C.: Office of Naval Intelligence, 1947),* 5.

51. Ibid., 5–6.

52. Ibid., 8.

53. Ibid.

54. Organized into four distinct groups, the twenty-five squadrons were to be composed of three mixed coastal wings (each with a single close-reconnaissance squadron, a long-range reconnaissance squadron, and a multipurpose squadron with bombs, mines, and torpedoes); two shipborne wings (each made up of two seaplane squadrons); three mixed aircraft carrier wings (each one comprising a fighter, multipurpose, and Stuka squadron); and three seaplane coastal squadrons. Adapted from Gaul, "The Development of the Naval Air Force," 2.

55. The sixty-two-squadron program totaled some 800 planes in twenty-nine multipurpose, nine flying boat, three long-range reconnaissance, six long-range bomber, seven shipborne, and twelve carrier-borne squadrons; see G. Bildlingmaier, "Der Grundlagen für die Zusammenarbeit Luftwaffe/Kriegsmarine und ihre Erprobung in den ersten Kriegsmonaten," in *Die Entwicklung des Flottenkommandos, Beiträge zur Wehrforschung,* vol. 4, ed. Arbeitskreis für Wehrforschung (Darmstadt: Wehr und Wissen, 1964), 78–79; Gaul, "The Development of the Naval Air Force," 4.

56. *Generalstab der Luftwaffe. Nr. 3244/38 gKdos. 1Abt. (III). Betr.: Konzentriertes Flugzeugmuster-Programm, Berlin, den 7.11.1938,* reproduced in Bildlingmaier, "Der Grundlagen für die Zusammenarbeit Luftwaffe/Kriegsmarine," 108–9; K. A. Maier, "Einsatzvorstellungen und Lagebeurteilungen der Luftwaffe und der Marine bis Kriegsbeginn: I. Totaler Krieg und operativer Luftkrieg," in *Das Deutsche Reich und der Zweite Weltkrieg,* vol. 2, 60–61.

57. Gaul, "The Development of the Naval Air Force," 6.

58. Boog, "Luftwaffe Support of the German Navy," 305.

59. W. Green, *Warplanes of the Third Reich* (London: Macdonald and Jane's, 1970), 336.

60. The most notable example is R. H. Fredette, *The Sky on Fire: The First Battle of Britain, 1917–1918 and the Birth of the Royal Air Force* (Washington, D.C.: Smithsonian Institution Press, 1991), 273. Fredette based his conclusions on a negative post–Great War analysis by Major F. von Bülow in Public Records Office, Britain, AIR1/711/27/13/2214, "Air Raids on Great Britain Carried out by Bombing Squadron No. 3 *(Bogohl 3).* May 1917 to May 1918" (1927). Perhaps a survey of the largely ambivalent German Great War aviation classics would have balanced this view. See G. P. Neumann, *The*

German Air Force in the Great War, trans. J. E. Gurdon (London: Hodder and Stoughton, n.d.; originally published as *Die Deutschen Luftstreitkräfte im Weltkriege,* 1920), 157–91; *General der Infanterie* E. W. von Höppner, *Germany's War in the Air* (unabridged and unpublished English translation; originally published as *Deutschlands Kreig in der Luft,* 1921), 76–78, 104.

61. Australian War Memorial [hereafter AWM] 54 432/4/103: *The Douhet Theory and Its Application to the Present War (1944) (Translated by the Air Ministry A.H.B.6., November 1946. Translation VII/11),* 3–7.

62. Ibid., 2; E. Emme, "The Genesis of Nazi *Luftpolitik,* 1933–1935," *Air Power Historian* 5, no. 1 (January 1959): 21; L. Barker and B. F. Cooling, "Developments Before World War II," in *Case Studies in the Achievement of Air Superiority,* ed. B. F. Cooling (Washington, D.C.: Center for Air Force History USAF, 1994), 10–11.

63. E. L. Homze, *Arming the Luftwaffe* (Lincoln: University of Nebraska Press, 1976), 121–22.

64. E. L. Homze, "The Luftwaffe's Failure to Develop a Heavy Bomber Before World War II," *Aerospace Historian* (March 1977): 20–21.

65. Ibid.

66. Ibid., 21.

67. W. Murray, "The Luftwaffe Before the Second World War," *Journal of Strategic Studies* 4 (September 1981): 265.

68. Ibid.

69. Homze, *Arming the Luftwaffe,* 60.

70. Ibid., 122.

71. Ibid.

72. Ibid.

73. Ibid.

74. Ibid.

75. J. R. Smith and A. L. Kay, *German Aircraft of the Second World War* (London: Putnam, 1989), 412.

76. Green, *Warplanes of the Third Reich,* 504–10. Of course the Germans developed longer-range aircraft as the war progressed, such as the four-engined Junkers Ju 290 and six-engined 390, which were successors to the Ju 90; the Messerschmitt Me 264, dubbed the *Amerika-Bomber;* and very long-range versions of the Condor. Nevertheless, all these aircraft entered the war either too late or in too few numbers to significantly play a part in the war at sea.

77. The short quote is taken from the otherwise excellent study by R. Suchenwirth, *Historical Turning Points in the German Air Force War Effort,* USAF Historical Studies No. 189 (New York: Arno Press, 1968).

78. A good portion of this argument owes itself to W. Murray's analysis of the Germans' situation in the prewar period in "Luftwaffe Against Poland," in *Case Studies in the Achievement of Air Superiority,* 70–71.

79. Ibid.

80. Ibid., 71.

81. For a discussion of the effect of the Reich's resource shortage and its importance to German military planning, see B. H. Klein, *Germany's Economic Preparations for War* (Cambridge, Mass.: Harvard University Press, 1959), 76–82.

82. Ibid., 227.

83. D. Irving, *The Rise and Fall of the Luftwaffe: The Life of Luftwaffe Marshal Erhard Milch* (London: Futura, 1976), 54.

84. Homze, "Luftwaffe's Failure to Develop a Heavy Bomber," 25.

85. E. Heinkel, *He1000* (London: Hutchinson, 1956), 185; R. Overy, "From 'Uralbomber' to 'Amerikabomber,'" *Journal of Strategic Studies* 1 (1979): 173.

86. Homze, *Arming the Luftwaffe*, 127.

87. Overy, "From 'Uralbomber' to 'Amerikabomber,'" 157.

88. Murray, "Luftwaffe Before the Second World War," 262.

89. W. Baumbach, *The Life and Death of the Luftwaffe* (Newport Beach, Calif.: Noontide Press, 1991), 212; Green, *Warplanes of the Third Reich*, 343–44.

90. Irving, *Rise and Fall of the Luftwaffe*, 64–65; that German planners were thinking about the problems associated with air attacks can be seen in NA T971/3/6: *Chef 1. Abt., Luftkriegführung gegen England, 22.11.39*. Interestingly, it would appear that the map at the end of the document showing "attack targets for the Luftwaffe in England" has been incorrectly inserted here by the cataloger (who scribbled at the top of the map that it should be added to this file), since it contains flight details not only from the German coast but also from France and Norway, a highly unlikely scenario in late 1939, when Norway was still excluded from Hitler's plans, let alone Luftwaffe considerations. Moreover, the document makes no reference to flights from Norway or France in the text.

91. Homze, *Arming the Luftwaffe*, 167.

92. Ibid.; interestingly, the concept of requiring a large bomber to be able to dive was not uniquely German, as RAF planners were also toying with the idea; E. R. Hooton, "Axis Aircraft at the Outbreak of War," in *Aircraft of the Second World War*, series ed. P. Jarrett (London: Putnam, 1997), 16.

93. A. Price, *Combat Development in World War Two: Bomber Aircraft* (London: Arms and Armour, 1989), 34.

94. Homze, *Arming the Luftwaffe*, 167.

95. Smith and Kay, *German Aircraft of the Second World War*, 281.

96. M. Cooper, *The German Air Force: An Anatomy of Failure* (London: Jane's, 1981), 272.

97. AWM 54 423/4/103: *Address by the Reichsmarschall Goering to the Representatives of the German Aircraft Industry, 13th September 1942 (Translated by Air Ministry, A.H.B.6, 8 Ocotober 1948. Translation VII/78)*, 6–7.

98. Baumbach, *Life and Death of the Luftwaffe*, 212.

99. Green, *Warplanes of the Third Reich*, 343–44.

100. G. Hümmelchen, *Die deutsche Seeflieger 1935–1945* (Munich: Wehrwissenschaftliche Berichte 9, 1976), 18; Bildlingmaier, "Der Grundlagen für die Zusammenarbeit Luftwaffe/Kriegsmarine," 81–83.

101. The 27 January Protocol is reproduced in Bildlingmaier, "Der Grundlagen für die Zusammenarbeit Luftwaffe/Kriegsmarine," 109–10.

102. These units numbered nine long-range reconnaissance, twelve multipurpose, twelve carrier-borne, and two shipborne squadrons; Gaul, "The Development of the Naval Air Force," 6.

103. Hümmelchen, *Die deutsche Seeflieger*, 19; Boog, "Luftwaffe Support of the German Navy," 306.

104. NA RG 457/743: *German Naval Air 1933 to 1945*, 11.

105. Maier, "Totaler Krieg und operativer Luftkrieg," 65.

106. Ibid., 55.

107. Even these obsolete forces the navy would consistently battle to retain; see P. E. Schramm, gen. ed., *Kriegstagebuch des Oberkommandos der Wehrmacht 1940–1941 (Wehrmachtführungsstab), Band 1* [hereafter *KTB OKW*] (Frankfurt am Main: Bernard & Graefe Verlag für Wehrwesen, 1961), 10 September 1940.

108. *Genst. d. Lw./Gen. Qu./6. Abt. (Organisationstafeln des Ob. d. L.),* reproduced in Bildlingmaier, "Der Grundlagen für die Zusammenarbeit Luftwaffe/Kriegsmarine," 109; cf. W. Gaul, "German Air Force Successes in Operations Against Enemy Shipping in the Channel, Off the East Coast of Britain and the North Sea Between April and December 1940," in *Essays by German Officers,* 9.

109. Bildlingmaier, "Der Grundlagen für die Zusammenarbeit Luftwaffe/Kriegsmarine," 110–11.

110. Gaul, "German Air Force Successes," 10.

111. *KTB, Skl,* 9 October 1940; Hümmelchen, *Die deutsche Seeflieger,* 61.

112. NA T1022/1756: *Oberkommando der Kriegsmarine, 1 Skl-Teil D Luftlage. Meldung Genst. Luftwaffe, 10.10.39. 0800 Uhr;* Gaul, "German Air Force Successes," 13; Hümmelchen, *Die deutsche Seeflieger,* 60–61.

113. Gaul, "German Air Force Successes," 13; Hümmelchen, *Die deutsche Seeflieger,* 61; NA T1022/1756: *Oberkommando der Kriegsmarine, 1 Skl-Teil D Luftlage. Meldung Genst. Luftwaffe, 10.10.39. 0800 Uhr.*

114. NA T1022/1756: *Oberkommando der Kriegsmarine, 1 Skl-Teil D Luftlage. Meldung Genst. Luftwaffe, 10.10.39. 0800 Uhr; KTB, Skl,* 9 October 1939.

115. Bildlingmaier, "Der Grundlagen für die Zusammenarbeit Luftwaffe/Kriegsmarine," 95–97; NA T1022/1756: *Oberkommando der Kriegsmarine, 1 Skl-Teil D Luftlage. Meldung Genst. Luftwaffe, 22.10.39. 0800 Uhr.*

116. *KTB, Skl,* 21 October 1939.

117. Ibid., 22 February 1940.

118. Ibid.

119. NA T1022/1756: *Oberkommando der Kriegsmarine, 1 Skl-Teil D Luftlage. Meldung Genst. Luftwaffe, 23.10.39. 0800 Uhr. "Morgenmeldung Fliegerkorps X 0735 Uhr über den Verlauf am 22.2.1940."*

120. *KTB, Skl,* 23, 24, 26 February 1940.

121. Gaul, "German Air Force Successes," 21.

122. *KTB, Skl,* 26 February 1940.

123. Gaul, "German Air Force Successes," 21.

124. Boog, "Luftwaffe Support of the German Navy," 307.

125. For the battle over the control of mines and torpedoes, see *KTB OKW,* 1 October 1940; *KTB, Skl,* 23, 26 February 1940; *Fuehrer Conferences,* 3 December 1940, Annex 2.

126. AWM54 423/4/103: *Operation "Sea-Lion" (Translations of 12 Top-Secret directives for the invasion of Britain, signed by Hitler, Keitel and Jodl in July, August, September and October, 1940. Translated by Air Ministry, A.H.B.6, February 1947. Translation VII/21).*

127. Ibid.

128. A. F. Wilt, *War from the Top: German and British Military Decision Making During World War II* (Bloomington: Indiana University Press, 1990), 146.

129. Ibid.

130. Hubatsch, *Hitlers Weisungen,* 61–65.

131. AWM54 423/4/103: *Operation "Sea Lion."*

132. Wilt, *War from the Top,* 148.

133. Ibid.

134. Ibid.

135. NA T971/1: *Oberkommando der Luftwaffe, Chef des Generalstabes, Nr. 16/45 gKdos (8.Abt.-II). Vorstudien zur Luftkriegsgeschichte, Heft 11: Der Luftkrieg gegen England 1940/41, Bearbeiter: Oberstleutnant von Hesler, Karlsbad, den. 31.12. 1943;* NA T971/3/224: *Vortraege und Besprechung mit dem Reichsmarschall. Besprechung Reichsmarschall am 21.7.40: "II Verschärfter Luftkreig gegen England."*

136. NA T971/1: *Oberkommando der Luftwaffe, Chef des Generalstabes, Nr. 16/45 gKdos (8.Abt.-II). Vorstudien zur Luftkriegsgeschichte, Heft 11: Der Luftkrieg gegen England 1940/41, Bearbeiter: Oberstleutnant von Hesler, Karlsbad, den. 31.12. 1943. Anlage: Kriegsgeliederung der Luftflotten 2, 3 und 5 am 13. August 1940.*

137. These were Stab/AufklGr 22, 2(F)AufklGrObdl, 1(F)/120, and 1(F)/121.

138. Luftflotten 2 and 3: 875 He 111s, Ju 88s, and Do 17s, 406 Ju 87s, 282 Bf 110s, and 813 Bf 109s; Cooper, *German Air Force,* 133.

139. Wilt, *War from the Top,* 148–49.

140. An excellent chronicle compiled from the *Kriegstagebücher* of Luftlotten 2, 3, and 5 of the Luftflotte's air war against Britain and used here is NA T321/54: *Luftkrieg gegen England, Gefechtskalender ab 1.8.40–31.3.41.*

141. NA T971/1: *Oberkommando der Luftwaffe, Chef des Generalstabes, Nr. 16/45 gKdos (8.Abt.-II). Vorstudien zur Luftkriegsgeschichte, Heft 11: Der Luftkrieg gegen England 1940/41, Bearbeiter: Oberstleutnant von Hesler, Karlsbad, den. 31.12. 1943.*

142. C. Bekker, *Angriffshöhe 4000: Ein Kriegstagebuch der deutschen Luftwaffe 1939–1945* (Grafelfing vor München: Urbes Verlag Hans Jürgen Hansen, 1964), 156. The distances in Bekker's original German publication are well short of the actual distances involved, but in the English edition these were corrected reasonably accurately; see Bekker, *The Luftwaffe Diaries* (New York: Doubleday, 1968), 156, 157.

143. B. Norman, *Luftwaffe over the North: Episodes in an Air War, 1939–1943* (London: Leo Cooper, 1993), 62.

144. Bekker, *Angriffshöhe 4000,* 157.

145. *KTB OKW,* 15 August 1940; D. Wood and D. Dempster, *The Narrow Margin: The Battle of Britain and the Rise of Air Power, 1930–1940* (London: Tri-Service Press, 1990), 204; Shores, 354.

146. R. Hough and D. Richards, *The Battle of Britain: The Jubilee History* (London: Hodder and Stoughton, 1989), 173.

147. Ibid.

148. F. Mason, *Battle over Britain* (London: Amadeus, 1990), 200.

149. P. Townsend, *Duel of Eagles* (London: Weidenfeld and Nicolson, 1970), 318.

150. Bekker, *Angriffshöhe 4000,* 158; Townsend, *Duel of Eagles,* 318.

151. Bekker, *Angriffshöhe 4000,* 158.

152. Norman, *Luftwaffe over the North,* 66–67.

153. NA T1022/1756: *Oberkommando der Kriegsmarine, 1 Skl-Teil D Luftlage 1 August bis 31 September 1940. Eingegangene Meldungen Generalstab Luftwaffe während des, 15.8.40;* NA T971/1: *Oberkommando der Luftwaffe, Chef des Generalstabes, Nr. 16/ 45 gKdos (8.Abt.-II). Vorstudien zur Luftkriegsgeschichte, Heft 11: Der Luftkrieg gegen*

England 1940/41, Bearbeiter: Oberstleutnant von Hesler, Karlsbad, den. 31.12. 1943, 12; N. Gelb, *Scramble: A Narrative History of the Battle of Britain* (London: Michael Joseph, 1986), 118.

154. NA T971/1: *Oberkommando der Luftwaffe, Chef des Generalstabes, Nr. 16/45 gKdos (8.Abt.-II). Vorstudien zur Luftkriegsgeschichte, Heft 11: Der Luftkrieg gegen England 1940/41, Bearbeiter: Oberstleutnant von Hesler, Karlsbad, den. 31.12. 1943*, 12.

155. Wood and Dempster, *Narrow Margin*, 204.

156. NA T971/1: *Oberkommando der Luftwaffe, Chef des Generalstabes, Nr. 16/45 gKdos (8.Abt.-II). Vorstudien zur Luftkriegsgeschichte, Heft 11: Der Luftkrieg gegen England 1940/41, Bearbeiter: Oberstleutnant von Hesler, Karlsbad, den. 31.12. 1943*, 15–16; NA T971/3/224: *Vortraege und Besprechung mit dem Reichsmarschall. KTB, OKL, 6.9.40;* NA T971/3/224: *Vortraege und Besprechung mit dem Reichsmarschall. Fuhrungstab Ia, den 29 August 1940.*

157. Luftflotte 5 was ordered to take part in some night raids over northern England and Scotland, but these never equaled the air fleet's effort of 15 August. See NA T971/60: *Besprechung am 19.8.1940 in Karinhall. Aufgaben der Luftflotten für die nächtsten Tage*, in which orders are given for a night raid on Glasgow; and NA T321/54: *Luftkrieg gegen England, Gefechtskalender ab 1.8.40–31.3.41*, for details of Luftflotte 5's continued meager contribution to future attacks on Glasgow.

158. Hough and Richards, *Battle of Britain*, 174.

159. *KTB OKW*, 5 September 1940.

160. Irving, *Rise and Fall of the Luftwaffe*, 106; Wilt, *War from the Top*, 73.

161. AWM54 423/4/103: *Operation "Sea-Lion."*

162. Ibid. It does appear, though, that he had already decided not to go through with the invasion at a much earlier date; for a discussion of this and a detailed account of the reasons behind it, see NA T971/3/18: *Maj. Rauch, Bericht über das im Jahr 1940 geplant gewesere Englandunternehmen (deckname Seelöwe), Strub den. 30 Juli 1945.* This report on Operation *Seelöwe* was written by Major Rauch in July 1945 while in an OKL POW camp in Berchtesgaden. Rauch's insight into the planned invasion of Britain is based on his position as liaison officer to Headquarters Army Group "A" *Generalfeldmarschall* von Rundstedt in Germaine-en-Laye near Paris in the second half of 1940.

163. R. Higham, "The Royal Air Force and the Battle of Britain," in *Case Studies in the Achievement of Air Superiority*, 135.

164. Ibid.

165. H. Boog, "The Luftwaffe and the Battle of Britain," in *The Battle Re-thought: A Symposium on the Battle of Britain*, ed. H. Probert and S. Cox (Shrewsbury: Airlife, 1991), 27.

166. AWM54 423/4/103: *The Course of the Air War Against England (Two studies prepared by the German Historical Branch, 22 November 1939 and 7 July 1944. Translated by Air Ministry, A.H.B.6, May 1947. Translation VII/26).*

167. M. Domarus, *Hitler, Reden und Proklamationen 1932 bis 1945. Teil II Untergang*, vol. 3 (Leonberg: Pamminger and Partner, 1988), 1580.

168. Higham, "Royal Air Force and the Battle of Britain," 138.

169. W. Murray, *Strategy for Defeat: The Luftwaffe, 1933–1945* (Maxwell Air Force Base, Ala.: Air University Press, 1983), 52.

170. P. Calvocoressi, G. Wint, and J. Pritchard, *Total War: The Causes and Courses of the Second World War* (New York: Pantheon Books, 1989), 148–49, 515; G. V. Or-

ange, "A Broad Margin: The Battle of Britain North of Watford," in *Defending Northern Skies, 1915–1995,* ed. A. F. C. Hunter (Newcastle: Royal Air Force Historical Society, 1995), 66–67; Wilt, *War from the Top,* 151; K. Klee, *Operation "Sea Lion" and the Role Planned for the Luftwaffe,* USAF Historical Studies No. 157 (Manhattan, Kans.: MA/AH, c. 1980), 272.

171. A. Kesselring, *The Memoirs of Field Marshal Kesselring* (London: Greenhill Books, 1988), 76; AWM54 423/4/103: A. Galland, *The Battle of Britain by General Adolf Galland (1940–41) (Translated by Air Ministry, A.H.B.6, February 1953. Translation VII/ 121),* 8.

172. Suchenwirth, *Historical Turning Points in the German Air Force War Effort,* 43. Suchenwirth based this assessment on postwar discussions with senior German officers; J. Ray, *The Battle of Britain: New Perspectives* (London: Arms and Armour, 1994), 36.

173. Suchenwirth, *Historical Turning Points in the German Air Force War Effort,* 67.

174. Ibid., 43.

175. Wilt, *War from the Top,* 149–50.

176. Smith and Kay, *German Aircraft of the Second World War,* 260, 418.

177. R. J. Overy, *The Air War, 1939–1945* (London: Europa, 1980), 113.

178. Ibid.

179. Smith and Kay, *German Aircraft of the Second World War,* 282.

180. Ibid., 289, 306.

181. Higham, "Royal Air Force and the Battle of Britain," 119.

182. Ibid., 130.

183. Ibid.

184. Ibid.

185. Smith and Kay, *German Aircraft of the Second World War,* 285.

186. Ibid., 287–88.

187. Irving, *Rise and Fall of the Luftwaffe,* 94.

188. Ibid.

189. D. van der Vat, *The Atlantic Campaign: The Great Struggle at Sea, 1939–1945* (New York: Harper and Row, 1988), 81; NA T971/48: *Dula, Hptm., Luftkriegsakademie. Die Bedeutung der Seefernaufklärung für die U.Bootkriegsführung, Berlin 5.4.1944,* 13.

190. Gaul, "German Air Force Successes," 6.

191. Ibid.

192. NA T971/48: *Dula, Hptm., Luftkriegsakademie. Die Bedeutung der Seefernaufklärung für die U.Bootkriegsführung, Berlin 5.4.1944,* 5.

193. Ibid., 8.

194. Doenitz, *Memoirs,* 134.

195. *Bdu, KTB,* 14 December 1940; Doenitz, *Memoirs,* 135.

196. Smith and Kay, *German Aircraft of the Second World War,* 202; AWM54 423/ 4/103: *The Operational Use of the Luftwaffe in the War at Sea, 1939–43 (A study prepared by the German Air Historical Branch, 8th Abteilung, January, 1944. Translated by the Air Ministry, A.H.B.6, October 1950. Translation VII/102),* 4.

197. The liner was subsequently sunk by a U-boat; AWM54 423/4/103: *The Operational Use of the Luftwaffe in the War at Sea, 1939–43,* 4.

198. K. Poolman, *Focke-Wulf Condor: Scourge of the Atlantic* (London: Macdonald and Jane's 1978), 44; Overy, *Air War,* 39.

199. *KTB OKW,* 6 January; *Fuehrer Conferences,* 4 February 1941, Annex 2, "Air Naval Units."

200. *Fuehrer Conferences,* 27 December 1940, Annex 2 "Urgent Demands of the Navy on the Air Force," and 3 December 1940, Annex 3 "Reflections Concerning the Conduct of the War Against Britain (Air Reconnaissance for Naval Warfare)."

201. N. Miller, *War at Sea: A Naval History of World War II* (London: Scribner, 1995), 171–72.

202. *BdU, KTB,* 7 Jauanry 1941.

203. Ibid., 8 February 1941; G. Hessler, *The German U-Boat War in the Atlantic,* vol. 1, *1939–1945* (London: HMSO, 1989), 67.

204. *BdU, KTB,* 9 February 1941.

205. Ibid., 19 February 1941.

206. Hubatsch, *Hitlers Weisungen,* 100–103.

207. Boog, "Luftwaffe Support of the German Navy," 311.

208. Hubatsch, *Hitlers Weisungen,* 100–103.

209. Boog, "Luftwaffe Support of the German Navy," 308.

210. Hessler, *German U-Boat War in the Atlantic,* 1:68.

211. *BdU, KTB,* 19 February 1941.

212. Ibid.

213. Ibid., 21 February 1941.

214. Hessler, *German U-Boat War in the Atlantic,* 1:68.

215. *BdU, KTB,* 19 February 1941.

216. Ibid., 26 February 1941.

217. Ibid., 2 March 1941.

218. W. S. Churchill, *The Second World War,* vol. 3, *The Grand Alliance* (London: Cassell, 1950), 107; F. H. Hinsley, *British Intelligence in the Second World War: Its Influence on Strategy and Operations,* vol. 1 (London: HMSO, 1979), 329–30.

219. At a stretch the Condor could reach up to 4,410 kilometers; Smith and Kay, *German Aircraft of the Second World War,* 207, 289; Green, *Warplanes of the Third Reich,* 232, 344.

220. Doenitz, *Memoirs,* 139.

221. Hessler, *German U-Boat War in the Atlantic,* 1:69.

222. Doenitz, *Memoirs,* 139.

223. J. Terraine, *Business in Great Waters: The U-Boat Wars, 1916–1945* (London: Leo Cooper, 1989), 261.

224. Ibid.

225. Churchill, *Second World War,* 3:112; Overy, *Air War,* 39.

226. For a contemporary assessment of the slow deployment of the FW-200 Condor, see USAFHRA 512. 6314A: *April 1943, Notes on the German Air Force (Air Ministry, Air Publication, April 1943. Second edition),* 10–11.

227. M. Milner, "The Battle of the Atlantic," *Journal of Strategic Studies* 13 (March 1990): 47, 49.

228. AWM54 423/4/103: *The Battle of Britain by General Adolf Galland (1940–41),* 18.

229. Overy, *Air War,* 39; cf. J. S. Corum, *The Luftwaffe: Creating the Operational Air War, 1918–1940* (Lawrence: University Press of Kansas, 1997), 282.

230. This possibility was foreseen as early as a November 1939 in a secret report, AWM54: *Proposal for the Conduct of Air Warfare Against Britain (This report was presented by General Schmid of the German Air Force Operations Staff, Intelligence, 22 November 1939. Translated by Air Ministry, A.H.B.6, June 1947. Translation VII/30).*

231. E. Weichold, "A Survey from the Naval Point of View of the Organization of the German Air Force for Operations over the Sea," in *Essays by German Officers*, 12–13; NA T971/48: *Dula, Hptm., Luftkriegsakademie. Die Bedeutung der Seefernaufklärung für die U.Bootkriegsführung, Berlin 5.4.1944*, 11–12.

232. G. Till, "The Battle of the Atlantic as History," in *The Battle of the Atlantic*, 589.

233. An interview with Gr Adm Karl Doenitz, Ko Adm Gerhard Wagner, "The U-Boat Campaign Against US-UK Shipping," in *World War II German Military Studies*, vol. 2, pt. 2, *The Ethint Series*, 2.

234. Doenitz, *Memoirs*, 269.

235. Ibid., 270.

236. AWM54 423/4/103: *Report of a Conference held by Reichsmarschall Goering on 22 February 1943 (Translated by Air Ministry, A.H.B.6, 18 March 1949. Translation VII/85)*, 5.

237. Weichold, "Survey from the Naval Point of View," 14–15.

238. Green, *Warplanes of the Third Reich*, 360.

239. Ibid.

240. R. Probert, "Allied Land-Based Anti-submarine Warfare," in *The Battle of the Atlantic*, 379.

241. Ibid., 373.

242. Weichold, "Survey from the Naval Point of View," 13.

243. Milner, "Battle of the Atlantic," 48; Till, "Battle of the Atlantic as History," 586.

244. Till, "Battle of the Atlantic as History," 587.

245. *BdU,KTB*, 23 May 1943; J. Terraine, *The Right of the Line: The Royal Air Force in the European War, 1939–1945* (London: Hodder and Stoughton, 1985), 449.

246. *BdU, KTB*, 13 November 1943; S. Neitzel, "The Deployment of U-Boats," in *The Battle of the Atlantic*, 295–96; Terraine, *Business in Great Waters*, 754–55 n. 21.

247. AWM54 423/4/103: *Report of a Conference held by Reichsmarschall Goering on 22 February 1943*, 7.

248. Overy, "From 'Uralbomber' to 'Amerikabomber,'" 173.

6. LUFTFLOTTE 5 VERSUS ARTIC CONVOYS

1. M. Domarus, *Hitler, Reden und Proklamationen 1932 bis 1945. Teil II Untergang*, vol. 4, (Leonberg: Pamminger and Partner, 1988), 1664.

2. W. Hubatsch, *Hitlers Weisungen für die Kriegführung 1939–1945: Dokumente des Oberkommandos der Wehrmacht* (Koblenz: Bernard & Graefe, 1983), 84–88.

3. USAFHRA K113.309/3: *Verteilung der Fliegerverbände auf verschiedenen Kampffronten. Stand 20.6.1941;* H. Plocher, *The German Air Force Versus Russia, 1941*, USAF Historical Studies No. 153 (Montgomery, Ala.: USAF Historical Division, Research Institute, Air University, 1965), 219–20.

4. USAFHRA K113.309/3: *Gliederung der Luftflotte 5. Stand: bei Beginn des Ostfeldzuges.*

5. Plocher, *German Air Force Versus Russia, 1941,* 32.

6. Ibid., 34, 190; cf. *Halder, Kriegstagebuch,* 12 September 1941.

7. NA T971/26: *Europäische Beiträge zur Geschichte des Weltkrieges II, Heft 3: "Der Kreig in der Luft,"* 26, 29–30; Plocher, *German Air Force Versus Russia, 1941,* 33–34; O. Anttonen and H. Valtonen, *Luftwaffe Suomessa-in Finaland 1941–1944* (Helsinki: Vantaa-Lento, 1976), 15.

8. USAFHRA K113.309/3: *Der Luftkrieg im Osten gegen Russland 1941 (Aus einer Studie der 8.Abteilung, 1943/1944;* USAFHRA K113.309/3: *Oberkommando der Wehrmacht, Nr.44355/41 g.K.Chefs.WFSt/Abt.L(I Op.). Weisungen an den Wehrmachtsbefehlshaber Norwegen ueber seine Aufgaben im Fall "Barbarossa." F.H.Qu., den 7.4.41.*

9. E. F. Ziemke, *The German Northern Theater of Operations, 1940–1955,* Pamphlet No. 20-271 (Washington, D.C.: Department of the Army, 1959), 317.

10. For army strength and organization on 22 June 1941 see ibid., 137–38.

11. W. Erfurth, *Warfare in the Far North* (Washington, D.C.: Center of Military History, United States Army, 1987), 10–12.

12. Ibid., 12–13.

13. Ibid.

14. For this and Stumpff's headquarter transfer, see Ziemke, *German Northern Theater,* 236.

15. *KTB OKW,* 8, 15 March 1941; USAFHRA K113.305: *Oberkommando der Wehrmacht, Nr. 00469 gKdos. WFst./Abt.L (I Op.). Bezug: Chef OKW/WFSt./Abt. L(IV) Nr. 0321/40 g. v.25.7.40. Kampfanweisungen fuer die Verteidigung Norwegens, F.H.Qu., den 26,3,41.*

16. Ziemke, *German Northern Theater,* 215; NA T1022/3995: *Kriegstagebuch des Admiral Nordmeer,* 26 December 1941.

17. *KTB OKW,* 28 December 1941; *KTB Skl,* 27 December 1941; NA T1022/3995: *Kriegstagebuch des Admiral Nordmeer,* 27 December 1941; Ziemke, *German Northern Theater,* 215–16.

18. *Fuehrer Conferences,* 29 December 1941; later fears even concerned a possible British landing in Jutland; see NA T321/173: *Aktenvermerk Nr 1. Anl.7 zu Chef Genst Lfl.5 Nr.1/42 gKdos.*

19. *KTB Skl,* 30 December, 2, 3, 6 January 1941.

20. *Fuehrer Conferences,* 29 December 1941.

21. *KTB Skl,* 29 December 1941; *Fuehrer Conferences,* 29 December 1941, 12 January 1942.

22. *Fuehrer Conferences,* 12 January 1992.

23. Sweden was implicated in these mechanizations, and consequently German planners began examining the need to invade Norway's eastern neighbor in 1942; see W. Hubatsch, "Operation *Polarfuchs:* Ein strategischer Schubladenentwurf," *Wehr-Wissenschaftliche Rundschau,* 1 (January 1956): 11–19.

24. J. Terraine, *Business in Great Waters: The U-Boat Wars, 1916–1945* (London: Leo Cooper, 1989), 727 n. 13.

25. For Norwegian coastal defenses, see USAFHRA K113.305: *Ausbau der Gefestigungen vom Atlantik und Norwegen. Aus den Fuehrer-Protokollen Februar–Mai 1942*

(Reichsminister Speer), 6; a good overview is provided by A. Hillgruber's commentary, "VI. Die Verteidigungsmaßnahmen im Norden und Westen Europas, 1 Norwegen-Dänemark," to the *KTB OKW, 1. Januar 1942–31.Dezember 1942*, vol. 2, 122–26.

26. *KTB Skl*, 22 January 1942; Ziemke, *German Northern Theater*, 216.

27. Two concise discussions of Churchill's *Jupiter* plans and used as the basis for this discussion are found in P. Salmon, ed., *Britain and Norway in the Second World War* (London: HMSO, 1995): H. P. Willmot, "Operation *Jupiter* and Possible Landings in Norway," 97–108; and E. Grannes, "Operation *Jupiter:* A Norwegian perspective," 109–16.

28. Grannes, "Operation *Jupiter,*" 111.

29. Willmott, "Operation *Jupiter* and Possible Landings in Norway," 101.

30. Grannes, "Operation *Jupiter,*" 112.

31. *KTB Skl*, 27 May 1942.

32. For orders, signals, and reports concerning the breakthrough, see NA T971/37: *Vorbereitung, Unternehmen "Donnerkeil" Kanaldurchbruch, 26.1.42–11.2.42.*

33. *KTB Skl*, 2 January 1941.

34. NA T1022/3995: *Kriegstagebuch des Admiral Nordmeer*, 27 December 1941.

35. *KTB Skl*, 30 December 1941.

36. Ibid., 6 January 1942.

37. Ibid., 7, 8 January 1941.

38. NA RG457/94–99: *G.C. & C.S. History*, vol. 23, *Northern Waters*, 58.

39. *KTB Skl*, 24 January 1942.

40. *Fuehrer Conferences*, 22 January 1942.

41. *KTB Skl*, 31 January 1942.

42. NA RG457/94–99: *G.C. & C.S. Naval History*, vol. 23, *Northern Waters*, 171.

43. NA T971/48/756: *Genst.d.Lw., 8.Abt. Nr. 35/44 gKdos. (II). Studien zum Luftkrieg, Heft3: Gedanken zum Einsatz der Luftwaffe im Luftkrieg über See*, 46.

44. NA T1022/3996: *Kriegstagebuch des Admiral Nordmeer*, 5 March 1942; *KTB Skl*, 5 March 1942.

45. K. Assmann and W. Gaul, "Die deutsche Kriegfuehrung gegen den english-russischen Geleitverkehr im Nordmeer 1941–1945," in *Essays by German Officers and Officials About World War II* (Wilmington Del.: Scholarly Resources in cooperation with the U. S. Naval Historical Center, n.d.), 20.

46. B. B. Schofield, *The Russian Convoys* (London: Pan, 1964), 37.

47. NA T1022/3996: *Kriegstagebuch des Admiral Nordmeer*, 12 March 1942.

48. The meteorologic and topographic description of the Far North and polar waters has been drawn from the following: NA T321/239: *Luftgeographisches Einzelheft: Europäische Polarländer (Herausgegeben vom Generalstab der Luftwaffe, Berlin 1941)*; USAFHSO 512.277B: *List of Airfields, Landing Grounds, and Seaplane Bases: Norway (Air Ministry, October 1st, 1943)*; Schofield, *Russian Convoys*, xvi–xv; R. Woodman, *Arctic Convoys, 1941–1945* (London: John Murray, 1994), xiv–xvii.

49. Schofield, *Russian Convoys*, xv.

50. Ibid.

51. NA T321/239: *Luftgeographisches Einzelheft: Europäische Polarländer (Herausgegeben vom Generalstab der Luftwaffe, Berlin 1941)*.

52. Ibid.

53. W. Baumbach, *Life and Death of the Luftwaffe* (Newport Beach, Calif.: Noontide Press, 1991), 90.

54. *Fuehrer Conferences*, 14 March 1942.

55. For details on the expected completion date for *Graf Zeppelin* and the adaptation of aircraft for this vessel, see *Fuehrer Conferences*, April 1942; regarding the latter point, cf. an earlier document, NA T1022/3349: *Generalluftzeugmeister, LC 2 Nr. 1968/ 41 gKdos. Besprechungs-Niederschrift. Betr.: Ausrüstungs des Flugzeugträgers "Graf Zeppelin." Vorg.: Besprechung am 28.9.41. Berlin, den 30. Sept. 1941.*

56. E. Weichold, "The Importance of the Aircraft Carrier in the War at Sea, 1939–45, Based on the Experiences of the German and Italian Navies," in *Essays by German Officers*, 8–9.

57. *Fuehrer Conferences*, 16 April 1942.

58. Ibid., 14 May, 17 June 1942.

59. W. Rahn, "Der Seekrieg im Atlantik und Nordmeer, IV: Operationen an der europäischen Nordflanke," in *Das Deutsche Reich und der Zweite Weltkrieg*, vol. 6, *Die globale Krieg, Die Ausweitung zum Weltkrieg und der Wechsel der Initiative*, ed. H. Boog et al. (Stuttgart: Deutsche Verlags-Anstalt, 1990), 411; Ziemke, *German Northern Theater*, 237.

60. NA T1022/3996: *Kriegstagebuch des Admiral Nordmeer*, 15 March 1942.

61. NA T1022/3996: *1935 Uhr Eingang Fernschreiben: SSD nachr. Adm. Nordmeer, SSD Gr. Nord, SSD nachr.Adm.Norw.-gKdos.- Zur Unterrichtung nachstehende Weisung Ob.d.L. Führungsstab an Luftwaffe 5 für die Fortsetzung der Luft-Kriegsführung. Anlage 11 zu Kriegstagebuch des Admiral Nordmeer*, 15 March 1942.

62. *KTB Skl*, 15 March 1942.

63. NA T1022/3996: *1935 Uhr Eingang Fernschreiben: SSD nachr. Adm. Nordmeer, SSD Gr. Nord, SSD nachr.Adm.Norw.-gKdos.- Zur Unterrichtung nachstehende Weisung Ob.d.L. Führungsstab an Luftwaffe 5 für die Fortsetzung der Luft-Kriegsführung. Anlage 11 zu Kriegstagebuch des Admiral Nordmeer*, 15 March 1942.

64. USAFHRA K113.305: *Zuteilung von fliegenden Verbänden an die Luftwaffe 5 (Norwegen) (Stand 10.1.1942, 14.2 1942 and 14.3.1942) (Aus den in England befindlichen Lagekarten).*

65. NA T1022/3996: *Lagebetrachtung, Kriegstagebuch des Admiral Nordmeer*, 21 April 1942.

66. NA T1022/3996: *Zusammenfassende Betrachtung der Operationen vom 29.4. bis 5.5.1942, Kriegstagebuch des Admiral Nordmeer*, 13 May 1942.

67. AWM54 423/4/103: *German Air Attacks on PQ Convoys. Extracts from the War Diaries of Luftflotte 5, dated May–September, 1942 (Translated by the Air Ministry, A.H.B.6., 10th January, 1948. Translation VII/60)*, 27 May 1945.

68. USAFHRA K113.309/3/7: *W. Kluemper, Der Einsatz des KG 26 als Torpedotäger in Norwegen* (n.d.), 1.

69. AHB, *The Rise and Fall of the German Air Force, 1933–1945* (London: Arms and Armour Press, 1983), 112–14; Baumbach, *Life and Death of the Luftwaffe*, 93.

70. NA T1022/1758: *Oberkommando der Kriegsmarine, 1 Skl-Teil D Luftlage. Eingegangene Meldungen Generalstab Luftwaffe während des 27.5.42.*

71. AWM54 423/4/103: *German Air Attacks on PQ Convoys. Extracts from the War Diaries of Luftflotte 5*, 27 May 1945.

72. *KTB Skl*, 28 May 1942.

73. Ibid., 27 May 1942.

74. NA T971/6: *Die Kampfuehrung der Luftflotte 5 in Norwegen 1942 (Quellen: KTB des Gefechtsstabes im Kemi, Ergaenzungsbaende des KTB der Luftflotte 5; Akten 66758, 66759, 66760, 66761).*

75. AHB, *Rise and Fall of the German Air Force*, 114.

76. USAFHRA K113.305: *Seenotdienst in Norwegen (Aus den amtlischen Truppengliederung des Luftflottenkommando 5. Teilgebiet Norwegen. Sammlung Karlsruhe);* USAFHRA 519.601B-4: *Air Staff Post Hostilities Intelligence Requirements on the German Air Force, Tactical Employment (Section IVG), 15 October, 1945.* This postwar report, some of which appears to have been translated from a late 1942 or early 1943 Luftwaffe guide, examines the employment of the Luftwaffe's Sea Rescue Organization; see also NA RG 457/54: *Der Reichsminister der Luftfahrt und Oberbefehlshaber der Luftwaffe, Chef des Nachrichtenverbindungswesens. Abt.3(V) Nr.8352/41 (K) geh. Nachrichtenbestimmungen für den Seenotdienst der Luftwaffe im Krieg (25.8.41).*

77. G. Hümmelchen, *Die deutsche Seeflieger 1935–1945* (Munich: Wehrwissenschaftliche Berichte 9, 1976), 145–47; H. Plocher, *The German Air Force versus Russia, 1942,* USAF Historical Studies No. 154 (USAF Historical Division, Reseach Institute, Air University, 1966), 38.

78. Hümmelchen, *Die deutsche Seeflieger,* 147.

79. NA T971/6: *Die Kampfuehrung der Luftflotte 5 in Norwegen 1942 (Quellen: KTB des Gefechtsstabes im Kemi, Ergaenzungsbaende des KTB der Luftflotte 5; Akten 66758, 66759, 66760, 66761),* 9–10.

80. AWM54 423/4/103: *German Air Attacks on PQ Convoys. Extracts from the War Diaries of Luftflotte 5,* 30 May 1945.

81. These details are from Hümmelchen, *Die deutsche Seeflieger,* 146.

82. AWM54 423/4/103: *German Air Attacks on PQ Convoys. Extracts from the War Diaries of Luftflotte 5,* 29 May 1945.

83. Anttonen and Valtonen, *Luftwaffe Suomessa-in Finaland,* 17.

84. USAFHRA K113.309/3/5: *Die Luftflotte 4, Luftwaffen-Kommando Ost, Luftflotte 1 und 5 im strategischen Luftkrieg von Anfang des Jahres bis zur Mitte 1942,* 8; NA T1022/1756: *Oberkommando der Kriegsmarine, 1 Skl-Teil D Luftlage. Eingegangene Meldungen Generalstab Luftwaffe während des 28.5.42.*

85. AWM54 423/4/103: *German Air Attacks on PQ Convoys. Extracts from the War Diaries of Luftflotte 5,* 27 May 1945.

86. Historical Section, Naval Staff, Admiralty, *Arctic Convoys, 1941–1942* (November 1954), 172; AHB, 114; Assman and Gaul, "Die deutsche Kriegfuehrung gegen den englisch-russischen Geleitverkehr," 34, 37–38.

87. For background appreciation of the situation, see Schniewind's detailed memorandum of 30 May: NA T1022/1791: *Befehlshaber der Schlachtschiffe. B. Nr. gKdos. 375/42 Chefsache. Operative Verwendung der Flottenstreitkräfte im Nordraum. An Bord, den 30.Mai 1942.* This memorandum and a good deal of the documents pertaining to *Rösselsprung* are contained in an indexed file on the operation in the War Diary German Navy, NA T1022/1791: *1 Skl-1942 Heft C: Handakten für besondere Operationen: "Rösselsprung."*

88. C. Bekker, *Hitler's Naval War* (New York: Kensington, 1978), 273–74.

89. NA T1022/1791: *Oberkommando der Kriegsmarine. Skl.I Op 1103/42 Gkds.Chefs. Vortragsnotiz Unternehmung "Rösselsprung." Berlin, den 9. Juni 1942; Fuehrer Conferences,* Appendix Operation Rösselsprung, 15 June 1942.

90. Woodman, *Artic Convoys,* 193.

91. *KTB Skl,* 8, 19 June 1942.

92. Ibid., 19 June 1942.

93. Ibid., 1 June 1942; NA T1022/3996: *Kriegstagebuch des Admiral Nordmeer,* 13 May 1942.

94. *KTB Skl,* 8 June 1942.

95. Ibid., 9 June 1942; see also NA T1022/3948: *Kriegstagebuch, Marinegruppenkommandos Nord, Anlage 23 a zum K.T.B. Gruppe Nord v. 1–15.6.1942. Abschrift. Fernschreiben vom 10.6.1942 00.27 Uhr;* and NA T1022/3948: *Kriegstagebuch, Marinegruppenkommandos Nord, Anlage Nr. 24 zum K.T.B. Gruppe Nord v. 1 bis 15.6.1942. MKYG 0637 10.6.1942 2023 Uhr.*

96. *KTB Skl,* 9 June 1942.

97. Ibid., 10 June 1942.

98. *Fuehrer Conferences,* 15 June 1942.

99. Woodham, *Arctic Convoys,* 193.

100. D. Irving, *The Destruction of Convoy PQ 17* (London: Cassell, 1968), 26.

101. NA T1022/3948: *Kriegstagebuch, Marinegruppenkommandos Nord, Anlage Nr. 31 zum K.T.B. Gruppe Nord v. 1 bis 15.6.1942.*

102. *KTB Skl,* 29 May, 1 June 1942.

103. Ibid., 18 June 1942.

104. Ibid., 23 June 1942.

105. Ibid., 18 June 1942.

106. AWM54 423/4/103: *German Air Attacks on PQ Convoys. Extracts from the War Diaries of Luftflotte 5,* "Complete report on the operations against PQ 17," 5.

107. NA T1022/1791: *Handakte Ib: "Rösselsprung." Anl. zum KTB. Teil C. Anlagen Nr. 5: 14457/42 Gkds, Auslaufbefehl für U-Boote, 10.6.1942.*

108. Irving, *Destruction of Convoy PQ 17,* 46.

109. Ibid.

110. Ibid., 41.

111. Ibid., 35.

112. "The Admiralty's Instructions of 27 June 1942" are reproduced in full in Appendix 1 of ibid., 303–4.

113. *Kriegstagebuch des Oberkommandos der Wehrmacht,* 4 July 1942; NA T1022/1758: *Oberkommando der Kriegsmarine, 1 Skl-Teil D Luftlage. Eingegangene Meldungen Generalstab der Luftwaffe während 4.7.42;* NA T1022/1791: *1 Skl-1942 Heft C: Handakten für besondere Operationen: "Rösselsprung,"* 57; Irving, *Destruction of Convoy PQ 17,* 83–85.

114. AWM 54 423/4/103: *German Air Attacks on PQ Convoys. Extracts from the War Diaries of Luftflotte 5,* 4 July 1942; NA T1022/1791: *1 Skl-1942 Heft C: Handakten für besondere Operationen: "Rösselsprung,"* 36.

115. Irving, *Destruction of Convoy PQ 17,* 97.

116. Ibid., 103.

117. NA T1022/1758: *Oberkommando der Kriegsmarine, 1 Skl-Teil D Luftlage. Eingegangene Meldungen Generalstab der Luftwaffe während 4.7.42I; KTB OKW,* 4 July 1942. Later claims for the 4 July torpedo attack were lower but still in excess of what was actually achieved; see the final summary of KüFlGr 706 reconnaissance activities during the operations against PQ 17 in NA T1022/3438: *Küstenfliegergruppe 706, Feldpostnummer B 19559, Luftgaupostamt Berlin. B.Nr. 3567/42 geheim. Betr.: Gefechtsbericht K.Fl.Gruppe 706 und Staffeln über Aufklärung gegen P.Qu. 17 am 30.6. bis 7.7.1942,* 20–22.

118. *KTB Skl,* 4 July 1942.

119. Ibid.; Irving, *Destruction of Convoy PQ 17,* 97.

120. Irving, *Destruction of Convoy PQ 17,* 167.

121. *KTB Skl,* 5 July 1942.

122. Ibid., 7 July 1942.

123. Ibid., 5 July 1942.

124. AWM54 432/4/103: *German Air Attacks on PQ Convoys. Extracts from the War Diaries of Luftflotte 5,* "Complete report on the operations against PQ 17," 7.

125. Some of the attacks made by *Luftflotte 5* and all of those by U-boats on 5 July can be found in NA T1022/1791: *1 Skl-1942 Heft C: Handakten für besondere Operationen: "Rösselsprung,"* 65–70.

126. Ibid., 70–71.

127. Ibid.

128. Ibid., 130–31.

129. Irving, *Destruction of Convoy PQ 17,* 170.

130. Ibid., 177.

131. *Kriegstagebuch des Oberkommandos der Wehrmacht,* 5 July 1942; Irving, *Destruction of Convoy PQ 17,* 171.

132. Irving, *Destruction of Convoy PQ 17,* 179.

133. Woodman, *Arctic Convoys,* 223.

134. *KTB Skl,* 6 July 1942.

135. NA T1022/1791: *1 Skl-1942 Heft C: Handakten für besondere Operationen: "Rösselsprung,"* 90; "Complete report on the operations against PQ 17," in AWM54 432/4/103: *German Air Attacks on PQ Convoys. Extracts from the War Diaries of Luftflotte 5,* 6.

136. *KTB, OKW,* 10 July 1942.

137. Woodham, *Arctic Convoys,* 244.

138. NA T1022/1791: *1 Skl-1942 Heft C: Handakten für besondere Operationen: "Rösselsprung,"* 105.

139. AWM54 423/4/103: *German Air Attacks on PQ Convoys. Extracts from the War Diaries of Luftflotte 5,* 10 July 1942.

140. Ibid.

141. Ibid., "Complete report on the operations against PQ 17," 7.

142. This excludes a number of auxiliary vessels sunk.

143. AWM54 432/4/103: *German Air Attacks on PQ Convoys. Extracts from the War Diaries of Luftflotte 5,* "Complete report on the operations against PQ 17"; E. R. Hooton, *Eagle in Flames: The Fall of the Luftwaffe* (London: Arms and Armour, 1997), 63.

144. Woodman, *Arctic Convoys,* 224–25; Schofield, *Russian Convoys,* 91.

145. Schofield, *Russian Convoys,* 69.

146. AWM54 432/4/103: *German Air Attacks on PQ Convoys. Extracts from the War Diaries of Luftflotte 5,* 7 September 1942.

147. A detailed account of the torpedo units' involvement in attacks against PQ 18 can be found in USAFHRA K113.309/3/7: *W. Kluemper, Der Einsatz des KG 26 als Torpedotäger in Norwegen.*

148. *KTB, OKW,* 13 September 1942.

149. NA T971/6: *Die Kampffuehrung der Luftflotte 5 in Norwegen 1942,* 14.

150. Ibid., 14; M. Cooper, *The German Air Force: An Anatomy of Failure* (London: Jane's, 1981), 245; Woodman, *Arctic Convoys*, 280.

151. NA T971/34: *Genst.d.Lw 8.Abt. Nr 35/44 gKdos. (II). Studien zum Luftkrieg, Heft 3. Gedanken zum Einsatz der Luftwaffe im Luftkrieg über See*, 47; Hooton, *Eagle in Flames*, 63; Assmann and Gaul, "Die deutsche Kriegfuehrung gegen den english-russischen Geleitverkehr," 53.

152. AHB, 115.

153. NA T971/34: *Genst.d.Lw 8.Abt. Nr 35/44 gKdos. (II). Studien zum Luftkrieg, Heft 3. Gedanken zum Einsatz der Luftwaffe im Luftkrieg über See*, 48; Hooton, *Eagle in Flames*, 63.

7. SLOW DEATH, 1943-1945

1. USAFHRA T971/18: *Tätigkeit der Luftflotte 5 im Nord-Ostraum 1942–43*, 7.

2. E. F. Ziemke, *The German Northern Theater of Operations, 1940–1945*, Pamphlet No. 20-271 (Washington, D.C.: Department of the Army, 1959), 240–41.

3. C. Barnett, *Engage the Enemy More Closely: The Royal Navy in the Second World War* (London: Norton, 1991), 731.

4. K. Doenitz, *Memoirs: Ten Years and Twenty Days* (Annapolis, Md.: Naval Institute, 1990), 372–73.

5. Ibid., 373.

6. USAFHRA 519.601 B-4: *Air Staff Post Hostilities Intelligence Requirements on German Air Force. Appendix V: Attitude Towards an Independent Naval Air Force—Admiral Schniewind C of S German Navy.*

7. NA T971/48/933: *Seekriegsleitung, B.Nr. 1.Skl. 3233/43 gK Chefs. Betr.: Luftaufklärung in Nordsee und Nordmeer. Berlin, den 3. Nov. 43.*

8. S. Roskill, *The War at Sea*, vol. 3, *The Offensive*, pt. 1, *1 June 1943–31 May 1944* (London: HMSO, 1960), 102; S. E. Morison, *History of United States Naval War Operations in World War II*, vol. 10, *The Atlantic Battle Won, May 1943–May 1945* (Boston: Little, Brown, 1964), 231–33.

9. E. R. Hooton, *Eagle in Flames: The Fall of Luftwaffe* (London: Arms and Armour, 1997), 64; P. Lundeberg, "Allied Co-operation," in *The Battle of the Atlantic 1939–1945*, ed. S. Howarth and D. Law (Annapolis, Md.: Naval Institute, 1994), 252–65; Stegemann, "Der-U-boot-Krieg," 363.

10. NA T971/48/933: *Seekriegsleitung, B.Nr. 1.Skl. 3233/43 gK Chefs. Betr.: Luftaufklärung in Nordsee und Nordmeer. Berlin, den 3. Nov. 43.*

11. NA T971/48/1029: *Abschrift. Marinegruppenkommando Nord. & Flottekommando. B.Nr. gKdos.Chefs 640/43 C. An des Luftflottenkommando 5 Oslo/Nowegen, den 30.Juni 1943.* Part of a file containing correspondence between Maringruppenkommando Nord and Luftflotte 5 over the use of bombers for reconnaissance.

12. NA T971/48/1029: *Abschrift. 1.Skl. 1885/43 gK Chefs. An Ob.d.L. Führungstab Robinson I z.H. Herrn Generalleutnant Meister. Berlin, d.28.7.43.*

13. USAFHRA K113.305: *Norwegian—10. Juli 1943;* the figures given here should be used cautiously, since they were compiled after the war for the Karlsruhe Collection of Luftwaffe documents from enemy-prepared strength charts. More accurate figures

can be found in a Von Rohden Collection file, NA T971/47/38: *Verlust, Verbrauch und Bestandszahlen und Monatsmeldungen, August 1943–November 1944*. Overall, this more accurate material prepared by the Luftwaffe's own 6. Abteilung has higher figures for all types of aircraft (but particularly fighters) deployed in Norway. Nevertheless, the rise and fall in operational strengths over time between the two sources is relatively consistent and supports the overall points being made in the text. Since, therefore, the information contained in this latter set of documents does not cover the complete period under discussion, I have chosen to rely on the former for consistency's sake; for the structure of the air fleet in this period, see NA T321/230: *Truppengliederung des Lfl.Kdos.5, Stand vom 1.5.1943*.

14. NA RG457/94–99: *G. C. & S. C. Naval Histories*, vol. 6, *The German Navy— Communications, Appendix C, The German Naval Meteorological Service*, 232; for a discussion of German meteorologic intelligence, see D. Syrett, "German Meteorological Intelligence from the Arctic and North Atlantic, 1940–1945," *Mariner's Mirror* 71 (August 1985): 325–33.

15. USAFHRA 512.62512M-92: *Air Ministry/U.S.A.F.E. Intelligence Report Number 92. The German Meteorological Service in War, Appendix X: Weather Reconnaissance Staffeln (Westas) 1942 and 1945*. This seventy-two-page document was prepared by Rudolf Benkendorff, Director OKL Meteorological Service.

16. Ibid., 51; USAFHRA 519.601B-14: *Air Staff Post Hostilities Intelligence Requirements of the German Air Force: GAF Meteorological Service (Section XIV)*, 49.

17. NA RG457/94–99: *G. C. & S. C. Naval Histories*, vol. 6, *The German Navy— Communications, Appendix C, The German Naval Meteorological Service*, 252.

18. Ibid., 237.

19. A handful of Ultra decrypts related to this subject are to be found, along with translations of German operational orders for the establishment of bases in Greenland and an interrogation report of a German prisoner captured in Greenland, in NA RG457/622: *Joint Intelligence Staff, Memorandum of Request: Enemy Activity in Greenland, 3 February 1945*.

20. NA RG457/94–99: *G. C. & S. C. Naval Histories*, vol. 6, *The German Navy— Communications, Appendix C, The German Naval Meteorological Service*, 241.

21. B. Philpott, *German Maritime Aircraft* (Cambridge: Patrick Stephens, 1981), 11.

22. For details on the process involved, see NA T321/173: *Verschrift fur Beölung U-boot und Flugboot*.

23. NA RG 457/177: *CX/MSS/SALU West 824, Week 22–28/8/43. Summary of G.A.F. Offensive, Bomber, Recon and Coastal Operations in the Areas of Luftflotte 3 and Luftflotte 5*.

24. *KTB Skl*, 18 December 1943.

25. Ibid., 12, 15 December 1943.

26. Ibid., 15 December 1943.

27. Ibid., 23 December 1943.

28. Ibid.

29. Ibid.

30. Ibid.

31. Ibid., 24 December 1943.

32. C. Bekker, *Hitler's Naval War* (New York: Kensington, 1978), 342.

33. *KTB Skl*, 24 December 1943.

34. Ibid., 25 December 1943.

35. Bekker, *Hitler's Naval War,* 347.

36. Doenitz, *Memoirs,* 375–76.

37. Bekker, *Hitler's Naval War,* 358.

38. *KTB Skl,* 26 December 1943.

39. Bekker, *Hitler's Naval War,* 356.

40. *KTB Skl,* 26 December 1943.

41. Ibid.

42. Bekker, *Hitler's Naval War,* 357.

43. Ibid.

44. J. Winton, *The Death of the Scharnhorst* (Strettington, Chichester: Antony Bird, 1983), 94; Bekker, *Hitler's Naval War,* 358.

45. *KTB Skl,* 26 December 1943; NA T971/37: *Analge 15b: Abschrift (Fernschreiben) an Ob.d.L. Robinson Ic. Endkampf "Scharnhorst." Luftflottenkommando 5, Fuhr. Abt. Ic Nr. 5749143 gKdos, in Der Einfluß der Luftwaffe auf die Seekriegsführung (erläutert an Beispielen), Karlsbad, den 14.10.1944.*

46. Historical Section, Naval Staff, Admiralty, *Battle Summary No. 24: Sinking of the "Scharnhorst," 26th December 1943* (June 1944), 17.

47. *KTB Skl,* 28 December 1943.

48. Ibid., 27 December 1943.

49. Hooton, *Eagle in Flames,* 269–71.

50. H. Boog, "Luftwaffe Support of the German Navy," in *The Battle of the Atlantic,* 314; Hooton, *Eagle in Flames,* 64.

51. W. Green, *Warplanes of the Third Reich* (London: Macdonald and Jane's, 1970), 346; H. Boog, "'Josephine' and the Northern Flank," *Intelligence and National Security* 4 (January 1989): 141.

52. A. Price, *The Last Year of the Luftwaffe, May 1944 to May 1945* (London: Arms and Armour, 1991), 181.

53. AWM54 423/4/103: *Report of a Conference held by Reichsmarschall Goering on 22 February 1943 (Translated by the Air Ministry, A.H.B.6, 18th March, 1949. Translation VII/85).*

54. Price, *Last Year of the Luftwaffe,* 20, 28.

55. Hooton, *Eagle in Flames,* 75 n. 68.

56. Ibid., 64.

57. USAFHRA K113.305: *Zuteilung von fliegenden Verbaenden an die Luftflotte 5. (Norwegen, Stand 10.4.1943).*

58. USAFHRA K113.305: *Luftflotten 5 (Norwegen)—20 October 1943, and 10. November 1943 (Aus den England befindlichen Lagekarten);* Hooton, *Eagle in Flames,* 64–65.

59. USAFHRA 520.332: *Eighth Air Force, Mission No. 75. Target: Heroya I, Trondheim I. Date of Raid: 24 July 1943, Part 1—1st Wing, Heroya—Magnesium, Aluminum and Nitrate Works,* 2.

60. USAFHRA 520.332: *Eighth Air Force, Mission No. 75. Target: Heroya I, Trondheim I. Date of Raid: 24 July 1943, Enemy Tactics;* W. F. Craven and J. L. Cate, *The Army Air Forces in World War II,* vol. 2, *Europe, Torch to Pointblank, August 1942 to December 1943* (Washington, D.C.: Office of Air Force History, 1983), 674–75; for radar along the Norwegian coast, see USAFHRA 519.601 B-4: *The German Air Force Aircraft Warning and Fighter Control System: Radar in Norway,* 396.

61. USAFHRA 520.332: *Eighth Air Force, Mission No. 75. Target: Heroya I, Trondheim I. Date of Raid: 24 July 1943.*

62. Craven and Cate, *Army Air Forces in World War II*, 2:675–76.

63. Ibid., 676; for a contemporary assessment of the effectiveness of such raids on Germany's U-boat pens, see USAFHRA 178.26–29: *J.I.C. 246/4, 24 January 1945, Bombing of U-boat Assembly Yards and Operating Bases.*

64. Craven and Cate, *Army Air Forces in World War II*, 2:682.

65. USAFHRA 520.332: *Eighth Air Force, Operation No. 131, 16 November, 1943, Rjukan, Knaben.*

66. Of course the "Me 109" here is more correctly known and cited as the Bf 109, USAFHRA 520.332: *Eighth Air Force, Operations No. 132, 18 November, 1943, Kjeller;* A. Lang, "Die Aktion *Weserübung.* Deutsch-norwegische Geschichte im Spannungsfeld zwischen Emotion und Erkenntnis," in *Ideen und Strategien 1940: Ausgewählte Operation und deren militärgeschichtliche Aufarbeitung,* ed. Militärgeschichtlichen Forschungsamt (Herford: E. S. Mittler & Sohn, 1990), 119.

67. These figures are taken from M. Middlebrook and C. Everitt, *The Bomber Command War Diaries: An Operational Reference Book, 1939–1945* (New York: Viking, 1985), 593–94, 609; a less indiscriminate raid was made on the same site on 12 January 1945 without the loss of civilian life (650).

68. These figures are taken from ibid., passim.

69. USAFHRA K113.309.3/15–18: *Jagdeinsatze Lw.Kdo.West, Lw.Kdo.Suedost, Kdr.Gen.d.d.Lw. in Norwegen (West) und Kdr.Gen.d.d.Lw. in Italaien i.J.1944. H.Qu., den 16.2.1945;* USAFHRA K113.309.3/15–18/893: *Der Ablauf der der Kämpf an der Ostfront, 1. Januar 1944–30.6.1944 (Zusammenstellung der 8. kriegswissenschaftliche Abteilung).*

70. Hooton, *Eagle in Flames*, 65.

71. *KTB OKW, Bd. 4, 9. Abschnitt: Der nördliche Kriegsschauplatz (Finnland, Norwegen, Dänemark),* 917.

72. USAFHRA 506.6191–1: *Detailed Interrogation Report, Notes on German Activities in Norway: IV Feldwerft Abt (Mot) Arkt (22 März 45).*

73. A good account surrounding Ehrler's role in the disaster can be found in W. Girbig, *Jagdgeschwader 5 "Eismeerjäger"* (Stuttgart: Motorbuch, 1975), 255–66; Hooton, *Eagles in Flames*, 65.

74. S. Roskill, *The War at Sea,* vol. 3, *The Offensive,* pt. 2, *1 June 1944–14 August 1945* (London: HMSO, 1961), 169.

75. W. Hubatsch, *Hitlers Weisungen für die Kriegführung 1939–1945: Dokumente des Oberkommandos der Wehrmacht* (Koblenz: Bernard & Graefe, 1983), 233–38.

76. Allied plans for *Fortitude North* and *South* are reproduced in J. Mendelsohn, ed., *Covert Warfare: Intelligence, Counterintelligence, and Military Deception During the World War II Era,* vol. 15, *Basic Deception and the Normandy Invasion* (London: Garland, 1989).

77. D. Kahn, *Hitler's Spies: German Military Intelligence in World War II* (New York: Macmillan, 1979), 310; Boog, "'Josephine' and the Northern Flank," 139; F. H. Hinsley, *British Intelligence in the Second World War,* vol. 5, *Strategic Deception* (London: HMSO, 1990), 188.

78. Boog, "'Josephine' and the Northern Flank," 139; cf. K.-J. Müller, "A German Perspective on Allied Deception Operations in the Second World War," and T. L. Cubbage,

"The Success of Operation Fortitude: Hesketh's History of Strategic Deception," both in *Strategic and Operational Deception*, ed. M. Handel (London: Frank Cass, 1987), 316–22, 327–46.

79. *KTB OKW, Bd. 4*, 918; Boog, "'Josephine' and the Northern Flank," 140.

80. USAFHRA K113.305: *OKL 2382(452) Der Reichsmarschall des Grossdeutschen Reiches und Oberbefehlshaber der Luftwaffe, Nr. 9050/44 gKdos Chefsache (FueSt. Ia). Betr.: "Drohende Gefahr Nord." H.Qu., 6.1.44.*

81. *Luftwaffe Befehlshaber Mitte (Gen.d. Lw. in Dänemark)* was part of what would become known as Luftflotte Reich and responsible for the defense of the Germany; see Hooton, *Eagle in Flames*, 260–61.

82. USAFHRA K113.305: *OKL 2382(452) Der Reichsmarschall des Grossdeutschen Reiches und Oberbefehlshaber der Luftwaffe, Nr. 9050/44 gKdos Chefsache (FueSt. Ia). Betr.: "Drohende Gefahr Nord." H.Qu., 6.1.44.*

83. USAFHRA T971/14: *Der Verbrauch von Flugbetriebstoff im Vergleich zu den vorhandenen Vorräten;* M. Cooper, *The German Air Force: An Anatomy of Failure* (London: Jane's, 1981), 349.

84. Cooper, *German Air Force*, 349.

85. USAFHRA T971/14: *Der Verbrauch von Flugbetriebstoff im Vergleich zu den vorhandenen Vorräten.*

86. A. Price, *Combat Development in World War Two: Bomber Aircraft* (London: Arms and Armour, 1989), 96.

87. Ibid., 129.

88. Boog, "'Josephine' and the Northern Flank," 153.

89. *KTB Skl*, 8, 20, 24, 29 October 1944.

90. J. F. Gebhardt, *The Petsamo-Kirkenes Operation: Soviet Breakthrough and Pursuit in the Arctic, October 1944* (Fort Leavenworth, Kans.: Combat Studies Institute, U.S. Army Command and General Staff College, 1990).

91. *KTB OKW, Bd. 4*, 905, 908.

92. Boog, "'Josephine' and the Northern Flank," 150, 159 n.102; *KTB Skl*, 27 October 1944; F. H. Hinsley, *British Intelligence in the Second World War: Its Influence on Strategy and Operations*, vol. 3, pt. 2 (London: HMSO, 1988), 491–92; Price, *Combat Development in World War II*, 122.

93. Hinsley, *British Intelligence*, vol. 3, pt. 2, 494; Boog, "'Josephine' and the Northern Flank," 150.

94. A *General der Luftwaffe in Finland* was also established but was of course abandoned when the Finns withdrew from the Axis cause in August 1944.

95. Hinsley, *British Intelligence*, vol. 3, pt. 2, 495.

96. Ibid.

97. Ibid.

98. *Fuehrer Conferences*, 1 December 1944.

99. *KTB Skl*, 2 March 1945.

100. Fears of a "northern redoubt" (as opposed to a southern "Alpine redoubt") in northern Germany, Denmark, and Norway were based more on the Allies' overactive imagination than any real German intentions; see J. Ehrman, *Grand Strategy*, vol. 6, *October 1944–August 1945* (London, HMSO, 1956), 147–48; R. Bennett, *Ultra in the West: The Normandy Campaign, 1944–45* (London: Hutchinson, 1979), 236.

101. *Fuehrer Conferences*, 10 March 1945.

102. *KTB Skl*, 4 March 1945.

103. Ziemke, *German Northern Theater*, 312.

104. P. Nordeide, ed., "The Black Friday: The Air Battle over Forde Fjord 9th February 1945" (unpublished pamphlet, trans. M. L Iverson and O. L. Iversen, Sydney, 1986), 18.

105. Ibid., 21.

106. *KTB Skl*, 11 February 1945.

107. Ibid., 26 March 1945.

108. Roskill, *War at Sea*, vol. 3, pt. 2, 172.

109. Ibid.

110. The Germans also had an unusually large amount of heating oil in Norway compared with other areas, some 34,000 tons; see *KTB Skl*, 27 March 1945.

111. USAFHRA K113.309.3/15–18: *Betriebstoffmangel bzw. Transportschwierigkeiten Februar 1945 hindert fliegerischen Einsatz und Ausbildung (Aus dem Kriegstagebuch des Oberkommandos der deutschen Luftwaffe)*, 13 February 1945.

112. Ibid., 15 February 1945.

113. Ibid.

114. USAFHRA T971/14: *Gen.Qu.6.Abt. Bezug: Anforderung Intelligence Service v.12.6.45 (Ergänzung zur Ausarbeitung Gen.Qu.6.Abt.v.17.6.45). Betr.: Entwicklung der Flugkraftstofflage der deutschen Luftwaffe. 25.6.1945. Anlage 1: Gen.Qu.4.Abt.(I). Flugkraftstofflage, Stand 10.April 1945, 1800; KTB Skl*, 11 February 1945.

115. USAFHRA T971.14: *Gen.Qu.6.Abt. Bezug: Anforderung Intelligence Service v.12.6.45 (Ergünzung zur Ausarbeitung Gen.Qu.6.Abt.v.17.6.45). Betr.: Entwicklung der Flugkraftstofflage der deutschen Luftwaffe. 25.6.1945.*

116. USAFHRA T971.14: *Gen.Qu.6.Abt. Bezug: Anforderung Intelligence Service v.12.6.45 (Ergünzung zur Ausarbeitung Gen.Qu.6.Abt.v.17.6.45). Betr.: Entwicklung der Flugkraftstofflage der deutschen Luftwaffe. 25.6.1945. Anlage 4: Gen.Qu.4.Abt.(I). Flugkraftstofflage, Stand 23.4.45. Rob. 4, den 26.April 1945.*

117. *KTB Skl*, 7 February 1945.

118. USAFHRA K113.309.3/15–18: *Unterstützung der Kriegsmarine 1945 (Auszug aus dem Kriegstagebuch des Oberkommandos der Luftwaffe)*, 10 February 1945.

119. *KTB Skl*, 7 February 1945.

120. Ibid., 10 February 1945; Roskill, *War at Sea*, vol. 3, pt. 2, 255.

121. Ibid.

122. Ibid., 257 n.1; V. E. Tarrant, *The Last Year of the Kriegsmarine, May 1944–May 1945* (Annapolis, Md.: Naval Institute Press, 1994), 153.

123. USAFHRA K113.309.3/15–18: *Unterstützung der Kriegsmarine 1945 (Auszug aus dem Kriegstagebuch des Oberkommandos der Luftwaffe)*, 11, 12 April 1945; one further eastbound and one westbound convoy were undertaken after the war's end; Roskill, *War at Sea*, vol. 3, pt. 2, 261.

124. ibid., 262.

CONCLUSION

1. USAFHRA 512.621: *Jodl, "Norway,"* 6.

2. W. Hubatsch, *"Weserübung." Die deutsche Besetzung von Dänemark und Norwegen 1940* (Göttingen: Musterschmidt Verlag, 1960), 353.

3. USAFHRA K113.305: *Norwegen (Aus einer Bearbeitung des Nachkriegs-projekts von Rohden. "Europaeische Beitraege zur Geschichte des Weltkriegs II. 1939/194. Luftkrieg, Heft 14, Seite 114–171). "Das Ringen um Norwegen,"* 13 n. 1.

4. USAFHRA 512.621: *Jodl, "Norway,"* 6.

5. M. Cooper, *The German Air Force: An Anatomy of Failure* (London: Jane's, 1981), 111.

6. E. R. Hooton, *Phoenix Triumphant: The Rise and Rise of the Luftwaffe* (London: Arms and Armour, 1997), 237.

7. J. S. Corum, "The German Campaign in Norway 1940 as a Joint Operation" (paper presented at the conference of the Society for Military History, Montgomery, Alabama, April 1997), 21; cf. R. D. Hooker and C. Coglianese, "Operation Weserübung and the Origins of Joint Warfare," *Joint Force Quarterly* 1 (1993): 100–111.

8. E. H. Stevens, ed., *Trial of Nikolaus von Falkenhorst* (London: William Hodge, 1949), 257.

9. E. F. Ziemke, *The German Northern Theater of Operations 1940–1945*, Pamphlet No. 20-271 (Washington, D.C.: Department of the Army, 1959), 32; for a lengthy discussion of this report, see H.-M. Ottmer, "Das Unternahmen *"Weserübung.* Die Besetzung Dänemarks und Norwegens durch die deutsche Wehrmacht im April 1940. Vorgeschichte, Vorbereitung und Durchführung der Landeunternehmungen in Norwegen," in *Ideen und Strategien 1940. Ausgewählte Operationen und deren militärgeschichtliche Aufarbeitung,* ed. Militärgeschichtlichen Forchungsamt (Herford und Bonn: E. S. Mittler & Sohn, 1991), 146–49.

10. S. W. Mitcham, *Men of the Luftwaffe* (Novato, Calif.: Presidio Press, 1988), 79; Hooton, *Phoenix Triumphant,* 236. One of the few general works on the Luftwaffe to praise Milch's effort is Cooper, *German Air Force,* 110–11.

11. *Milch Tagebuch,* 25 April 1940.

12. Ibid., 16, 26 April, 1 May 1940.

13. Quoted in D. Irving, *The Rise and Fall of the Luftwaffe: The Life of Luftwaffe Marshal Erhard Milch* (London: Futura, 1976), 88.

14. *IMT,* 9, 316.

15. J. S. A. Hayward, *Stopped at Stalingrad: The Luftwaffe and Hitler's Defeat in the East, 1942–1943* (Lawrence: University Press of Kansas, 1998), 320.

16. Corum, "The German Campaign in Norway," 21.

17. N. Below, *Als Hitlers Adjutant, 1937–45* (Mainz: Hase & Koehler, 1980), 227–28.

18. R. Woodman, *Arctic Conveys, 1941–1945* (London: John Murray, 1994), 443.

19. B. B. Schofield, *The Russian Convoys* (London: Pan, 1964), 221.

Select Bibliography

Adams, J. *The Doomed Expedition: The Campaign in Norway, 1940.* London: Leo Cooper, 1989.

Air Ministry, Great Britain. *The Rise and Fall of the German Air Force, 1933–1945.* London: Arms and Armour, 1983.

Assmann, K. *The German Campaign in Norway.* London: Naval Staff Admiralty, 1948.

Barnett, C. *Engage the Enemy More Closely: The Royal Navy in the Second World War.* New York: Norton, 1991.

Baumbach, W. *The Life and Death of the Luftwaffe.* Newport Beach, Calif.: Noontide Press, 1991.

Bekker, C. *Angriffshöhe 4000: Ein Kriegstagebuch der deutschen Luftwaffe 1939–1945.* Gräfelfing vor München: Urbes Verlag Hans Jürgen Hansen, 1964.

———. *Hitler's Naval War.* New York: Kensington, 1978.

———. *The Luftwaffe Diaries.* New York: Doubleday, 1968.

Below, N. *Als Hitlers Adjutant, 1937–45.* Mainz: Hase & Koehler, 1980.

Bennett, R. *Behind the Battle: Intelligence in the War with Germany, 1939–45.* London: Sinclear-Stevenson, 1994.

———. *Ultra in the West: The Normandy Campaign, 1944–45.* London: Hutchinson, 1979.

Bildlingmaier, G. "Der Grundlagen für die Zusammenarbeit Luftwaffe/Kriegsmarine und ihre Erprobung in den ersten Kriegsmonaten." In *Die Entwicklung des Flottenkommandos, Beiträge zur Wehrforschung,* vol. 4, ed. Arbeitskreis für Wehrforschung. Darmstadt: Wehr und Wissen, 1964.

Bittner, D. F. *The Lion and the White Falcon: Britain and Iceland in the World War II Era.* Hamden, Conn.: Archon, 1983.

Boog, H. "'Josephine' and the Northern Flank." *Intelligence and National Security* 4 (January 1989): 137–60.

———. "The Luftwaffe and the Battle of Britain." In *The Battle Re-thought: A Symposium on the Battle of Britain,* ed. H. Probert and S. Cox, 18–32. Shrewsbury: Airlife, 1991.

Boog, H., et al. *Das Deutsche Reich und der Zweite Weltkrieg.* Vol. 6, *Die globale Krieg, Die Ausweitung zum Weltkrieg und der Wechsel der Initiative.* Stuttgart: Deutsche Verlags-Anstalt 1990.

Brett-Smith, R. *Hitler's Generals.* San Rafael, Calif.: Presidio, 1985.

Bryant, A. *The Turn of the Tide: A Study Based on the Diaries and Autobiographical Notes of Field Marshal the Viscount Alanbrooke.* London: Collins, 1957.

Butler, J. R. M. *Grand Strategy.* Vol. 2, *September 1939–June 1941.* London: HMSO, 1957.

Churchill, W. S. *The Second World War.* Vol. 3, *The Grand Alliance.* London: Cassell, 1950.

Cooling, B. F., ed. *Case Studies in the Achievement of Air Superiority.* Washington, D.C.: Center for Air Force History USAF, 1994.

Cooper, M. *The German Air Force: An Anatomy of Failure.* London: Jane's, 1981.

Corum, J. S. "The German Campaign in Norway 1940 as a Joint Operation." Paper presented at the conference of the Society for Military History, Montgomery, Alabama, April 1997.

———. *The Luftwaffe: Creating the Operational Air War, 1918–1940.* Lawrence: University Press of Kansas, 1997.

Craven W. F., and J. L. Cate. *The Army Air Forces in World War II.* Vol. 2, *Europe, Torch to Pointblank, August 1942 to December 1943.* Washington, D.C.: Office of Air Force History, 1983.

Dean, M. *The Royal Air Force and Two World Wars.* London: Cassell, 1979.

Derry, T. K. *The Campaign in Norway.* London: HMSO, 1952.

Dilks, D. "Great Britain and Scandinavia in the 'Phony War.'" *Scandinavian Journal of History* 2 (1977): 29–51.

Doenitz, K. *Memoirs: Ten Years and Twenty Days.* Annapolis, Md.: Naval Institute, 1990.

Domarus, M. *Hitler: Reden und Proklamationen 1932 bis 1945. Kommentiert von einem deutschen Zeitgenossen. Teil I Triumph, Zweiter Band 1935–1938. Teil II Untergang, Dritter Band 1939–1940.* Leonberg: Pamminger and Partner, 1988.

Ehrman, J. *Grand Strategy.* Vol. 6, *October 1944–August 1945.* London: HMSO, 1956.

Erfurth, W. *Warfare in the Far North.* Washington, D.C.: Center of Military History, United States Army, 1987.

Essays by German Officers and Officials About World War II. Wilmington, Del.: Scholarly Resources in cooperation with the U.S. Naval Historical Center, n.d.

Fritz, M. *German Steel and Swedish Iron Ore, 1939–1945.* Göteborg: Publications of the Institute of Economic History of the Göteborg University, 1974.

Gebhardt, J. F. *The Petsamo-Kirkenes Operation: Soviet Breakthrough and Pursuit in the Arctic, October 1944.* Fort Leavenworth, Kans.: Combat Studies Institute, U.S. Army Command and General Staff College, 1990.

Gelb, N. *Scramble: A Narrative History of the Battle of Britain.* London: Michael Joseph, 1986.

Gemzell, C. *Organization, Conflict, and Innovation: A Study of German Naval Strategic Planning, 1888–1940.* Lund: Esselte Studium, 1973.

———. *Raeder, Hitler und Skandinavien: Der Kampf für einen maritimen Operationsplan.* Lund: CWK Gleerup, 1965.

Gilbert, M. *The Churchill War Papers.* Vol. 1, *At the Admiralty September, 1939–May 1940.* London: Norton, 1993.

Girbig, W. *Jagdgeschwader 5 "Eismeerjäger."* Stuttgart: Motorbuch, 1975.

Goulter, C. J. M. *A Forgotten Offensive: Royal Air Force Coastal Command's Anti-shipping Campaign, 1940–1945.* London: Frank Cass, 1995.

Green, W. *Warplanes of the Third Reich.* London: Macdonald and Jane's, 1970.

Gupf, P. *Luftwaffe von Sieg zu Sieg, von Norwegen bis Kreta. Mit Unterstützung des Oberbefehlshabers der Luftwaffe.* Berlin: Deutschen, 1941.

Halder, F. *Halder, Kriegstagebuch: Tägliche Aufzeichungen des Chefs des Generalstabes des Heeres 1939–1945.* 3 vols. Stuttgart: Kohlhmmer, 1962, 1964.

Halpern, P. G. *A Naval History of World War I.* Annapolis: Naval Institute Press, 1994.

Handel, M., ed. *Strategic and Operational Deception.* London: Frank Cass, 1987.

Harvey, M. *Scandinavian Misadventure: The Campaign in Norway, 1940.* Tunbridge Wells, Kent: Spellmount, 1990.

Hayward, J. S. A. "Hitler's Quest for Oil: The Impact of Economic Considerations on Military Strategy, 1941–42." *Journal of Strategic Studies* 18, no. 4 (December 1995): 94–135.

————. *Stopped at Stalingrad: The Luftwaffe and Hitler's Defeat in the East, 1942–1943.* Lawrence: University Press of Kansas, 1998.

Heinkel, E. *He1000.* London: Hutchinson, 1956.

Herwig, H. H. "The Failure of German Sea Power, 1914–1945: Mahan, Tirpitz, and Raeder Reconsidered." *International History Review* 10 (February 1988): 68–105.

Hessler, G. *The German U-Boat War in the Atlantic, 1939–1945.* 2 vols. London: HMSO, 1989.

Hinsley, F. H. *British Intelligence in the Second World War: Its Influence on Strategy and Operations.* Vol. 1. Vol. 3, pt. 2. Vol. 5, Strategic Deception. London: HMSO, 1979, 1988, 1990.

Historical Section, Naval Staff, Admiralty. *Arctic Convoys, 1941–1942.* November 1954.

————. *Battle Summary No. 24: Sinking of the "Scharnhorst," 26th December 1943.* June 1944.

Hitler, A. *Mein Kampf.* Munich: Franz Eher Nachfolger, 1933.

Homze, E. L. *Arming the Luftwaffe.* Lincoln: University of Nebraska Press, 1976.

————. "The Luftwaffe's Failure to Develop a Heavy Bomber Before World War II." *Aerospace Historian,* March 1977, 20–26.

Hooker, R. D., and C. Coglianese. "Operation Weserübung and the Origins of Joint Warfare." *Joint Force Quarterly* 1 (1993): 100–111.

Hooton, E. R. *Eagle in Flames: The Fall of the Luftwaffe.* London: Arms and Armour, 1997.

————. *Phoenix Triumphant: The Rise and Rise of the Luftwaffe.* London: Arms and Armour, 1994.

Hough, R., and D. Richards. *The Battle of Britain: The Jubilee History.* London: Hodder and Stoughton, 1989.

Howarth, S., and D. Law, eds. *The Battle of the Atlantic, 1939–1945.* Annapolis, Md.: Naval Institute, 1994.

Hubatsch, W. *Hitlers Weisungen für die Kriegführung 1939–1945: Dokumente des Oberkommandos der Wehrmacht.* Koblenz: Bernard & Graefe, 1983.

————. "Problems of the Norwegian Campaign, 1940." *RUSI Journal* 103 (1958): 336–45.

————. *"Weserübung." Die deutsche Besetzung von Dänemark und Norwegen 1940.* Göttingen: Musterschmidt Verlag, 1960.

Hümmelchen, G. *Die deutsche Seeflieger 1935–1945.* Munich: Wehrwissenschaftliche Berichte 9, 1976.

Irving, D. *The Destruction of Convoy PQ 17.* London: Cassell, 1968.

———. *Göring: A Biography.* London: Macmillan, 1989.

———. *Hitler's War.* London: Focal Point, 1991.

———. *The Rise and Fall of the Luftwaffe: The Life of Luftwaffe Marshal Erhard Milch.* London: Futura, 1976.

Jacobsen, H. *National-sozialistische Außenpolitik, 1933–1938.* Frankfurt am Main: Alfred Metzner, 1968.

Jäger, J. "Sweden's Iron Ore Exports to Germany, 1933–1944: A Reply to Rolf Karlbom's Article on the Same Subject." *Scandinavian Economic History Review* 15 (1967): 139–47.

Kahn, D. *Hitler's Spies: German Military Intelligence in World War II.* New York: Macmillan, 1978.

Karlbom, R. "Sweden's Iron Ore Exports to Germany, 1933–1944." *Scandinavian Economic History Review* 13 (1965): 65–93.

Kersaudy, F. *Norway 1940.* London: Collins, 1990.

Kesselring, A. *The Memoirs of Field Marshal Kesselring.* London: Greenhill Books, 1988.

Klee, K. *Operation "Sea Lion" and the Role Planned for the Luftwaffe.* USAF Historical Studies No. 157. Manhattan, Kans.: MA/AH, c. 1980.

Klein, B. H. *Germany's Economic Preparations for War.* Cambridge, Mass.: Harvard University Press, 1959.

Koch, H.-A. *Flak: Die Geschichte der deutschen Flakartillerie 1935–1945.* Bad Nauheim: Hans-Henning Podzun, 1954.

Kühn, V. *Deutsche Fallschrimjäger im Zweiten Weltkrieg.* Stuttgart: Motorbuch, 1977.

Kurowski, F. *Generaloberst Dietl. Deutscher Heerführer am Polarkreis.* Berg am Starnberger See: Verlagsgemeinschaft Berg, 1990.

Lang, A. "Die Aktion *Weserübung.* Deutsch-norwegische Geschichte im Spannungsfeld zwischen Emotion und Erkenntnis." In *Ideen und Strategian 1940: Ausgewählte Operation und deren militärgeschichtliche Aufarbeitung,* ed. Militärgeschichtlichen Forschungsamt, 107–37. Herford: E. S. Mittler & Sohn, 1990.

Lee, A. *The German Air Force.* London: Duckworth, 1946.

Lewin, R. *Ultra Goes to War: The Secret Story.* London: Hutchinson, 1978.

Liddell Hart, B. *History of the Second World War.* London: Cassell, 1970.

Loewenstern, E. *Luftwaffe über dem Feind.* Berlin: Wjlhelm Limpert, 1941.

Loock, H.-D. "Nordeuropa zwischen Außenpolitik und 'großermanisher' Innenpolitik." In *Hitler, Deutschland und die Mächte: Materialien zur Außenpolitik des Dritten Reiches,* ed. M. Funke, 684–707. Kronberg: Athenäum 1978.

———. *Quisling, Rosenberg und Terboven. Zur Vorgeschichte und Geschichte der nationalsozialistischen Revolution in Norwegen.* Stuttgart: Deutsche Verlags-Anstalt, 1970.

———. "*Weserübung:* A Step Towards the Greater German Reich." *Scandinavian Journal of History* 2 (1977): 67–88.

MacClure, V. *Gladiators over Norway.* London: Allen, 1942.

MacIntyre, D. *Narvik.* London: Evans Brothers, 1959.

Macleod, R., ed. *The Ironside Diaries, 1937–1940.* London: Constable, 1962.

Maier, K. A., et al., eds. *Das Deutsche Reich und der Zweite Weltkrieg*. Vol. 2, *Die Errichtung der Hegemonie auf dem europäischen Kontinent*. Stuttgart: Deutsche Verlags-Anstalt, 1979.

Mason, F. *Battle over Britain*. London: Amadeus, 1990.

Mendelsohn, J., ed. *Covert Warfare: Intelligence, Counterintelligence, and Military Deception During the World War II Era*. Vol. 15, *Basic Deception and the Normandy Invasion*. London: Garland, 1989.

Messerschmidt, M., et al. *Germany and the Second World War*. Vol. 1, *The Build-up of German Aggression*. Oxford: Clarendon Press, 1990.

Middlebrook, M., and C. Everitt. *The Bomber Command War Diaries: An Operational Reference Book, 1939–1945*. New York: Viking, 1985.

Miller, N. *War at Sea: A Naval History of World War II*. London: Scribner, 1995.

Milner, M. "The Battle of the Atlantic." *Journal of Strategic Studies* 13 (March 1990): 45–66.

Milward, A. S. "Could Sweden Have Stopped the Second World War?" *Scandinavian Economic History Review* 15 (1967): 127–38.

———. *The Fascist Economy in Norway*. Oxford: Clarendon Press, 1972.

Mitcham, S. W. *Men of the Luftwaffe*. Novato, Calif.: Presidio Press, 1988.

Morison, S. E. *History of United States Naval War Operations in World War II*. Vol. 10, *The Atlantic Battle Won, May 1943–May 1945*. Boston: Little, Brown, 1964.

Morzik, F. *German Air Force Airlift Operations*. USAF Historical Studies No. 167. New York: Arno Press, 1968.

Moulton, J. L. *The Norwegian Campaign of 1940: A Study of Warfare in Three Dimensions*. London: Eyre and Spottiswoode, 1966.

Murray, W. "The Luftwaffe Before the Second World War: A Mission, A Strategy?" *Journal of Strategic Studies* 4 (September 1981): 261–70.

———. *Strategy for Defeat: The Luftwaffe, 1933–1945*. Maxwell Air Force Base, Ala.: Air University Press, 1983.

Nazi Conspiracy and Aggression. Washington, D.C.: U.S. Government Printing Office, 1946.

Nordeide, P., ed. "The Black Friday: The Air Battle over Forde Fjord 9th February 1945." Unpublished pamphlet. Trans. M. L. and O. L. Iversen. Sydney, 1986.

Norman, B. *Luftwaffe over the North: Episodes in an Air War, 1939–1943*. London: Leo Cooper, 1993.

Oberkommando der Wehrmacht. *Kampf um Norwegen*. Berlin: Zeitgeschichte-Verlag Wilhelm Andermann, 1940.

Orange, G. V. "A Broad Margin: The Battle of Britain North of Watford." In *Defending Northern Skies, 1915–1995*, ed. A. F. C. Hunter, 56–72. Newcastle: Royal Air Force Historical Society, 1995.

Ottmer, H.-M. "Skandinavien in den marinestrategischen Planungen der Reichs- bzw. Kriegsmarine." In *Neutralität und totalitäre Aggression: Nordeuropa und die Großmächte im Zweiten Weltkrieg*, ed. R. Bohn et al., 49–72. Stuttgart: Franz Steiner, 1991.

———. "Das Unternehmen *Weserübung*. Die Besetzung Dänemarks und Norwegens durch die deutsche Wehrmacht im April 1940. Vorgeschichte, Vorbereitung und Durchführung der Landeunternehmungen in Norwegen." In *Ideen und Strategien 1940. Ausgewählte Operationen und deren militärgeschichtliche Aufarbeitung*, ed.

Militärgeschichtlichen Forschungsamt, 67–106. Herford: E. S. Mittler & Sohn, 1991.

———. *"Weserübung." Der deutsche Angriff auf Dänemark und Norwegen im April 1940.* Munich: R. Oldenbourg, 1994.

Overy, R. J. *The Air War, 1939–1945.* London: Europa, 1980.

———. "From 'Uralbomber' to 'Amerikabomber.'" *Journal of Strategic Studies* 1 (1979): 154–78.

Philbin, T. R. *The Lure of Neptune: German-Soviet Naval Collaboration and Ambitions, 1919–1941.* Columbia: University of South Carolina, 1994.

Philpott, B. *German Maritime Aircraft.* Cambridge: Patrick Stephens, 1981.

Picker, H., ed. *Hitlers Tischgespräche im Führerhauptquartier.* Berlin: Ullstein, 1993.

Plocher, H. *The German Air Force Versus Russia, 1941.* USAF Historical Studies No. 153. Montgomery, Ala.: USAF Historical Division, Research Institute, Air University, 1965.

———. *The German Air Force Versus Russia, 1942.* USAF Historical Studies No. 154. Montgomery, Ala.: USAF Historical Division, Research Institute, Air University, 1966.

Price, A. *Combat Development in World War Two: Bomber Aircraft.* London: Arms and Armour, 1989.

———. *The Last Year of the Luftwaffe, May 1944 to May 1945.* London: Arms and Armour, 1991.

Quisling, V. *Russia and Ourselves.* London: Hodder and Stoughton, 1931.

Raeder, E. *Struggle for the Sea.* London: William Kimber, 1959.

Ray, J. *The Battle of Britain: New Perspectives.* London: Arms and Armour, 1994.

Reuth, R. G. *Joseph Goebbels Tagebücher.* 4 vols. *1940–1942.* Munich: Piper, 1992.

Richards, D. *The Hardest Victory: RAF Bomber Command in the Second World War.* London: Hodder and Stoughton, 1994.

———. *Royal Air Force, 1939–1945,* Vol. 1, *The Fight at Odds.* London: HMSO, 1953.

Riste, O. "Sea Power, Air Power, and Weserübung." Paper presented to the International Commission for Military History, Washington, D.C., August 1975.

Rosenberg, A. *Der Mythus des 20 Jahrhunderts.* Munich: Hoheneichen, 1933.

Roskill, S. *The War at Sea.* 3 vols. London: HMSO, 1954–1961.

Salewski, M. "Basis Nord: Eine fast vergessene Episode aus dem Zweiten Weltkrieg." *Schiff und Zeit* 3 (1976): 11–17.

———. *Die deutsche Seekriegsleitung 1935–45.* Vol. 1, *1935–1941.* Frankfurt am Main: Bernard & Graefe, 1970.

———. "Germany and North Norway: Strategy and Ideology." In *Narvik 1940: Five-Nation War in the High North,* ed. K. Rommetveit, 36–44. Oslo: Institutt for Forvarsstudier, 1991.

Salmon. P., ed. *Britain and Norway in the Second World War.* London: HMSO, 1995.

Schofield, B. B. *The Russian Convoys.* London: Pan, 1964.

Schramm, P. E., gen. ed. *Kriegstagebuch des Oberkommandos der Wehrmacht 1940–1941. Wehrmachtführungsstab.* Vols. 1–4. Frankfurt am Main: Bernard & Graefe Verlag für Wehrwesen, 1961–1965.

Seraphim, H.-G., ed. *Das politisches Tagebuch Alfred Rosenbergs, 1934/35 und 1939/40.* Munich: Deutscher Taschenbuch, 1964.

Shores, C. *Fledgling Eagles: The Complete Account of Air Operations During the Phoney War and the Norwegian Campaign, 1940.* London: Grub Street, 1991.

Smith, J. R., and A. L. Kay. *German Aircraft of the Second World War*. London: Putnam, 1989.

Speer, A. *Inside the Third Reich*. London: Weidenfeld and Nicolson, 1970.

Suchenwirth, R. *Historical Turning Points in the German Air Force War Effort*. USAF Historical Studies No. 189. New York: Arno Press, 1968.

Tarnstrom, R. L. *The Sword of Scandinavia*. Lindsborg, Kans.: Trogen Books, 1996.

Tarrant, V. E. *The Last Year of the Kriegsmarine, May 1944–May 1945*. Annapolis, Md.: Naval Institute Press, 1994.

———. *The U-boat Offensive, 1914–1918*. London: Arms and Armour, 1989.

Terraine, J. *Business in Great Waters: The U-Boat Wars, 1916–1945*. London: Leo Cooper, 1989.

———. *The Right of the Line: The Royal Air Force in the European War, 1939–1945*. London: Hodder and Stoughton, 1985.

Thies, J. *Architekt der Weltherrschaft: Die "Endziele" Hitlers*. Düsseldorf: Droste, 1976.

Townsend, P. *Duel of Eagles*. London: Weidenfeld and Nicolson, 1970.

Trial of Major War Criminals by the International Military Tribunal Sitting at Nuremberg, Germany. Nuremberg: International Military Tribunal, 1947–1949.

United States Strategic Bombing Survey: The Effects of Strategic Bombing on the German War Economy. N.p.: Overall Economic Effects Division, 1945.

U.S. Department of State. *Documents on German Foreign Policy, 1918–1945*. Series D. Washington, D.C.: U.S. Government Printing Office, 1956.

Vat, D., van der. *The Atlantic Campaign: The Great Struggle at Sea, 1939–1945*. New York: Harper and Row, 1988.

Waller, J. H. *The Unseen War in Europe: Espionage and Conspiracy in the Second World War*. New York: Random House, 1996.

Warlimont, W. *Inside Hitler's Headquarters, 1939–45*. London: Weidenfeld and Nicolson, 1964.

Wegener, W. *The Naval Strategy of the World War*. Ed. and trans. H. H. Herwig. Annapolis, Md.: Naval Institute, 1989.

Weinberg, G. L. *A World at Arms: A Global History of World War II*. Cambridge: Cambridge University Press, 1994.

———, ed. *Hitlers zweites Buch: Ein Dockument aus dem Jahr 1928*. Stuttgart: Deutsche, 1961.

Winton, J. *Carrier Glorious: The Life and Death of an Aircraft Carrier*. London: Leo Cooper, 1986.

———. *The Death of the Scharnhorst*. Strettington, Chichester: Antony Bird, 1983.

Wood, D., and D. Dempster. *The Narrow Margin: The Battle of Britain and the Rise of Air Power, 1930–1940*. London: Tri-Service Press, 1990.

Woodman, R. *Arctic Convoys, 1941–1945*. London: John Murray, 1994.

World War II German Military Studies. London: Garland, 1979.

Ziemke, E. F. "The German Decision to Invade Norway and Denmark." In *Command Decisions*, ed. K. R. Greenfield, 49–72. Washington, D.C.: Office of the Chief of Military History, United States Army, 1960.

———. *The German Northern Theater of Operations, 1940–1945*. Pamphlet No. 20–271, Washington, D.C.: Department of the Army, 1959.

Index